WITHDRAWN
HARVARD LIBRARY
WITHDRAWN

Holy Russia, Sacred Israel

Holy Russia,

JEWISH-CHRISTIAN ENCOUNTERS IN RUSSIAN RELIGIOUS THOUGHT

Sacred Israel

DOMINIC RUBIN

ACADEMIC
STUDIES
PRESS

Library of Congress Cataloging-in-Publication Data

Rubin, Dominic, 1972-
  Holy Russia, sacred Israel : Jewish-Christian encounters in Russian religious thought / Dominic Rubin.
    p. cm.
  Includes bibliographical references and index.
  ISBN 978-1-934843-79-6 (hardback)
  1. Judaism--Russia--History. 2. Judaism--Soviet Union--History. 3. Russia--Religion. 4. Soviet Union--Religion. 5. Judaism--Relations--Christianity. 6. Christianity and other religions--Judaism. I. Title.
  BM331.R83 2010
  296.0947--dc22
                    2010017687

Copyright © 2010 Academic Studies Press
All rights reserved
ISBN 978-1-934843-79-6 (hardback)

Cover and book design by Adell Medovoy

Published by Academic Studies Press in 2010

28 Montfern Avenue
Brighton, MA 02135, USA
press@academicstudiespress.com
www.academicstudiespress.com

Contents

Preface 9

CHAPTER ONE: SOLOVIEV'S JUDEO-RUSSIAN WISDOM 13
    Introduction: Russian Jewry in the time of Soloviev 15
    Soloviev's general development 24
    Soloviev, the Jews and Judaism 29
        The flawed wholeness of the Jewish nation 29
        The encounter with J.Rabinowitz 36
        Judaism, Judeo-Christianity and the Law 40
        Talmudic Judaism and integral Christianity 43
    Sophia (Soph-Jah) and Judaic/Christian pan(en)theism 47
    Jewish responses to Soloviev 53

CHAPTER TWO: BULGAKOV AND THE SACRED BLOOD OF JEWRY 59
    Bulgakov: wrestling with Soloviev's heritage 61
    The Jews in Bulgakov's thought: a preview of the main problem 66
    Judaism and the Old Testament in Bulgakov's early philosophy 69
        Two Cities (1906-1910) 70
        The Unfading Light (1917) 74
        Bulgakov and Kabbalah 80
    Bulgakov and Jewry (1): in Russia – the shadow of the Revolution 82
        An early essay in Christian Zionism (1915) 82
        The paradox of Bulgakov's anti-Semitism 91
        Bulgakov's recollections of the 1905 and 1917 Revolutions 101
    Bulgakov and Jewry (2): in exile – the shadow of the Holocaust 105
        The Biblical conception of blood and nation 108
        Sophiology and sacred blood 112
        The blood-chosenness of the Jews after Christ 123
        The collective fate of Israel and the remnant 127
    A critical development of Bulgakov's ideas 134
        A Messianic Jewish reading of Bulgakov? 134
        A (covert) two-covenant reading of Bulgakov? Judas, Saul, and Paul 138
    Conclusion 147
        Bulgakov in two contemporary Russian-Jewish interpretations 149

CHAPTER THREE: N. BERDYAEV, M. GERSHENZON AND L. SHESTOV: JEWISH AND RUSSIAN NIHILISTS OF THE SPIRIT 153
    The three pessimists 155
    Berdyaev and Gershenzon 157
        Nicolai Berdyaev 157
        Mikhail Gershenzon 161

Between Slavophilism and Bolshevism 165
   Berdyaev and Gershenzon on Slavophilism 165
   Gershenzon, Berdyaev and the Bolshevik Revolution 174
   Gershenzon and Vyacheslav Ivanov after the Revolution 177
1922: Berdyaev and Gershenzon on history 183
   Berdyaev on history and Jewry 184
   Gershenzon and Jewish destiny 188
   Pushkin-Ahasuerus 188
   Apotheosis of Jewishness: Gershenzon against Land, Torah and People 191
   The 'Judaization' of Berdyaev 197
Lev Shestov 200
   Shestov on Gershenzon 203
   Shestov on Buber and Judaism 205
   Shestov on Berdyaev 207
Shestov, Bulgakov and Steinberg 211
   Bulgakov on Shestov: 'fideist without faith' 212
   Steinberg on Shestov: reveal the 'black man' 214
Judaism beyond the Pale: superseding both Testaments 220
   Gershenzon and Shestov – differences and similarities 220
   V.V.Zenkovsky: the dialectic of Jewry and Christianity 225

CHAPTER FOUR: VASILY ROZANOV (AND PAVEL FLORENSKY) 227
'Sinful slave Vasily....' 229
Rozanov's intellectual development. 236
Early Rozanov: Judaism over Christianity 246
   "Judaism" (1903) 246
   The immanent church of conciliar Jewry 249
   1.Circumcision 249
   2.Sabbath 254
   3.Mikveh 258
   Astarte, Egypt and Judaism 262
   The agonies of Marcionism 262
Middle Rozanov: Russia expels the Jew within 267
   Two Jewish encounters in the Beilis years 271
   Mikhail Gershenzon 271
   Aaron Steinberg 283
   Rozanov's Judeophobic outpourings (1911-1914) 288
Florensky: Rozanov's secret helper 294
   Florensky's Jewish writings 298
   Ritual murder and the eucharist 301
   The flaw in Florensky's two-tiered logic 304
   Florensky, Romans 11 and Jewish blood 307
   Florensky's 'Kabbalistic scholarship' 312
Florensky: the broader context 313
   Occultism and magic 313
   Political totalitarianism 315
   Katsis and Florensky's 'Christian exegesis' 317

Florensky's position in Russian religious thought	319
Name-worship and symbolism	322
Iosef Davydovich Levin: "I met Florensky once...."	326
Christianity and anti-Semitism: final words	330

CHAPTER FIVE: L. KARSAVIN AND A. STEINBERG: RUSSIA AND ISRAEL SYMPHONICALLY INTERWINED 335

Two friends, two worlds	337
Eurasianism, Volphila, Autonomism	342
The Karsavin-Steinberg exchange	347
Karsavin	347
Steinberg	360
Inflected philosophy: Jews and Russians among the Greeks	367
Steinberg, Jewishness and philosophy: How strange that I am a Jew.	367
Jewishness and Russianness in philosophy	378
Jewish Platonized Kantianism	379
Steinberg and Jewishness in philosophy	386
The boundaries between the believer and the world	391
Core and periphery, Orthodoxy and Revolution	391
The case of Georgy Fedotov	393
The case of Alexander Meier	396
Karsavin: rootless Christianity	399
"A Study in Apologetics"	400
Karsavin: experiencing the Jewish vision of God (Poem on Death)	410
The tortured Jewess	410
Contrary couples	412
Karsavin's and Steinberg's triadology	417
Israel and the living God	422
The end of the Poem on Death	428
The Inquisitor and the Jewess-'conversa'	429
The final drama	432
The role of the Jewess in the final drama	435
Jews and personality	436
Final years: London, Lithuania, Siberia	439
Abez and a final Jewish encounter	441
Death and burial	442

CHAPTER SIX: SEMYON FRANK: FROM *russkiy yevrei* TO *russkiy yevropeetz* 445

Frank: the Jew as universal man	447
Frank's philosophy	455
Frank and Gershenzon	462
Frank's universalism	463
Frank and Gershenzon from Landmarks to Revolution	469
Gershenzon and Frank: the wisdom of Pushkin	472
Pushkin between Frank and Gershenzon	473
Pushkin's message for contemporary Russia	475

      Russian-Jewish Wisdom 482
  Frank and German-Jewish philosophy 485
      Cohen and Frank 486
      Frank and Cohen on suffering 490
      Frank and Rosenzweig 495
      The argument of The Star and Frank's critique 496
      The Star 496
      The critique 498
      Evaluation of Frank's critique 500
      Frank and O.Goldberg 507
  Conclusion 508

CONCLUSION: SOLOVIEV'S HEIRS: THE THIRD GENERATION 511
Alexander Men: Bulgakovian Judeo-Christianity? 511
The polemic against Men's Jewish Christianity 514
      N.Feingold and S.Lyosov 514
      Men in the context of post-Auschwitz theology 516
      Benevich: no Jew, no gentile – no Russian? 520
Conclusion: Russian Orthodoxy and Jewish-Christian dialogue – a note 522

BIBLIOGRAPHY 527

INDEX 547

Preface

This book has personal roots. An earlier fascination with and immersion in Hasidic theosophy triggered in me a shock of recognition when I started to become familiar with Russian religious thought. This was firstly through the books of Sergei Bulgakov. On picking up his *Sophia: The Divine Wisdom*, I was struck by the parallels with the panentheistic thought of the Habad and Breslov schools of Jewish mysticism, and began to wonder whether the similarity was mere coincidence. Some time later, at a monastery in Jerusalem with a group of Russian pilgrims, a member of the group had selected another text of Bulgakov for discussion, one germane to the location of the pilgrimage. That text was Zion, and as I listened to the text being read out loud, my curiosity increased by several degrees: so, Russian religious philosophers had thought in some depths about their Jewish neighbors in the Russian empire.

Shortly after returning from Jerusalem, I met Fr. Vasile Mihoc, a Romanian Orthodox priest with an interest in Jewish-Christian relations, at a lecture he was giving about Maximus the Confessor. I unwittingly monopolized his attention by asking some questions about Judaism, and it emerged that we were both intrigued by the same questions. Shortly afterwards, I approached him with a two-page summary of a book I thought might attract the interest of people other than ourselves. His assurance that the theme was worthwhile and interesting set me off on the path to filling out the summary with content. Over three years, the book and my conceptions of the subject evolved rather exponentially.

Being by education neither a specialist in Russian studies nor, technically speaking in philosophy or theology, the learning gradient was rather steep. My theological education was in large part down to Fr. Georgy Kotchetkov, the rector of St. Philaret's Orthodox Christian Institute in Moscow. Fr. Christopher Hill, a priest at St. Andrew's monastery in Moscow, was another source of inspiration, and he generously loaned me significant chunks of his library. Dr. Marion Wyse read draughts of each chapter and offered extremely helpful comments. Georgia Williams did likewise, and was another source of theological enlightenment and friendship in the three years that the book was being germinated. I am also grateful to Fr. Fyodor Ludengoff, both for personal conversations and for inviting me to teach Old Testament at his church in Novoperedelkino, where parishioners' questions about Judaism and the Old Testament drove me to investigate the patristic perspective on some of the questions raised as the book progressed. Students and teachers at St. Philarets, including Lev Shipman, Olga Sushkova, Grigory Gutner, Lyuba Brisker, Semyon Zeidenberg, and Victor Kott also provided friendship and food for thought. I also spent many hours talking to Andrei Iljichev, a fellow amateur theologian (and, unlike me, professional computer specialist), and his input was invaluable. Finally, Bill Bloom helped me with some intractable word-processing subtlties.

I subtitled the book "Jewish-Christian encounters" because I did not want to write a strictly comprehensive academic history, but to focus on the personal element of Russian thought, mixing the "high" and the "low," i.e. dense theology as well as conversations, fall-outs, chance meetings and so on, which are the stuff of life and often as, or more, revealing than dense treatises. Nonetheless, having selected the people through whom a certain story would be told, I did decide, as matters progressed, to devote serious attention to particular texts of these authors. The result is sometimes sustained literary exegesis, which again, I tried to relate to the author and the historical circumstances in which he was writing.

As far as the selection of the authors is concerned, I chose those Russian religious thinkers who are influential today in Russian church consciousness, and whose influence has penetrated in translation into Western theology as well. The other selection criterion was, of course, that they had written considerably on the Jewish question and had had Jewish friendships which were germane to their work. Obviously Bulgakov, Florensky and Berdyaev are well-known to English-speaking readers interested in Orthodoxy. (Even here a difference can be observed: the last named thinker is a veritable cultural hero in Russia, while he is at best a rather musty name from the distant past in the West, in academic circles at least). Rozanov and Karsavin and perhaps even Frank, however, will be new names to some whose interest is more in theology than Russian literature or philosophy. Other minor characters quickly joined the cast, whose relationship to theology and even philosophy was marginal, and yet whose creativity was highly illuminating for theology. This led to my own discovery of the fascinating influence of literary, cultural and political activity on theology in the Russian context.

The pride of attention has certainly been devoted to the Christian aspect of these Christian-Jewish encounters. This applies particularly to Aaron Steinberg: more space is given over to Karsavin in the chapter devoted to them. One conclusion I have come to is that, for me at least, this study for the most part only raises questions concerning the relationship and nature of Jewish and Christian philosophy and theology, and that for the investigation to go deeper, one would have to examine the Jewish context much more thoroughly than has been done here, especially in the sections concerning Steinberg – whose work deserves to be explored further and disseminated far more widely.

I am also conscious that, despite the length of the study, in many ways it is not as thorough and systematic as it could be. This is partly because I chose to concentrate on a small number of figures. However, another reason is that, living in Russia, my access to scholarly literature in English and even some Russian texts of the Russian emigration has not been completely satisfactory. (The most obvious aspect of this was the need to read certain English books in belated Russian translations). There are thus no doubt gaps in the literature. However, I hope that a certain critical mass was achieved so that my conclusions can survive these omissions. And despite these gaps, I hope that the work as it stands can provide food for thought and further research among interested readers.

The book is intended to fulfill different functions. In addition to exploring how Russian religious thinkers thought about Jews and Judaism, I wanted to sketch a history of this thought for theological readers (both Jewish and Christian) who do not know Russian and are not familiar with the Orthodox tradition: hence at times the rather extensive presentation. My hope is that readers theologically more experienced than myself can gain enough access to the material to develop their own analyses and critiques – which may well differ from mine. Next, I was interested in how this thought is being received now in the Russian, Jewish and Christian camps. Finally, I wanted to engage in what these thinkers had to say on a personal level – and in this endeavor, it must be said that my conclusions are still evolving and not always free of ambiguity.

Before moving on to the matter at hand, I would like to thank my wife, Maria, who helped with the editing, discussed at length some of the chapters with me, and helped with tricky linguistic, literary and cultural moments. Most importantly of all, she expressed her faith in me by giving me the space and time to work for very long stretches uninterrupted by the mischievous attempted incursions into my domain of the younger generation. She also tolerated rather well the notable changes in my mood as I immersed myself first in one powerful personality, and then another, becoming first Bulgakovian, then Karsavianian, and so on in turn.

I dedicate the book to her and hope that it will help us in our common spiritual development.

ONE

Soloviev's Judeo-Russian Wisdom

One

Introduction: Russian Jewry in the time of Soloviev

The religious philosophers who are going to be investigated in this study can all rightfully be called the heirs of Vladimir Soloviev. This is true of their philosophical orientation, as well as their attitude towards Judaism. Although Soloviev lived for a mere forty seven years, by the time of his death he had achieved a legendary status in Russian philosophy and literature. However, it was not merely his philosophic and literary output that made Soloviev significant: as a personality, both in character and physical appearance, he came to embody the Russian God-seeker for the following generation, the generation of the bright new twentieth century.

In terms of his relationship to Judaism, Soloviev lived through a critical time in the fortunes of Russian Jewry. At his birth, just over half a century had passed since Russia had incorporated one million Jews within her borders with the annexation of Belarus, Lithuania and Ukraine in 1772, 1793, and 1795 – the spoils of the divided Polish kingdom. Before then, according to the statutes, Jews had been forbidden from living in Russia, as being "enemies of Christ;" since the so-called "Judaizing" heresy of the fifteenth and sixteenth centuries they had little direct impact on Russia's consciousness. By the beginning of Soloviev's life, the number of Russian Jews had increased from a million to two and a half million; by his death even that number would have doubled and the status of Russian Jews would have changed radically.

Two years after he was born, Alexander II came to power. In the 1860s, the new tsar initiated a series of political reforms in Russian society (including most famously, the emancipation of the serfs in 1861). These included reversing some of the discriminatory legislation against Jews, who were now permitted to receive a Russian secondary and university education and live in Russian cities outside the Pale of Settlement. This was an about-turn as regards the harsh policies of his father, Nicolas I, one of whose measures had been the introduction of twenty five year military service for Jews of twelve years and older (a law that was repealed by Alexander)[1].

During Alexander's reign, Jews began to assimilate into Russian society. Many of them became involved in Russian political movements; the presence of Jews among the professions rose sharply, as well as in finance and academia, and significant Jewish communities grew up in St Petersburg, Moscow and Odessa. It was during this time that Russia's "Jewish question" took on a different coloring.

---

[1] Cf. Feliks Kandel', *Kniga vremyon i sobytii: istorii russkykh yevreev, 1.* Moscow, Gesharim: 2002. Ch.12 tells the harrowing story of these recruits, who were often as young as 7 or 8, and who were often forcibly converted whilst serving. 30, 000 Jews were "Christianized" in this way during Nicolas I's reign.

Under Alexander I, the government's reaction to the unprecedented number of Jews in Russian lands had been an optimistic policy of Christian mission and conversion. As the defender of Orthodoxy, the tsar aimed to foster the good will and subsequent conversion of Jewish communities by founding such societies as "The Society of Israelite Christians" for the support of Jewish converts. He also made the conduct of "ritual trials" for the investigation of so-called Jewish ritual murders of Christian children illegal. This was combined, however, with efforts to ban Jewish books, such as the Talmud and Zohar, which would delay the Christian enlightenment of the new population.

The effort was fairly half-hearted, however, and produced little effect. The next tsar, Nicolas I, then adopted a policy of oppressing the Jews through military conscription – pursuing by different means a similar aim to his predecessor: to hasten the "improvement," assimilation and disappearance of this suddenly sprung-up community of "Christ's enemies" on Russian soil[2].

It was only under Alexander II – who was to become for Jews, as well as for serfs, the "liberator tsar" – that for certain sections of the population, the status of Jews began to approach what had already long been the norm in Western Europe. Nonetheless, these reformist measures were also ultimately undertaken to benefit Russian society, which had suffered an economic and ideological setback after the defeat of Russia by Western powers in the Crimean war. The measures only allowed certain classes of Jews, namely merchants, manufacturers and artisans to settle outside the Pale, with the express aim of improving the economic conditions of the interior provinces; the vast majority of poverty-stricken Jews in the Pale were unaffected by the new legislation – and many of these would turn to radical political movements to vent their frustration.

As with other reforms of Alexander the effects of Jewish "liberation" were mixed. In the 1860s and 1870s, which overlapped with Soloviev's formative intellectual years, the reforms and the subsequent emergence of russified Jews at all levels of society provoked a backlash. These years coincided with the second wave of Slavophile philosophy, whose main proponents were Konstantin Aksakov and Yuri Samarin.

Whereas in the first wave of Slavophilism in the 1830s and 1840s, Jews had been sealed off from Russian cultural life, the rise of Russian-language Jewish papers and the appearance of Jews in the cities of the interior evoked a new type of reaction to Jews in Russian thought. Jews became a visible symbol of Alexander's reformist policies, and thus as in Western Europe, a target for conservatives who associated their freedom with the demise of old forms of power and belief.

Until then, Russian reactions to Jews had consisted of abstract theological images of Jews as "God-killers" and "enemies of Christ," drawn from Byzantine tradition. To this, it is true, had been added the Judaizing heresy that had spread from Novgorod and Pskov to Moscow in the fifteenth century, seducing among

---

[2] Brian Horowitz, p.c., remarks that recent research (by Petrovsky-Shern and Michael Stanislawski) reveals that Nicolas I was not as oppressive and cruel as previously imagined: his aim was, in principle, benign: to modernize the new population.

other members of the court, Grand Duke Ivan, who placed Judaizing bishops in charge of the Kremlin's cathedral. While the heresy's link with actual Jews was tenuous after its beginnings, and the heresy's Old Testament reformism was an old and constant tendency within Christianity itself, its very name[3] connected religious heresy and political sabotage with the image of Jews in the Russian imagination at a formative moment in Russian history.

To this anti-Judaism (or perhaps more accurately anti-anti-Trinitarian Christianity[4]), was added from Polish Catholicism the idea of Jews as religious fanatics and exploiters of the peasants – the latter especially was a favorite theme of Dostoevsky in his 1860s entries in his *Diary of a Writer*.

However, an entirely new note was added to this predominantly religious Russian anti-Judaism by Ivan Aksakov, the publicist brother of the Slavophile writer. From his reading of the French and German press, Aksakov took the modern Western European idea of a world conspiracy of the Jewish *race*. He also propagated the idea that the Jewish religion and race (the two were inextricable) were inherently hostile and opposed to Christianity.

However, Aksakov himself presents an interesting microcosm of the changes in perception towards Jews during the reign of Alexander II. He moved from the more traditional Russian anti-Judaism to the new-fangled Western anti-Semitism. In 1867, he wrote an article[5] reacting skeptically to the recent granting of rights to Jews. However, even though the article argues for the need to "emancipate" Russians from Jewish economic oppressors, the main thrust is that Jews need to be treated as a religion and not as a nationality. For Aksakov, it is unjust that Jews are granted the privileges to convene rabbinical courts and assemblies, rights which no one would think of granting to Lutherans or Catholics.

In that article, Aksakov supports "the sincerity of progressive Jews" who "who wish to merge with Russians, to earn the name of Russians of the Mosaic faith, to separate from their fanatical co-religionists," thus escaping the rabbis who are suppressing their own people. In other words, Aksakov's argument is with Judaism and not with Jews who wish to emancipate themselves, as he sees it, from that religion.

---

[3] In Old Russian, the heresy is called *zhidovstvuyshaya yeres*. The old Russian word "zhid" later became pejorative, and at least from the early nineteenth century corresponds in most cases to "Yid" or "kike." In later chapters, we will see how the use of *zhid* versus *yevrei* (non-pejorative 'Jew') continued to have a variety of emotional connotations in the work of nineteenth and twentieth century religious writers' reactions to the Jewish question.

[4] The hostility to heretical Christian sects, combated as religious and political enemies, often translated into attitudes towards the new "alien entity," Judaism. There were also, for example, blood libels against Christian sectarians – which resembled those brought against Jews. Cf. L.Katsis (2006) for a discussion of attitudes to Jews and Christian sectarians.

[5] Ivan Aksakov, "Ne ob emansipatsii yevreev sleduet tolkovat', a ob emansipatsii russkyx ot yevreev," in Rus' 15 July, 1867.

In 1883, however, his rhetoric has changed[6]. The intervening years had seen a rise in the number of Jews joining radical movements, from the populists to the social democrats. In addition, Alexander II, the great reformer, had been assassinated by such radicals, one of whom was a Jew. Now the new conception of a merciless world conspiracy of the Jewish people is developed. Judaism and Jewry are inseparable, and Judaism is "utilitarian" in ethics and "anti-mystical" in spirit – epithets associated with political and religious philosophies that were anathema to Slavophilism. Further, Russian liberals and radicals are all automatically Judophiles, identifying gladly with an ideology, which whether they are fully aware of it or not, undermines Russia and Christianity. They thereby play into the hands of the Jews, who influence them through their control of the press and the stock-exchange.

In examining the attitude of Russian religious thinkers to Judaism and Jews, both Aksakov's new anti-Semitism and the layers of that more archaic Russian anti-Judaism need to be kept in mind – as they continue to feed into the consciousness of all these figures from Soloviev to Karsavin, and even the Jewish-born Semyon Frank. A figure who combined the "new" and the "old" anti-Semitism was Dostoevsky, whose influence on Russian religious thought was as iconic as that of Soloviev. To a significant extent, these religious philosophers derive their basic principles for judging Judaism by swinging sometimes unpredictably between these two foundational personalities.

Soloviev himself reacted with repugnance to the new anti-Semitism, as we shall shortly see: it was a major reason for his break with the new hard-nosed nationalist "young" Slavophilism and the stimulus for a counter-active new type of Russian philo-Semitism. Nonetheless, Soloviev's celebrated philo-Semitism cannot be understood without bearing in mind that it too has deep traditional Russian Christian roots.

In this sense, the figure of St.Philaret of Moscow (1782-1867) is useful for comparison. His life and service in the church stretched from the incorporation of Jews into the empire until Alexander's reforms, and he outlived the four emperors who laid the foundations of Russia's policy to the Jews. In a certain sense, Philaret was friendly to Jews and supported Jewish rights.

In one sermon on Good Friday[7], he made it clear that the Jews were not responsible for crucifying Christ, for as the Savior Himself said: "They know not what they do." He intervened with Alexander I to soften the decree to ban all Jewish books. He persuaded Nicolas I to allow a Jewish secondary school in Riga a degree of self-determination, rather than having the school answer to the local bishop. And he argued for a loosening of the laws of

---

[6] Ivan Aksakov, "Vozzvaniye Kremyo, obrashennoe k yevream ot litsa 'Vsemirnirnogo Izrail'skogo Soyuza'," in Rus', 1. Nov.1883.

[7] Metropolitan Philaret (Drozdov), "Iz 'Slova v Velikuyu pyatnitsu,'" in Willem J. Vavilon i Ierusalim. Blizhnevostochnii konflikt v svete Biblii. Edited by D Radyshevski, 9-11. Moscow-Jerusalem: MCF, 2002.

travel for Jews outside of the Pale of Settlement[8].

All of these incidents have a twist, however: Philaret's beneficence towards Jews was part of that early optimistic groundswell of enthusiasm that believed the newly incorporated Jewish population would soon convert to Christianity. The reason he argued for a relaxation on the ban of Jewish books was that it demonstrated the problematic non-unity of Jewish tradition, and might thus weaken Jewish belief. The secondary school was to be granted independence, as Christian heavy-handedness would alienate Jews from Christianity. He concerned himself with Jewish travel rights when a scrupulous observance of the discriminatory laws interfered with the desire of several Jews to be baptized outside the Pale.

Philaret was a dynamic and, in his time, controversial figure, in the Russian Church. It was he who pioneered the translation of the Slavonic Bible into Russian, and issued the first Russian catechetical handbook for the spreading of the faith. Both of these measures met with opposition from conservative churchmen. It was also his evangelical zeal in a sometimes staid church that led him to embrace converted Jews and find a place for them in seminaries teaching Hebrew and Judaism and translating the liturgy and New Testament into Hebrew – all with the ultimate aim of spearheading that mission to the Jews of which Nicolas I had fondly but idly dreamed.

Thus, Philaret took the sudden intersection of Jewish and Russian fate with utmost zeal and seriousness, and was concerned for Jewish destiny. But, of course, this "philo-Semitism" came from a viewpoint that could hardly be regarded as amicable or beneficial by Jews concerned for their own interests.

Nonetheless, this makes him a precursor of Soloviev. The latter was more sympathetic to and interested in Judaism, and fought for Jews' rights regardless of whether they were considering conversion. And yet, Soloviev never hid his belief that what he desired above all was the same as Philaret: that which he saw as ultimately being best for Jews, their embrace of Christ.

This Christian philo-Semitism is met in other figures who fall outside the remit of this book, as they do not belong to the stream of Russian religious thought. They combined their ardent faith in Christ with a concern for the Jewish people. Often the doleful history of Russian anti-Semitism, replete with acts of discrimination, violence and persecution carried out in the name of the state religion of the empire, has led to an assumption that Russian Orthodox figures, especially conservative ones, were anti-Semitic by default.

While the imbalance of power between Jews and Christians before Alexander II, and to a large extent after his reforms, meant that many of these figures held unconscious prejudices with regard to Jews, the actions and opinions of several of the most outstanding figures in the Russian Church of the nineteenth and twentieth centuries refute an excessively hasty judgment about anti-Semitism in the church hierarchy.

---

[8]   For these incidents, cf. Konstantin Gavrilkin, "Mitropolit Filaret (Drozdov) i yevrei," in Kontinent No.111. (2002).

St. Theophan the Recluse (1815-1894), along with St.Philaret, one of the major figures involved in church education in the nineteenth century, argued for the judicious use of the Hebrew Bible alongside the traditional Septuagint in training Orthodox lay and clergy in the faith[9]. His interpretation on the ninth to eleventh "Jewish" chapters of St.Paul's letter to the Romans is also outspokenly generous to the Jews[10]. His reading of this key passage, which we will encounter time and again in the work of Russian religious philosophers, holds that Jews continue to be God's chosen people, who have been temporarily excluded only in order to bring truth to the gentiles. The small number of Jews who accepted Christ in Paul's time brought about the foundation of world Christianity. "What then," asks Theophan, "will happen when they all believe?" For "of all the nations, none can fulfill better than them God's intentions for the salvation of people." Hence "it is impossible not to care for them and worry about them."

Another example is John of Kronstadt, who has earned a reputation as an anti-Semite due to the use that was made of his name by right-wing organizations at the end of his life[11]: and yet he delivered a sermon in reaction to the 1903 Kishinev pogrom sharply condemning the "satanic" violence of the pogromites, and urging his "Russian brothers" to act in accordance with the spirit of humility and patience and respect innocent Jewish life[12].

Metropolitan Anthony Khrapovitsky, who became the head of the conservative, monarchist Russian Church Abroad in exile on several occasions met rabbles intent on committing a pogrom and by his spiritual authority persuaded them to turn back. In 1905, the strict and conservative Kiev priest, Mikhail Yedlinsky (1859-1937)[13], went out at the head of a religious procession

---

[9] Metropolitan Theophan. *O mere upotrebleniya yevreiskogo nynyeshnogo teksta, po-ukazaniyu tserkovnoy praktiki*, in Tserkovniy Vestnik, 1876, No.23, 12 June: 1-5.

[10] Metroplitan Theophan. "Iz tolkovaniya na XI Poslaniya k Rimlyanam svyatogo apostola Pavla," in Willem J. *Vavilon i Ierusalim. Blizhnevostochnii konflikt v svete Biblii*, ed. D.Radyshevski. Moscow-Jerusalem: MCF, 2002.

[11] For more details on the distortion of John of Krontstadt's teachings by his self-proclaimed followers, the "Johannites," cf. Nadezhda Kitsenko. *Svaytoi nashego vremeni: otets Ioann Kronshtadtskii i russkii narod.* (Moscow: Novoe Literaturnoe Obozrenie, 2006).

[12] "O how thunderously Christ would have forbidden the Kishinev thugs from killing Jewish townsmen and from smashing and destroying their property. Do you know, Russian brothers, of what spirit you are? Do not offend anybody for any reason. Love your enemies, bless those who curse you, bless those who hate you, and pray for those who offend you (Mt.5:44). That is my short Gospel word, Russian brothers, on account of the bloody massacres of the Jews and their children, who are guilty of nothing. Amen." The quote from Matthew may imply that Jews are somehow "enemies;" for John of Kronstadt, in a certain theological senses that was the case – but as the entire context makes clear, in terms of action and peaceful co-habitation Jews are fellow townsmen, to be equally respected as Russian brothers, and moreover they are not "guilty" of anything – such as the murder of Christ etc.

[13] He was imprisoned and shot by Stalin in 1937. He did charitable work among

to confront a mob intent on committing violence in the Jewish quarter, and forced them to disband.

There are odder stories too, like that of Mikhail Pavlovich Polyanovskii, a general in the army of Alexander II[14]. In his love for the Jews, he imagined the day when an Orthodox Jewish Church would be founded, so that Jews could be Christian without losing their culture and identity. In fact, Polyanovskii was born into a poor Jewish family and seized by the Cantonists when he was seven. Losing contact for many years with his Jewish family, and climbing higher up the echelons of the army, he eventually became a sincerely believing Christian, and yet never lost his loyalty to the Jewish people.

In one man there were combined two deeply different experiences: that of a persecuted minority and that of the ruling majority. According to rabbinic law, he was quite literally a *tinoq shenishbah*[15], i.e. an apostate from Judaism who cannot be blamed as he apostasized against his will. And yet Polyanovskii resisted that judgment, embracing his new faith with utter devotion, which owed nothing to the desire to find a place in Russian society.

Thus, although the abhorrent position of the new Jewish minority in the Russian Christian empire very often led to the compromising of the Christian religion, there were cases of sincere belief by Christians in the theological superiority of their faith to that of the Jews, which did not lead to attacks – verbal or physical – on the humanity of the latter.

After the assassination of Alexander II, the Russian Church lost much of its zeal for converting the Jews. What came afterwards highlights that for all the heavy-handedness of Philaret's approach, it was well-intentioned. For the new Ober-Procurator of the Holy Synod, Konstantin Pobedonostsev[16], changed the missionizing policy of the Russian Church towards Jewry, replacing it with defensiveness. In the last years of the nineteenth century and the first decade of the twentieth century, Russia became an unenviable centre of anti-Semitic propaganda, manufactured by church figures close to the government, often converted Jews who – unlike Polyanovskii – had a psychotic hatred of their past lives[17].

---

workers in Kiev. Cf. Anotoly Zhurakovsky, *My dolzhny vsyo preterpet' radi Khrista: zhizn', podvig i trudy svyashchenika Anatoliya Zhurakovskogo* (Moscow: PSTGU, 2008).

[14] Archbishop Ioann Shakhovskoy, *Ustanovlenie yedinstva* (Moscow: Sretinskii Monastyr, 2006), 184.

[15] Heb.: "a child who is captured."

[16] He was famous for his dictum that the ideal solution to the Jewish question would be for "one third to die, one third to emigrate, and one third to assimilate without trace." Less than four decades after he made this remark, one third of the Jews in the territory of the former Pale of Settlement did indeed "die" in the Nazi genocide.

[17] One such early figure was Yakov Brafman (1825-1879), baptized in 1858. He was more extreme that Aksakov in his creation of an anti-Semitic cocktail that would eventually be used by the author of *The Protocols of the Elders of Zion*: world conspiracy, rabbinic misanthropy, blood libel, calumny of the Talmud. (His grandson was the

Nonetheless, even with the growing fear of revolution infecting church circles that new defensiveness often expressed itself – in contradistinction to Aksakov's first stage – as a tolerance, and sometimes even admiration[18], for traditional Jewry and Judaism and a distaste for emancipated liberal Jews, whom traditional church figures now associated with radicalism. This support for traditional Jewry, which to some extent was a recognition of the stalemate in the attempt at conversion, often coincided with the interests and beliefs of traditional Jewish leaders themselves. The latter were just as keen to stop the assimilation of their youth and their infatuation with atheistic ideas.

In the remainder of this chapter and throughout this book, we will focus on one aspect of Russian Jewish-Christian relations in the period after Alexander II's assassination and up to the middle of the twentieth century. In terms of the number of individuals considered here, and indeed the layer of Russian society to which they belonged, this encounter among the Russian "spiritual intelligentsia" is objectively rather narrow. And yet encounters which passed "undigested" in the wider society were analyzed in depth by these figures in terms of the new theologies and philosophies they were trying to forge.

In addition, these figures have once again attracted lively interest in the Russian Orthodox church in post-Soviet Russia, as well as in other non-Russian and non-Orthodox churches. Their heritage continues to be absorbed and debated, and their relevance can be assessed simply by considering the large quantities of their books being printed and sold in contemporary Russia – in commercial as well as church bookshops.

Unfortunately, as regards the Jewish question, there is little critical evaluation of this material which includes a spectrum of views from Soloviev's philo-Semitism to Rozanov's Judeophobia. In the explosion of liberty since the disintegration of communism, it is also common to find in Moscow bookshops tomes arguing for a re-opening of the case against Mendel Beilis and the canonization of Andrei Yushchinsky[19] standing next to scholarly volumes by

---

poet Vladislav Khodasevich, on whom cf. ch.3 for his attempts to make amends for the anti-Semitism of his grandfather by translating Hebrew poets into Russian).

[18] Nicanor, Bishop of Kherson and Odessa (1883-1890), gave a sermon on the consecration of the church of the Odessa commercial college in whose building "Russians not only of the Christian but also the Mosaic law" had enthusiastically participated, where he draws detailed parallels between Judaism and Christianity, and refers to Jews as brothers of Christians, not only in spirit but in flesh and vice versa. Others contrasted the enthusiastic observance by Jews of Jewish law and festivals with the lax observance by Christians of church holidays and practices. Archbishop Nicanor, "Iz poucheniya pri osvyashchenii tserkvi Odesskogo komercheskogo uchilishcha," in Willem J. *Vavilon i Ierusalim. Blizhnevostochnii konflikt v svete Biblii*, edited by D.Radyshevski, (Moscow-Jerusalem: MCF, 2002), 20-23.

[19] The boy allegedly ritually murdered by Beilis and shadowy Jewish associates, but even before the trial known to have been murdered by members of a criminal gang whose secrets he had become privy to. Cf.ch.4 for details and a discussion of Rozanov's and Florensky's writings connected to the "Beilis affair" as it came to be

Jewish authors on aspects of Russian-Jewish history. However, some of that chaotic mix of attitudes to the "Jewish question" is not unknown within the writings of Silver Age[20] authors themselves – Rozanov, of course, being the most obvious example. Thus part of the aim of this book is to evaluate these writings both in their original context and as they can speak to us now.

For an Orthodox Christian, finally, there is another question that must be addressed. This is the relationship of Russian religious philosophy to Christian theology. In this sense, these thinkers' writings on Judaism, the Old Testament and contemporary Jewry are often situated in the cross-roads between traditional Christian dogma, Russian and European ideology about Jewry (which had its origins in a range of social, economic and cultural developments), and the neo-pagan tendencies of the turn-of-the-century symbolist literary movement[21].

The Jewish question sometimes enables dissections to be made that in other areas of thought are subtler and trickier to perform: as we will see in the chapter on Pavel Florensky, many thinkers had long been worried by Gnostic and even occultist tendencies in this priest-philosopher's thought. The discovery of letters written to Rozanov during the Beilis trial reveal that he also embraced a racist anti-Semitism, which he attempted to derive and justify from a reading of select Old and New Testament passages. Here clearly, the pseudo-Christian justification of the "new anti-Semitism" can be shown to be incompatible even with the, by comparison, benign *religious* anti-Judaism of the church fathers.

The appraisal of Russian religious philosophy through the lens of the Jewish question also raises philosophical questions: can there be a "national" philosophy as the term Russian philosophy indicates? If so, how does it differ from Jewish philosophy?

The four (or three and half) Jewish thinkers examined here (Gershenzon, Steinberg, Shestov – and Frank, for certain purposes) are also interesting from the point of view of Jewish history. All of them were Jews who benefited from Alexander II's reforms, joining the mass influx of Jews into the Russian professional class. Thus their stories comprise an aspect of Russian-Jewish history. As the term "Russian-Jewish" indicates, however, in entering Russian society to an extent that was impossible for their parents, they also became deeply Russified. Thus the question of what is Russian and Jewish in their thought arises again in sharper form.

---

called, by analogy with the earlier Dreyfus Affair in France.

[20] The Silver Age refers to the flourishing of Russian literature, poetry and religious thought during the last two decades of the nineteenth century until the Russian Revolution. The "Golden Age" would then be that explosion of literary genius starting from Pushkin and running till Dostoevsky.

[21] We draw on the judgments of several contemporary Russian philosophers and religious thinkers to evaluate Silver Age thought, who judge by philosophical as well as "Christian" criteria. For a purely "Christian" judgment on Soloviev, Berdyaev, and Shestov by a recent Church figure, cf. Hieromonakh Dmitri (Zakharov), *Vsyo obretaet smysl*, Moscow: Fond "Khristianskaya zhizn," 2000 – pp.109-123.

Again, the examination of four Russian-Jewish intellectuals is objectively a small number. Nonetheless, they were representative of that section of Jewry that chose embrace of Russian culture over Zionism, bundism, emigration, radical politics or the practice of Judaism in one or another form. As such, theirs is a Jewish story – even if for them the Jewish and Russian influenced each other to such an extent that they became indistinguishable at times.

Still, as in political and economic life, so in intellectual life the boundaries between the Russian and Jewish depended on who was doing the drawing. While for some, political radicalism was archetypically and dangerously Jewish, and for others quintessentially Russian in spirit – so in philosophy, metaphysical immanentism – to take a case in point – was for some[22] a dangerous Jewish error and for others the very expression of the Eastern Russian religious spirit. In contrast, for others it was transcendentalism that was labeled accordingly. Even in philosophy, then, it would seem that Jews were both "communists" and "capitalists," i.e. bearers of seemingly incompatible traits.

With this background in mind, we will turn to a more detailed consideration of Vladimir Soloviev, the father of Russian religious philosophy and the – not always heeded – conscience of the intelligentsia when it came to the Jewish question of Russia.

Soloviev's general development

Soloviev's life can be conveniently divided into three stages, coinciding approximately with the seventies, eighties and nineties of the nineteenth century[23]. We will outline these stages briefly, before seeing how his writings on Jews and Judaism form a part of this development.

In his first stage, Soloviev embraced the early Slavophiles' attempt to find a new synthesis of human knowledge, which following Khomiakov, he called "integral knowledge" (*tselnoe znaniye*). His Moscow University dissertation, *The Crisis of Western Philosophy: Against the Positivists* was published in 1873. It was in fact his own attempt to overcome the crisis of faith he had undergone during his last years at school, when he had identified as an atheist and a nihilist.

The 1860s in Russia had seen the flourishing of positivism, materialism and utilitarianism in the works of radicals and nihilists such as N.K.Mikhailovsky (1842-1904), D.I.Pisarev (1840-1868), the radical democrat and materialist N.G. Chernyshevsky (1828-1889), as well as in the liberal ideology of Westernizers

---

[22] As we will see the charge of "immanentism" was in fact not directed at Jews in Russian philosophy: this was deemed Jewish by orthodox Protestants reacting to Spinozism in German romanticism. Russian philosophers considered a transcendental view of the deity Jewish.

[23] Frank sees Soloviev as going through three stages, Vasilenko through four; Marina Kostalevsky emphasizes the continuity that existed between the different stages. (Cf. Marina Kostalevsky, *Dostoevsky and Soloviev. The Art of Integral Vision*. New Haven: Yale University Press, 1997.)

such as P.L. Lavrov and A.Herzen. Both the second-wave Slavophiles, and in the same spirit, Soloviev, went back to Khomiakov and Kireevsky to find a Russian answer to this crisis of faith.

In two ways, Soloviev's emergence into philosophy preempted the later development of his heirs. They too all passed through an infatuation with philosophical materialism, most often of the Marxist variety. In addition, Soloviev's initial philosophical inspiration – as had been the case with the early Slavophiles – was deeply indebted to the German romanticist-idealists such as Hegel, Schopenhauer, Hartmann and Schelling. However, for present purposes the most significant hero in Soloviev's gallery of philosophers, whom he called "my first philosophical love" was Spinoza.

Already in his first descriptions[24] of all-unity, Spinoza's monistic influence is strongly felt in Soloviev's characterization of all-unity as consisting of an absolute and true being – "absolute substance," the "all-unified first principle," the *hen kai pan*[25] – that embraces and generates out of its "positive nothingness" that "real being" which is the physical-sensual world. Human thought must move from a rational understanding of this lower real being to a mystical intuition of this upper but connected absolute being, and thus merge with the truly essential, or God.

Of course, these pantheistic elements are found in Schelling and Hegel as well – but there too, the sometimes covert influence of Spinoza can be felt.[26]

---

[24] *The Crisis of Western Philosophy* (1874), *The Philosophical Principles of Integral Knowledge* (1877), *The Lectures on God-Manhood* (1878) and *The Critique of Abstract Principles* (1880). For these early essays, see Vladimir Soloviev, *Sobranie sochineniy. Tom 1,* edited by Ernst L. Radlow. St Petersburg, 1901.

[25] Gk. "One and all."

[26] Yirmiyahu Yovel's excellent study on Spinoza (and other Spanish-Dutch-Jewish thinkers) shows how deep his influence was on German figures such as Hegel and Feuerbach. (Yirmiyahu Yovel, *Spinoza and Other Heretics. The Marrano of Reason*; and Yirmiyahu Yovel, *Spinoza and Other Heretics. The Adventures of Immanence.* Princeton, Princeton University Press: 1989.) Yovel also sees Spinoza as the first "secular" Jew in history, and uncovers how his Marrano heritage, with its skepticism regarding both a recently discarded Catholicism and an unenthusiastically re-embraced Judaism, was instrumental in shaping his pantheistic, critical worldview, intended as an alternative to both mainstream religions. As we will see, Spinoza's "immanentist Jewish" influence can be felt quite distinctively in Soloviev, as well as in Frank, Karsavin and Florensky. It should also be remembered, however, (taking Yovel in a somewhat different direction) that underlying Spinoza's surface Rationalism and "secularism," there is a powerful alternative religiosity, which is what was most admired by the Solovievian school. It may not be far wrong to see this, too, as an – albeit highly individualistic – expression of Jewish religiosity, consisting in a thirst for the unity of God and Being, which shares the same reformist and mystical tendencies as the Kabbalistic theosophy that was being developed by other exiled Spanish Jews at the same time (such as Luria and Cordovero). Cf. below for more on Spinozism, Kabbalism and Soloviev.

Soloviev's new and self-proclaimed *Russian* "integral knowledge," even at its inception, thus shares with German mysticism a direct genealogy that leads to the monism of the heterodox Amsterdam Jew.

At this stage of his development, the discovery of Jewish affinities was not high on Soloviev's agenda. Indeed, the purpose of Soloviev's Russian all-unity had a specifically Christian apologetic purpose. Christianity was to be instrumental in the attainment of this integral knowledge, and at the same time Soloviev saw his life as being devoted to the task, as he wrote to his fiancée, of "raising Christianity from blind traditional faith to the level of rational conviction" by creating a new Christian philosophy whose credibility would help overcome the fashion for atheism and materialism.

In the 1870s Soloviev's all-unity had a Russian angle that was also taken from the Slavophiles. The attainment of integral knowledge would be realized through the Messianic task of Russian Christianity: the Russian Church's historic mission was to overcome the split between East and West, thus realizing all-unity on earth, due to the special nature of Russia and her people as intermediaries between the East and the West. For in Russia the Eastern tendency to despotism and the Western tendency towards rampant individualism are harmoniously avoided.

The Slavophile orientation of Soloviev's first stage of development is not contradicted by the fact that he includes Kabbalistic terminology in the construction of his new Christian philosophy. It was in *The Philosophical Principles of Integral Knowledge* that Soloviev used the term "Ein Sof" (Heb. "without end, infinite") to describe the "positive nothingness" of the ground of being, i.e. to construct an apophatic theology of the unknowability of the Divine essence before creation. In the same period, he was also developing the Kabbalistic term "Adam Kadmon" (Heb. "primordial man/Adam") to describe the supernal man, or Logos, who was an intermediary between the unknowable divinity (the Ein Sof) and the world. Finally, it was in this first stage that Soloviev was developing the concept that was to prove his greatest heirloom: the concept of Sophia-Chochma (the Divine wisdom). This in particular was to become an intimate part of his mystical and literary life due to the famous three visions he had of a mysterious woman, whom he identified as her embodiment– a subject, however, that we will treat at greater length below.

One needs to see Soloviev's early Kabbalistic "activism" in the proper light. At this Christian-Slavophile stage of his development, it would be wrong to see this as a drawing close to Jewish sources and a special openness to Judaism and Jewry. As Burmistrov points out[27], while Soloviev undoubtedly did study Kabbalistic texts in translation and in Hebrew at this time, these concepts were also to be found in Jacob Boehme and Emmanuel Swedenborg, Western European mystics for whose work Soloviev had the greatest admiration. In

---

[27] Konstantin Burmistrov, "The interpretation of Kabbalah in early 20th-Century Russian Philosophy. Soloviev, Bulgakov, Florenskii, Losev," in *East European Jewish Affairs*, Vol.37, No.2, August 2007:157-187.

addition, Soloviev significantly changed the concept of the Ein Sof and Adam Kadmon, so that it is clear that Kabbalah was merely a secondary source for his own Christian inspiration, to be adapted as necessary[28]. In that sense, Soloviev's interest in Kabbalah in the 1870s was part of the broader trend among the Russian intelligentsia of the time to dabble in Kabbalah, theosophy, occultism and masonry.

Still, even if Soloviev's Kabbalistic sources in the seventies were received to some extent through secondary sources, Boehme and Swedenborg themselves were part of that trend of Christian kabbalah whose roots went back to a very genuine immersion in Jewish mystical sources in the Renaissance. Soloviev may thus have been quite some way "downstream" from these originals, but – as with the influence of Spinoza, both in direct form and through "Spinozised" German romanticism – this first stage of Soloviev's development laid a convert Judaic ground in his thinking, which he would later appropriate when he did in fact turn consciously to Russia's "Jewish question."

Just such a reorientation was marked by Soloviev's second stage of development, which began with a serious revision of his idealization of Russia. The change of mind was triggered by the events that followed on from the assassination of Alexander II, a period which ushered in a mood of gloom throughout Russia. It was also the beginning of the long history of anti-Jewish violence that would last until the Civil War: pogroms broke out in Kherson, Odessa and Kiev in the wake of the assassination.

There was a new aspect to the violence, however. The authorities were confused as to the meaning of the pogroms, and feared most of all that they were part of the same revolutionary terrorism that had killed Alexander II and of which the new tsar was terrified. The government thus decided to appropriate the outbreaks for its own purposes, and a commission was launched into what peculiar practices of the Jews could have provoked such behavior on the part of Christian peasants[29]. The government, in other words, was quick to put itself on

---

[28] Burmistrov writes that Soloviev Christianized these Kabbalistic concepts, as did the Renaissance Christian Kabbalists. To an extent this is true. But it needs to be kept in mind that in a serious sense, all these Christian Kabbalists (Mirandello de Pico, Boehme, Swedenborg, and Soloviev) departed significantly from Christian dogma in creating their theosophic science. In Boehme and in some places in Soloviev, the Ein Sof becomes a divine essence that precedes the persons of the Trinity; Soloviev also equated Adam Kadmon with Christ and with the Logos, differentiating these three from the historical Jesus. Both these undogmatic moves led to the creation of what one might call a "trans-Christian" theosophy, in the sense that it holds that all humans have Christ-ian/ "Adam-Kadmonic" souls. As we will see later, this more open, less dogmatic "trans-Christianity" was also attractive to Jews interested in Russian philosophy (such as S.Frank, and one might add Osip Mandelstam, who was attracted by Florensky's sophianic philosophy). In this sense, this "trans-Christianizing" of more orthodox Christian dogma can be said to be, in indirect origin, Judaic.

[29] John Klier and Shlomo Lambroza, ed., *Pogroms: anti-Jewish violence in modern*

the side of the *pogromshchiki* and disperse any revolutionary use the violence could be put to. This would set a grim precedent. Under Alexander III and then Nicholas II, government-sponsored or -tolerated anti-Semitic propaganda assumed the time-honored role of deflecting attention from the inadequacies of the ruling regime.

On the other hand, the assassination of Alexander II gave Soloviev the opportunity to test his idea that Russia was a prototype of harmonious Christian all-unity by making a plea in 1881 to Alexander III to forgive his father's assassins. That plea was rejected, however, and he was forbidden from lecturing at Moscow University. Although the ban was only temporary, such was Soloviev's disillusionment that he immediately resigned his post.

In the coming years, this disillusionment only deepened. The closing of ranks of Slavophiles such as Aksakov with the government in a rampant condoning of anti-Jewish violence in the coming years left a bad taste in Soloviev's mouth. He now began to view the Slavophile idealization of Russia as idolatrous: admiration for the Christian faith of the simple Russian people had turned into an uncritical faith in the people themselves, whatever they may do or believe.

He thus began to look Westwards for Christian inspiration, and there followed nearly a decade in which Soloviev tried to realize his vision of human and church unity by engaging in a campaign for the unification of the Eastern Orthodox and Roman Catholic Churches. In so doing, he was trying to put into practice the ideas which he had previously outlined in theory: the concept of pan-unity, god-manhood, and Christian theocracy under the influence of Divine Wisdom.

For Soloviev, the Jewish Question in the heightened form it had taken in the eighties fitted organically into this stage of his quest: the split between Orthodox and Catholic which he was trying by means of active "Christian politics" to heal was a consequence of the earlier schism in the church between Jewish and gentile Christians. It was for him a fact of great significance that Providence had placed the greatest concentration of Jews in the world at the divide between the Christian East and West (the Pale of Settlement, which lay between Catholic Poland and Orthodox Russia). Thus, as he saw it, if the East-West schism could be healed, the healing of the Jewish Question would surely follow.

Soloviev threw himself into a decade-long one-man campaign to overcome that schism. Perhaps the most dramatic moment in that struggle was his approach through a Croat bishop to Pope Leo XIII with a scheme for a reconciliation with Eastern Orthodoxy under the aegis of Alexander III. The pope, however, on learning of Soloviev's idea was not convinced[30], and in the coming years Soloviev's enthusiasm for his theocratic project ground to a halt. We will dwell

---

Russian history, 39.

[30] As Frank recounts, Pope Leo XIII said: 'Bella idea, ma fuor d'un miracolo, e cosa impossibile.' (A beautiful idea but short of a miracle, impossible to carry out.) Semyon Frank, introduction to *A Solovyov Anthology*, edited by S.Frank (London: The Saint Austin Press, 2001), 18-19.

more on Soloviev's second stage when we consider his Jewish writings.

This failure ushered in the third stage of Soloviev's development, which also coincided with the death of the woman he was intimately, though fruitlessly involved with. This was a period of pessimism as far as the grand goals of the previous two decades were concerned. According to Frank, it was a period of disillusionment with official Christianity whether in Eastern or Western guise. Having denounced Eastern Orthodox Caesaropapism and Western Catholic legalism, Soloviev saw himself as above any institutional church.

However, Frank's reading of Soloviev's final stage of development is not the only one. Soloviev's peripatetic lifestyle, which included legendary acts of generosity that often left him penniless, contributed to his early death, and it is not fully clear in what further direction his thought would have developed. As a result, his heritage was divided in different ways. Frank's description of Soloviev's final stage curiously mirrors his own: he too had become to believe that the true church could not be found within the boundaries of any earthly denomination. Catholics for their part became convinced that Soloviev's Roman turn in the 1880s had left a permanent imprint and that he died a confessing member of the Catholic Church[31].

Others, such as Alexander Blok, would later see the true meaning of Soloviev's legacy in his political theocracy. On this reading, Soloviev was a herald of the Scythian movement that Blok and others founded in revolutionary Russia as a spiritual complement to Bolshevism. For Bulgakov and Berdyaev, Soloviev on the contrary had been prophesying against the type of Godless cataclysm that the Russian revolution represented.

A contemporary interpreter, L.Vasilenko[32], takes the view that the final period of Soloviev's life was marked by a sober recognition that his one-man campaign to rectify all the wrongs of universal Christendom were mistaken and that, for all her faults, the Russian Orthodox Church was his mother-church and the ultimate repository of truth. This interpretation, in fact, has much to recommend it, and this new theological realism is reflected in his depiction of the Jews in his final work, the "Short Story of the Anti-Christ," which will be discussed below.

Soloviev, the Jews and Judaism
The flawed wholeness of the Jewish nation
Soloviev's Jewish essays belong to his second ecumenical-"theocratic" stage, being written in the 1880s. The two main works on which we will comment are: "The Jews and the Christian Question" (1884) and "The Talmud and the Recent Polemical Literature about it in Austria and Germany" (1885).

---

[31] This belief that Soloviev became a Catholic is decisively refuted by Frank, but was believed by among other Hans Urs von Balthasar.
[32] L.I. Vasilenko, *Vvedenie v russkuyu religioznuyu filofiyu*. (Moscow: PSTGU, 2006), ch.6.

Soloviev also touched on Jewish issues, especially as they related to the concept of spiritual nationhood which was to be a model for Russia, in other major works produced at this time: "The National Question in Russia" (1883), "The Great Dispute and Christian politics" (1883) and "The Philosophy of Biblical Theocracy" (1886). Another significant article is "The New Testament Israel," written in December 1885, and detailing Soloviev's reactions to the "Messianic Jewish" community of J.Rabinowitz.

As Judith Kornblatt[33] has convincingly demonstrated, Soloviev's writings on the Jewish question in this period are not merely incidental to his philosophy but a grindstone on which he sharpened his whole world view. The works on Judaism were produced simultaneously with the works in which he developed the key concepts of his philosophy: the concept of integral wholeness (*tsel'nost'*); the difference between positive nationhood (*narodnost'*) and negative nationalism (*natzionalism*); and theocracy (*teokratia*) and godmanhood (*bogochelovechestvo*). It was also during this period that he began his intensive study of Hebrew and Jewish sources, and they were to provide him with additional tools to forge an alternative vision of Russia and the world than those provided by Slavophile thought.[34]

This deepening of his acquaintance with Jewish sources was aided by his friendship with Faival Gets, who became his Hebrew instructor: from 1879 the two studied Bible and Talmud in Hebrew in the traditional pairwise Yeshiva manner. And yet, odd as it may seem, Burmistrov makes a good point when he writes that "Soloviev's Jewish studies prevented him from becoming acquainted with genuine Jewish mysticism." This is because Gets was a *maskil*, that is, a representative of the rational enlightenment trend in nineteenth century Jewish thought, and frowned on the irrational Kabbalah.

Again, one can qualify this by pointing out that while Soloviev's acquaintance with Gets may have not deepened his contact with genuine Kabbalah, from the point of view of his own self-identity and "Jewish" consciousness (he once told Nicolai Lossky "I am a Jew"), these studies exerted a great influence. One can take Burmistrov's point even further: as we will see, Gets' maskilic influence seems to have steered Soloviev away from the non-rationalistic parts of the Talmud as well, so that even in this respect, one may question the genuiness of Soloviev's Jewish knowledge[35]. But the same judgment applies: regardless of content, Soloviev's

---

[33] Judith Kornblatt, "Vladimir Soloviev on Spiritual Nationhood, Russia and the Jews," *Russian Review* 56/2 (1997): 157-77. In the following two paragraphs I draw on several of her insights.

[34] Hamutal Bar-Yosef even refers to Soloviev's absorption of Jewish sources as his "attempt to bring Russian Christianity nearer to Judaism, and even to Judaize Christianity." There might be something in this. The reader can judge from what is presented below. Hamutal Bar-Yosef, "The Jewish reception of Vladimir Solovyov." In *Vladimir Solovyov: Reconciler and Polemicist*, ed. Ewert von Zweerde, (Peeters, Lewen, 2000), section 4.

[35] An interesting – though also biased – "corrective" to this is Rozanov, who approaches

contact with his Jewish teacher and his studying of Jewish texts certainly convinced Soloviev that he was engaged in a Jewish project[36], which was connected to his revision of Western as well as Russian philosophical trends.

Turning next to these Jewish texts of the 1880s, one sees that immersion in Jewish esoteric knowledge and personal friendship with his Jewish teacher continued to co-exist with the harsh rhetoric of traditional Christian anti-Judaism. To a certain extent, the above qualifications explain this: Soloviev's fairly standard belief of the time that Kabbalah was not related to genuine Judaism would not have been significantly corrected by Gets; and his previous Slavophile convictions could not be sloughed off in one go. Thus Soloviev's reading of Jewish texts is undoubtedly a part of his internal self-definition, so that his reading of Jewish texts and the "Jewish question" contain much traditional Russian and Christian "reading into" to the material – with the result that hostile and sympathetic reactions sometimes co-exist uneasily.

In "The Jews and the Christian Question," Soloviev expounded his famous idea that there is no "Jewish question" as such in Russia; rather the failure of Russians to treat Jews justly constitutes a burning "Christian question," which concerns the problematic failure of Christians to live up to the demands of their religion. Nonetheless, Soloviev takes it for granted that Jewish suffering is a result of their rejection of Christianity and the fact that they have "not subordinated carnal reason to the knowledge of the truth."

In a pattern which recalls what we saw in Philaret and Theophan, the concern for and defense of Jews is combined with a recognition of their faults and their need for redemption. Soloviev, like Theophan, weaves into his essay Paul's letters to the Romans, which he interprets in a similarly optimistic light, as far as the ultimate eschatological fate of Jewry is concerned, for: "The best elements among the Jews will enter the Christian theocracy, and the worst will remain outside, and only at the end, having suffered retribution in accordance with God's justice, shall be saved through His mercy – for St Paul's words that 'all Israel shall be saved' are sure."

Meanwhile, Jewish suffering – while not to be further inflamed by Christians who have rejected the Gospel call to mercy – has a certain divine logic, as the Jews "did not want to understand the Cross of Christ, and so for the last eighteen centuries they have against their will been bearing their own heavy cross.... The Cross of Christ...demanded of the Jewish people a twofold effort: first, to renounce their national egotism, and secondly, to renounce temporarily their worldly strivings and their attachment to worldly welfare...."

Thus, in one sense, Soloviev's anti-Jewish rhetoric draws on the same sources as were used by Judeophobes such as Aksakov – whose influence in the Russian press Soloviev was trying to counter. Both Aksakov and Soloviev were

---

Judaism initially through the most non-rational parts of the Talmud, then being translated into Russian by Pereferkovich. Cf. ch.4.

[36] This self-consciousness would have an objective influence on his heirs, who were not necessarily in a position to judge Jewish genuineness.

in agreement that the Jews displayed "national egotism" and an "attachment to worldly welfare." It would seem that they only differed in their proposed reaction to this: Soloviev recommended Christian forbearance and love; Aksakov a limitation of rights and further confinement for this threat to Russia's interests.

However, in the same essay, Soloviev adds a different note to this Christian anti-Judaism, when he tries to answer the question of why, given all their faults, the Jews were chosen by God. Importantly, his reading of *Romans* implies a belief that the Jews *continue* to be chosen. On this theological point, he is at one with Theophan, and at odds with the Judeophobes – who could not countenance the idea that Russia's enemies could have a place, and a central one, in God's scheme for human salvation[37].

In answering this question, Soloviev widens the gap between himself and the so-called Christian Judeophobes. For he goes on to outline a theory of the national character of the Jews, which – in contrast to the previous negative rhetoric – shows why the Jews, in Theophan's words, "can fulfill...God's intentions for the salvation of people" better than all other nations. For like Theophan, Soloviev was convinced that God's election of the Jews was not random, but deliberate.

Within Christian writings on Jewry, this is an important distinction: as we will have reason to see in detail in later chapters, all Orthodox Christian thought that bases itself on the New Testament and patristic writings cannot but see in Jewish exile a divine punishment. In this, in fact, it is no different from traditional Orthodox Jewish theology. However, when Christian thinkers take the concept of divine Jewish punishment back before the time of Christ, they thereby undermine the roots of their own Old Testament, and anti-Judaism quickly turns into anti-Semitism.

Soloviev, unlike the nationalists, avoids this. His conviction is that the recipients of the Old Testament revelation must have attracted God's favor for a special reason. To think otherwise would be to distort the image of God, for God's revelations cannot be arbitrary, still less can they be forced on humanity. Instead, humanity must be capable of responding to God if its freedom is to be preserved. This brings Soloviev to the important theme of human personality, and in the case of the Jews the characteristics of their national personality.

The three traits Soloviev attributes to the Jews are intended to answer this old question, and they are: innate faith or religiosity; an intense and self-conscious personality; and "sacred materialism." In combination, these produce

---

[37] It is possible to read to read Romans 9-11 as meaning that the Jews are no longer chosen. A certain amount of theological good will is needed to interpret these chapters in favor of Jewish chosenness, as well as a theological framework to imagine how such chosenness combines with the existence of the Church, who is the New Israel. This will be discussed in more length in later chapters. For examples of "non-chosen" readings of Romans, cf. especially the discussion on Florensky in the second part of ch.4.

the right positive national character which made the Jews suitable to receive Divine revelation[38].

The first trait is self-explanatory. The second trait Soloviev explains as follows: Jews are extremely self-aware and self-assertive in their national, family and personal lives. This strength of self was necessary for receiving Revelation so as to avoid the "annihilation of man in universal divinity" (as happened among the Indians) and to allow "personal interaction between the divine and the human self." This healthy respect for self induced Abraham while he was still living among pagans, to become discontented with the worship of objects lower than man and to seek "for a personal and moral God, faith in whom would not be humiliating to man."

Thus the Jew sought God and God revealed Himself to him[39]. The Jewish personality was thus able avoid "the two extreme errors of paganism in which man is either engulfed by the deity (India) or the Deity itself becomes the reflection of man (in Greece and Rome)," and thus Judaism constituted an entirely new religion in world history.

Only in this new Jewish religion are "both sides…equally preserved throughout – both the human and the divine." This *tsel'nost'* (integrity, wholeness) of the Jewish character is what makes God-manhood possible, i.e. a meeting

---

[38] It should be added that Soloviev already departs from anti-Judaist or anti-Semitic premises of some classic Christian writings by maintaining that Jews, for the most part, still possess these traits which made and thus still make them a "God-bearing nation." This will be discussed further below.

[39] Interestingly this account of Abraham's discovery of monotheistic faith seems to accord with the account in Midrash Bereshith Rabba. Again, Soloviev bases his reasoning not on the Fathers or other Christian sources, but goes straight to Jewish writings. This will be seen later in the defense against conversion he puts into the mouth of an imaginary Jew in *The Talmud and recent polemical literature*. Another example of this is in *The History and Future of Theocracy* where, searching for an image of Divine light, he uses the story of the burning bush in Exodus. Kornblatt points out ("Soloviev on Nationhood," fn.24) that Soloviev passes the many patristic references to divine light and goes straight to the Old Testament as the source of this image of unconsumed union with God. However, Kornblatt's observation needs to be modified: the burning bush was also a key text in patristic exegesis, as a symbol of the divine nature not consuming the human nature of Christ, as well as of the Mother of God, who bore Christ without being consumed by the divinity dwelling within her. This trope also appears regularly in the Orthodox liturgy, especially on holidays associated with the Mother of God. So though Soloviev reads the Old Testament keenly, he also reads it patristically and liturgically. St Augustine of Hippo also saw Jacob's struggle with the angel as a model for the believer grasping hold of God aggressively; other fathers, too, see the struggle as God's manifestation to Jacob according to his understanding, and Jacob's faithful grasping of the divine revelation (cf. Mark Sheridan, ed. *Bibleiskie kommentarii otsov tserkvi i drugikh avtorov I-VIII vekov. Vetkhi zavet. II. Kniga Bytiya 12-50*. Transl. A.Bogatyrev and others. (Moscow: Germenevtika, 2005), 270-8.) Thus Soloviev's characterization of the "pro-active" nature of Jewry has patristic precedents.

and reconciliation of the Divine in which both enter into the closest proximity, yet without division or confusion[40]. The term *tsel'nost'*, not coincidentally, is the same word Soloviev used in *Philosophical Principles* to refer to the new whole knowledge that must replace abstract European thought. And God-Manhood was the ideal to which this knowledge should strive.

Already, it is clear that Jewish history and, more, the Jewish national character, provide a model for the aspirations of other nations – and the paradigm of the divine incarnation that will redeem humanity. Of interest, too, is the fact that the very egotism which Soloviev, along with the Judeophobes, had detected in Jews, is now given a positive twist: God *needs* to be sought out by a "pushy" and inquisitive humanity if He is to reveal Himself. Here, Soloviev's conception of the bestowal of grace is closer to the Eastern Christian idea that man must make efforts to prepare himself for God's revelation, rather than the Augustinian view that prevailed in the West, whereby grace is bestowed inscrutably on entirely sinful creatures.

The third Jewish national trait is sacred materialism. This is explained by Soloviev as the practical bent of Jews, their reluctance to engage in fruitless speculative philosophizing and to always insist on a practical fruit of any endeavor. (Again, the overlapping with Soloviev's critique of European philosophy makes it clear through what prism he was viewing Jews). Such religious materialism (which is not the negative practical or scientific-philosophical materialism, he hastens to add) also shuns any artificial division of the world into categories of body/soul, or spirit/matter. Rather "the whole religious history of the Jews may be said to have been directed towards preparing for the God of Israel not only holy souls but holy bodies as well," hence all the Mosaic laws aimed at purification. And this is why the Word was incarnated among the Jews – for besides "a holy and virginal soul, a pure and holy body was needed for God to be made man."

All this is deeply flattering for Jews, no doubt! And in many respects, this description of the Jewish character, while prone to the faults of any gross generalization, and while obviously shaped by Soloviev's own interests, draws as we saw on Jewish sources and is in keeping with at least the Jewish self-perception to be found in rabbinic texts and in self-defining Jewish anti-Christian polemic. In that sense it is a fair portrait. The picture becomes less immediately flattering to Jews, at first sight, when Soloviev turns to his portrait of post-Christic Jewry, starting with the question of why, given this commendable national character, the Jews rejected the God incarnate, who was the summation of their yearnings and the apogee of their religion.

---

[40] Soloviev deliberately uses the formulations of Chalcedonian Christology, when discussing the human-divine encounter of Old Testament Jews and God, as he sees it as on a continuum with the later revelation of Christ. Hence his use of the term Judeo-Christian is not merely an accommodating label, but expresses a belief that Judaism and Christianity are in essence compatible (see more below). Probably Soloviev's habit of calling himself a Jew is intended in the same spirit to denote his image of himself as essentially and deeply Christ-ian (and Christ for him was the ultimate Jew).

Soloviev's answer is couched in the harsh-sounding language quoted earlier. But not surprisingly the harshness is mitigated by several factors. For a start, Soloviev's philosophic all-unity leads him to dismiss the traditional dichotomy which holds that it is the carnal and sensuous nature of the Jews which blinded them to the truth of Christ, leading them to wish for a this-worldly political Messiah. The rhetoric of "carnal" and this-worldly Israel, to which he himself had subscribed earlier, was used by the Judeophobes to "explain" Jewish engagement in radical politics and the liberal quest for an expansion of civil rights to Jews and other minorities.

However, given that Soloviev's philosophy places a positive accent on the "carnal," he rejects this approach. The idea that Jews desire an earthly paradise compared to the other-worldly "kingdom not of this world" preached by this Christ also sits ill with Soloviev's main project of this decade: the quest for a reconciliation of Eastern and Western Christianity that would culminate in a theocracy on earth.

Instead, Soloviev avers the opposite: the incarnation (as the etymology suggests[41]) made God *more* perceptible to the senses, and so one would presume to carnal Israel. So the problem cannot lie there. Rather, Soloviev posits that a disharmony in the triad of Jewish characteristics blocked Jewish acceptance of Christ.

Soloviev was a great admirer of Plato (his last unfinished work was a life of Plato) and the analogies with Plato's three-tiered harmonious personality come immediately to mind. In this case the overdeveloped aspect of the national character was the impatient practicality of the Jews' sacred materialism. The Jews were – and still are, as Soloviev shows by quoting at length a Passover prayer from the Siddur for the rebuilding of the Temple – highly impatient for God to manifest Himself on earth. They thus share the Christian desire for the Kingdom of Heaven to appear on earth. It was only in the means to attain this goal that they differed.

Their desire for quick tangible results meant that they could not understand the circuitous route of the Cross, of ascetic denial, of withdrawal in order to draw close to that goal: "they wanted to obtain from without by formal testament, that which has to be gained by suffering, through a hard and complex process of inner division and moral struggle." That is, they rejected not God Incarnate (as the Jewish crowds who followed Jesus show) as many maintain, and not even the Trinity, but the Cross: "They sought union with God through an external conditional agreement and not through inner deification by means of the Cross, by means of moral achievement and personal and national self-renunciation."

Once again, their developed sense of the real, the practical, the possible led them to be skeptical of the idea of the salvation of "humankind." The concrete concept of the nation they understood, but universal brotherhood seemed too abstract. For "humanity from the time of Babel has become an abstract idea

---

[41] Soloviev does not make the connection between "carnal" and "incarnation," but it is the sort of etymological insight of which Russian thinkers are fond!

and does not exist as a concrete self-contained whole. Therefore the Jews, who had not subordinated carnal reason to the knowledge of the truth, in picturing to themselves the Kingdom of God, naturally stopped at the confines of their own nation..." They grasped the idea of God-manhood, but limited it to their own nation.

A further twist in Soloviev's analysis of Jewry that takes him away from the Judeophobes is his drawing of a parallel between the disharmonious aspects of Christ-rejecting Jewry and the nationalists of his own nation. In the Christian tradition, there is nothing novel in an apologist insisting that he and his audience are best described by the sinners in the Old and the New Testaments. But for those publicists who used the sinner/saint rhetoric of the Bible to paint themselves white and their opponents black – as might seem obvious to do with regard to the Jews of the Bible and the contemporary Jewish question – this was an unsettling departure.

Thus for Soloviev, his condemnation of the Jews at the time of Christ is at the same time a condemnation of contemporary Russian Slavophiles and nationalists. A year earlier, he had written in "The National Question in Russia:" "The assertion of one's own exclusive mission, idolizing one's own nationhood is the point of view of ancient Judaism, and by accepting that point of view, Christians fall back into Old Testamental Judaism."[42]

Here it was members of the Russian nation who, by exalting Russia's role in the world excessively, had cut themselves off from world history. Soloviev went on: a true sense of nationhood is not a sin; but that nationhood must travel the way of the Cross, surrendering itself to the universal good. Otherwise it turns into blind and narrow nationalism. Thus the real "Jews" for Soloviev do not reside in the Pale, but at the heart of Russian government in Moscow[43].

The encounter with J.Rabinowitz

As far as contemporary Jews – in the literal sense – are concerned, Soloviev's vision for them comes out of his vision of a theocratic pan-unity of the nations. As he expressed this vision towards the end of "The Jews and the Christian Question:" "...Christian universalism aims not at destroying the national peculiarities of each nation but, on the contrary, at strengthening the

---

[42] "Morality and Politics: Russia's Historical Responsibilities" in *The National Question in Russia* (1883), quoted in Kornblatt *Vladimir Soloviev on Spiritual Nationhood, Russia and the Jews*, p.174.

[43] Notice that this analysis still ascribes negative value to the term "Jew." In Bulgakov, and to an even greater extent Florensky, this "philosemitic" defense, thus easily relapses into an equation of "contemporary Jew" with "negative symbolic materialist-Jew" – and with Trotsky in the Kremlin in 1917 the idea that "real contemporary Jews" have re-assumed the role of "Old Testament materialist-nationalist Jews" becomes surprisingly easy to hold. Thus the proposition "Soloviev=philo-Semite and Dostoevsky=anti-Semite" comes to be blurred somewhat with respect to the first term.

national spirit through purifying it from all leaven of egotism." And a little later: "All nations are only equal before the Gospel in the sense in which, for instance, in a state all citizens are equal before the law; this does not in the least prevent different grades and kinds of citizens having special rights arising from special duties...thus there is no necessary contradiction between the theocratic ideas of Judaism and Christianity..."

In one sense, this constitutes another departure from the general policy of the Russian government since the end of the eighteenth century: Soloviev believes that Judaism and the Jewish people contain many positive characteristics which can guide them in their future development. In another sense, however, Soloviev agrees with the thrust of Russian policy towards the Jews: for he, too, wishes to reform and improve them. However, he believes that the impetus for reformation can come from within the still divinely chosen nation itself.

Jews, according to Soloviev's vision, should pursue their old dream of bringing the Divine down to earth, of becoming "spiritual matter" and "material spirit," but they should combine this and achieve this through faith in and action in the name of the Messiah who has already come, and who has already achieved the ultimate meeting of Divine and human, without division or confusion.

That there need be "no necessary contradiction between the theocratic ideas of Judaism and Christianity," and that there can be "different grades and kinds of citizens" in the Universal Church implies that the Jewish nation can somehow accept Christ while maintaining its national identity, along with its special characteristics and talents – restored to a rightful balance once the ascetic path of the Cross has been collectively taken.

In fact, in 1884 a Jew from Kishinev, former rabbi Joseph Rabinowitz, attracted Soloviev's attention as incarnating precisely this vision. Soloviev rushed to express his support for him in an article written at the end of 1885. By this time, the construction of Rabinowitz's Jewish-Christian prayer hall had been completed and more than two hundred Kishinevan Jews began holding services in the building, at the centre of which stood an altar that held a Torah scroll bearing the Hebrew inscription: "The end of the Law is the Messiah (Rm.10.4)."

Rabinowitz was an unlikely candidate to become one of the first "Messianic" Jews in modern history. He had been a rabbi, a Jewish scholar, and respected member of the Jewish community. In 1882, he traveled to Palestine as part of a commission of Jewish communal leaders to investigate the possibilities for Jewish emigration there. The visit was a direct reaction to the pogroms of 1881, which had convinced him, like many Jews in the south-western provinces, that there could be no future for Jews in Russia as the campaign for rights had hit a brick wall in the policy of the new government.

When he returned, his solution to the Jewish question had turned from Zionism, emigration and the strengthening of Judaism, to the very same proposal advocated by the new arch-conservative Ober-Procurator of the Holy Synod, and by preceding Russian governments: conversion to Christianity.

His about-turn had been triggered by a conversion experience on the

Mount of Olives, when in his words "the prince of life, the Lord Jesus Christ, showed Himself to me as the Divine Messiah, and when I came down from the mountain, I felt that my soul had been reborn to a new life."[44] From that time on, he dedicated himself to his two loves, the first of which was Christ, and the second of which continued to be the Jewish people.

Rabinowitz's endeavors to form a Jewish-Christian congregation were supported by the Russian government, and church figures including Pobedonostsev himself, and the Kishinev municipality gave its permission for the building of the church. Initially, Rabinovitz's response dovetailed with this support. He expressed his belief in Russia in an article quoted in Soloviev's own piece dedicated to defending him: "Western Christianity has given Jews the chance to become acquainted with the Gospel, - it has been translated there excellently into Hebrew – and Eastern Christianity, whose protector Russia is, is destined to give them a chance to build a church."

Nonetheless, Rabinowitz's approach had detractors among Russian Orthodox Christians, who saw in it a Protestant version of Christianity. This was not helped by the fact that Rabinowitz had received financial support from a prominent English missionary and philanthropist. And indeed in March, 1885, Rabinowitz himself was baptized in Leipzig into the Lutheran church. Even that step had been a difficult one, and Rabinowitz insisted that his baptism bear a resemblance to the Jewish *tvila*, or immersion, ceremony. After his baptism as a Protestant, Pobedonostsev withdrew his support for Rabinowitz, accusing him of ungratefully turning his back on the support the Russian Church had given.

Soloviev's article was written nine months after Rabinowitz's baptism, which in no way diminished his support for the ex-rabbi and his community of Christian Jews. However, Soloviev's position was based not on an exaggerated ecumenical indifference to confessional boundaries. Even during his "Roman" diversion, and his greatest disillusionment with the Eastern caesaro-papism, Soloviev had maintained a love for his native church which – despite the rumors – prevented him from becoming a Catholic. This is clear in his attitude to Rabinowitz.

Soloviev states in his article about "The New Testament Israel" that the full Christian truth is contained in the Orthodox church. He also agrees with the critics that Rabinowitz's thirteen principles of Jewish-Christian faith (modeled as replacements of Maimonides' principles of the Jewish faith) depart from the full depth of Christian Orthodoxy. To those who see Protestantism in this, however, Soloviev compares the fledgling Jewish-Christian congregation and Protestantism to two trains moving in opposite directions that pass each other by in the same place: the Protestants, having been a part of the body of the Church have moved away from the truth; the Jewish-Christians, having never been a part of the Church, should be seen as moving towards it.

Thus Soloviev makes a plea of tolerance for Rabinowitz's absence of dogmatic precision concerning questions which arose only centuries into the history of

---

[44] Rabinowitz, as quoted by Soloviev in "Novozavetniy Izrail," in *Rus'* No.24.(1885):7-9 and No.25 (1885):6-7.

the Church. In all essential points concerning the belief in the saving power of Christ, the resurrection and the kingdom of God, Rabinowitz is true to those first confessions of faith that the early Jewish disciples and apostles made. They are thus treading the path of those early Jewish Christians who came to Christ through the Law and the Prophets, and found in Jesus not just a general savior of humanity's sins, but also the national redeemer of his people who saves them from historical misfortunes.

Further, argues Soloviev, while for Christians born in the Church, obedience to Christ means obedience to the Church, for a Jew not born in the Church obedience to Christ means following the prophetic meaning of the Old Testament. This is different from those Christian sects which broke from the Church and formed their own rules; Jews were never a part of that Church and the fluidity of the Jewish Christian community reflects the early nature of the Church itself.

Soloviev's ends his essay with an appeal to Gregory the Theologian's plea in the fourth century for a broad-minded approach concerning doctrinal differences. Gregory had written that mature Christians who were confident in their faith should allow for differences of doctrinal formulations in fellow-Christians whose behavior showed them to be sincere believers, urging them to "confess the nature under different names, which you most respect, and we will heal you like weak patients, even hiding the other thing for your pleasure. For it is shameful…to be healthy in soul and place emphasis on sounds…Confess in the Trinity one Divinity, or if you like, one nature: and I will ask of you from the Spirit the word God."

In the same way, Russian Orthodox Christians should continue to be forgiving of immaturities in Rabinowitz's community, for only through a forgiving overlooking of errors can they give a chance for the Jewish Church to be grafted back onto the solid trunk of the universal church, from which so many dried branches have fallen aside.

It is thus clear that Soloviev's article pleading for tolerance of Rabinowitz's endeavor is of a piece with his intended meeting with Pope Leo XIII: it was an attempt to heal humanity by recreating that all-unity that had existed in the church before the Jewish-Christian, and then Eastern-Western schism sundered the body of Christ.

Indeed, although it did not receive the attention of the latter effort, Soloviev's support of Rabinowitz was more central than his plans for Christian reconciliation, for the schism there was theologically more central to the health of Christianity. This is demonstrated by Soloviev's choice of metaphor for the re-grafting of Jewry back onto the body of Christ: the trunk of that tree, as the metaphor taken from *Romans* suggests, was after all Christ the Jew and his Jewish disciples.

Thus for a time at least, Rabinowitz, Soloviev and the Russian government were united in their aims of advancing humanity through their support of Jewish Christian enlightenment. However, Rabinowitz died in 1889, and his community did not draw any closer to the Orthodox Church. Nor, obviously, did it turn out to be the nucleus from which a Jewish Christianity would radiate outwards and transform the other five million of Rabinowitz's co-religionists. In that sense, Soloviev's one chance to see a concrete result of his support of Judeo-Christianity turned out to be as disappointing for this global dreamer as his attempt at rapprochement with Catholicism. In addition, the Russian government's adroit turning of its back on Rabinowitz after his Protestant baptism must have been a further cause of disillusionment for Soloviev with Russian Orthodoxy.

Judaism, Judeo-Christianity and the Law

While Soloviev had supported Rabinowitz's Judeo-Christianity, it is important to notice that he was not an advocate of what is nowadays called "Messianic Judaism." This "Jewish Christianity" started as, and has remained, Protestant in orientation, and is dedicated to some combination of Torah observance and Christian belief. In some forms, it is also hostile to central Christian dogmas and symbols, including the Cross. Its very name indicates that it sees itself not as a form of Christianity, but rather a form of Judaism – from which much of its religious ritual is drawn.

Rabinowitz himself was extremely emphatic in his belief that "the end of the Law is the Messiah," and he rather chillingly referred to rabbinic Jews as being enslaved to the "knight of this world" and the "father of lies," expressions which he took as referring to the Talmud. Thus his insistence on a Jewish baptism rite was not due to some attempt to create a Jewish-Christian *halakha*, pace Messianic Judaism, but a deference to the original Jewish spirit of Christianity.

Soloviev generally shared this orientation. For him, Judaism was a "bad law," one which had not attained to the level of the New Law of Christ, which advocated a higher moral standard, i.e. the requirement to forgive one's enemies, and to put others' interests over one's own. By comparison with this Jewish law was narrow and self-regarding. Nonetheless, Soloviev's belief in the unique personality of the Jewish people led him to envisage their preservation within the community of Christian nations, and this is a vision which is not only consistent with Theophan's briefly stated comments on *Romans*: it would be developed and extended at some length by admirers of Soloviev, like Sergei Bulgakov and Lev Karsavin.

However, Soloviev's vision for Jewish Christianity differed from Rabinowitz's in one important respect. Soloviev had a very real belief in the body of Christ on earth and its infallibility, even though at times he came to believe that this church could be found in a combination of the Roman and Eastern churches[45]. Thus

---

[45] After the proclamation of the doctrine of papal infallibility in 1870, Soloviev for a time accepted it. The Eastern doctrine of infallibility holds that the church as a whole, through its councils, will arrive at the truth. However, without going into details of Soloviev's changing attitude to Orthodoxy and Catholicism, it is clear that at no time did he abandon the idea of an earthly community of believers with a visible hierarchy who were the body of Christ on earth, and the individualist orientation of Protestantism whereby each believer is his own priest was alien to him.

he states quite clearly his hope that Rabinowitz's community will in the course of time draw closer and closer to Orthodox Christian dogmas and practices. Everything else is a temporary aberration that must be tolerated only out of Christian love, in order to further that end. Rabinowitz, for his part, seemed to envisage a much greater freedom of his Jewish Church, which is why he may have been drawn to Protestantism.

Given this downgrading of Judaism, another rather surprising difference between Rabinowitz and Soloviev is the latter's laudatory article written in defense of the Talmud in 1885. If Soloviev was so convinced that Judaism was a "bad law," what good could he have to say about Judaism's central legalistic document?

There are several points which will help clarify this dilemma. Firstly, Soloviev was performing a civil duty in defending the Talmud. He could not stand by and see a persecuted and powerless minority deprived of its religious freedom, or tolerate vicious attacks on the Jews' sacred writings, especially given the atmosphere of anti-Jewish violence in Russia.

Secondly, in examining the Talmud – which he had studied with Getz – Soloviev focused almost exclusively on *Pirkei Avot*, the one tractate of sixty three Talmudic tractates that does not have religious law as its subject. Here, too, his purpose was apologetic: this was not a time to be highlighting (perceived) inadequacies.

The final point, however, is theologically more serious and relates to the course of Soloviev's general development. As we saw, on Vasilenko's interpretation, Soloviev had given up on his theocratic project after the failures of the 80s. His final work, "A Short Story of the Anti-Christ," is conspicuously lacking in the philosophical premises that he had developed in the previous two decades: there is no discussion of divine-humanity, whole personality, or most importantly, all-unity. This abandonment of "theocratic activism" seems to have been accompanied by a corresponding change in views regarding Jewry.

If we posit more continuity between Soloviev's different stages, we can see him as simultaneously holding two not completely exclusive positions in the 1880s, one of which would eventually gain the upper hand. So, while he held out hopes for an East-West reconciliation and a rebirth of Judeo-Christianity, perhaps a more sober part of his consciousness realized that even if this scenario were to be achieved in his lifetime, the question of how to relate to those who had not yet joined the reunified divine-human church still stood.

In that sense, his defense of the Talmud was not purely apologetic: it was also a recognition that non-Christian Jews had a connection to God and that Judaism had some legitimacy. After the failure of the reunion, that position eclipsed the previous optimistic one in the 90s – though even then, there may have been traces of that optimism remaining.

In the "Short Story of the Anti-Christ," the forcing of church unity by human means is presented as a temptation of the anti-Christ, a human emperor who effects a miraculous union between Protestants, Catholics and Orthodox, to which the majority of Christians joyously submit, based on the lordship of the emperor himself and the power of the anti-Pope whom he appoints. It is certainly possible that this is a bleak commentary on his own earlier attempt to bring about a meeting between Alexander III and Pope Leo XIII, and a repudiation thereof.

Later in the "Story," the true Pope Peter (Catholic) and Elder John (Orthodox), having been struck down by the Emperor but then miraculously resurrected, together with Professor Pauli, the representative of German Protestantism, effect a far less ostentatious reunion, based not on imperial fiat but mutual love and love of Christ, near Mount Sinai in the Arabian desert, where they are joined by a small number of believers – compared to the number of "superficial Christians."

The role of the Jews in this "post-theocratic" story seems to confirm the idea of a new tolerance for rabbinical Judaism. At first, the Jews side with the anti-Christ, but then abandon him, turn to the defense of the true Pope and Patriarch, and march on Jerusalem, determined to sacrifice themselves to the death in order to defeat the anti-Christ. As the crowd of faithful Jews reaches Jerusalem, Christ appears from on high to initiate His thousand-year reign over the faithful, both Jews and Gentiles.

A significant detail here is the reason that Soloviev gives for the switch of Jewish loyalties from the anti-Christ to Christ: they are enraged on discovering that the anti-Christ is a renegade Jew who is not even circumcised as the Law of Moses requires. In other words, at the end time, continued Jewish devotion to the Mosaic law is the herald of the final salvation and the foundation of the Kingdom of Heaven on earth under the thousand year reign of Christ. The anti-Christ, moreover, although he is a Jew is a Jew who has violated his religion.

As mentioned, this is not a complete disjuncture from some of his earlier statements in "The Jews and the Christian Question." There Judaism is presented as lower than Christianity, but Jews are also praised for fulfilling their law (after all they do not persecute Christians), while Christians are hypocrites in respect to their higher law. Nonetheless, the idea in the "Short Story" that even at the end of time, Jewry will still not have accepted Christianity does represent a pessimistic step compared to his hopes for Rabinowitz.

One could say that, drawing close to the end of his life, Soloviev was suffering from the same weariness that the Russian government as a whole had experienced in regard to its initial high hopes of a reformation and baptism of the Jews. The conversion project, in other words, is shunted off until the end-time. In addition, the representation of the anti-Christ as a secular Jew is not so distant from conservative Christians who had decided that religious Jews – for all that they were not Christians – were to be supported over secular Jewish youth who were entering the radical parties[46].

---

[46] Incidentally, this demonization of secular Jewry in the person of the uncircumcised Jewish anti-Christ is part of a general Russian conservative Christian stance which favors religious over secular Jewry. Again, Florensky's and Bulgakov's belief that

However, this analysis of the "Short Story" is somewhat preemptive. Turning to the defense of the Talmud in the context in which it was written, namely in the middle of Soloviev's theocratic optimism, the defense of Jewish Talmudic ethics could also be fitted in with the support of Judeo-Christianity. For as Soloviev sees it, Talmudic ethics are complementary to Christian ethics, and the crucial difference of Judaism lies rather in its metaphysical than its ethical content. This confirms Soloviev's near-contemporary statement that "there is no necessary contradiction between the theocratic ideas of Judaism and Christianity," and can be seen as part of a vision in which a new Jewish Christianity retains ethical aspects of "Old Testament" Judaism.

Still, Soloviev's defense of that Old Testament Judaism is so thorough that at times it reads like an apology for Judaism *per se*, and only the faintest of philosophical threads keeps the reader from thinking that perhaps it would not be such a bad thing, after all, if Jews did not convert to Christianity before the end time. To that extent, his apology for the Talmud cannot be fully reconciled with those more traditional moments where Soloviev downgraded Judaism. This can be seen by looking at that article in more detail.

Talmudic Judaism and integral Christianity
Soloviev starts "The Talmud and the recent polemical literature about it in Austria and Germany," which was written in same year as his defense of the Talmud-hating Rabinowitz, with a maxim for the rules of engagement: "In the evaluation of the Talmud and Talmudic Judaism below we have tried primarily to follow the higher rule of Judeo-Christian[47] morality: do unto others as you would wish them to do unto you." What follows bears this out to such an extent that even a recent Jewish commentator has herself noted "he glosses over those passages that do indeed suggest a kind of militant exclusivity."[48]

That said, Soloviev is on his habitually provocative good form. He makes some points about the relationship between Judaism and Christianity, which were only to be made again in the flourishing of scholarship in the second half of the twentieth century that led to the rediscovery of the Jewish Jesus[49].

Firstly, carrying on from his rejection of the idea of a "carnal" Judaism, he sets out to demolish the usual distinction between Pharisaic, law-bound

---

"Yids" (i.e. secular Jews) had taken over the Kremlin and undermined Sacred Russia in 1917, while at first glance, a betrayal of Soloviev's philo-Semitic heritage, can also be seen as displaying a continuity with this aspect of Soloviev's Jewish analysis. See further discussion in ch.2. with regard to Bulgakov's Solovievian and Dostoevskian traits.

[47] The very use of the term "Judeo-Christian" contrasts with Aksakov's argument that Judaism is completely incompatible with Christianity.
[48] Kornblatt, Nationhood, 167.
[49] Cf. G.Vermes, who spearheaded the modern search for the Jewish Jesus in, for example, *Jesus the Jew*. London: William Collins and Son, 1973, and *The Changing Faces of Jesus*. London:Penguin Books, 2000.

Judaism and grace-filled Christianity. Revising the usual pejorative meaning of Pharisaism in Christian discourse, Soloviev argues that Jesus' Christianity is in fact closer in spirit to Pharisaism than to the Essenes, who are the usual candidates for proximity.

He quotes Jesus' saying: "The scribes and Pharisees are sitting in the seat of Moses. Everything they tell you, observe and do, but do not act as they act: for they speak and do not act," to show that Jesus agreed with the Pharisaic message, and only criticized the Pharisees for not living up to it themselves. Jesus' arguments with the Pharisees only prove that they had a common language to engage in discussion. It was because they were prominent and influential members of society who were essentially in tune with his message that Jesus chose them as partners for dialogue rather than any other group.

Unfortunately, Soloviev writes, Christians still not have lived up to Christ's maxim to do as the Pharisees tell people to do, let alone living up to His second maxim to go beyond the righteousness of the Pharisees. "The Pharisees, at least in principle, permitted no division between life, law and action. On the contrary, their constant efforts were directed so that all human deeds would be a fulfillment of the Law of God. This they taught and about this Christ said: 'Observe and do.' Since then we have succeeded in making into a principle the contradiction between the requirements of religion and the conditions of social life, between the Divine commandments and our whole sphere of activity."

Soloviev concludes strikingly: "This is why Pharisaism, consolidated into Talmudism, has not been and cannot not be invalidated by historical Christianity." So, Talmudism lives and has every right to, and moreover can provide a lesson for Christians in the practice of righteousness, which was to occupy Soloviev in his later years more than the program to embrace all humanity in the pan-Unity of the church.

As before, though in a more detailed way, Soloviev is pointing to a model of the tsel'ny'/integral approach to life, for which he was striving and campaigning. He finds it now, of all places, not in Holy Russia where the Slavophiles were looking for tsel'nost', but among the despised Jews of the Pale.

But if this is so, perhaps some sort of mass conversion to Talmudic Judaism is required for Russia, some sort of revival of the Khazar kingdom? Soloviev catches himself in time. Ultimately, he wants to demonstrate that there *is* a difference between Judaism and Christianity, but is insistent that it does not lie in the usual glib assurance from the Christian side that Christianity is ethically superior to Judaism, or that Christians are more spiritual than carnal Jews (a canard Soloviev refutes in the same way as he did in "The Jews and the Christian Question").

Soloviev offers the following quotations: "The righteous man shall live by his faith" and "Do not do unto others what you would not have them do to you."[50] Then, probably expecting a certain degree of surprise among his less

---

[50] The negative phrasing of the Golden Rule, and the contrast with Jesus' maxim "Love your enemies" are sometimes said to distinguish Christian from Jewish ethics.

informed Christian readers, he contends that these *Talmudic* maxims clearly show that "between the legalism of the Talmud and New Testament morality, founded on faith and altruism, there is no contradiction." Instead, "the principle argument between Christianity and Judaism consists not in the ethical, but in the religious-metaphysical sphere, in the question about the divine-human meaning and redeeming sacrifice of Christ."

In sum, in Soloviev's view Talmudism and Christianity are compatible and the former is often a surer path to righteousness than the latter. In this essay, Soloviev does not expand much on the metaphysical-religious difference. But from his previous writings, we understand that Christianity is, despite all this, the ultimate path for all humanity, including the Jewish nation, because only Christianity has a vision – given from on high – of how the whole of humanity can intimately fulfill its dreams and unite with God, without confusion or division, in a process of deification.

This is the process of the gathering of all nations, their *integration*, with all aspects of their lives, into the Universal Church. Those who bear the name Christian are guilty of disintegration, of separating out the elements of personal piety and political life, of placing nation higher than Church, so that one hand does not know what the other is doing, and in this way they betray, disrupt and fragment the Christian vision. And on the other hand, it is true that "Talmudists and the people they lead have often forgotten the ideal-moral views of their *aggadas*[51] and become bogged down in the formal legalisms of the *halakha*[52], so that law and formal truth have often got the upper hand over mercy (*hesed*) and internal truth (*emet*)."

As for persuading the Jews to enter with their nation into the Universal Church, to become flesh and bone with deified humanity unified round the God-Man, Soloviev gives the last word to an imaginary but very convincing Jew who feels himself unable to take this step for several reasons.

It is worth briefly paraphrasing a part of this Jewish refutation: "Firstly, the 'Universal Church' is so divided that even if we Jews wanted to join you, we would not know where to start. So in the absence of a real Messianic kingdom now, we have little reason to abandon our own hoped for Messianic kingdom. Then again,

---

Unfortunately, Soloviev does not deal with these obvious objections. This is a polemical issue. In fact, in Jewish sources there are voices which call for a man to pray for the repentance of sinners, to refrain from cursing one's enemy, to refrain from hatred of any of God's creatures. There is also the "Prayer before lying down to sleep" which starts: "Master of the Universe, I hereby forgive anyone who angered or antagonized or sinned against me..." Rabbi Nosson Scherman, *The Complete ArtScroll Siddur. Week/Sabbath/Festival*. co-edited by Rabbi M.Zlotowitz and Rabbi Sheah Brander, (Brooklyn: Mesorah Publications Ltd, 1984), 289. Cf. also: "Praying for the Downfall of the Wicked," in Louis Jacobs, *Judaism and Theology. Essays on the Jewish religion*. London (Valentine Mitchell, 2005), 144-159, 144 ff. A deeper discussion of this matter will be conducted elsewhere.

[51] The narrative-homiletic parts of Jewish writings.
[52] Jewish law.

we Jews judge a tree not by the size of its trunk or the beauty of its branches, but by the taste of its fruits: wonderful and abstract theologizing cannot convince us in the absence of deeds to back it up – and there is no point saying that one must judge Christianity on theoretical grounds alone, and not be too harsh on the practitioners, because after all a religion should be a system of life.

"If you point to Christian fruits such as the abolition of slavery, we have to reply that this was achieved in an age when Christianity was in decline. And compared to the feeble palliative measures against slavery taken in Church canons, our own Mosaic law thirteen hundred years ago already decreed the Sabbatical and Jubilee years for the release of slaves and the help of the destitute. Our own sages taught us that life is built on three things: teaching, the divine service and active love. All of them are interconnected, and cannot be disconnected without sacrificing the truth. So if your life and deeds do not conform to your liturgy and teachings, then even if we accept the truth of the former, we want no part in your religion – it is an incomplete truth."

The Jewish refutation goes on for two pages. It is certainly cogent enough to give Christians pause before they open their mouths to preach some theological truth to a Jew or any one else for that matter – if they do not examine their own deeds first. The Talmudic Jew is the heir, for Soloviev, of Biblical righteousness and faith. The Talmud has preserved the Jewish nation with the characteristics which made them freely choose and be chosen by God. That they do not choose now to take their national mission to the next level, transcending though not abolishing the national, is ascribed in "The Jews and the Christian Question" to an imbalance in that noble character. But in his essay on the Talmud, Soloviev does not mention this explanation.

Rather he attributes Jewish reluctance to fulfill their national vocation once and for all to the poor witness of the Gentile nations – an appropriate emphasis, given that he is responding to anti-Semitic calumny. As such Talmudic Jewry "stands as a living reproach to the Christian world…We cannot force the Jews to abandon the laws of the Talmud, but it is always within our power to apply to Jewry itself the commandments of the Gospel."

In concluding this examination of Soloviev's views, we can only reiterate that this defense of Judaism is not fully consistent with his other anti-Judaic rhetoric. Furthermore, the thin account of Christianity's remaining metaphysical superiority over Judaism seems to suffer from precisely that lack of concreteness which the imaginary Jew accuses it of.

However, off the page, Soloviev's answer to such an accusation in the 1880s was clear: his campaign to unite the church, if successful, would have solved at least one of the imaginary Jew's dilemmas, which in fact was a dilemma for Rabinowitz: which of the many branches of the so-called universal Church to enter.

There is a final irony in Soloviev's picture of Talmudic Judaism as a model of religion-state unity, and the integration of social and spiritual life. In an obvious sense, this ideal of Christian theocracy contradicts Christ's saying "Render unto Caesar's that which is Caesar's and unto God that which is God's." That saying would form the basis of a fundamental Church-state duality in Christian history, which was absent in the pagan Roman empire, as well as in Judaism and Islam (for all the attempts by different parties in the Christian East and West to implement caesaropapism or papocaesarism).

Among Soloviev's heirs, there were three thinkers who reacted in different ways to this vision of theocratic Christianity. Semyon Frank rejected it, on the grounds of Christ's saying. In his opinion to theocratize Christianity would be to impose turn free grace into enslaving law. (It is perhaps not a coincidence that he was born, as a Jew, "under the yoke of the Law")[53].

The other thinker, Pavel Florensky built a vision of all-unity that resembled this vision in its desire to church all aspects of life – in a way that might be called Talmudic. The irony is that this Christianization of everything was accompanied by a rabid anti-Semitism.

The third thinker, Nicolai Berdyaev, came to see the desire to build a theocracy on earth as a peculiarly Jewish temptation that must be averted at all costs. He was consistent, however, in rejecting this tendency in Soloviev as well.

Sophia (Soph-Jah) and Judaic/Christian pan(en)theism

One extremely important aspect of Soloviev's thought that has so far been only been mentioned in passing is the place of Sophia, or the Divine Wisdom, in his philosophy and poetry.

Soloviev came across the term Sophia, or *Hokhma* in Hebrew, as early as 1875, during a research trip to London while he was a student at the Moscow Spiritual Academy[54]. In all likelihood he found a Latin translation[55] of the Zohar there, as his Hebrew at this stage was probably not good enough to make study in that language possible. (Later on, Soloviev's studies with Faivel Gets greatly improved his command of the language, so that his later use of Jewish mystical texts and understanding of Judaism are more sophisticated).

A year after his trip to the British Musem, Soloviev was writing an article in French called "Sophie," in which using Kabbalistic play on the Hebrew words

---

[53] For example, cf. Semyon Frank, "Tserkov' i mir. Blagodat' i zakon." Put' No.8. (1927):3-20.
[54] This fascination with Jewish sources was not unique at that time: there was a trend in the reign of Alexander II for mystical societies as well as interest in and translation of Jewish texts. In this sense, Soloviev also fits into another line of Christian thinkers (starting at least from St. Jerome) who have turned to the Jews for "Jewish truth," as well as to sharpen their understanding of Christian truth, starting with Jerome and Justin Martyr and continuing through to the Christian kabbalists of the Renaissance.
[55] Possibly Christian Knorr von Rosenroth's *Kabbalah Denudata*, according to Stremooukhoff; footnote 14 in Judith Kornblatt, "Androgynous Sophia and the Jewish Kabbalah," Slavic Review 50/3 (1991):487-496.

he derived the Greek word for wisdom, Sophia, from the two Hebrew words Soph (End) and Jah (the name of God). This makes Sophia "the End of God," the principle which connects God's transcendence with his immanence in the soul of man. Thus in this work, rather as in both Jewish and Christian Kabbalah, as well as in neo-Platonism, Wisdom is an intermediary between God and the world.

This, of course, is deeply problematic from the view of the traditional Jewish and Christian view of the creation of the world from nothing. The idea that the principle of the world is connected to the essence of God, while upgrading the world and enabling an approach of "sacred materialism" (which Soloviev, and in different ways his followers, would later praise in Judaism), also leads to heterodox pantheism. This was a theological time-bomb that Soloviev would leave to his heirs, some of whom would reject his "sophianic" account of the world, and others of whom (especially Bulgakov) would devote their lives to trying to render more Orthodox – with questionable success. A recent commentator, Hamutal Bar-Yosef[56], has seen in Soloviev's use of sophianic motifs an attempt "to bring Russian Christianity nearer to Judaism, and even to Judaize Christianity." This accords with Kornblatt's investigation into Soloviev's use of Kabbalistic motifs, and her contention that key aspects of Soloviev's worldview owe much to his construction of a "softer" version of Slavophilism out of Jewish elements.

Still, as we intimated above, it would be premature to attribute both Soloviev's politics and his mystical metaphysics entirely to the philosopher's philosemitism. Burmistrov points out that some of Soloviev's Kabbalistic concepts, such as Adam Kadmon, Sophia and Ein Sof, may owe more to his reading of Christian Kabbalists and even theosophists like Swedenborg, whose link with Jewish Kabbalah was even more tenuous. Furthermore, Faival Gets, as we saw, would not have been a great influence as far as Jewish mysticism was concerned.

Nonetheless, even if Soloviev was imbibing Judaic influence in already Christianized form (through theosophy and Christian Kabbalah), the influence is certainly there. At this point, however, it may help to point to an even deeper link between the Christian and Judaic elements in Soloviev's thought, one with far older historical roots. We can theorise that the Judaization of Soloviev's worldview was successful because of his philosophy's deeper compatibility with the Eastern Christian mysticism of Church Fathers like Gregory of Nyssa and Maxim the Confessor, who also inspired Soloviev[57]. This thought in turn has a close relationship with a certain stream of Jewish theology.

It has often been noted that Byzantine theology and medieval Jewish philosophy share more than Byzantine and Western Christian theology[58].

---

[56] Hamutal Bar-Yosef, "The Jewish reception of Vladimir Solovyov," In *Vladimir Solovyov: Reconciler and Polemicist*, ed. Ewert von Zweerde, Peeters, Lewen, 2000.

[57] And conversely, as we shall argue later, the Jewishness of Russian philosophy made it amenable to Russian Jewish philosophers.

[58] A.Altman, "Judaism and world philosophy," cited in George Pappadimitriou, *Maimonid i Palama o Boge*. (Moscow: Put', 2003), 77-78.

This has been explained by the influence of the apophatic thought of John of Damascus (7th century) on early Arab philosophy, which later played a key role in shaping the thought of luminaries like Moses Maimonides. G.Papadimitriou devoted a study to exploring the similarities between Maimonides and the greatest thinker of medieval Byzantium, St. Gregory Palamas. He highlighted how both thinkers made a distinction between God's unknowable essence and his energies or activities, (a distinction which is ultimately traceable to John of Damascus): God's energies are the means by which He interacts with the world and becomes known to man; however both construct their conception of God so that changes in these energies and the divine will do not detract from the ultimate unity, unchangeability and unknowability of God's essence.

This distinction between divine essence and activities is already embryonically present in Gregory of Nyssa and Maximus the Confessor. It may well have passed from Maimonides into the thought of Abulafia and thus into medieval Kabbalah. So, in drawing on Kabbalah, Soloviev was drawing on a thought-system that had genealogical links with the early Eastern Christian mysticism already familiar to him. And, of course, John of Damascus' emphasis on the unknowbality of God arose out of that theologian's own need to bring the intellectualizing deity of Greek philosophy, which he had inherited from Plotinus and Proclus, closer to the mysterious God of the Jewish Bible.

In others words, although at present researchers are not agreed as to the extent of the "purity" of Soloviev's Kabbalistic sources, even if he transposed directly from Hebrew sources, this in itself would not rule out a common Judeo-Christian genealogical similarity and compatibility.

As it happens, however, Soloviev and those who continued and developed his sophiology were often accused – by fellow Christians – of heterodoxy. The classic case is the dispute between V.Lossky and Bulgakov: the former accused the latter of compromising the Orthodox theology of the Church Fathers with pantheistic tendencies. This might polemically be attributed to extraneous Kabbalistic influence. However, leaving aside the fact that Eastern Christian thought itself had on several occasions to fight pantheism, it should be noted that the conflict between mystical pantheism and a more orthodox emphasis on transcendence also played itself out in the Jewish environment, in not dissimilar categories – thus pointing to further similarities in Eastern Christian and Jewish thought. For Hasidic thinkers, who adapted the Kabbalah in a more pantheistic direction, also fell under suspicion of heterodoxy[59]. Indeed, the Kabbalah itself was once

---

[59] Cf. Louis Jacobs, *A Jewish Theology*. (London: Berman House Inc., 1973), 35-37. "Not long after the rise of Hasidism, this doctrine [panentheism, DR] was severely attacked by the traditional defenders of Jewish monotheism. It was claimed that the panentheistic doctrine tends to obliterate the demarcation lines between the holy and the unholy, between good and evil." L.Karsavin (cf. ch.5 of the present book) outlined a doctrine of all-unity that develops many of the themes of Soloviev; in particular he extends the focus on erotic love as a path to the divine, and was so taken by the Oneness of being, that he attracted exactly the same charges of moral

described by Solomon Maimon, as "nothing but expanded Spinozism"[60].

One reason why Soloviev's adaptation of Eastern Christian mysticism blended with (Judaic as well as Christianized) Kabbalah might recapitulate a tendency found in Hasidic adaptations of Jewish mystical philosophy can perhaps be sought in R.Elior's characterization of Hasidism as belonging to the general movement of European romanticism of the late eighteenth century[61]. L. Jacobs also remarks that Hasidism extended a tendency already developed in the Kabbalah itself to lessen the apophatic strictness of its Maimonidean neo-Platonist sources concerning the unknowbality of God's essence[62]. Romanticism, of course, was well-known for its rebellion against rationalism and for its philosophies of immanence. It seems, then, that Soloviev and the Hasidic masters were thus both romanticizing, and to an extent popularizing, some of the more stringent doctrines of their cognate mystical tradition[63]. The result is a surprising similarity in tone and content of Jewish Hasidic writings and Christian sophiological writings – a similarity rarely noted, and due to political and historical circumstances of the time, as we will later see, hardly likely to be considered an enviable comparison.

In that sense, what Bar-Yosef refers to as Soloviev's "Judaizing" tendency can be seen as having multiple parentage: there is indeed Judaic input, but this is also a function of his own native Eastern Christian heritage, as well of the Romantic strain in European thought that had spread to Russia in the form of German Idealism[64].

---

relativism and blurring of ethical boundaries. (For more on Jewish conceptions of immanence and transcendence and apophatic theology, cf. A Jewish Theology, ch.4 and Jacobs, Louis. *Judaism and Theology. Essays on the Jewish religion*. (London: Valentine Mitchell, 2005), ch.2: "The *via negativa* in Jewish thought."

[60] See ch.5 for further discussion of Maimon and Spinozism in the German Enlightenment.

[61] Rachel Elior, *The Mystical Origins of Hasidism*. Oxford/Portland, Oregon: The Littman Library of Jewish Civilization, 2006.

[62] *A Jewish theology*, 27: "The 'unification of God' means, therefore, for many of the medieval thinkers, the complete refinement of the God concept so as to negate from it all multiplicity. This led to severe abstraction, to great austerity in the formulation of the God concept, to which the rise of the Kabbalah can be seen as a reaction."

[63] It is beyond the remit of this study to investigate how Hasidism and sophiology made innovations to their inherited traditions, but in passing we can note that Hasidic thought was no less bold than sophiology in its idea that through the divine commandments a Jew can partake not just in the lower aspects of divinity but in the divine *essence* itself – certainly something neither Maimonides (or Palamas) could have countenanced, and which is a radical and provocative development of the idea of the Ein Sof, meant to depict that unknowable part of the Godhead utterly removed from the reality of the lower spheres of creation.

[64] Above we mentioned Y. Yoval's thesis about Spinoza as the first secular Jew, who introduced a critical philosophy of immanence into early modern Western philosophy. What we are saying about Soloviev's relationship to the Jewish and

Of course, Soloviev added much that was purely his own. Thus, in a way which departs from both Jewish and Renaissance Christian Kabbalah, Soloviev conceived of Ein Sof as the essence of God that precedes the sephirot Keter, Chochma (Sophia) and Bina, and these are then equated with the three Persons of the Trinity. This doctrine would imply that the divine essence precedes the Persons. And here, undoubtedly, Soloviev's fusion of Kabbalah, theosophy and German mysticism results in a doctrine which departs markedly from Orthodox Christian dogma. There, the Persons share equally in the divine essence; the separation of essence and Persons recalls more Jacob Bohme's Urgrund, the pure divinity that precedes the divine Persons. This separation is continued in Bulgakov's own doctrine of Sophia, the divine essence; and we can perhaps also see S.Frank's unfathomable Deity as being related to the unfathomable Ein Sof[65].

Furthermore, these three sephirot are elsewhere described by Soloviev as being not equal but hierarchical. Consequently, if the identification with the Trinity is taken seriously, one would get a Plotinus-like graded "trinity." Further, as regards Adam Kadmon, in two places Soloviev equates the supernal man with the Logos and Christ – but later implies in a diagram that the historical man Jesus is different from all these[66]. Once again, it is not surprising that Soloviev's new Christian philosophy earned the skepticism of more mainstream Christian theologians.

However, in terms of Soloviev's influence on posterity, one of the most important points to remember is that his conception of Sophia, whatever its exact inspiration, soon became much more than an abstract theological doctrine. Three times in his life Soloviev had encounters with a mysterious otherworldly woman whom he would come to identify as the embodiment of the divine Wisdom. The first vision had come to him as a boy of thirteen when he was playing outside away from the care of his nanny. The second occurred in the Reading Room of the British Museum where he was examining a Kabbalistic manuscript, and the extraordinary woman instructed Soloviev to take himself to Egypt. Having done so, he was graced with his third vision of

---

Christian tradition can be applied back to Soloviev's predecessor, Spinoza. The latter's "secular Jewish" philosophy of immanence and God-world unity is, after all, not purely Judaic in origin, even on Yovel's analysis. Rather, it emerged out of the gap, or intersection, between Catholic-Christian and Judaic tradition (among the Marranos), and was a *critique* of both, as well as being an heir to both (as well as to the Hellenistic tradition). Likewise, Soloviev both inherits Orthodox and Judaic elements in his thought, but remolds them critically in his own way. Thus to say (*pace* Bar-Yosef) that Soloviev "softens" the Christian through the Judaic is perhaps to miss this: in fact he softens ("immanentizes") more orthodox transcendentalist tendencies in *both* the traditions he inherits (rather as Hasidism did with Maimonideanism).

65   Cf. ch.6 for more discussion of Frank.
66   For a summary of Soloviev's Kabbalistic doctrine, cf. Burmistrov. The explanation of how this differs from Christian dogma (rather than Jewish Kabbalistic norms, which is Burmistrov's concern) is mine.

the woman he now tacitly identified as Sophia[67] in the desert.

In the coming years, he would try to articulate the theological meaning of Sophia: in different works, she was variously: the "world soul;" the higher intellectual force in God, which contains the image of that which the world should become; the guarantee of the process of the becoming of all-unity on earth; the divine rational essence of the three hypostases, but also it seems, in some discussions, a person in her own right, a fourth divine hypostasis; the mediator between God and the world, who emerged after God's self-limitation (another Kabbalistic concept).

These personal mystical experiences, which had their roots initially in rather academic contemplation, took this Eastern Christian/Judaic mysticism out of the realm of religion and into that of literature, when Soloviev put pen to paper to describe his encounters in poetry. His poems dedicated to Sophia would be a powerful influence on the symbolist poetry and prose of Andrei Bely and Alexander Blok, for whom "the beautiful lady" came to symbolize the eternal feminine in the world, mother nature, Eros, and the pagan antiquity of the Russian land.

Indeed, Soloviev's merging of theology with the literary and philosophic crafts through his sophianic vision would set another important precedent for his heirs, in whom the Word, or Logos, as often as not refers to human artistic and literary creativity as to the Second Person of the Trinity. In this way, not just the boundaries between man and God were narrowed, but art and religion and literature were brought together in a heady fusion – in a way that gave Russian religious philosophy a potentially ecumenical, universal air that permitted those of no faith, those of a new faith, those of Christian faith, and finally – as in the case of Aaron Steinberg or Jacob Gordin – those of Jewish faith to participate in it.

Thus Soloviev, acting as medium to different traditions, opened the gates to the Russian "Silver Age" of Spirit-inspired literature and literary-philosophical God-seeking, continuing to guide it even after his death. This endeavor was an inspiration to his direct Russian and Russian-Jewish heirs. In the latter category, we can place Semyon Frank, whose work will be examined in the final chapter of this book. However, he also had an indirect influence on those Jews, who reacting in their own way to the pogroms and repressions of the last two decades of the nineteenth century, placed their hopes in a revival of Jewish life in Palestine. In the next section, we will consider the nature of this influence.

Soloviev died on July 31st, 1900 at the estate of his friend, Count Evgeny Trubetzkoy. The latter recounted how before his death he recited a psalm in Hebrew and prayed for the Jewish people. What the nature of this prayer was is not known.

Perhaps it was a prayer for the conversion of the Jewish people to Christ,

---

67 Soloviev describes these meetings in a poem called Three Encounters, which rather typically for Soloviev is written in a humorous, ironic almost parodic vein, verging occasionally on the self-mocking when the incongruity of the visions is considered.

after the model of Rabinowitz. But considering the overall spirit of his work, perhaps it was a prayer that the Jewish people might find a worthy inspiration in the deeds of Christian individuals and nations that would inspire them to recognize in Jesus Christ their own national redeemer. These hopes would be two sides of the same coin for one who considered the Jewish question a Christian question.

Perhaps, on the other hand, it was a prayer that rabbinic Jews might receive understanding from Christians of the deeply integrated and ethical spirituality of their religion, so helping Christians behave as the Jewish Messiah would have wished towards His people. Or perhaps it was a prayer that the Jews might find the strength to faithfully observe the tenets of their religion until the time came for them to fulfill their appointed role in hastening on the Second Coming of Christ.

Whatever the nature of the final words he uttered for the Jews, there are good grounds in his works for attributing all of these somewhat divergent meanings to his understanding of a question which obviously took pride of place in his heart – so much so, that as N.O.Lossky recalled, Soloviev often referred to *himself* as Jew.[68]

Jewish responses to Soloviev

Obviously, not all Jews would have agreed in seeing in the gentile philosopher from a privileged Russian background a *bona fide* Jew. Nonetheless, Soloviev's Jewish aspirations were not entirely solipsistic, as can be seen in the reactions of "real" Russian Jews to his work and person.

One of the most abiding testimonies to Soloviev's living relationship not just with Judaism and the "Old Testament" in the abstract, but with his Jewish contemporaries is the eulogies and memorials we find on his death in the Jewish press and Jewish literature. There is also the influence that Soloviev had on the work of Jewish cultural figures.

Yehuda Leib Kantor writing an obituary in Hebrew in *Ha-Dor* praised Solovyov's love for the Jews, and attributed it to his personality, the generosity of which he illustrates through several examples. He also praised his courage in battling the Slavophiles. The outstanding Jewish historian, Simon Dubnow, gave Solovyov a place of honor in his *World History of the Jewish People* (Russian 1936-1939), highlighting his article written against anti-Semitism in the press in 1890. Nahman Syrkin, a leading Socialist Zionist, wrote an article in 1902 called "V.Solovyov and his Attitude to the Jewish Question and the Jews" where he recounted Solovyov's admiration of the Jewish way of life.

This is to say nothing of Faivel Getz's "Recollections of V.Solovyov's Attitude Toward the Jews," in which Soloviev's Hebrew and Talmud teacher recalls with devotion their twenty year friendship. In the Russian-Jewish press in general, the image of Soloviev as one of the *hassidei umot ha-olam* (righteous gentiles)

---

[68] Nicolai Lossky, *Istoria russkoi filosofii*. Moscow: Akademicheskii Proiekt, 2007.

was propagated. In several synagogues, prayers were recited for the peace of his soul. Adolph Landau, editor of the Russian-Jewish paper *Voskhod*, wrote: "He died not only for science, not only for Russian society, he also died for Judaism and the Jews, with whom he sympathized and collaborated, and to whom he dedicated his work."

The Jewish response was not confined to eulogies and memorials. The contemporary Israeli scholar, Hamutal Bar-Yosef[69], shows that Soloviev influenced the work of a number of leading literary and religious Jewish figures. It is instructive to mention some of the most prominent of these.

Rabbi Yizhak Ha-Cohen Kook (1865-1935), the first Ashkenazi rabbi of pre-State Israel, and himself a well-known mystic with hotly contended views, used Soloviev's views to encourage Jewish self-belief among Zionist pioneers in Russia. H.N. Bialik, the first Jewish national poet, turned to the Talmud as a source of national revival rather than the Biblical sources then favored by Zionists: Bar-Yosef argues that this was in part due to the new respect in which the Talmud was held in Russia after Soloviev's famous essay defending it.[70] Bialik's poetry was also influenced directly by Soloviev's own poetry and by the Symbolist movement which Soloviev spearheaded.

Then there is the figure of rabbi Shmuel Alexandrov, a mystic and a Zionist, who corresponded with Ahad Ha'Am (the pen-name of Asher Ginsberg[71]) and Rabbi Kook: he preached the idea that in the eschatological future the Jewish commandments would be abrogated to be replaced by "superior Divine Wisdom." The gentile wellsprings of his inspiration were Schelling and "the great sage Vladimir Soloviev." Soloviev's doctrine of Sophiology also influenced the two major Russian-born poets of pre-State Israel, Avraham Shlonsky (1900-1973) and Natan Alterman (1910-1970).

On the other hand, it would create a false picture not to mention the critical Jewish reactions to Soloviev. Asher Ginsberg (alias Ahad Ha'Am[72]), the main proponent of cultural Zionism[73] and one of the most influential of Zionist

---

[69] The following references all come from her articles: Hamutal Bar-Yosef, "Recreating Jewish identity in Bialik's poems: the Russian context," http://www.bgu.ac.il/~baryosef/Eng/research/jewish_identity.htm ; and Hamutal Bar-Yosef, "The Jewish reception of Vladimir Solovyov," in *Vladimir Solovyov: Reconciler and Polemicist*, ed. Ewert von Zweerde, (Peeters, Lewen, 2000).

[70] As a result of his essay, N.Pereferkovich translated parts of the Mishna and Tosefta into Russian in from 1900-1910. Soloviev himself published and wrote the introduction to David Ginzburg's article on Kabbala in the collection *Voprosy filosofii i psikhologii* (1896).

[71] Ahad Ha'am means "one of the people" (Hebrew).

[72] His *nom de plume* means "one of the people."

[73] The strain of Zionism which argued that Jewish settlement in Palestine should not replace diaspora Jewry but serve as a cultural centre to revive world Jewry culturally (through the revival of modern Hebrew) and spiritually. He critiqued Herzl's political Zionism on the grounds that it was negatively conceived, as a response to anti-Semitism, and would run out of steam if Jews feeling to Palestine had nothing

thinkers, took issue with Soloviev's contention[74] that the Jewish national spirit is individualistic and materialistic. He also argued that Judaism is based on "objective justice" that strives for the redemption of the nation and not just, as in Christianity, the individual. Christian altruism, he writes in the same essay, is merely inverted egotism, presumably because of this vested interest in getting oneself to Heaven. Jewish justice, on the other hand is based on the principle of "Love your fellow as yourself," and he quotes Soloviev as a writer who argued that international relationships should be based on this Jewish principle.

Bar-Yosef points out that Ginsberg was engaged to a certain extent in a polemic against Jews who were taking too vicarious and too positive an interest in the study of early Christianity, attempting to bring it back into the Jewish experience. At the turn of the century throughout the Pale of Settlement there existed mixed Jewish-gentile discussion groups where the local intelligentsia discussed in a free spirit all sorts of topics of mutual interest from religion to revolution. In those circles some of the taboos against Christianity were relaxed, and Ahad Ha'am was perhaps concerned to reassert the superiority of Judaism over the newly attractive Christianity[75].

It might be argued in Soloviev's defense that Ahad Ha'am is not entirely fair to the philosopher, whose main concern was to steer Christianity away from such an individualistic preoccupation and to struggle for precisely the idea of universal Christian community, composed of free and integrated nations – an idea, which in fairness, comes out of Christianity's Jewish heritage. However, Ahad Ha'am's defensive approach to Soloviev's outreach to Judaism, perceived as an attempt to blur the boundaries between Judaism and Christianity, is understandable in a situation where Christianity was associated with a majority culture often for the most part hostile to the Jews and which for reasons often tainted by impure motives was drawing Jews away from their own people and culture.[76]

A similar criticism was heard from Dr Shemaryahu Levin. Displaying more understanding of Soloviev than Ha'am, he writes: "Had the writer [Soloviev] taken as an example not the nationality that seeks to swallow everything [i.e.

---

of the cultural or spiritual to nourish them once they got there.

[74] Ahad ha-Am, "Al Shtei Ha-Se'ipim," in *The Collected Writings of Ahad ha-Am*. Jerusalem: The Jewish Publishing House, 1956.

[75] Especially after 1905, when the government conceded constitutional reforms as a result of the revolution, there was a rise in the number of Jews converting to Christianity out of conviction. After the 1917 Revolution, a similar pattern was repeated. Cf. chs.4 and 5.

[76] In another article (Hamutal Bar-Yosef, "Jewish-Christian relations in Modern Hebrew and Yiddish literature: A preliminary sketch." http://www.bgu.ac.il/~baryosef/Eng/research/jewish_christian.htm), Bar-Yosef gives a fascinating and dismaying picture of the often traumatic reaction of especially pre-State Hebrew writers (some of whom had survived pogroms, and later the Holocaust) to European Christian culture in general. Israeli literature and Israelis in general are only recently beginning to respond to Christianity with a neutrality unshadowed by such experiences.

Russia], but the nationality of people who do not wish to be swallowed up [the Jews], then maybe he would have been spared the effort of seeking the third idea [to mediate between cosmopolitanism and aggressive nationalism]…which is already included in these people's nationality."

Simon Dubnow, cited earlier, was troubled by similar concerns. But essentially he was more sympathetic to Soloviev and saw the philosopher as having left room for the preservation of the nationality of both the big and the small nation in the distinction between *narodnost'* as a positive force and *national'nost'* as a negative force. Dubnow gives further precision to these terms, distinguishing between "oppressive nationalism" and "emancipatory nationalism," adding that the national struggle of the weak is only positive if it does not itself become oppressive in turn[77]. His own rejection of Zionism for Jewish cultural autonomy in Europe was founded on such a fear of Jewish nationalism turning aggressive[78].

A critique from a different direction came from the poet Avraham Shlonsky, who while influenced by Soloviev's sophiology criticized Russian symbolism's "panicky ideological retreat to mysticism" and championed political involvement – in his case Zionist activity. However, the example of Shmuel Alexandrov and Rabbi Kook demonstrate that not all Jews were so skeptical about the combination of nationalism, mysticism and a universalist understanding of both. It should also be remembered that the symbolists often turned political in the case of the 1917 Revolution, seeing it as a concrete implementation of their spiritual ideals – the prime example being Andrei Bely.

Bar-Yosef ends her essay on Soloviev with this call: "Soloviev opened a channel of Jewish-Christian mutual interest. Ironically this channel was blocked by two historical forces which were hostile to both Judaism and Christianity: the Soviet and Nazi regimes. It is only now, half a century later after the Holocaust's Jewish trauma and about a decade after the end of the Soviet regime, that we can begin to examine it again."

Perhaps even now, given the recentness of the last-named disaster and its lingering influence on contemporary Russia and the Russian Church, the time is too soon for free dialogue to take place. But one can only concur, that imperfect as the efforts may be, they should be initiated.

Another factor which evidently overshadows "Jewish-Christian mutual interest" is the fear of both sides of losing their own identity. In another essay[79] Bar-Yosef shows that the interest of Hebrew and Yiddish writers in the Jewish Jesus and in other Christian figures like Mary and John the Baptist which took

---

[77] For more on Dubnow, and his Jewish follower Aaron Steinberg (also a philosopher of Russian all-unity), cf. ch.5.

[78] Dubnow later worked with Aaron Steinberg, the subject of ch.5. Steinberg was a Russian-Jewish philosopher of all-unity, albeit it more in the Dostoevskian than the Solovievian tradition, though there is of course significant overlap.

[79] "Jewish-Christian relations in Modern Hebrew and Yiddish literature: A preliminary sketch."

place in the first two decades of the twentieth century among writers as well as artists (Marc Chagall is the most prominent example) could lead to a reaction of shock and repellence on the Jewish side: Sholem Asch, the Yiddish writer most well-known outside of Jewish circles before Isaac Bashevis Singer, went a step too far in his novel *Mary* – Christianity is presented so attractively there in contrast to Judaism that for a long time he could not find a translator. This looks like the converse problem of Soloviev's infatuation with the Talmud, where the philosopher verges on an abandonment of his own earlier "mission to the Jews."

Another example was the Yiddish poet Itsik Manger, who wrote a collection of poems called "Ballads, Poems of Christ and Poems of the Baal Shem" where Christian and Hassidic Jewish symbols have permeated deep into the consciousness of the poet – rather like a verbal equivalent of Chagall's paintings. In contrast, the national poet Bialik[80], while immersed in Russian and sophianic imagery due to the Solovievian influence transmitted through symbolism, took great care to draw a distancing line of irony in his poem *The Scroll of Fire*: redemption through the love of a woman and self-sacrifice to all-unity are presented as false Christian symbols alien to the spirit and future of Judaism[81].

This drawing close of Christianity and Judaism is, obviously, a theme found in Soloviev's works, specifically in his qualified endorsement of Rabinowitz's Jewish Christianity. Among his heirs, those who would be most drawn to the idea of Jewish-Christian "fusion" were Sergei Bulgakov and Lev Karsavin. Both of them were attracted to the idea of a revived Judeo-Christianity, and Bulgakov especially, saw the possibility of such a revival as the sign of the apocalyptic times in which they were living. However, just as Bialik and Shlonsky were cautious in their absorption of certain elements of Soloviev's Christian philosophy, Bulgakov and Karsavin experienced a similar deep ambiguity and unease at the form that that the Judaic element in this hybrid might take.

Finally, in assessing Soloviev's writings on Judaism, one should always be cautious in assigning success and failure. For almost two thousand years Christians saw the exile of Jews as proof of the truth of Christianity. The ingathering of Jews to the State of Israel certainly puts a question-mark alongside that *theologoumenon*. But, likewise, to maintain that the State of Israel fulfills Judaism's, or for that matter, Christianity's deepest Messianic

---

[80] The very idea of a national poet-prophet as Bialik, somewhat against his will at first, was to become to the fledgling Israeli nation, is a role taken from Russian culture.

[81] For further details, cf:, Hamutal Bar-Yosef, "Recreating Jewish identity in Bialik's poems: the Russian context." http://www.bgu.ac.il/~baryosef/Eng/research/jewish_identity.htm ; Hamutal Bar-Yosef, "Jewish-Christian relations in Modern Hebrew and Yiddish literature: A preliminary sketch." http://www.bgu.ac.il/~baryosef/Eng/research/jewish_christian.htm ; and Hamutal Bar-Yosef, "Sophiology and the Concept of Femininity in Russian Symbolism and in Modern Hebrew Poetry." In *Modern Jewish Studies* 2/1, (2003): 59-78.

yearnings would be dangerous and confused[82].

The same is true in judging Soloviev. His Christian politics may have met with failure at the obvious level. But the contemporary Russian Orthodox thinker, Vasilenko, while cautioning against some of Soloviev's more exotic ideas (the soul as a pre-existing Leibnizian monad; sexual love as the surest way to communicate with the female, sophianic Divine[83]; Sophia as a goddess who must rule over the universe), rightly concludes that "whoever approaches all-unity with understanding will never consider Orthodoxy something local, weak or isolated from world Christianity and the problems of the contemporary world."

In the following chapters, we will investigate how Soloviev's heirs used his heritage to understand the problems of their contemporary world. This was a world which lived up to the apocalyptic expectations that traumatized Soloviev on the cusp of the twentieth century. In the half century that followed his premature death, both the Jewish and Russian peoples were to experience revolution, genocide, World War, exile and incarceration – often shoulder to shoulder – and Soloviev's linking of the Jewish and Russian spirit was to provide a paradigm for those of his fellow-thinkers drawn into that era of upheaval.

---

[82] In the Russian Christian context, "Kabbalistic Messianism" may be said to have taken a revolutionary eschatological form in the quasi-Solovievian revolutionism of Blok and Bely; in the Jewish Israeli context, "Kabbalistic Messianism" has often displayed dangerous political eschatological tendencies in the heritage of the above-mentioned Rabbi Kook, and religious Zionism. Yeshayahu Leibowitz, in particular has made this point regarding Kookian religious Zionism. (cf. Yeshayu Leibowitz, *Judaism, Human Values and the Jewish State*. Ed. Eliezer Goldman. Cambridge: Harvard University Press, 1995, pp. 111-113.) It is a point worth bearing in mind when we come to consider the polemic about eschatologism in Judaism and Christianity in Russian religious thought in the run-up to the October Revolution. In ch.2, we will see how a Kookian Zionist reads Bulgakov sympathetically, showing how Russian Jewish and Christian "theosophical Messianism" can meet in the contemporary context.

[83] This theme is found particularly in Lev Karsavin, cf.ch.5.

Two

Bulgakov and the sacred blood of Jewry

Two

Bulgakov: wrestling with Soloviev's heritage

The first "spiritual child" of Soloviev whom we will consider is Sergei Bulgakov. To begin with we will trace the general development of the man who has been called "arguably the greatest Orthodox theologian of the twentieth century" and the "greatest Orthodox theologian since Gregory Palamas,"[1] paying attention to his links with Soloviev. Then, we will turn to his treatment of the Jewish question in its various forms.

As the superlative epithets just quoted show, Bulgakov is a figure of monumental importance in modern Orthodox theology. Although many would qualify the high praise given him by his admirers due to significant disagreements with key aspects of his theological outlook, this does not detract from the fact that a central position in Orthodox thought is occupied by Bulgakov, whose extensively stated views on the Jewish question would thus be of interest even if they did occupy the crucial role in his theology that he attributed to them.

In 1890, the last decade of Soloviev's life, Sergei Bulgakov was only a twenty-one-year old youth, just finishing his gymnasium education. In 1895, he was nearing the end of his studies at Moscow university, where he had become an adherent of "legal Marxism." By 1900, he had written two works on Marxist economics: *Markets in capitalist production* and *Capitalism and agriculture* – not, one would imagine, a very prepossessing start for a future world-famous theologian.

---

[1] Catherine Evtuhov, "Bulgakov, Sergei Nikolayevich," in Encyclopedia of Russian History. The Gale Group Inc. 2004. *Encyclopedia.com*. (October 4, 2009). http://www.encyclopedia.com/doc/1G2-3404100184.html; and Constantin Andronikov, the translator of Bulgakov's works into French (quoted in Krassen Stanchev, "Sergei Bulgakov and the spirit of capitalism," in *Journal of Markets and Morality*, Volume 11, number 1, Spring 2008.) Boris Jakim, Bulgakov's most recent English translator, refers to him as "the twentieth century's most profound Orthodox systematic theologian" (Introduction to Sergei Bulgakov, *The Lamb of God*, translated by Boris Jakim. (Michigan: Eerdmans, 2008), p.x.) On the other hand, another notable French heir of Russian theology, Olivier Clément, maintained that the 20th century saw only three great theologians: Fr. Dumitru Staniloae (a Romanian), Fr. Justin Popovich (a Serbian), and Vladimir Lossky. The latter was Clément's own teacher, and the main critic of the orthodoxy of Bulgakov's thought. Clément's vs. Evtuhov's and Andronikov's evaluations show that Bulgakov's status within Orthodoxy still has not been resolved, due to his sophiology, which will be examined below. (As we will see in the chapter on Berdyaev, another contemporary Orthodox figure assigns the epithet of "greatest Orthodox theologian since Palamas" to Berdyaev – a sign of the enthusiasm Russian thought continues to inspire in (some parts of) the contemporary Russian Orthodox Church; though such an evaluation, I believe, would be far rarer.)

However, that was soon to change – in a pattern that recapitulated Soloviev's own move from materialism to religion. Having relocated to Kiev to take up a position as a lecturer in politics and law at the technical university there, Bulgakov became interested in Kantian philosophy and moved his orientation from "Marxism to Idealism" (as the title of an anthology he edited at the time was called). In 1902, he finally discovered Soloviev with a vengeance, and in 1903 he wrote an article called "What can the philosophy of Vladimir Soloviev give to contemporary consciousness?"[2]

In this and a string of other articles, Bulgakov first hammered out the foundations of his own vision of Christianity: he was particularly drawn to Soloviev's personality and his commitment to a universal Christianity, as well as his emphasis on Christian politics. Whereas Soloviev's Christian action had taken the form of a theocratic vision of unity between the Christian churches, Bulgakov at first linked the concept of Christian politics to a fusion of socialism and Christianity, in an attempt to weld together two aspects of his life that still struggled within him.

Although the 1905 Revolution graphically brought home to him just how unsympathetic the beliefs and deeds of the radical faction were to his new mentality[3], he continued to believe that Soloviev's vision was best implemented in a combination of Christianity and social action. He even presented himself for election as a representative of his native region at the first state Duma[4] in 1907. Having been selected, he stood on a non-party platform, representing something that he called Christian socialism, a socialism that would be free of atheism, and filled with Orthodoxy, the "Russian socialism" as Dostoyevsky had called it.

This was the first of many positions that Bulgakov would defend in his life that attracted controversy and misunderstanding. For in the categories of the time, it was taken for granted that if a member of the Duma professed Orthodoxy, then his political outlook was conservative and monarchist; and if he professed socialism, then he was *ipso facto* against the old order. In fact, Bulgakov soon came to see the sense of this dichotomy, and while he could never fully accept the polarity of Christianity and social action, he later rejected his naïve blend of opposites in the strongest terms, calling his project of that time "social-idiotism." Others, like Blok and Bely, however, would only much later, and under the tragic pressure of the events of the second Revolution, come to a similar judgment about the infelicity of spiritual politics in the Solovievan style – as they saw it[5].

---

[2] Sergei Bulgakov, "Chto dayot sovremennomu soznaniyu filosofia Vladimira Solovieva?" in *Voprosy filosofii i psykhologii*, No.66 (1903).

[3] Later, we will quote extracts from Bulgakov's diary that describe his reaction to the first Russian revolution.

[4] One of the constitutional concessions ceded by the government after the 1905 Revolution.

[5] The writers Blok and Bely, and the poet novelist-philosopher Dmitri Merezhkovsky were at the heart of the symbolist movement, and all interepted Soloviev's mysticism in a revolutionary way – as a call to create a new Christian Kingdom of

Bulgakov's stint in real politics, though, was an effective catalyst in speeding up that disillusionment, and by the end of the decade, he was turning to another aspect of Soloviev's heritage, one that would also get him into deep waters of a different sort in the coming years: sophiology. 1912 was the year in which Bulgakov first outlined his thoughts on Sophia, in a book called *The Philosophy of Economics*. Now political action was to be much gentler and slower, and connected to "mystical action," namely the "sophianization" of the world.

In 1917, Bulgakov developed this idea in *The Unfading Light*. By then, a veritable metamorphosis had occurred in the soul of the former Marxist and devotee of Kantianism: by the time the October Revolution was drawing near, Bulgakov was embracing a mystical religious concept of the Russian monarchy, with extreme reverence for the Tsar as office and as a person, despite his personal failings. As he saw it, the soul of Russia and the monarchy of Russia were intertwined: the fall of one would mean the fall of the other. Much of his energy was taken up now with uncovering the essentially atheistic, anti-religious, even demonic character of his former Marxist beliefs, and that of the radicals intent on implementing that ideology in Russia. As we will see, this gradual "sophianization" of his thought was to have a radical impact on his evaluation of Jewry and Judaism as well, casting at first a negative but then a positive light on his attitudes[6].

The year after the Revolution, Bulgakov was ordained to the priesthood, succumbing as he put it, to the call of his Levitical blood[7]. This signaled in an even more obvious way his complete opposition to the new Soviet regime, to whom he was now an official enemy[8]. But the priesthood would also put him

---

God on earth. Bulgakov, and Soloviev's nephew Sergei Soloviev, came to repudiate this approach. In fact, this millenarianism came to be seen as Judaic by Bulgakov, as we will see in the next section.

[6] Ch.4 discusses how the mysticism of Pavel Florensky was connected to his attitude towards Jews. In the 1910s Bulgakov and Florensky were very close, and both were working on a sophiology that would bring Soloviev closer to Orthodoxy. Florensky's return to the Church from an atheist youth was more rapid than Bulgakov's; though eleven years younger than him, he was ordained to the priesthood in 1913, five years earlier than his friend. Florensky's and Bulgakov's Sophia-oriented all-unity with its conservative social and political outlook led to a number of similarities in their evaluation of Judaism and Jewry. The most obvious difference is that Florensky's "Judeology" was uncompromisingly anti-Semitic; the nature of Bulgakov's thoughts on Judaism will become clear shortly.

[7] In the sense of continuing the priesthood of his father and grandfather. This is an interesting observation, given his thoughts on blood, nation and Judaism discussed below. He even writes, "I was a Jew from Jews" (p.48) of his pure Levitical lineage, echoing St. Paul's language, and reminiscent of Soloviev's self-image as a "Jew." Incidentally, present at his ordination were two Jewish friends who will be the subject of the next chapter, Mikhail Gershenzon and Lev Shestov.

[8] As a priest in Soviet Russia, he had to forthwith resign his teaching position at Moscow University, and he moved back to the Ukraine where he was second priest

into opposition with aspects of his own intellectual past, and not just Marxism and materialism. While the teaching of Sophia would remain close to his heart, Bulgakov came to reject the philosophical enterprise *per se*, so that Soloviev's vision of an integrated philosophy came to seem to him a mistaken enterprise. More and more, he began to mine his thought, as he put it, from the Eucharistic cup. Theology, and not philosophy, would be his path henceforth.

In his last philosophical work, aptly titled *The Tragedy of Philosophy* (1921), he writes of the exhaustion of philosophy, and its failure to live up to its essentially religious roots and inspiration. In sum, "the history of philosophy can be shown to be and interpreted as religious heresiology." In its place must come theology, based on religious experience, which needs to be shored up against subjectivity and individualism by being brought into harmony with Church tradition. As such anything that lay outside of that tradition could have no place in Christianity. If Christianity was to be living and new, it would have to find a way forward into the future without philosophy.

Certainly Western attempts to improve Christianity - the Renaissance, the Reformation and humanism – were more and more to be considered by Bulgakov to be part of that same heretical tradition as philosophy. But ironically, his own attempt to expand and reapply the Tradition for the salvation of contemporary man through an extension and deepening of Soloviev's sophiology, was itself to be branded heresy,[9] and some have questioned whether Bulgakov escaped from philosophy at all, seeing in his work the German Romanticism of Hegel and Schelling[10].

Interestingly, at this time Bulgakov was also recapitulating another phase of his early spiritual mentor: the temptations of Catholicism. Even though he was at this point immersed in his Russianness, including a Slavophile-tinted distrust of the West, and was a monarchist in mourning, in another sense he was confronted by a similar situation as Soloviev: the seeming weakness of his native Russian church, and its inability to hold its own in the world, a fact which contrasted with the perceived strength and organization of the Roman church in the West.

Living through the Civil War as it raged in all its bloodiness and brutality in the Ukraine from 1918-1922, seeing the Church attacked from within (by the collaborationist Living Church) and without (by the Bolsheviks), Bulgakov came close to despair and believed that the Russian Church did not have the resources to survive its first persecution on native soil. Only the organizing principle of the Papacy could save Christ's church, and he wrote a series of articles in which he struggled with these questions[11].

By the time of his exile in 1923, though, he had overcome this temptation[12],

---

at the Alexander Nevsky Cathedral in Kiev.
[9] For details, see the discussion in the section on sophiology below.
[10] This is a charge that has been made against other Russian religious thinkers like Frank, Florensky, and Karsavlin, and will be discussed at the relevant places.
[11] *U sten Khersonisa* (manuscript, Yalta, 1923) reprinted in *Simvol*, Paris, 1991, No.25.
[12] On the first stage of his exile, he resided briefly in Constantinople, he was subjected

and although he never consider himself anti-Catholic, it may be said that by the time he settled in Paris he had a great confidence in what Orthodoxy could give to the West, suffering as he saw it from humanism, atheistic socialism, the distortion of the Papacy and the consequent Reformation, as well as another temptation that he himself had overcome, scientism[13].

However, these years in the Ukraine will form a central focus of our examination of Bulgakov below, for a different reason: there he was subject to another temptation, that of anti-Semitism. The former Pale of Settlement in which he was living had been abolished by decree of the the Provisional government on March 20, 1917 and the Soviet regime's continuation of a pro-Jewish policy caused many Jews to experience sympathy for the Bolsheviks. Thus Bulgakov and Jewry – at least as he perceived it – found themselves on different sides of the political barricades. Given the apocalyptic nature of that political struggle, and the mystical turn of Bulgakov's mind, for him that opposition soon exploded beyond politics and into theology.

In 1923, the regime expelled Bulgakov as an undesirable, a decision which spared him the harsher sentences that would be handed out to dissidents after Lenin's death. Arriving in Paris along with many other expellees, he threw himself into organizing Orthodox life among the Russian émigré community, and also representing Orthodoxy in ecumenical dialogue with Protestants and Catholics.

He helped found the St Sergius Institute, which opened in Paris in 1925 with Bulgakov as its rector. He also took a guiding role in the formation of the Russian Christian Youth Movement[14]. Both the institute and the movement were

---

to Jesuit missionizing, which actually helped him to overcome his infatuation for good. Thenceforth, he was to look at his Roman temptation as a necessary dialectical stage in his developing conception of the Church, and as a "preventative inoculation" for the future. Bulgakov's development contrasts interestingly with that of Sergei Soloviev, the philosopher's nephew, who had been close to his uncle at the end of his life, and a central figure in the dissemination of his heritage. Initially, S.Soloviev was, like Bulgakov, close to the spirit of the 'new religious consciousness' preached in Soloviev's name by the symbolists: Bely (to become S.Soloviev's brother-in-law), Blok (S.Soloviev's second cousin), and Merezhkovsky. Then, like Bulgakov, he rejected the unchristian elements of Merezhkovsky's 'third testament' and the neo-pagan veneration of Sophia. He was ordained an Orthodox priest, but after the Revolution he converted to Catholicism, eventually being ordained a Catholic priest. Later, he suffered psychological traumas which eventually led to his death. (Further reading: P.P.Gaidenko, "Vladimir Soloviev i filosofia serebraynogo veka," ch.10 on S.Soloviev.)

[13] In *Svet Nevecherniy* (*The Unfading Light*), he refers to his liberation due to his growing faith from "a panicky fear of…scientism and its Sanhedrin." (It will be noted, in passing, how *Sanhedrin* is a negative term – by default. This is indicative of the general unthinking atmosphere of anti-Jewishness in which not just Russia, but the whole of Christian Europe was soaked).

[14] Many well-known Orthodox figures in the West were graduates of the Institute or the Youth Movement, and some were Bulgakov's spiritual children, for example: Lev

to become a beacon of Orthodoxy in the West: Soloviev had once expressed the regret that Khomiakov, the leading Christian Slavophile, had never founded a school, a deficiency that Soloviev himself did not rectify. In that sense, Bulgakov answered a need, and though by that time, there was much in Soloviev's heritage that Bulgakov could not accept, the ties that connected them were in many ways still strong.

Bulgakov was prolific both in his old role as a philosopher and then in his new role as theologian. His purely theological works start with *The Burning Bush* (1927), which explores aspects of the Orthodox veneration of the Mother of God. Later works treat miracles[15], angels[16], and the power of the Name of Christ[17]. The culmination of Bulgakov's theological work is the trilogy exploring the Divine-humanity[18], whose last volume *The Bride of the Lamb*, which is heavy in sophiological content, was published at the same time as his final essays on the Jewish Question, during the Second World War.

Bulgakov died in 1944, after suffering for three years from throat cancer. Those who were present at his death-bed reported how his face shone after death and those who saw him lying in repose were filled with a great sense of inner peace.

The Jews in Bulgakov's thought: a preview of the main problem

Having looked at Bulgakov's general development, it is time to focus on his evolving attitudes to Jews and Judaism. The nature of our treatment will be shaped by a problem which ultimately confronts the reader of these writings. Broadly

---

Zander, Paul Evdokimov, Nicolai Afanasiev (who was present at Vatican II and had some influence on the "return to the Fathers" movement in Catholicism), Mother Maria Skobtsova, and the nun and original icon-painter Joanna Reitlinger. Another giant of Orthodoxy in the West, Metropolitan Anthony of Sourozh, first came into contact with Bulgakov in the Youth Movement. During Soviet times, he was greatly revered in Russia by underground Christians (as he still is after the fall of the regime), so that Bulgakov's influence extended indirectly back to his homeland. Bulgakov himself is widely studied today in Russia, though controversy continues to surround his sophiology.

[15] Sergei Bulgakov, *O chudesakh yevangelskikh*. Moscow: Russkiy Put', 1994.

[16] *Lestvitsa yakovleva*, in Sergei Bulgakov, *Malaya trilogia. (Kupina neopalimaya. Drug zhenikha. Lestvitsa Iakovlya.)* Moscow: Obshchedostupniy pravoslavnii universitet, osnovannii protoiereem Aleksandrom Menem, 2008.

[17] Sergei Bulgakov, *Filosofia imeni*, Moscow: Nauka, 1998.

[18] Consisting of 3 volumes: *The Lamb of God* (1933), devoted to Christology; *The Comforter* (1935) devoted to pneumatology; and *The Bride of the Lamb* (1942), devoted to anthropology, or the doctrine of the church – ecclesiology – understood as Sophia. Two of these volumes are available in an English translation by Boris Jakim: Bulgakov, Sergei. *The Bride of the Lamb*. Translated by Boris Jakim. Michigan. Eerdmans, 2002; Bulgakov, Sergei. *The Lamb of God*. Translated by Boris Jakim. Michigan: Eerdmans, 2008.

speaking, if we divide Bulgakov's writings on Judaism into two periods[19], those that preceded his exile from Russia and those that followed it, it emerges that the early writings are rather sympathetic to Judaism, while the latter are peppered with some truly breath-taking anti-Semitic statements – which nonetheless are intermingled with a very rich and suggestive theological approach that in outline is potentially very "philo-Semitic."

But it is not just the question of Bulgakov's anti-Semitism, if such it is[20]. There is another related problem, which we will try to bring out in presenting these writings: this is that the crimes that Bulgakov accuses (contemporary) Jews of in his later writings are laid at the feet of Christians and Russians in his earlier writings, and there Jews are said to be innocent of these crimes. Thus, regardless of the content or truth of Bulgakov's claims, there is a logical problem here. How did it come about that Jews are suddenly accused of faults which they were not associated with before?

To preempt a bit, the concrete charges are as follows. In the early writings, Old Testament Judaism is seen as holy because its purity serves to lay the ground for the Incarnation of Christ. After the Incarnation, this purity is exclusivist and legalistic and thus inappropriate. Likewise, the Jewish impatience for the Messiah and the end-time is praiseworthy before Christ, but foolishness afterwards. Nonetheless, Bulgakov makes clear in these earlier writings that after the Incarnation eschatological speculation and behavior came from the early Christians and later Christian sects awaiting the Second Coming. And in one passage, he makes clear that the source of these speculations and strivings was Jewish Apocalyptic writings – but in translation into gentile languages. For these writings had been dropped from the rabbinic Biblical canon, did not exist in Hebrew and were thus not influential in Talmudic Judaism.

In these earlier writings, Bulgakov further develops a thesis that modern socialist and communist movements are rooted in Christian sectarian aberrations. Thus the ultimately bloody and inhuman attempt to create a paradise on earth – as in Soviet Russia – can be traced to Christian apocalyptic heresies. Russian communists have maintained their Christian faith, but in perverted form. In at least one work, Bulgakov sees some hope in the genetic connection of communism to Christianity: there is the possibility that atheism can morph back into true belief.

Now we see the contradiction clearly with the later writings. One of the most striking features there is that the blame for the apocalyptic Russian revolution is for the most part shifted onto Jewish shoulders. Contemporary Jews are now accused of attempting to murder Holy Russia; and Jewry, Jewish religion and Jewish "consciousness" are depicted variously as "parasitic," "poisonous," "corrupt" and "materialistic."

Bulgakov's earlier exemption of Talmudic Judaism from the sin of

---

[19] This division ignores overlapping tendencies in both periods and will be qualified in the next section.

[20] There is some disagreement about this among different people as we will see.

eschatological paradise-mongering leads us to wonder how Jews became involved in revolutionary activity against Holy Russia. But instead of addressing this problem, Bulgakov pays almost no attention to Judaism, or to religious-secular distinctions within Jewry. Instead he ascribes all the dangerous propensities of an undifferentiated Jewry to "Jewish consciousness."

It is clear that Bulgakov's approach is heavily influenced by classical Christian attitudes to Judaism, overlaid with a very Russian suspicion of Judaism and Jews. If Bulgakov had added nothing new to the classical supersessionist approach, if he had not tried to immerse himself scripturally in the full paradox of the "mystery of Israel," then he could have avoided this contradiction with a dry formalism: the Jews were chosen in the Old Testament; but after the Incarnation they lost their chosenness and became vessels of evil such as communism. But as we will see, Bulgakov constantly explodes out of this formalism and his own original theology – as is often the case – shatters conventions. The reader of these works thus comes face to face with powerful currents that seem to be tugging in opposite directions. For example: Bulgakov the castigator of Jewish revolutionaries simultaneously declares that Jews are closer to God than gentiles and rejects the classical doctrine of Christian supersessionism as utterly unbiblical.

From the perspective of Christian theology in the twentieth century what is enthralling about these writings is how close in spirit they are to Karl Barth's theology of the Jews. The great Protestant theologian also declared that Jews were holier than gentiles. At the same time, he made many deeply anti-Semitic statements in his theology. He even confessed: "I am decidedly not a philosemite, in that in personal encounters with living Jews (even Jewish Christians), I have always so long as I can remember, had to suppress a totally irrational aversion…"[21] As we will see, this is finds an echo in some of Bulgakov's attitudes.

Barth and Bulgakov were both writing their Jewish essays during the Second World War. Whether Bulgakov was influenced by Barth, I cannot say.[22] His theology of Jews is so organically linked to his general theology that even if there had been some influence, it could only have been of the surface.

---

[21] Karl Barth, Letters: 1961-1968, quoted in Michael Wyschogrod, *Abraham's Promise: Judaism and Jewish-Christian Relations,* (Michigan: William B. Eerdmans Publishing Company, 2004), 235.

[22] Bulgakov was aware of Barth's work, of course. In 1934, he mentions his work in a couple of pages in an article devoted to "voices of Christian conscience in Germany." While admiring Barth's resistance to Nazism, perhaps not surprisingly he is critical of Barth's main axes of concern: "fear of God" and "salvation of the soul." He sees these concerns as leaving no room for the problem of attributing Christian meaning to the world; further he sees in Barth a one-sided denunciation of all forms of historical Christianity, with the result that he allows no non-German Christian to offer an alternative approach to the situation of Christianity in Germany. This, for Bulgakov, represents a pride-filled radicalism, which almost brings him to an extremism as unbalanced as that of his poisonous opponents. Among German Christian resistance to Nazism, Bulgakov prefers Friedrich Heiler. Cf. Sergei Bulgakov, "Golosa khristianskoi sovesti v Germanii," in *Put'* No.43, 1934: 62-71.

The discovery of such temporal and temperamental neighbors in thought is exciting. A Jewish theologian, Michael Wyschogrod, who is an admirer of Barth remarked: "It may be an exaggeration to say that statements such as these [of Barth's on the Jews] cannot be found in the writings of any other contemporary Christian theologians. But if they exist, they cannot easily be found, and in any case, are probably not as clear as those of Barth."[23] The fact is that such writings do exist. They can be easily found, but only in Russian. Whether they are as clear as Barth, readers can judge for themselves. Certainly, the parallel is not exact. There are other local factors which make Bulgakov different. However, here the comparison is merely suggested and not developed.

It will be our task in the coming sections to see how Bulgakov came to his paradoxical conclusions. After that, we will engage in an exploration of some of the fruitful contradictions in his writings, trying to develop Bulgakov's insights in other – hopefully still Bulgakovian – directions.

To begin with, we will add more detail to this sketch of Bulgakov's early writings on Jews and the Old Testament. Secondly, we will look at the question of Bulgakov's anti-Semitism, the biographical factors which probably influenced him and the reactions to this of Jews and non-Jews of the time. Thirdly, we will examine the development of Bulgakov's "sophiology," which played a role in deepening his understanding of the Jewish question and is probably responsible for his "Barthian" evaluation of the contemporary Jewish people. We will then look in some depth at his war-time writings on Jewry so that the reader without Russian can gain access to these essays. Finally, we will go back to an earlier essay on Russian destiny and use it as a spring-board to critique the inconsistencies and develop some of the latent insights in Bulgakov's work. We will round off by considering certain contemporary Jewish reactions to Bulgakov.

Judaism and the Old Testament in Bulgakov's early philosophy

What we referred to above as Bulgakov's "early pre-exilic writings" on Judaism appear in *Two Cities*, a collection of essays written in Moscow between 1906 and 1910, and *The Unfading Light,* a philosophical-theological work that appeared in 1917. Another "early" work that appears between these two is the essay "Zion," written in 1915 for the collection *Shchit'* (Shield). These may be contrasted for their absence of any harsh rhetoric against Jews with his "later post-exilic" Jewish essays, which were written in 1941 and 1942 in Paris. There the anti-Jewish rhetoric is extremely harsh, although the theological analysis of Jewry builds on earlier insights and is overall sympathetic to Jewry.

Before looking at the early writings, a proviso is in order. The clear-cut division into early and late Jewish writings is too rigid, for the periods overlap. Firstly, the post-exilic 1931 essay, "Judas: Apostle-Traitor" contains anti-Russian rhetoric and is "soft" on Jews – that is, while the subject would seem to present

---

[23] Michael Wyschogrod, *Abraham's Promise: Judaism and Jewish-Christian Relations,* 221.

opportunities for finger-pointing at Jewish involvement in Bolshevism, these are bypassed. The essay thus continues an analysis first broached in *Two Cities* of a sectarian-Christian origin of modern eschatological politics. Secondly, our analysis of the early writings on Old Testament Jewry must be supplemented by reference to Bulgakov's *Autobiographical Fragments*, especially those parts that tell of his experiences and reactions to the Russian Revolution. Here we encounter early anti-Jewish sentiments that will only resurface again in the late 1941-2 essays.

Thus the "early" period really stretches from 1906 to 1931, while the "late" 1941-2 period has roots that go back into the period of revolution and Civil War (1917-1923). In this section we will look at the relevant parts of *Two Cities* (1906-1910) and the *Unfading Light* (1917). Then we will examine "Zion" (1915). Finally, we will make our first attempt to understand Bulgakov's anti-Semitism by looking at his autobiographical musings that concern his last years in Russia before his exile in 1923. We will touch on the "early-late" essay on Judas, but a real engagement with that work will only come at the end of the chapter – for reasons that will become clear.

Two Cities (1906-1910)
In *Two Cities*, Bulgakov is really discussing the Old Testament and the people of the Old Testament, rather than contemporary Jews, from a perspective that is shaped by his own transition from Marxism to Christianity. Rather as with Karl Barth, Bulgakov is stating a thesis that was stated in similar form in the West, this time by Karl Lowith. Lowith's book *The Meaning of History*, however, appeared in 1959, a full half century after Bulgakov (and other Russians like Berdyaev) were making the link between Christian chiliastic movements and early socialism[24].

In his introductory essay to the recent Russian reprint of *Dva Grada* (*Two Cities*), Yu. N. Davydov summarizes three elements of the main thesis that unites the different essays in this volume[25]. The first element is Bulgakov's *structural* analysis of the intelligentsia's atheistic religion of "human-divinity"[26] derived from Feuerbach, Compte and Marx; the second is a *genetic* analysis of this paradoxical religion, which finds the origin of this modern "religion" in the Christian chiliasm of the Middle Ages, with its "mirage of an earthly city, beckoning and seducing, but deceiving." The genetic analysis, as we will see shortly, ultimately traces this religion all the way back to the "Judaic apocalyptic" of the first century before Christ. The third element of these essays is the attempt to give meaning to the "tragic event of the first Russian

---

[24] One should not forget that Merezhkovsky's chiliastic pretensions must have contributed to Bulgakov's equation of a distorted Christianity and social-revolutionary impulses: after all, at the start of the 20th century he and Bulgakov were both attracted to revolution, socialism, Marxism and a "new Christianity" – which Bulgakov would shrug off, one by one.
[25] Sergei Bulgakov, *Dva Grada*. (Moscow: Astrel', 2008), 35-36.
[26] The atheistic distortion of Christian "divine-humanity."

revolution [in 1905] and the role played in it by the Russia intelligentsia."

From our perspective, what is of most compelling interest is the role played in Bulgakov's analysis by Judaic apocalyptic. Bulgakov begins his section on "The general nature of Judaic apocalyptic" by listing the apocalyptic books, a number of which form part of the Orthodox Biblical canon. Straightaway, we encounter a fact which will have repercussions for Bulgakov's whole analysis of Judaism and Jewry. For having listed the canonical and non-canonical apocalyptic books, he comments: "Finally, rabbinic theology, the Talmud, ancient Jewish prayers (the Shmoneh-Esreh, Havienu, Kaddish and Musaph) contain a number of petitions of an eschatological character." In a footnote, he comments: "Ignorance of Hebrew and the complexity of the Talmudic literature have not permitted me to become acquainted with this literature in the original,"[27] and in fact there is no further discussion of rabbinic Apocalypse.

A couple of pages later, however, the reason for this omission becomes clear. As Bulgakov writes: "After the destruction of Jerusalem and the fall of Judea, apocalyptic writings came under suspicion in the ruling circles of Jewry, and afterwards were completely expelled from use, being completely replaced by Talmudic wisdom. But then they reappear in Christian communities and become the favorite reading in several primarily 'barbarian' churches, in whose languages are preserved for us many monuments of apocalyptic writing, as well as in the Slavonic East (the 'Slavonic Enoch'!)."

This must be borne in mind whenever we encounter the phrase "Judaic apocalyptic" in these essays: they exclude rabbinic writings, which for Bulgakov are mainly quietistic on this front. The interesting parallels which Bulgakov draws between apocalyptic motifs and modern sociology are thus analogies between non-rabbinic Jewish literature as mediated through Christian thought.

This corresponds to the needs of Bulgakov at this period. The 1905 Revolution played the single biggest role in convincing him of the mistakenness of his Marxist and socialist sympathies, and *Two Cities* reflects his pondering on the meaning of this event, as Davydov points out. As we will see in his *Autobiographical Fragments* later, as well as in a later 1914 essay, *The Russian Tragedy*, at this stage Bulgakov sees Russian revolutionary activity as the poisonous fruit of the Russian intelligentsia's alienation from Christianity and a sincere feeling for Russia and Russian history. Dostoyevsky's analysis of the Russian "devils," possessed by demonic atheism, is gradually given philosophical and metaphysical flesh by Bulgakov in the years from 1905 to 1917. And Jews, as yet, play no part in this.

The stepping stones on the path to Russian revolutionary demonism are as follows. First, there are the writings produced by Jews under Greek and then Roman rule, in the epoch of "the unfeasible, desperate struggle of a small nation for its political and religious existence, first with the Greek and then the Roman eagle...." These writings envisage deliverance by God or a national Messiah from the nation's oppression, and Bulgakov admits that the Gospels and early

---

[27] *Dva Grada*, 349, fn.2.

Christianity are to some extent imbued with their spirit (as in the "May Your Kingdom come" of the Lord's prayer).

Next, the real heirs to the desire for a deceptive paradise on earth can be found in the chiliastic sects of Western Europe: "Throughout the whole of the Middle Ages, along with the main stream of Catholicism, which saw the victory of the Augustinian world-view equating the Catholic Church with the thousand year kingdom, there is the formation of opposing sectarian movements of a clear chiliastic character, not to mention a quite often revolutionary-communist nature...So in Italy the spiritual teaching of Joachim del Flore quickly turned into the revolutionary-chiliastic teaching of Segarelli and Dolcino, who led a peasant movement."[28] Other examples are given by Bulgakov, culminating in the Puritans of the English Civil War.

Finally, the socialistic-revolutionary orientation of chiliasm was given new philosophical expression by Marx, who drew on Feuerbach, a quote from whom serves as an epithet to the whole volume: *Homo homini deus est*[29]. Other contributing streams were Fourier and Saint-Simon, with their socialist communes in France.

Before looking at Marx and Bulgakov's evaluation of his Jewishness, it is worth looking at the ingenious way in which Bulgakov draws a "genetic" parallel between pre-Christian Jewish apocalyptic writings and contemporary scientific socialism. In his view, apocalyptic writings differ from the books of the prophets; for the latter "the perspective of the future...is not revealed in its general lawfulness, but within the bounds of a specific historical horizon, and this explains the conditional nature of prophecies and their relative character... as well as the contradictory nature of their sometimes conflicting images, so that it is impossible to understand them without some indications that give a sense of the history of the epoch... this feature of prophecies completely prevents them from being taking as oracles for predicting future events...and makes them alive, concrete, historical..."

Apocalyptic writing, meanwhile, does "not want to fit in with place and time, it strives for an abstract objectivity, and so ideas which appear in the first century before Christ are deliberately ascribed to Enoch...To depict the whole of world history as a succession and struggle of a few apocalyptic beasts...is the same sort boldness of logical abstraction and symbolism which we have in our contemporary sociological concepts..."

Feuerbach's ultimate "immanentization" of God, i.e. his claim that God is merely a projection of human thought, allows Marxism to replicate the schematic nature of apocalyptic writings within a context where God has been replaced by humanity and by internal laws of human history. The result is that the "role of *deus ex machina* which facilitates the transition to chiliasm [in Judaic apocalyptic]...is played by the 'laws' of development of society or the growth of productive forces, which first lay the ground for this transition, and then through

---

[28] *Dva Grada*, 393.
[29] Man to man is a god.

the well-known maturity of the process, by virtue of its 'internal and inevitable dialectic', necessitate the transition to socialism...Thus the role once assigned to the messiah or directly to the Divinity is here ascribed to the impersonal, and in significant measure, mythological abstract pantheistic concept of 'the law of development of productive forces'..."

The parallel with crude, clunky, self-assured and ahistorical apocalyptic is complete: "The chosen people, the bearer of the Messianic idea, or as in later Christian sectarianism, the people of the 'holy ones', is replaced by the 'proletariat' with a special proletarian spirit and a special revolutionary mission. What is more, this chosenness is defined now not by internal self-definition as a necessary condition of Messianic election, but by the external factor of membership in the proletariat, by participation in the manufacturing process, which is a sign of social class....The Messianic sufferings and the final pangs here correspond to the inevitable and, according to the 'theory of impoverishment', constantly progressing unification of the national masses, accompanied by the growth of class antagonisms..."

Again, it is necessary to reiterate that this schematic, oracular, artificially law-bound and this-worldly distortion of sacred inspiration is a feature of non-rabbinic Jewish apocalyptic and is primarily seen in Christian movements. Perhaps the only hint that later this historical distinction will be ignored in a rather rough-shod manner is a hint in the last quoted text: membership of the chosen people by external factors rather than internal spirit looks like an exclusive property of the Jewish people both before and after Christ. In this detail we glimpse an intimation of what is to come: for in his 1941-2 essays, Bulgakov will simply transfer pre-Christian Jewish apocalyptic features wholesale onto contemporary Jewry.

Nonetheless, there is another point worth remembering here, and it is a sign of Bulgakov's multi-facetedness, the difficulty of pinning him down. For even in the midst of criticizing the apocalyptic tendency in these early essays, Bulgakov refuses to condemn it completely[30]. He contends that it would be wrong to merely propose an abstract dogmatic interpretation of eschatology for Christianity that is diametrically opposed to socialism's immanent eschatology. Instead, Christianity requires an "eschatology capable of feeling the truth of the chiliastic idea, and along with this not only the limits of that idea, but its *own* limits." This was to lead Bulgakov on to a search for Christian socialism and Christian social activism, which despite his disappointments with practical politics, he never entirely abandoned.

Finally, in considering Bulgakov's thought in *Two Cities* as it relates to the Jewish question, his opinions about Marx in *Karl Marx as a religious type (his relationship to L.Feurebach's religion of human-divinity)*[31] must be examined. Bulgakov disapproves of Marx not just as a thinker but as a person. (He emphasizes

---

[30] His constant grasping of both sides of the coin is perhaps the imprint of his early Marxist immersion in dialectics.
[31] One of the essays in the collection; written in 1906, it appeared in two Moscow journals in 1906 and 1907.

how the two aspects are connected). By nature, he contends, Marx was an atheist for whom the essentially spiritual Hegel (whose philosophy Bulgakov is keen to defend) was merely an excuse to pin his prejudices on. Once this philosophical exterior is stripped off, one can see Marx for what he is: a mean-spirited, hyper-rationalistic and confrontational character with an intuitive hatred of God.

The important point here, once again, is that this is not linked to Marx's Jewishness; rather the opposite. In this essay Bulgakov expresses revulsion at the Jewish Marx's anti-Semitism: "The Jewish question for Marx is a question about the 'interest-charging Yid'…Marx's writings on the Jewish question produce a most repellent impression on me. Nowhere does this icy, blind, one-tracked rationalism appear in such naked form as here." Marx's attitude towards Jews is for Bulgakov another prime example of Marx's inadequate personality. The latter is also the reason why his socialism does not come from love of humanity, or even pity, but simply out of cold and materialistic logic, and a pathological hatred of God and religion.

The spirit of the character of Marx as a man is what has been disseminated throughout Europe, and is visible in the fractured, enemy-hungry nature of socialist and communist circles, who preach and disagree with each other with misplaced religious zeal. Marx's crass blindness to religion[32] is what makes him incapable of seeing, as Bruno Bauer had obviously seen, that the Jewish question is "at its root religious, a question about the relationship between Jewry and Christianity [which] primarily defines the historical fates of Jewry. The world role of Jewry in the history of capitalism is only the empirical casing of the particular religious psychology of Jewry."

All this proves once more that Bulgakov at this stage has no axe to grind when it comes to Jews. In the essay on Marx, he only hints at the dimensions that must be brought to bear on the Jewish Question, but for Bulgakov that analysis will be many years in coming.

The Unfading Light (1917)
Our next look at Judaism in Bulgakov's early thought takes us to his 1917 book, *Svet Nevecherniy* (The Unfading Light), which like *Two Cities* was also written at a time of Russian revolution[33]. Bulgakov is already well on his way to

---

[32] Another goal of the essay on Marx is to show to show that despite his protestation, Marx owed took very little of substance from Hegel, for whose idealism Bulgakov had respect. Hegel was merely window-dressing to give credibility to his theories. Instead it was Feuerbach who was the real, though deliberately concealed, source by which Marx could give voice to his natural religious atheism.

[33] It is not surprising that Bulgakov writes in *Dva grada*: "Our ear is especially sensitive when it listens to the beating of the historical pulse of albeit distant but similar epochs…apocalyptic literature has become in part a historical mirror for our epoch as well, it has an affinity with this burning and trembling contemporary age, it has become for us a means of spiritual orientation." This will become more true as the century progresses.

his theological transformation, following the principle that the key to reality is theology. In this work, moreover, he continues to deepen the "sophianic" aspect of his thought which he had sketched in *The Philosophy of Economy* (1913), through an engagement with European mystical philosophy and theology. We will return to this in a later section. There are two points of interest in *The Unfading Light* for our theme. The first is Bulgakov's first outline of a theology of Judaism. The second, and more obscure point, concerns some brief comments of Bulgakov's about the Jewish Kabbalah.

Bulgakov's picture of Judaism here fits the classical Christian approach which sees Old Testament Judaism as preparatory of Christianity. Nonetheless, Bulgakov is concerned to refute German Idealist and Protestant conceptions of Old Testament religion, which underemphasize its richness and divine inspiration. His opponent in this debate is the philosopher Schelling, who contended that pre-Christian paganism was a religion of the Son, while the Judaism of the Old Testament was Father-based. The implication was that Judaism in the Old Testament and even more so after it was inferior to Christianity[34].

Bulgakov's position differs from Schelling's, and indeed from the standard orthodox interpretation of the relationship between the Old Testament and paganism. He insists that the full Trinitarian divinity was immanent in both paganism and the Old Testament[35]. Here we see the high value Bulgakov places

---

[34] Again, this argument is implicitly directed at Merezhkovsky.

[35] The place of "paganism" will be discussed repeatedly in this and other chapters. Bulgakov's high evaluation of paganism comes out of the same symbolist dynamic as embraced by Soloviev and Merezhkovsky, as well as Florensky and Rozanov (cf. ch.4, present book) – that is, it is part of a history of "Russian" paganism, which has folk roots. But there is also a broader dynamic of the Christian relationship to paganism. In this sense, on the one hand, it could be argued that Bulgakov is unorthodox in attributing to paganism the fullness of Trinitarian knowledge, albeit in blurred form. On the other hand, as early as Tertullian, Christians vacillated between a belief that pagan wisdom was Christian wisdom before Christ ("The soul is by nature Christian" in his apology to the pagans "On the testimony of the soul") and a belief that Christianity was radically disjunct ("credibile est, quia ineptum est" in "De Carne Christe"); cf. Tertullian, *De Carne Christi,* edited and translated by Ernest Evans. (London: S.P.C.K., 1956); and Tertullian, *On the Testimony of the Soul and on the 'Prescription' of Heretics*, translated into English by T.Herbert Bindley. London: S.P.C.K., 1914. A little later, in the sixth to the seventh centuries, a similar struggle over the relationship between paganism and Christian thought took place in the work of Maximus the Confessor. A. Louth analyses how the Neo-platonic and cyclic-pagan (i.e. the world is repetitive, not linear; nature not history is primary) elements in the "cosmic" theology of pseudo-Dionysius and Origen were stripped of their cyclic and world-denying elements by Maximus the Confessor, who nonetheless retained a Christian reverence for divine immanence in nature (Cf. Andrew Louth, *Maximus the Confessor*. Oxford: Routledge, 1996). Similar struggles took place in the Byzantine Middle Ages between defenders of the Christian use of Plato and Aristotle, and denigrators. Ultimately, Bulgakov's self-confessedly pagan cosmism must be seen as being the latest attempt of the Christian mindset to ponder

on paganism, for its ability to respond to the divine wisdom, Sophia, which is the foundation or entelechy of the natural world[36]. For Bulgakov the Trinity is imprinted in the natural world and accessible to the pagan worshipper in the "sophianicity" of the nature.

But Old Testament Judaism also had access to the pre-Incarnate Logos. Bulgakov therefore seeks to refute Schelling's claim that paganism was superior to Judaism and Jewry, which for the German philosopher was a mere means for the incarnation of a Christ, Who was inherently more comprehensible to the gentiles than the Jews. Bulgakov comments of Schelling's approach that "in these judgments is seen, for all their restraint, the characteristic German religious anti-Semitism." We see the same tendency we noted in Bulgakov's essay on Marx: a painedness at expressions of anti-Semitism and wish to distance himself from such sentiments.

However, this condemnation of anti-Semitism seems to be compromised – depending on what position one ultimately takes – by Bulgakov's immediately following analysis of the role of Judaism in the divine economy that does not differ greatly from Schelling in its attribution of inherent worth to that religion. A reminder of Soloviev's position is instructive here: he saw Judaism as being a golden mean between Indian self-dissolving mysticism and Greco-Roman humanistic projection of an overly assertive self onto the deity. The Jewish religion in the Old Testament was already for him a perfect balance of heaven and earth, as was the Jewish national character, and this was the reason why God chose the Jews as bearers of revelation and then incarnation. Subtle distortions in the harmonious Jewish character resulted in the rejection of Christ, but much of Jewish creativity, including the Talmud is still ethically fruitful.

In contrast, Bulgakov goes on to sketch a picture of Old Testament Judaism, which shows it to be imbalanced even *before* the Jews' rejection of Christ. The equivalence between paganism and Old Testament comes into play here. Before Christ, Judaism leaned excessively in the direction of a transcendent conception of the Divinity, while paganism leaned excessively towards immanence. Only with the Incarnation of Christ was the perfect blend of the two achieved. This is

---

the meaning of contemporary non-Christian worldviews, and to make Christianity "ever new" by finding the Christian kernel in secular wisdom. Whether Bulgakov succeeded in creating a new Maximian synthesis for our times, or whether he did not shuck off the Romantic-symbolist-decadent garments of his earlier thought, would require a separate treatment. Certainly, it should be remembered that, as we will see in the chapter on Rozanov, Bulgakov set very clear limits to his own "re-valuation" of paganism, and was conscious of the excessive folk-Russian and thus non-Christian paganism of his friend, Fr.Pavel Florensky (which included occultism and magic). Nonetheless, Bulgakov's own drawing of the line did not satisfy critics such as V.Lossky and G.Florovsky. In ch.4 we will consider an updating of that charge in S.S.Khoruzhy's argument that Bulgakov's sophiology was also a part of the same pagan neo-Platonism as Florensky's and the younger A.Losev's. See below for Bulgakov on Egyptian paganism, and further comments.

[36] See the section on sophiology later in this chapter.

a rather unusual position. Bulgakov wants to say that paganism contained much that was positive, perhaps as much as the Old Testament.

For him, it is not just the Incarnate Word that is lacking in the Old Testament revelation, but also some of the true insights of paganism – such as "the mystery of the pre-vision of the mother of God in the feminine goddesses of paganism," or the hints of incarnation and resurrection that can be found in Greek and Egyptian fertility cults of dying and rising gods (Osiris, Orpheus). He admits that there was much falsehood mixed in with pre-Christian paganism, and this is why Old Testament Jewry had to be weaned away from it, and then reject it with excessive severity in its true and false totality, for "Judaism could only be tempted by paganism and from time to time fall ill with it, so as in being healed once more even more strictly and, of course, even more unfairly, to relate to the harmful infection. Let us recall that even the apostles themselves at the beginning had to overcome with some difficulty their prejudice against the 'uncircumcised."

Again, a little oddly, Bulgakov seems to imply that the Church tradition's rejection of paganism is not wholly in keeping with this insight into the truths of paganism, but "has been passed on from Judaism to Christianity by apologetes right up to the present day. Even now they look at paganism with the eyes of Judaism, although there is no ban in Christianity like that in Old Testament religion, and if there is, it is completely different."

For Bulgakov, Judaism's suppression of the pagan element through the Law had unfortunate consequences for Old Testament religion, as well as for the Jewish people: "Dressed up in divine sanction, the law became an isolating fence which served to separate Judaism from the rest of the world. Because the faith of Israel was not a religion of a good and merciful Father of all people, she did not wish to and could not become international and supranational. Nationalism, and that of the most burning and exclusive kind, was contained in its very essence, in the idea of the chosenness of only one nation; compared with Judaism the religious nationalism of paganism was broad and tolerant. Therefore between different religions it was possible to merge, to have 'syncretism'…"

The claim is, therefore, that the Old Testament did not know even God the Father, *contra* Schelling. Instead God revealed Himself as a dim and undifferentiated Divinity, whose Trinitarian nature was blurred in the same way that three peaks will blend into one mountain when seen from a distance. Thus, in his own way, Bulgakov downgrades the Old Testament to the level of, if not below, that of the gentile pagan cults[37].

He continues this analysis by making clear that the Old Testament's holiness was limited to the temporary function it was designed to play: "in the confines of the Law, in the 'shadow of future goods', in an atmosphere of pure and untainted monotheism to nourish the earthly ancestors of the Savior, to prepare the appearance of the Most Pure Mother of God, as well as the Forerunners of the Lord, John the Baptist and Joseph the Betrothed of Mary. In them were merged

---

[37] Rozanov (at least before 1911) had equated paganism and Judaism, to the advantage of the latter. Cf. ch.4.

the living threads of the whole of believing, righteous Judaism, as is testified in the Gospel genealogies of the Savior. When this holy and God-chosen birth had been prepared in Judaism, the Law had completed its deed: 'When the fullness of time came, God sent His Son, Who was born of a woman, submitted to the law, in order to redeem those under the law, so that we could receive the status of sons (Gal.4.3-5).'"[38]

Thus Bulgakov converges on the classical position that the Old Testament is redundant for the Christian who lives under the New Testament. However, he arrives at this point by somewhat unconventional means. His argument with Schelling also foreshadows his later view that the Jews as a people can make the transition from the Old to the New Testament without losing their nationhood. If for Schelling, "the Jews should have disappeared after Christ…they were *nothing else* but bearers of the future…," Bulgakov is not in such a rush to hurry the Jews off the stage of world history. Instead, he wants them to stay and open up to the world, to the fuller Sophianic revelation given in Christ. That is, he differentiates Jewry and Judaism.

Still the old problem of how much in the Old Testament is "juridical purity" that can be dispensed with after Christ's coming and how much has a more enduring worth also haunts this book. For elsewhere in *The Unfading Light*, Bulgakov shows other sides to his enthusiasm for the Old Testament. This is especially true in his high evaluation of Old Testament prophecy and priesthood.

Bulgakov was to be ordained to the priesthood only a year after this book was published. Perhaps remembering his time as an altar-server in his father's church[39], however, he makes intimate and personal references to the sacredness

---

[38] Sergei Bulgakov, *Svet Nevecherniy*. (Moscow: Respublika, 1994), 288.

[39] Bulgakov's work drew on his fond memories of service in his father's church, to which he even traced his infatuation with Sophia: "Here in the Sophia Church of the Assumption, I was born and defined as a venerator of Sophia, the Wisdom of God, and as a venerator of Saint Sergey of Radonezh…And here I was defined as a Russian, a son of my people and my mother – the Russian land, which I learned to feel and love on this little hill of Saint Sergey and in this little humble-minded cemetery." In Sergei Bulgakov, *Avtobiograficheskiye zametki*, (Paris, YMCA-Press, 1991), 14. Another suggestive influence on Bulgakov's sophiology might be Russian folk wisdom. Bulgakov's contemporary and colleague in Paris, Russian Church historian and political activist, G.P.Fedotov (on whom more in ch.5), wrote an article in 1935 on Russian *dukhovniye stikhi*. These were folk-religious songs sung by wandering minstrels at markets and fairs; theirs roots go back at least to the 17th century, although they were not written down until the 19th century. They mix a near-pagan veneration for the earth with Orthodox Christian motifs and symbols, in a way that is strikingly similar to some of Bulgakov's own theological insights. For example: "the wild winds come from the divine bloods;" "the world-people [who sprung] from Adam;" "Making flesh the Spirit of God/In the damp earth…;" "flow, you rivers, where God has commanded" (which sounds like an Old Testament Psalm); "split open, damp earth mother/Into four, four directions/Swallow up the serpent's blood/Do not let us perish." And most suggestively: "When the Yids crucified Christ/

of the priestly task, drawing on Moses' experience on Mount Sinai and Jacob's struggle with the angle to capture the awe of the liturgy. "In priesthood human nature crosses the flaming fire of the cherubic sword that separates the Holy Throne, and the priest is separated from the people by that curtain of fire, as Moses was on Mt. Sinai." Then in words that are closer to Soloviev's description of the strong personality of the Jewish people which fitted them for revelation, he adds: "But this itself means that a person needs a focusing of human energies (not by chance does the priesthood, like the levitical rank, require physical and spiritual perfection), for a person joining the display of angelic service still remains himself, obliged to exert his very humanity in this service..."

The requirements of the Law regarding priestly fitness are directly applied to the priests of the New Testament. This is surely more than theoretical. Bulgakov at this point must have been burning with the thought of his intended ordination. Elsewhere, in the book he talks of the blood of animals in the Old Testament sacrificial system[40] as linked closely to Christ's sacrificial blood. Again, his autobiographical comments about the call of his "levitical blood" show how personal the Old Testament was for him. Later, in fact, the theme of blood will become a central one in his meditations on Jewish destiny.

Another image of the priesthood is Jacob-Israel himself. "The theurgic act [of priestly service] in this respect calls to mind the struggle of the mysterious Unknown man with Jacob, who forced a blessing from Him, although He wounded his rib [sic] in the process." The figure who is the emblem of the Jewish people becomes Bulgakov's own model. This ability to immerse himself in Scripture, we will see later, gives him an ability to formulate intuitions about Jewry, which in some respects at least are very similar to the Jewish rabbinic formulations.

From all this we gain the impression that while the Trinity may have been "blurred" like the outline of three distant mountains, the divine presence in the Old Testament was far from distant or ineffective. This impression is backed up by certain hints Bulgakov drops in his discussion of the Jewish Kabbalah.

Then the divine mother Theotokos wept/ Dropping tears into the damp earth/ And from this grew up weeping-grass." (Weeping-grass is the folk-name for a type of grass; the earth is often equated with Mary, the Mother of God, or *Bogoroditsa*: thus the Earth gives birth to the *narod*, as Mary gives birth to Christ.) Fedotov points out that though these *stikhi* are replete with both pagan and Orthodox imagery, they do in fact stay on the right side of the divide: that is, while the winds and other elements are metaphorically "aspects" of God, the poets restrain themselves from out-and-out pantheism with a clear recognition that God is the creator and ultimately *above* the earth. Perhaps we can say the same of Bulgakov, who would have been familiar with *stikhi*, and of course with the remaining folk-wisdom of the people among whom he grew up in rural Russia. [G.P.Fedotov, "Mat'-zemlya: k religioznoy kosmologii russkogo naroda," in *Put'*, No.46, 1935.]

[40] *Svet*, 296.

Bulgakov and Kabbalah

The brief discussion on "Jewish mysticism: the Kabbalah" comes within the general discussion of mysticism in the first part of *The Unfading Light*.[41] Once again, as with his discussion of Jewish apocalyptic, Bulgakov notes (perhaps comparing himself regretfully to Soloviev in this respect) that his understanding of Kabbalistic concepts is hampered by the fact that "unfortunately I do not know Hebrew," and he relies on German and French translations and commentaries to the Zohar. The most interesting part of the essay is a hint dropped in his discussion of the apophatic theology of the Kabbalah that mystical Judaism may have a concept of the Divine nature of "the Son of Man" figure that appears on its pages.

In the midst of a discussion of the Ein Soph[42], for some reason Bulgakov takes exception to the contention of his scholarly source, Professor Muretov, that "the Son of Man" is not recognized as divine in the Zohar. Bulgakov quotes the professor's own discussion of the relevant extracts from the Zohar: " 'The first revealer and most common bearer of the characteristics of the predicateless Ein, Metatron, the first-born divine son, standing at the head of all the other Sephirot, and controlling them,' to whom is assimilated all the attributes of Jehovah, 'the name of whom is like the name of God,'....notwithstanding his superiority to all the other Sephirot, by no means possesses the Divine nature....thus Metatron often receives the name 'creatus.'"

Bulgakov comments stiffly: "This opinion of Professor Muretov needs checking and in any case seems arguable." Is he implying that the professor's own quotes about "the first-born divine son" argue for a Kabbalistic doctrine of a fully divine Son of Man? The discussion is conducted within the confines of a long footnote[43] and in the main text Bulgakov comments that interpretation of the Kabbalistic doctrine of the deity is "excessively difficult," so one cannot be sure.

Elsewhere in *The Unfading Light*, Bulgakov criticizes Soloviev's identification of Sophia with either the sphere of Chochma or Malkhut, and argues that Sophia is better identified with the Shekhina or the Glory of the Lord (Kavod). Again, Bulgakov has high praise for the Kabbalistic insights about Sophia: "The Kabbalah draws close to Christianity, and also clarifies the Old Testament doctrine of Sophia."

Two final doctrines that Bulgakov treated in this work were that of the Primordial Man, or Adam Kadmon, and the Kabbalistic view of sex. In the former doctrine, Bulgakov saw a link between Adam Kadmon and the Heavenly Man Christ, who contains within Himself all of humanity, for every person "belongs to the corpus of the mystic human organism." He concludes: "The idea of the person as a microcosm, which has been expressed many times in the philosophical and mystical literature of ancient and modern times, has nowhere received such a

---

[41] Ibid. p.120, in Part One: The Divine Nothing. Figures looked at are: Plato, Aristotle, Plotinus, Philo, a wide range of Church fathers, Nicolas of Cusa, German mystics like Meister Eckhardt, and Kant's "negative theology."

[42] The Infinite aspect of God which played a role in Soloviev's mysticism.

[43] Ibid, p.122.

profound interpretation as in Kabbalah." Later, we will see that Bulgakov developed this Kabbalistic concept in his own doctrine of the relationship between Adam, humanity and Jewry, the chosen people – sympathy for Jewish mystical doctrine evidently spilling over into sympathy for the people who produced such sages and mystics.

Finally, as far as sex is concerned, Bulgakov saw in the Kabbalistic focus on the sacredness of sex a welcome correction to Soloviev's erotic mysticism, which however was marked by a tortured ambiguity about sexuality in favor of Platonic abstention. In this regard, while Bulgakov does not mention Merezhkovsky, he too would be included in a polemic against prurience in matters of sex. Thus Bulgakov draws close to, and may have been influenced by, Rozanov's "philosophy of sex," and later we will examine correspondence between the two which sheds light on their similarities and differences.

To conclude, it is interesting to note that in terms of Bulgakov's knowledge of the Kabbalah, a recent commentator, K.Burmistrov,[44] has argued that of all his contemparies Bulgakov's readings were closest to the original and that he "was remarkably free of such occult distortions as was prevalent in his times. In this respect, he was unique, as the relationship to Jewish mysticism that he represented had died out by the eighteenth century." Thus Burmistrov sees in Bulgakov a typological connection to the scholarly Christian Kabbalah started by the first researchers of the Renaissance, and which was distorted by the occultists and theosophists who came after them[45].

To sum up, in *The Unfading Light* there are two conflicting tendencies: a great enthusiasm for the Old Testament, coupled with the conviction that the Old Testament as Law has served its purpose. This account is in essence the traditional Orthodox account that Christ is prefigured in the Law. Like Orthodox Christians before and after him, Bulgakov searches the Law for hints of Christ. However, as Bulgakov will say in a later work "spiritual birth…does not revoke but presupposes mankind's natural birth"[46]: that is, sometimes Bulgakov seems willing to embrace so much of the pre-figuring details of the Old Law that they saturate his sensibility and call into question the idea that the Law has been revoked (I have in mind, for

---

[44] Konstantin Burmistrov, "The interpretation of Kabbalah in early 20th-Century Russian Philosophy. Soloviev, Bulgakov, Florenskii, Losev," in *East European Jewish Affairs*, Vol.37, No.2, August 2007:157-187. Bulgakov's Kabbalistic "faithfulness" was obviously a result of examination of translated secondary sources, and perhaps a mystical flair of his own. However, unlike Florensky, Bulgakov was entirely above-board about his use of secondary sources and his ignorance of Hebrew. Cf.ch.4 for Florensky and Kabbalah.

[45] Of course, faithfulness to Jewish originals of the Kabbalah is not the same thing as faithfulness to Orthodox Christian dogma, and later we will examine criticisms of Bulgakov made on that front.

[46] Sergei Bulgakov, *The Holy Grail and the Eucharist,* translated by Boris Jakim, (New York: Lindisfarne Books, 1997), 37.

example, his comments about the nature of priesthood; later we will see this in his "theology of blood"). One gets a sense that the New need not replace the Old Testament, but can be superimposed on it.

While for a Protestant, this may seem like an accusation, it surely would not have seemed so to Bulgakov. It is intrinsically connected with the idea, also only hinted at in this book, that the people to whom the Old Law was given, the Jews, are also not replaced.

Of course, as we saw, there is another strand here: while the Church recognizes in Socrates and Aristotle "Christians before Christ," Bulgakov with his understanding of the divine Wisdom as permeating paganism stretches this understanding well beyond the conventional boundaries. For him ultimately, Christianity contains within itself all the physical, natural richness that was to be found in Judaism and paganism.[47] The operative idea here is "contains" – rather than rejects or replaces. Nonetheless, there is a tension between the idea that Judaism contains riches and even deep theological insights and the rather conventional dismissal of its value after Christ. This tendency is excoriated by Bulgakov's own avowed weak knowledge of Hebrew and rabbinic Judaism. What is a hair-crack in these early writings will, I believe, turn into a veritable fault-line in the later writings.

With these ambiguities firmly in place, we can turn to Bulgakov's first essay devoted exclusively a contemporary Jewish theme.

Bulgakov and Jewry (1): in Russia – the shadow of the Revolution
An early essay in Christian Zionism (1915)
The first essay where Bulgakov addresses himself to the contemporary Jewish situation, rather than to Judaism as it intersects with his own developing thought is "Zion," written in 1915. It was elicited by Maxim Gorky for the collection *Shchit'* (*Shield*), of which he was chief editor. This was a collection of articles by

---

[47] Another example of this is his positive attitude towards the Egyptian cult of the dead in *Svet*: the complex liturgy and rituals to assure the body's resurrection, the myth of Osiris whose body is reassembled by Isis and resurrected by Gor, Osiris's son, all bring to mind for Bulgakov the somewhat eccentric Russian philosopher, Nicolai Fyodorov's call for sons to resurrect their fathers in order to achieve universal brotherhood. In this Bulgakov draws close to Rozanov's reverence for pagan cults (cf. ch.4 for similarities, but also disagreements between Rozanov and Bulgakov on the Old Testament and paganism). Indeed Merezhkovsky and Rozanov both used the term "sacred flesh," which is cognate with the epithet often given to Bulgakov's philosophy of "sacred materialism." Two decades later, Bulgakov would in fact refer to Christianity by the simple and revealing epithet "Judeo-paganism" (in "Nekotoriye cherty religioznogo mirovozreniya L.I.Shestova," Sovromeniye Zapiski, No.68, Paris, 1939.) For another very similar view on Judaism and Jewry written before Bulgakov's later Jewish writings but self-confessedly inspired by Bulgakov, cf. Vladimir Ilyin, "Khristos i Izrail'," in *Put'* No.11 (1928):59-75.

Jewish and non-Jewish writers on Jewish themes from different perspectives.[48] The collection to which Bulgakov contributed was part of his effort to support Russia's beleaguered Jewish community during the First World War, when charges of treachery and cowardice were being hurled at Jews whose communities on the Western front of the Empire were being criss-crossed by German battle-lines. As a result of this hostility, there were also a number of pogroms.

The collection also came out two years after the conclusion of the "Beilis affair" in 1913. The St.Petersburg Religious-Philosophical Society had voted at the end of the year to exclude Vasily Rozanov from its ranks, as a punishment for his publication of vehemently Judeophobic articles in the right-wing press. The person who forwarded the proposal was none other than D.Merezhkovsky[49], Rozanov's co-founder of the Society, and along with him, the godfather of the new religious movement, whose first meetings had taken place in his own house in St Petersburg. Thus support for the Jewish cause became a way to demonstrate moral sensitivity, as well as re-assert an ongoing belief in the contribution of the "new religious consciousness" to the political shape of Russia.

Not all proponents of the new consciousness were convinced that their cause was best served by support of Mendel Beilis and Western Russian Jewry.

---

[48] A little known fact about Gorky, the Soviet Union's first official writer and darling of the new regime after the Revolution, was his extreme philo-Semitism. As a youth of 16 in 1881, he witnessed the first pogrom on central Russian soil in Nizhny Novgorod. He lived for a time with a Jewish family, acting as a *shabbas-goy*, and grew to love and admire the Jewish family lifestyle. He had wide personal contacts with Zionist and religious Jewish leaders and founded an organization for the study of Jewish life. In the early years of the Soviet Union he intervened with the authorities to help the National Jewish theater, ha-Bima, as well as to help Zionist leaders escape the country. See Mitsuakaro Akao, "'Yevreiski' vopros kak russkii. (Obshchestvennoe dvizhenie russkykh pisatiley v zashchitu yevreev v posledniye desyatiletie tsarskoi Rossii.)" (http://src-h.slav.hokudai.ac.jp/coe21/publish/no17_ses/11akao.pdf), 226. Akao also analyses Tolstoy's "universalist" indifference to the Jewish question.

[49] Merezhkovsky was a leading novelist, poet, thinker and a pioneer in the search for a "New Christianity," which for him could only develop as a Third Testament of the Spirit, outside the stifling bounds of the historical church. In the first decade of the 20th century, Bulgakov belonged to the same circle as him, but in the second decade their paths diverged as Merezhkovsky became more hostile to orthodox Christianity, and trod further the path of neo-paganism. In emigration, Merezhkovsky's hatred of communism led him to sympathize with fascism; in 1939 he met with Mussolini, and in 1941 he made a speech on the radio in support of "the heroic deed that Germany has taken upon itself in the holy crusade against Bolshevism." Though not enthusiastic about Hitler, he chose him over Stalin as the force to support in the War. Cf. ch3. for Berdyaev's support of Stalin in similar circumstances, a decision which also shocked the émigré community; cf. ch.6 for more on the Russian émigré community's flirtation with fascism; and ch.5 for the deep affinity of Florensky's political and religious views with German fascism. (Cf., also: Volkogonova, Olga. "Religiozny anarkhizm D. Merezhkovskogo." At: http://www.philosophy.ru/library/volk/merez.html#_fn1).

Much of this consciousness was linked to a spiritual nationalism that often took an exclusive attitude towards Jewry. It drew, that is, more on Ivan Aksakov and Fyodor Dostoevsky than on Vladimir Soloviev. Moreover even the contributions to *Shield* mixed elements of antipathy towards Jewry, so that the equation *Shield*-contributor and philo-Semite would be hasty.

For allegiances were sometimes complex: Rozanov, before his Beilis Judeophobia had written much that was positive about Jews. Merezhkovsky himself later drew close to fascism in emigration. Another interesting case is Nicolai Berdyaev, who was close to Bulgakov in many ways. His article "On Jewry" was turned down by Gorky for being anti-Semitic[50], and it ended up being reprinted in the "anti-Shield" anthology: "Israel in the past, present and future." Again, the forward to this openly anti-Semitic anthology was written by another spiritual ally of Bulgakov and key figure in the movement for the "regeneration" of Russian Christianity, Pavel Florensky[51].

In sum, Bulgakov's contribution to *Shield* could not have been predicted just by looking at the views of his close associates, and as we will see, despite the generally philo-Semitic tone of the article, much of the ambiguity we have already traced in his scholarly works is present between the lines there too. But even if Bulgakov's philo-Semitism in these years had been of Soloviovian proportions[52], it could hardly have competed with Gorky's pro-Jewish feelings.

For Gorky, as Akao points out[53], philo-Semitism was the other side of the coin of Russian self-hatred: Russians were backward, Asiatic, lazy, brutal and indifferent to their fellow man[54]. Jews are the opposite of all this, and Jewish wisdom is superior to all others. In this, he calls to mind Lenin's assertion that if you scratched an intelligent Russian, you would find a Jew. Both attitudes were symptomatic of a general uneasiness with self among the Russian intelligentsia, fighting as self-appointed guardians of the people, but separated from the people in nearly all aspects of their lives. The Jewish question often exacerbated this unease.

In this respect, before turning to Bulgakov's essay, it is instructive to get a feel for the times by considering Merezhkovsky's contribution, which gives clear articulation to the dilemma of the Russian intellectual in relation to the Jewish question. For him it took the form of an unpleasant compulsion from above to be nice to Jews:

"That is why we say to the nationalists: Stop trampling on the rights of other nationalities, so that we can have a right to be Russian, so we can show our

---

[50] In ch.3 we examine Berdyaev's evolving attitude to Jewry, and his friendship with two Russian-Jewish thinkers.
[51] Cf. ch.4 for comments on Florensky's Introduction.
[52] And we already saw that Soloviev's philo-Semitism also contains complex contradictions which causes him to overlap in part with Aksakov.
[53] Ibid.
[54] It is ironic to consider that Zionist, Reform, enlightened, and radical Jews leveled exactly these kinds of adjectives at their Orthodox co-religionists.

national face with honor, as a human face and not as an animal face. Stop being Judophobes, so that we can stop being Judophiles...otherwise it is acceptable to talk about attraction, but not about dislike." In this extract, we can already see the potential crossing of lines: it is as if public dignity and duty have persuaded Merezhkovsky to throw in his lot with "Shield." But there is a sense that he looks wistfully across the battle-lines to "Israel in the past...," quite ready and capable of contributing some lines to their cause as well.

In sum, the nationalists by their denigration of Jews are preventing their ultimate conversion to Christianity – a viewpoint that we saw held by St.Philaret. As Merezhkovsky puts it: "The Jews' lack of rights means the silence of Christians. The external force imposed on them means an internal force pressing on us. We are forbidden to separate Christianity from Judaism, because that would mean, as a Jew expressed it, to introduce a new Pale of Settlement. First of all, destroy the physical Pale, and then it might be possible to talk about the spiritual Pale. But while that has not been done, the truth of Christianity before Judaism and Jewry will remain in vain."[55] Philo-semitism is thus a tool in the promotion of Merezhkovsky's "new" Christianity.

Bulgakov's essay is much bolder than Merezhkovsky's: in three pages he outlines a theology of Christian Zionism which is quite surprising for the Russian context[56]. From the very first paragraph, in fact, he refuses to draw a line, to demarcate a Pale of Settlement, between Judaism and Christianity, between Russian Christians and Russian Jews.

The deepest aspirations of Orthodox Christians for Bulgakov converge with the deepest aspirations of Jews. Just as Russian Orthodox Christians yearn to see a cross atop the Hagia Sophia in the now Muslim Constantinople and the Holy Sepulchre reclaimed from the hands of non-believers, so "the question of Palestine and the settlement of Israel on the land given and promised to her by God should hold a similar significance for the Jewish and the Christian heart (I thrice emphasize that 'and')." In this way, Bulgakov manages to combine nationalist Russian sentiments (concerning the expansion of the empire to Turkey) with a genuinely enthusiastic effort to feel the excitement of the Zionist dream for Jews.

---

[55] *Shchit*, pp.136-8.

[56] Again, it is instructive to remember that anti-Semites could be Zionists; the difference is a matter of motive and tone. Across the ideological divide, Florensky was writing in his preface to "Israel in the past...:" "No! I say to you – 'no'. I am more frightened of 'just so' kikes. Any nation lives in its own particular Pale of Settlement; any nation sits in its ghetto. Let the Jews then also, the ones who say 'it's all right by me', and the one with 'payyos', get for themselves some sort of territory somewhere on the earth and arrange for themselves their kingdom, their ghetto, any of them that want to, but just let them leave us in peace." For discussion of Florensky and his relationship to Rozanov, cf.ch.4. It would be as well to remember that, despite this "divide," during these years Bulgakov maintained warm personal relations with both Rozanov and Florensky, and that in many respects their worldviews converged.

The year is already 1915, and as we will see in more detail shortly, Bulgakov is now a great admirer of the monarchy and a believer in the sacred Christian destiny of Russia. As the First World War rages, he sees a chance for Russia to assert a Christian role in the world, defeating a Germany whose Christian roots have been distorted by the Reformation and Enlightenment. Evidently, the idea that Germany's ally, Ottoman Turkey, might likewise suffer defeat is entertained, with the consequent perspective that a cross will indeed soon top the Ayia Sophia.

This is all an updated version of the Slavophile philosophy of Khomiakov, Leontiev and Danilevsky to which Dostoevsky – whom Bulgakov quotes in the essay – was also heir. Thus, while on the one hand it is surprising that Slavophilism in the twentieth century can combine with nascent Zionism, on the other hand there is a certain logic here: this is the epoch of grandiose European colonial dreams. Just as Protestant Great Britain sponsored the Biblical vision of the Return of the Jews to a land that now lay in the remit of her vast empire, so a Russian monarchist sweeps up the Jews into his own vision of Christian Europe.

Nonetheless, within the Russian Orthodox church of the time this was a marginal opinion, and certain members of the hierarchy would later be opposed to Zionism not just for theological reasons but for political reasons: there was a distinct threat that the Zionist colony as a British protectorate could do harm to the interests of Russia, also seen as the main defender of the Orthodox world.[57]

Furthermore, Bulgakov defends Zionism by appealing to the prophecies of Isaiah and Ezekiel. "And it will come to pass in that day: the Lord will raise his hand a second time to ransom the remnant of his people, from those still left, from Assyria, from Egypt, from Pathros, Cush and Elam, from Shinar, Hamath and the islands of the Sea. He will hoist a sign for the nations and assemble the outcasts of Israel; he will gather the scattered people of Judah from the four corners of the earth. (Is.11.10-12);" and "After many days you will receive your orders; in the final years you will enter the land, which has been saved from the sword, gathered from many nations, unto the mountains of Israel, which were in constant desolation, but now its inhabitants will be returned from the nations, and they will all live in safety (Ez.38.8)."

These are "our common prophecies, Jewish and Christian: are they really nearing fulfillment now?" he asks. The eschatological tone is one which we will encounter again in Bulgakov's reaction to the events of the Second World War, and the Jewish role then. Again, for an Orthodox Christian tradition used to seeking Christ in the Old Testament and interpreting the elements of the Law and the details of Israelite history as typological pointers to the Incarnation, Bulgakov's willingness to read Isaiah and Ezekiel as referring not to the Christian's return to

---

[57] Cf. Oleg Budinitsky, *Rossiskie yevrei mezhdu krasnymi i byelami (1917-1920)* (Russian Jewry between the Reds and the Whites). Moscow: Rosspen, 2006, ch.9: "Problema vossozdaniya yevreiskogo gosudarstva v Palestine, Russkaya pravoslavnaya tserkov' i 'belaya' diplomatiya."

the Promised Land of Christ, but quite literally to the return of the Jews to the Land of Israel must be considered original.

One should also bear in mind that Bulgakov was free to choose any topic for Gorky's collection: that he was attracted to the subject of Zionism is already revealing. Bulgakov, as we saw in his essay on chiliasm, firmly believed a Christian should react to his times, and not retreat to mere dogmatic formulas, but engage in his society, and constantly make the Gospel message new (and even revolutionary[58]). The events of the Revolution, the First World War, the Second World War, the exile and dispersion of so many Russian Orthodox to Western Europe were all for Bulgakov signs of God's hand, and he sought in his theology to uncover the meaning of these contemporary events; the eternal had to be made concrete. His Zionism fits squarely into this cast of mind.

Bulgakov's Zionism also fits in with what we saw of his keen sense of the realities of the Old Testament: the blood-sacrifices of old, the prescriptions regarding priestly purity, the figures of Moses and Jacob are all alive for him in the near-contemporary work *The Unfading Light*. In "Zion" he gives us a glimpse of his attitude to the living people of the Old Testament, whose national movement he supports. In a certain sense, this essay adds a counterpoint to those moments where the Old Testament is portrayed as already fulfilled.

But the key passage here that shapes Bulgakov's attitude to post-Christic Jewry is St Paul's comments on Jewish destiny in Romans 9-11. He quotes Romans 11.25-26: "I do not want to leave you, brothers, in ignorance of this mystery, that a hardening has come over Israel in part until the time when the gentiles have wholly come in. And so all Israel will be saved, as it is written: 'the Redeemer shall come forth from Israel and will remove misfortune from Jacob.'" As with Soloviev, Bulgakov's attitude to Jewry is shaped by Paul's "prophecy" (for so he reads it) that "all Israel will be saved." And this is the root of his support for Zionism: it is a means of preserving Jewry until the end time.

To this effect, he quotes Jewish writers on Zionism. A Dr. Tzolshan writes: "There are only two ways of preserving Jews for Jewry: external persecution or the cessation of the diaspora." The opinion of the better known Austrian Zionist, Arthur Ruppin, that Zionism will be "the seed of national crystallization" is also cited approvingly. Bulgakov aligns himself with the cultural Zionist tendency (best typified by Ahad Ha'am), which saw Palestine not as a place for all Jews to emigrate to, but merely as the centre of the independent national revival of Jewish language and culture.

Of course, Bulgakov had his own ideas of what Jewish national regeneration should look like. The chance to dwell on the land alone, in proximity to the sacred remains of Abraham, Isaac and Jacob, and there to listen to the voice of religious consciousness should lead to a self-cleansing and self-testing of Israel, that will culminate in an embracing of Christ. Until that happens, the national movement which has so far based itself on the national and cultural-ethnographic principle is doomed to mediocrity.

---

[58] See the extract from his *Autobiographical Fragments*, below.

Such a principle would be demeaning for any nation. For the Jewish nation, above all, only a spiritual foundation can be the real basis of its national regeneration. Here Bulgakov looks for support to Dostoevsky, the same writer whose philosophy he had appealed to to cast light on the Russian tragedy.[59] The great novelist, who for a certain type of intellectual had achieved the status of prophet in the succeeding generation[60], declared in his Writer's diary: "It's impossible to imagine a Jew without God....Not only that, I do not believe in educated Jewish atheists"[61].

Thus Bulgakov's support for Zionism is mixed. A drawback of Zionism is this cultural-ethnographic orientation, and "the greatest difficulty for Zionism is now the fact that it is not within its strength to bring back the lost faith of its fathers." This statement contains an ambiguity: evidently it cannot express a regret that Jewry embrace "the lost faith of its fathers" for Bulgakov has expressed a hope that Zionism will eventually culminate in faith in Christ. And yet that is what it seems to imply at first glance: if Zionism could combine with religious Judaism, it might have more depth.

So while Bulgakov comes out in support of Zionism he has reservations about its secular foundations. In a sense, this puts us in mind of Jewish Zionists like Rabbi A.I. Kook[62], the Russian-born mystic who was one of the few religious figures to put his weight behind the Zionist endeavor. For him, the socialist secular foundations of the movement and the involvement in it of Jews who had turned their back on Judaism was justified by the idea that God was using these Jews for an ultimately religious aim. We will return to this ambiguity in more depth later[63].

---

[59] Sergei Bulgakov, "Russkaya tragedia," *Russkaya Mysl'*, Bk.IV.(1914): 1-26.

[60] For Bulgakov, Berdyaev, Struve, Frank, Vy. Ivanov and several other Silver Age religious philosophers an essay declaring the prophetic status of Dostoevsky was almost mandatory. An irreverent exception to this is Lev Shestov, for more details on whom see chapter 3.

[61] Leo Tolstoy held a similar opinion. In a discussion about the Russian-Jewish writer Lev Shestov (Lev Isaakovich Schwartzmann), when someone raised the question of Shestov being a Jew, Tolstoy firmly asserted: "No, he's not a Jew. He does not believe in God," – despite of course, all ethnic considerations to the contrary. This was a response to Shestov's earlier skeptical writings; later Shestov's writings took on a religious cast. But of course, we see in both Tolstoy and Dostoevsky a rather arrogant propensity to define Jews without any consultation with the party under discussion, and in accordance with their own criteria. Bulgakov is not free from this fault either, as we will discuss below.

[62] Rabbi HaCohen Kook was the first Ashkenazi chief rabbi of the British Mandate of Palestine. He believed in maintaining connections with secular Zionist settlements in order to bring them closer to an Orthodox Jewish lifestyle. At the time of the writing of this essay, he was living in London, acting as a rabbi to the predominantly Russian émigré Jewish community in the East End.

[63] Some Russian Israelis have become involved in Kookian religious Zionism, such as Pinchas Polonski, whose work we will quote intermittently later. We will also

Bulgakov, in similar Kookian vein, ends his essay on a note of optimism inspired by the prophecies of Isaiah and Ezekiel he has just quoted: "And in this time, when the rays of the future are shining, there appears hope for the possibility of a new way of posing the eternal question. O, let us hope it does not deceive!"

This then is the Bulgakov of 1915: a conservative Russian Orthodox philosopher who believes that "the destiny of the Christian world is connected with the spiritual destiny of Israel in a mysterious and unalterable way." The imperial Christian destiny of Russia is connected with the revival of God's ancient people, all the more evidently in that the majority of Zionists are Russian Jews[64]. All the philo-Semitic hints of his other essays are cashed out in full here – so it would seem.

And yet there are clues, open and hidden, that this is not the full picture. The obvious fact is that like Soloviev, Bulgakov sees Zionism as a prelude to the conversion of the Jews. This is connected to the fact that, as he will outline a couple of years later in *The Unfading Light*, Judaism has seen its day: thus the spiritual basis that is necessary for the national movement of the Jews cannot as for Kook be rabbinic Judaism, but must be something else – which, however, the Jews must discover of their own accord, with a freedom for which territorial and political integrity can serve as the nourishing soil.

The hidden clues are exposed by reading this essay in conjunction with the later diary entries and war-time essays. There is one phrase towards the beginning of "Zion" which gains a whole new meaning when read retrospectively.

---

look at Raya Epstein, who also has a Kookian orientation, and writes explicitly and approvingly of Bulgakov. As we have already partly seen, there are complex genetic and typological links that bind Kookian Kabbalistic "theo-politics" and Russian Christian religious thought.

[64] Not surprisingly, the combination of Slavophile-like glorification of Russia's destiny does not automatically lead to philo-Semitism and Zionism. This is worth bearing in mind to get a historical grip on Bulgakov's position. So for example, another leading light of Russian religious philosophy and émigré life, P.B.Struve, who like Bulgakov had also taken part in Constitutional Democratic politics and then also drifted towards monarchist conservatism, took a different approach to the Jewish question: the Jews should be more like the Germans, he believed, contributing to Russian culture but then assimilating into Russia and no longer constituting a separate entity. (His own ancestors were German). On the other hand, he also insisted that the Russian intelligentsia should assert its ethnic Russianness, and not lose its identity in a non-ethnically state-defined Russianness that encompassed all the nationalities of the empire (i.e. should remain *russkoe*, not becoming *rossiskoe* – the Russian terms capture approximately what would be understood by contrasting *English* with *British*). See Budnitsky (2006), 345. To my mind, there is a distinct double standard here. Cf.ch.6 for more on Struve and his close friendship with S.Frank, who was a Jew who followed a "Struvian" path of assimilation, down to conversion to Orthodox Christianity.

Praising the Zionists, Bulgakov writes: "It is not a worldly calculation for power, wealth and influence that guides those representatives of the Jewish people who rightly see in the overcoming of 'golus', the diaspora or dispersion, the basis of a spiritual rebirth of their nation and thirst not just for liberation from the Pale of Settlement, or new rights in the diaspora, but settlement, and the right to determine their own lives."

At first glance this can be read as ringing endorsement of the Jewish national movement and wholesale praise for the Jewish people. But when one looks at the anti-Jewish rhetoric of the "late" Bulgakov, one is compelled to read the first sentence with a contrastive accent: "It is not a worldly calculation for power.... that influences *this* section of Jewry....." What other reading is allowed once takes into account phrases from the war-time essays such as the following: "Jewry in its lowest degenerateness, predatoriness, love of power, self-importance, self-assertiveness...enacted...an extremely significant violence against Russia and especially against Holy Rus, which was an attempt at the spiritual murder of Russia."?

The other major clue that the picture is not quite as rosily philo-Semitic as first appears is Bulgakov's invocation of Soloviev in the same breath as Dostoevsky. The essay starts with an epithet from Dostoevsky and in addition to the passage quoted above contains another extract from the Writer's diary where the writer talks of the Jew's "instinctively irrepressible attraction to Palestine" which legend has it will culminate in their final return to that land. Immediately following this quote, we find Soloviev's final "Short Story of the Anti-Christ" brought as evidence of the philosopher's similar instinct that at the end of days the Jews will be dwelling in Palestine, where they will rise up against the anti-Christ.

The oddity of appealing to Soloviev and Dostoevsky cannot be expressed better than in these comments of Shimon Markish, a contemporary Russian-Jewish writer: "I must admit that I cannot understand how it is possible to start with Vladimir Soloviev and – literally within the space of a page – end with Dostoevsky. I can see no logic or common sense in this."[65] Here Markish is talking of another essay that appeared in *Shield*, written by the symbolist poet Vyacheslav Ivanov – who develops a basically philo-Semitic argument in terms drawn from Soloviev and Dostoevsky[66].

Markish's astonishment at Ivanov's juxtaposition of the writer and philosopher is due to the fact that Soloviev was a well-known philo-Semite and Dostoevsky a notorious anti-Semite[67]. Evidently, for at least one Russian Jew of the second

---

[65] In Markish, Shimon. "Vyacheslav Ivanov i yevreistvo." Paper delivered at the memorial colloquium for Vyacheslav Ivanov at Geneva University (10-11 December, 1982).

[66] Vyacheslav Ivanov, "K ideologii yevreiskogo voprosa," in *Shchit*, Moscow, 1915. This essay will be discussed briefly in ch.3.

[67] It is worth recalling the context in which Bulgakov's quotes of Dostoevsky originally occurred. They are from his journalistic *Dnevnik Pisatelya* (Writer's Diary), in which he paints a picture of the Pale Jew as a cynical exploiter of the Russian masses. The

half of the twentieth century, appealing to such contradictory witnesses is highly anomalous. This merely confirms the sense that Rozanov's notorious "switching" when it came to the Jewish question could be found in less marked forms elsewhere, and that the lines between *Shield* and "Israel in the past..." did not exclude subterranean contact.

Nonetheless, not everyone within the same cultural sphere has seen the anomaly – and the answer to this question determines whether or not Bulgakov is for a given person anti-Semitic or not. It is this question that we will take up in the coming section.

The paradox of Bulgakov's anti-Semitism: between Soloviev and Dostoyevsky

The controversy over Bulgakov's anti-Semitism can be dated quite precisely to the year 1920. Bulgakov was living in the Crimea, and serving as a priest there as well as working as a professor of economics and theology at Tavra University. An extraordinary charge began circulating among his former acquaintances, the Russian Jewish community in exile, and the White movement in exile, that Bulgakov had become a far-right agitator for anti-Semitism, going so far as to write pamphlets and posters that were distributed on the walls of Crimean cities inciting the masses to pogroms. This was no abstract matter of theology now: between 1918 and 1920 the civil-war-ravaged Ukraine became scene to the worst anti-Jewish atrocities in Jewish history before the Holocaust.[68] The testimonies come from different sources.

---

quote about "educated Russian Jews" being atheists is embedded in a long tirade against the Yids (he reproaches Jews for taking offense at this basically friendly term), who he maintains whine and groan about the awfulness of their predicament while controlling all the stock-exchanges and political institutions of the world. The "educated Russian Jew" for Dostoevsky seems to be a particular offense, guilty of giving himself airs, and pointlessly distancing himself from the general Yiddery from which he has sprung. Dostoevsky finally comes out grudgingly in support of equal rights for Jews in the empire, as a matter of Christian principle; however, typically, he quickly adds that there is good reason to fear the abuse to which the Jews will put this Christian concession, using it for more domination and exploitation. That Bulgakov can merely abstract from this context and use extracts in support of his Zionism is, as Markish says of Ivanov, puzzling at the very least, and shows a very thick skin, or at least short-sightedness, where Jewish sensibilities are concerned. This is scarcely diminished by the fact that Bulgakov on another occasion (*Russkaya Tragedia*, Russkaya Mysl', 1914, kn.IV, 1-26) did distance himself from Dostoevsky's right wing views; but he was also convinced that this flaw in the writer's make-up did not impede his genius, and that furthermore the writer was aware of this flaw and both struggled against it, as well as mining insights out of it into the fate of Russia. For another insight into Dostoevsky's relation to Jews, cf. the correspondence between Abraham Uri Kovner and Dostoevsky, which can be found in Lucy Davidovicz, *The Golden Tradition: Jewish Life and Thought in Eastern Europe*, ch.38. "I confess to Dostoevsky." New York: Syracuse University Press, 1996.

68 Budnitsky, *Rossiskie yevrei mezhdu krasnymi i byelami*, 7-8: "During the Civil War

It should be said in advance that no pamphlets or posters from the period survive. Thus before beginning this discussion, I will extract some sections from his wartime essays which express the sort of opinions which could have given rise to the shocked reactions of Bulgakov's contemporaries in 1920. They seem to correspond to what these contemporaries were describing. As this section proceeds, we will examine these testimonies, then look at Bulgakov's diary entries for the period (written in exile three to six years after the Revolution and Civil War). Finally, we will attempt to define the nature of Bulgakov's anti-Semitism. (At the end of this chapter, we will also consider reactions to Bulgakov's Jewish writings among contemporary Russian Jews).

The extracts which should guide the reader in their assessment are the following:

> Jewry, as such, is a force which demands submission to itself, and in point of fact obtains it in the most varied situations, and the weakest among the other nations are not in a position to resist, although they sometimes react to this with paroxysms of impotent rage – in pogroms, and generally in the loss of political and spiritual civility towards the Jews, though at the same time seeming to be guilty against their will, or as it were apologetically. However genuine equality and equal rights are never achieved by this. The notorious "international" character of the Jewish "anti-race" makes her stronger and better armed against any other nation confined within the limits of a national existence.[69]

> Not by this theology [Judaism] does Jewry influence the world, although this, together with the building of synagogues also expresses the national character. As a religion, Judaism is now naturally conscious of itself as in opposition to Christianity. But it is not in this way that it is possible to identify the religious consciousness of Jewry, inasmuch as it possible to speak of it at all. But here it expresses itself either negatively, as a factual abandonment of religious faith, or as a militant atheism, which does not stop short of persecuting religion, which in point of fact means Christianity.[70]

> German racism reproduces in itself Judean messianism, which is the opponent and rival of Christianity from its very first beginnings...[Nazism contains the same seeds as the zealotistic movements of early Judaism:

---

of 1918-1920 in Russia, Russian Jewry underwent a tragedy commensurate with the Khmelnitsky disaster and exceeded only by the Holocaust...the bloodiest of the pogroms took place in the Ukraine in 1919 and the beginning of 1920. The statistics in the literature vary from 60,000 to 200,000 murdered victims as well as those who died from wounds. To these victims must be added tens of thousands of persons who were maimed, raped and robbed."

[69] *Racism and Jewry*, p.28.
[70] Ibid, p.31.

nationalism and socialism. Jewish messianism, national Judaism] can with the same readiness be found both in the Talmud and in Marx and in all the other representatives of socialism and Bolshevism. In general, social utopianism of different stripes in our days is a specific degeneration of ancient Jewish messianism, in which the Messiah is a social-revolutionary leader, able to realize the earthly kingdom, a sort of führer of national socialism on the soil of Judaism.[71]

Christians must realize a Christian relationship to Jewry even when a consequence of this will be that a dominant position for Jewry will be created in the world. Christians should not be afraid of this, because this is the only way to overcome Jewry, not from without but from within.[72]

Jewry is in general, and especially in Russia, in a struggle with the Christian foundations of European culture[73]

The political and historical fate of Israel condemns it to parasitism.[74]

A Prusso-Jewish outcome....Hitler, Stalin, Rosenberg, Trotsky in their identity....[75]

And not 'holy Israel' but strong-willed Jewry showed itself as a power in Bolshevism, in the suffocation of the Russian people.[76]

Jewry in its lowest degenerateness, predatoriness, love of power, self-importance, self-assertiveness, through the means of Bolshevism enacted if – in comparison to the Tatar yoke – not a chronologically long (though a quarter of a century is not a short period for such tortures), then an extremely significant – in terms of results – violence against Russia and especially against Holy Rus, which was an attempt to spiritually and physically suffocate her....In its objective meaning this (the Jewish Bolshevist yoke) was an attempt at the spiritual murder of Russia, which by God's mercy, was left with inadequate means.[77]

....Israel is a laboratory of all sorts of poisons, poisoning the world, and in particular Christian humanity. On the other hand, it is a nation of prophets, in whom the spirit of prophecy has not ebbed and whose religious element

---

[71] Ibid,, p.34.
[72] Ibid, p.35.
[73] *The Coming Fates of the World: The Jewish Question*, p.41.
[74] Ibid, 44.
[75] *The Fates of Russia, Germany and Jewry*, p.49.
[76] Ibid, p.52.
[77] Ibid, p.55.

has not weakened. However in a state of blindness it is Christianity without Christ and even against Christ, however in search of and hoping only for Him.[78]

...Israel has armed itself with the weapons of the Prince of this world, and occupies his seat. All the invincibility of the element of Jewry, its giftedness and strength, being directed to earthly lordship, is expressed in the cult of the golden calf, known to it from the beginning in its Old Testament temptation at the foot of mount Sinai. The power of money, of Mammon, is the worldwide power of Jewry. This indisputable fact does not contradict the fact that a significant portion, perhaps the majority of Jews up to the present time live in deep poverty, and need, and a struggle for existence, which finds no natural solution for itself in the absence of their own country, through an Ahasuerus-like diaspora, a state of 'eternal Jew'.[79]

These sentiments which are expressed openly in 1941-1942 are very likely the product of Bulgakov's last years in Russia, as the constant reference to Bolshevism makes clear[80]. The large (but not seriously disproportionate to their numbers in the general population[81]) numbers of Jews in revolutionary movements before and during the Revolution was the main context for Bulgakov's meditation on Jewish fate. As we saw, these thoughts lay for the most part dormant, until the Nazi attempt to annihilate Jewry provoked Bulgakov to ponder on the events of those days, as well as the unfolding atrocities of the later period.

---

[78] *Christianity Without Israel*, p.70.
[79] Ibid, 69.
[80] Given that Bulgakov had been living in Western Europe for twenty years by this point, this assertion may seem debatable. It is certainly possible that other factors entered into his evaluation of Jewry; however, it seems that to some extent for the Russian exiles the concerns of twenty years ago continued to be experienced with the same vividness, exile acting as a sort of preservative. Put another way, just as founder populations have a disproportionate influence on the language and culture of an emergent society which no later immigrants can match, foundational experiences (for Bulgakov Russia and the Russian Revolution) can exert disproportionate influence on the absorption and interpretation of later experience (for Bulgakov his life in exile). The rise of Stalin and refusal of the Soviet Union to melt away can only have deepened and renewed his despair about Bolshevism.
[81] See for example Semyon Reznik, *Vmeste ili vroz': sudba yevreev v Rossii*; O.Budnitski: *Rossiskie yevrei mezhdu krasnymi i byelami*, ch.2; or *Istoria yevreev Rossii* (Projekt Vsemirnogo kongressa russkoyazychnogo yevreistva), ch.11. for evidence that Jewish involvement in the Revolution was not of the dimensions that Bulgakov imagines. Reznik's book is a careful critique of similar accusations brought by Solzhenitsyn in his book *Dvesti let vmeste* (Two Hundred Years Together). Other studies of Jewish involvement in revolutionary movements include Erich Haberer's *Jews and Revolution in nineteenth century Russia* and Jonathan Frankel's *Prophecy and Politics: Socialism, Nationalism and the Russian Jews 1862-1917*.

While Bulgakov did not see in the Nazi persecution a reason to mitigate the harshness of his judgment of Jewry for its involvement in Bolshevism, there are signs of a change of heart, as we will discuss in the relevant section. In fact, these negative quotes, selected for illustrative purposes, are embedded in a larger theological context that strives to work out a benign approach to Judaism from a Solovievan Christian perspective.

Thus one can say that these quotes belong not so much to the later period as to that traumatic time before exile in the Ukraine. And in this sense, they give further grist to the thesis proposed above: that the dividing-line between support for Jews and denigration of Jews was highly unstable. Bulgakov, full of empathy and tolerance for Jewry in *Shield* 1915, was repeating sentiments that recapitulate to the word the violently anti-Semitic sentiments of Florensky in "Israel in the past..." in the same year, and Rozanov between 1911-1913[82].

What then triggered the *volte-face*, or if one looks at it a different way, brought to the surface simmering mistrust and hostility[83]?

The first public accusation against Bulgakov appeared in the Jewish exilic paper *Evreiskaya Tribuna* (Jewish Tribune) claiming that Bulgakov had posted calls to pogroms on the walls of Crimean cities, and that the "philosopher and priest, scientist and monk, with his writer's authority and monk's cap is giving strength to the black deeds of the apparachiks of the Osvag[84] and the zealous police captains and the dark, violent...mob..."

Bulgakov's friend and colleague M.O. Gershenzon, who had collaborated with him on the pivotal *Landmarks* project[85], was a Russian Jew deeply sympathetic to Russian culture, and indeed a Slavophile of sorts. He too picked up on the rumors: "I knew that...he kept out of politics," he wrote in 1923 to another Russian Jew of similar sympathies, Lev Shestov[86]. "...But K[amenev] did not listen to my assurances; in the end he announced: don't you know, that B[ulgakov] has written a call to Jewish pogroms, which have been posted around all the cities of the Crimea. I answered, of course, that this was a stunning lie, that B was not capable of that. And he says to me: Rodichev himself has confirmed this fact in his foreign newspaper..."[87]

---

[82] Cf.ch.4 for the closeness of the language.

[83] Certainly, part of the answer was the general instability of the times: we will see other baffling transformations – that of M.Gershenzon from a Slavopile to a Bolshevik (or so it seemed); and of N.Berdyaev from an anti-Soviet to a supporter of Soviet power. P.Florensky also seemed to go from a monarchist to a covert admirer of Soviet totalitarianism.

[84] The propaganda agency of the White movement.

[85] Incidentally the *Landmarks* project was a liberal-conservative religious-cultural critique of the socialist intelligentsia in Russia. Three of the seven contributing members (Frank, Gershenzon, Izgoev-Lange) were Jews – a fact which contradicts the equation Jew = Bolshevik later favored by Bulgakov himself. *Landmarks* will be analysed in some detail in ch.4, and further in ch.6.

[86] See chapter 4 for more on Gershenzon and Shestov.

[87] Letters of M.O. Gershenzon to L. Shestov (1920-1925), quoted in *Issledovaniya po-*

Gershenzon's shock is understandable: how could Bulgakov have turned from Christian Zionist to right-wing agitator in seven years? Gershenzon, it should be noted, was present – along with the recipient of this letter, another non-baptized Jew, Lev Shestov, at Bulgakov's ordination in Moscow a mere *two years* earlier[88]. Gershenzon himself came from Kishinev in the Pale of Settlement, scene in 1903 of one of the worst Russian pogroms to date.

More light is shed on this matter by four non-Jewish sources: the journalist G.N.Rakovsky; the Hebrew scholar and renowned church intellectual, A.N.Kartashev; V.A. Maklakov, the ambassador of non-Soviet Russia in Paris; and an anonymous writer of an article about Bulgakov's visit to Simferopol in 1919.[89]

Rakovsky testified that: "the clergy from the autumn of 1920 began to engage in "particularly furious monarchic agitation," establishing "days of repentance with three day fasts." The dark masses were electrified by "the pogrom-rousing sermons and speeches of Bishop Veniamin, S. Bulgakov, Malakhov, members of 'national communities' and so on." Vostokov called for the shattering of Jewish skulls. However, the reliability of this testimony is called into question by Vostokov's own memoirs, where he testified that Bishop Veniamin in fact asked him to desist from his sermons against Jews as they were leading many astray. If Rakovsky's journalism was the source of the rumor against Bulgakov, it too may well have been false.

The second and more reliable witness is V.A. Maklakov, who had been sent on a mission to the Ukraine by P.N. Vengel, the general of the White Russian army. His task was to try to curb the widespread and vicious anti-Semitism of the White movement in Russia. One of the main offenders was the above-mentioned Fr. Vladimir Vostokov, who was giving inflammatory anti-Semitic sermons throughout the Crimea and was something of a perverse attraction for the population, who flocked to hear and be mesmerized by his hate-filled rhetoric. The curious fact about Vostokov, in light of Bulgakov's case, is that while he lived in Moscow he had embraced extremely liberal views. Due to his criticism of Rasputin, he had been exiled to the Ukraine and once there had metamorphosed into a reactionary firebrand.[90]

Maklakov, troubled by rumors of his propagandizing activity, met with Bulgakov, a former colleague of his at Moscow University with whom he had shared a right Kadet[91] political orientation. The account he gave of this meeting in a letter to the Russian ambassador in Washington is worth quoting extensively:

---

istoriyi russkoy mysli, ezhegodnik, St Petersburg, Aliteia Press, 1997.

[88] As Bulgakov recounts in the same chapter of his *Autobiographical Fragments* that we will examine below.

[89] The following details are drawn from Oleg V. Budinitsky, *Rossiskie yevrei mezhdu krasnymi i byelami (1917-1920)*. (Moscow: Rosspen, 2006): pp.267-274.

[90] Some attributed this to the murder of his daughter by Bolsheviks, but it seems that he only learnt of the murder after he had already started preaching.

[91] The term refers to participants in the Constitutional Democratic party. Maklakov and Bulgakov had belonged to its conservative wing; both had been jokingly referred to as the "black-hundreders of the Kadet party."

"Bulgakov is a firm opponent of the pogroms and in this sense recognizes that Vostokov's sermons, while not incitement to pogroms – he denies that – could nonetheless call forth unchristian and very dangerous feelings in the masses. He is cultured enough to recognize that; on the other hand, Bulgakov might give support to a far more dangerous, and I would say, obsolete tendency of the government to look with complete satisfaction towards a policy of self-defense against Jewry; I would not be surprised if Bulgakov encouraged, if not a Pale of Settlement, then a ban on Jews entering government service, as well as other deprivation of rights."

More extraordinary than this is Maklakov's testimony that when he tried to enlist Bulgakov's support in preventing the dissemination of a document addressed to the people concerning Jewish participation in Bolshevism which would have had provocative consequences, Bulgakov replied: "I wrote it myself."

Where does the truth of the matter lie? Opinions divided immediately. Another contributor to the same *Evreiskaya Tribuna*, the well-known Russian Orthodox church figure and Biblical scholar, A.V. Kartashev, reacted with indignity to the rumors about the posting of calls to pogroms. For him "there was not a minute's doubt that this was the usual illiteracy of informants talking about something they have no essential understanding of. Bulgakov has become a monarchist. Such a move for a Solovievan theocrat contains nothing unusual in itself…The vulgar link between monarchism and anti-Semitism is in any case not applicable to such a noble, lofty expression of Russian culture as is evident in the personality of S.N.Bulgakov."[92]

Finally, another witness of Bulgakov's life in the Crimea in those years enables us to go some way to resolving the contradiction between the image of a pogrom-inciting rabble-rouser and a thoroughly eirenic Solovievan philosopher who could not have uttered a single provocation against Jewish Bolsheviks. This is the anonymous writer of an article about Bulgakov's visit to Simferopol, which was published in a White newspaper shortly after the event under the title: "Vegetus: A week of Bulgakov."[93]

The writer was present at the Tavra diocesan conference, which took place in

---

[92] Quoted in O.V.Budnitsky, *Rossiskie yevrei mezhdu krasnymi i byelami (1917-1920)*. Moscow: Rosspen, 2006, pp. 272-3. Original article: A.V.Kartashev, "Antisemitizm i russkaya tserkov," in Yevreiskaya Tribuna, 1920, 3 December. Both writers were not present in Crimea and are thus second-hand witnesses. Kartashev's defense of Bulgakov is, I would venture, somewhat compromised by the fact that he had a clearly apologetic function in defending the Russian Church from charges of anti-Semitism. In this sense, Maklakov's testimony is stronger, clashing as it does with the self-interest he must have felt in wishing to defend supporters of his own movement. Budnitsky himself comments in a footnote (fn.155, p. 156) that "Bulgakov's anti-Semitism was most certainly not 'sudden'…" as the Jewish contributor to the Tribune had supposed; in support Budnitsky points to Bulgakov's "Agoniya," which will be discussed below.

[93] Vegetus. A week about Bulgakov. Velikaya Rossiya. Rostov-na-Donu. No.339. Wednesday 6 (19). November 1919. No.2.

Simferopol in autumn, 1919. Bulgakov, newly ordained and serving at a church on the south coast of the Crimea, gave presentations almost every evening of the conference, producing an inspirational impression among the beleaguered Christians of the Civil War-ravaged region.

In addition to addressing the diocesan conference, Bulgakov also gave talks at the Tavra University "Society of philosophical, social, and historical learning." One talk was dedicated to "Three," a discussion of the mystical nature of power and a united Russia – which no doubt was well-received by the more monarchist members of the audience. After another presentation, however, "some socialists were offended on account of Chernyshevsky; and in Jewish circles a rumor started up that Bulgakov had come to initiate a Jewish pogrom…"

In that talk, Bulgakov had lectured on "the spiritual roots of Bolshevism." Repeating the theses we have already examined, Bulgakov traced Bolshevism to the rationalistic philosophy of the eighteenth century, and in Russian society pointed the finger at "the conceptual founders of contemporary Bolshevism – the leaders of the radical and socialist intelligentsia of the 19th century – Belinski, Herzen, Dobrolyobov, Chernishevsky, and in many ways, Tolstoy." Hence, the offense of the socialists.

However, a new note has crept into the explanation, and it was this which no doubt caused offense among Jews, for Bulgakov now referred to another ingredient: "the mystical hopes of a Godless paradise on earth of the Jerusalem Bolsheviks two thousand years ago." In terms of our present commentary, it is noticeable that this judgment of the "Jerusalem Bolsheviks" shares an affinity with the phrases extracted from his later wartime writings. It differs, however, from his earlier comments regarding pacifist rabbinism and pre-rabbinic apocalyptism that we noted in *Two Cities*. It also differs from those comments in the odd contention that the Jews in time of Jesus were atheists; evidently, Bulgakov was imbuing ancient history with contemporary relevance.

Still, it is hardly likely that this theological slight would have led to charges that Bulgakov was posting pogrom-inciting posters round the Crimea. The writer of "Vegetus" sheds light on this too. During a discussion about how Orthodox Christians could resist the rise of sectarian tendencies in the Church, as well as the atheist propaganda of the Bolsheviks, "there was a proposal to start a missionary effort, to carry out energetic propaganda by means of publishing and dissemination of brochures and pamphlets. In respect of this question, Bulgakov expressed himself at the conference. While not denying the necessity for propaganda and mission, he showed that the best form of propaganda was not negative but positive, and urgently called on the clergy to deepen and confirm their own faith….."

By the time Maklakov met with Bulgakov, however, we can surmise that Bulgakov had decided to take up the suggestion of using pamphlets to defend against sectarianism and Bolshevism. An additional clue as to the nature of these pamphlets comes from the fact that the session in which Bulgakov had talked about "Jerusalem Bosheviks" was chaired by Bishop Veniamin (Fedchenkov), mentioned above. Whether or not Rakovsky's assertions that Fedchenkov gave anti-Semitic sermons is true, it is a fact that the bishop wrote to Rozanov after Beilis' acquittal in 1913 and Rozanov's exclusion from the Religious-Philosophical Society congratulating him on his "martyrdom" for the cause of truth[94]. Bulgakov's speech was, in turn, delivered to the Tavra branch of the Religious-Philosophical Society.

All this leads to the conclusion that Bulgakov disseminated pamphlets warning of the spiritual dangers of Jewish Bolshevism in apocalyptic language. For as he had said at the speech on spiritual Bolshevism, "everything in contemporary life hints more and more at the struggle of Christ and the anti-Christ." Thus, Russians needed to rediscover the heritage of Pushkin, Lermontov, Tyuchev, Dostoevsky, the Slavophiles – and Soloviev.

The inclusion of Soloviev is interesting. According to the writer of "Vegetus," Bulgakov's speech on Holy Russia was couched "partly in the style of Soloviev's Tale of the Anti-Christ." In that tale, of course, the godless Jews had dedicated themselves to the Anti-Christ at the endtime. Thus, although we have maintained that Bulgakov's anti-Semitic leanings owe more to Dostoevsky, there is also a sense in which Soloviev too provided a language for an apocalyptic identification of Jewry and dangerous anti-Christian tendencies. In other words, while in "normal" times, neither Soloviev nor Bulgakov would have wished to make that charge concrete, in the turbulent times of the Civil War, such comments were incendiary.

A glimpse of the toll that the times were taking on Bulgakov is also discernible in a comment of Maklakov that Bulgakov showed a vivid interest in the former's Masonic connections, and was hungry for information that might confirm or disconfirm his suspicions of a world-wide Jewish conspiracy[95].

Yet another clue as to how Bulgakov could have shifted sides from the writer of "Zion" to the writer of anti-Jewish pamphlets is given by Bulgakov himself, in a comment Bulgakov made regarding his own character[96]: "I never had an interest

---

[94] Leonid Katsis, *Krovavy navet i russkaya mysl: istoriko-teologicheskoe issledovanie dela Beilisa*, (Moscow: Gesharim/Mosty kultury, 2006), 277-8.

[95] S.Y. Witte, a senior minister in the government of Nicolas II, and one of the few pro-Jewish officials there provides another backdrop against which to understand Bulgakov. While he opposed the discriminatory policies of the government, he himself was incredibly naïve with respect to Jewish realia, and indeed to the political realia of the revolutionary movement. He lumped together Constitutional Democrats (Kadets) with anarchists, calling them all bombers, murders, and bandits. As for the Jews, he believed that Jewish leaders in the West should tell their fellow tribesmen to stop engaging in Revolutionary activity – revealing a childish belief that Jewry is an internationally co-ordinated organization under the control of a central cabal. (As Reznik, 136 quotes and analyses Witte). It really seems to be the case that it was not so much malice as almost unbelievable naivety shading into incompetence in the person of a government minister responsible for administering the empire in the twentieth century that is behind these opinions.

[96] In the preface to the chapter "5 years: 1917-1922" of his *Autobiographical Fragments*

or a taste for the concrete, for reality, that is the nature of my weakness and what is characteristic of me. Events were always perceived by me in the form of threads of sound and color of a certain shade and intensity, but I didn't have the ability or the taste to decompose them into something concrete."

This is an enlightening self-portrait. Bulgakov is very much the deep thinker who sees far into the distance, sketches broad apocalyptic canvases, and can do nothing but mix the grand tones of theology with the events of daily life. This leads at times to inspiring prophetic insight – but at other times, it leads to a short-sighted inattention to, inadmissible fudgings of, crucial distinctions on the ground-beneath-one's-feet of real life.[97]

Thus I believe that Bulgakov has so absorbed the Old Testament tirades against the Chosen People, the Johanine reproaches against the Jews, that he can apply them to contemporary Jews *en masse* by a simple sleight of hand. Again, as we saw, he traced Soviet communism back to Jewish apocalyptic – and his lack of "interest or…taste for the concrete, for reality" which was "the nature of [his] weakness" meant that Jewish involvement with Bolshevism in the Crimea became a chapter straight off the pages of the ancient books.

In this way, he ignored his own insight that rabbinic Judaism had disowned the apocalyptic heritage of the past more than Christianity. He was guilty of not "decomposing…into something concrete" his own flashes of insight. And of course, when thousands of Jews were being torn to pieces (sometimes literally) in his own vicinity, this short-sightedness is inexcusable. A more "concrete" analysis, it might be said, would have laid the blame for Jewish involvement in *Russian* communism on precisely these appropriated and then heretically interpreted Jewish texts[98].

Bulgakov's reaction to Vostokov's sermons (which on occasions caused the crowd of listeners to scream out "Beat up the Yids!") – that they were not incitement to pogroms, but merely a possible cause of unchristian feelings – also seems to be an inadmissible hair-splitting reservation about the meaning of "incitement," given the widespread violence against Jews taking place outside the Church's walls[99].

(p.405).

[97] Thankfully, unlike Witte, Bulgakov was not a government minister!

[98] Indeed, in other places, Bulgakov has much to say about the poisonous nature of Russian communism. However, he never makes the step of blaming the Russians for corrupting the Jews, a step that would perhaps have seemed perverse to him. However, Rozanov – in his philo-Semitic upswings – made precisely that connection.

[99] A propagandistic song among supporters of the Whites should make clear the close connection in some elements of the populace between patriotism, sacred Orthodoxy and the duty to do violence to Jews:
Vypim my za krest svyatoi
I za liturgiyu
I za lozung, 'Byey zhidov
I spasai Rossiyu.'
(Let's drink to the holy cross/And to the liturgy,/And to the slogan "Beat the Yids/

In sum, Bulgakov's approach is evidence that the Church's own teaching on the Jews – even the most Solovievianly philoSemitic of them – could fuse all too easily with a limited political viewpoint, no matter how sophisticated in other respects Bulgakov's political-cultural analyses were. For the fact of the matter, even now under-recognized in Russia, is that Jews were involved in liberal and conservative political movements in the years before the Revolution, and were not communists to a man – to state the obvious, which unfortunately has become unobvious for some. Moreover, the most "visible" Jews who were the easiest targets for pogrom-makers were those in religious garb: and religious Jews by definition were opposed to the Bolshevik revolution.

Somewhere in the back of his mind, Bulgakov must have harbored such distinctions – else friendship with Jews like Gershenzon, Frank, and Shestov would have been impossible. But the concrete, the composite, the complex tended to be exploded into one burst of holistic brightness when history triggered an emotional response in Bulgakov. We can see this by following his inner development from Marxist to monarchist as he recounts it in deeply personal tones in his *Autobiographical Fragments*, to which we will now turn.

Bulgakov's recollections of the 1905 and 1917 Revolutions

His account of the years from 1905-1917 affords a glimpse of how Bulgakov's transformation from materialist Marxist to Orthodox monarchist, which proceeded not so much gradually as in fits and bounds, was not simply an abstract intellectual transformation. Rather it was an emotional-spiritual metamorphosis that impacted on his whole self-identity, as he found himself allied with forces and tendencies in the life of Russia that as yet provided an uncomfortable fit for the former professor of economics. As he himself noted, the Bulgakov that

---

And save Russia. Cf. Budnitsky 2006, p.234.) This unpleasant ditty captures more than a hundred tomes the extent to which nationalism, folk culture, and the core elements of the Christian faith can be combined into a demonic cocktail which some have taken for the real McCoy. The question of how Christian such anti-Semitism is will be discussed in ch.4. A useful historical insight into the position of Jews in the Ukraine during the time of Bulgakov's stay can be found in chapter 10 of Praisman L. and Kipnis M. main author and ed. *Istoria yevreev v Rossii*. Moscow: Lekhaim, 2005. Praisman shows that many Jews enlisted in the White volunteer army and were keen to fight Bolshevism. Increasingly, from 1919 onwards the Whites rejected Jewish officers and discouraged Jewish infantry from enlisting. Cossack battalions perpetrated many pogroms, and on entering villages would ignore Communists and seek out Jews for violence. Thus the propagandistic White equation that Jews are communists became reversed: *only* Jews were communists, for the purposes of "recrimination." Bulgakov's idea of "Jerusalem Bolsheviks" must be seen as part of this inaccurate oversight of Jews who did not welcome Bolshevism, and worse, of that tendency which turned into a self-fulfilling prophecy – by excluding Jews from the anti-communist resistance, the Whites lost an important element of support in the non-Russian population and by their atrocities drove Jews towards acceptance of the Bolshevik reality.

emerged at the end of this period was a unique combination of so many opposing tendencies that people were often at a loss to categorize him – as we have already seen.

His disillusionment with socialism and his embrace of Christianity are depicted as happening almost within the space of a single day, during the 1905 revolution. Bulgakov describes the events vividly in a chapter of his *Autobiographical Fragments* called 'Agony'[100].

As the title suggests, these years were experienced for him as the Christ-like death of sacred Russia. He is in Kiev when the 1905 revolution breaks. Taking part in a vulgar, boorish and violent demonstration in the centre of town, Bulgakov suddenly comes to feel the spiritual dryness and anti-Christian spirit of the demonstrators and the demonstration. On the way there he had joined in with the bravaderie of the revolutionaries, who had put red ribbons and rosettes in their button-holes. When he gets home, Bulgakov throws the red rosette he had been wearing in his own button-hole into the toilet. He is alone and empty. He opens the Gospel to look for a word of guidance and finds the words: This type of demon you can only cast out through prayer and fasting. He ponders: "But then the presence of this type of demon was already clear to me, from it on the evening of the same day pogroms began in Kiev, only in the black camp this time, and without red ribbons in buttonholes." He leaves behind his social-revolutionary fervor, and the vanity of coupling it to Christian hopes. Instead, from now on, he begins to develop a respect for the tsar[101], for nationality, for Orthodoxy.

What is interesting in this last quote is the way Bulgakov's impressions of the "black" camp and the "red" camp are identical. From his own point of view, the distinction between socialist-communist and extreme right nationalism is trivial. Perhaps there is something in this, as the history of the twentieth century would later show, but it is the same sort of ethereal elision of political realities which we see in his later reactions to Jews.

Bulgakov goes on to recount how his own peculiar point of view does indeed put him at odds with the various parties springing up around him. He is aware that his new and growing monarchism puts him into the same camp, superficially, as the right wing, the conservatives, and even the *pogromshiki*, "who," he writes later in the same chapter, "are a clique of Moscow reactionaries embracing despotism under the mask of conservatism. The *pogromshiki* raised their heads and formed their own fighting bands. And, still, they professed Orthodoxy and nationality, which I too then confessed, and I felt myself in almost tragic loneliness in my own camp."

The account of these years was written in Istanbul (*Tsargrad* in Bulgakov's

---

[100] Sergei Bukgakov, *Avtobiograficheskiye zametki*. (Paris, YMCA-Press, 1991): Pyat' Let – Agoniya, pp.73-93.

[101] Two quotes will give a taste of the cataclysmic nature of his political-religious conversion: "In my student days I dreamed of regicide (lit. 'tsaricide')...(p.408)," while after his transformation: "I loved the Tsar, I wanted Russia with the Tsar, and without the Tsar Russia was for me not even Russia (p.406)."

nomenclature) in 1923, and perhaps in order to reply to the likes of Gershenzon, Maklakov and the unsympathetic writer of the Jewish Tribune, he is keen to make clear that "in my enthusiasm for the power of the tsar there was not (and never has been) any element of police black-hundreds sympathy, and I did not become any closer to the right wing...." Far from it: Bulgakov accuses the Slavophiles, the *pochviniki*[102], of harking back to the past, and rejecting the responsibility of the future. They are also complicit in the Revolution. Orientation towards the future is for Bulgakov a Christian duty; "for Christ said, 'Behold, I create everything anew'...And this religious-revolutionary, apocalyptic feeling of 'interuptedness'... allies me intrinsically with revolution and even – *horribile dictu* – with Russian bolshevism...But this 'revolutionariness' in the Russian soul has been so indissolubly linked to Gadarene[103] demonism that from the national-political and cultural point of view it can only be suicidal."[104]

And yet Bulgakov's reassurances that he never shared "black-hundreds sympathy" is typically compromised when he comes to describe the second October Revolution, some twelve years, which is experienced by him as Russia's final sacred agony and crucifixion:

> It was the Lenten week of Prostration before the Cross. Everyone of course had forgotten about this, and I had the most heavy premonition about this symbolic coincidence. However, my whole thought and care (alas! powerless and ineffective) was about Him, about the Anointed. What was happening with Him? Would he retain the throne? And if so, then maybe he would be reconciled with the responsible ministeries....Afterwards, rumors began to circulate about a forced abdication: this is what I had expected, because I knew in my heart how there in the heart of the revolution, it was the Tsar that they especially hated, how there they did not want a constitution, but precisely to topple the Tsar, and what *Yids* were giving directions...And then, one piece of news after another: the Tsar had abdicated. Simultaneously, there appeared more news in the papers about 'Alexander Theodorovich' (in the new Yid terminology, with which it was impossible to reconcile oneself): the royal children were sick with measles....I was suffocated by final tears of helplessness...

---

[102] Advocates of a return to the *pochva*, soil, of Russia, who shared similar views to the Slavophiles, and some of whose leading figures embraced anti-Semitic views.

[103] A reference to the demon-possessed Gadarene swine in Mt.8.28 that rushed off the cliff into the sea after Jesus had expelled them from a possessed man. This Gospel episode was the source of the title of Dostoevsky's *The Devils*, and Bulgakov developed Dostoevsky's thesis that Russian communism was a type of anti-Christian demonic possession.

[104] Berdyaev's reaction to the Revolution reflects a similar ambiguity as to how to greet this new force in Russian life, although there are major differences in their approaches; see next chapter.

At the climax of Russia's agony, and his own agony, Bulgakov loses his Soloviovian sympathy for the Jews and turns on them with Dostoevskian bitterness. But again, it would be simplifying matters to see this as a sudden about-turn from tolerance to hatred. That ambiguity was present in all his works, and circumstances have merely elicited a preponderance of enmity.

Once he has finally been exiled, the resentment and the rancor against the red Yids[105] is mixed in with something sweeter, with a note of tolerant fascination, that nonetheless is not without a taste of bitterness. Traveling on a steamer across the Black Sea to Constaninople, he is in his very exile – irony of ironies – crowded out by emigrating Jews to whom he pays great attention:

> Our steamer that was full of emigrating Jews, doleful, caricatures, but still ciphers of the Old Testament, suddenly entered into communication with another steamer, standing alongside it *en route* from Rumania to Palestine: it was full of Jews moving to Palestine. We also had an enthusiast of that matter, and a conversation started in ancient Hebrew, and then the large though not very harmonious choir from their ship for a long time sang their national songs, and with the fading day the words of the song faded quietly. Lord, how touching it all was: from the Bolshevik Palestine to this Palestine? And they're everywhere! And the next day there appeared their fellows from Constantinople, after which a Jewish society sent gifts (they spare some for us too – an amusing anecdote here!), and here they are at home. What an ability to penetrate everywhere, what indissolubility, this people has: they travel – old people and children, in winter, to America and Palestine, quite sure of themselves, without getting lost, noisy, funny and touching. The chosen people, and together with that rejected, and *sacer*, in both senses of the word[106].

---

[105] The word translated "Yid" is in Russian *zhid*. In modern Russian, it is pejorative and offensive. In Slavonic, it was closer to being a straightforward word for Jew. Hence the Judaizing heresy of the 16th century is called *"zhidovstvuyushchaya,"* discussed in ch.1. Because of the political percussions of that heresy, we can surmise that for Bulgakov there was an obvious connection between Yids and regicide. Because there is no "Yid(dish)izing" heresy in English, in a sense the word in Russian, if taken with a dash of Slavonicism, is less crude and offensive, though this depends on context. In Gogol's stories about the Ukraine, for instance, the word *zhid* is used as a synonym for Jew, where Jews are being referred to neutrally – though this is meant to echo the peasants' attitudes to Jews and all that entails, so that it is probably mistaken to speak of complete neutrality. One could say that *zhid* ranges from light, patronizing caricature to violent, offensive epithet, with historical-political context often unconsciously determining the meaning. In ch.4, we discuss Florensky's consciously applied distinction between *zhid* and *yevrei*: the former denoted secularized, radical, cosmopolitan Jew; the latter, a Jew still rooted in his albeit mistaken Judaic culture. The latter is also preferable as wishing to remain in the Pale; the former are most threatening for their desire to join (and for Florensky undermine) Russian culture through integration, and worst of all, intermarriage.

[106] "Homo sacer" in Roman law means both a "sacred man" and an "accursed man,"

In Bulgakov's diary, the next and final mention of Jews will also be aboard a ship, this time when he is on a visit to America. The date is 1931. Bulgakov is already living in Paris. He makes his first trip to America on the *Europa*. "Somewhere I read in Zombart," he writes, "America is a Jewish land. And now, sitting on the German steamer *Europa*, with a flag with a swastika, I am surrounded by Jewish travelers, amid this northern jargon of the German tongue, when I hear the nasal American as an exception, my heart jumps a bit for joy…Meanwhile I still feel the human mediocrity, the Philistinism. I haven't yet seen…a single intelligent face, although there is the well-known minimum of decency…But I won't yet trust to my first impressions, which are all tending in one direction – the factual conquest by Israel of the world…"

In this, we are reminded of Barth's words, which however are filled with a greater self-consciousness in this regard: "I have always, so long as I can remember, had to suppress a totally irrational aversion [to Jews]…." One can only conclude that these sentiments in Barth and Bulgakov are themselves part of that very "mystery of Israel," with which Bulgakov was grappling.

The next time Bulgakov takes up the theme of Jews and Jewry, the subject will be overshadowed by the sign of that same swastika which topped the *Europa*. Bulgakov's essays, written in German-occupied Paris, do not neatly and cleanly resolve the tensions which we have just examined. But one gets the feeling that just as Russian Orthodoxy for Bulgakov was taking on a universal and essential form, freed from its national ground in exile, so that the secondary was becoming distinguished from the primary, the merely ethnic from the universal, part of this process is Bulgakov working out a truly Christian approach – as Soloviev in less troubled times attempted to do – to the Jews and the Jewish question. Some of the scars of Russian-Jewish interaction from the old land are still there, but Bulgakov will begin to penetrate into these matters with a depth that ultimately transcends local origins.

Bulgakov and Jewry (2): in exile – the shadow of the Holocaust

The war-time writings comprise four works written at the end of 1941 and the beginning of 1942. They are: "Racism and Jewry" (December 1941); "The Destiny of Israel as the Cross of the Mother of God," a sermon delivered on the Feast of the Dormition, 1941; "Racism and Christianity," written in 1942; "The Genealogy of Christ," "The Mystery of Israel," and "Christianity without Israel," short connected pieces written in 1942. The Germans had already invaded Paris. As if living in an enemy-occupied city, a city of exile moreover, were not enough torment, Bulgakov himself was suffering from the throat cancer that would lead to his death in 1944.

The essays are filled with a realization of the action of God in history, with the

---

who can be killed by anyone who finds him.

fate of God's people highlighting once again the struggle of the transcendent forces of good and evil on the immanent stage of human history. His own disciples, as we saw, Mother Maria and Father Klepinin and others, were struggling to bring aid to Jews and others whom the Nazis were persecuting in Paris. Bulgakov heroically continued his own work despite all hardships. And one aspect of this work was to hammer out a response to Nazi anti-Semitism, to formulate an answer to where the place of this persecuted people of God lay in God's plans for humanity. It was, as Mother Maria, shortly to go to her own death in Ravensbruck, said a "time of the martyrs. We would all wear the star of David, if we were brave enough."[107]

Of course, for the Russian exile Bulgakov, a meditation on the fates of Jewry could not but turn into a meditation on the fate of Russia. And shortly after the breath-taking Stalin-Hitler pact earlier in the year, it was natural for Bulgakov to contemplate the higher meaning of the lethal struggle between Russia and Germany taking place on the soil of Europe. Not a few Russian exiles (the earlier quoted Merezhkovsky, now in exile in Germany) turned to Nazi Germany with new attention after this pact, hoping that Hitler would be the savior of Russia-in-exile, defeating the Soviet usurper and returning the long-suffering intelligentsia to their beloved homeland under a new regime. It is a measure of Bulgakov's integrity that the pain of exile in no way compromised his feel for evil, and he devotes great effort to uncovering the heretical, pagan, anti-Christian essence of the Nazi ideology, while also deploring as a shame to European civilization the unprecedented respectability of anti-Semitism among the Nazis and others of his contemporaries who were now sheltering under their ideological protection.

As we saw above, Bulgakov himself still has harsh words to say about Jewry. However, he recognizes that his argument with Jewry is of an altogether different order from that of the Nazis. Bulgakov's argument is religious: Jewish rejection of Christ has distorted their entire existence, but there is hope and indeed assurance of redemption. Those Jews who embrace Christ can escape the tragedy of Jewish history. While they may share the persecution of their non-believing brothers, theirs will be a redemptive Christian suffering.

Nazi ideology, on the other hand, condemns the Jews *in essentia* on racial grounds so that a change of faith makes no difference to racial identity. It is this aspect of Nazi anti-Semitism that Bulgakov is concerned to combat. And his main avenue of attack is the claim that this ideology is essentially anti-Christian.

Thus, just as Bulgakov had before cut through to the essence of socialism by exposing its theological underbelly, in "Racism and Jewry" – the first essay we will examine – his task is to root out the pseudo-mystical seeds of Nazi ideology and expose them as the purloined and distorted fruit of Christianity: blood, race, nation, chosenness – yes, all these come from the Bible, but they have been paganized and distorted.

His argument constitutes an interesting reply to those who use the same facts to point to a continuum between Nazism and Christianity and I believe the argument holds water. However, this argument obviously does not suffice

---

[107] Cf. Sergei Haeckel, *Mat' Maria*. YMCA Press 1992, Paris.

to remove all doubts that Christianity is guilty of fostering a different type of violence against Jews, of the type that Vostokov's demagoguery encouraged in the Ukraine in 1920. Nor is the argument intended to absolve Christianity of the charge of anti-Semitism *in toto*. When all is said and done, we will see that one of the lingering insights from these essays of Bulgakov's is that if Jewry has been distorted by its rejection of Christ, Christianity has been irremediably damaged by its own rejection of the Jews.

Nazi anti-Semitism, with its appropriation of Biblical language and its Messianic claims to be the third empire that would last for a thousand years (just as Orthodox Moscow had claimed to be the third Rome) must have come as somewhat of a shock to Bulgakov. It triggered an outpouring of hurried thinking (these essays have a rough-and-ready feel), whose goal is to restate the relationship between Christianity and Judaism in a way that is free of any of the Nazi poison.

In other words, Bulgakov wanted to avoid that pernicious route chosen, for example by those churches which welcomed the Nazis and accommodated their anti-Semitism with ease. And perhaps, closer to hand, he wished to distance himself from a Russian anti-Semitism that veered uncomfortably close to the language and tone of Nazi anti-Semitism[108].

As we look in more detail at Bulgakov's analyses in what follows, it will become apparent that many of his insights depend on the "sophiological" theology he had been developing at least since his 1912 book, *The Philosophy of Economy*.

---

[108] A Russian aristocrat, Baron A.V. Meller-Zakomelsky, tried to create a Russian fascist movement in Berlin before the war. He wanted to adapt Eurasianism to create a quasi-Slavophile racist ideology. As Eurasianism contains many ideas of Russian religious thought, the resulting blend at first blush makes it look as if there is an affinity between racism and mystical Christianity, as the following quote indicates: "This path inevitably leads to the race question. After all, personality is a psychophysical category. Nation, people, tribe – as symphonic personalities – have a body and a spirit. The link between spirit and blood, between the idea of a nation and its race is one of the givens of life. A realist has no right to close his eyes to that given. An ideocrat who refuses to reckon with the racial concept remains an abstract, groundless rationalist." (Letter to P.N.Savitsky, 1934, in A. Sobolev, *O Russkoy Filosofii*. St Petersburg: Mir, 2008.) See further discussion in ibid. ch.5 on Karsavin, Trubetzkoy and Eurasianism. A more troubling parallel, for Bulgakov's own conscience, was the racial anti-Semitism of his friend and fellow sophiologist, Fr.P.Florensky. His 1913 collaboration with Rozanov on "sophianic" anti-Semitic propaganda was known to Zinaida Gippius in Paris in 1925; his collaboration on "Israel in the past..." was public knowledge. (Cf. ch.4, present book). By the time Bulgakov left Russia, he had come to distance himself from the pagan and occult elements in Florensky's thought, reproaching himself for formerly believing them to be true to Orthodoxy. Thus Bulgakov's essays can partly be seen as continued attempts to assure himself that in this area his thinking was not poisoned with the same defects as troubled him in Florensky. This chapter does not explore the parallels between Florensky's and Bulgakov's Judeologies, but such an article surely needs to be written – and it would have to focus on the crucial focus that each thinker gives to blood in his exposition of the meaning of Jewish existence.

In fact, much of his theology of Jews and Judaism draws heavily on sophiology. For it was precisely during the nineteen thirties that Bulgakov brought his ideas about Sophia into mature form. However, we will delay giving an account of what exactly sophiology is and how it developed in Bulgakov's thought, until the reader has had time to absorb a concrete analysis where it plays a role. Only then is there sense in giving a sketch of some of the more metaphysical components of this theory.

The Biblical conception of blood and nation ("Racism and Jewry," 1941)

Bulgakov denounces the Nazi principle that racial purity, established through the blood, is the key to humanity, as being crass and materialistic. Nazism offers a seeming pluralism for humanity in its vision of many bloods, but in fact the ideology dictates that only one blood type is to count, German blood. German blood is the highest blood type of humanity, the apotheosis of human development. Germans are thus the Chosen Nation. Bulgakov detects in all this an envious reworking, and a dishonest distortion of Biblical concepts.

In the Bible, blood and nation are in fact ontologically important concepts. They are fundamental to the Biblical vision: there it is stated that "the blood is the life" and the Chosen Nation and its correlate, the nations of the world, are intrinsic units in God's interaction with humanity (he quotes: "all the nations will come and bow before you" [Rev.14.4]; and "in the past he allowed the nations to go their own way [Acts 14.16];" also, the 70 apostles symbolize the nations of the world). Bulgakov thus sets out to redeem these concepts from the abuse and distortion they have undergone in Nazi ideology, bringing worthy concepts back into proper use. His key is sophiology, which for the moment the reader can understand simply as referring to the immanent presence of God in the material world in the form of the Divine Wisdom – which itself takes different forms.

One obvious form of God's immanence in the world is God's presence in the world in the Body of Christ, the Church. In the Church there is a "multi-uniform"[109] relationship between humanity and nation. Nations blend into a shared humanity, while preserving the uniqueness of their personalities. But in racism, the nation stands between the individual and humanity and defines the type of person. In Christianity, however, the nation is the specific medium through which an individual can express their underlying *universal* humanity. Furthermore, nations in Christianity, although they "differ quantitatively and qualitatively due to their fates" are certainly "not a closed-off unity, on the contrary between them at all

---

[109] "Multitude in unity" is how Boris Jakim translates the term *mnogo-edinstvo*. The term is cognate with all-unity, vse-edinstvo, which Soloviev first introduces into Russian philosophy. Bulgakov, as we will see, is fond of these compound words (there is dual unity (*dvu-edinstvo*), triple unity (*tryokh-edinstvo*)) which denote the freedom, yet determination, of parts within an organic whole. The model for these different degrees of multitude in unity is the three-in-one unity of the Holy Trinity, and the two natures of Christ in one person.

times there is an ongoing process…of mixing of blood and cultures."

In addition, blood in the Old and New Testaments, is also not a limiting and exclusive concept, but the very key to universalism. It is not a materialistic concept, matter fatalistically defining personality[110], but a mystical concept: blood is where spirit and matter meet, which is the meaning of blood in Biblical theology: it is the fusion of the "breath of life" breathed by God into the material "dust of the earth (=Adam):" blood is where dust and divine breath cohere, in the same way that later divinity and humanity will cohere in the person of Christ.

Paganism, to which Nazi ideology looks, has only a weak conception of the universality of humanity, and that in its late Stoic phase. Nazism is, furthermore, from this perspective a heresy: it removes the divine breath from the blood, idolizing the blood which is the container of the breath, as a principle in itself. Without the breath, blood loses its universality. The blood ceases to have "a connecting, mediating meaning of an environment in which the incarnate human spirit is revealed."

Having clarified the Christian meaning of blood and nation, Bulgakov turns to what these concepts mean for the Jewish nation – both before and after Christ. The chosen people before Christ were the ancestors of Christ. In them the pan-human, Adamic soul had a uniqueness; before Christ "a certain biological absoluteness exists in the chosen people, the ancestors of the Savior and his relatives by blood, in the race of the Mother of God. This is the blood and soul of the whole humanity in its multiple unity." And it was this blood of the Chosen People that flowed in the veins of the Godman. The Old Testament Jewish nation was chosen to "realize the human path of divine incarnation, the genealogy of Christ.…From this flows the utterly special…'nationalism' of Israel: she is not one of many nations, but unique – God's nation… By its chosenness the People of God is not excluded from but is included in humanity, as its very heart and concentration."

Thus Bulgakov is full of praise for Jewish chosenness. But in the next paragraph[111], he goes on to state that after the Incarnation "the Old Testament nationalism of unique chosenness gradually melts in the rays of Christ's sun: yet there remains a place for multiple and various national expressions…but they are all, at least potentially, of equal worth in the face of Christ's incarnation.…

---

[110] As we will see, Florensky's sophiological theory allowed for the possibility that Jewish characteristics were indeed fatalistically and tragically transmitted through poisonous blood into the pure nations of the world. For Rozanov, too, Jews and blood are connected, but in a different way: the Jewish thirst for sacrificial blood in animals, which is transferred to the ritual murder of gentiles. Bulgakov himself does not acknowledge these aspects of Russian thought, and indeed in places he assumes an innocence in the Russian attitude towards Jews compared to the German attitude that is unfortunately lacking in self-criticism. Nonetheless, as in 1915, whether in conscious or subconscious reaction against this tradition, he emancipates himself from this medieval-modern Russian blend of anti-Semitism.

[111] p.19.

The question of nations and nationalities is not made empty, but receives a new meaning….." This looks like a contradiction at first: the Jews are chosen by God, "by blood," "with a certain biological absoluteness." How then can all the nations of the world be of equal status to the Jews, also be chosen by blood after Christ's coming? How can it be that "this uniqueness of Israel among all the nations passes along with the fulfillment of this calling, with the coming of the Messiah"?

The answer of course is that blood is not an independent principle, but is the locus where the divine spirit or breath is incarnated; blood derives its holiness by being a vessel for this spirit. The real principle of humanity, by another name, is personality (*lichnost'*): in contrast to "blood" this word has connotations of abstractness, spirituality. But these are inadequate dichotomies: rightly understood, personality "lives, not only spiritually… but also mentally and corporeally, because in this unification of spirituality and mental-corporeality, in the incarnation of the spirit, humanity consists." Thus the blood-chosenness of Israel gradually moves to the pagans – brought to them by workers for salvation born into the Chosen Nation.

A new spirit is transforming the blood of those of the Old Covenant and those of the New Covenant. All bloods are chosen by this spirit. As Bulgakov will emphasize elsewhere, while the nations of the world are infused with chosenness, it is also the case that the chosenness of Israel, of Jewry persists, except that now it is one chosenness among many. In the new, expanded post-Christic situation, "this incarnatedness[112] of the spirit, assuming a specific personal quality, gives life its multifarious character. In it there is a place for family, race, nation, each on its own terms and with its special character." Thus according to Bulgakov, the blood does not annihilate the spirit (as in Nazism). However, nor does the spirit suppress the blood: this would be the case with an overly universalistic conception of Christianity, where national identity – especially Jewish - is erased entirely[113].

Interestingly, as the number of hair-raising quotes from the work in our sample extracts above shows, it is in this essay, "Racism and Jewry," that Bulgakov's language reaches some of its more disturbing dimensions. This is partly due to the fact that Bulgakov engages here so closely in a reading of Nazism's chief propagandist, Alfred Rosenberg[114], that even as he strives to refute him some of the flavor of the language rubs off onto his own work. Hence talk of

---

[112] In this *expanded* incarnatedness, one might add.

[113] Here there is an implicit contrast – alluded to elsewhere in Bulgakov's thinking – between the multitude-in-unity of the Eastern Orthodox churches and the centrally imposed unity (uniformity) of the Roman Catholic church.

[114] Interestingly, Rosenberg (born in 1893, two decades after Bulgakov, and thus a contemporary of Florensky, Karsavin, and Steinberg) was a Baltic German, born in Estonia and educated in Moscow. He was a supporter of the Whites during the Revolution, and after their defeat he moved to Germany. For those who believe that Nazi anti-Semitism is utterly disjunct from Russian anti-Judaism, these facts should cause a rethink. Cf. further thoughts on the connection between Rosenberg, Vasily Rozanov and P.Florensky in ch.4.

the "notorious 'international' character of the Jewish 'anti-race'."

If we look at the works of Bulgakov and other Russian religious philosophers[115] between the World Wars, however, we are reminded that talk of the Aryan, Slavic and Semitic spirits was all the fashion, a fusion of the relatively new sciences of philology and anthropology. What to us now seems like dangerous pseudo-science after Hitler, then had a certain respectability before his monstrous distortions of these concepts.

Nevertheless, even here Bulgakov manages to extract a positive meaning in the application of these concepts to Jewry, which constitute another plank of his argument with racism. The internationalism and assimilation-without-integration which Rosenberg denounces as the most pernicious traits of the Jewish virus, the Jewish anti-race, are given a completely new evaluation by Bulgakov.

Firstly, Jewry's elasticity and inability to be assimilated is a function of Paul's prophecy in Romans 9-11 that "all Israel will be saved." The features which prevent Jewry from disappearing are God's way of preserving her for the final redemption.

But secondly, these very traits are what enabled the Jewish apostles of Christ to spread His word: they dispersed internationally without losing their identity, instead imprinting their Jewish identity on the nations of Europe. "Christ baptizes and teaches all the nations, and the fulfillment of the commandments (to go out and baptize the nations), which already presupposes that well-known assimilation, begins from the first centuries of the Church's existence. Then – and in a well-known sense similar to now – that assimilation along with internationalism took place, according to which in the Church of Christ there 'is no Greek, no Jew, no barbarian and no Scythian', but Christ is in all. However, this unification in Christ not only does not cancel the mystical and historical force of the fact that Israel is united by certain bonds of spiritual marriage with the whole of humanity, but it confirms it."[116]

Europe should thus be grateful to Rosenberg's "anti-race." And in fact, she should mourn the disappearance of Jewry due to assimilation, for the bond between Jewry and Christian Europe is being eroded by European de-Christianization. The process of secularization itself is leading to the disappearance of Jewry, and destabilizing Jewry in turn, unleashing within her those negative attributes of which he will complain amply elsewhere.

We see here a rare moment where Bulgakov thus actually lays the primary blame for European (Russian or Western) troubles on Europe rather than Jewry, and sees Jewry as the victim of Europe. Unfortunately in later essays, he does not pursue this logic, for there is a definite logic here: after all his general analysis of European/Russian integration (which had highlighted the Reformation and Enlightenment as the cause of the rot) had always got along well without reference to the Jews. It would follow from this that Jews stranded in a disintegrating

---

[115] For example, Berdyaev in *The Meaning of History*, where he talks of the Aryan and Semitic spirit.

[116] "Racism and Jewry," p.29.

Europe would become prey to those same forces of decay.

As we will see later, however, the outlines of a clear analysis of the relationship between post-Enlightenment Europe and Jewish secularization is soon drowned out by emotion later in this essay, and then elsewhere. Thus while Bulgakov sees a spiritual meaning in the internationalism and non-assimilation of Jewry, which makes them – in his celebrated phrase – "the axis of world history," and a blessing to the world, in many points he finally concurs that on the surface at least, the Jewish anti-race has been a dangerous poison for Europe, so that one seems to see the ground of difference between Rosenberg and Bulgakov suddenly close up without warning. As a result, one is again left wondering whether Bugakov's convincing deconstruction of racial anti-Semitism is enough to inoculate Christianity against a similar infection.

One of the fruitful contradictions in Bulgakov's work, however, is how he himself tries to reconcile these morbid conclusions with a Christian attitude to Jewry. The key here will be the application of his own mystical theology, sophiology, to the Jewish question, especially as it relates to the concepts of blood and nation that he has just examined.

Sophiology and sacred blood

These ponderings on blood and nation were not elicited initially by his encounter with the Jewish Question. They have deep roots in his early work. A particularly interesting precedent in this respect are the two extraordinary meditations on *The Holy Grail* and *The Eucharist*[117], which he had written in 1930.

In *The Holy Grail*, he focuses on the passage in John 19:34: "one of the soldiers with a spear pierced his side and forthwith came there out blood and water." Bulgakov points out that this blood and water are different from the blood and flesh that Christ offers to his disciples at the Last Supper, and in which Christians continue to receive communion at the Eucharist. These were not separated from Christ's body when he ascended to the Father; they are a part of this glorified body, or humanity, of Christ. Meanwhile, the blood and water that flowed out of Christ's body at Golgotha were received by the world. They entered the world and remained in the world, turning the world into a Grail for the bodily presence of Christ. Thus the words of Christ that "I will be with you until the end of time" are made true: the Ascension did not signal the complete departure of Christ in his humanity from the world. In addition to Christ's continuing presence in His Comforting Spirit, He continues to dwell in humanity and the world in a humanity which is not personalized[118].

---

[117] Which have been translated by Boris Jakim, Lindisfarne Press.

[118] See shortly below for what this means. Incidentally, The Holy Grail was written in 1932, and published in Berdyaev's journal *Put'*. G.P. Fedotov's article on Russian folk-Orthodox veneration of Mother-Earth appeared in the same journal three years later. As we pointed out in an earlier footnote, the sacredness of the earth, its role as a quasi-Mother of God, its reception of the tears of the people-mankind and so on, all show deep affinities to Bulgakov's thoughts in *The Holy Grail* and can thus be seen as

The above exegesis and dogmatic development of John 19:34 is a good example of Bulgakov's mature sophiological thinking. It was this very "theory" of Sophia which attracted so much controversy round Bulgakov during and after his lifetime. In 1935, Metropolitan Sergius of Moscow (later to be elected Patriarch in 1943) condemned Bulgakov's sophiology; then in 1937, a synod of Orthodox bishops followed suit at Karlovtsi in Yugoslavia. In the same year a synodal commission convened by Metropolitan Eulogy in Paris exonerated Bulgakov of any charges of heresy. However, Fr. Georgy Florovsky and the theologian Vladimir Lossky were unconvinced by the exoneration[119].

For a time, many parts of the Russian Church (barring the Parisian jurisdiction, of course) were of the opinion that the question of Bulgakov's sophiology was settled: it was a modernist aberration. However, due to the split nature of the Church none of the condemnations of Bulgakov had canonical effect. Recently, an influential figure in the Moscow Patriarchy (which has since re-established communion with ROCA), Bishop Hilarion Alfeev, has called for a re-evaluation and deeper exploration of Bulgakov's works, commenting that "it is necessary today to recover the intuitions and the spiritual journey of one of [sophiology's] most ardent defenders, Father Sergius Bulgakov." Regarding the condemnation by Lossky and Metropolitan Sergius, he adds that "criticisms of Bulgakov's 'sophiology' were far from exhausting or closing the argument, but only the first phase in a discussion which has not yet gained momentum."[120] Within the Paris "school" of theology, such explorations have already been ongoing. Antoine Arjakovsky usefully summarizes some of the contemporary work which continues and develops Bulgakov's sophiological insights: he mentions Fr. Boris Bobrinskoy's *The Mystery of the Trinity*, as well as the work of Paul Valliere, Olivier Clément and Paul Evdokimov.[121]

---

another clear source of his sophiology. (Of course, he was the first to recognize this link, but this puts flesh on that recognition).

[119] Entering into the finer points of theology, were the politics of the émigré Russian church: at stake was the extent to which the Moscow Patriarchy had compromised itself with the Soviet government. Deciding that the compromise had gone too far, some members of the Moscow Patriarch formed The Russian Church Abroad (or ROCA, headed by Metropolitan Khrapovitsky), while Metropolitan Eulogy left the Moscow Patriarch for the jurisdiction of the Constantinopolitan Patriarch. Behind these ecclesial decisions lay theological differences: the ROCA was conservative theologically and monarchist politically. Bulgakov's writings were viewed in advance with extreme suspicion by such people, as unorthodox, Gnostic, and destructive of the faith of simple, true believers. Bulgakov became a symbol of what was seen as the modernizing, ecumenical and Gnostic sect of the Constantinopolitan church in Paris. However, criticism came from closer quarters, too: Florovsky was a close friend and one-time colleague of Bulgakov in Paris; he thus had more sympathy with Bulgakov. For him, the main problem with sophiology was that it was "unpatristic" and thus also compromising of true Orthodoxy. For more detail, see below.

[120] Bishop Hilarion Alfeev, official website: http://orthodoxeurope.org/page/11/1/1.aspx

[121] Antoine Arjakovsky, "The Sophiology of Father Sergius Bulgakov and Contemporary

Here the question is more concrete: in what way does sophiology bear on Bulgakov's theology of the Jews? One way of answering this question is to say, in brief, that it allows Bulgakov – and any who wish to follow him – to appreciate what Soloviev called the "sacred materialism" of Jewish history and Judaism. Let us explore how this is so.

Sophiology for Bulgakov was a way of giving doctrinal expression to his intuition that God was deeply present in the world. Further, all aspects of the world are woven of the same fabric and intimately linked to one another. In other words, Bulgakov was an enthusiastic believer in Soloviev's idea of the "all-unity" of the world. More than this, in his spiritual life – as we saw – he very early on developed a sense that this immanence of God was connected with the Divine wisdom, or Sophia. Bulgakov believed that this sense of Sophia was very Orthodox and very Russian. But he thought that Soloviev's doctrine of Sophia had drifted into individualistic speculation, and had been expressed in a less than felicitous manner. Among other things, he wished to correct the pantheistic leaning of Soloviev's thought, so that God Himself was not swallowed up in the definition of All-Unity. He also saw himself as purging the doctrine of Sophia of Gnostic and Western mystical borrowings (from Jakob Boehme, for example), and as placing it on thoroughly Orthodox foundations. Early Russian icons of Sophia, the cathedrals dedicated to Sophia in Kiev, Novgorod and Constantinople were evidence for Bulgakov of the ancient Orthodox roots of the doctrine of Sophia. The Biblical sources out of which Bulgakov mined his insights were the famous passages in Proverbs (especially Proverbs 8.22-31), read in tandem with the account of creation in Genesis. The Church fathers' talk of divine "logoi" (in Athanasius, Maximus the Confessor, and John of Damascus) were further material for his doctrine.

At first[122], Sophia is considered the soul of the world, the end to which all things move, that very fabric and goal which gives the world its all-unity, *natura naturans* to *natura naturata*. In these earlier works, Bulgakov also talks of a heavenly and earthly Sophia. The heavenly Sophia is associated with the Logos, the second person of the Trinity; however in relation to the Logos, the active principle of creation, she is said to be passive. Of course, this is somewhat undefined. It is only later[123] that Bulgakov gives his final, his boldest and his clearest formulation regarding Sophia and her relation with the divine. Now Sophia is equated with the Divine nature itself, the essence or *ousia*, of the Divinity, the Trinity. But the dual nature of Sophia is preserved: this now refers to the Divine nature as it is manifested within the Trinity, and the Divine nature

---

Western Theology," paper presented at the Sergius Bulgakov conference at the Russian House of Emigration, Moscow, Russia, March, 2001.

[122] In earlier works like *The Philosophy of Economy* and *The Unfading Light*, written in 1912 and 1917 respectively

[123] In the trilogy *On the Divine-Humanity*, and in a special work aimed at clarifying his sophiology to his critics, *Sophia: The Divine Wisdom;* the latter has appeared in English as *Sophia. The wisdom of God. An outline of sophiology*, translated by Boris Jakim. Lindisfarne Press, 1993.

outside the life of the Trinity (the earthly Sophia).

This revolutionary step takes us to the heart of what sophiology means for Bulgakov, and it is the step that his opponents found least acceptable. In works written from the thirties on (including the works on the Jewish question), this conception of Sophia as the divine nature will be applied to different theological topics, such as the creation of the world and man, Mary the Mother of God, the Church, and as we saw the blood of the Grail. It becomes an inextricable part of Bulgakov's creative output. This doctrine really gives flesh to Bulgakov's belief that God and the world, in a carefully defined sense, share the same nature[124].

In *The Holy Grail*, we see this in Bulgakov's belief that the world has become – after Christ's crucifixion and piercing – a Holy Grail, a sacred container of the (non-Eucharistic) Holy Blood[125]. In this, Bulgakov is reacting against what he sees as the Manicheistic dualism which maintains that the acts of salvation are tangential to the world, isolated and to some extent incomprehensible flashes of other-worldly light that intrude into the world. Christ does not "dip into" the world in his humanity and then rapidly depart again, leaving us in darkness. We do not partake of the Eucharist, momentarily partaking in something outside of the world, and then fall back into the God-alienated world. Rather, the events of salvation transform this very world so that it is thereafter a permanent container of Divinity – whether we have eyes to see this or not.

But precisely *transformation* of the world – rather than entrance into and escape from the world – presupposes that the world in its nature is capable of being transformed. For this, it must have an affinity to the divine. True, the world is fallen and therefore the transformation proceeds in stages, moving towards an ultimate end. But each of these transformative steps, as recounted in the Biblical history of salvation, builds on the sophianic receptivity of the world. Thus, as we will see in more detail later, God comes into the world and receives His humanity from Mary. But what is this humanity? It is the blood that has been passed on through the generations of Mary's Jewish forebears. Due to the intimate connection of the material world to the nature of God, although this blood precedes the Incarnation, it still has a measure of sacredness, a rootedness in the divine Sophia, which enables it to be a vessel to receive God. Ultimately, it is this blood – this Jewish blood – that falls onto the ground at Golgotha and continues to dwell in the world, while the rest of Christ's humanity is glorified in heaven.[126]

Two words of warning should be added immediately. Firstly, Bulgakov is not saying that God and the world are one. Secondly, he is not saying that the world is already Divine. This would mean that God and man would have

---

[124] See below for how Bulgakov tries to avoid the charge of pantheism in this respect.
[125] The flowing of water in this blood is a sign for Bulgakov that the essential element of the world, water, has become sanctified; this part symbolizes the sanctification of the whole.
[126] Again, this is the "dual-unity" of Christ's split humanity; at the Second Coming it will be reunited; or rather, earth and heaven merging will bring the sundered bloods together again.

to do nothing more to save it. Rather God and the world are in the following relationship: Bulgakov described the Divine nature as overflowing the bounds of its Trinitarian life. Within the Trinity, Sophia is always personalized – in a unique way – by each of the three persons of the Trinity. But in an act of love, the divine Sophia overflows into the nothingness outside the Trinity. That is, Sophia abandons her personal hypostatized being in the Trinity and loses her hypostatizedness in an act of self-emptying, or *kenosis*, and bestows herself on the nothingness of which Genesis speaks. But this unhypostasized Sophia is already different from Sophia as she exists within the Trinity: in saying this Bulgakov draws a line between the divine (sophianic) foundation of what will become the world, which to be sure has deep roots in divinity, but is other than divine – and Trinitarian divinity[127].

The Biblical history of the transformation of the world has its parallel, or deeper explanation, in the idea of the re-unification of the lower worldly Sophia with the higher Trinitarian Sophia. And this is the process which takes place through human history, and culminates according to Christian hopes, in the state when God will be truly "all in all." This re-unification of the lower, non-personalized Sophia takes place through the agency of man. Human creatures, unlike the created world of nature, also have a sophianic foundation: but this sophianic nature appears in a personalized form within man. This is the significance of the Biblical detail that God breathes into man, and creates a being who is "like one of Us." God's sophianic nature is "replicated" in a hypostasized form within man. Thus humans have personal being, humans are – in Bulgakov's expression – God's "co-I's," gods by grace, co-gods.[128] As beings in whom is found God's sophianic nature in *personal* form, humans can help the impersonal, "emptied out" sophianic element in nature to take on personal form, to realize itself personally. Put another way, man's task is to raise the world, to help God, as it were retrieve a part of Himself.[129] Humanization of the world (an aspect that Bulgakov looked at in his philosophy of economics) is thus divinization of the world.

Had it not been for man's Fall, this re-unification could have taken place by virtue of man's personalized sophianic nature. However the Fall caused a misalignment in that nature, which could only be rectified by the Incarnation. When the second person of the Trinity is incarnated in Jesus Christ, this

---

[127] Sometimes he refers to the divine hypostatized nature within the Trinity as *ousia*, and to non-personal nature outside of the Trinity as *Sophia*.

[128] See *The Bride of the Lamb*, ch.1.4 for this and other inspiring exegeses of the creation account in Genesis.

[129] The phrasing in this sentence is mine, but I hope it does not do violence to Bulgkov's thoughts as expressed in The Bride of the Lamb, esp. ch.1.4. The affinity with Jewish kabbalistic and especially Hassidic thought are rather striking here: cf. *tikkun 'olam* (mending the world) through the observant Jew's gathering of the sparks of primal creation; also the idea current in Jewish mystical (and sometime midrashic) thought that God needs man to be complete.

intended unification of created and divine Sophia is once again made possible. For Christ unites within His Person the created, human Sophia and the eternal, divine Sophia. Here, sophiology plays its main role for Bulgakov in providing a "full dogmatic elucidation" of the doctrine of Divine-humanity. Human beings, by joining themselves to Christ, by becoming one body with Him, partake in a nature – which they to a lesser extent possess in natural form – which is a restored created Sophia, a created Sophia which is brought into intimate unity with the divine Sophia. Thus united in the body of Christ, mankind once again can set about redeeming, which is to say personalizing, the fallen world. Towards the end of *The Holy Grail*, as in *The Philosophy of Economy*, Bulgakov waxes quite lyrical about the creative social and economic transformation of nature that the Christian human can perform on the world. "What is ignited in man," after the Incarnation, "is the idea of universal human action, the idea that 'the common task', of 'progress', of the City of God on earth, which by no means contradicts the idea of the Heavenly Jerusalem, but on the contrary is the earthly 'place' for the Heavenly Jerusalem, the historical correlate of eschatology…This is the idea…of Christ's thousand year kingdom on earth."[130]

The explication of the doctrine of Divine-humanity by means of sophiology is the pinnacle of Bulgakov's theology. Earlier we said that Bulgakov's sophiology allowed him to appreciate, or perhaps better, to partake of that Soloviovian Jewish "sacred materialism." This is seen in Bulgakov's sensitivity to the whole issue of blood. In *The Grail*, again, he draws attention to how according to the instructions in Levitucus the priest was to take the blood for the sin-offering and anoint the horns of the altar with *some* of it (Bulgakov's emphasis). The rest he poured away at the bottom of the altar. For Bulgakov (who, we remember, talked of his Levitical blood and, as in *The Unfading Light*, so now in *The Grail* often refers to his own priestly duties and rituals at the Christian altar as a way of gaining a deeper understanding of the Christian mystery), this has an exact parallel in the way that some of Christ's blood is poured away at the foot of the Cross – with the same redemptive function. Bulgakov finds further support for the importance of blood in the Christian sacrifice in the letter to the Hebrews, which was addressed to priests of the Jewish Temple, familiar with the blood offerings there. There it was animal blood; here it is the god-man's sophianically human blood – poured out not just once, but once and forevermore.

This is not the only instance of Bulgakov's sophianic "sacred materialism." Elsewhere, he writes of how the Orthodox service of the Divine Liturgy makes full use of the richness of the world's sensual beauty: colors, scents, metals, materials are brought in to worship the divine. This shows how Christian service can raise the impersonal but covertly divine aspects of the created world to the level of personal worship of God. Nature, emphasizes Bulgakov,[131] is alive; and all life is Divine: as a prayer often repeated in Orthodox worship says, life is a

---

[130] *Holy Grail*, Jakim, p.57.
[131] *The Bride of the Lamb*, p.81.

gift of the Holy Spirit, Who is addressed as The Giver of Life.[132] As we saw in our earlier discussions, however, Bulgakov extends this sacred materialism to an appreciation of aspects of paganism. The doctrine of the creaturely Sophia captures not just the sacredness of the Old Testament ritual: pre-Christian, pagan religious veneration of the Eternal Feminine in nature as seen in the cult of the Great Mother, and the worship of Demeter, Isis, Cybele, and Ishtar was also a blurred and distorted feeling for the sophianicity of the world, the divine roots of natural beauty.[133]

This brings us to another important area in which Bulgakov's sophiology influenced his reception of Church dogma: his perception of Mary, the Mother of God. Bulgakov, sensitive to critics, had stopped calling Sophia a "fourth hypostasis," or as he had occasionally done in early work, a "goddess." Sophia was now the non-personalized nature of God at the foundation of the world. But Sophia, while not a hypostasis, is "hypostasizable," meaning the extra-Trinitarian impersonal creaturely divine nature can be given personal form. Mary, among all humans striving to personalize Sophia, is the highest creaturely hypostatic expression of Sophia, and as such "the highest of all creatures, She abounds *at the boundary* of heaven and creation. She is the peak of the world which touches heaven."[134] Furthermore: whenever a Christian at baptism "puts on Christ," he at the same time "puts on" the Mother of God, for the incarnate Logos is always incarnated through the Holy Spirit in the human nature of Mary. And Mary empties herself (*kenosis* again), makes herself transparent to the Logos. The Logos in His incarnation is always Jesus-Mary, a dual-unity (yet another aspect of the shimmering fabric of "multitude in unity"). Mary, as she contains Christ – as in the Icon of the Sign where Christ is shown as if in Mary's womb – is the Church, the creaturely Sophia containing within herself the Divine Sophia.

It is this sophianic understanding of Mary that enters into Bulgakov's thoughts about Judaism. In "Racism and Christianity" (1942)[135], he adds a qualification to his thesis that Nazism is distorted Christianity. For Bulgakov Protestantism in a sense had (echoing Ruether this time) already laid the groundwork for racism, but not because of Christology or supersessionism, but rather because the Reformers had abolished the veneration of Mary, the feminine Sophianic element in the Church: "…a specific feature characteristic of Protestantism is precisely its lack of feeling for the Divine Motherhood as the Eternal Feminine and the basis of the Church. The element of a male principle and of masculinity, so emphasized by Sauer in Prussianness and in Germanness in general, has a parallel in the general absence of the principle of the Mother of God in the Protestant world-view." Bulgakov points out that *das ewig Weiblich* (the eternal feminine) was known to Goethe and Romanticism, but is crushed under the heel of the German boot

---

[132] The prayer "O Heavenly Comforter."
[133] We will see later how this re-evaluation of paganism influences Bulgakov's understanding of the Old Testament and Judaism.
[134] Bride.
[135] pp.20-21.

by the racists, whose "world view...idealises the Archangel Michael and his host of warriors" and forgets the feminine principle. Before the war, Bulgakov had campaigned at ecumenical meetings for the churches to recognize Mary as the sponsor of Church unity for this very reason. The Church without Mary lacks her very essence.

Russian Orthodoxy, by contrast, as well as the Russian nation is tenderer, more feminine, and due to its awareness of Mary, - and as Bulgakov emphasizes, Mary's Jewish humanity – can respond more humanely to Jewish humanity. It should be said that this is an interesting thesis. Somewhat worrying for this idea, however, is the fact that in the late thirties and during the war there flourished in Romania an Orthodox anti-Semitism with strong fascist overtones and receptivity to Nazism, which penetrated into the higher ranks of the Church hierarchy. There was also an anti-Semitic Orthodox brotherhood of the Archangel Michael.[136] Orthodox self-congratulation on this front would thus be premature; veneration of Mary does not automatically inoculate against anti-Semitism[137].

Before carrying on with an examination of Bulgakov's other sophiologically informed writings on the Jewish issue, three points remain to be made. The first concerns Bulgakov's sophiological "social activism." The second concerns the interesting parallel of Bulgakov's sophiology with certain Kabbalistic-Hasidic doctrines. The third concerns the criticisms made by Florovsky of Bulgakov's sophiology.

A little earlier, we quoted Bulgakov's idea in the Grail that a Christian must partake in the redemption of the world, in the building of "the City of God on

---

[136] For an overview of Romanian anti-Semitism, much of it replete with explicit Orthodox Christian themes and sentiments, during the Second World War, cf. Paul Shapiro, "Faith, Murder, Resurrection. The Iron Guard and the Romanian Orthodox Church," in *AntiSemitism, Christian Ambivalence, and the Holocaust*, ed. Kevin P. Spicer. Bloomington: Indiana University Press, 2007.

[137] In "The fates of Russia, Germany and Jewry," Bulgakov remarks that Russians were never seriously tempted by racism. There was "the Union of the Russian People," the concept of the "true Russian people" but for Bulgakov none of this was a serious threat to the Russian soul. Instead, the corruption of Russian society before the Revolution was the fault of Russians, but the fatal turn of Bolshevism was primarily a Jewish crime against Russia. The more one finds out about the pogroms by Russians (and Belorussians and Ukrainians) against Jews during the First World War, then the Civil War, and finally the collaboration during the Second World War with the invading German forces in anti-Semitic atrocities, the less convincing this exoneration of "feminine" Russia seems. This is compounded when one considers Bulgakov's own brush with temptation during the Civil War and to a lesser extent that of a thinker like Berdyaev (for whom, see chapter three). In another sense, the fact that the White movement – with its exclusivist definition of Russianness that may have developed into fascism had it won the Civil War – was unable to convince the masses may be an ironic testimony that Bulgakov's observations hold some truth. But for this to be so, Bolshevist universalism would have to be made a Russian trait.

earth, which by no means contradicts the idea of the Heavenly Jerusalem, but on the contrary is the earthly 'place' for the Heavenly Jerusalem', the historical correlate of eschatology." This is an interesting remark in light of Bulgakov's feeling (expressed both earlier than this work, and later) that Marxists and socialist revolutionaries, including particularly Jews, had been too precipitate in building paradise on earth. Is this not an indication that social justice and its implementation is also a Christian task?

This may indeed be an inconsistency in Bulgakov. However, the phrase "the common task" is taken from Nicolai Fyodorov's work *The Philosophy of the Common Task*. In that book, Fyodorov stated his eccentric belief that mankind should develop the technology to resurrect the dead, so hastening the unity of humanity. In a footnote, Bulgakov comments: "It is in this sort of 'active Christianity' that Fyodorov sees to be the 'common task' of humanity...whose commencement will already begin to overcome the 'unbrotherly' human-is-a-wolf-to-human relationship that has dominated humanity throughout history."

Thus, though Bulgakov makes reference to "regulation of nature" as a Christian task, and to a hastening of the earthly reign of Christ, this most likely still has spiritual – perhaps an agricultural-pastoral communitarian – dimension that is far removed from the social program of Marxism. The idea that Bulgakov is appealing to the prophetic ideals of social justice and perhaps a restructuring of society, would be misplaced, given the general context of Bulgakov's development[138]. Fyodorov's "goals," after all, would hardly be compatible with that type of sober social program.[139]

The second point in this sketch of Bulgakov's sophiology is how reminiscent it is of certain Kabbalistic-Hasidic doctrines. The exiled *Shekhina*, or feminine presence of God, is said to be reunited with the male aspect of God through the observant Jew's performance of the Commandments. Bulgakov talks of the raising of the lower Sophia to unite with the upper Sophia through Christian activism. Hasidic thought talks of how God's commandments single out elements of the fallen material world and raise them up to God by means of the observant Jew's obedience. Thus a "secular" cow-hide becomes sacred when the rituals are administered to transform it into a scroll of the Holy Torah: the material becomes spiritualized. Bulgakov's talk of how the lower divine elements of the natural world can be incorporated into divine worship is strikingly reminiscent of this. In sum, there is distinctively "Jewish feel" to Bulgakov's theology, right

---

[138] However, at the end of this chapter, we look at his essay on "Judas Apostle-Traitor," written a year later. Here, while by no means condoning Soviet communists, he has words of understanding and even hope that their zeal has its roots in a worthy religious instinct. Perhaps, here too, there is a recognition that while Soviet communism was obviously incompatible with the Church, there was *some* affinity, and that the Church would be failing if she did not articulate her own social doctrine.

[139] Perhaps Bulgakov is even hinting at the role of Christian brotherhoods, such as his own St Sophia brotherhood, in creating islands of redeemed life on earth, that can serve as preludes to the coming of Christ.

down to his deep respect for the principle of blood, which as he correctly intuits, is still of great import in Judaism. Orthodox Judaism, after all, yearns and prays thrice daily for a restoration of the blood sacrifices of old; and the prohibition on the consumption of blood is still strictly enforced[140]. This "Jewish" element was no doubt partly filtered into his thought through Soloviev, who had studied the Kabbalah directly in Hebrew[141]. However, its roots also lie in his own reworking of themes stated in a Gnostic-pagan way by Merezhkovsky, Rozanov and Florensky, all of whom struggled with the relation of their new mystical knowledge to "old" historic Christianity[142].

Thirdly, it is necessary to state briefly the chief criticism[143] that was aimed at Bulgakov's sophiology. Florovsky[144] called into question Bulgakov's claim that sophiology existed in embryonic form among the Church Fathers, and that his own sophiology was an organic and necessary development of their theology[145]. Instead, for Florovsky, the patristic doctrine of creation and the divine *logoi*[146] were quite different. Writers like John of Damascus and Athanasius the Great made a crucial distinction in the divinity between nature (*ousia* – Greek; or *substantia* – in Latin) and will (voluntas). The *nature* of God is associated with the generation of the Son and the Spirit from the Father; the *will* of God is associated with the creation of the world. In the act of creation God already acts as a Trinity,

---

[140] As it is, indeed, in Orthodox Christianity – though not in a "halakhic" sense.

[141] The comments in ch.1 concerning the complex interactive relationship between Kabbalah, Hassidic mysticism, Eastern Christian theology and German idealism also apply for Bulgakov too.

[142] While the success of Bulgakov's Christianization of sophiology is still a controversial question, there is no doubt that his project was far closer to Christian Orthodoxy than Merezhkovsky or Rozanov, who openly rejected historic Christianity, or Florensky, who resembles these two but differs from them in his belief that his system also fell within the bounds of Orthodoxy.

[143] That is, the serious, rather than polemical, or "political" criticism.

[144] A similar criticism regarding Bulgakov's pantheism is made in less acute form by Coplestone in Frederick Coplestone, *Russian religious philosophy. Selected aspects.* (Search Press/Notre Dame, 1988), 97. Coplestone concludes that Bulgakov cannot be exonerated from the charge of pantheism. He reasons as follows: if Sophia is the nature of God and Sophia is the idea of the world, then the nature of the world and God are one, But if Sophia is lower than God, but also the nature of God, then the nature of God is lower than God – which is contradictory. Or if there is a higher Sophia, which is one with God, and a lower Sophia which is not distinct from creation, then again, it would seem that creation is not distinct from God. At the very least, "it is not altogether a simple matter to distinguish clearly between the panentheism which Bulgakov affirms, and the pantheism which he rejects."

[145] Florovsky, *Creation and Redemption,* The Collected Works, Vol. III., as cited in Sergeev, *Divine Wisdom and the Trinity: A 20th century controversy in Orthodox theology,* paper presented at the World Congress of Philosophy in Boston, August 1998.

[146] Space does not permit a discussion of Florovsky's analysis of the *logoi*.

not according to separate hypostases[147]. The nature of God cannot be associated with anything created, as God's sophianic nature is for Bulgakov. All acts of will, and indeed thought, all acts of God, all "energies" (in Palamas' terminology[148]), are external to the internal generation of the Trinity, to the mystery of the Divine nature, or *ousia*. Involving the divine nature in creation would be to introduce a notion of change into the essence of the Divinity, which is impossible. This was echoed in Lossky's criticism of sophiology: for him Bulgakov's sophiology departed from the apophatic silence which was the only fitting response to the internal life of the Godhead, trying to prize open its secrets by ungrounded speculation. Like Florovsky, Lossky lays the blame for this on the influence of German Idealism, itself a late incarnation of the Protestant Reformationist heresy[149].

Bulgakov was well aware of these criticisms and responded to them. He was in full agreement that he had abolished the nature/will distinction as applied to God's creative act. He went further, maintaining that the distinction itself was a fatuous scholasticism which had no place in theology. For this distinction is intended to preserve God's freedom – in this case, his freedom not to create the world. Creation is said not to be a consequence of his nature, but of his will. God is thus depicted as having the choice not to create the world. For His act of creation was an inscrutable act of will.

For Bulgakov, far from increasing the splendor of God, this projects onto God anthropomorphically aspects of our limited human psychology: for Bulgakov, God who is and has all does not *have* a will, which is an instrument of striving and a desiring[150]. The nature/will distinction gives rise to occasionalism, that is, the doctrine that God is always intervening in the world, that world events and laws are themselves inscrutable in that they arise constantly from God's free and unfathomable invention. It also seems to imply that God's nature contains necessity, while His will does not. In contrast to this demeaning picture of the world's relationship to God, and of an odd dichotomy between freedom and necessity, nature and will in the Divinity, Bulgakov finds the nature of the world to be rooted deeply in the intimate nature of God: as such the natural world, as

---

[147] Bulgakov does indeed write of how different hypostases are involved in different aspects of creation; for example, he writes that "The male hypostasis exists in the image of the hypostasis of the Logos, while the female hypostasis exists in the image of the hypostasis of the Holy Spirit," and this "corresponds to the fundamental fact that the Son of God was humanized into the male nature, while the hypostatic descent of the Holy Spirit took place into the female nature of the Most Holy Mother of God." *Bride of the Lamb*, 89.

[148] In ch.4, we outline another criticism of pantheistic tendencies in sophiology and in Russian symbolism as a whole (made by S.S.Khoruzhy), showing the relationship between the 1911-1913 "name-worshiping" controversy and the distortion of Palamite theology among Silver Age philosophers (mainly Bulgakov, Florensky and Losev) at that time and onward.

[149] This is ironical, given Bulgakov's own critical approach to Protestantism and Western Christianity in general.

[150] *Bride*, 32.

well as the events of salvation are not merely incomprehensible intrusions into our created darkness of the apophatically unknowable God (unknowable even in revelation if Augustine and others of this ilk are to be believed) – rather, nature and revelation, which are both intimately linked are imbued with a recurring and repetitive pattern, a mellifluous unity, which Bulgakov's theological works constantly strive to uncover. Sophiology is thus a rejection of divine arbitrariness, of occasionalism, and of voluntarism – all distorted tendencies of Catholic and Protestant theology, which sophiology is meant to overcome[151].

However, it is probably best to leave the debate at this stage, as it is a topic worthy of an entire book. But as Alfeev intimated, the proper debate over sophiology has surely not been had yet[152]. The above sketch is intended to show how Bulgakov's doctrine of the intimate relation of world to God's nature is not an arcane metaphysical abstraction. Its concreteness, its boldness, its ability to inspire and produce new Christian insights is seen most sharply, I believe, in Bulgakov's Biblical exegesis: and he is always extremely precise in his reading of verses. With this in mind, we will continue to look at his other wartime essays on the Jews.

The blood-chosenness of the Jews after Christ

We saw, then, how in "Racism and Jewry" Bulgakov had outlined a Biblical theory of nation and blood, based on the sophiological insight that the blood is sacred matter, and as such the potential bearer of spirit. The Jewish disciples had transferred to pagan blood the divine spirit, so that the nations of the world could now participate in the very blood-chosenness which had been the prerogative of the Jews before.

The question now arises: What place then do post-Christic Jews occupy in

---

[151] Recently the Greek patristics scholar, Nikolaos Asproulis, has argued that Florovsky's Palamite-inspired neo-patristic synthesis itself suffers from pantheistic tendencies, on the grounds that the Palamite energy-essence distinction fails to adequately separate God and world. He recommends a return to a more personalistic and less ontology-oriented theology, that would be based on the Cappadocian fathers. Given the enormous respect for Palamas in the contemporary Orthodox world, if Asproulis is correct in seeing little difference between the higher Sophia/lower Sophia distinction and the essence/energy distinction (and Arjakovsky also equates the two, seeing this as a positive result), then Orthodox theology even in its most "mainstream forms" may have a serious problem with pantheism, that goes well beyond Bulgakov! (Cf. Nikolaos Asproulis, "Creation and creaturehood. The neo-patristic alternative worldview of totalitarianism (all-unity, universalism). A brief approach to G.Florovsky's theology." Paper read at the conference on All-Unity and Universalism, Bose, Italy, 22-25 October, 2009.)

[152] Again, however, S.S.Khoruzhy's books and articles are a good start to this debate: cf. Sergei Khoruzhy, *Posle pereryva. Puti Russkoy Filosofii.* Saint Petersburg: 'Aleteia', 1994 (including a chapter on Bulgakov); *Opyty iz russkoy dukhovnoy traditsii.* (Moscow: Parad, 2005); and *O starom i novom.* (St. Petersburg: 'Aleteia', 2000). We will consider some of his insights in ch.4.

this re-Christianized, "sophiologized" theory of blood? What is to become of their own blood and nationhood, now that chosenness has been expanded to include the nations? How, if it does, does Jewish chosenness function now? These, of course, are the key questions for a Christian theologian interested in Jewish-Christian relations. In the various war-time essays with their loosely connected sub-sections, Bulgakov hammers out an answer. This answer is not systematic, but there are certain themes and insights that recur. Perhaps the most convenient way of assessing Bulgakov's answer is to summarize these themes, drawing on these different essays, and then to analyze each one of them, allowing Bulgakov to speak where possible, so as to avoid being falsely schematic.

Bulgakov's most startling ideas can be put as follows, then. Firstly, the Jewish people is still chosen: the Jews, by the brute fact of their descent from Abraham, have a blood-chosenness which makes them closer to God than to other nations. Secondly, there is a saving fact in the blood-relatedness of the Jews to Jesus Christ and His Mother, both before the Incarnation and after: just as Christ gathered into himself and saved Old Testament Israel through his genealogy, He will again incorporate Jewry into Himself at his Second Coming, so that "all Israel will be saved." Thirdly, in a related point, attempts to destroy the Jews are madness and cannot succeed because, according to Revelation, the heralds of Christ's second coming will be blood Jews – to attack Jews is to risk the death of these salvational descendants, imperiling the whole world. Fourthly, the Jewish people is judged collectively by God, and this is its tragedy: though only a fraction of the people, its leaders, condemned Christ, Jewry has been collectively punished for deicide ever since. Fifthly, another point where Bulgakov shocks conventional sensibilities, Christians should not preach Christianity to Jews: the latter know it better than the gentiles, and Christianity is too weak and compromised by anti-Semitism to make such preaching meaningful. Sixthly, there is a sacred remnant in Jewry which will lead to its salvation and the salvation of the whole world, through a regenerated Christianity, whose hub will be a new Judeo-Christianity.

The first three points are all closely related. In "The Destiny of Israel as the Cross of the Mother of God," a sermon delivered when the Nazi persecution of the Jews had moved from brutal discrimination to genocide, Bulgakov uses the figure of the Mother of God, so beloved in Orthodoxy, to underline how intimately connected Jewry is to Christianity. Mary feels the pain of the world and is the great protector and interceder for sinful humanity with her Son. But Mary was born a Jewess and remains, even after her assumption a Jewess[153]: thus she feels especial pain and sympathy for the fate of her own people, and suffers multiply for them. She smarts at their rejection of her Son; at her Son's harsh words directed at them; and at her own resulting estrangement from her people. No one can desire more the return of Jewry to their Messiah, her Son. All who add to the pain of Jewry offend and pain the Mother of God.

In "Christianity Without Israel," and the "Genealogy of Christ," Bulgakov

---

[153] Bulgakov underlines that Mary is in a sense "more Jewish" than Christ, in the sense that both her parents belong to that people.

deepens and extends this idea. In the latter essay, Bulgakov sets out to prove how the divine nature of Christ the man spills backwards (and forwards) onto those humans – the Jews – who played a role in bringing His humanity into the world. Moreover, if Jews are divine, God in a sense is also Jewish!

Examining Luke's genealogy of Christ, Bulgakov reminds us how Christ is said to be descended not only from Abraham and David (as in Matthew) but also from Adam. Adam in turn is called "son of God."[154] Retrospectively, Luke's genealogy thus includes Adam in the Jewish people: he is the ancestor of Christ the Jew. More, God himself is brought into the genealogy so that image of God in which God created man is the image of a Jew. The Chalcedonian formula concerning Christ's full humanity and full divinity gives dogmatic content to the idea that Christ's Jewish humanity is an intimate part of the Divine. Jews then are stamped intimately with the Divine image, the image of Christ; and the nations of the world if they unite with Christ also partake in Jewishness, "the co-Jewishness of all humanity in Him."[155]

The message for the persecutors of the Jews is clear: not persecution but reverence should be the order of the day. For it would seem that Jews' ties to divinity are innate, and that of the gentiles is adopted through a Jew, Jesus Christ.[156] So much so that "Israel even in its backsliding has not ceased to be the chosen people, the relation of Christ and his Most Pure Mother, and this blood relation is not interrupted and does not stop even after the birth of Christ.... this is a fact which one needs to ponder and grasp with all one's strength, in its dogmatic meaning as it applies to the fate of Israel."[157]

In "The Mystery of Israel," the point is put from a slightly different angle. There Bulgakov points out that in the Gospel genealogies "the personal ancestors of the Savior are only representatives for the whole of their nation, the bearer of holy blood, which serves such a sacred mystery...," so that "Israel, as the Old Testament Church, belongs to Christ, is His body, His Old Testament humanity, which becomes also His New Testament humanity, is included into the Church of Christ by virtue of the Incarnation itself." That is, there is an identity between the whole of Israel (not just Christ's personal ancestors) and Christ; the former is incorporated into the latter[158].

Bulgakov starts the essay with a meditation on the Massacre of the Infants by Herod: these infants are commemorated as martyrs by the Church. This shows

---

[154] Luke 3.23ff.

[155] "The Genealogy of Christ," p.68.

[156] Bulgakov thus seems to be putting forward an idea of some special spiritual Jewishness which is reminiscent of Hasidism's concept of an ontologically special Jewish soul, as well as of Rosenzweig's belief that Jews are closer to God than gentiles. This will be explored below.

[157] "The Persecution of Israel."

[158] This adds an interesting take on the dispute about the identity of the Suffering Servant in Isaiah 51. Jewish exegesis maintains the Servant represents Israel, Christian that he represents Christ. But if Israel is Christ, both are correct.

that the Church dogmatically recognizes that pre-Christic Israel is incorporated into Christ, becomes part of Christ. Israel is the vessel for the Incarnation, the link leading to the Godman: in the case of the Infants, they are recognized as martyrs who die in the place of the infant Christ, giving their lives for the ultimate incarnation of Christ[159]. The ultimate symbol of this incorporation of Israel into Christ is the Virgin Mary, who "is…venerated by the Church as having given humanity to the Godman, not only in her personal capacity, but as the New Eve, the Daughter and Mother of the Chosen People."

Christ took his humanity from the whole of Israel, through the Virgin Mary, and He thus has "a unity and organic connection – bodily, cultural and spiritual with the whole Jewish nation. In this, the chosenness of the Chosen People is not annulled by all its backslidings, individual and national…" as the Old Testament amply shows. And Bulgakov adds another tantalizing hint: "This inclusion is completed not only here on earth, but also beyond this earthly life, by virtue of 'the preaching in Hell', so to speak, of Hell's baptism beyond the grave."

Finally, in "Christianity Without Israel" Bulgakov voices the idea that the special comforter of the Jewish people is not so much Mary, as his Dormition sermon stated, but Christ Himself: the Mother of God's Assumption does not mean her absence from earth; instead she is even said to appear on earth and share in human suffering. So Christ's redeeming sacrifice on the Cross cannot be seen as a one-off; rather it is a continuing sacrifice, that repeats itself through historical time, with Christ suffering constantly with humanity, and "especially with the Chosen People, with whom He is so emphatically connected." This springs from Bulgakov's conviction that the blood of Christ spilt at the foot of the Cross continues to abide in the world, continues to flow forth, the remnant of Christ's continuing crucifixion on earth. Here, that blood is explicitly recognized to be Jewish blood. The equation, and the message for Jewry's persecutors, is graphic: the persecutors of Jewry are literally re-crucifying Christ. Bulgakov has expressed a very Chagalesque insight here[160].

A natural consequence of the continued relationship of Jews to Christ and His Mother, and their continued chosenness, is that out of their loins will come

---

[159] The question that constantly hovers before the mind in this context is whether the Church can recognize Jewish children and adults slaughtered as members of the carnal Israel *after* Christ as martyrs for Christ: one might contend that these Jews were scapegoats for Christians who might otherwise have died instead of the Jews. Certainly, Hitler's anti-Christianity never had a chance to turn fully genocidal due to the efforts he exerted in massacring Jews. The question is discussed more fully below.

[160] It is interesting to read "The Eucharist" in tandem with "Christianity without Israel:" then the blood that spilt at the foot of the Cross is the same blood as flows in Jewish veins today. The persecutors of Israel spill Christ's blood. It is also interesting to compare this with Florensky's idea that Jewish blood is demonic; and interesting, too, to consider that Florensky gets this interpretation only at the cost of a darkly Marcionite reading of both the Old Testament and a Gnostic reading of the New Testament.cf.ch.4.

Elijah and the two witnesses mentioned in Revelations,[161] the heralds of Christ's Second Coming. Those who attack the Jews thus risk "trampling on the tender shoots of the Coming One that are blooming from under the soil."[162] This thought is developed in an essay discussing the collective fates of Germany, Russia and Jewry. The threatened attack Bulgakov has in mind is not just the German persecution of the Jews, but the danger Bulgakov fears that the Russian people will succumb to a demonic spirit and turn on the Jews with a massive pogrom designed as revenge for the "Jewish pogrom" perpetrated against Russia. This could have the effect of crushing the "holy remnants" lying dormant in Jewry out of which this new force will spring.

Bulgakov was not far wrong in this: only Stalin's death in 1953 prevented him from bringing into effect a full-scale persecution of Soviet Jewry. Bulgakov's understanding of that psychology was no doubt honed by what he saw and felt himself in the Ukraine during the Civil War.

The collective fate of Israel and the remnant

This brings us directly to Bulgakov's second group of insights: the sacred remnant of Jewry; Jewry's collective fate; and the weakness of historical Christianity vis-à-vis its witness to the Jews. What Bulgakov says about these matters can, at least initially, be stated briefly:

Israel has been condemned collectively by God for the sins of its leadership in condemning Christ to death. Nonetheless, there is a sacred remnant among Jewry who believe in Christ and who thus, as individuals, are innocent. Due to Israel's tragic fate, however, they must share the lot of their unbelieving brothers and sisters. Their death at the hands of Jewry's persecutors can serve as an atoning sacrifice for Israel's sin. Indeed, Bulgakov hints, and Mother Maria and her circle state it more explicitly, that the grand clash between nations that is the Second World War, with its concomitant persecution of the Jews, bears all the marks of the end-time when the innocent Christ-loving martyrs of Israel can bring about the redemption of their nation, and thus of Christianity as a whole, and the world. "In historical Christianity will appear a new force," Bulgakov writes, "which becomes its spiritual core, as it was in its first days: Judeo-Christianity." Of the ongoing Holocaust, he writes in "The Coming Fates of the World, The Jewish Question:" "But it has, should have, a fitting meaning for Jewry as well, inasmuch as it is deprived of earthly success, the kingdom of this world with its power. Its fate is becoming a martyrology, a Cross-bearing, which however is being fulfilled not with Christ, and not in His name. But let us believe that it is a calling and an education for this."

Bulgakov thus converges on the same "Holocaust theology" as Edith Stein, who went to her death in Auschwitz as a cross-bearer on behalf of her Jewish people. In her words: "I spoke with the Savior to tell him that I realized it was

---

[161] Rev.11.13: "But I shall send my two witnesses to prophesy for twelve hundred and sixty days wearing sackcloth…"

[162] "The Fates of Russia, Germany and Jewry," p.60.

his Cross that was now being laid upon the Jewish people, that the few who understood this had the responsibility of carrying it in the name of all…;" "This is the shadow of the cross that falls upon my people! Oh, if they would only realize! This is the fulfillment of the curse which my people have called down upon themselves!;" "I understood the Cross as the destiny of God's people, which was beginning to be apparent at the time (1933)…;" "I firmly believe that the Lord has accepted my life as an offering for all. It is important for me to keep Queen Esther in mind and remember how she was separated from her people just so that she could intercede for them before the king…"[163]

The two ideas of the remnant of Israel and the unity of Israel are intimately linked for Bulgakov. That is, God's people are so closely connected that what one member does has immediate repercussions for his neighbor. Therefore, Israel shares a collective destiny. There is an upside and a downside of this. The guilt of those leaders who condemned Christ to death spreads over the whole nation, and includes those who rejected that decision. But, as with Edith Stein, the merit of a small core of Jewry who turn to Christ, also runs through the tightly bound nation, and washes away the guilt.

In Bulgakov's words: "…according to the word of the Lord, this guilt lies on the shoulders both of those who accept the guilt, as of those who do not accept it, and even of those to whom it is alien…in its falling away Israel is both guilty and not guilty…but the gifts and choosing remain irrevocable…" due to the fact that "the most mysterious aspect of the fate of Israel remains its unity. Thanks to this, the guilt of only one part, the leaders, becomes the fate of the whole nation, and this part speaks on behalf of the people, calling upon themselves the curses of Christ-murder and Christ-enmity. But this unity has another side: all Israel will be saved through the salvation of her 'holy remnant', though until that time this remnant is also hidden in Israel's falling away."[164]

And elsewhere: "But amid this persecuted and suffering Israel we cannot but distinguish between those who act blindly and in their turn persecute the Church and crucify Christ, and that chosen part of the 'holy remnant', who are persecuted along with Israel, but at the same time are persecuted for Christ, like the infants of Bethlehem. We have in mind that Judeo-Christianity which already exists in its rudiments… To these rudimentary chosen of Christ is given the difficulty of a double cross: of their Christianity[165] in relation to their persecutors, as of their Christianity in relation to their blood-relatives, who are not related brothers in belief, to their people, who reject Christ. Their lot is truly prophetic, and together with it is a martyr's lot. To them is given to be crucified for Christ and with

---

[163] Quotes from various sources on Edith Stein in Roy Schoemann, *Salvation is from the Jews. The role of Judaism in salvational history from Abraham to the Second Coming.* (San Francisco: Ignatius Press, 2003), 160-2.

[164] "The Mystery of Israel," pp.67-8.

[165] *Sic*, though is it not (also) their Jewishness which is a provocation to their Nazi persecutors?

Christ....In them is being revealed the strength of the One who is coming."[166]

In other words, Israel before and after Christ, as God's people, is a nation where each member is inextricably linked to the other, in a tight-knit holy body, united by one precious blood. In this sense, Bulgakov has penetrated to the heart of the rabbis' own perception of Israel as an indivisible spiritual unity, where each member is beholden to the other.[167]

In fact, Bulgakov's "theology of blood" enables him to take with full seriousness the rabbinic idea of Israel's "election of the flesh." The idea of an election by flesh is, to some extent, more paradoxical than Christianity's "election of the spirit" – and it is a paradox that, as we saw earlier in looking at Wyschogrod, is not easy for Jews themselves to come to terms with. Orthodox Jews who see Jewishness as inextricably linked to the covenant at Sinai and the observance of its six hundred and thirteen divine commandments are nonetheless forced to recognize that on one level, at least, they are no more Jewish than an atheist born of a Jewish mother with no connection to Judaism.

Given the oddness of this idea of election by the flesh of the seed of Abraham, it is perhaps not surprising that Bulgakov's driving idea contains, here and there, splinters of contradiction. The neat Steinerian picture painted above is of an overwhelming mass of Christ-rejecting Jews who have been punished for deicide. Their fate is offset by Jewish Christians, whose deaths will redeem their blood-brothers. And yet: there are hints elsewhere that amid the mass of non-Christian Jews there are further distinctions.

Firstly, in the events of the Holocaust, Jewry's "fate is becoming a martyrology, a Cross-bearing, which however is being fulfilled not with Christ, and not in His name. But let us believe that it is a calling and an education for this." This implies that even non-Christian Jews who die as Jews are dying a meaningful, redemptive death. This would make sense given that the blood that is spilt in the death of these Jews is the same blood as Christ's – an idea that is at the heart of Bulgakov's sophianic theology.

Secondly, we find phrases such as the following: "Bolshevism is precisely a Jewish pogrom carried out precisely by Jewish power – an awful victory of Satan over Jewry, carried out by means of Jewry. One can say that this is the historical suicide of Jewry, but only in the sense that it was carried out on earthly Israel, which betrayed its calling."[168] "Till now Jewry has remained in a state of

---

[166] "Christianity Without Israel," p.72.
[167] E.g. Jacob Shochet, *Chassidic Dimensions* (New York: Kehot Publication Society, 1990), 54: "Midrashic interpretation of the Biblical injunction 'You shall be unto Me a Kingdom of Priests and a Holy Nation': the singular tense of 'Holy Nation' teaches that all of Israel is as one body and one soul. As any one of them sins, all are affected; as any one of them is afflicted, all of them feel it." This is a summary of Talmudic and Midrashic thoughts, to be found at *Mechilta deRashby* on Exodus 19.6; *Yerushalmi Nedarim* 9.4; as well as of Hassidic interpretations such as *Reishit Hochma* on Exodus 19.6.
[168] "The fates of Russia, Germany and Jewry," p.60.

subservience to the golden calf and falling away from the faith, even in the God of Israel." And: "One can say that Jewry in Russia, finding itself under Jewish power, has no true friend..."[169]

On the basis of these statements, the contemporary Russian-Israeli scholar Raya Epstein[170] would be justified in concluding that Bulgakov envisaged a section of Jewry that "found in Marxism a quasi-religious substitute for their authentic religion that they had abandoned and betrayed." That is, these extracts seems to envision a different division of Jewry than the apostate/Christian divide. Instead we have those who have apostatized from the God of Israel, turning to the Golden calf or to power-mongering, and those who have stayed and remained true to the God of Israel, i.e. by implication, to their rabbinic faith, "their authentic religion." The latter are presented as the more virtuous part of Israel, which is somehow true to itself, as opposed to those renegade Jews who do not fulfill Jewry's historical destiny – though, of course, not as virtuous as the "remnant" of Jewish Christians.

It must be said without further ado that these are not minor divergences from the previous picture. They present – or rather, seemingly accidentally let slip the possibility of – an extremely different analysis of Jewish fate than the Steinerian one. Jewry is now divided into three: apostate Jews who consciously reject Christ; the "sacred remnant" among Jewry who consciously accept Christ; and "earthly Israel" which continues to fulfill its calling to worship the God of Israel. All of them share a mysterious unity of the flesh.

Indeed, I think it would be fair to say that Bulgakov's discovery of the unity of Israel, which is a genuine and piercing insight, leads to an eclipse of these distinctions. The weakest distinction, the one that falls into the crack between the two others, is that third element of the equation, "religious" Jewry. The reason for this seems clear. Bulgakov's lack of knowledge of Hebrew, his lack of familiarity with rabbinic sources, his lack of acquaintance with contemporary Judaism and religious Jews were all evident – and by his own admission – in his work from *Two Cities* (1906-10) up to *The Unfading Light* (1917). It is an interesting question what significance that third blurred "pillar" of Jewry could have if taken seriously in Bulgakov's analysis. We will return to this question in a later section.

Finally, we come to Bulgakov's remaining idea, the surprising thesis that historical Christianity is too weak to be a competent witness of Christ to Jewry. Christians must thus refrain from trying to missionize among Jews. All this is stated in the context of Bulgakov's eschatological analysis of the events of World War Two given in "The fates of Russia, Germany and Jewry."

In this essay Bulgakov states that "The main point of the present war is its Jewish aspect, though how is not clear. Hitler and Rosenberg are the greatest publicists of this truth, though. Perhaps this final persecution is a signal of

---

[169] "The fates of Russia, Germany and Jewry."

[170] For more on Epstein and her interpretation of Bulgakov, see the Conclusion of the chapter.

the coming conversion of the Jews. This persecution could also be the final punishment for Jewry's crime against Russia (via Bolshevism)."

Immediately, we encounter that itching paradox of Bulgakov's anti-Semitism. For whatever he seems to give to the Jews with one hand, he takes away with the other. He recognizes the weakness of Christianity, he announces in what must be a shock for many that Christians must not preach to Jews, but he couches all this in an analysis of Jewry that seems to be a model of the anti-Semitism it wishes to denounce.

For a start, of the three elements of Jewry he has delineated elsewhere, in this analysis only one – the Bolshevik atheist element – is deemed to be representative of Israel. Germany's invasion of Russia is then seen as punishment of Bolshevik Jewry – with the other two innocent elements of Jewry suffering along with the guilty due to the mysterious unity of Israel.

This analysis makes Bulgakov's call for a "Christian relationship to the Jewish question" – the language is Soloviev's – rather hard to fulfill. Not surprisingly it is directly connected with the anti-Semitism he detects – and contributes to – in Christianity. The only context could be that of following Christ's commandment to love one's enemies. And the way Bulgakov paints it (I refer the reader to the extracts quoted at the end of the previous section), these are particularly horrendous and vicious enemies. But this is hardly the sort of love for Jewry that we found in Soloviev.

Again, we can appeal to the two strands in Bulgakov's make-up: here Dostoevsky again wins out over Soloviev. The latter turned his back on the popularized Slavophile-nationalist vision of Russia. Bulgakov sees the war precisely through this prism. Russia is "the entelechia of world history, its real axis, and this has always been known by the Russian soul." Germany's current goal of being the prime mover of history is a pseudo-Messianic pretension. It "has decided that chosenness and uniqueness belongs precisely to itself," putting it into genocidally envious conflict with Jewry.

Russia's Messianic calling, on the other hand, is genuine. Russians are "out of all the historical peoples…indisputably called to the coming revelation…" Russia is suited to its eschatological task due to its femininity, which manifests itself in *sobornost'* (conciliarity). Unlike with Germany, Russia's Messianic mission does not – in principle – bring it into conflict with Jewry. The latter is – despite the distortion consequent on rejection of Christ – potentially a creative, masculine people who can help Russia fulfill its goal of spreading Orthodox Christianity to the world. The current war, Bulgakov believes, could be the event that realigns the fates of all these key nations: Jews will become Christian and take an assisting role in helping a victorious Russia spread the Gospel.

The real turmoil of the war, its underlying metaphysical ground, is thus for Bulgakov not the movement of armies across the soil of Europe. It is the movement taking place in the souls of men, or rather, of nations. As in the First World War, Bulgakov hopes that Russian victory will have a spiritual aspect. And the Holocaust is God's way of rousing the soul of his still chosen people, his firstborn Israel, to participate in the eschatological times that will follow this war. Persecution will goad Israel into renouncing the fruits of this world, will force them to Golgotha, where they can finally embrace the Messiah they rejected so long ago.

Precisely amid the apocalyptic turmoil of the War, a special process is taking place in Jewry. But "this internal process for Christians and non-Jews in general remains hidden and mysterious. It is unnecessary and forbidden to missionize to Jewry, to convince them of the truth of Christianity, in its soul the devil directly, face to face, struggles with Christ, as in the soul of Judas. And it is also necessary to recognize that contemporary 'historical', non-'apocalyptic' Christianity is without strength and helpless for such a task, has no fire for it which could inflame Israel[171]. Christianity itself needs to be taught a Christian relationship to the Jewish question, to find it for itself. It is in spiritual captivity to anti-Semitism and itself does not know by what new revelation 'of the first resurrection' the Judeo-Christianity of the future will display itself."

Thus Bulgakov states a "Holocaust theology" of sorts. It must be said that it is a rather Russocentric approach, a theodicy of the murder of the Chosen People in which sacred Russia plays the axial role. Jewry is being decimated for the crimes of its Bolshevik leaders, the new killers of the Russian Christ. But this decimation is God's instrument to bring His people to Christ, so that they can help the Christ-nation, Russia. While there may be a divine justice in this murder of Jewry, Christians are certainly in a compromised position as well. For they have failed to kindle Jewry's spirit with Christ, and through their own lack of love for the Jews have abandoned God's nation. Most damningly of all, they are no longer reliable witnesses for Christ.

What is one to make of this analysis of Jewry? Firstly, there is the audacity in giving such a cut-and-dry theodicy: God kills Jews in Germany because of the Bolshevik commissars in Russia. Another Russian philosopher, Semyon Frank, pointed out that in a sense theodicies are impossible: for to explain evil is in a sense to justify evil. Even if it were true that Russia were the Christ-nation, in whose Gospel-preaching efforts a penitent Jewry could assist after having been brought to Christ through their suffering, Dostoevsky's question is still pertinent: is this magnificent end justified if it comes about through the tears of a suffering child (not to mention thousands of children)? To state this so schematically is immediately to undermine the persuasiveness of this vision[172]. The only solution to evil is to act against it – which, it must be said Bulgakov's followers did in relation to the persecuted Jews of Paris.

---

[171] In ch.3, we will see a very concrete instance of Bulgakov's implementation of his own advice to be discrete in preaching Christianity to Jews, when we look at his friendship with Lev Shestov.

[172] Cf.ch.6 for Frank's own reaction to the slaughters of the First and Second World Wars. We argue there that his German-Jewish background saved him from the jingoism displayed by Bulgakov and other Russian philosophers towards Germany in both wars.

Secondly, the call to a Christian relationship to Jews can surely only be tested by the criterion of love: but to see the worst elements of Jewry as representative of the nation is to have eyes wide open to the faults of a person, which is surely not a sign of love.

Thirdly, the idea that 60,000-200,000 murdered in the pogroms of the Civil War was not "punishment" enough of Jewry shows a worrying indifference to mass murder.

Finally, the whole theodicy is undermined again by a refusal to stick by the terms of the analysis. For no sooner has Bulgakov pinpointed the corrupt element in Jewry as Bolshevik commissars than we learn that "the Jewish influence, most obvious in banking and finance, but [also evident] in science, the arts and the press must be recognized, as well as its tendency to destroy anything with which it does not agree."[173] Once again, Bulgakov displays his lack of "interest or...taste for the concrete, for reality." He elides Jewish communism, Jewish capitalism, Marx, the Talmud, Jewish apocalyptic, Bar Kockhba's revolt, Jewish rejection of Christ, into one homogenous whole. All the careful distinctions collapse. All that is left of good in Jewry is a handful of Jewish Christians. Is the "sacred remnant" of Jewry, one wonders, really to be determined by examining whether a given Jew holds a baptismal certificate?

So on one level, Bulgakov's analysis of Jewry and its relationship to Christianity is highly disappointing, unconvincing and even primitive.

But on another level, as one reads these writings a central conviction begins to emerge, that Bulgakov is struggling to articulate something of incredible importance. The contradictions, the backslidings, the lashes of emotion, the reductionism, all these give color and depth to the truth that is emerging. If it had been stated in a more clinical way, in a more logical way, perhaps it would have lacked such persuasiveness. For Bulgakov's attraction to Jewry, his yearning for a redeemed Jewry, is coupled with his repulsion and distaste for Jewry. And the latter is a sign of the high standards that Bulgakov, true to the Bible, sets for Jewry – the high standards and the tragic punishments that befall Israel when she fails to reach them.

This conviction is stated mostly plainly in an essay entitled "Christianity Without Israel." The title itself expresses the poignancy of Bulgakov's belief. This is quite simply that: "Christianity without Judeo-Christianity cannot realize itself fully, remains incomplete. It can only reach its fullness in conjunction with Judeo-Christianity, as it existed in the apostolic church, because this latter was just that.... With the disappearance of the Jerusalem church, Jewry has been victimized by the Christian nations, which is its tragedy..."

All the vitriol, all the pain, all the anger – it seems that this is all frustrated hope, frustrated desire that the Jewish heart of Christianity come back into the bosom of Christianity. For all the talk of Russia being the entelechia of world history, Bulgakov misses Jewry. Perhaps that is why *whatever* Jews do outside the

[173] *The fates of Russia, Germany and Jewry*, p.42.

orbit of Christianity is for Bulgakov ultimately poisonous. Perhaps that is why his attempts to draw fine distinctions break down.

In what follows, we will try to revive these distinctions, dragging them out from under the rubble of contradictions.

A critical development of Bulgakov's ideas

To reiterate: Bulgakov gives two analyses of Jewry. The "surface" analysis holds straightforwardly that Jewry is divided into, firstly, an unredeemed, Christ-rejecting mass that is attracted by and involved in all the evils of this fallen world from capitalism to Bolshevism; and secondly, a small "sacred remnant" of Jews who have embraced Christ and can redeem the other half of Jewry.

The below-the-surface analysis, which is dropped in throwaway phrases, hints at something different. There is another component to Jewry, which is Holy Israel, the observer of the Torah and the venerator of the God of Israel. In Bulgakov's thinking as it stands, there is no room for this analysis to develop.

This is because if one looks a little closer at this hint with Bulgakovian eyes, one will soon discover that religious Jewry has, after all, rejected Christ, and that Judaism is a religion of purity and legalistic narrowness, which contrasts with Christian freedom. To a certain extent this is right: the nineteenth blessing of one of Judaism's central prayers, the *Shemoneh Esreh*[174], is in fact a curse directed at Jewish heretics, under which rubric is included Jewish Christians. At the heart of religious Judaism, then, there is indeed a basic antipathy to Christianity. Nonetheless, I believe that it would not depart from the spirit of Bulgakov's work to propose an approach to religious Judaism which is tolerant, with a characteristically paradoxical Bulgakovian sort of tolerance. I will return to this point in a section examining "Judas: the Apostle-Traitor."

There is another approach to Judaism in Bulgakov, which is also below-the-surface and is no sooner mentioned than it slips into the deep again. This analysis is also similarly short of space to develop in Bulgakov's thinking as it stands. It is this "covert" alternative approach to Judaism that I will address first.

A Messianic Jewish reading of Bulgakov?

When Bulgakov talks of a revived Judeo-Christianity which will be the new heart of an eschatological Christianity, what does he have in mind? At first, it would seem that he could not have meant what we now refer to as "Messianic Judaism," that is, a Christianity that tries to combine elements of rabbinic Judaism and to foster a separate community of Jewish Christians.

This is because Bulgakov's estimation of rabbinic Judaism, and indeed of Old Testament Judaism is so low. Further, he has no time for Jewish exclusiveness,

---

[174] The prayer means "eighteen (benedictions)", though in reality there are nineteen benedictions, including the one against heretics added in order to exclude Jewish-Christians and other heretics from the synagogue.

and Jewish isolation and separation from gentiles.

Judaism, for example, receives short shrift in "Racism and Jewry:" "Not by [Judaism] does Jewry influence the world, although this, together with the building of synagogues also expresses the national character. As a religion, Judaism is now naturally conscious of itself as in opposition to Christianity. But it is not in this way that it is possible to identify the religious consciousness of Jewry, inasmuch as it possible to speak of it at all. But here it expresses itself either negatively, as a factual abandonment of religious faith, or as a militant atheism, which does not stop short of persecuting religion, which in point of fact means Christianity." Judaism here is merely one ingredient in the larger obnoxious "Jewish religious consciousness," and it barely receives a mention. It is almost not "possible to speak of it all." That is, Judaism barely merits the title religion. In another place, it is called parasitic – defining itself in combat with Christianity.

But this is all rather surprising, when taken in the context of Bulgakov's insistence on the carnal affinity of Christ and the Jewish people, before and after the Incarnation. Christ, after all, is said to have "a unity and an organic connection – *bodily, cultural and spiritual* [italics DR] with the whole Jewish nation."[175] But unfortunately, all we hear of in Bulgakov is the bodily unity with Christ. What, we are within our rights to ask, has happened to the cultural and spiritual unity Bulgakov identifies theoretically?

This is potentially extremely damaging to Bulgakov's whole approach to Jewry. To highlight the affinity of Jewry with Christ, but then to assert that it is only an impotent and dormant blood-affinity confronts the risk of sliding into racism[176]. We saw how Bulgakov contrasted the Christian notion of blood with that of the Nazis. The latter is purely materialistic, the former is spiritual. But for Bulgakov, Jewry's "voice of the blood in all its strength" cries unanimously of Christ "Crucify Him!"[177]. Jews are Jews by blood, and it seems that with that blood they inherit this rejection of Christ. This, however, verges on the racism which maintains that it is the blood which determines the person. As Bulgakov's analysis now stands, Jewish blood has no spirit in it, merely an inherited parasitic voice. The blood determines the Jewish person. Moreover, it is a blood from which one would want to escape if such is the voice that cries out in it. But how could one wish to escape the blood of Christ?

The question which arises then is the following: if Jews accept Christ, should they abandon their Jewishness? Bulgakov's answer to this is clearly: no. For, as we have just seen, he yearns to see a Judeo-Christianity "as it existed in the apostolic church, because this latter was just that," a type of Christianity which would resemble the early Jerusalem church, whose disappearance he mourns. But has Bulgakov thought about what this would mean? After all, the members of the Jerusalem church visited the Temple, were circumcised, and observed the Law.

---

[175] *The genealogy of Christ*.
[176] Which is exactly what happened to Florensky's sophiological blood-analysis of Jewry.
[177] "Racism and Jewry," p.32.

That is, like Christ, they were Torah-observant members of the Jewish people.

Of course, this is an old chestnut. Two thousand years later, is it appropriate for Jewish converts to observe the Torah in the way the Jamesian church did? Entering into the question is an interpretation of Paul: was he polemically arguing against Law-observance only for gentiles, while leaving it open for Jewish Christians to be Torah-observant, or was he in principle against Torah-observance by Jewish Christians too?

Leaving those complex questions aside, if we focus simply on the spirit of Bulgakov's approach we sense a new contribution to the debate. If we take him more seriously than he took his own suggestions about Judeo-Christianity, we should read what he writes very closely: "Israel even in its backsliding has not ceased to be the Chosen People, the relation of Christ and his Most Pure Mother, and this blood relation is not interrupted and does not stop even after the birth of Christ....this is a fact which one needs to ponder and grasp with all one's strength, in its dogmatic meaning as it applies to the fate of Israel."[178]

Indeed: what is the dogmatic meaning of Jewry's link with Christ, culturally and spiritually, as well as bodily – especially for those Jews who "have put on Christ"? The Orthodox Church is meant to act with *sobornost'* (conciliarity, *gatheredness*). The Jerusalem church gathered together to decide whether gentile Christians needed to observe the Torah. But did the gentile churches ever gather, along with Jewish Christians, to decide in conciliarity whether Jewish Christians need not observe the Law? But then is their polemic against Torah Christianity for Jews canonical? The gap that Bulgakov senses with aching certainty at the heart of Christianity arises in exactly that place[179].

Going further down this route, we remember another side to Bulgakov. When he is not restating the classical Christian doctrine about the purity of the Law, he is brimming with admiration for the Old Testament. Bulgakov, who sensed so keenly the "sophianic" aspect of pagan religion seems to have missed sophianicity in the Old Testament and Judaism. The Festival of Unleavened Bread, the Festival of Booths, the Festival of Weeks, are seen by scholars as agricultural festivals all taken over from the natives of Canaan, or Israel's own pre-Sinaitic nomadic past – and transformed in the worship of Yahweh. The Sabbath year for the Land – what could be more sophianic than this respect due to the mother of the nation? The celebration of the Sabbath Queen in Judaism is another case in point.

True, Bulgakov at one point in "The Fates of Russia, Germany and Israel" writes that what "was revealed in the depth of Jewish mysticism as sophianicity must be recognized as the incarnated Logos, the Divine Strength and Wisdom." This recalls the passage in *The Unfading Light* where Bulgakov seemed to argue

---

[178] "The persecution of Israel."

[179] Fr. Vasili Mihoc is perhaps the only Orthodox figure today who is asking these kinds of questions. He is the only Orthodox representative of the organization Jerusalem Council 2, which argues for a meeting of another Jerusalem council which would admit Jews to the church *as* Jews. Cf.ch.5, for a discussion of Karsavin's view on Judeo-Christianity; and ch.7, for a discussion of Alexander Men.

for a doctrine of a Divine Son of God hidden in the depth of the Kabbalah. This is a rare recognition of the religious value of Judaism. But here the question is not of giving value to Judaism as such – but of detecting in it elements which Jewish Christians can continue to cleave to after their embrace of Christianity.

Surely the culture and spirit into which God chose to be incarnated must contain something worthy of preservation for the blood descendants of the Incarnated God? Surely, the religion of the Old Testament – even if its function was to preserve Jewry until Christ – was not a meaningless collection of random precepts and half-baked laws? That is, *pace* Soloviev, just as God's choice of the Jews was deliberate and based on their natural characteristics, surely the religion God then revealed to the Jews must have had some lasting meaning?

Again, in *The Grail*, Bulgakov had written: "True, Christ brought a new Godsonhood for God's children, who are born not of flesh and blood but of water and of the Spirit from God. However, this *spiritual* birth too does not revoke but presupposes mankind's natural birth and natural life, though it crowns this birth and life with God's grace. In other words, we must ask whether Christ's Ascension breaks his natural connection with us according to humanity…or whether after His Ascension, Christ still belongs to *our* earthly humanity…"[180] As we know, Bulgakov's answer to this question was that Christ's humanity was still present on earth after the Ascension, and can incorporate elements of our natural humanity. This is part of his sophiological idea that nature and the world contain a divine principle. Christ, as it were, does not have to start from scratch: Bulgakov allows for a sanctification of human culture, and of inanimate nature, as they are incorporated into Christ's divine-human body, the Church.

In the case of the Jews, however, the "natural" basis of their culture is the very culture out of which the humanity of Christ was hewn. The "natural blood" of the Jews is the very blood which Christ took for his own. Again, in *The Grail* Bulgakov had written of how humanity, even that portion of it that is not consciously part of the Church is transformed by that "left-behind" blood of Christ, receiving a new power.[181] But that Golgothan blood, Bulgakov has shown us, is precisely Jewish blood! How by this logic can a Jew who accepts Christ turn his back on his blood? Or on his culture, the original receptacle of the Godman?

To conclude, it might seem odd to contend that it is a natural development of Bulgakov's own insights to take the step towards "Messianic Judaism," considering that he denigrated the Law and the Jewish religion so harshly. Certainly, a "Messianic Judaism" which simply tacked Christ onto existent rabbinic Judaism would in all likelihood have been considered a grotesque error by Bulgakov. Also, given that the blood-nations of the world have been filled with the Spirit, and given that blood is now a receptacle of the universal spirit of the New Adam, a "Messianic Judaism" which insisted on strict isolation and bans on intermarriage with non-Jewish Christians would also contradict Bulgakov's sophiological spirit.

---

[180] *Grail*, 37.
[181] *Grail*, 57.

Of course, the question was not explicitly raised, still less answered by Bulgakov. Nonetheless, the idea that the "remnant" may be a core of Christ-believing Jews who combine their belief in Christ with a sophianic, mystical, Christ-centred reworking of Jewish religion, culture and language, is not a completely far-fetched reading of Bulgakov. If such a Judeo-Christian core could achieve historical continuity, while maintaining a flexible openness to the gentile Christian Church, this could only add to what Bulgakov called the "multitude in unity" of the New Adam, the unity in diversity of human nations in the Body of Christ, the Church.

The thought arises that a natural locus for such a revived Judeo-Christianity would be that Jewish State for which Bulgakov in 1915 initially held out such high hopes. There, where the national festivals of Judaism have to some extent taken on a cultural rather than a halakhic dimension[182], where the old connection with the "mother-land of Israel" has been revived, perhaps the time is ripe for a sophianically reborn Judeo-Christianity? Only time can tell.

In the next section, we will once again go against the grain of Bulgakov's surface meaning and try and tease out another, perhaps even more paradoxical, reading of the Jewish Question.

Above we read how Bulgakov insisted that "it is unnecessary and forbidden to missionize to Jewry, to convince them of the truth of Christianity, in its soul the devil directly, face to face, struggles with Christ, as in the soul of Judas." It should not be surprising that Bulgakov compares Jewry with the figure of Christ's betrayer. What is very surprising, however, is that Bulgakov could write a whole essay about "Judas The Apostle-Traitor" and make minimal reference to the Jewish people. Instead, as we will see the nation with whom Bulgakov compares Judas is his own native land and people. It is Russia and the Russian nation that is named the apostle-traitor. Jews, though, do make an entrance.

Among the intriguing aspects of this essay is the fact that we catch a glimpse of how a "Christian relationship to the Jewish question," that is, one that is informed with love, is possible. When Bulgakov deals with the treachery of his own beloved nation, he is far more forgiving, strives far harder to see the good, to exculpate and wish for the best. This is not true when he writes of Jewry, for whom the worst elements are always representative. It is tempting, and given the subject, natural therefore, to transfer these more benign insights from Russia to Jewry and see what happens – and this is what we will do.

A (covert) two-covenant reading of Bulgakov? Judas, Saul, and Paul
The essay[183], a psychological, historical, critical and dogmatic exploration of

---

[182] And surely Bulgakov's sophiological spirit would hardly be compatible with a halakhic Judeo-Christianity.
[183] The essay was published in two sections: Sergei Bulgakov, "Iuda Iskariot Apostol Predatel' (dogmaticheskaya)," in *Put'* No.27, (1931): 3-42; and Sergei Bulgakov, "Iuda

Judas, contains the idea that Judas' character and his crimes in their darkness and zealousness contain within themselves the seeds of redemption. Comparing Russia to Judas, on the basis that she is a Christian nation who has betrayed her heritage, Bulgakov expresses the hope that even the non-Christian zeal of the Soviet leaders could be counted in their favor, come judgment day.

Regardless of the originality of Bulgakov's interpretation of Judas, the essay is rather anomalous in its complete absence of any rhetoric of blame-laying for the Revolution on the Jews. His diary entries and the war-time essays put the bulk of responsibility for Bolshevism on the Jews, or the Yids. But here Bulgakov faces up squarely to the role of Russians in the Revolution. The reasons for this anomaly are not clear; nor is it clear why the more obvious link between Judas and Jewry is not made, except fleetingly.

The real interest of this essay for us now, however, is that it provides a way of looking at that unstable third pillar of Jewry that we identified in Bulgakov's thought above: religious Jewry. We saw that Bulgakov is vaguely aware that religious Jewry comprises an element of Israel that is true to its destiny and to the God of Israel. And we have already pointed out that ignoring Judaism as a serious component of Jewry can slide into racism, into viewing Jews as a blood-nation without any spirit, so that this aspect of Bulgakov's approach needs correction.

But there is another important aspect here, which shows that his approach not only needs, but demands correction. For Bulgakov yearns for a Judeo-Christianity. He points out that Jewry must never, and can never, be destroyed for out of her loins will spring the witnesses of the end days. But there is a glaringly obvious correlate of this assertion which Bulgakov misses. That which preserves Jewry as an entity through history is: the Law. Jewish blood is Jewish because of the Law which separates Jewry from the nations, and which insists on a ban against intermarriage – absent conversion – with gentiles. Jewish Bolsheviks and Jewish Christians and Jewish bourgeois, whatever their degree of identification as religious Jews, are Jewish by virtue of the fact of their parents' or grandparents' adherence to some form of religious Judaism, in a form that forbids intermarriage. The result of all this is that some positive valuation must be made of the Law: after all it plays a role in bringing about the Second Coming.

But one must go further. The Law is not simply some instrument for keeping Jews around until they produce the necessary persons for Christian redemption. That would hardly go beyond the idea that Judaism is simply about blood-purity for its own sake. Nor would it improve on the idea that Jewish blood is completely without a serious ideology or spirit, but merely parasitic on Christianity.

Thus it must be recognized that the preservation of Jewish blood by Jews is not racism, not an empty ideology but has its own deep spirit. That spirit,

---

Iskariot Apostol Predatel' (istoricheskaya)," *Put'* No.26, (1931): 3-60. It also appears in Sergei Bulgakov, *Put' parizhskogo bogosloviya*. (Moscow: Khram svyatoi muchenitsy Tatiany pri MGU, 2007), 291-364. In citations, I will refer to page numbers in the latter version, citing the essay in English as "Judas Iscariot, Apostle-Traitor."

for the overwhelming portion of Jewish history since Christ, has been rabbinic Judaism. For the rabbis, Jewish blood purity only makes sense in the context of preserving Yahweh's chosen nation. Without the worship of Yahweh, Jewish blood for the rabbis means nothing. *This* is the spiritual principle of Jewry, its voice of the blood, in the true Bulgakovian sense. Proof lies in the fact that a change to Judaism's spiritual principle, for example determining Jewishness by patrilineality or matrilineality, or changes in conversion rituals, changes the very composition of the Jewish nation, Jewish blood. For religious Jews too, we must say that the spirit determines the blood and not *vice versa*, with the nation being driven to cursed greed by the inevitable cry of its blood – as Bulgakov intimates[184].

On the other hand, having established this positive revision of his approach to religious Jewry and its role, we can admit with Bulgakov that rabbinic, Law-based Judaism in its essence is indeed opposed to the recognition of Christ as God, the Second Person of the Trinity. And so we are left with a paradox. The zealous followers of the Law are the core from which the saving remnant of Jewry and indeed of the world and Christianity will come. The Law, no more than the Jewry which it preserves, cannot be abolished if Elijah and the heralds of the Second Coming are to be born and play their role. However, this same Law and its followers are adamantly opposed to Christ and Christianity.

And this is where Bulgakov's analysis of Judas is so helpful. For it is just such a rich paradox that Bulgakov tackles when he compares the fate of Russia to Judas, the paradoxically named Apostle-Traitor. He concludes that hidden in Judas is a potential Saul, that is, a persecutor of Christ who might turn around and become Paul.

At one point Bulgakov writes: "But this unity [of Israel] has another side: all Israel will be saved through the salvation of her 'holy remnant', though until

---

[184] Oddly enough, a famous contemporary of Bulgakov's manages to come to a positive evaluation of Judaism without any fuss and bother. This is Metropolitan Anthony Khrapovitsky, who lived in the Ukraine at the same time as Bulgakov and later became the head of the Russian Orthodox Church Outside of Russia. Despite their difference in outlook, Bulgakov and Khrapovitsky shared a conservative monarchist orientation, and an aversion to the radicalism and liberalism that threatened traditional Russia. In a short essay analyzing the Jewish question from Biblical sources (*Yevreisky vopros i svyataya Bibliya*, pp.884-900, Sobraniye Sochinenii, tom 1) Khrapovisky encourages Jews to remain faithful to their religion instead of joining the ranks of the revolutionaries, adding that Russian Christians can only be friends to such Jews, while they must be hostile to their faithless co-religionists. Khrapovitsky even expresses praise for rabbinic learning and Jewish philosophers like Maimonides. If Jews genuinely cannot find it within themselves to believe in Christ, adherence to the Torah is easily a second best option. Khrapovitsky was also active in intervening to stop pogroms and in preaching against anti-Semitism. Why one man could find value in Judaism and another not perhaps boils down to the mystery of personality.

that time this remnant is also hidden in Israel's falling away." The language is suggestive: the "sacred remnant" is currently "hidden." But if this "sacred remnant" is straightforwardly identified with a scattering of Jewish Christians, why is the remnant hidden? Surely, it is immediately obvious who is a baptized Jew and who is not. This hints at an interpretation by which it is far harder for Christian eyes to make out the salvational remnant in Jewry, for it is hidden deeply in the folds of Israel's falling away and is not transparent to Christian understanding.

Just such a mysterious and intriguing understanding of Russia's fate, and the fate of the apostle-traitor, was developed by Bulgakov in the essay to be discussed.

Let us now turn to this essay and see how Bulgakov's analysis of Russian destiny provides a model for an analysis of Jewish destiny.

First of all, it is worth first recapitulating Bulgakov's depiction of Judas to understand what Bulgakov means when he talks of Russia as a Judas nation.

Judas is the apostle-traitor. This title embodies an unbearable paradox and contradiction. For almost all Christian theologians, a simplistic emphasis on Judas' treachery and thievery ends all discussion. But Bulgakov throughout the essay puts more and more emphasis on Judas' apostleship, his worthiness and chosenness for this role by Christ, and he tries to tease out all the clues in the gospels to build up a portrait of the apostle who betrayed his Divine master.

Bulgakov also reminds the reader constantly of how the other apostles failed: Peter was called Satan by Christ, James and John were seduced by a desire for high rank in the kingdom, Thomas doubted the Resurrection, none of the apostles understood till the end the nature of the spiritual kingdom that Jesus was preaching, and all of them fled in cowardice at Jesus' trial,– except, points out Bulgakov, Judas who returned to the high priests after the trial to return the silver coins, despite the risk that they could turn on him now as an ally of Christ.

In the same way, Bulgakov sees a positive motive in the betrayal: Judas betrayed Christ out of burning love for his master. Judas saw a reluctance in the master to reveal himself in his full glory, and believed that he needed to be provoked into showing himself as the Messiah. Arrest by his enemies would lead Jesus to call upon the angels and strike them down. This was his obsession by the apocalyptic vision of an earthly kingdom of God, a Jewish sovereign state free of Romans and their lackeys[185].

---

[185] Bulgakov's Judas emerges as embodying traits that are not dissimilar from certain nationalist tendencies in pre-State Zionism, such as Jabotinsky's Revisionism. Jabotinsky's right-wing nationalist Zionism had its roots, incidentally, in his experience of anti-Semitism after the Kishinev pogroms and during the Beilis affair, which precipitated his turn from Russian-language journalist-novelist to Jewish nationalist. Bulgakov's own 1915 support for Zionism as a benign tendency in Jewish life sits uncomfortably with his later distaste for Jewish "self-assertiveness," as he saw it, and seems to ignore the militant potential of the Jewish national movement, not to

Bulgakov shows how the temptation of a worldly kingdom, while present for the other disciples, was particularly strong in the personality of Judas. Bulgakov painstakingly extracts hints from the gospels to build up a picture of this personality, and he emphasizes the positive nature of Judas' personal traits, which made him a natural choice as a disciple. Judas was special: he was the only Judean in the band of apostles, thus connected like Christ to the line of David. He was a city-dweller, thus more sophisticated than the other disciples, who were Galilean fishermen peasants. He was a proletarian, thus he knew the oppression of the Jewish people more closely than them. He was a man whose mind ruled his heart – unlike the other disciples, who were simple folk. And he had a useful familiarity with money and business, which is why he was entrusted with the common purse. In short, he was an organizer: what better person could there be to stage the final revelation of the new Messiah?

In this portrait, we are straight away put in mind of the profile Bulgakov will later paint of the Russian Jewish revolutionaries who tried to destroy Russia. But at this stage of his essay, Bulgakov does not draw the parallel. Instead, it is the similarity of the *Russian* people to Judas that Bulgakov mentions: it is the Russian nation who was chosen for apostleship by Christ and then betrayed Him for the thirty coins of economic paradise. Nonetheless, this portrait of Judas will double for the Jews later on, which is not surprising. As Bulgakov makes clear, the mystery of the apostle-traitor for him holds the key to two theological dilemmas often neglected in the history of theological thought: the interaction of personality and fate in the unfolding of world-history; and the action of God from within the world and outside the world (the lower sophianic/immanent and higher sophianic/transcendent aspects of God's relationship with man and the world) – which Bulgakov argues have often been reduced to sterile formulas about predestination, double or single, in Western theology.

With expert skill, Bulgakov shows how Judas zealously pursued his goal of helping Jesus to help himself, giving suppleness to the contradictory signals in the different gospels about Judas' person and motives. Even as Jesus handed over the morsel of bread to Judas at the last supper (as Evdikimov will say, following his teacher's insight, thus taking a morsel of the Divine Body out into the outermost darkness), Judas had persuaded himself that his master was "in the know" about his intentions, that he loved Judas more than all the others, that he was entrusting him secretly with this delicate mission. And why not? Given his special character, this would only be appropriate. Only after the scourging, the hanging on the Cross, the death of Christ did Judas finally understand that

---

mention its often anti-religious orientation. There is certainly an inconsistency here – partly this is Bulgakov's fault, partly it is due to the richness and complexity of Jewish life options at this time. Despite its inconsistency, I believe that Bulgakov's thought continues to be rich and suggestive. (For another thinker who made an implicit connection between the 66 a.d. Jewish Revolt and the 1917 Russian Revolution, cf. Metropolitan Anthony Khrapovitsky, *Khristos spasitel' i yevreiskaya revolyutsia. Religiozno-istoricheskii ocherk*. St Petersburg: 'Literarturniy Vestnik', 1993.)

Christ, without giving up a single one of the miraculous powers he had displayed to heal the sick and raise the dead, could choose not to use these powers against this world. Only then did Judas understand that his loving zeal, his keen organizational flair to pull off the biggest scoop in sacred history, were acts of gross miscomprehension and savage treachery. And then, with courage and impetuousness, Judas goes back into the mouth of the lion, to the high priests, and returns the coins of betrayal.

Thus Judas, whose story Bulgakov fully admits "makes clear [...] the whole history of the world and man, as it is revealed in the Word of God, especially in the history of the Chosen People [, which is] an unceasing struggle of God with its fatal sinfulness" is unmistakably a Jew, urban, zealous, the great organizer and doer, – and a hero, right till the end. What goes wrong? Judas kills himself. That is, he enacts punishment on himself. His pride, his impatience, his taking everything into his own hands once again have not abated. And so, despite Christ's love for him (Judas was right about that), he condemns himself without even turning to that Master whom he has betrayed. He kills himself, the self which God had lovingly crafted to be a companion for His Son, in a great arrogance of judgment.

This then is Bulgakov's Judas. Bulgakov ponders on the dogmatic implications of his Judas, but it is meditations about how the type of Judas can be embodied in the destiny of a nation that are more pertinent here. Here we see how Bulgakov takes the lessons to be learned from Judas to heart, deriving not just illumination into the theological problem of predestination, but a personal lesson for Russia, Russians, and the Russian who writes about Judas. Indeed, Bulgakov writes that Judas' blend of apostleship and treachery is a temptation for the believer, which could lead him like Job to question God's actions[186]. Normally, this is a paradox from which it would be decent to turn away one's gaze, not probing into the mysteries of Providence. But this cannot be as "it has become unavoidable, it has been made our own fate, not personal, but national."[187]

And here Bulgakov states those principles which will guide him in his later analysis of the "fates of Jewry." The only surprising point is that, while in the later essays, Bulgakov will not hesitate to put much of the guilt for the Russian Revolution onto Jewish treachery and parasitism, here reference to the Judas-Jewry connection is slight and tangential. The person of Judas instead is mirrored in the history of Russia, not directly, but as a spiritual principle, for while it is "forbidden...to directly compare the fates of separate personalities and whole nations, it is yet possible to place side by side...those spiritual principles which are revealed in them as an internal law of their life." After all, nations in the Old

---

[186] Bulgakov draws and develops a parallel between Satan asking God's permission to tempt Job, and Judas being used by the Devil as another conduit to bring about the downfall of Christ. He sees in both the paradox of God's seeming permission of evil, as well as the way in which evil-doers eventually become instrumental in bringing about a higher good. Intriguingly, Bulgakov refers to as this as an instance of Hegel's "cunning of reason" ("Judas Iscariot, Apostle-Traitor," p.352).

[187] "Judas Iscariot – Apostle-Traitor," p.353.

Testament were called after the names of individuals: Assur, Israel, Amalek were people and then nations, who took their fates from their founders. The twelve apostles stood in for the twelve tribes of Israel, and the seventy apostles for the seventy nations of the world. Likewise, Russia took its apostolic stamp from John.

But to this has been added now "the dark and burning spirit of Judas." But how, asks Bulgakov, can we make sense of two apostolic callings of Russia?[188] Perhaps by quantity – some, "a small remnant," remain true to the Johanine calling, while more have followed Judas? But this would be to assume that there are two parts of the nation which have nothing in common, to "cancel the nation as a spiritual and historical unity, having its common fate." Bulgakov explores two not wholly consistent answers to this dilemma, which mirror the answers we examined for Jewry.

On the one hand, Bulgakov seems by this analogy to be implying that the Johanine righteous remnant of martyrs and confessors who are keeping the faith in Soviet Russia will be the key to the salvation of the greater nation. This is a foretaste of his idea of Jewry's "sacred remnant" that we examined above[189]. But he does not develop this.

Instead, he begins to unfold a more fascinating and paradoxical vision of Russia's future, suggesting that Russia's new Judas-like apostleship (which it seems represents the whole nation) can be transformed by forces internal to the apostle-traitor himself. For "religious temptation can have a positive meaning… "[190] leading to greater self-knowledge and knowledge of one's dependence on God. "In the scales of Divine truth…human souls look different than when they are viewed by us from the outside. Isn't this what the Book of Job talks about, his friends' judgment over him, and God's judgment? And will not they be justified on Christ's judgment day who did not know Christ but yet served Him? Our homeland is now experiencing the temptation of Judas…it is betraying and crucifying Christ, and the crucified Christ is glorified in the martyrs and confessors…But this fight against Christ – precisely in its very struggle against God – preserves its religious character, stamped with the spirit of the persecutor Saul, who oppressed God's church…"

In other words Bulgakov's sympathetic portrait of Judas allows him now to find in the apostle-traitor's depth the same well-meant zeal which would be seen in the Pharisee Saul, and then transformed, in Saint Paul. Judas' outcome was not predestined in the crude sense. His intentions, wrapped in the Judaic apocalyptic Bulgakov analyzed as the roots of socialism more than two decades before, were after all benign. Judas can become a new Paul: and here lies the hope for Russia.

Thus, at the end of this essay Bulgakov sees the hope of Russian salvation not in those who have remained true to Christ, but in the misplaced zeal of

---

[188] The same question can be asked of Jewry: who is really representative – Jewish Bolsheviks, the "religious pillar," or secular Jews?
[189] i.e. the idea that the sacred remnant is straightforwardly Jewish Christians.
[190] Ibid.pp. 360-361.

those who are serving atheism with all their strength. Bulgakov's sympathetic portrait of Judas turns him upside down in comparison to more two-dimensional traditional appraisals of the apostle-traitor. So: those at the helm of Soviet communism are indeed seen by Bulgakov as Judases: but Judases who hold in their soul the possibility of Russia's Christ-embracing future: "in Judas more essential and unshatterable must be reckoned not his treachery, but his apostleship. He disowned the first by repenting, and the second is inseparable from him even in his fall. Apostleship also cannot be taken away from the Russian people…"[191]

This is an extraordinary reading of Judas, and indeed of Russian history. From the point of view of the present discussion, what is surprising and somewhat hurtful is the contrast Bulgakov's analysis of Russian Bolshevism presents to his picture of Jewish Bolshevism. In Russian Bolshevism, Bulgakov sees godlessness and a deceptive belief in earthly paradise. But Russian Bolshevism's very zealousness becomes for him a redeeming quality, the zeal of a Saul on the road to Damascus. In this there are clear continuities with those sentiments expressed in his diary: "And this religious-revolutionary, apocalyptic feeling of 'interuptedness'… allies me intrinsically with revolution and even – *horrible dictu* – with Russian

---

[191] Ibid.pp. 363. The idea that Russia is irrevocably chosen puts Bulgakov in the tradition of Slavophile Messianism. The sophiological inflection of his analysis in which the entire people has a fleshly stamp of apostolic chosenness which, presumably, all who are born into it inherit, borders on a risky linking of nationality and belief which would make Orthodoxy an automatic attribute of Russianness. Nonetheless, it would be artificial to ignore the deep influence a person's culture plays in shaping their most intimate beliefs, and Bulgakov avoids chauvinism by his emphasis on the openness of the nation to new influences and new blood (people). The impression, though, is that Bulgakov, like Soloviev, has very much Judaized his reading of Russian destiny. He admits to this Judaizing tendency, as we have seen; nonetheless, this "carnal Judaizing" does partially feed into the charge – so close to the surface of Russian consciousness – that there is something a little too Old Testament, i.e. too *zhidovstvuyushchi*, in this analysis; cf. ch.4, discussion of Khoruzhy's detection of Judaizing elements in Silver Age neo-Platonism. (On the other hand, the identification of nation and Orthodoxy in a similar way can be found in less controversial and more "mainstream" modern Orthodox thinkers, among Russians and non-Russians. As regards the latter, cf. Justin Popovich and Nicolai Velimirovich, both canonized by the Serbian Orthodox Church. The latter, in particular, in *Through the Prison Window*, writes of Europe as a Christian continent which has betrayed its chosenness, in terms very similar to Bulgakov. Many have seen Velimirovich as anti-Semitic, for his denunciation of ancient Jewish treachery against Christ – but it should be borne in mind that his rhetoric against secular, Enlightenment-influenced Europeans as contemporary "Jewish traitors," i.e. a Chosen (Christian) People who have rejected their Chosenness, is far sharper than his remarks about Jews, so that most of his anti-Jewish remarks are in fact anti-European and not directed against "Jews" per se at all. As in Bulgakov, there is a "Judaic" bond – almost genealogical – between Europe and Christian faith. Cf. Svyatitel' Nicolai Serbskii, *Skvoz' tyuremnoe okno*. Moscow: Izdatel'stvo Moskovskogo Podvorya Svyato-Troitskoy Sergievoy Lavry, 2006.)

bolshevism..." One writer, S.A. Levitsky, tellingly wrote of Bulgakov's transition from Marxist to Christian using the following words: "In those years (1901-1906)...a spiritual turn-around takes place in him. From Saul he becomes Paul. Bulgakov leaves the ranks of the social-democratic party and becomes rather a member of the constitutional-monarchic party."[192] This insightful description can serve to remind us of the deep autobiographical roots in this analysis of Judas.

Given that earlier in his diary, and then later in the war-time essays, Bulgakov had analyzed Bolshevism as an alien Jewish (or at best Jewish-German) imposition on Russia, another oddness of this essay is the analysis of Bolshevism here as entirely Russian. This is really quite a puzzle.

Thus it does not take much effort – given Bolshevism, given Judas, given Bulgakov – to shift from thinking about a Russian apostle-traitor, to a Jewish apostle-traitor. Indeed Bulgakov, as we saw briefly, links Israel and Russia intimately in his mind[193]. He believed that the Jewish people could find their greatest ally in the Russian nation. In terms of spiritual destiny, he believed that Russia and Israel were the true pair, even though many pointed to America as the real homeland of the Jews.

Taking Bulgakov on his own terms, then, it is hard to resist applying all that he says about Judas "who makes clear...especially the history of the Chosen People" to the nation most associated with the name of the apostle-traitor – Israel.

What is the parallel, explicitly stated? Looking at Jewry with the eyes of love and hope with which Bulgakov gazed at the Soviet Russia that had so disappointed him and yet was so native to him, still flesh of his flesh, and in a hidden way akin to his spirit, we would see the most representative element of Jewry in that "third pillar," namely religious Jewry. This is the part of Jewry whose blood is akin to Christ's, whose culture was the culture into which Christ was born, whose language Christ spoke, and in whose land Christ lived.

Out of the loins of this section of Jewry will come Elijah and the two witnesses. Thus Torah-observant Jewry is the mysteriously *hidden* sacred remnant of Jewry, the very last place a Christian looks to redemption, but precisely the locus out of which redemption must spring, and which is thus

---

[192] Sergei Levitsky, *Ocherki po istorii russkoy philosofii* (Moscow:Kanon, 1996).One might argue that he not only left behind Marxism, but then had to overcome the temptation of a sectarian "new Christianity" with chiliastic pretensions to found the Kingdom of God on earth, which he rejected in moving away from Merezhkovsky's influence.

[193] In a sense, therefore, while our present task is to read Jewry in the light of Russia, one could just as well go back over the war-time essays and read Russia in the light of Jewry. For if one were to read this essay from a more "Judeocentric" perspective, what would be interesting is how Judaic ideas continue to shape Russian thinkers' ideas of their own nationhood. Bulgakov is anxious to emphasize that the (Judaic) mantle of Messiah-nation belongs to Russia and not Germany. Unlike the Nazis (and other European nations who have coveted the title of Chosen People since the Reformation) his innovation – in places, at least – is to believe that Jews can continue to be a Messiah-nation, too; furthermore, the presence of Jews in Russia is not a contradiction, but a confirmation of, Russia's Messianic status.

preserved – for all its rejection of Christ – by God's love. Is there not in this a consistency with Bulgakov's brief, though undeveloped, characterization of religious Jewry? Bulgakov's point about Russian Judases could ring true of the Christ-less followers of the Law: "And will not they be justified on Christ's judgment day who did not know Christ but yet served Him?"[194] through their well-meant devotion to the God of Israel, and their devotion to Israel itself? As Bulgakov looked at the Bolsheviks, who thirsted for social justice, so a Christian can look at observant Jewry, with its thirst for redemption – recognizing, too, that they are necessary for the redemption of the world.

In closing this discussion of the Russian and Jewish Judases, it should be said that there is no particular necessity to choose between the two different interpretations of that Jewish sacred remnant. Bulgakov leans very much towards Gregory of Nyssa's position that all will be saved, including the Devil. Therefore, the idea that the sacred remnant is "Messianic Jews," as proposed in the preceding section can go together with the idea there is another portion of Jewry, zealots of the Law who reject Christ, but who will also be rewarded for having avoided the sin of lukewarm indifferentism. This dichotomy is more in keeping with Bulgakov's own words about Russian fate: resurrection will come both from the Johanine remnant of believers (read: Judeo-Christians, "Messianic" or otherwise); but also from the Judas commissars (read: Zionist Orthodox Jews[195] in the Jewish State). Both are, each in their different ways, seen from different perspectives, tools of God's salvation, perhaps in different stages of "hiddenness."

Conclusion

We have thus come to the end of our examination of Bulgakov's "Judeology." Though only a fraction of his output was devoted to exclusively Jewish questions, these writings mirror much in Bulgakov's evolution from a young Solovievan philosopher of neo-Christianity to a mature theologian of Sophia, whose work continues to inspire many.

While, of course, one of the great undecided questions in the study of Bulgakov is the place of Sophia in Orthodox theology, from the narrower perspective of this chapter, another controversial issue which Bulgakov left to his spiritual heirs was the – for him – closely related question of how Christianity should relate to a crying absence in her very heart. For if the divine-human Church should embrace all of humanity, where is that foundation-stone of humanity, Jewry?

Bulgakov's proposal that there must be a new Judeo-Christianity was, of course, not entirely novel – Soloviev had wrestled with the same question in his

---

[194] Did not Bulgakov himself hint at a knowledge of the Son of God in contemporary Judaism when he seems to argue that the Kabbalah contains an – albeit obscurely expressed – doctrine of the fully divine Son of Man?

[195] I choose the category of Zionist Orthodox Jews partly in response to one such contemporary reading of Bulgakov which I discuss shortly below.

essay on Rabinowich, and Alexander I founded a society for Israelite Christians that he thought would be the kernel of a mass influx of Jews into the Church. Nonetheless, Bulgakov's own grappling with this issue is profounder than Soloviev's, even though it is enmeshed in contradictions, some of them inherent in the issue itself, which goes to the very heart of the mystery of Christ – as Bulgakov makes clear.

Later in this book, we will look at the thought of Lev Karsavin, who in some ways converged on Bulgakov's vision of a Judeo-Christianity[196]. And we will have reason to return to this aspect of Bulgakov's thought in the conclusion, when we consider Alexander Men. His thought was not only indebted to Soloviev and Bulgakov. His position as the (Jewish-born) priest of a parish with an unprecedentedly large number of Jewish Christians gave his thought on this issue a relevance which affects his admirers today.

As far as Bulgakov's anti-Semitism is concerned, one gets a sense that as with his contemporary "immunizing dose" of Catholicism during the Civil War, he overcame it and used his illness to good effect. Bulgakov was a devoted patriot, a religious mystic and a monarchist: these are factors which in Russia have often gone hand in hand with anti-Semitism, and the case of Florensky provides an eery counterfactual to Bulgakov's possible development. Leaving aside complex theological formulations, one of the key differences between Bulgakov's and Florensky's writings on Jewry is that the former passed through hate to love, and the latter ended with hate[197].

Furthermore, Jewry awoke in Bulgakov a self-reflective strain of thought, causing him to ponder on the transnational nature of Christianity. His meditations on Judas, in which Jewry hovers in the background, also inspired him to a piercing critique of Russian destiny and awoke in him mercy, albeit without concession to their ideology, for the regime that had expelled him from his beloved homeland.

Finally, as with several Russian thinkers, his own experience of exile deepened his sympathy with Jewry, and gave him a sense of the chosenness of Jewry which can add new dimensions to our understanding of St.Paul's meditation on Jewish destiny in his letter to the Romans.

Interestingly, these aspects of Bulgakov have recently found sympathy in the writings of two contemporary Russian Jews, and it might be appropriate in rounding off this chapter to add further perspective to the debate, as it continues in contemporary

---

[196] L.I.Vasilenko stated the view that Karsavin rejected the possibility of a Judeo-Christianity due to the fact that as a historian he was more aware of the inappropriateness of such a vision: "Fr. Sergei was not a historian, but he could have taken note of the fact that the Judeo-Christian community in Jerusalem, headed by James the brother of the Lord, where the norms of piety accepted by Jews in those days were rigidly observed, was nationally defined. Some years after the martyr's death of James it did not preserve the purity of faith and lost its significance." Cf.L.I. Vasilenko, *Vvedenie v russkuyu religioznuyu filosofiyu* (Moscow: PSTGU, 2006),307. However, Karsavin's views on this issue were more complex, cf.ch.5.

[197] At least as far as Jews were concerned, cf. ch.4.

form, about Bulgakov's attitude to the Jews by glancing at these opinions[198].

Bulgakov in two contemporary Russian-Jewish interpretations
One reaction is that of the Russian-American Jewish scientist, Yuri Okunev, who has written a book on the meaning of Jewish history called *The Axis of World History*[199]. The phrase is taken from Bulgakov (and ultimately Soloviev's) characterization of Jewish destiny.

In the opening chapters of the book, Okunev devotes a section to "Bulgakov's Law," which he derives using a direct quotation from an essay that we examined above: this is the iron-clad historical law that anyone who persecutes the Jews will call down inevitable disaster and defeat upon their heads. For Okunev, this conviction of Bulgakov's is taken as more evidence of Bulgakov's lofty and prophetic status. What is interesting is that the same essay from which this phrase is taken is also rife with the sort of anti-Jewish rhetoric we encountered earlier. But to Okunev, this simply does not seem to count.

Another thinker of Russian-Soviet background, the Israeli historian Raya (Raisa) Epstein, in her article "Israel and the post-Zionists: a nation at risk" also enthuses about Bulgakov[200]. However, she is aware of the charge of anti-Semitism that has been leveled against Bulgakov and takes time to refute it with some indignity. In this she repeats the attitude of Kartashev, writing in 1920 in the Berlin Jewish Tribune.

"This intellectual priest," she writes, "very sharply criticized the Jews who participated in the Bolshevik Revolution. His explanation for their utopian-messianic radicalism was that, having essentially religious souls, they found in Marxism a quasi-religious substitute for their authentic religion that they had abandoned and betrayed. He was regarded by many assimilated Jews as one of the fathers of Russian intellectual anti-Semitism. This is a gross misconception."

Epstein in fact uses Bulgakov to support her own ideological struggle against the hegemony in Israel, as she perceives it, of American-style individualist liberal democracy in favor of a "patriotic, nationalist" model of democracy that she sees as being closer to the European model and more in keeping with true and unashamed Zionist ideology. In addition, Bulgakov becomes a spokesman in Epstein for the place of national religion in the political arena.

This is an extremely interesting approach. In one sense Epstein, the religious Zionist, has understood Bulgakov perfectly and is absolutely aware that he would not have supported her final step in favor of Jewish religious and political

---

[198] As far as other non-Jewish readers of Bulgakov on Judaism are concerned, Nikita Struve, a professor at the St. Sergius Institute in Paris has written a summary and appraisal of these articles called "S.Bulgakov et la question juive," but I have not been able to get hold of the article. Another reader is Rowan Williams, in *Sergii Bulgakov: Towards a Russian Political Theology*. According to Williams, Struve exempts Bulgakov of the charge of anti-Semitism; Williams' feelings are more mixed.

[199] Yuri Okunev, *Os' vsemirnoi istorii*. Moscow: Isskustvo Rossii, 2004.

[200] Raya Epstein, "Post-Zionism and democracy," in *Israel and the post-Zionists: a nation at risk*, edited by Shlomo Sharan. Sussex Academic Press with ACPR publishers, 2003.

independence, with no regard for Christianity. But, as we have seen, Bulgakov's enthusiasm for the Russian monarchy as a mainstay of the nation's soul, as well as his mystical dissatisfaction with *laissez-faire* political and economic liberalism makes Epstein's translation of Bulgakov into the contemporary Israeli context highly plausible and indeed fascinating. It stands as another example of the influence Russian thought continues to have in the post-Soviet era on Jewish and Israeli reality, just as it once did in the early days of Zionism.

In another sense, though, it might seem that Epstein has crucially misunderstood Bulgakov. Jews for Bulgakov do have religious souls, but their behavior was not a result of their abandoning their "authentic religion." Bulgakov's eventual explanation of Jewish Bolshevism and its relationship to Judaism is, unfortunately, not as logical as that – as we demonstrated above.

And yet we also saw that, looked at from another angle, Epstein may not be that far off the mark: our own claim was that the covert logic of Bulgakov's thought demands some sort of recognition of Judaism and Jewry on its own "sacred materialist" terms. The above reading, if taken seriously, would align us in a very real sense with Raya Epstein. For the fact is that in contemporary Judaism, Orthodox Judaism has become something of a "sacred remnant." If in Bulgakov's day, Russian Jewry was for the most part traditionally observant, nowadays Orthodox Judaism is numerically in grave decline. In Israel, where Epstein is writing, the shape of the constitution bears the stamp of its secular, socialist origins. When she argues for a holistic-religious identity for the Jewish State, she is arguing for a strengthening of the core of religious Jewry and Judaism.

Therefore, in a paradoxical way, Epstein perhaps converges more fully with Bulgakov than seems the case at first glance: a "sacred remnant" of Orthodox Judaism in Israel, as repugnant to Christianity as this may be (to adopt frank Bulgakovian speech!), might nonetheless have attracted Bulgakov's approval – for this Saul can, as Bulgakov did on a personal level, one day, at the given time, transform in the twinkling of an eye into Paul.

So perhaps it should not be surprising to see a "hawkish" Zionist ideology justifying itself by reference to Bulgakov's political theology. In fact, perhaps the line from Bulgakov to Israeli politics is less surprising than, for example, the resurgence of interest in Bulgakov evinced by Rowan Williams' 1999 compilation of Bulgakov's earlier political-economic works, which bears the subtitle "Towards a Russian political theology," and is aimed at "those seeking a radical or Christian alternative to state socialism and the free market"[201]. Of course, Epstein's

---

[201] From the back-cover of Williams' volume. Williams, though, comments on "the impossibility of secular socialism – and implicitly, I think, the impossibility of secular politics overall for Bulgakov." Perhaps it would be more accurate to say, then, that the essays Williams has edited have more chance of having a concrete impact in the Israeli situation than that of Williams' own cultural context, namely, the British multicultural liberal polity. And this is due to the fact that Epstein is not just ideologically related to Bulgakov, but through successive waves of Russian-Jewish immigration, "genetically" related to him.

Bulgakovian political holism must provoke the same questions that Bulgakov's original political mysticism did: only this time these would concern not the place of minorities in the Russian Christian empire, but the place of minorities in the Israeli Jewish state.

One final point that is of interest concerns Epstein's tolerance for Bulgakov's "very sharp criticism" of Jewry. Perhaps, this might be due her Russian background. However, that explanation fails for Markish. Another factor, then, which might explain why Epstein is so warmly receptive to Bulgakov – and so ready to overlook his harsh rhetoric – is her own religious and political convictions, which bring her so close to the Russian Christian.

In this regard, while I have argued that Bulgakov's opinions were irresponsibly expressed given the atmosphere in Crimea during the Civil War, it is interesting to look at a contemporary Jewish theologian's criticism of secular Jewry, non-Russian this time. This is Michael Wyschogrod, whom we quoted in connection with his interest in Karl Barth.

Wyschogrod, in an essay called "Divine Election and Commandments" is defending the Jewish idea of an "election of the flesh" of the seed of Abraham, as against the Christian "election of the spirit." In the course of defining what this means, he notes the paradox that religious Jews are thrown together into a state of election with secular Jews simply by the fact of birth. He notes how hard it is for religious Jews committed to a divine covenant to live in necessary community with those who deny God's very existence, or who give Jewishness a completely opposite meaning – insisting, however, on the necessity of so living, as this is God's will. In one passage Wyschogrod writes the following:

> I also observe the 'Jewish' organizations, heavy with money and access to the media of public communication that only money can buy, for whom the Jew's relationship with God is a topic of very little interest. Instead, they are busy with such projects as the eradication of all manifestations of Christianity from American public life…to which they object…not so much because they are Christian as because they are religious and take seriously the Word of God as a genuine event in human history. They issue pronouncements on public issues, such as the birth control controversy, without even mentioning the rabbinic view of the matter, as if the Jewish point of view were self-evidently identical with the ideology of the social sciences or the liberalism of the *New York Post*.

Wyschogrod is on the "liberal" wing of Modern Orthodox Judaism[202]. Much harsher rhetoric can be found against secular Jewry by ultra-Orthodox figures – but it would never be published, still less in a non-Jewish language for non-Jews to read. But it can be seen that this criticism of secular Jewry, as with Epstein, overlaps with Bulgakov's criticism of atheistic Bolshevik Jews in the Russia of his time. In other words, some of Bulgakov's anti-Semitic rhetoric is clearly

---

[202] Liberal, that is, in his willingness to engage in dialogue with Christian theology.

anti-secular rhetoric – although unfortunately this is not always clear, even to Bulgakov himself, it would seem[203].

In sum, Epstein and Okunev show that Bulgakov can still find a resonance among Russian Jews. Wyschogrod shows that, while there are undoubtedly anti-Semitic elements in Bulgakov, this is not to say that all his criticism of some sections of Jewry is automatically off the mark. With Epstein and Wyschogrod, we can agree that some of it is to the point. But is there anything prophetic in criticizing the faults of others? Is that not too easy? Perhaps Wyschogrod goes too far when he remarks of Barth's criticisms of Jewry that "it is not for gentiles to see the sins of Israel. It is not for gentiles to call Israel to its mission, to feel morally superior to it." After all, Israel is still human and part of the human community – and the gentiles are also chosen now, according to the Christian. The Christian would recognize that it is not for a Christian to feel superior to *anyone*, while recognizing the particular dangers superiority has in regard to the people of Israel.

Still, as we saw, Bulgakov would come to concur fully with the sentiments expressed a little later by Wyschogrod in his essay: "But woe unto those gentiles who become the rod of God's chastisement of Israel, the instrument of this anger, the satisfied bystanders of the punishment." While I believe he had this awareness in the Crimea, it seems that at times he teetered on the brink of being a "satisfied bystander" of the "punishment" that the godless Jews were receiving, and even succumbed to the temptation to contribute to this retribution.

However, his own exile, and then the horrors of the Nazi period would bring him to a realization of just how inadmissible such a position was. Among the Russian thinkers, in fact, he was one of a small number who expressed himself on the emerging Holocaust. This, as well as the rich suggestiveness of his concern for the "Jewish question," indicates that his writings have not lost their relevance for Christians today, both inside his native Russia and outside it.

---

[203] There was a Jewish section of the communist party in the Ukraine in 1920, the Yevsekstia, which imposed a ban on Hebrew activity in Russia. Their hounding of Zionists was one of the factors that caused Bialik to finally leave Odessa for Palestine. (See Hamutal Bar-Yosef, "Bialik and the Russian Revolutions," in *Jews in Eastern Europe* 1(29)(1996):5-31.).In this sense, one atheistic-Bolshevik part of Jewry did indeed persecute another part. However, whether this fact mitigates Bulgakov's pamphleteering is another question. That Bulgakov was to some extent aware of these nuances, and supported the Zionists over the Bolsheviks, is evident, however, and could lend support Epstein's reading.

THREE

N. Berdyaev, M. Gershenzon and L. Shestov:
Jewish and Russian nihilists of the Spirit

Three

The three pessimists

As the First World War dragged on, the Russian "spiritual intelligentsia" was divided as to what meaning it held for the future of their country. Many believed a victory would lead to a reassertion of Russia and its deepest values. A new Russian era in European and world history would be initiated. The defeat of Germany would be a defeat of militarism, materialism and positivism. What values Russia would offer in its place depended on where the intellectual stood on the philosophical-political spectrum. However, not everyone was so convinced of the benefits of war.

The writer Yevgeniya Gertsyk in her *Recollections*[1] divided her circle into two groups: pessimists and optimists. The latter included symbolist poet Vyacheslav Ivanov, Sergei Bulgakov and philosopher Vladimir Ern. The former included historian-critic Mikhail Gershenzon, philosopher-writer Lev Shestov, and the Christian philosopher Nicolai Berdyaev.

Lev Shestov lost his son in the fighting. For him the War was thus a time of personal loss and world-shaking gloom. Berdyaev, too, though he had started off in synchrony with the jingoism of his circle also began to see the destruction as senseless and to doubt the possibility of a Russian victory. In particular, he began to fear that a defeat by Germany would mean a disastrous victory for Bolshevism.

By 1916, Gershenzon – a sensitive, deeply intelligent and generous man whose house on the Arbat hosted a cultural salon for all manner of cultural figures – had become disenchanted in quite a different way. He went from optimism about the fighting to stark rejection of it. On one occasion, he blurted out to the poet Bely: "Down with the war!" He expressed the view that deserters should be welcomed back, that Russia should pull out of this capitalist farce.

Gershenzon had been the editor and organizer of the sensation-producing *Landmarks* anthology of 1909. His own contribution had contained a phrase that provoked a minor uproar: "*In our current situation*, we [the intelligentsia] cannot even start dreaming of merging with the people – we should fear them more than all the punishments handed out by the authorities and bless the powers that be, who alone with their bayonets and prisons are still protecting us from the wrath of the people."

This was taken by the left-leaning intelligentsia to be some sort of reactionary-conservative blessing of tsarist autocracy, and it sounded very strange coming from a Jew – especially one born in Kishinev, scene of two devastating pogroms in 1903 and 1905[2], that had been stirred up and condoned

---

[1] Yevgeniya Gertsyk, *Vospominaniya*. Paris: YMCA-Press, 1973.
[2] It is true that Gershenzon left Kishinev in the late 1880s, but he continued to visit his mother and one can assume he continued to feel touched by events in his home-town.

by populist right-wing papers and political organizations.

But in 1917, it was the turn of his fellow *Landmarks* contributors to be shocked when – in a seemingly inexplicable *volte-face* – he came out in favor of the October Revolution and the Bolsheviks, throwing himself into cultural activity in support of the new Soviet state (among other things, he organized the Union of Writers). The following year, under the editorship of Piotr Struve, all the former contributors produced a new collection condemning the Revolution, *From the Depth*[3]. Gershenzon was noticeable by his absence.

Berdyaev, who had been a regular visitor to Gershenzon's house, became estranged from him. Gershenzon's daughter and granddaughter testified in their memoirs that the main reason for the fall-out was Berdyaev's anti-Semitism[4].

Lev Shestov, meanwhile, had been approached by Anatoly Lunacharsky, the new Soviet minister of culture with an offer to publish his latest book. A symbolic half-page in the preface outlining his support for Marxism would be mandatory, but other than that the book would be off the press in no time.

Many thought that Shestov (born Lev-Judah Shwartzmann) would agree. His rebellious spirit, his nihilistic rejection of old values, his belief in the "Scythian" nature of Russia, and his indifference to the War made him seem like a perfect potential neophyte for the new Soviet cultural reality. But Shestov turned Lunacharsky down in a blink and moved back to his native Kiev to escape unpleasant repercussions. Bulgakov found him a job teaching at the University alongside him.

All three of the "pessimists," Berdyaev, Shestov and Gershenzon had been close friends before the Revolution. While Gershenzon and Berdyaev fell out, relations remained untouched otherwise. As we saw, in 1923 it was Gershenzon who wrote to Shestov in Berlin expressing disbelief about reports of Bulgakov's anti-Semitic activity in the Crimea. And Shestov continued to enjoy a deep friendship with Berdyaev – and this despite the fact that Berdyaev often reproached him with Jewish nihilism, and urged him to solve his problems through conversion to Christianity.

The question arises as to how true Berdyaev's (and others') belief was that Gershenzon's Jewishness was a contributing factor in his support of the Revolution and Bolshevik ideology. Likewise, although Shestov did not support the Soviets, Berdyaev found Shestov's self-styled philosophy of "groundlessness" and irrationalism to be a fruit of the same Jewish rejection of values that he had detected in Gershenzon. Another question that needs answering is why Shestov and Berdyaev maintained deep respect and sympathy for each other,

---

[3] *Landmarks* (Rus. Vekhi) and *From the Depths* (Rus. Iz glubiny) will be cited below from: A. Yakovleva, edit. *Vekhi. Iz Glubiny*. Moscow: Pravda, 1991.

[4] As the discussion below shows, this judgment is certainly an oversimplification. However, the pressure-boiler of the Revolution and the agonizing dilemma over whether or not to support the Bolshevik coup in October 1917 certainly put an unnatural strain on the concept of Jewishness at this time, and it is telling that Gershenzon's family chose to formulate the break in these terms.

while similar rhetoric shattered the ties with Gershenzon.[5]

To answer these questions, we will start by examining the beliefs of Berdyaev and Gershenzon, and then consider the rather unique figure of Lev Shestov.

Berdyaev and Gershenzon
Nicolai Berdyaev

Nicolai Berdyaev was born three years later than Sergei Bulgakov into a military-aristocratic family in Kiev with French and Polish roots. He followed a similar intellectual trajectory to Bulgakov, passing from Marxism through Idealism to Christian belief. Although close to Bulgakov – the two associated so closely in Moscow in the fist decade of the twentieth century that they were known as the Dioscurus brothers – there were important differences between them, both in terms of their personalities and their beliefs.

Berdyaev never became a monarchist and reacted with amused skepticism to Bulgakov's growing respect for the tsar and Holy Russia – a difference which caused a certain amount of tension between the two friends. In addition, the philosophical outlook he developed after passing through his Kantian phase was of a personalistic, existentialist variety. Christianity for him came to be a matter of deep, inner choice by each individual and the embrace of Christ was a personal liberation.

This can be seen in what each man took from Soloviev's philosophy. Bulgakov was attracted by the idea of all-unity and made it his life's task to develop and correct the doctrine of Sophia. Berdyaev, however, rejected this mystical aspect of Soloviev's heritage with impatience – seeing it as metaphysical mumbo-jumbo. He took instead for his inspiration the concept of the god-man, which he gave a Christian humanist reading, seeing in it an insight into the complete freedom and uniqueness of each human personality.

More attractive to him in his first Christian awakening was Merezhkovsky's reworking of Christianity: inspired by and inspiring the aesthetics of the symbolist movement, Merekhovsky's circle believed that the twentieth century demanded a revived Christianity that would be a Third Testament, embracing the way of the Spirit rather than the Father or the Son. Merezhkovsky and his wife Zinaida Gippius even went to the extent of inventing a new Eucharistic ritual, where he presided over the communicants[6].

---

[5] One of the *Landmarks* and *From the Depths* contributors who remained in touch with Gershenzon after the Revolution was Semyon Frank, one of the other two Jewish contributors (in addition to Izgoev-Lange) to the collection – despite his conversion to Christianity in 1913 and rejection of the anti-Christian utopian nihilism of the Revolution. We will consider their relationship in the chapter on Frank. (Izgoev-Lange also subsequently converted to Christianity).

[6] In one ritual, a converted Jew and Jewess mixed pin-pricks of their own blood with water and distributed it to the assembled. This became a plank of scandal during the Beilis trial, Russia's most notorious twentieth century case of the blood libel against

While Berdyaev later reacted against the arbitrary and stylized nature of what he came to see as a distortion of Christianity, for the first decade of the twentieth century he was an enthusiastic admirer of Merezhkovsky, and even in 1916 was writing admiringly of the liberating possibilities of Merezhkovsky's "chiliasm of the intelligentsia" which had introduced a thirst for "a common life in the Spirit, a collective ecstasy" into the deadened Church of the time[7].

This emphasis on the freedom of the Spirit remained very much a part of his later more Orthodox belief. Indeed, this inspiration by the Spirit was shared by Mikhail Gershenzon and the writer Andrey Bely. The latter looked to Gershenzon as an intellectual mentor, and – to give an idea of the ties that bound Berdyaev and Gershenzon in the first decade of the twentieth century – while Berdyaev reacted cautiously to some of Bely's Gnostic excesses, he too hailed Bely as a prophet of the Russian soul.

Another aspect of Berdyaev's developing thought which makes his fall-out with Gershenzon less predictable is that after his discovery of Christianity, Berdyaev refused to play the role of penitent neophyte turning his back on his past and bowing to the Church's authority in every matter. He liked to think that, in contrast to other returnees, he had not become a pious straight man[8] but remained his old non-conformist self.

Certainly his emphasis on the call of the Spirit and personal freedom, as opposed to a Bulgakovian sophianic concept of the mystical body of believers, often made it difficult for him to fit in with the hierarchical and conservative Russian Church of which he had become a member. His personality and philosophy made the idea of belonging to *any* collective a strain on his imagination – certainly, unlike with Bulgakov, there would be no talk of a Holy Christian Russia, or indeed of any holy nation, be it Byzantium – or as we will see later, the Jews.

Thus he frequently criticized what many believers would have seen as fundamental institutions of the Church, and was renowned for standing by his conscience over the demands of unassimilated ecclesiastical dogma: he always refused, for example, to accept the notion of eternal damnation. For this reason, the contention of a recent scholar[9] that the otherwise progressive Berdyaev's hostile

---

Jews. This incident and Rozanov's involvement in it will be discussed in the chapter on Rozanov and Florensky.

[7] N.A.Berdyaev. "Tipy religioznoy mysly v Rossii"//Sobr. Soch. Paris, 1989, p.500. Berdyaev's praise of chiliasm in 1916 is ironic: in the following years he would link Judaism and chiliasm as a reproach to the former in the same way as Bulgakov.

[8] The same Yevgeniya Gertsyk recalls that "he never lost his sense of humor after his conversion" and they would often share a smile over "the supremely pious Novoselov and Bulgakov."

[9] E.Y Fedotova, "Vzglyady N.Berdyaeva na 'yevreiskii vopros', ix sootnesenie s traditsionnym khristianskim bogosloviem i novymi issledovaniyami," in *N.A.Berdyaev i yedinstvo Yevropeiskogo dukha*, edited by V.Porus, 132-142, (Moscow: Biblieisko-bogoslovskii Institut sv. Apostola Andreya,2007).

expressions regarding Jews and Judaism were a result of a neophyte enthusiasm in Church matters are highly implausible. Other reasons must be sought.

Even well into his Christian phase he continued to buckle against conformity. "Official Orthodoxy," he wrote on one occasion, having in mind the Russian church, "long ago became a pernicious, anti-Christian heresy."[10] Monks, monasteries and the church hierarchy were "funereal," and provoked melancholy and sadness in him. This was linked to his Merezhkovskian belief that the asceticism of historical church Christianity needed to be superseded by a new erotic ethic which would include aspects of ancient pagan fertility cults – though, like the Merezhkovskys this combined with a distaste for the institution of marriage: Berdyaev, like Bely and Blok, had a Platonic relationship with his wife[11].

Not surprisingly he attracted the condemnation of church figures, to whom he was more of a puzzle than Merezhkovsky. The latter rejected official Christianity in full, and believed his own (Platonic) ménage-a-trois[12] and the Religious-Philosophical Society that emerged from it would form the kernel of a new church of the Third Testament[13]. Berdyaev, however, eventually came to place his hopes in the Orthodox Church, but combined this new belief with elements of his old Merezhkovskian Gnosticism.

Thus one priest berated Berdyaev for showing wholesale contempt for Russian Orthodoxy: "If in the heat of the moment you had reproved one or another hierarch, or one or another phenomenon in Russian Church life, that would not have been offensive – righteous anger, no matter how severe, is always understandable…But your article is not full of righteous anger, but of contempt and judgment of the whole Russian Church – the question involuntarily occurs to me: are you with the Church, or are you against her?"[14]

This outspokenness – which he gave vent to in public and private – was characteristic of Berdyaev: he often expressed himself harshly and categorically, in a way which provoked Bulgakov to invent a verb to describe these outbursts

---

[10] Berdyaev, *Sobraniye Sochenenii* 3, "Tipy religioznoy mysly v Rossii," cited in in V.Vasilenko, *Vvedenie*, 267.

[11] His wife, in fact, though baptized, was of Jewish origin – though this seems not to have effected his pronouncements on Jews and Jewry. (Of course, such a judgment is rather difficult to make, the more so given the distance in time and lack, for me at least, of more information about their relationship).

[12] The third member was Filosofov. The Platonic nature of the threesome was comprised by Merezhkovsky himself, who on at least one occasion, succumbed to the temptations of female admirers and brought them into his church of the sacred flesh through a form of non-Platonic communion.

[13] Merezhkovsky drew a parallel between pagan and Christian "trinities:" in Canaan and Egypt there was Baal (Father)/Astarte(Mother)/Adonis(Son). Christianity's Trinity had been imperfectly realized in history, and the third member of the Trinity was looked upon by Merezhkovsky sometimes as a mother, who feminizes masculine Judaism and Christianity, or as a figure who contained both sexual polarities, and would thus transcend sex in a new type of love.

[14] Priest S. Chetverikov, in Vasilenko (2006): 268.

of self-assertive truth-telling: *berdyaevsvovat'*, or to Berdyaevize.

This is not an accident: for Berdyaev the connection between truth and personal experience was inextricable and much of his philosophy welled up from within him. The uniqueness of the human personality was the cornerstone of this philosophy. He held that no institution, secular or sacred, and any fact, sociological or scientific or historical, can explain away or reduce the uniqueness and mystery of the human personality.

Further, it is from the human personality that the new and inexplicable springs into the world, in defiance of any natural laws – and in defiance, in fact, of God Himself. For both God and humans have their origins in the "pre-divine" abyss from which freedom springs – an idea which he took from the German mystic, Meister Ekhardt.

And, in Berdyaev's solution of the problem of theodicy, God thus has no control over the evil that freedom gives rise to. Personality, and the freedom of personality, are supreme for Berdyaev. Even "God waits for the revelation of creativity from man...," and as a result, traditional Christian thought needs to shift emphasis away from the supremacy of God, for: "Not only does man need God, but God needs man."[15]

Both of these beliefs once again owe much to his earlier involvement with Merezhkovsky. The latter had argued that the new religious consciousness must dialectically incorporate the opposite tendencies of past spirituality: Christianity and paganism, spirit and flesh, heaven and earth must all be transcended in a synthesis which combines them. As late as 1916 Berdyaev had written approvingly of Merezhkovsky's belief that the new consciousness must even mix Christ and anti-Christ, so as to give man "his final religious freedom"[16].

These doctrines are every bit as controversial as Bulgakov's sophiology – in fact, they clash with Orthodox doctrine in an even more obvious way. Still, Berdyaev was an inspiration to intellectuals estranged from the Church: he seemed to demonstrate that one could keep one's integrity while being a believer. And, for all the idiosyncracies of his philosophical declarations, Berdyaev did take his Christian faith – and its importance for his vision of Russia – with utmost seriousness.

After his emigration to the West, in fact, Berdyaev found himself in the odd position of being looked to as a spokesman for the Orthodox viewpoint, and as a typical religious Russian – among Western Europeans, of course, who sometimes took his heterodoxy and wild prophetic stance as par for the course for someone from the exotic East. This troubled Berdyaev[17], not least because

---

[15] Quotes from *The Meaning of the Creative Act*.

[16] Berdyaev, Sub specie aeternitatis, p.343, quoted in Gaidenko 2008, p.336-7. See Gaidenko for further discussion of the link between Merezhkovsky and Berdyaev. P.P. Gaidenko, *Vladimir Soloviev i filosofia serebryanogo veka*. Moscow: Progress-traditsia, 2001.

[17] Cf. on this, Gyorgy Fedotov, "Berdyaev Myslitel'," first published in Novii Zhurnal, XIX, New York, 1948. Also at: http://russianway.rchgi.spb.ru./Berdyaev/46_Fedotov.pdf

it led people to pay less attention to the content of his philosophy. Indeed, as a philosopher he sank into oblivion in the West after his death.

Within his own church, the reception was less warm: Anthony Khrapovitsky once called Berdyaev a "prisoner of freedom" due to his exaltation of freedom over God and the effects it had on his philosophy and life. On the other hand, in Russia Berdyaev belonged to the parish of Alexei Mechev, the priest-elder who founded a brotherhood in the heart of communist Moscow and always defended Berdyaev's freedom of expression.

In emigration, he also remained a faithful parishioner of the Moscow Patriarchate. And today, the dictum of S.Levitsky that "he violated the letter of Christian dogma, but always remained faithful to the spirit of Christianity"[18] seems to be broadly accepted: both in liberal and conservative church circles, his books are widely read and he has even been compared for theological originality to the great Orthodox theologian and saint, Gregory Palamas.[19]

However, as we will see below, it was not just church figures who were made uneasy by Berdyaev. He was engaged in a decades-long argument with Lev Shestov as to the philosophical integrity of his thought. In the debate about objectivity and subjectivity in the pursuit of religious knowledge, it is not surprising that the discussion turned to the deepest Jewish and Christian identities of these two Russian "God-seekers." It was a "sharp but friendly" discussion that was unsatisfactorily resolved only by Shestov's death.

Mikhail Gershenzon
Turning to Gershenzon, we can observe certain similarities in the interests of the historian and the religious philosopher. Certainly, in that crucial time "between the revolutions"[20] both were immersed in the brave new world of the Moscow intelligentsia. That is to say, both men to a greater or lesser extent, exercised the vocation of intellectual in the prophetic mode, whereby the writing of books was simultaneously an inspiration by the Spirit and a searching out of the destinies of Russia.

Mikhail Gershenzon, like Berdyaev, was born on the south western fringe of the Russian empire, and like him was geographically and ethnically removed from the Russian heartland. However, his journey to Moscow and the world of Russian literature, history, philosophy and meditations on the fate of Russia was much more twisted and lengthy and his emergence there more surprising.

As a Jew from an Orthodox family, there were financial and administrative barriers to his desire for an intellectual career. Jews were not allowed to reside or study in Moscow without invitation – unless they were baptized. When

---

[18] S.Levitsky, *Ocherki po-istorii russkoy filosofii*.
[19] Gyorgy Kochetkov, "Genii Berdyaeva i Tserkov." Paper presented at the First Berdyaev Lectures, Kiev, 28 May, 1991.
[20] The title of Andrey Bely's reminiscences (Andrei Bely, "Vospominaniya.Mezhdu dvukh revolyutsii." In *Andrei Bely. Izbrannaya proza*, ed. L.A. Smirnova, 297-439. Moscow: Sovietskaya Rossia, 1988.)

Gershenzon, in miraculous defiance of the Jewish quota was offered a place at Moscow University in 1889, his father did not believe in the "miracle" and thinking he had reneged on his religion cut off his allowance. Gershenzon's four years of study in the classics and philosophy faculties were thus marred by serious financial difficulties[21].

After graduating with honors and seeing his thesis published, these difficulties did not end – once again despite his brilliant performance, unless he became a Christian, there was no chance of receiving a professorship. Thus in the nineties, Gershenzon set off on the perilous path of a freelance scholar and publicist. While his growing success reconciled his family to his choice of a literary career, his mother continued to insist that her son show her his passport on every home visit to assure herself that he had not converted.

Gershenzon never did abandon Judaism for Christianity. But this family pressure and his childhood schooling in a *cheder* where "a cruel medieval regime reigned" soured his relationship with the religion of his fathers. Indeed, his whole upbringing in a traditional Jewish environment provoked him to comment that he was "born and grew up in darkness"[22]. His move beyond the Pale to metropolitan Russia was a partial rejection of that "Judaic darkness." And yet, formally, he was true to the letter of his promise to his mother, if not to the spirit: even the woman he would marry, though an Orthodox Christian, was Jewish by birth.[23] Thus, Gershenzon retained some form of Jewishness without the concurrent burden of Judaism. However, it was to Russia – if not to Russian Christianity – that he increasingly looked for sustenance of the spirit.

This quest was facilitated when, in the years before the turn of the century, he changed his field of interest from classical history and philology due to meetings with M.F.Orlov and N.A.Ogerova-Tuchkova[24]. The former was the grandson of noted political thinker and Decembrist, E.N. Orlov; the latter was the daughter of

---

[21] The poet, Vladislav Khodasevich in his recollections of Gershenzon, recounts how the "miracle" had a more prosaic explanation: most Jews were keen to enroll in other faculties; Gershenzon was the only Jew who applied to the philological faculty, and thus automatically fell within quota levels. (Vladislav Khodasevich, "Gershenzon," in Khodasevich V. *Nekropol': Vospominaniya*, 56-63. Brussels: Les éditions Petropolis, 1939.)

[22] Quote from Vy.Ivanov, *Sobraniye sochineniye*, Brussels, 1979 – in V. Prokurina, "M.O. Gershenzon – istorik kultury," introduction to Gershenzon M.O. *Griboedovskaya Moskva. P.Y.Chaadaev. Ocherki Proshlogo*, (Moscow: Moskovskii rabochii, 1989), 3-26.

[23] Maria Goldenweizer, herself from a prestigious Kishinov family of legal scholars and musicians. Gershenzon's rejection of Judaism with a retention of Jewishness was not an uncommon option for Russified Jewish intellectuals. Mandelstam also rejected what he called the "Judaic chaos" of his childhood, but married Jewish and later would incorporate "Jewish rhythms" into his poetry. See ch.5 for further brief comments about Mandelstam.

[24] For this and later descriptions of Gershenzon's development I draw on V.Prokurina, above, and Evgeny Rashkovsky, *Istorik Mikhail Gershenzon*. Novy Mir No.10, (2001).

another noted Decembrist A.A.Tuchkov, the second wife of N.P.Ogarev and the common-law wife of Russia's most renowned political philosopher, A.I.Herzen. Gershenzon was accepted as an intimate member of their intellectual circles and they opened up to him their family archives, consisting of the letters, memoirs and books of their ancestors dating back to the time after the Napoleonic War. This, of course, was the period when Russian was penetrated by French ideas and underwent an all too brief Enlightenment before Nicolas I put the lid on liberalism with his arrest and exile of the Decembrists.

Gershenzon, who was already fascinated by Carlyle's depiction of history as wrought out of the personalities of men, and captivated by the historical fiction of Tolstoy, saw a whole new path of inspiration open up for him. Over the first decade of the twentieth century, he began to produce works dedicated to the men of the 1820s and 1830s, the first Russian socialists, free-thinkers and political mystics on the right (such as Kireevsky) and the left (such as Chaadaev). He combined scrupulous use of the archives with imaginative flair to reconstruct Russia's birth as a modern nation, often coming to original conclusions that conflicted with accepted interpretations.

Gershenzon was fascinated by psychological conflicts in men and historical situations: in Turgenev's diaries he examined the split between the writer's organic reason and his discursive, logical thought. He championed his view that if a person embraces Nature, then he will be exempted from slavery: we see here already a glimpse of how the philosophical-religious worldview of this Russian liberal had political repercussions – a pattern that would be repeated in Gershenzon's own philosophical and political struggles. Also significant is Gershenzon's admiration for Turgenev's pantheistic view of the world: this was to be a bone of contention in Berdyaev's reaction to Gershenzon's work.

In 1914, he published another tour-de-force, *Griboedov's Moscow*. This time, using the archives of the Rimski-Korsakov family from the 1810s and 1820s, Gershenzon blended letters and diaries into a beautifully written semi-novelistic reconstruction of the age, once again inspired by the spirit of Tolstoy, whose *War and Peace* can be felt in the background. Tolstoy had died four years previously, an event which marked Gershenzon deeply.

Gershenzon's historical research fed into his own philosophical meditations and his meditations on contemporary Russia. He was the first to admit this. He believed that through art and literature, as well as the historian's craft, the divine Spirit-Logos worked in mankind. In 1909, he advised Bely to put aside political activity and focus on finishing his novel *The Silver Dove* on the grounds that creative development was a more pressing type of transformation, and indeed a prerequisite for political change.

Still, the relationship between his area of research, nineteenth century Russia, and his own twentieth century Russia – between what some admiringly called Gershenzonian Moscow and Griboedovan Moscow – was problematic, and even tragic and this is nowhere more evident than in his *Landmarks* article, *Creative Self-Consciousness*, and the reaction it provoked.

In that essay, he described the tragic genealogy of the Russian intelligentsia, into which he had by a series of strokes of good fortune landed himself. They were the descendants, as he put it so succinctly, of the "serf-owning Voltairean" freethinkers he was studying. Now, as then, the Russian intelligentsia belonged to a class that preached freedom but personified bourgeois or aristocratic alienation from the people.

Due to this alienation, Gershenzon wrote, in the phrase that would cause such a furore, "we cannot even start dreaming of merging with the people – we should fear them more than all the punishments handed out by the authorities" – because just as in the days of Populist, liberal landowners the spirit of the intelligentsia and the spirit of the masses, who were still the virtual slaves of the former, were at loggerheads.

Gershenzon added a clarifying note to the second edition of *Landmarks*, explaining that he was not justifying the oppressive measures of the tsarist regime, but simply pointing out that the distorted consciousness of the intelligentsia would condemn them to be hated by the masses as long as they did not look within themselves to find the source of a different spiritual existence, one which would reconcile them with the people to whom they were constantly preaching. (Gershenzon believed that Bely's literary activity was just such a project of intellectual spiritual self-recreation – and so far more useful than practical politicking).

For the people (*narod*) was still in touch with that "general consciousness of humanity [that] does not err," and which Gershenzon saw as a "a sort of indescribable mutual interaction of consciousness and sensual personality….." The intelligentsia, however, was all intellect without live consciousness, and had lost contact with the dynamic cosmic-divine energy that fills all life with its will from the lowest beings to the highest.

As a result the *narod* "does not see in us people: we are human-like monsters, people without God in our soul – and the *narod* is right, because just as electricity is observed at the contact of two oppositely charged bodies, so the divine spark appears only at the conjunction point of personal will and consciousness, which with us have not been brought into contact at all. That is why the *narod* does not sense in us people, and does not understand us and hates us."

However, Gershenzon's explanation of his "non-reactionary" intent did not pacify his critics. Petr Struve and Semyon Frank were two fellow *Landmarkers* who were unsympathetic to his idealization of the masses, which they considered a naïve point of view that could only hinder Russia's future with its failure to see that the uneducated and inert masses were also a large part of Russia's problems[25]. And his view of the "God-bearing" masses – derived in part from his reading of Tolstoy and the Slavophiles – would ignite his other great disagreement with Berdyaev, also a fellow-*Landmarker*. Finally, in 1917 his seeming metamorphosis from Slavophile to Bolshevik would complete his

---

[25] For further detail on Struve's and Frank's disagreement with Gershenzon, see ch.6.

exclusion from the *Landmarks* circle's follow-up volume *From the Depths*.

In all of this, Gershenzon himself was torn in his attitude to the past, the Russian past, that is, by which he derived his own genealogy as a Moscow intellectual. (It was still some years before he would try to work out where his own Jewish past fitted into this picture.) As he wrote to his brother, in *Griboedov's Moscow* one of his tasks, paradoxically, had been to highlight the "spiritual wholeness" in what was agreed by most to be the "sinful and empty" environment of self-satisfied aristocratic Moscow of balls and soirees of the 1820s.

Indeed, it seems that he had become tragically seduced by his historian's craft into escaping the present. As he wrote later to his brother: "How I envy the men of the 20s and 30s, with what insatiable rapture I examined those pictures in which their comfortable and unhurried existence is depicted. Reading their recollections, their books, I became a part of their life – and, really, I don't know, probably that is why the magic aroma of Pushkin is for me like an eternally living echo of that lost paradise!"[26]

Contemporary life, meanwhile, was for him "a world of shadows, instability, disharmony." Old Russia was undergoing a fatal, bloody death along with the whole of Europe. Here there is a tragic dissonance: admiration for a traditional past, coupled with realization that the seeds of rot were sown in that past. What could one do in such a dilemma?

More and more, Gershenzon began to use his meditations on the past to draw out a philosophy for the present. What Rashkovsky refers to as Gershenzon's "second hermeneutic," his forging of a philosophy of the spirit for the present, was undertaken after the Revolution[27]. The transition from his first academic historical-descriptive-imaginative hermeneutic to a practical philosophical-religious hermeneutic was constructed using the figure of Alexander Pushkin – recast as a prophet. But the seeds for Gershenzon's revolutionary religion of the Spirit-Word had been prepared out of other sources as well, including the studies of Chaadaev, Samarin, Kireevsky, Herzen, and Turgenev.

Between Slavophilism and Bolshevism
Berdyaev and Gershenzon on Slavophilism

Perhaps the best way to understand the fall-out that occurred between Berdyaev and Gershenzon is to compare one of the latter's "Slavophile" essays with his *Landmarks* essay. It then becomes clear that Gershenzon's "second hermeneutic," i.e. that post-Revolutionary phase of creativity in which the historian devoted himself to outlining his own worldview, was not so very different after all from his first hermeneutic, in which he was supposedly engaged in objective historical research. Some of the mystery of the Slavophile-Bolshevik shock will also become more understandable.

---

[26] Quoted by Proscurina, p.21.
[27] Evgeny Rashkovsky, *Istorik Mikhail Gershenzon*. Novy Mir, 2001, No.10.

The most revealing essay is that on Ivan Kireevsky, written in 1908, the year in which Gershenzon was organzing the *Landmarks* volume. By giving a brief outline of Kireevsky's thought and comparing it with Gershenzon's own portrait of man and thinker, it will become clear what was historical research and what were already the seeds of Gershenzon's own private philosophy.

Kireevsky was seen by many as the founding figure of Slavophilism. Many of its key concepts were first articulated by him, albeit in compressed format as his output was not great. It was Kireevsky who first contrasted Western and Russian Christianity: the Papacy with its formal, authoritarian religion had prevented the deep dissemination of Christian values among the divided, barbarian tribes of Europe. By contrast, Russia's non-warring Slavic communities had absorbed the more holistic message of Byzantine Christianity in such a way that it had become an intimate part of their daily existence.

Unfortunately the Western Enlightenment, for Kireevsky, had created a gulf between the German- and French-educated Russian aristocracy and the people, whose worldview continued to be determined by holistic Eastern Orthodoxy. The key to Russia's regeneration thus lay in the reform of the education system: the model for this should be the work of the Eastern Church Fathers in transforming pagan philosophy into a system of Christian thought. For Christianity, philosophy could not be an end in itself, but merely an intermediary between science and faith, explaining the one to the other. As a result, Kireevsky believed that reason, while important if it recognized its limits, must be subservient to faith.

The reconstitution of philosophy should be reflected in the remaking of the individual and society. Seeing as the individual, unlike in the Western conception, can only gain salvation through his immersion in the organic whole of society, society's roots needed to be assured by a new unity of the Church and the world.

The Church consists of the divine and the human: the latter is the changing implementation of the former's eternal truth; however, the Church also needs to be developed in accordance with the new educational goals of society to form an organic unity. Thus for society to be whole, there must be a true synergy of Church and society.

Once this is the case, the inner transformation of the individual can take place: into his soul will flow the truths from the divine-human organism of the Church. However, if the Orthodox Church and Orthodox values are not built into society then "striving for the earthly…will become the ruling characteristic of the moral world."[28]

In part five of his essay, Gershenzon summarizes Kireevsky's essential doctrine as consisting of three insights. Firstly: a person contains an emotional core, a supra-conscious sphere, which is responsible for the management of the personality; secondly, this core organizes his spiritual life from his feelings to his faith convictions and is "unified-essential," "unified-cosmic" or "divine;" thirdly,

---

[28] I.V. Kireevsky, Poln.sobr.soch.T1,p.237, quoted in M. Maslin, edit.*Istoria russkoi filosofii. Uchebnik dlya vuzov.* (Moscow: KDU, 2008), p.144.

a person's work on himself should consist of building his internal personality, so that he brings himself under one will and the division between feeling and consciousness disappear, with the result that no one feeling asserts itself against a will which is always true to itself.

Such a unified, wholesome personality will then have access to "unified knowledge" which differs from merely rational knowledge. Through such psychological restructuring – which is called the "attainment of belief" – a person becomes open again to the cosmic rhythms of nature: "The main character of believing thought is in the striving to gather all the separate parts of the soul into one force, to search for that internal focus of being where will and reason, and feeling and conscience, and the beautiful and the true and the wonderful….and the whole volume of the mind merge into one living unity and in this way the essential personality of a man is re-established in its original undividedness."

In part six of his essay, Gershenzon addresses the reader (and future critics like Berdyaev, as it turns out), who might be surprised at a certain disconnect between Gershenzon's Kireevsky and the Christian Slavophile they thought they knew.

Gershenzon explains: "….in this solidly linked chain of deductions [of his summary of Kireevsky's philosophy], there is absent in fact that which it would be natural to see as the very foundation of Kireevsky's worldview: Christ and Christianity are absent. They do not have necessary places in this chain….for nothing can allow us to know in advance what form the truth will take in an illuminated soul. We can only say: in striving for wholeness, pay attention to the relationship of the world to your unlocked soul, and you will recognize the truth: but to assert that this truth will turn out to be precisely such and such a definition of confession, such and such a dogma – is obviously arbitrary."

In the rest of the section, Gershenzon further argues that Kireevsky's views on Russian history as being indebted to Christianity for its development are mistakes that the modern historian can only find laughable[29]. Furthermore, his insistence on Christianity as having a role to play in the development of man is due to "deep prejudices" arising from his emotional family background and his religious upbringing. These "distortions" by Kireevsky of his own work are "deep mistakes." Instead, "having discovered the main law of perfecting oneself, precisely the internal construction of the soul, he should have transmitted it to people in a pure form, strong only in its metaphysical truth, without prejudicing the forms in which the spirit should flow forth in the future." The true importance of Kireevsky in fact lies in the way he anticipated the American psychologist Myers' theory of the subconscious and Nietzsche's concept of

---

[29] "The direct line in which Kireevsky…reduces the whole of Western history to three elements….can only fill the contemporary historian with horror…Who now believes that the [Russian] Church 'guided the composition of society as the spirit directs the composition of the body', that she 'invisibly led the government to the implementation of higher Christian foundations', that with us there reigns 'wholeness of being'….?"

living creativity and his criticism of abstract philosophy.

It can be seen, then, that Gershenzon focuses entirely on Kireevsky's description of the human personality, deliberately rejecting the thinker's political and metaphysical grounding of this conception. What is particularly interesting, however, is that this remodeled Kireevskian doctrine of the "purified" holistic personality makes a central appearance in his own *Landmarks* essay a year later – where it is presented as the goal of the intelligentsia's own striving, and where once again, it is seen as being in conflict with political activism, which is an undesirable and damaging pseudo-religion.

The criticism of Frank and Struve can now be understood, especially that of the former. Frank had seen Gershenzon's "Creative Selfconsciousness" as some sort of Tolstovian mystical anarchism, and it is easy see why. For once the Christian and social content of Kireevsky's doctrine is removed, the "holistic" personality seems mysteriously to derive its entire beneficent power from within itself, through an unspecified access to general cosmic energies, or "divinity."

Kireevsky, by contrast, had insisted that unless the individual personality is connected to the Church it is condemned to a mere "striving for the earthly," for the Church – the divine-human organism – is the individual's source of contact with the divine. Gershenzon's depiction of an entirely inward-looking individual whose task is to adapt to the surges of cosmic essence that well up from his subconscious has a solipsistic, and indeed positivistic-scientific feel[30], that is absent in Kireevsky's more integrated, historical doctrine.

Nonetheless, Gershenzon's doctrine of "creative self-consciousness" preserves Kireevsky's idealization of the *narod*. As in Kireevsky, so in Gershenzon the Russian people is perceived as having a holistic consciousness that is "in tune" with reality. However, in Kireevsky the source of the harmony is the Church and centuries of exposure to the doctrines of the Byzantine ecclesiastical structure. In Gershenzon, the source of such harmony is at first perplexing: if "creative self-consciousness," as the label implies, is such a difficult state to achieve, it seems odd that the vast masses of Russia have somehow magically attained that state, while the educated have failed.

Here, however is the key: in his *Landmarks* essay, Gershenzon emphasizes how the complex beliefs of the intelligentsia have taken them away from a natural harmony and simplicity. For Gershenzon, as for Tolstoy, enlightenment seems to be more a function of the people's freedom from any education or artifice whatsoever, a sort of Rousseauesque primitive state of grace and innate simplicity. Of course, such optimistic idealization of human nature is far from

---

[30] In his later developments of his own philosophy, Gershenzon is fond of metaphors that describe the inner workings of the personality in engineering and factory terms: cogs, wheels, components, departments etc (in, e.g. *The Sermon on the Mount*). He is also fond of biological metaphors. All this makes his philosophy close to that branching of a branching of pan-unity that is Russian cosmism, (thinkers such as Tsiolkvsoky and Vernadsky).

Christianity's belief that mankind is fallen and this is precisely why the Orthodox Church looked askance at Tolstoy's cheerful anarchism.

To be fair, these themes of popular enlightenment and the casting off of the intelligentsia's educational background do of course have their equivalents in Kireevsky; however, they have been so worked over, both in Gershenzon's essay on Kireevsky (which is less excusable)[31], as well as in his own statement of belief that they are only distantly cognate. In fact, as we will see, this optimistic belief in the people's naïve purity, coupled with concomitant pessimism as regards the intelligentsia, is the linking factor between what one might call Gershenzon's early "quasi-Slavophilism" and his later "quasi-Bolshevism," which to many seemed inexplicable.

Turning to the reaction of one such baffled critic, Berdyaev, we observe a development that runs from initial acceptance, to qualified dissent, to ultimate rejection of Gershenzon's various positions from the Slavophile essays to the declaration of support for the Bolsheviks.

At the time of *Landmarks*, Berdyaev's own spiritual anarchism made him a natural ally of Gershenzon. Nor was the latter's Slavophile rhetoric alien to Berdyaev, and indeed he initially interpreted it more favorably than Frank and Struve. Even after 1917, when Berdyaev and Gershenzon were corresponding with each other about the latter's embrace of the Bolsheviks, Berdyaev remonstrated: "the most critical article written against the revolutionary intelligentsia belongs to you...this obligates you. How could it be that at the moment of the revolution, when the former forces have been unchained and those same ideas and feelings which you mercilessly criticized have been thrown to the dark masses....you have lost all your spiritual baggage, swim with the current and use street language foreign to you? And you begin to cry out the words about 'the bourgeois', 'counter-revolution'...and so forth."[32]

Berdyaev's later shock must have been partly due to his own misinterpretation of Gershenzon's *Landmarks* article, but also due to an inherent ambiguity in the article itself. The call to the spirit, and the call to the intelligentsia to embrace spiritual values by looking to the people was part of a rhetoric familiar in symbolist circles, so that it must have seemed they were all speaking the same language. Unlike Frank and Struve, it seems that Berdyaev interpreted Gershenzon's Kireevskian language as a different dialect of his own.

For Berdyaev himself had not been immune to a similar idealization of the people, and indeed in his first Christian stirrings he had concurred with Merezhkovsky that Christianity needed to be revived through greater contact

---

[31] B.Horowitz judiciously concludes that "if Gershenzon's task is, as he himself defined it, 'historical' in nature...then Gershenzon cannot be excused in completely purifying Slavophilism of its Russian Orthodox elements, and Berdiaev's criticisms, while one-sided in favor of a Russian Orthodox interpretation, are justified." Brian Horowitz, "A Jewish-Christian Rift in Twentieth-Century Russian Philosophy: N.A. Berdiaev and M.O.Gershenzon," in *Russian Review*, vol.53, October (1994): 497-514.

[32] Berdyaev to Gershenzon, 29 Sept. 1917, in Horowitz, 510.

with its neglected pagan sources. These could often be found in the semi-pagan folk Orthodoxy of the peasants.

A similar tendency – involving a greater or lesser degree of reworking of Christian sources – was expressed by Rozanov, Bulgakov, Ivanov, and Bely. Rozanov looked to ancient Egyptian paganism as an inspiration for a more concrete, less abstract Christianity, and Bulgakov's own emphasis on the beauty of the natural world, specifically the landscapes of "Mother Russia," as an integral part of Christian sensibility was a product of the same yearning.

Vyacheslav Ivanov, a close friend of Gershenzon, for his part looked to ancient Greece (through the filter of Nietzsche) to develop his influential theory of artistic creativity. The poet transcends subjectivity through an Apollian ascent of the imagination, and a return to the masses in a Dionysian descent. True artists, on this theory, even transcend objectivity: they depict the real, but only as a force to be overcome and transformed. For Ivanov, Bely was such an artist – and both Gershenzon and Berdyaev had waxed lyrical about Bely's discovery of new cosmic rhythms in the world. Bely himself, under Gershenzon's tutelage considered himself to be the vehicle of the spiritual regeneration and birth of a higher humanity.[33]

So far, so good: however, even at the time of *Landmarks* Berdyaev was beginning to diverge from Ivanov, Gershenzon and Bely as to what the nature of this spiritual inspiration should be. More and more, he was beginning to reject a general or quasi-pagan spirituality in favor of an explicitly identified and pure Christian spirituality. However, this had not yet become a point of principle for him and the Christian rhetoric in his own *Landmarks* contribution is not strong. Indeed, he is very close to Gershenzon's position there that the transformation of Russia must take place through an unspecified inner spiritual change in individuals – a proposition with which two other contributors strongly disagreed, insisting on the need for legal reforms that would build on the concessions of 1905.

It was in 1910, the year immediately after *Landmarks* came out, that Berdyaev began to weave into his rhetoric of spiritual anarchism the Solovievian note of Christian theocracy, thus explicitly opening up the rift that would culminate in 1917. The change can be seen initially in his new evaluation of Bely.

In that year Berdyaev reviewed Bely's *Silver Dove*. While full of praise for the novel *qua* novel, he was critical of Bely's implicit philosophy. The content of this criticism could just as well have been directed at Gershenzon, whom Bely referred to as the "godfather of my novels" due to his creative consultation and encouragement in their writing. Indeed much of that philosophy has a Gershenzonian flavor. It is thus worth quoting this critique at some length:

---

[33] Cf. Victor Terras, *A History of Russian Literature* (New Haven and London: Yale University Press, 1991), 93. Terras, p.393. It is in these early strains of 'revolutionary spirituality' such as Bely's and Ivanov's that the key to Gershenzon's later political switch from seeming conservative to Bolshevik sympathizer can be found. Both Bely and Ivanov also supported the Revolution, and Berdyaev also fell out with Ivanov.

In his philosophical consciousness, A. Bely is as uprooted from the Logos as he is in his mysticism.....Discipline of will and the discipline of consciousness³⁴ cannot be achieved by the methods of critical philosophy or via occultism, but can only be grasped in the depth of one's soul, in its unity with the Logos of the Church....Bely is too much the Slavophile and too much the Westernizer. He is drawn to the Eastern mystical element, and to the ineffable mysticism of the Western image. But the ineffable Western mysticism denies that basic religious truth that mysticism is expressed in the Word-Logos. Mysticism that cannot be expressed in the Word is against the Church and anti-religious...As a philosopher A. Bely remains unconnected to the universal Logos. This disconnectedness plunges him into endless pessimism.³⁵

Thus now, for Berdyaev inner transformation through the Spirit is not only an inadequate response to the Russian intellectual materialism *Landmarks* had criticized, but it too is false path if it does not go through Christ. In fact, as the title of the review indicates, Berdyaev coined a name for this new false path that had sprung up alongside the Marxist-materialist deception: he labeled Bely's Gnostic-occult spiritualism "the Russian temptation"³⁶.

---

34   Both, as we have seen, Gershenzonian motifs from his reading of Kireevsky.

35   Sobrananie sochinenii, tom III: *Tipy religioznoy mysli v Rossii*: Russky Soblazn (Po-povodu 'Serebryanogo golobya' A. Belogo.), p.407. Another figure not mentioned by Berdyaev here but crucial to an understanding of Berdyaev and Gershenzon is D.Merezhkovsky. As we saw briefly in ch.2, his "third testament" included a belief in a revolutionary Christianity that would implement the Kingdom of Heaven on earth – precisely the sort of vision that Berdyaev will later identify as Judaic, although Merezhkovsky believed his program came out of rejecting the Old Testament religion of the Father (Judaism), and even the outdated New Testament of the Son ("old" Christianity), for the apocalyptic religion of the Spirit ("new" Christianity).

36   It is interesting that he calls such views a "*Russian temptation.*" It would, of course, be possible to contend that Gershenzon had seduced Bely into a particularly *Jewish* temptation here, that of a non-denominational heterodoxy of the Logos – but this would be to ignore similar tendencies in the other figures mentioned. Still, Blok did make similar insinuations at a later period of Bely's intellectual development, toying with the idea that his misguided interest in theosophy may be due to the Jew Steiner's malign influence. Another Jew close to Blok and Bely, Steinberg, persuaded him that in fact Rudolph Steiner was not Jewish. In light of this keenness to detect anti-Russian Jewish ideologies, the figure of Blok is interesting in another respect: Blok went well beyond Bely or Gershenzon in his assault on Christian sensibilities: his shocking poem "Twelve" almost as good as equated the new Christianity with Bolshevist bloodletting. And this is to say nothing of Rozanov's anti-Christian blasphemies, also in the name of a heterodox (or downright heretical) revived Christianity of the flesh. Rozanov, though trampling on Christian Orthodoxy himself, also went through a phase of blaming Russia's ills on the Jewish worldview.

Berdyaev next turned his critical sights on Gershenzon himself. This engagement arose due to his own burgeoning interest in the Slavophiles. Whereas earlier he had praised Gershenzon's work[37] on them, in the light of his more overt Christian orientation, he began to reevaluate his colleague's work on this period of Russian thought. The main point of contention was Gershenzon's belief that Khomiakov was an unoriginal thinker who was mostly indebted to Kireevsky – which is why he had excluded him from his studies. This was unforgivable for Berdyaev, who in 1912 was to publish a book devoted exclusively to Khomiakov, "a knight of the Russian Orthodox church," and for him the central figure of Slavophilism.

More unacceptable still were Gershenzon's motives for doing so. In an article responding to similar accusation by Petr Struve, Gershenzon had reiterated the justification briefly presented in his article on Kireevsky for excluding Christianity from his presentation of the Slavophiles. His motives, he wrote there, were "to husk the authentic core, the eternal religious truth, to cleanse it of its Slavophile skin…, and clearly to explain it as simply as possible"[38]. That is, he wished to update Slavophile ideology, and present it as a spiritual panacea for post-1905 Russia.

Berdyaev agreed that one might "husk" Slavophilism of its monarchist elements, without which the ideology would not suffer. He himself at this stage viewed the monarchy as a temporary stopgap before the complete dissolution of the State that would be heralded after the required inner Christian transformation of the Russian people. After this a spiritual enlightened anarchy would prevail. But he was, therefore, utterly insistent that "it is impossible to cleanse Slavophilism of the universal truth of Christianity," and that to do so would be to distort its essence.

Of course, we have already seen that as Gershenzon was aware, his historical work was certainly not disinterested, any more than Berdyaev's was. Both of them would no doubt have agreed that "objectivity," even if achievable, was not the ultimate task of historical research. Although Gershenzon was less inclined to play the prophet than Berdyaev, intellectual work and prophecy were generally agreed to be mutually binding commitments for the Russian intelligentsia of the period.

Still, it was precisely in this pivotal year that Gershenzon was becoming aware of just how problematic it was for a Jew to don the mantle of Russian prophet, while drawing on authors steeped in Christian and Russian national themes.

It was in this year that he made the acquaintance of the notorious Judophile/Judophobe Russian master of letters, Vasily Rozanov, and started

---

More on Rozanov in ch.4; on Blok and Bely in ch.5.

[37] Here and further on on this section, I draw on Horowitz's neat summary of Berdyaev's attitude to the Slavophiles and his reception of Gershenzon's work on them in *A Jewish-Christian Rift in Twentieth-Century Russian Philosophy*.

[38] In Horowitz, 505.

a correspondence with him. Revolving to a significant extent as it did round issues of Jewish identity, Gershenzon began to reevaluate the meaning of his Jewishness[39].

In another letter of the same year to A.G.Gornfeld, we hear a new note of self-awareness, triggered by other similarly skeptical reactions to his work on the Slavophiles: "I feel myself a human being and a Jew and I do it all *sub specie humanitatis*; but it is true that I love something in Russia, very tenderly and powerfully love it. Recently I have had occasion more than once to hear ironic comments: Gershen(zon) the Slavophile, a clumsy joke, but I am fed up with it..."

However, later in the same letter, Gershenzon is forced to recognize the justice of these jibes, some of which were no doubt sympathetic and humorous, but – certainly in the case of Rozanov – some of which must have been hostile. For he comes to a recognition that his Jewishness does indeed combine oddly with the contemporary Slavophilism he had been trying to forge in his books: "I feel that my psychology is completely Jewish and I completely share the viewpoint of Chukovsky and Bely and others, i.e. I am certain that I am not in a state to understand Russians intimately. Thus I scrupulously avoid such themes (in contrast to Aikhenvald[40], for example). All my work in the area of Russian literature has eternal themes for its subject – general human themes."

There is a certain pathos in this conclusion: seeing a barrier to complete immersion in Russianness, he nonetheless continues to immerse himself in Russianness, but *sub specie humanitatis*. If by this, he had intended to dodge accusations that his Jewishness blocked or distorted a true understanding of the "Russian soul," then the sad irony is that he achieved an opposite result: it was precisely his universalization of Russian themes that was seen as most unacceptably Jewish by Berdyaev and others[41].

For his former *Landmarks* colleagues, terms such as Logos, Spirit and

---

[39] We will focus on Rozanov and Gershenzon's correspondence with him in ch.4.

[40] For more on Aikhenvald in connection with Semyon Frank, see ch.6.

[41] As a non-Russian non-contemporary observer, I personally find Gershenzon's Slavophile idealization of the God-bearing Russian masses particularly difficult to understand in light of what he must have known about the ready participation of the Russian *narod* in pogroms like those that took place in Kishinev. Of course Jewish *narodniki* had their own explanations about the temporary reactionary tendencies of their people, so this is not exceptional. Nonetheless, the more intelligent and more Christian Slavophiles (like Kireevsky, Khomiakov) were prevented by a certain wise Christian pessimism from idealizing the half-paganized Russian masses too much; in addition their awareness of Orthodoxy's universal roots in Byzantium and ultimately Judea also protected them against excessive Russophilia. It is thus surprising that Gershenzon would have chosen the less sophisticated aspects of Slavophilism to create his idealized picture of a cosmically aware common people. In that sense, his universalization and de-Christianization of Slavophilism had a paradoxically narrowing effect on the doctrine.

tvorchestvo (creativity), could not be used with impunity: they had to be connected back to their Christian roots – even if, in the case of Berdyaev, the resulting fusion still attracted criticisms of idiosyncracy and heterodoxy by more conventionally Orthodox Christian figures.

Gershenzon, Berdyaev and the Bolshevik Revolution

Of course, these historiosophical disputes were academic compared to the demands that the October Revolution made of Russian intellectuals. It was in this period that what might until then have remained "academic" criticisms of Gershenzon's historical work took on a far more urgent meaning. Scientific work, ethnic-religious identity and political partisanship formed a potent mix after the events of 1917.

It was Lev Shestov, who mockingly pondered on how it was possible for Berdyaev to change his metaphysical commitments several times before breakfast without it having any real impact on anyone, while a man would be extremely careful before he switched political orientation[42]. As usual this was as much a dig at metaphysics as at Berdyaev, and the scenario of Gershenzon and Berdyaev in 1917 somewhat belies this cavalier attitude to metaphysics.

Berdyaev's Christian anarchism and individualism blended with Christian theocracy meant that for him the Revolution, as Horowitz puts it, became "a religious question" – in much the same way as it was for Bulgakov. The atheist nature of the Soviet regime meant that he would have no truck with it, for it had set itself against the earthly church as well as Berdyaev's own more subjective belief in the Christian anarchistic transformation of Russia.

Rather to Berdyaev's shock, however, Gershenzon's peculiarly apolitical doctrine of an inner transformation of consciousness, which drew on many of the same spiritual sources as Berdyaev's own, found room for the Revolution as a working of "the Spirit."

This divergence did not become immediately apparent. In the period before the Revolution, Berdyaev and Gershenzon were still running parallel in their reactions to events. In the first two years of the First World War, they both agreed that the war served a useful purpose in destroying "bourgeois" German complacency. Berdyaev declared in a letter to Gershenzon in 1914: "The genuine world can only be reached through war. The bourgeois world isn't worth a thing, it was a lie. Now my whole soul desires victory over the Germans." Gershenzon wrote an article in the same year in which he commented on the unexpectedly high-minded "scorn for the things of this world" among German industrialists in pursuit of their war aims[43].

This contempt for bourgeois European existence is revealing: it can be

---

[42] Lev Shestov, "Poxvala gluposti." *Fakeli*, kn.II. (1907).

[43] Berdiaev to Gershenzon, 22 July 1914, Gershenzon papers, M.Gershenzon, "Vtoroi god voiny," *Birzhevye-vedomosti*, 28 June 1915. Quoted in Horowitz, p.507. In this section, I draw several times on the quotations from this correspondence quoted by Horowitz in his article.

traced to both men's worship of the Spirit over the comforts of the flesh and an anarchistic dissatisfaction with the order of this world. Indeed, in terms of traditional dichotomies, one might say that the other-worldliness of both thinkers had Christian roots. The difference was that Berdyaev proclaimed his Christian allegiance, while the underground Gnostic Christian spirituality of Gershenzon had been, to use his word again, husked of overt terminological connections with its Christian origins[44].

However, on Gershenzon's analysis the otherworldly benefits of the war were indirect: the war itself was being fought in the name of rationalism, an ideology that analyses and compartmentalizes holistic nature in order to rip benefits from her. His ensuing disillusion with the war thus follows naturally from this viewpoint. Berdyaev, though, saw the war in a Hegelian light: through conflict it encouraged the individualization of each nation, while covertly fostering a universal unity of all nations. This complacent analysis of mass slaughter was only brought up short by the sudden realization in 1917 that a Russian defeat would in all likelihood facilitate the victory of the atheistic Bolsheviks.

When that did indeed happen, Gershenzon welcomed the Bolsheviks as "the party of the heart," who put the "humiliated, tortured people, in whom the feeling of human pride...had so violently appeared" above abstract "values" like "statehood, holism and the might of Russia."[45] The October Revolution seemed to be that event for which his soul had been so painfully waiting for almost a decade. Indeed, the Bolshevik's sacrificial rejection of victory in a capitalist, nationalistic war fit Gershenzon's conceptions of self-denial, rejection of rationalism and an embrace of holistic consciousness that would transcend nation and class.

It is true that Gershenzon was nuanced in his support of the Bolsheviks: he recognized that there were good people on both sides of the catastrophic divide, and neither was he unaware of violent elements among the party. As he underlined to Berdyaev in a letter, he deliberately refrained from publishing articles in support of the Bolsheviks so as not to inflame an already incendiary situation.

Berdyaev, meanwhile, had no such reservations and threw himself wholeheartedly into journalistic condemnations of the Revolution. For a while he drew close to conservative right forces and even published articles in the journal *Narodopravstvo*, which carried anti-Semitic articles. Gershenzon, on learning of this, found Berdyaev guilty by association.[46]

---

[44] This picture of the covert Christianity of Gershenzon's thought will be confirmed when we examine his meditation on Jewish fate later.

[45] Gershenzon, letters to Berdiaev, 29,30 September 1917 in Horowitz.

[46] Gershenzon wrote to his wife in October 1917: "'Narodopravsto' is an anti-Semitic paper: Khodasevich has quit its editorial board as a sign of protest....N.A. (Berdyaev) has fallen into vile company and unbeknown to himself has become the poet laureate of big industry and black hundreds extremism. Now they are saying there that Shestov, me and Bely are dangerous as we are spreading a despicable and base Bolshevism...What a nasty bunch!" For this and other extracts from

Both men continued to live in Moscow until Berdyaev was exiled in 1922. However, Berdyaev's collaboration on an anti-Semitic paper[47], his belief that the Bolsheviks were a force of anti-Christian evil, and his belief that Russia must return to its Christian identity if that evil were to be averted had the effect of estranging Gershenzon. The two "spiritual anarchists" had lost their common language; what had seemed to unite them now divided them.

Gershenzon wrote in 1922 to their common friend Lev Shestov that although they continued to bump into one another at cultural events they barely exchanged words. A telling phrase in the letter is his observation that "the Berdyaevs live the same way they used to, and not too badly....just as before on Tuesdays they have 'Church come-alongs', as I called them, with lectures on mystical, Church and national themes."[48]

The sense of alienation is palpable in this brief description: for Gershenzon there is something musty, churchy, retrograde about Berdyaev's interests – as if he had gone over to the flabby bourgeois they had both despised and was dabbling in the petty hobbies of a dead era. Doubtless, there is also that sense of exclusion: the Jew who, as Rozanov had reminded him throughout their correspondence, just could not "get" Russia with its mystical, national and Church themes.

Gershenzon's correspondence cf.http://www.krotov.info/spravki/persons/20person/gershnzn.html Human relations have a certain illogic: after all, Bely was not so far in his attitude to the Revolution from his friend Aaron Steinberg – and Berdyaev congratulated the latter on his book on Dostoevsky in 1923. It should be recalled, however, that Berdyaev was quarrelsome and fiery by nature. He quarreled several times with Shestov, and with Gershenzon regarding Slavophilism and the meaning of the First World War. Given that he made up with Shestov, one suspects that it was Gershenzon's sense of offense that prevented reconciliation in this case. This is confirmed by the fact that Berdyaev expressed regret for his break with Gershenzon in his autobiography – and by his own realization that their positions were not as far apart as his brief rightist infatuation made him think at the time. To that extent, Gershenzon's claim that Berdyaev was acting out of motives "unbeknown to himself" seems quite accurate.

[47] That the incredible pressures of the Revolution brought latent tensions to the boil which might otherwise have been non-fatal is evident if we remember that in 1915, Berdyaev had published "On Jewry" in the anti-Semitic anthology "Israel in the past, present and future," with no fatal impact to their friendship. In addition, Berdyaev was expressing admiration for Russia's chiliastic sects as late as 1916, and praising Merezhkovsky for his enthusiasm about creating a Kingdom of God that would not just be confined to earth (as in Judaism) or heaven (as in Christianity) but would be manifest in both. (For further details, cf. ch.8 "Anarkhicheskiy personalizm Nikolaya Berdyaeva" and ch.9 "D.S.Merezhkovskiy: apokalipsis 'vseokrushayushchey religioznoy revolutsii'" in P.P. Gaidenko, *Vladimir Soloviev i filosofia serebryanogo veka*. (Moscow: Progress-traditsia, 2001), ch.8.) The Revolution brought an about-turn on that front too – at least until he returned to his own propensity for chiliasm after the Second World War (see below).

[48] Gershenzon to Shestov, 23.4.1922, quoted in Horowitz (1994).

In that sense, Berdyaev and Gershenzon conformed well to each other's stereotypes: Gershenzon for Berdyaev was a Jew whose universalization of Russia had in fact undermined its flesh-and-blood concrete identity. As we will see shortly, Berdyaev was already then beginning to develop the idea, which we saw in Bulgakov, that the false utopianism of the Revolution was a particularly Jewish temptation. Thus while he never explicitly accused Gershenzon of this peccadillo, one can speculate that he must have been tempted to explain his former spiritual ally's strange about-turn at this time in these terms.

On the other hand, for Gershenzon, Berdyaev must have seemed like a man who did not have the courage to follow the Spirit into the more difficult and lofty terrain of self-negation and was still clinging to meaningless constructs of the past. But we will see more of how each one framed the events which had separated them in philosophical terms when we consider Berdyaev's *Meaning of History* and Gershenzon's *Destiny of the Jewish People* below.

It should be said, meanwhile, that Lev Shestov, the recipient of the above letter, probably managed to preserve his friendship with both of them through his occupation of a third position. By his own admission, politics did not much interest him. But in this situation his adogmatism demanded that he repudiate equally the positions espoused by both Gershenzon and Berdyaev.

Berdyaev's Hegelian justification of war must have been anathema to Shestov: later he would focus on Dostoevsky's parable of the parents who torture their child to death, and the challenge this must eternally pose for any metaphysically conceived theodicy. In effect, Berdyaev's attempt to glorify war through a philosophical scheme must have meant neatly justifying the death of Shestov's own son in that war.

On the other hand, the Marxists with their idea of bloodshed in the name of progress must have seemed to him no less Hegelianly monstrous, a grotesque "anthropodicy." This is why he so promptly rejected any compromise with Lunacharsky and his Marxist overtures. Nonetheless, Shestov in his refusal to occupy any positive ground was closer to Gershenzon, although as will become clear even his nihilism was not stringent enough for him.

Gershenzon and Vyacheslav Ivanov after the Revolution
In the summer of 1920, Gershenzon and the poet Vyacheslav Ivanov shared a room at a Moscow sanatorium for workers in science and literature. A philosophical discussion in epistolary format, published in 1921 under the title *A correspondence from two corners*, was started by Ivanov[49], which gives an insight into how Gershenzon was faring two and half years later in the new Russia he had embraced.

Ivanov and Gershenzon were certainly not unique among Russian non-Marxist intellectuals in welcoming the Revolution. As we will see in more detail

---

[49] Gershenzon later wrote to Shestov saying that he had not wanted to engage in the correspondence at all, but was pressured into it by Ivanov.

in chapter five, loosely Christian anarchists like Alexander Meier embraced a similar position. His belief was that, while mistaken in its materialist ideology, the Bolsheviks' goals were praiseworthy: their pursuit of social justice and a restructuring of a deeply imbalanced and sick society had hidden religious roots, and should be supported.

Like Gershenzon and Ivanov, Meier believed that with time the Bolsheviks would abandon their materialism, and that meanwhile the fruit of their actions could be appreciated. Spiritual activists could help this transformation by their presence in Russia and the example of their work and their communities. The Orthodox Jewish brothers Aaron and Isaac Steinberg are striking examples of this faith in a combination of old spirituality and new social activism: the former worked with Bely and Blok at the Free Spiritual Academy in Petrograd; the latter became minister of justice in Lenin's first government[50].

The public epistolary exchange between Gershenzon and Ivanov provides an interesting contrast to the hidden exchange of letters between Berdyaev and Gershenzon a couple of years earlier. It too is a type of Jewish-Christian dialogue. And yet both men hint only obliquely at Gershenzon's Jewishness. This seems to be out of a delicate sense of tact on Ivanov's part, and a function of Gershenzon's own rejection of any cultural affiliation, Jewish or Russian[51].

Ivanov was a self-declared philo-Semite on the Solovievian model. In his short article[52] in the 1915 *Shield* anthology in support of Russia's Jews, he had declared that a Christian must not just be a *philo*-Semite: the more he comes to know his own Christian tradition, he must be a Semite himself, a spiritual Semite. For the Church is the body of Christ, and Christ is physically descended from Abraham, and thus a Christian is descended from Abraham. Like the Temple curtains, this Abrahamic body of the Church split down the middle after Christ's coming: both halves resent each other and simultaneously yearn for reunion with each other. Both have expressed unworthy hatred to each other. But the Church's hatred of Jewry has always been out of concern that she has not lived up to the true "spirit of Jewry," which she claims to represent. The resentment of Jewry, for her part, is really a lover's offense, what the Hellenes call anti-Eros.

Jews stand as a test of the truth of Christianity. Once Christians shine with Christ's truth, then Jews will be convinced that there is no other Messiah to wait for; and if Christians do shine with that truth, Jews will cease to be an irritant –

---

[50] Berdyaev himself was later to express regret for his hasty condemnation of Gershenzon and Ivanov, recognizing that the charge of collaboration with the atheist Soviet regime was premature: "the Soviet structure at that time was still not completely worked out…and it was impossible yet to call it totalitarian." (In *Samopoznanie*). We will return to this question below.

[51] N.O.Lossky in his *History of Russian Philosophy*, also refers to the exchange as one between two Russian men of letters, completely overlooking the Jewish angle. Zenkovsky was another Russian Christian philosopher who, like Berdyaev, focused on Gershenzon's Jewishness in evaluating his attitude to Christianity. See below.

[52] Vyacheslav Ivanov, "K ideologii yevreiskogo voprosa," in *Shchit'*, Moscow, 1915.

for love conquers fear. The article ends, as we saw in chapter two, with a quote from Dostoevsky – a "so-called anti-Semite" – advocating a Christian attitude towards Jews.

In condensed format, and replete with the symbolistic sharpness characteristic of a poet, this anticipates Bulgakov's own absorption of Soloviev's teaching on Jews. However, at least in this period, Ivanov was to follow the spirit of this doctrine more closely than Bulgakov as his dialogue "between corners" with Gershenzon shows.

Of course, one of the ties that bound them, that was as strong as and perhaps stronger than their Jewish and Christian identities, was their love of Russian literature. If Ivanov painted himself as a "son of Abraham" in 1915, it is as a "son of Russia" that he presents himself initially to his neighbor – as well as addressing his neighbor as such: "We Russians," he writes to Gershenzon, the pronoun displaying an entire world of trust and affection, "have always been… fugitives…." And then: "You, of course, are flesh of our flesh and bone of our bone part of our intelligentsia, no matter how much you revolt against it; I myself am barely so: rather I am only half a son of the Russian soil…and I am half a foreigner, from the disciples of Sais, where race and tribe are forgotten…"

Ivanov's tact, and no doubt genuine belief, consists in seeing Gershenzon as his Russian brother. Gershenzon's failings are then not the failings of a Jew, but rather of a Russian who has taken a false turn in Russia's destiny. We recall here Berdyaev's own characterization of Bely's Gnosticism as a "Russian temptation" – a metric, however, he did not apply in his analysis of Gershenzon. For Ivanov, however, Gershenzon's "temptation" is to believe in Tolstoy instead of Dostoevsky.

In 1912, Ivanov had written an essay called "Tolstoy and Culture," in which he had condemned the writer's vision as simplistic, rationalistic and full of a "moral utilitarianism" that was hostile to Dionysius, art and spirituality. In Gershenzon's infatuation with Tolstoy, Ivanov sees something equally dangerous: the desire to simplify history, to merge with nature, to put down Rousseauesque roots in the earth and abandon the roots of culture[53]. Dostoevsky, meanwhile, "knew that the road to simplicity goes through complexity. The road to simplicity through forgetting is a false path." Thus even though Gershenzon might "understandably be repelled by Dostoevsky"[54], only the latter's vision of an entry into culture is

---

[53] Tolstoy, as we saw, was indifferent to the national question, particularly as it concerned the Jews. This led to a certain indifference to Jews bordering on anti-Semitism. Gershenzon, as we will see later, actually recapitulates such an attitude, so that Ivanov's comparison is perceptive.

[54] Is this a recognition on Ivanov's part that Dostoevsky's anti-Semitism might be hard for a Jew to stomach? Even if this is the case, Ivanov's contrast of Tolstoy and Dostoevsky as exemplars of different spiritual philosophies is interesting as regards the Jewish question too. As Akao discusses, Tolstoy's individualist ethic rejected the notion of national or group interests. Thus, Tolstoy was irritated by demands for Jewish rights. He preferred to see people as individuals, stripped of national

true: the soul must die a fiery death before it is reborn.

Gershenzon, however, is not persuaded and clings to his nihilism and his condemnation of culture. Throughout the letters, he expresses a weariness with scholarship, study and knowledge and a keenness to throw off the clothes of civilization and "throw himself into Lethe." All Ivanov's defenses of values, of the Church and morality and so on, are defenses of abstract entities that have far outlived their original inspiration in the bosom of the personality for whom they were many centuries ago a genuine inspiration of the Spirit.

Ivanov too believes that culture can be a deadweight from the past, unless the individual dies and is resurrected with Christ. But Gershenzon refuses to embrace any old symbols that come from without and not from within. He refuses to buy into Ivanov's optimism that ancient European culture can return to its sources and be revitalized. He sees a contradiction in Ivanov's contention that culture will provide redemption through a natural historical development and an immanent teleology, but that nonetheless the individual must die to culture: if culture is so naturally redemptive, surely these propositions contradict each other – the death of the individual means that he will cease to work within the saving streams of culture, so that the latter will falter. To the end, Gershenzon insists on a rejection of all values, "those poisons of culture that have entered the blood and polluted the very sources of the spiritual life."

A faint echo of Jewish-Christian motifs is present in the rhetoric of both. Ivanov declares that, having escaped from the heavy fleshpots of Egypt, Gershenzon is a wanderer stuck in the desert and cannot enter the Promised Land, though he stands on Mt. Nebo. Still, he sees in Gershenzon's nihilism a worthy prophetic spirit, a Mosaic critique of Egyptian paganism, a Biblical iconoclasm. All this is said without compromising Ivanov's assertion that Gershenzon is a Russian; he does not state explicitly that the desert wanderer is, literally, a Jew, rather than a symbolic one. But if the symbolic and literal Jew do merge, then both – in keeping with his philo-Semitic agenda of 1915 – are still evaluated positively.

Gershenzon's expression of his Jewishness is equally understated and ambiguous. In several places, his rhetoric borrows a lofty Judaic tone, but then just as radically casts it away. "I say to Perun," thunders Gershenzon in the sixth letter, "you are an ancient idol, not God. I feel God to be invisible

---

belonging – with the result that he harbored a sort of Enlightenment hostility towards Jewry as a nation. Dostoevsky, however, despite vicious enmity towards Jewry, still saw in the collective fate of Jewry something special. The Orthodox Jew, Aaron Steinberg, even considered Dostoevsky's worldview to be the most "Old Testament," the most congenial to Judaism, among all the Russian writers – and he made Dostoevsky the corner-stone of his own philosophical system. In this sense, Gershenzon's embrace of Tolstoy's vision is understandable in one who held negative opinions about Judaism and Jewish national survival. (For Akao on Tolstoy, cf. Mitsuakaro Akao, "'Yevreiski' vopros kak russkii. (Obshchestvennoe dvizhenie russkykh pisatiley v zashchitu yevreev v poslednie desyatiletie tsarskoi Rossii.)" at http://src-h.slav.hokudai.ac.jp/coe21/publish/no17_ses/11akao.pdf).

and omnipresent; but you still try to assure me that this idol is a symbol of my Divinity, and that I just have to comprehend its signs and it will fully replace my God. But though it is indeed very interesting, and you expose very profoundly its symbolic nature – I am willing to listen without end, I am almost convinced by you – still, its appearance is so terrifying and contrary to my feeling that I cannot control myself. I remember all the victims that we brought him…. terrible, bloody victims!"

If one reads this with the eyes of a Christian looking at the writings of a Jew, as perhaps Berdyaev or Zenkovsky would have done, it seems as if Gershenzon is equating Christian European culture with the idolatry of ancient Russia, and advocating in its place a return to pure monotheism. It seems, for all the world, as if Christian culture is a Perun to whom the "terrible bloody victims" of countless Jews who refused to conform to its dictates have been offered up in pogroms, inquisitions and expulsions. One cannot help feeling that the shadow of tsarist Russian anti-Semitism is indeed present in these denunciations. The barrier, however, to making this the overt interpretation of these words is the little "we" in "all the victims we brought him" – which indicates that Gershenzon has in mind not just religious culture but other disciplines that rest on values: science, art, history and so on, in which Gershenzon had avidly participated as a Russian *intelligent*.

Thus while Gershenzon's rejection of Ivanov's siren call for him to join the ranks of culture again have a definite Judaic flavor, it is quite clear that Gershenzon is not setting up Jewry or Judaism as a pure alternative to culture, as an entity that has escaped the ravages of culture[55]. Nor would we expect him to, knowing of his equally negative pronouncements about the "darkness" of the culture that bore him.

Still, Gershenzon hints that, despite Ivanov's generous inclusion of him among the native sons of the Russian land, he too like Ivanov belongs there even less, and has another side to him. By day, he is a Russian intellectual engaged in academic activity. By night, however, a different side of him opens up:

> In the depths of my consciousness I live otherwise. For many years already, insistently and unstoppably a secret voice sounds to me from there: not this, not this! Some other will in me is repelled by culture, from everything that is done and spoken about around me. This is boring and unnecessary for it, it is like a fight of ghosts, rebelling in the wilderness; it knows another world, sees another life, which does not yet exist on earth…and this voice I recognize as the voice of my genuine 'I'. I live like a foreigner assimilating in another country; I am loved by the natives and love them myself…I feel their sicknesses and joys, but still I know myself to be an alien, secretly I

---

[55] As we will see later, Gershenzon was probably more pessimistic about Jewish culture and religion than about non-Jewish culture. Knowing this, any remaining ambiguity about a Gershenzonian defense of Judaism in *From two corners* is expunged completely.

pine for the fields of my native land, for her different spring, for the smell of her flowers and the speech of her women.

Who then is this alien living in a foreign land? Gershenzon here immerses his reader in a typical symbolist dynamic: he draws his tropes from the real world but uses them to point to a higher reality, just as Ivanov did in his poems. Undoubtedly these tropes are heavy with the history of his own Jewishness: Gershenzon, as a Jew, was legally a foreigner in Russia; the Pale of Settlement was indeed – before the Revolution – jurisdictionally a different zone to central Russia. The "natives" did indeed love him – though some hated him. He had indeed assimilated extremely well. And the truth was that his native land was not really Russian Moscow but Jewish Kishinev, with its traditional Orthodox, Yiddish life.

And yet, of course, the symbolic intent would be destroyed and reversed if the trope were to replace the higher reality[56]. The "real" native land is, of course, not Kishinev, which was a place of darkness for Gershenzon, and which he had always yearned to escape. It is certainly not Palestine, for Gershenzon was a vehement anti-Zionist and an anti-nationalist, whatever the stripe. Perhaps then, if Russia, Kishinev and Palestine are not his native land, then it is beyond this earth in the realm of the Spirit? But that cannot be; Gershenzon assures Ivanov only that it "does not *yet* exist on earth."

It seems that even in 1920, Gershenzon preserved a belief that the Revolution would create, if not paradise on earth, then at least a "native land" where Gershenzon could dwell with other like-minded individuals. Again, in letter six, Gershenzon expresses his thoughts about the Revolution, which seem to confirm this reading.

Part of the goal of the Revolution was to abolish illiteracy in the proletariat. Gershenzon's own cultural activity involved disseminating creativity to the masses through his organization of the Union of Writers. He concedes to Ivanov that this is also a struggle for culture, and that the proletariat is being fed those values about which he has just been complaining to Ivanov.

Gershenzon's solution to this dilemma is dialectical – somewhat oddly for one who has criticized such philosophical moves in Ivanov. He sees in the first stage of the Revolution an inclusion of the excluded, which will be a stage to a later revolt against values: "Maybe (and I actually think so) the proletariat itself is sincerely mistaken: it thinks these values are necessary for it in and of themselves, while in actual fact they are necessary to it only as a means for other achievements…[for] what we see in the Revolution says nothing about the distant evaluation and plan with which the Spirit called it into life."

Gershenzon here appeals to the theory of "the heterogeneity of goals:" the

---

[56] In ch.4, we will see that Florensky's interpretation of Judaism and Christianity can be considered just such a failed symbolist dynamic: instead of seeing Old Testament tropes as symbols of a higher reality, Florensky constantly seeks to demote them to references to a lower reality: animal sacrifice is really code for human sacrifice and so on. Cf. discussion of Florensky's "two-tiered logic" in ch.4.

goal selected by the conscious mind is only the first step on the path determined by the Spirit; after that consciousness sees itself deceived at every step of the way – for in its realization of its ultimate aims, "the goal determined by consciousness…is transformed or replaced by another one utterly different to the first; and so on, link after link…"

Although Shestov was later to praise Gershenzon for sticking to his nihilistic, anti-metaphysical guns in *From Two Corners* and resisting Ivanov's metaphysical overtures, it seems he read the correspondence selectively (as was often the case with Shestov). While Gershenzon denies that he was influenced by Hegel or Nietzsche, this last declaration of a belief in "the heterogeneity of goals" distinctly recalls Hegel's "cunning of history."

Frankly, it has all the notorious looseness of the Hegelian approach, in much the same way as the Marxism of the Bolsheviks: in the present case, it enables Gershenzon to be reconciled with policies and events in Revolutionary Russia which stood in stark opposition to his own beliefs and desires. Thus the Soviet education of the peasants in values and a culture that he rejected is still seen as a first step on the way to the building the "homeland" that he was yearning for. His own participation in that project was thus dialectically justified.

Thus, in 1920, it would seem that Gershenzon was still a supporter of the Revolution. He believed that the Spirit had called it into being and in unfathomable ways would coax it to yield fruit on earth, and not in heaven. To state the matter in this way is to bring to mind Bulgakov's later thesis about the carnal Judaic desire for this-worldly paradise – which Berdyaev takes up in a different key. However, we saw how Bulgakov's thesis hit a rock wall of contradiction: all his examples of Judaic apocalypse were taken from Christian history.

Here, finally, we have a Jew who supports the Revolution in idiosyncratic Gnostic terms. And yet, this seems to only further confirm the flaws in Bulgakov's analysis: for Gershenzon's religion of the Spirit seems to be welded out of the Slavophiles, Tolstoy, Bely and Turgenev. It is also shares roots with Merezhkovsky and Berdyaev's own "neo-Christianity."[57] And as we shall see shortly, for Gershenzon this Spirit – even when it moves in Jewish history – distinctly rejects the ethos of traditional, Law-bound Judaism.

1922: Berdyaev and Gershenzon on history

Berdyaev's exchange of opinions with Gershenzon was less explicit than Ivanov's. After their correspondence faltered to a halt in 1917, there was no further dialogue. Five years later, however, both men produced books which examined the "Jewish question." Gershenzon's was a short work entitled *The Destiny of the Jewish people*[58]; Berdyaev's thoughts can be found in a chapter

---

[57] Berdyaev's term.
[58] Mikhail Gershenzon, *Sudby yevreiskogo naroda*, Berlin, 1927. Also reprinted in *Tajna izrailja*. 'Yevreiskii vopros v russkoi religioznoi mysli kontsa XIX-pervoi polovinoi XX

dedicated to Jewry in *The Meaning of History*.

Assuming that the thoughts expressed there are a fruit of meditations going back to 1917 and before, the estrangement between the two becomes even more comprehensible. For Berdyaev's depiction of the role of the Jews in world history after Christ departs from the more conciliatory line adopted by Soloviev, Bulgakov and Ivanov. And Gershenzon's analysis of Jewish destiny, couched as it is in the Gnostic spirituality which Berdyaev had sharply rejected in his own development, must have been anathema to Berdyaev. Nonetheless, it will become clear that behind this seemingly stark dichotomy between the two, a case can be made that there is more that binds than separates their philosophies of history.

Berdyaev on history and Jewry

In *The Meaning of History* Berdyaev states that the key to the historian's art consists in grasping the historical thing-in-itself. A person gains access to this essence by discovering it within the layers of his own personality, where the outer events of history are recapitulated inwardly. Thus "it should be possible for man to apprehend history within himself; he should be able for example, to discover within himself the profoundest strata of the Hellenic world and thus grasp the essentials of Greek history. Similarly, the historian must discover within himself the deep strata of Jewish history before he can grasp its essential nature." Berdyaev performs this exercise in his book and he lays out his conclusions regarding the Greek and Jewish historical essences, reaching the following conclusions.

The Greeks never developed a historical sense because they were obsessed by perfect beauty and necessary form. Because historical events are not repeatable, history as the flow of contingent events was alien to the Greek metaphysical mindset – as it was to the Indian. The Semites, by contrast, were dualists – which for Berdyaev is positive: they wished to see the action of the metaphysical, their other-worldly God, in the affairs of this world. And thus, "the Jews were the first to have an inkling of a philosophy of history."

Nonetheless, the Jewish Old Testament contains only "an inkling" of such a philosophy, as it sees God's participation in contingent human affairs as random and utterly transcendent. It was only the coming of Christ that proved once and for all that the Divine did not just guide history from afar, but that our history in its deepest (Kantianly noumenal) essence is actually a reflection of events in the life of God. Christ's earthly life was a struggle against evil, and this struggle was a continuation on earth of God's struggle against the evil that arises out of the pre-eternal Abyss (Boehme's Ungrund). Christ thus made transparent in history the inner life of God.

The Jewish idea that God intervenes in history and their expectation of some final apocalyptic intervention were thus partly right. But little did the Jews know that this apocalyptic event would not be some this-worldly consummation of history, some final great *historical* event, but the coming to earth of God's

---

vv. (St Petersburg, Sophia: 1993), 468-497.

Son to reveal that the heavenly and the earthly are one and the same drama. As a result of the Incarnation, "man began to liberate himself... from the Jewish subservience to God as a remote and menacing and wrathful power which it was terrifying and dangerous for man to meet...."

Moreover, after the Incarnation, a continued expectation of a future Divine intervention is meaningless. The incarnation, crucifixion and resurrection reveal the Divine life on earth and transfigure human understanding: they thus deliver humans from any need for historical intervention by the Divine. In fact, Christ's victory over death takes place *outside* history. And the fruits of human creativity, likewise, can only be preserved outside history. Man can now join Christ in his creative struggle over evil: but just as Christ in this world was not victorious, dying on the Cross, so man's creative triumphs cannot be of this world.

This leads to the important conclusion that the Jews are no longer chosen. Indeed, Berdyaev states that Jews who await a separate Messiah are now awaiting the anti-Christ. Anyone who rejects Christ rejects the thesis that history has already reached its consummation and that all progress must be ahistorical. A continued belief in some intervention from above that will have repercussions in history and on earth is a false eschatology, the desire to build paradise on earth.

The clearest example of such false utopianism is, of course, the Soviet Union, from whence Berdyaev had just been expelled. However, he also mentions Byzantine theocracy, the papacy, the Renaissance, Hegel, Compte, Spencer and Marx as examples of ideologues and ideologies that have clung to a belief in God's continuing immanent action in history.

Thus Berdyaev has harsh words for Jewry, its false chosenness and its desire for the anti-Christ[59]. Jewish attempts to find justice within history ignore the fact that "human destiny as expressed in historical time admits of no resolution within the historical framework" and that "the metaphysics of history teach that what is insoluble within the historical framework may be solved [only] outside it." In false Jewish eschatology is "is the basis of the revolutionary character of the religious consciousness of Jewry. A Jew easily becomes a revolutionary and a socialist. Jews accept the false myth that at the basis of history lies the exploitation of man by man....Among Jews this idea of earthly bounty was not secular or worldly, but religious and theocratic."[60]

Gershenzon, if he read Berdyaev's *Meaning of History*, may have been repelled by the anti-Jewish sentiment expressed there and found confirmation

---

[59] Berdyaev, while seemingly less conciliatory than Soloviev towards Jewry, nonetheless converges on Soloviev's final depiction of the Jewish expectation of the anti-Christ in the latter's final *Short Story of Anti-Christ*.

[60] Here we run into the very same problem that we saw with Bulgakov's analysis: Berdyaev blames Judaism for Jewish revolutionary activity, but all his examples of false eschatology come from Western European Christian history, and no examples of Jewish revolutionary activity are produced. Evidently in the atmosphere of the Russian emigration after the Revolution, it was taken for granted that Jews were revolutionaries. Later, Berdyaev questioned this stereotype.

of the anti-Semitic nature of Berdyaev's beloved "mystical, national and church" themes so ardently discussed at his Tuesday "Church come-alongs"[61].

[61] There is the question of how familiar Gershenzon would have been with these views. Here a complication arises. Berdyaev expressed similar views about Jewry in his fourth letter of *Filosofia neravenstva* (*The philosophy of inequality*). This letter, addressed to the Soviet government in 1918, criticized their policy of offering equal rights to all nationalities as a mistake which ignored the mystical-biological essences of the different peoples. Especially in regard to Jewry, Berdyaev took issue with the equalization of Jewry, which would lead to the salvation of the man but the disappearance of that falsely universalized man as a Jew. This clearly anti-liberal perspective shows Berdyaev to fall at that time into the conservative camp – among both Jews and Christians – who were in favor of preserving Jewish uniqueness even at the cost of individual human rights. There is one phrase in this letter which is particularly interesting: "Jewry is stronger than all your teachings…Jewry exists in the world in order to prove to all the nations the existence of the secret of nationality and the secret of religion. In truth, both philo-Semites and anti-Semites judge too easily and superficially. One needs to approach this question very deeply. In this nation one can sense the struggle of God in history. Jewry has its mission in world history and this mission crosses the boundary of the national mission." The interest lies in the fact that it echoes almost word for word a phrase of Pavel Florensky in his preface to the anti-Semitic collection "Israel in the past, present and future…," where he writes of Judephobes and Judophiles both being right, but also due to insufficient depth of understanding, both wrong. As we saw in ch.2, Berdyaev wrote an article for *Shchit'*, which having been rejected by Gorky, he included in "Israel in the past….." I have not been able to locate that article, but it is possible to surmise that it would have combined elements from *Filosofia istoria*, so close to Florensky's comments, and *The Meaning of History*, whose hostile reading of Jewish religiosity would also fit the tone of that anthology. And yet, while negative about Jewish chiliasm and Jewish religion, Berdyaev's claim to place himself beyond the categories of philo-Semite and anti-Semite must be read more generously than the similar claim of Florensky – for in *Filosofia neravenstva*, he does see a positive dynamic in the survival of Jewry in the world, and though a conservative position, it is at root amicable to Jewry. All this raises the question again: what would Gershenzon have made of this? Why, given Berdyaev's collaboration on the anti-Semitic "Israel in the past….," did he not sever ties earlier? When we consider Gershenzon's friendship with Rozanov in ch.4, the answer will become clearer. However, to preempt, we can say that circumstance played a very great role. Berdyaev's position was nuanced and complex, not fitting easily into the category of philo- or anti-Semite, rather like the entire Solovievian inheritance. Absent pressing political and social circumstances, there is no reason why his views should have triggered an explosive reaction in Gershenzon, whose own views on Jewry and traditional Judaism were deeply ambiguous. It took the critical events of October 1917 to resolve that ambiguity into something far more confrontational, as was the case with Bulgakov. Incidentally, a Russian-Jewish thinker, P.A. Berlin, later critiqued Berdyaev's stance in *Filosofia ravenstva*: he contended that the policy of equality coincided with Jewry's interests, and that while he appreciated Berdyaev's religious orientation and attempt to get to the heart of the meaning of Jewish history, he should have remembered that governments deal with law not philosophy, and that

However, to put Gershenzon and Berdyaev on two different sides of a Jewish-Christian dichotomy would be wrong. Once again, in philosophical terms they seem to be on one side of the barricade. Berdyaev, like Gershenzon, is utterly pessimistic about culture: there is not a single epoch in European history that escapes his condemnation. Moreover, in terms of heterodoxy, Berdyaev's rejection of God's intervention in history goes against the general Christian belief in God's continuing action in history, both through the sacraments and in "secular" events. Finally, Berdyaev's almost Marcionite rejection of the Old Testament mentality is, as we will see, shared by Gershenzon, who was no less anxious to reject this aspect of his Judaic past in favor of something more "spiritual."

Berdyaev himself recognized that "…the metaphysical consciousness of the Old Adam continues to set up its barriers in the New Testament period of human history… The Christian consciousness has so far but inadequately applied this process of revaluation. It is true to say that the new revelation of Biblical truth was the contribution rather of great individual mystics like Jacob Boehme…than of the Christian philosophy in general."

In other words, Berdyaev realizes that along with the Old Testament, his philosophy of history must reject most of historical Christianity and rely on the insights of a few pantheistically inclined mystics. Again, it looks as if Gershenzon and Berdyaev have placed themselves in the camp of the Spirit – as against the camp of historical Judaism and Christianity.

In what, then, if anything does the opposition between Berdyaev and Gershenzon consist? For all his rebelliousness and nihilism, Berdyaev's aristocratic military background made him by temperament sympathetic to imperial Russia, and by his own admission he was drawn towards the White movement at the beginning of the Civil War. Gershenzon's background gave him a direct understanding of the dark side of Christian empire, which translated into support for the Soviet change of power.

Nonetheless, the crucial factor missed by Berdyaev as well as Bulgakov is that Gershenzon was not constrained by any Jewish religious belief in his (albeit nuanced) empathy for the new Marxist government. Further, it would be difficult to imagine that Gershenzon's individualistic religion of the Spirit could have been seen as posing a danger to Soviet ideology at that stage. Christianity, by contrast, as the former state religion of the empire, had an altogether different political aura.

However, this merely adds to the impression that it was not so much the content of Gershenzon's and Berdyaev's philosophy that translated into different reactions to the Revolution; rather it was extraneous facts concerning social

---

the Soviet government was not headed by Solovievs who might be able to implement the mystical approach sensitively. Instead, a politician who viewed the Jewish question mystically and biologically-philosophically was Hitler – with predictable consequences. P.A.Berlin,"Russkie mysliteli i yevrei." *Novy Zhurnal*, No.70. (1962).

background – and, perhaps, to take a Berdyaevan stance, the irreducible element of personality.

Shortly, we will see that even these remaining differences in outlook were to close up in a later stage of Berdyaev's development.

Gershenzon and Jewish destiny
Pushkin-Ahasuerus

In 1919, Gershenzon published two works on Pushkin, *The Wisdom of Pushkin*[62] and *The Vision of a Poet*. In 1922, he continued his thoughts on Pushkin in *Gulfstream*. In the same year, there appeared *Key to Faith* – a meditation on the Bible and history. Finally, he published *The Destiny of the Jewish People*.

This last work applies the philosophy of history developed in the previous works to Jewry. That philosophy developed out of his new technique of a "slow reading" of Pushkin, in which he payed attention to every line and syllable of his opus. Through this hermeneutic method, Gershenzon claimed to have come to know more about Pushkin than the poet knew about himself.

For the work of Pushkin, as far as Gershenzon was concerned, was prophetic and at the centre of Pushkin's prophetic activity was the Word, whose profoundest meanings are couched in images. Gershenzon's interpretation "[drew] out [the prophetic meaning] from the images," and he was aware that "brought out into the light of day, it will seem strange and perhaps unbelievable."

But that was because there were two Pushkins: one was the child of his time; the other is the eternal poet and creator, who "in creating, becomes transfigured; in his well-known European face step forth the dusty creases of Ahasuerus, from his eyes there stare out the heavy wisdom of millennia…"[63]

As with Berdyaev's objection to Gershenzon's Slavophilism, most Pushkin specialists of the time did indeed find Gershenzon's readings of Pushkin "unbelievable."[64] While Proscurina objects that his contemporaries missed the profundity of some of Gershenzon's insights, there is an analogy between Gershenzon's reading of the Slavophiles and Pushkin, which can be see initially in the striking way that – consciously or unconsciously – Gershenzon sees in Pushkin's face the features of Ahasuerus.

Later in the article, Gershenzon refers to Pushkin's "Arab" ancestry and "Eastern spirit" of thought. However, his comparison of the poet to Ahasuerus,

---

[62] This work will be examined and contrasted with Semyon Frank's interpretation of Pushkin in ch.6.
[63] Mikhail Gershenzon, *Izbrannoe. Tom 1. Mudrost' Pushkina*. Moscow: Gesharim/Mosty kultury, 2000), 19.
[64] Cf.Proscurina, 1989. His friend and admirer, Khodasevich, a poet who had also written on Pushkin, wrote: "The study of facts, it seems to me, were more a means for him to test conjectures than to extract material for conclusions. Quite often this has led to errors. His 'Wisdom of Pushkin' was to a well-known extent the 'Wisdom of Gershenzon.'" (Vladislav Khodasevich, "Gershenzon," in Khodasevich V. *Nekropol': Vospominaniya*, 56-63. Brussels: Les éditions Petropolis, 1939).

the type of the wandering Jew, more than anything confirms Khodasevich's observation that his "Wisdom of Pushkin" was more a "Wisdom of Gershenzon" – a charge which Gershenzon always vehemently denied.

Yet if even the Jewish writer Leib Yaffe[65] could see in Gershenzon "the appearance and mannerisms...of a shtetl rabbi" and his friend Khodasevich saw in him a "typical Jew" who gave the impression of "halting speech....[due to] the Jewish intonations of a Kishinev native," it seems rather remarkable that Gershenzon could remain unconscious that applying this popular Judaic trope[66] to Pushkin was perhaps not a genuine insight into the poet, but a projection onto him from himself.

Thus, if we apply Gershenzon's own somewhat impudent method of extracting meaning out of writers which they themselves were unaware of, we are bound to say that Gershenzon Judaized Pushkin in his own image, so as to mine from him insights which for all their non-correspondence to traditional Judaism could still be felt to be Jewish. In this way, Pushkin became a Hebrew prophet, and Gershenzon's promise to his mother never to convert was fulfilled, not only in letter but in spirit.[67]

Of course, it was equally crucial for Gershenzon's needs that this Ahasueran-Pushkinian philosophy transcend in ancientness even Judaism, and that the Bible be merely one element in its universal range. At its centre was the image of the universal human soul as fire, a doctrine traced back through Heraclitus, the Avesta and the Rig Veda. This soul-fire was the recipient of the Spirit-Word, or Word-Fire, which rushes through history inspiring mankind, but also burning away anything vain and useless.

Not only the ancient books testify to the power of the Word, but all great artists up to and after Pushkin manifest the eternal flame, the historical "Gulfstream," of the Spirit. Indeed, it is when history is at its most hopeless that the fiery word is seen blazing strongest and man must dedicate himself most zealously to the spiritual work of creativity – appropriate and comforting words for the year in which Lenin exiled the leading non-Marxist intellectuals from Russia, and Gershenzon's own faith in the direction of the Revolution was being challenged.

A special place in Gershenzon's philosophy of the Word-Spirit is reserved for historians. It is they who can uncover the direction in which the Word is calling humanity. Intense historical research reveals how "the experience of the

---

[65] Leib Yaffe, "Vladislav Khodasevich (iz moix vospominaniiy)," in Khodasevich V. *Iz yevreiskikh poetov*, 15-29. Moscow-Jerusalem: Gesharim, 1998.

[66] Years later, Bulgakov used this image to refer to Shestov in his obituary of the latter: Shestov was "something of Ahasuerus: he knocks on different windows, but only so as to continue on the same circular path." Sergei Bulgakov, "Nekotoriye cherty religioznogo mirovozzreniya L.I.Shestova," *Sovromeniye Zapiski*, No.68, Paris, 1939.

[67] We will see that a similar dynamic applies in Shestov's heterodox Judaic philosophizing by means of free-style midrash.

every day non-trivially comes together with the eternally unfulfilled moments of the internal spiritual self-definition of man."[68]

This, then, is the background for his essay on Jewish destiny. The latter can thus be seen as a call to the Jewish people by the prophet of the Word-Spirit. It is, in fact, Gershenzon's most sustained public effort to apply his prophetic insights to his native people "of the flesh." Perhaps, it was a final attempt to overcome his torment about having rejected Jewish life. As he had written to Gornfeld in 1910: "I feel Jewish both socially and subjectively-psychologically. As regards the first, as a matter of fact, recently (I must have got old) quite often I am tormented: I do not see any avenue into active participation in Jewish affairs."

In the years following this confession, Gershenzon did intervene in Jewish affairs on several occasions. In 1915, he wrote a plea concerning Jewish victims of the war-related violence taking place on the Western frontier[69]. Then in 1916, he wrote an essay on "The yoke and genius" of the Hebrew poet, Bialik[70]. Finally, between 1916 and 1918, he acted as an intermediary between the Zionist writer Leib Yaffe and Russian poets, in support of Yaffe's project of a Russian-Hebrew anthology of contemporary Hebrew writers.

In an introduction written for that collection, Gershenzon celebrated the revival of Hebrew and the poetry now being written in it, seeing it as a welcome departure from the lachrymose and sickly themes that had obsessed medieval Jewish writers. This emancipation of the Hebrew soul had returned a sense of dignity to Jews, and given Jews a way to express the Jewish Spirit in a way that now corresponded to "the entire depths of the flourishing human spirit." Later, Khodasevich recalled that their period of intense collaboration on this Russian-Hebrew project, was looked back on by both of them with great fondness.

In 1922 Khodasevich even wrote to Yaffe expressing joy that his former collaborator had finally realized his dream of emigrating to "his Palestine… to engage in his cherished and beloved task," and informing him that "many times Gershenzon and myself have envied you." He added: "Ha! If only I had the money – how I would then travel to Palestine."[71]

Yaffe, for his part, had welcomed Gershenzon's involvement in a Jewish project. "Not so very long ago, he was sitting at home in his attic and he knew nothing about our people… With the deftness of a rabbi he pored over his studies and labored, only his studies were Russian history, the Decembrists, research

---

[68] Rashkovsky in Evgeny Rashkovsky, "Istorik Mikhail Gershenzon," in Novy Mir No.10, (2001).

[69] Mikhail Gershenzon, "Delo pravdy i razuma!" Nevskii alamanakh. Zhertvam voiny. Petrodgrad, 1915.

[70] 'Yarmo i genii' (o Byalike) – Yevreiskaya zhizn', 1916. One of Bialik's most famous poems 'On the slaughter' was about the pogrom in Gershenzon's hometown of Kishinev. In that poem, Bialik outraged Jewish sensibilities by criticizing the passivity of the pogrom's victims.

[71] Leib Yaffe, "Vladislav Khodasevich (iz moix vospominaniiy)," in Khodasevich V. *Iz yevreiskikh poetov*, 15-29. Moscow-Jerusalem: Gesharim, 1998.

into the poetry of Pushkin and the problems of Russian literature."[72] Thus Yaffe felt that in some sense, he had contributed to Gershenzon's Jewish awakening.

It is thus with some shock that one reads the "Jewishly revived" Gershenzon's final essay on Jewish destiny and marvels at the complexity of his personality. For if one separates out from the philosophy expressed there a concrete call to action to his fellow Jews, the message can be distilled as follows: of all tendencies in Jewish life, the Zionist is the most cruelly mistaken and misleading. The true path for a Jew to follow is to assimilate himself out of existence, so that he dissolves without a physical trace among greater humanity.

Gershenzon's essay received a fairly cold reception among Russian Christians[73]. However, the reaction among most sectors of Jewry can be imagined: with uncanny precision, Gershenzon moves from treading on the toes of the Zionists to rebutting the religious and cultural advocates of Jewish identity. If Russian intellectual opinion had stood aghast at his interpretations of Pushkin and the "cosmic" Slavophiles, it was now the turn of Jewish intellectuals to be left breathless.

Apotheosis of Jewishness: Gershenzon against Land, Torah and People

Gershenzon starts *The Destiny of the Jewish People* with a well-meant, fraternal polemic against Zionism, which is a bowing before "the Moloch of European nationalism." As a Jew, as a member of "a family at a crossroads", he addresses himself first and foremost to the Zionists for the simple reason that their advocacy of return to Palestine embodied a completely opposite reading of Jewish history to his own. For him, the Diaspora and not settlement on the Land contained the key to the meaning of Jewish fate. Again, if we remember that Bulgakov and Berdyaev generally favored the Zionist movement, we are struck by the irony that it was Gershenzon who gave the less "worldly" analysis of Jewish fate than his Christian counterparts.

Very early on, Gershenzon makes it clear that, as for world history, so for Jewish history destinies are determined by the Spirit. In this case, it is the "Jewish Spirit" or "Will" that drove Jews off the Land two millennia ago, and since then the Jewish people has matured. The Zionist dream of a return is thus contrary to the Spirit, for to return would be to "swaddle a mature nation and lay it in a cradle"[74].

---

[72] Ibid.
[73] If Zenkovsky's 1938 reference in *Historiosophical Themes* is anything to go by (Vassily Zenkovsky, "Na temy istoriosofii," in *Sovremmenie zapiski* No 69. (1939):280-293.) The easy way in which he drops a reference to Gershenzon's essay gives the impression that it was familiar to the emigrant community. We will look at Zenkovsky's reaction to the essay below.
[74] The question arises what the relationship is between the "Jewish Spirit," or "Will" and the world Word-Spirit that rushes like a gulfstream through the affairs of humanity in general. Does every nation have a spirit? Or is the Spirit one and embodied severally in different nations? Gershenzon's essays are not philosophical tracts and

In fact, the Jewish nation was born in exile – in Egypt. But even after it moved into the land, its history was disastrous – as the division of Judah and Samaria and the destruction of the Temple show. In exile, of course, the tragedies that befell the Jewish people were manifold. Nonetheless, Gershenzon again sees in all these disasters the deliberate work of the "Spirit"[75].

The crucial question arises then: why did the Spirit engineer these misfortunes. For Gershenzon is quite explicit that it was the Jewish Spirit who "…by a secret signal…summoned Titus to destroy its kingdom, the Crusaders to massacre its sons in Worms and Kologne, Philip to expel them from Spain, and the Kishinev mob to destroy their homes."

The answer, which Gershenzon himself confesses to find so strange that "I can hardly bring myself to express it," is that the Spirit wishes to develop in Jewry "an indifference to permanence." The Spirit of the nation gives land, language, temple, law, king, custom, profession, in fact every conceivable aspect of life to the Jews – and then engineers its violent removal, in order to break the attachment of the Jews to worldly goods, which are the bread and butter of the rest of humanity.

The repeated process of exile and resettlement up to the destruction of the Second Temple were a boiling and refining process, a straining away of unwanted elements (who assimilated in exile), until a pure residue was attained that would be ready for the last exile, ready to embody in each and every member of the Jewish nation the special task of Jewish creativity[76], which would necessarily be fulfilled in the Diaspora.

For once the Jews' physical ties to the land were broken, the Spirit set about weaning Jews away from their religion and peoplehoood, those final all-too-human crutches that the rest of mankind feels to be indispensable.

At this point, Gershenzon addresses his Jewish readers and invites them like himself to take the final step suggested by the Spirit and reject Torah and 'am yisrael: "Do you feel attracted to Torah? Tear yourself away. Do you feel eternally settled in Jewry – leave it behind. Your spirit must become as homeless as your body." Only thus can the upward movement of the Spirit be fulfilled for: "You were once in the flesh a citizen of the Cannanite kingdom, now you are a citizen of the universe; you were in the spirit dedicated to Torah and a citizen of Jewry; be dedicated to no one, a citizen of spiritual humanity. I will not leave you anything except your daily bread and family love, so that you can live."

---

do not offer answers to these questions. For this reason, they are unpersuasive for those not already immersed in a similar world-view. Given the radical nature of this world-view, it is thus not surprising that Gershenzon did not persuade many.

[75] Once again, though Gershenzon denied to Ivanov that he was influenced by Hegel this thesis contains a note of Hegelian complaceny: the real is rational and the rational is real. Whatever happened in Jewish history happened for the good and one cannot go backwards in time against the grain of the Spirit.

[76] Already we can see that, as with Berdyaev, "creativity" (*tvorchestvo*) and Spirit are the key elements of human religiosity.

Of course, Judaism's rites are the final barrier to Jewry's complete assimilation and Gershenzon is aware of this and ready to accept Jewry's ultimate physical dissolution. For if and when Jewry disappears completely, the Spirit of Jewry will remain. This is the inevitable triumph of the Spirit, and nothing the Zionists do to cage the spirit by trying to mummify the body of Jewry can change this.

Looking around him, Gershenzon already sees the future in the lives of assimilated European Jews like himself. The Viennese journalist[77], the bourgeois businessman in Petersburg, the Jewish merchant and professor, are all types of the Jewish spirit, separated from the Jewish body by four generations of assimilation away from the community. They are characterized by a radical and utter skepticism towards the values of their ambient culture, which they pretend to believe in, but inside themselves they instead have a great emptiness which is utterly separated from all that surrounds them in the world.

This is the emptiness left by the cruel Jewish God, who filled them with the wonderful spectacle of religion with all its picturesque festivals, and then undermined it – now theatre and literature and scholarship cannot fill this void, cannot compare with it in intensity. But precisely this skeptical emptiness is the last stage of Jewish emancipation. The Jew is spiritually empty.

Finally, Gershezon asks: Why was this liberation necessary? What purpose did this history of the Jews from Egypt and Canaan through Assyria and Rome to Russia and Europe serve? His answer, befitting for a Jewishly empty nihilist, is that no one can say for sure.

Only the negative aspects of the liberation can be seen: the fruits of the Spirit are invisible. But the result is that Jews so liberated have become "lowly in spirit." "Maybe," speculates Gershenzon in his concluding thoughts, "they will be the first to enter the Kingdom of spiritual freedom; maybe the last will of Jewry can be seen in the words that were once pronounced out of its depth: 'Blessed are the lowly in spirit, for theirs is the Kingdom of Heaven. Blessed are those who thirst and hunger for truth, for they shall be sated.' They have been sated with a food which the world has not yet tasted, for all worldly values are like sham victuals." The final words of the essay are: "The Jewish kingdom is not of this world."

It should be apparent just how much this picture of the "Jewish Spirit" shares with Berdyaev. Gershenzon also uses the term "Jewish Spirit" with a dual meaning: there is a good manifestation of the Jewish spirit and a bad one. In his polemic with retrograde Zionists, he is saying that Jews who defend their people, and their "earthly kingdom" in Palestine are carnal, anti-Spiritual and this-worldly. They have missed the direction in which history is moving.

But this agrees step by step with Berdyaev analysis of the "Jewish Spirit:" it is falsely eschatological, missing the essential meaning of history and strives always for this world. The real fruits of history, as for Gershenzon, cannot

---

[77] An odd choice, as Herzl was a Viennese journalist.

be seen in the success of this world, but can only be perceived in that other invisible world.

In addition, Gershenzon accuses the Zionist program of normalization of the Jewish people as "selling the birthright of chosenness for a pot of lentils." And yet Jewish chosenness consists precisely in recognizing that the Jewish people and religion must disappear, leaving only a "Jewish Spirit" which can be incarnated in Jew and non-Jew alike. While not exact, this is not far from Berdyaev's idea that the Jews have fulfilled their mission and have no earthly role to play: their heritage has entered into Christianity.

In fact, given that Gershenzon's philosophy of Jewish history finds nothing worth preserving in Jewry it is hard to resist the conclusion that, if this had been written by a non-Jew, it would be straightforwardly labeled anti-Semitic. The only reservation one might have in this respect is that while Gershenzon converges finally on the anti-Semitic stereotype of the Jew and the "Jewish Spirit" as rootless, spiritually empty, skeptical, cosmopolitan and nihilist, he puts an approving tick in the box beside this category rather than a vituperatively hateful cross.

Gershenzon's final unacknowledged quote from the Gospel even seems to collapse his "new Judaism" with the message preached by Christ: the kingdom "not of this world" is, in fact, "the Jewish kingdom." In its own way, this is a spiritual-anarchistic revision not only of the author's inherited "fleshly" Judaism, but of historical Christianity, whose practitioners had always been so convinced of its inherent and superior spirituality.

In fact, Gershenzon expanded this theme in an essay which was to have a fate peculiarly illustrative of its author's development. The essay was called *The Sermon on the Mount*. It had been commissioned by E.Y.Belitsky for a collection to be called "Russian thinkers." Gershenzon's essay would give a statement of his worldview, and Belitsky (who edited a Berlin-Petrograd journal called *Epoch*) would help in its publication. The other co-authors whom Belitsky proposed were Andrey Bely, Lev Shestov – and Nicolai Berdyaev[78].

The mere mention of Berdyaev's name, however, caused Gershenzon to withdraw his article, which he then included in an anthology of his own works, also to be published under the auspices of *Epoch*. However, the Soviet censorship removed so much material that eventually Gershenzon decided not to include the mutilated remainder. The article has only recently become available in Russia.

It is perhaps not an accident that Belitsky, unaware of the enmity that had arisen between Berdyaev and Gershenzon, should have grouped the two authors together. In his "final testimony," Gershenzon continues that anarchistic and personalistic critique of organized religion, which is at the heart of his idiosyncratic philosophy – and which draws from the same wild-spirited rebelliousness which

---

[78] See further details in V.Proscurina, "Neizadannaya statya M.O.Gershenzona." Simvol 28 (1992).

made Berdyaev the object of suspicion among his fellow Christian believers, for all that he ended up pitted against Gershenzon as Christian against Jew.

In his "Sermon on the Mount"[79], Gershenzon focuses on Christ's words that the "lowly in spirit" are blessed. The interpretation he gives these words is, not surprisingly, no more Orthodox than his interpretation of Judaism[80]. For Gershenzon, Christ is above all calling on men to empty themselves of all dogma and doctrine, and to become utterly empty – lowly – of belief. Only then can man be open to the flow of cosmic energy, the cosmic will, which fills all men who do not parcel, hoard and stifle it. The lowly in sprit are ignorant of any fossilized "Truth" and alien to dogmas, which are merely elemental forces torn from their permanent movement and forced into solid format by human beings.

Thus, in a way which – as we will see below – echoes his co-author to-have-been, Lev Shestov, Gershenzon uses the books of the Bible, both Jewish and Christian, to critique what he sees as the fossilized and degenerate religious descendants of the Book of books: contemporary Jews and Christians.

Gershenzon's final "Sermon" does not actually add much to the philosophy which implicitly hovers between the lines of his *Landmarks* article. The intervening thirteen years have not changed his basic belief in a universal cosmic consciousness, or will, which can flow uninterruptedly into the human heart if only it is does not succumb to "cold" reason but remains open to the "heat" of nature. However, the context has changed. Now the passion of Gershenzon's cosmic religion for change, and constant dissolution and dynamism, thrills to the disruptive events ("the great quakes of our days which have no equal in the past") unleashed in the new Soviet Russia, for: "the path that leads to where the compass points is fearsome. It is said: 'Where your treasure is, there lies your heart.' If your heart is not to harden that is where you must go. Because the Spirit is the essence of life and life is constant motion."

Thus Gershenzon accepts the dissolution of Russia with the same strength of spirit, the same openness to cosmic energy, with which he had decided to bear the dissolution of his own Jewish people.

Of course, in retrospect, it is perhaps just as well that the intended anthology coupling Berdyaev and Gershenzon did not come to pass. Very probably, Berdyaev's reaction to his Jewish colleague's cosmic-revolutionary interpretation of the words of the founder of Christianity may have provoked yet another scandal – even though in practice Gershenzon's rhetoric was louder than his bite[81].

---

[79] Mikhail Gershenzon, "Nagornaya propoved," in *Simvol* 28 (1992).

[80] The Soviet censorship probably detected a covert attack on its own religion in Gershenzon condemnation of "those sated with the truth, all the politicians, political activists, philanthropists, professors and directors of schools, certain in their truth...."

[81] For all of Gershenzon's strong language, primary practice of what he preached consisted in acts of kindness and generosity to friends struggling under the pressures of those years. And secondly, the political conclusions that he made on the basis of his

However, once again, it is worth asking whether the Berdyaevan and Gershenzonian worldviews were so entirely at odds. It is true that Gershenzon's optimism about the accessibility of God, the goodness of human and world nature, and the general progressive direction of the "Spirit" are in a sense filled with a Jewish optimism[82]. Christianity's emphasis on the world's immersion in evil and the radical means – the death of God – needed to rectify this certainly provide a contrast on this score.

Nonetheless, two points need to be made here. Firstly, Berdyaev also idealized human creativity as a solution of the world's evil – in a way which also departs from a traditional Christian devaluation of the world and man's potential. And secondly, in looking for the source of this "Jewish optimism," we would be more justified in finding it – as Vyacheslav Ivanov and Semyon Frank did – in Gershenzon's admiration of Tolstoy, rather than in some distant memory of his *cheder* lessons.

In other words, once again, the source of Gershenzon's "cosmism" and the Revolutionary tincture it acquired are peculiarly Russian. The same can probably be said of Gershenzon's belief in the Spirit – which seems most cognate to the Spirit envisioned in the neo-Christianity of Merezhkovsky and the early Berdyaev.[83] Thus it seems that if there was a Jewish-Christian rift (to use Horowitz's term[84]) between Gershenzon and Berdyaev, it took place outside the camps of either Jewish or Christian Orthodoxy on peculiarly Russian ground[85].

---

cosmic religion seem rather tame and unapocalyptic by comparison with some of his bold slogans earlier in the article. At one point in the *Sermon* he states: "From this flow completely practical values. The new creation of great realms is bad; the dissolution of what was forcefully forged together is good. A republic is better than a monarchy, a federal arrangement better than a centralized republic; and the smaller the federal units, the better. Everything that leads to the greater enclosedness of the nation is bad; and growing commercial, spiritual and personal communication between them is good. The integration of trade, production and capital into companies is bad; productive and consumer cooperatives, the limitation of the law of inheritance is good." Hardly a program for the annihilation of the bourgeois and their religious lackeys!

[82] For more on philosophical "Jewish optimism", see ch.7 on Herman Cohen, Franz Rosenzweig and Semyon Frank.

[83] A common criticism of Merezhkovsky and Berdyaev by Russian Orthodox thinkers was precisely that they were reviving the medieval Catholic heresy of Johannes Flores, whose concept of epochs of the Father, Son and Spirit tore asunder the unity of the Trinity, all the person of whom act in full harmony. A similar absolutization of the Spirit at the cost of Christian Orthodoxy is found in Boehme, Hegel, Schleiermacher, Schopenhauer – all of whom influenced Berdyaev and other Russians.

[84] The title of Horowitz (1994)'s article: "A Jewish-Christian rift in Twentieth-Century Russian philosophy…"

[85] After considering the philosophy of Shestov, we will have a more precise feeling about the geographical lay-out of this ground and will then be able to return to the question of Berdyaev's and Gershenzon's similar yet conflicting interpretations of the 'Jewish spirit'.

Such a contention probably receives its most convincing proof in the subsequent intellectual development of Berdyaev himself.

The 'Judaization'[86] of Berdyaev
When Berdyaev returned to the theme of Jewry, Russia and the meaning of history in the thirties, he had changed his mind about several matters.

In *The Jewish Question as a Christian Question*, he tried to soften the rather stringent tone he had used against Jews in *The Meaning of History*. He divides anti-Semitism into social, political, racial and religious anti-Semitism and maintains that only the latter (which is in effect anti-Judaism) is permissible. Moreover, "The only one who has a spiritual right to Christian anti-Semitism is he who will love and not hate Jews, will oppose the Jewish spirit through his Christian spirit. Such is the paradox of the Jewish question as a Christian question." This, of course, is simply a restatement of Soloviev's position.

In the later *Christianity and anti-Semitism* (1938), Berdyaev is evidently still wrestling with his conscience. Here he takes pains to refute the idea the Jews were particularly active in the Revolution, as of course many in the Russian émigré community believed – including, as we have seen, himself. He also comments that those Jews who did take part in the Revolution often acted out of worthy motives, such as a concern for the poor and justice. In this comment, we can detect the ghost of Gershenzon, whom he came to feel he had treated unfairly.

But the most radical about-turn in Berdyaev's thinking can be found in his last work, *The Russian Idea*. Written immediately after the Soviet contribution to the defeat of Germany, this book resonates with Berdyaev's re-evaluation of Soviet Russia as a force not entirely for the bad, as he had so uncompromisingly argued before – and even, in a dialectical way, as containing tendencies and forces of great good.

The argument of the book is that what is best and most unique about the Russian spirit is its eschatological and apocalyptic orientation. This is the root of the active nature of Russian Christianity compared to the passive, ahistorical Western version which is content to shift redemption beyond the bounds of time. It was also the inspiration behind the conceptually worthy ideas which fired the Revolution. A range of figures on the left and right of politics, both religious and non-religious, are grouped together to provide examples of this manifestation of the "Russian idea."

---

[86] As we explain below, Berdyaev's "Judaization" could just as well be called his re-chiliasticization or re-millinerianisation, meaning that he returned to his Merezhkovskian belief in a Kingdom of God's will "on heaven as it is on earth." Another theme which we have not explored here is the parallels that were made by Russian writers (including Rozanov) between Russia's Christian sects and Judaism. Often sectarians were accused of ritual murders, unusual sexual practices and duplicitous allegiance to the government. Many of these themes were transferred when Russians came to write about Jews and Judaism, most notoriously in the case of the blood libel. For further discussion of this, cf. L.Katsis, *Krovavy Navet i russkaya mysl*, ch.10.

Among these figures is Lenin, whose Russian brand of communism shows how "the Russian messianic idea has been transferred in an unreligious and anti-religious form, [so that what] has taken place [is] a similar perversion of the seeking after the kingdom...But for Russian people, regardless of the temptations to which they have given in, the denial of the greatness and glory of this world is very characteristic....Greatness and glory are a sin and temptation, much more so than for Western people....Lenin, with his crudeness and lack of any polish, any theatricality, with his simpleness, bordering on cynicism, is a typical Russian person."

Berdyaev goes on to express implicit approval of Lenin's genetic connection with the ascetic Russian spirit of world-denial, and the Russian belief that "The Kingdom of Heaven is the transfiguration of the world, not only the transfiguration of the individual person, but also a transfiguration of the social and the cosmic."[87] By contrast, Konstanin Leontiev's passive conception of the Apocalypse is criticized for shying away from such an active transformation of the world: "a person can do nothing, he can only save his soul"[88].

But perhaps the most striking instance of Berdyaev's new infatuation with active, society-transforming apocalypticism is in his interpretation of Soloviev. He takes the philosopher to task for abandoning in his final *Story of the Anti-Christ* his previous theocratic ideas, and his awareness of the transformation of human history by the God-man, in favor of a passive scenario where redemption takes place beyond the bounds of history. This final tale "as it were, justified the most counter-revolutionary and obscurantist apocalyptic theories."[89] Now, it seems, the metric of evaluation is whether Soloviev's eschatological spirit is in harmony with the goals of the Revolution.

There is one further passage in *The Russian Idea*, where the full ambiguity over the relationship of eschatology to this world is put in terms which almost exactly echo those of his estranged friend so many years ago. One feels that if the word "Russian" were replaced by the word "Jewish," it could serve as a fitting prologue to Gershenzon's essay on Jewish destiny and essence.

"Eschatological striving," writes Berdyaev, "belongs to the structure of the Russian soul. Wandering (vagabondism) is a very Russian phenomenon, unknown in such a degree in the West. The wanderer roams over the whole of the unencompassable Russian land, never settles and never becomes attached to anything. The wanderer searches for truth, for the Kingdom of God, he is oriented into the distance. The wanderer does not have a permanent city on this earth, he is oriented towards the City that is Coming. The popular element always turned up from its midst wanderers."

In these lines we seem to be reading a paeon to the Russian Ahasuerus: and while Berdyaev does not make explicit the parallel between Russian and Jewish

---

[87] Nicolai Berdyaev, *Russkaya Ideya*, (St.Petersburg: Azbuka-klassika, 2008), 237.
[88] Ibid, 249.
[89] Ibid, 250.

wandering, one feels that the pain of exile had awakened in this Russian some chords familiar to the Jew in *galut*,[90] replete with the temptation to overcome that exile by any means possible – in this case a desperate desire to see good in the Soviet Union.

Berdyaev continues the above passage with examples of archetypical Russian wanderers: "But by their spirit wanderers were the most creative spirits of Russian culture, Gogol, Dostoevsky, Tolstoy, Soloviev were wanderers, and so was the whole Revolutionary intelligentsia." Again, distinctions are blurred: the religious philosopher, the reactionary novelist, and the materialist Marxist intellectual – against which he had so bitterly fought before – are all put on a par as exemplars of the best in Russian spiritual culture.

In sum, eschatology, rootless wandering, social activism, impatience for the end time are now the best fruits of the "Russian spirit." Two decades earlier, they had been, alternatively, a "Russian *temptation*," or the cursed fruits of the "Jewish spirit." From a certain point of view, this should not be surprising: even in 1922, despite Berdyaev's disagreement with Gershenzon, there were numerous points of subterranean contact. Furthermore, in *The Russian Idea* Berdyaev again praises the vigor of Russian Christian sectarians, returning belatedly in this way towards his earlier admiration for Bely and the sectarian spirituality seductively depicted in the latter's *Silver Dove*. The fact that admiration for Judaism coincides with a reevaluation of Christian sectarianism should be no surprise: Judaism was often interpreted in Russian thought in terms first applied to its own heretical offshoots[91].

Berdyaev's newfound admiration for Soviet power attracted outrage in the émigré community; some of them thought he had simply gone senile. Among many who criticized him for this was his friend, Georgy Fedotov,[92] who accused him of giving into patriotic sentiments and presenting Soviet Russia as the morally superior liberator of the world from Fascist Germany, forgetting the moral equivalence of the two totalitarian regimes. Certainly, there is a sense of déjà vu. In 1917, his "whole soul" had prayed for the victory over Germany, but defeat then had forced him to modify his Hegelian philosophy of war. That philosophy makes a triumphant come-back under the new turn of world-events three decades later.

Fedotov recognizes this and does not just take issue with Berdyaev's new support of the Soviets. He objects to the whole thesis of the "Russian idea" as eschatological in nature, arguing that this was a distortion of Russian history and if it was to be found anywhere in Russian religiosity, it was primarily in Berdyaev: "Like many people of his generation," Fedotov continued, "he transfers over into Christian eschatology the revolutionary moods of the epoch. The eschatologism

---

[90] The parallel between Russian and Jewish exiles was explicitly recognized in different ways by Lev Karsavin and Nicolai Trubetzkoy, cf. 5.
[91] Cf. Katsis (2006), ch.10 for this, with special reference to Rozanov.
[92] Whose work we will look at more closely later.

of Berdyaev arises from completely other religio-psychological roots than the traditional, particularly Orthodox, Christian…the eschatology of Berdyaev is not a rejection of history, but rather the completion of it."[93]

Thus Berdyaev found himself being subjected to exactly the same criticism that he had so vehemently directed at falsely eschatological Jews in 1922, and at Gershenzon in particular in 1917. Belatedly, he experienced that same "Russian temptation" which he had so perceptively noted in Bely after the first Revolution. This, of course, only adds to the impression that Gershenzon, rather than suffering from a peculiarly Jewish temptation, had become prey to a Russian malaise – though it was undoubtedly compounded by his extreme rejection of his own Jewish roots. It also perhaps suggests that Berdyaev's earlier description of eschatologism in Jewish terms, by making it seem another man's malaise, had only laid the grounds for the dormant tendency to rear its head in another unrecognized form.

Lev Shestov

Berdyaev's friendship with another Jew from the Pale of Settlement who had turned into a star of the Russian cultural firmament[94] provides another interesting perspective on the emerging commentary on the "Jewish spirit" and the "Russian spirit."

Like Berdyaev, Shestov[95] was a native of Kiev, where he was born Lev-Judah Isaacovich Shwartzman[96] in 1866 into the family of a well-to-do Jewish businessman, who had built up a textile empire throughout Southern Russia. His initial foray into literature and philosophy was interrupted by the necessity to take control of this business shortly after he graduated from university. Below, we will examine how Shestov's natural distaste for business and consequent depression over this torturous distraction translated into complex feelings of ambiguity towards his family and its Jewish commercial orientation, as he came to see it.[97]

Another shadow that was cast over his early life was his relationship with two women. An affair with the family's servant-girl produced an illegitimate son,

---

[93] Fedotov, Gyorgy: "Berdyaev Myslitel'." Here quoted in the translation of Fr. Steven Janos: "Berdyaev the thinker, by Georgii P. Fedotov," at: http://www.chebucto.ns.ca/Philosophy/Sui-eneris/Berdyaev/essays/fedotov.htm

[94] Just as Rozanov was provoked to comment on the Jewishness of "Russia's greatest historian," so Shestov drew a somewhat acidic remark from Merezhkovsky: "a Jew, but what Russian he writes."

[95] Here the details of his life and work will only be sketched briefly as a good account exists in English by Bernard Martin and can be found at: shestov.by.ru /intro.html. This website also contains most of his works in English translation.

[96] His choice of pseudonym will be explained below.

[97] Again, the rebellion against Jewishness accompanied by attraction is reminiscent of Mandelstam, also born to a Jewish trading family, which he escaped for Russian letters.

Sergei Listopadov, who was killed in 1915 fighting against the Germans. In 1896, having moved to Rome after a nervous break-down triggered by his despair over his involvement in the business, Shestov then married Anna Berezovskaya, an Orthodox Christian Russian medical student. The marriage took place in Rome, as marriages between unbaptized Jews and Christians were forbidden in the Russian empire. In this respect, Shestov shared a family dynamic with Gershenzon and Rozanov, both of whose marriages were illegitimate in the eyes of the state[98].

However, there was an additional reason for secrecy: though Shestov's father had a reputation as a free-thinker he still held strictly to Jewish tradition and would not have accepted his son's marriage outside the faith. This was part of the reason why Shestov led a peripatetic life outside the borders of Russia, constantly hiding his marriage and children from his father.

Shestov's early works were published in quick succession after his first visit back to Russia in 1898. The first three works examined other authors' opinions in a clear, witty and sharp prose: *Shakespeare and his critic Brandeis* (1898); *Good in the Teaching of Tolstoy and Nietzsche: Philosophy and Preaching* (1900); and *Dostoevsky and Nietzsche: The Philosophy of Tragedy* (1903). In the writing of these works, Shestov became infatuated with Nietzsche's rebellion against metaphysics and abstract truth, and his first original work expressing his own beliefs was the aphoristic *Apotheosis of Groundlessness*, published in 1905, the year of the first Russian revolution.

With this work, Shestov established the reputation of a cynic and a nihilist. Nearly all the reviews of this work were negative. One critic commented that he would have understood if Shestov had written his works in reverse order. For Shestov's earlier embrace of Nietzsche in his favorable comparison of the German writer with Tolstoy had praised his demolition of vapid moralizing appeals to an abstract Good, and seen it as a call "to seek that which is *above* pity, *above* Good. We must seek God."[99] But then in *Apotheosis*, Shestov seemed to question even the value of God and to pour scorn on all values.

Berdyaev, in fact, had initially seen a positive value in Shestov's embrace of Nietzsche, and in the circles in which Shestov was now mixing, this was not unique. For Berdyaev, Frank and Bulgakov, Nietzsche too had acted as a trigger for a rebellion against German idealist philosophy. Nonetheless, it was to be a long time before Shestov was to propose anything positive in the ruins left by Nietzsche.

Later he was to take his destruction of metaphysics forward with a "Biblical,"

---

[98] This was one of the factors that attracted Rozanov to Gershenzon.

[99] This triggered one of his earliest polemics with a philosopher of all-unity, S. Trubetzkoy, who in the same year was defending his doctoral dissertation "The teaching about the Logos", in which he equates the Platonic Good with the Biblical God, a thesis which directly contradicts Shestov's already embryonic belief in the opposition of Athens and Jerusalem. For further discussion of Shestov and S.Trubetzkoy, cf. P.P. Gaidenko, *Vladimir Soloviev i filosofia serebryanogo veka*, p.132 ff.

fideistic philosophy that he developed in works such as *Gesthemane Night* (1924), on Pascal's philosophy, and his several essays devoted to Kierkegaard and Luther. This was to culminate in his final work, *Athens and Jerusalem* (1938).

Still, most of Shestov's circle, while welcoming a relief from the pessimism of his early works, continued to question whether Shestov's radical fideism with its rejection of all of Western philosophy, did in fact constitute a step forward. It was Berdyaev who articulated this criticism most stringently, linking it to Shestov's Jewishness.

Shestov himself maintained that his philosophy had not undergone a radical change. From very early on, his faith in the straightforwardness of life had been shattered by a life-changing experience of the closeness of death. He refused to elaborate on the exact nature of this experience, but it constantly animated his stubborn resistance against all and any rationalistic, verbal explanations of life that would seem to give life a logic and consistency, or enough coherency for its meaning to be transmitted between fellow men.

This worldview, which came to be dubbed irrationalist, is at the root of the philosophical exchange between Shestov and Berdyaev. It is also beneath Shestov's corresponding embrace of, coupled with sharp criticism of, his friend Gershenzon's life philosophy.

Shestov's work is very one-tracked. It is almost the case that one can open any of Shestov's books and, plunging into them *in medias res*, after several pages pick up the drift of his whole philosophy. In this sense, it is easy to get an idea of Shestov's understanding of the quarrel between Berdyaev and Gershenzon, and his quarrel with both of them, simply by reading the short reviews he wrote of each of his friends' works.

On the other hand, if one were to confine oneself solely to these reviews without any reference to Shestov's own biography, one would very soon encounter a seemingly impassable paradox as far as his contribution to the debate about a Jewish and Christian spirit in Russian philosophy is concerned.

For it emerges that on Shestov's reading, Gershenzon's interpretation of the Bible in *Gulfstream* and a *Key to Faith* is a continuation of the false Christian universalization of the mysterious "God Yahweh's" actions as recorded in the Bible, which "was so carefully preserved through the course of centuries by a small, ignorant people standing at a side from the great highway of history." A naïve reading of this statement might conclude that Shestov is defending the truth of Judaic particularity as against Gershenzon's misplaced "Christian spirit."

In his reviews of Berdyaev, however, Shestov takes exception to the latter's overemphasis of Jesus' historical environment, reproaching him with becoming "mired in the Judaic aspect of the Gospels." But this would seem to be an attack on Berdyaev's excessively Jewish approach to Christianity.

It seems then that Shestov must have been operating according to a different metric of what was Judaic and what Christian than Berdyaev or Gershenzon. Below, it will emerge what that metric was – as far as this can be ascertained, as different interpreters, both his contemporaries and those who came later, were often at odds as to Shestov's precise relation to Judaism and Christianity.

Indeed, this was not the only area where Shestov evoked confusion, frustration and, as often as not, censure. He was accused of misreading the greats of European literature in the "pilgrimage among souls" that he conducted in essay-like forays into a small pantheon of his favorite thinkers and cultural figures, who included Abraham, Job, Luther, Pascal, Dostoevsky, and Kierkegaard. However, we will return to these charges, as brought by Berdyaev, after we have considered Shestov's own thoughts on his two contemporaries. In exploring these thoughts, we will also unfold some more details of Shestov's "metric" (for it would do it a disservice to call it a system).

Shestov on Gershenzon

In his essay dedicated to Gershenzon[100] on his death, Shestov focused on two works: Gershenzon's correspondence with Ivanov in *Exchange from two corners*, and *Key to Faith*. As usual, Shestov's interpretation of these works and their meaning for Gershenzon's creative output as a whole say as much about Shestov as about Gershenzon. He thus evaluates the first work positively, and the second work negatively, following criteria that will soon become familiar.

In *Two Corners* Shestov found Gershenzon's apophatic silence on the meaning of God and spirit laudable. This corresponded to his own insistence that a personal truth, once couched in traditional philosophical language, is universalized and thereby immediately falsified. For Greek philosophy is replete with terminology and dialectic that dress subjective insights up in generalizing, logic-filled language and argumentation. This gives them the status of a necessity before which other men, encountering them, must bow.

On this view Ivanov, for Shestov, is a slave to Reason and wishes to force Gershenzon to submit to Reason as well. Seeing as reason cannot be resisted by reason, the only answer to dialectic subterfuge is, in effect, to say Boo! – or, more civilly, "I do not like what you are saying and do not wish to reply." This Gershenzon does to Shestov's satisfaction in this first work.

It is thus with horror that Shestov observes Gershenzon in *Key to Faith* laying his inner convictions about the Bible, the Spirit, and God before the public in language highly reminiscent of one of Shestov's arch-enemies of the mind, Hegel. And indeed, *Key to Faith* is fairly similar in content to Gershenzon's later meditations on Jewish fate, where as we saw quasi-Hegelian[101] language abounds.

Just as later, so in the earlier essay he quite literally spiritualizes the Bible. All the uncomfortable bits of the Old Testament are given an allegorical meaning. Among other things that irk Shestov is Gershenzon's re-interpretation of divine

---

[100] Lev Shestov, "O vechnoi knige: v pamyat' o M.O.Gershenzone (1869-1925)," in *Sovremenniye zapiski*, no. 24 (1925). The following quotes are all from this obituary.

[101] No self-respecting Russian philosopher (other than I.Ilyin) of course would openly admit to being a Hegelian.

punishment as not "falling upon the sinner from outside - it arises in the sinner himself... *Punishment is not a miracle* but the *natural fruit* of the spirit darkened by godlessness."

Again, Gershenzon insists that the deep meaning of passages that refer to the "fear of God" and to "walking before the countenance of God" is psychological. For Gershenzon, according to Shestov's interpretation, "the meaning of all these terms is one: renunciation of personal will. God requires only one thing - self-renunciation...Such is God's unalterable will - in other words, *such is the preestablished law of the world...* Personality as arbitrary will must be extinguished and become the recipient and executor of the divine commandment....The world will, in any case, finally conquer personality, i.e., perfectly inculcate its will in man; *the triumph of objective reason* over personal consciousness and self-will is inevitable. And this will be the Kingdom of God on earth that was proclaimed by the prophets."

All this is anathema to Shestov. In his works he reiterated time and again that the central passage in the Bible was the account of the Fall in Genesis. He interpreted the tasting of the fruit of the tree of knowledge of good and evil as a reference to the evils of philosophy. All philosophers, with rare exceptions, had preached that true knowledge consists not in changing the world or embracing life, but in accommodating oneself to the necessity of an imperfect life. The Stoics are merely representative examples of philosophy's general tendency to hoodwink men into calling truly Real only what they can control, and of dismissing as non-existent what they cannot, such as pain, injustice and evil.

Here Gershenzon fits Shestov's bill of ill-health with uncanny aptitude. Hegel had proclaimed that "the real is rational and the rational real" with typical Stoical self-deception. Gershenzon sees the Bible's kingdom of God as the submission of man and God to the inalterable law of the world. For man this involves a denial of his will to bring it in line with the dictates of the universal Spirit. But for God, too, this involves a submission to the Spirit: for the Spirit is the logic of world history, or the Logos, against which God Himself cannot utter a word[102].

For Shestov this corrupts what he sees as the only exception in world religion to this vision of cold reason: the Bible – which for him includes the Old and the New Testaments alike[103]. For only in the Bible is the deity depicted as changing his mind and behaving capriciously. Only in the book of Job does God experiment on his creatures, but then concede to His creature and at his request change the past – bringing it about that all that he had destroyed of Job's property and family were not destroyed.[104] This is the height of Biblical *chutzpah*:

---

[102] There is some truth in this analysis as regard *The Destiny of the Jewish People* as well: the relationship between the Spirit of the Jews and God is not clear: but certainly the former seems to act ever upwards with law-directedness, casting aside those too weak to keep up (those Jews who assimilated early in history).

[103] Shestov's elision of Old and New Testaments is also highly interesting and will be discussed below.

[104] It will soon become evident just how partial and erratic Shestov's reading of the Bible

for God can so confound the expectations of reason as to make the past not have happened.

The betrayal of the (Shestovianly) Biblical vision was started by Philo – who translated the book of the Jews into the language of the Greek Logos. Philo made God all dialectic, and banished the unique, unpredictable, national God of one ancient people. And Gershenzon is continuing the treacherous work of Philo, and his successors: Plotinus, Aquinas, Spinoza, Kant and Hegel. All of them believed not in the "God of Abraham, Isaac and Jacob" but in the "God of the philosophers" – as Pascal, one of a handful of Shestov's heroes, put it.

It thus becomes clear how Shestov separates the "good" from the "bad" in Gershenzon: as usual, the good is apophatic, the bad philosophic. The confusion starts due to the fact that Shestov implicitly conflates the bad with Christian universalism, so that one seems to verge on the equation that bad = philosophic = Christian.[105] Indeed, further confusion arises if one continues to think in standard dichotomies, and subconsciously or otherwise fills out the equation further as: good = non-philosophic = Judaic. It is precisely this equation that the review on Berdyaev demonstrates to be false, as will be shown shortly.

In the meantime, however, Shestov's analysis at least partly converges with the one proposed above of Gershenzon as a thinker who was more colored by the Gnostic Christian spirit of Russian symbolism than by traditional Jewish sources.

Shestov on Buber and Judaism

Thus Gershenzon stands condemned as having Christianized the Jewish Bible. However, one would have an entirely false picture of Shestov's worldview if one were to walk away with the impression that his attack on Gershenzon entailed that he was a champion of Judaism.

After all, it would be a strange champion of Judaism who married an Orthodox Christian woman and hid the marriage from his traditional father for decades. It would be a strange champion of Judaism who did not observe any Jewish holidays and had serene contempt for the laws of *kashrut*[106]. And it would be a strange champion of Judaism who forgot the smattering of Hebrew he had picked up in his youth and read and quoted the Bible, New and Old Testament

---

is. Shestov always wrote that God restored his children to Job – but, as Bulgakov pointed out, this was not the case: God did not make the past as if it had never been, so that the original children never died. Instead, God blessed Job with new children, quite a different thing.

[105] As we will see in the chapter on Frank, such an equation was in fact proposed by Franz Rosenzweig.

[106] Steinberg recounts how Shestov said to him in Heidelberg over lunch once: "God forbid a drop of milk should fall in your meat soup. I do not believe in what a man eats." For him the childish fussiness about kashrut was a fitting analogy for Steinberg's fussy Germanic Kantianism as well. Cf. Aaron Steinberg, "Lev Shestov." In Steinberg A. *Druzya moikh rannikh let (1911-1928)*, ch.9. Paris: Syntaxis, 1991.

alike, entirely in Latin and Greek[107]. The same questions that arose in connection with Gershenzon concerning his relation to Judaism and Christianity now arise about Shestov.

The fact is that Shestov believed that it was not just Christianity that had been unfaithful to the Bible with mistress philosophy. For him, post-Biblical Judaism was just as guilty of this error. Shestov's rejection of his father's traditional Jewish lifestyle (and surname) speak more eloquently in this regard than his scattered writings on the subject. For he was much less forthcoming about the faults of Judaism.

Nonetheless, in addition to some comments in his essays on Berdyaev, there is also a review Shestov wrote of Buber's work[108] which makes this explicit, as well as some conversations recounted by Benjamin Fondane – the Romanian-Jewish writer, who was Shestov's one "disciple."

Shestov applauds Buber's return to the Biblical worldview. He also has praise, initially at least, for Buber's rediscovery of Hasidic wisdom. What he likes most about Buber's Hasidim is their untutored naïve ignorance, which is apparent in their legends. Particularly appealing is one story about how God put money in a woodchopper's pocket so he could buy food for the Sabbath celebration. Only a capricious Biblical God would break the laws of physics and intervene for one man at one time and place to fulfill a task that is fairly meaningless in the larger scheme of things[109].

At this point, one is beginning to think Shestov has gone all sentimental about traditional Jews in a way quite uncharacteristic of Russian Jewry – this was more a prerogative of Western European Jewish intellectuals safely removed from the *shtetl*. However, Shestov soon demonstrates that this is not the case.

He ultimately takes exception to a Hasidic doctrine regarding the origin of the soul of *tzadikim*. According to this belief, righteous souls escaped from Adam before he tasted of the tree of knowledge. Another Hasidic saying also alarms Shestov: "People suppose that they pray before God. But it is not so. For prayer itself is the essence of divinity."

---

[107] Shestov's works are scattered with Greek and Latin quotes from the classical authors. He maintained that he quoted the original precisely so as to ward off charges that he had "Shestovianized" the text. Still, it is odd that he quotes Isaiah and other prophets in Latin as proof of his faithfulness to the original. His brother-in-law Herman Lovsky recalled how Buber pointed out an inaccuracy in Shestov's use of Luther's German translation of the Latin Vulgate, which Buber objected changed the original Hebrew meaning. This was the epithet to his article about Spinoza, *Sons and stepsons of time*, which Buber had accepted for his journal *Creatur*. Shestov's over-emphasis on Latin and Greek seems to be part of his attempt to deracinate and universalize himself, noted by V. Paperny and others. This will be discussed further below.

[108] *Martin Buber*, Put' No.39, June 1933.

[109] This emphasis on capriciousness, unlawfulness, disconnectedness, subjectivity, hatred of systems and *logoi* not surprisingly made Shestov an enemy of the philosophy of all-unity – a philosophical trait he shared with Berdyaev.

The former doctrine implies that Hasidism believes in a perfect knowledge. That is, Hasidim also yearn for perfect gnosis of the world, not through the arbitrary and unpredictable intervention of the personal God but according to scientific, logical laws or their spiritual equivalent.

The latter saying looks to Shestov like a vision of prayer as Stoical meditation, rather than a direct address to the all-too-human God to grant the supplicant his urgent, willful and capricious needs. In sum, Hasidism too stands condemned of "Spinozism" and is a deviation from strict Biblical irrationalism.

That Shestov extended this view to Judaism in general is made clear in Fondane's 1936 article "Leon Chestov a la récherche du Judaisme perdu"[110] where he expounds Shestov's view that the Jews were seduced by the Greeks after prophetic times and embraced the autonomy of the law, so losing their Biblical relationship with God and reverting to an infantile stage of Kantian fallenness[111].

This is extremely important for understanding how Shestov, after excoriating Gershenzon for his Christianization of the Bible, could accuse Berdyaev of being too "Judaic" in his reading of the Gospel, as we will shortly see. It also explains why he did not practice Judaism, and why he read Genesis, Job, Isaiah, and the Gospels as one book proclaiming one – irrationalist – faith.

In this sense, Shestov really does occupy a quite unique, and as he recognized – not without some pride, one is tempted to think – a witheringly lonely position in the debate about Judaism and Christianity, the "Jewish spirit" and the "Christian spirit." For on Shestov's account, true "Biblical" religion is not to be found fully either in Judaism or in Christianity – regardless of denomination.

Shestov on Berdyaev

The dispute between Berdyaev and Shestov was carried on in personal correspondence[112] and conversations. It entered the public record in several articles that the two wrote about each other's work, of which we will focus only on four here. Shestov reviewed Berdyaev's philosophy as early as 1907, in *In praise of Folly*, and then again in the year of his death in *Gnosis and Existentialism: Nicolai Berdyaev*[113]. Berdyaev censured his friend in his 1936 *Lev Shestov and Kierkegaard*, and then in 1938 in more conciliatory tones after his friend's death

---

[110] Summarized in Gilla Eisenberg, *De la rue Rollin à la rue Agron, à Jérusalem*, http://fondane.com/Gilla%20Eisenberg.htm

[111] Shestov holds the exact opposite to Kant. Autonomy is a sign of immaturity, lack of faith; whereas of course for Kant autonomy was a sign that humans had made it into the adulthood of the species.

[112] Which is quoted in Shestov's daughter's account of her father's life: *Zhizn' L'va Shestova*, by N.Baranova-Shestova – quoted in P.Kuznetsov, *Lev Shestov i Nicolai Berdyaev: dva tipa russkoy religioznoy filosofii*. Logos, 2008.

[113] *Poxvala gluposti*, included in *Nachaly i kontsi*, 1908; *Gnosis i existentsialnaya filosofia* in *Sovremeniye Zapiski* 63, 1938. Shestov's works in Russian and English can be found on the website: http://shestov.by.ru

in *The fundamental idea of the philosophy of Lev Shestov*[114]. The latter was not just an intellectual evaluation, but also a homage to a friendship that had lasted for thirty five years.

Shestov and Berdyaev had first met in Moscow at a New Year banquet in 1903 and they remained extremely close until Shestov's death in Paris in 1938. Berdyaev said of Shestov that he was "perhaps my only friend, whom I consider one of the most remarkable and best of people I have had the fortune to meet in life."[115] Throughout these thirty five years, they "conducted a dialogue about God, good and evil, and knowledge. This dialogue has not infrequently been harsh, but it has been friendly as well…"[116]

Examples of "harshness" are not hard to find: after Shestov's 1923 book on Pascal's thought came out, Berdyaev wrote to him that through not understanding that Pascal's madness was a madness in Christ, he turns "grace into darkness and horror." Then in terms which echo Ivanov's reproach of Gershenzon but are several times blunter: "I see a 'way out' (which more than anything you rebel against), because I am a believing Christian…Both you and Sletzer[117], and all people of your spirit, rebel against anything which recognizes a positive spirit in life…"

At the beginning of their relationship Berdyaev told Shestov that the depression he was suffering from during the years of their early acquaintance in Russia was "the world grief of the Jews" speaking through him. It is thus not hard to see in Berdyaev's mention of "people of your spirit" a reference to nihilistic Jews.

However as in conversation and correspondence, so in print Shestov always responded to Berdyaev with the best form of defense: attack. At their very first meeting, in fact, it had been Shestov who had the table in laughter with his send-up of Berdyaev. When accused of harboring "the world-grief of the Jews," he also retorted: "Why the Jews? What's the plural for?" And turning Berdyaev's insistence on the uniqueness of the individual back on him, he insisted on answering for himself rather than having his literary and philosophical judgments made a function of a whole nation.

Berdyaev's assaults on Shestov's pessimism and nihilism are different to his reaction to Gershenzon. However, the accusation that Shestov has misread the Christian author Pascal, due to being filled with a "Jewish spirit" of nihilism, approaches his earlier charge concerning Gershenzon's misreading of the Slavophiles.

Shestov's reaction, however, was not apologetic: instead, as usual, he went on the offensive. In *Gnosis and Existential Philosophy*, his last refutation of

---

[114] Both Berdyaev's articles can be found in "Tipy religioznoy mysly v Rossii"// *Sobraniye. Sochenenii*. 3, Paris: YMCA-Press, 1989.
[115] In *Samosoznanie*. Moscow: 'Kniga', 1991.
[116] Nicolai Berdyaev, "Lev Shestov (po sluchayu ego semidesyatiletiya)," in *Put'*, No.50, (1935/6):50-52.
[117] Shestov's Jewish friend and translator.

Berdyaev's philosophy and its claims on him, he once again attacks the German metaphysical constructs which he saw Berdyaev as having covertly smuggled into his philosophy. Whereas before it was the "dialectical" idea of the God-man, Shestov now concentrates on Berdyaev's new focus on "pneumatocentricity" in his latest book *Spirit and Reality*.

However, he does it in such a way that it is clear he also wants to undermine Berdyaev's anti-Judaic rhetoric. Thus he takes time to refute the charge that the Incarnation is incomprehensible to a Jew, caught up in a transcendental conception of God. And then he goes one step further and attacks Berdyaev's own understanding of the real meaning of Christ's life.

One quote from Berdyaev's new book in particular attracts his attention: "The gospel is immersed in the Judaic human atmosphere… Jesus Christ does not withdraw at all from the manifold world, he does not renounce the sinful world… He lived among people, among publicans and sinners, he attended banquets…"

Of this Shestov writes disapprovingly: "Berdyaev might also have recalled how Jesus healed the sick, fed the hungry, restored sight to the blind, resurrected the dead, etc…. he could have tried at least to some degree to realize in the existential philosophy the idea: 'For God nothing is impossible.'"

In other words, Berdyaev's highlighting of the Judaic in Christ's life is a pandering to the belief that the ordinary, everyday, predictable, stable law-bound aspect of life has something deeply to commend it. But according to Shestov, the opposite is true. This is merely the deep, subconsciously ingrained and ineradicable pandering of Berdyaev – for all his protests – before the ethic of Kant and Hegel.

For Shestov sees the latters' influence in Berdyaev's Boehmian doctrine that God's power is limited by Nothingness and that Freedom antedates God: these are variations on the doctrine that God is bound by some sort of necessity. And Berdyaev's new emphasis on the Spirit, his discovery of pneumatocentricity – where before he was Christocentric, always speaking of the god-man – is more of the same: a shackling of God to the law-bound movements of a Hegelian-style dialectically evolving Spirit.

It thus turns out that Shestov is criticizing one and the same tendency in Gershenzon and Berdyaev: the presence of a philosophic framework which excludes and suppresses the capricious irrationality of God. In Gershenzon, however, Shestov labels this a "universalizing Christian" tendency; in Berdyaev it is a Judaic submission to the law of the everyday. Whether it is legitimate or helpful to give such different labels to the same phenomenon will be considered below.

Shestov criticizes Berdyaev's central doctrine of the god-man in similar terms: "in the two-member formula 'God-man' the emphasis is placed on the second member…[which] is ever more strongly and sharply emphasized…at the expense of the first member. So that in the measure that man grows and is enriched with independent content, God is correspondingly diminished and impoverished. He is impoverished to such a degree that the formula itself begins to lose its stability and threatens to be turned around: God-man is ready to be converted into man-god... I believe that I will be very close to the truth if I say that this possibility became a reality in the philosophy of German idealism."

Here, there is a more subtle counter-attack at play: first, Shestov makes the legitimate point that if God is powerless before the original nothingness, and if Christ the god-man is of one essence with God, then it is hard to imagine how Christ can overcome God's powerlessness in this world, when such a victory was impossible outside it. For Shestov, it looks as if this victory can thus only be due to the "man" element of the god-man.

Secondly, in the context of Russian philosophy, Shestov is accusing Berdyaev of the sin of German and Judaic humanism. The special virtue on which Russian god-seekers prided themselves was their freedom from Western European humanism: Berdyaev himself, along with Bulgakov, Frank[118], Struve, Ern, and Florensky among others all traced Western secularism back to the rationalism first of the Papacy then the Renaissance and Reformation. Due to the popularity of Kantianism with Jews in Germany and Russia, German Protestant idealism was also tarred with the brush of Judaic rationalism and legalism, i.e. a blindness to the Christian mystery.

Thus here, too, Shestov the Jew is covertly defending his Russian irrationalism and implying that Berdyaev is more Judaic than he is. The irony is that this charge did indeed come at a time when Berdyaev was softening towards the "Jewish spirit," highlighting the Judaic part of Jesus' heritage, regretting his treatment of Gershenzon, and embracing Judaic eschatology (with its laws of history and historical progress, another Shestovian bugbear). But Shestov pounces on this as a weakness, and it is as if he takes Berdyaev at his word: I, a born Jew, have more of the Christian spirit than you, a born gentile, and you have more of the *Jewish* spirit than me[119].

It is in this spirit that Shestov deftly parries another anti-Judaic punch thrown by Berdyaev: in *Lev Shestov and Kierkegaard*, Berdyaev had written that the Incarnation was a stumbling-block to Jews, and that Shestov's conception of God was so Judaically transcendent that he could not conceive of the deity becoming man (a theme familiar from *The Meaning of History*).

Now Shestov takes the time to rebut this below-the-belt swing. Far from

---

[118] Cf. chapter on Frank for this type of polemic in Frank's critique of Herman Cohen and Franz Rozenzweig.

[119] In his chapter on Jewish destiny in the *Meaning of History*, having defined the Jewish spirit, Berdyaev had contended - no doubt partly to ensure that the doctrine did not slip into racism - that Jews can be free of the Jewish spirit and gentiles can submit to it. Thus: "Racial anti-Semitism is completely infected with that deceitful Jewish spirit, against which it rises up. Hatred towards Jews is an unchristian feeling. Christians must relate to Jews Christianly. Within Christian history there constantly occurs the interaction of Judaistic and Hellenistic principles, which are indeed the main sources of our culture..."

being a radical idea, replies Shestov breezily, the Incarnation has become a cliché and it is all the rage to talk of the suffering God and the suffering man, and to see pagan religions as replete with pre-emptive notions of this sort. This is, once again, a sign of Berdyaev's Hegelianism: "for the philosophers the suffering God opens up the possibility of calling themselves *bona fide* Christians: herein is expressed, to speak in Hegel's words, the unity of the human and divine natures. Man is condemned to suffer, God is condemned to suffer - this is not a breach of the natural order of things, not a miracle, not a 'violence upon the spirit.'"[120]

Shestov goes further and considers it his duty to preach to Berdyaev about the real meaning of the crucifixion, which for Berdyaev has become bogged down in Judaic-Germanic rationalism. In contrast, real Christians (such as, by implication, Shestov) see the crucifixion, as interpreted by Luther: for "there is still one moment which Berdyaev almost passes over: God took upon Himself the sins of the world. Luther says, 'God sent His only begotten Son into the world and placed upon Him all the sins of all men, in that He said: Be thou Peter that denier, Paul that persecutor, blasphemer of God and doer of violence, David that adulterer, that sinner who ate the apple in Paradise, that thief on the cross; all in all, thou shalt be the person who committed the sins of all men.'"

Here Luther expresses perfectly for Shestov the idea that in Christ the denial of Peter and all the other sins are made not to have existed. *This* is miraculous Christianity, not Hegelian notions of the dialectic interaction of God and man according to laws superior to both of them.

Shestov, Bulgakov and Steinberg

Not surprisingly, Berdyaev had his own replies to these accusations. He was not convinced by Shestov's definition of faith: for him, faith was the start of the religious life; for Shestov it seemed to be the unattainable end. One is inclined to agree with this criticism, and in the above reviews, one gets a sense that Shestov is defending his precious irrationalist truth with some rather flashy rhetorical sleights of hand.

Just as before his defense of Judaic specificity in the face of Gershenzon's false universalizing turned out not to be a defense of Judaism after all, so here his righteous quotations from Luther did not culminate in any Christian commitment. Thus one gets the sense that they are indeed quotes, foils for warding off Berdyaev's attacks.

However, in the last section of this chapter we will broaden the trialogue between Berdyaev, Gershenzon and Shestov still further by bringing to bear two other interpreters of Shestov, one of whom we have already considered,

---

[120] In fact, this criticism undermines not only Berdyaev but Bulgakov, Florensky and other followers of pan-unity. In fact, as we will see, several Russian Orthodox thinkers (especially V.Lossky and G.Florovsky) also objected to what they saw as the excessive influence of Hegel on Russian religious thought.

Sergei Bulgakov, and the other of whom will be the subject of a later chapter: Aaron Steinberg. Their perspective will give a further insight into how Russian Christians and Jews of the time reacted to Shestov's shifting of the definitions of "Jewish" and "Christian."

Bulgakov on Shestov: 'fideist without faith'
Like Berdyaev, Bulgakov was friendly with Shestov for many years – though not as intimately. A striking difference in the exchange between Shestov and Bulgakov is that he was true to his later stated belief that it was forbidden to preach Christianity to the people of God. This becomes clear in Bulgakov's own review of Shestov's work in the year that he died.

Shortly before his death, Shestov had sent Bulgakov a copy of his final book, *Athens and Jerusalem*, and expressed a wish to discuss the relation between the Old and New Testament with him. Bulgakov, like Berdyaev, was of the opinion that Shestov's tragic "groundlessness" was due to his not having moved on from the Old to the New Testament. However, though truly desirous of knowing Shestov's attitude to Christ, he stated the matter extremely cautiously and periphrastically in his reply to his friend, not wishing to exert any pressure on him. When Shestov's death prevented a face-to-face meeting, Bulgakov expressed regret that he had not broached the matter more openly. This shows with what respect Bulgakov treated the personality of his Jewish friend.

In the article following his death[121], Bulgakov evaluates many aspects of Shestov's philosophy in a positive light and has nothing but the kindest words for the man.[122] He saw *Athens and Jerusalem* as a hopeful book, a sign that the faith that was in his heart was burning ever stronger. Indeed, Bulgakov comments that for him Shestov was ultimately a vindication of Paul's words in Romans 11. He must, of course, have been referring to Paul's saying that "all Israel will be saved." In other words, if we interpret this in conjunction with Bulgakov's Jewish writings, for him Shestov's last book was on the very edge of Christianity, and an expression of striving that testified to the living presence of Christ – albeit in a hidden way – in Shestov's soul.

At the same time, there is much in Shestov's philosophy that Bulgakov, like Berdyaev, cannot accept. In essence, Bulgakov pits his own "tragedy of philosophy" against Shestov's "philosophy of tragedy"[123]. Bulgakov had long since concluded that philosophy's central axioms of understanding can only come from religious dogma, and Shestov's philosophy of the absurd was devoted

---

[121] *Nekotoriye cherty religioznogo mirovozreniya L.I.Shestova*, Sovromeniye Zapiski, No.68, Paris, 1939.

[122] "It was impossible not to like him, even while completely not sharing his world-view…it was impossible not to take delight in meeting him…This can be explained, no doubt, by his wonderful large-heartedness, his captivating goodness and kindness."

[123] For another exploration of this, see V.Porus, *Tragediya filosofii i filosofiya tragedii (S.N.Bulgakov i L.I.Shestov)* in *U Kraya Kultury*, Moscow, Kanon, 2008.

to avoiding any dogmatism. But Shestov's prioritizing of (certain parts of) the Bible was itself a hidden dogmatism, according to Bulgakov. Refusal to spell out one's dogmatic axioms, a belief that one's system was completely devoid of axioms, could only be done at the cost of self-deception.

Further, once dogmas are accepted they must be thought through. "The existence of an unthought-through faith is as 'paradoxical' an invention as an enslaving rather than a liberating truth." Even if Shestov wants to mine his truth in Jerusalem, the road to Jerusalem thus lies unavoidably through Athens.[124]

In fact, Bulgakov's critique continued, the positing of a contradiction between Athens and Jerusalem is frivolous – and false, for "in order to realize the contents of this 'Jerusalemite' revelation, an effort of thought is required, just as thought is fertilized by the 'data' of faith. Shestov with lonely easy bypasses the wisdom writing of the Old Testament, as well as the fourth Gospel's Logos, as he declares his 'faith'...." That is, Shestov ignores the many moments of Athenian wisdom that are firmly lodged in the Hebrew Bible and the New Testament that he quotes for his own Jerusalemite purposes[125].

Shestov's eliding of the Old and New Testament may look like a successful "Judeo-Christian" fusion to some[126], continues Bulgakov. But he "cannot recognize this opinion as an expression of 'Judeo-Christian' (rather than Kierkegaardo-Shestovian) philosophy," which conceals its own type of "negative theology," "a negativity, in which however lies hidden a certain type of dogmatic doctrine."

In addition, Shestov in his "Judeo-Christianity" is ambiguous about the identity of Christ. Bulgakov sifts the moments when Shestov mentions Christ, and concludes that he ultimately evades the question: Who do men say that I am? Though there are passages where Shestov seems to assent to a belief that Jesus is God, these are mostly quotations from Luther or Pascal. The most maximal statement is when Shestov calls Christ "the most perfect of men" – thus showing that for him, Christ is still a man[127]. As a result, the Judeo-Christian blend is skewered in favor of the first element of the compound – which, of course,

---

[124] Bulgakov's position is reminiscent of Aristotle's own saying that "one must philosophize in order not to philosophize."

[125] S.L. Frank gives a similar critique of Shestov in *Russkoe Mirovozreniye*. "O L've Shestove (po-povodu yego novoy knigi 'Nachala I kontsi'")". He was another Russian Jew who had traveled a different path culminating in conversion to Orthodox Christianity. While appreciating Shestov's search for the truth, he berates his "mystical anarchism" and his fanatical faith in the impossibility of finding ideals, and his sacrifice of reason. As we will see, Frank himself believed in the limits of reason too: but he thought that reason could be transcended through a paradoxical leap into what he called the "unfathomable" ground of being. Cf. ch.6.

[126] Some have indeed seen his thought in that light.

[127] There is a passage where Shestov accuses someone of calling Christ a genius, where he comments that for this writer, Christ is a genius but only that. This rather obliquely implies that Christ is somehow more than man, but is a long way from an explicit recognition of his divinity.

brings Shestov's own charge against Berdyaev crashing back down on his head. For Bulgakov, this makes Shestov's "actual 'religious philosophy'…a philosophy of the veil: not the *Novum Testamentum in Vetere*, but *Vetus Testamentum supra Novum* – fideism without the main component of faith."[128]

Thus – as for Berdyaev – Shestov's philosophy was still that of the tragic wandering Jew, a paradoxical fideist without faith. Instead of faith in God become man, Shestov's strange faith was that God can do any amount of unnamed impossible things, whose nature remains beyond man's ken. However, the one divine feat that he does name – God's ability to make the past non-existent – Bulgakov rejects. Why would God change the past? That would be to destroy and annihilate his own creation. Instead, God transforms his creation in cooperation with his creatures.

Bulgakov also points out that Shestov's Biblical exegesis is dishonest here: God did not reverse the death of Job's children. He created new ones for him. Thus Shestov's strange theodicy comes from inside himself, and not from the Book to which he pretends to extend all authority.

In sum, Bulgakov's sober appraisal of Shestov's thought throws into serious doubt Shestov's counter-polemic against Berdyaev. One gets the feeling that Shestov's claim to be more Christian than Berdyaev and more Judaic than Gershenzon comes at the cost of emptying both terms of their historical meaning. Shestov did not subscribe to the article of belief Christians refer to when they talk of Christian faith, namely the belief that God in the second person of the Trinity became man. Berdyaev may have Germanized and humanized this belief but once the rhetoric has died away, it is not this key article of faith that Shestov holds dear.

Steinberg on Shestov: reveal the 'black man'
The other side of the coin concerns the Jewish reaction to Shestov, and the (ongoing) attempt to locate what is Jewish in his sensibility.

In a 1977 study of different Russian thinkers on Jewish themes, E.Glouberman[129] claimed that it was Shestov's conception of God as a principle that is opposed to necessity that was at the core of his Jewish thinking. A more recent commentator, V.Paperny, rightly points out that it is more likely Shestov took this from Luther and Pascal. One can, too, add that such a concept hardly

---

[128] i.e. Shestov sees not the New Testament in the Old and the Old Testament in the New (the maxim of patristic Biblical interpretation), but rather the Old Testament *above* the New Testament. Thus while striving for Pascal and Luther's fideism (faith above all), and imitating their cries of faith, the actual impossible, irrational content of that faith – that God became a man – is missing.

[129] Emmanuel Glouberman, *Feodor Dostoevsky, Vladimir Soloviev, Vassily Rozanov and Lev Shestov on Jewish and Old Testament themes*. Ann Arbor, 1977. Cited in Vladimir Paperny, "O 'natsional'noi pochve' filosofii L'va Shestova (midrash kak filosofskii metod)," in Moskovich W., Shvartzband S., and Alekseev A., eds. *Jews and Slavs*. Volume 1, 161-176. Nauka, Jerusalem-St.Petersburg. 1993.

divides Jewish and Christian conceptions of God, as both religions have produced thinkers who are closer to Aristotle's philosophical First Mover: Aquinas among Catholics, and Maimonides among Jews. Shestov himself, according to Fondane, during his reading of Maimonides in preparation for his Palestine trip of 1935 made the same point: Maimonides fitted classically into his paradigm of a Gnostic betrayer of God, due to his maxim that if reason and the Biblical text conflict it is necessary to choose reason.[130]

Paperny, for his part, sees Shestov's Jewishness in his anti-dialectic, concrete, anachronistic interpretation of a tightly limited "Scriptural canon" of greats. For Paperny this strongly recalls traditional midrash, right down to his preference for a forced meaning of a text over a plain meaning. Paperny's only reservation is that Shestov goes against the spirit of midrash in his preference for meanings which directly contradict the overt meaning of the Bible, and other authors in his canon, like Tolstoy. The gravest example is Shestov's fundamental conception of original sin (the temptations of philosophy for Shestov) irreversibly destroying man's access to God. This goes against the many stories and episodes in the Bible where man continues to meet directly with God after the Fall.

Paperny is not the only reader of Shestov to complain of this. What is interesting about Paperny's example is that, once again, we are reminded that Shestov's unknown and unknowable God is not the God of traditional Jewish tradition, or even much of the Bible, but a projection of his own sensibility. In fact, he had to distort the Biblical account (and ignore rabbinic and liturgical commentaries) in order to get his main authority to agree with him – although, as Paperny comments, he often managed to do this with a casuistic harmonizing logic reminiscent of midrash.

The most interesting attempt to grapple with Shestov's Jewish identity, however, is seen in his friend and younger contemporary Aaron Steinberg[131]. Although he was twenty six years younger than Shestov, the two of them became close. Steinberg ran the gamut of reactions to Shestov as well. At first he believed he was not connected to Judaism and then he came to appreciate his deep immersion in Jewishness.

This is quite literally the case. Steinberg became an admirer of Shestov's early works and wrote to him offering to be his German translator. When they first met on the platform of Heidelberg station in 1907, they missed each other at first. Steinberg simply had not expected a man with the Russian surname Shestov to be in appearance "a typical South Russian Jew." Shestov was surprised at how young Steinberg was, and afterward, shocked that he was Jewishly Orthodox.

Later, Steinberg's Russian academic colleagues[132], among them of course

---

[130] Benjamine Fondane, *Entretiens avec Leon Chestov*: Mars 1935, Chez Madame Lovtzki, soeur de Chestov. www.angelfire.com/nb/shestov/fon/f_1.html
[131] On whose own life and philosophy we will focus in chapter 5.
[132] The literary critic Ivanov-Razumnik thought Shestov's "groundlessness" was typical Jewish nihilism. But while he generally decried Jewish nihilists, for Shestov he made an exception: his permanent destructiveness has a prophetic role, keeps people eternally

Berdyaev, would insist on Shestov's philosophical Jewishness, and Steinberg would disagree, obviously finding the thesis that Jewishness and nihilism were linked distasteful.

Steinberg's opinion of the Jewish sources of Shestov's inspiration was changed primarily by contact with his family. His recollections of Shestov's father, mother and sister cast a serious doubt on Shestov's ingenuous disassociation from "the Jews."

One story in particular corroborates Paperny's idea that Shestov was influenced by midrash. One may doubt that he was Jewishly well-read enough to be familiar with midrash, but Steinberg's description of how the philosopher's father, Isaac Shwartzmann, put a young intellectual friend of his son's in his place casts light on Shestov's immersion in the atmosphere of traditional Jewish badinage.

Shestov, his father and some of Shestov's friends were on a train in Austria. The future art critic Evgeniy Lundberg was with them. Shwartzmann asked him what he was studying, and Lundberg replied with pride that he belonged to two faculties, theology and philosophy. To which, Shestov's father replied:

"Theology…words about God[133]. Ach, how interesting! Lyova[134] is always saying that philosophy is also the science of God, and now it turns out that there's another one about God, as you say. That's pretty hard to understand without a higher education." Thinking for some moments he then said: "Tell me, young man, you are a student of philosophy, of theology, and God knows what else, but do you know how geese sleep?" The confused young man did not know, so Shwartzmann enlightened him.

Geese, it turned out, sleep with their heads in the ground, and their wings over their heads. The reason is because their fat is on their backs. Chickens, on the other hand, fly up under the rooves of their coops – and that is because they have their fat on their bellies and in front. "Perhaps with you, young man, perhaps you haven't got your own fat, neither in front not behind, nor below, nor on top – so that's why you need philosophy, a warm hole in the ground – and theology, the warm word of God up above. Am I right?"[135]

One can certainly see where Shestov got his anti-metaphysical orientation from and his taste for concrete imagery. His father's influence can be seen in another anecdote that Steinberg recounts. Questioning his son on his new

---

"wakeful" as Isaiah and the prophets roused their people. It clears away rubble for rebuilding to begin. When reading the Old Testament once, Ivanov-Razumnik was surprised and delighted to recognize the plangent voice of his friend. See Steinberg's account of Ivanov-Razumnik and Shestov in Aaron Steinberg, "Lev Shestov," in Steinberg A. *Druzya moikh rannikh let (1911-1928)*, ch.9. Paris: Syntaxis, 1991.

[133] In Russian, *bogosloviye* – literally, God-word. Shestov's father apparently spoke fairly good Russian with a Yiddish accent.

[134] Diminutive for Lev.

[135] Steinberg speculated that Isaac Shwartzmann in turn got the information about fowl from his wife, who was much more informed about the niceties of farm life.

infatuation with Kierkegaard, he received the answer that according to the Dane Abraham's greatness lay in the fact that he really was willing to kill his son. To which his father replied straightaway: "Your new Rashi is simply a Judophobe.... Because of his like we had the Beilis trial in Kiev." He explained that on such an understanding, if the Jewish patriarch could shed his own son's blood, then it would be permissible to believe that Jews could shed others' blood for sacrificial purposes.

One can contest the insightfulness of Isaac Shwartzmann's home-spun wisdom. But what is more interesting is what it shows of Shestov's rootedness in Jewish sensibilities, including a deep skepticism about the very enterprise of abstract academic philosophy. This seems to go hand in hand with a certain proprietorial confidence in his right to interpret the Bible – the book of his own "small, ignorant people" as he referred to the Jews in writing about Gershenzon.

Shestov thus creates his own tradition of Jewish learned ignorance[136]: he often boasted that his philosophical originality was due to his never having studied philosophy professionally. The corollary of this, it seems, was his openness to a naïve folk-midrashic spirit of interpretation. By contrast, his fellow Russians "who arrived at Christianity through evolution absolutely cannot learn to pronounce the sacred words properly."[137]

Another facet of Shestov that emerges in Steinberg's recollections is that the philosopher was himself extremely conscious of his complex debt to his father. His very choice of a Russian *nom de plume* to replace the Jewish-sounding Shwartzmann encapsulated the devotion to and competition with his father[138]. He chose "Shestov," because it signaled a rejection of the commercial[139] element in the family, his dedication to science and literature, and the desire to *shesvovat'* (procede, march) in the opposite direction to his father. On another reading, he analysed "shestov" into three elements: sh-est-ov: "sh:" *Sh*wartmann junior; "est:" is (in Russian); "ov" father/patriarch (in Ashkenazic Hebrew). In sum, Lev Shwartmann is now patriarch of his family, replacing the old business despot.

---

[136] Semyon Frank used the term "docta ignorantia" for his own vision of trans- rather than anti-rational knowledge. This was connected to his reworking of Nicolas of Cusa's philosophy – for the latter *docta ignorantia* was a keystone of his philosophical approach.

[137] From *In Praise of Folly*, referring to Bulgakov, Merezhkovsky and Berdyaev. If it is true that he believed his Jewishness gave him a certain native license in Biblical matters, one should not rush to embrace his claim for the simple reason that he knew no Hebrew and, unlike Steinberg for example, had never been trained in that native wisdom.

[138] This, of course, is a red flag to a Freudian bull. And in fact, Shestov's sister, Fanya, was a devotee of Freud and spent hours regaling Steinberg with her analysis of her brother.

[139] "torg + shestvo" = commerce: Shestov took only the "shestvo" (the morphological ending), leaving behind the root morpheme "torg" = to trade.

The name thus started off as a rejection of his father with whom much of his early depression was associated: his time working for the family business was one of deep anxiety and depression. But the deliberate retention of the first letter, and the Hebrew element in its interpretation also signal Shestov's continuity with his Jewish roots, albeit through a paradoxical attempt to replace them.

This continuity surfaced, according to Steinberg, after the Beilis affair when Shestov was once again thrown face to face with his Jewishness. It also surfaced towards the end of his life when he received an invitation to lecture in the Zionist settlements in Palestine. When he was hesitating over whether to go or not, Steinberg urged him to reveal the "black man" (Shwartzmann) to the world, to respond to those friends, such as Berdyaev who had for years been calling him a Jew, to show to the world once again the Jew beneath the Russian persona.

Shestov did travel to Palestine (where his grandfather was buried on the Mount of Olives) and was spectacularly well-received. Three years later he completed his masterpiece *Athens and Jerusalem*, in which he pits sacred Jerusalem against philosophic Athens.

Like Bulgakov, Steinberg saw this final work as a move by Shestov towards a more traditional form of faith – only of a Jewish, not a Christian, variety. As he put it, towards the end of his life, his friend did indeed return to the "faith of his fathers…as he interpreted it."

But this "reclaiming of Shestov" for the Jews needs to be understood in the context of the times. Steinberg and Shestov had both been Eurasians[140] in the twenties. One of the tenets of the movement was that Jews and Russians were equally Asiatic and European, so that Russianness and Jewishness were complementary. Thus Steinberg, though traditionally observant, in terms of his beliefs had a very Russian understanding of what Shestov's return to his fathers might have meant.

In reality, Shestov's last book *Athens and Jerusalem* and his trip to Palestine probably did not add anything significantly different to Shestov's philosophy and identity. He had never completely rejected his Jewishness, and his philosophy also included a Judaism of his own making – which, perhaps for defensive purposes, he could equally well have described as a "genuine Christianity."

Indeed, other details tell against a sentimental *teshuvah*[141]. In the run-up to the trip Shestov complained sarcastically of the stilted Russian of the invitation, written by a Jewish "master of ceremonies for the English powers that be." He also grumbled about the stinginess of the travel stipend, complaining that he had never had any luck with Jews, and that his brother-in-law claimed that he was an anti-Semite.

In short, Shestov while deeply grounded in a very *haimishe*[142] Jewish

---

[140] An explanation of the origin and meaning of this movement is given in chapter 7.
[141] Heb. "return, repentance" – also used of estranged Jews returning to the Jewish religion.
[142] When Steinberg met Shestov's mother, he claimed that he had never met anybody so grounded as Shestov: she was a typical, proud, talkative Russian Jewish mother who

groundlessness and breathing the air of the "Russian spirit"[143], could never have returned to the "faith of his fathers" in any but the most idiosyncratic Shestovian sense. Credence can only be given to such a judgment if by "fathers" is meant his own "fathers" of faith – Pascal, Luther, Dostoevsky, Kierkegaard, Abraham, Job – in each of whom he found a kernel of the ancient Judaic deposit of faith that he detected in both testaments of the Bible.

This resolutely idiosyncratic statement of faith was a constant provocation to his more Orthodox Jewish and Christian friends. For example, Steinberg himself in his reminiscences is more than once riled by Shestov's person and philosophy, and accuses him of egotism, incoherence in his thought, selfish and vainglorious motivations in his philosophy, not to mention stinginess – a judgmental edge which is missing from his evaluations of his Russian friends. He even goes so far as to accuse the early Shestov of being a covert Hegelian – strong language indeed[144].

Moreover, although generously conceding that Shestov's philosophy has a Jewish element, it seems that he saw it as part of his task to ensure that this element developed into something more than the nihilistic Jewish element that had dominated him in his early years: it was Steinberg who encouraged him to accept the offer to travel to Palestine as a way of positive Jewish identification.

On another front, Steinberg's own religious identity provides a telling contrast to Shestov: the latter's contempt for the minutiae of Steinberg's ritual observance seems odd coming from a "Jerusalemite" philosopher who glorified the inscrutability of God's actions and edicts: it seems irrational for an irrationalist to ignore these particularistic, concrete elements in the Book he claimed as the foundation of his thought.

On the Christian front, we have already seen how Berdyaev criticized Shestov's philosophy and waited almost daily for his imminent baptism. Bulgakov likewise hoped for a resolution of his philosophy of tragedy through an embrace of Christianity. But somehow, Shestov saw it as part of his own sacred task to resist both Jewish and Christian overtures to step outside of his apophatic circle.

---

dominated and inspired and captivated her son. Shestov's sister was no less striking: a fanatical adept of Freud, who devoted long conversations to analyzing her brother in a psychoanalytic manner.

[143] Paperny shows how in his earlier work Shestov was a devotee of the idea of the unique Russian spirit. This continued in his support for Eurasianism and Scythianism (cf. ch.7) in the 20s. However, in exile he gradually emancipated himself from Russianness as he had earlier emancipated himself from Jewishness. Conversant and published in several European languages, he no longer "wandered" among Russian writers, but Western European philosophers. And his extensive display of Latin and Greek quotes proclaimed his entry into the ecumene.

[144] He writes that according to Shestov's implicit philosophy "the World Spirit had reached in its development the stage of dialectical self-destruction and then attained full self-consciousness in the adogmatic thought of Lev Shestov."

Judaism beyond the Pale: superseding both Testaments
Gershenzon and Shestov – differences and similarities

The conflict between Berdyaev and the two Russian-Jewish thinkers has raised a number of questions. Some of them will be taken up again when the circle is expanded to include other important participants in the debate about the place of religious affiliation in the search for truth. These are figures who have only been mentioned marginally such as Aaron Steinberg, Vasily Rozanov, Alexander Blok, and Andrey Bely, but also thinkers such as Lev Karsavin and Pavel Florensky.

Nevertheless, we can summarize here some observations of differences and similarities between the three figures just examined.

Starting with the similarities between Shestov and Gershenzon: Firstly, both men launched themselves into Russian culture partly as a way of escaping from their Jewish backgrounds about which they had negative feelings. Both of them searched for an archaic philosophy, one that would be ancient enough to overshoot and exclude the whole of Jewish history: Shestov went past Moses to Adam, Abraham and Job; Gershenzon to Heraclitus and "the most ancient tradition" of those who believed in the fiery nature of the soul.

Both of them built a religious philosophy out of a close "midrashic" reading of literature: Shestov started at the foot of the Russian greats, Tolstoy and Dostoevsky, but soon escaped to bigger pastures. Gershenzon always remained umbilically attached to his Slavophiles, and in the last years of his life to a curiously self-reflecting image of Pushkin, the ancient wandering Jew.

Both were deeply attracted by nihilism, and like their contemporary non-Jewish symbolists and Scythians, saw nothingness as a way of overcoming the decadence of the past and clearing a way for the new. Certainly, part of that decadence was the political situation of Russia on the eve of Revolution and they were barometers of the Russian intelligentsia's dissatisfaction with the old regime, perhaps more than the Jewish.

Nonetheless, a more concrete incarnation of the decadence of the old for both Shestov and Gershenzon was the external oppression of Jews in the Pale of Settlement, and perhaps even more importantly what they perceived as the internal stagnation of Judaism and Jewry. For Gershenzon Jewry had fulfilled its mission and must disappear; Shestov was less clear but knew that Judaism as much as Christianity had betrayed its deeper calling.

Whereas other Russian Jews reached into their own tradition to overcome the degeneration of the past, these Russian Jews turned initially to Russian culture as a source of renewal. And here they both encountered suspicion on the part of the natives. They were perceived by their closest intellectual collaborators, those who started off as their spiritual allies, as falsely universalizing that culture, and distorting its very essence through their refusal to embrace Christianity. Both of them, however, though resisting Christianity were deeply influenced by it.

As for their differences, an interesting indication is how each of them reacted to the accusations of their former allies. Gershenzon became estranged not only from Berdyaev, but from all the other *Landmarks* contributors. He also fell foul – as we will see in a later chapter – of another suspicious admirer, Vasily Rozanov. Their friendship suffered irrecoverably from Rozanov's Judophobia. Shestov was sturdier and despite equally aggressive anti-Jewish language from Berdyaev he stuck by his guns.

Perhaps the explanation is that Shestov found ground in his own groundlessness: he consciously embraced the role of Jewish prophet and outsider. He had thrown away first the solid ground of Judaism, then of the Russian spirit[145]. But he continued to write in the skeptical midrashic voice of his father, and really did become a second Shwartzmann patriarch. An important anchor, albeit through the filter of fideist Christian theology, was the Bible – which he still continued to see as his special patrimony.

Gershenzon, on the other hand, abandoned the "medieval cheder," which had scarred his attitude to Judaism more than Shestov. He was thus more beholden to Russia than Shestov. First the Slavophiles, then Tolstoy and Pushkin[146] were the well-springs of his spiritual identity. And yet, somehow, Russian and on a broader scale European culture did not really "live" for him, but filled him with a sense of deadness. He thus failed to launch himself beyond the orbit of either Russianness or Jewishness.

It is impossible to read a man's soul, especially from a distance. However, for Ivanov culture and literature were not merely academic: his studies of Dante and his infatuation with Italian medieval culture eventually culminated in his embrace of Catholicism. Thus Dante and Ivanov prostrated themselves before the same God. For Gershenzon, culture had become alienated from the cult (to use Florensky's terminology): it was thus a case of a living man examining a dead man's dead belief. It is thus perhaps not surprising that such studies felt for him like tired formalities.

In this sense, Aaron Steinberg presents an interesting contrast to Gershenzon, and to a lesser extent Shestov. While enamored of Russian (and to a lesser extent German) philosophical and literary culture, he was also immersed in Yiddish and Hebrew letters and an observant Jew, well-versed in the Talmud. The religious roots of culture were thus very much alive for him on all levels. He was therefore in a position to repudiate similar Russian attacks on his religious and ethnic identity[147].

---

[145] Paperny shows how Shestov at first identified as a Russian writer, but then as a "groundless" wanderer who drew from all and sundry. At the end of his life, he started reading the Vedas and Upanishads. However, he saw in them for the most part a repetition of European philosophical errors, and he stuck to his belief that the only original book was the Bible.

[146] The non-Russians William James and Thomas Carlyle also exerted significant influence on Gershenzon.

[147] Oddly enough, there is an even closer parallel: for he became another mentor, close

In all, Berdyaev identified three markers[148] of the "Jewish spirit:" national chosenness, this-worldly Messianism, and nihilism. As we have seen, Shestov and Gershenzon only really displayed the last "marker," and the previous two he admitted to be at least as much Russian as Jewish. Steinberg, although embracing a limited philosophical nihilism, also had a positive world-view. This demonstrates that the Jewish nihilism of the others was somehow connected to their tragic rejection of Judaism and estrangement from Jewry, rather than being a function of Judaism itself.

It should also be added that while Shestov and Gershenzon were indeed nihilistic, their nihilism was far more decorous as far as Christianity was concerned than Rozanov's and Blok's. Rozanov's rejection of values had as its main target "dark" Christianity; Blok's depiction of the Revolution being led by Christ and his twelve disciples was a patently blasphemous "regeneration" of an outdated Christianity. Compared to the Russian nihilists in their cultural circle, then, even on this score Shestov and Gershenzon were less overtly nihilistic as regards Christianity[149].

The reasons for this seem clear: firstly, despite great affection from their "own," both men were for the most part still perceived not only as non-Christian, but also as non-Russian[150]. If even Russian thinkers produced shock with their denigration of Christianity, the outrage at an attack by Jews can be imagined[151]. Secondly, while both may have linked Christianity with anti-Jewish prejudice, there was a reciprocal feeling that Christianity – at least in its historical Russian form – was not theirs to fight against; this was a task best left to people born in its remit who wished to escape from it or reform it.

Nonetheless, in the work of the two Russian-Jewish nihilists, there is a more covert resistance to Christianity.

In Gershenzon, this took the form of leaving Khomiakov out of his

---

friend and philosophical guide of Andrey Bely. As with Gershenzon, Bely was both inspired by Steinberg and served as his creative inspiration: Gershenzon's philosophy of the Word owed something to Bely, as did Steinberg's philosophy of the Logos – which was a central component of his own Judaic variant of the philosophy of pan-unity. For both, it seems, Bely was an incarnation of the native Russian Word, a path into Russian culture.

[148] There is the charge of "divine transcendence" as well. However, Gershenzon's philosophy is one of the immanence of the Spirit-word, and Shestov's fideistic God is more Lutheran than Jewish.

[149] As we saw, Berdyaev himself was not free from a certain literal nihilism in his own contention that God is under the power of Nothingness and does not intervene in this world before and after Christ. This is then followed by a conciliatory swing in the opposite – so-called Jewish – direction of eschatology

[150] Notwithstanding Ivanov's comments about Gershenzon being flesh of the flesh of the Russian intelligentsia.

[151] This is perhaps why Gershenzon only expressed his revisionist view of Christianity (*The Sermon on the Mount*) in Soviet Russia – which found it objectionable for different reasons.

account of the Slavophiles, quoting the words of Christ in his essay on Jewish destiny without attribution, and minimizing or explicitly excluding references to Christianity in Kireevsky and other Slavophiles in favor of a focus on the "cosmic" aspect of their religiosity.

In Shestov, it took the form of denying the uniqueness of Christianity, through erasing the distinction between the Old and the New Testaments. It also took the rhetorical form of appropriating the term "Christian" for his own use, so that his philosophy ends up as more "Christian" than Berdyaev's Germanic-Judaic philosophical confession of faith.

This overlaps with Gershenzon's own final reworking of Christ's Sermon on the Mount to serve as a condemnation of historical Christianity and an endorsement of a philosophy which is Gershenzon's own. This is part of a larger tendency in both Gershenzon and Shestov to resist Christian devaluation of Jews by appropriating Christian imagery and language for their own use. In both cases, however, this appropriation of "reconstituted" Christian language includes without argument the prior polemic of Christianity against the superseded old faith[152] of Judaism – a supersession they were happy to accept.

In other words, Shestov and Gershenzon, in joining the Russian intelligentsia's search for a "third testament" that would supersede Christianity, accepted the implicit downgrading of status that such an evolutionary spirituality ascribed to Judaism. But this also meant that, while adopting the premise that both Judaism and Christianity were superseded, they were enabled to participate in a licensed polemic against Christianity.

Indeed from the perspective that in the "new age," Christianity and Judaism were outmoded identities, they could sometimes write as if in the person of Christians. Gershenzon's *Landmarks* essay, for example, contains statements which are, strictly speaking, authorial inaccuracies: "We are for the people not even alien like the Turk or the Frenchman: he sees our human and precisely Russian face, but does not sense in it a human soul, and that is why they hate us with a passion…;" "From childhood, he [John Bunyan] knew that simple Gospel truth which all of us know as well…."

---

[152] A simple example of this can be found in Gershenzon's *Landmarks* article. His proposed new "creative self-consciousness" is contrasted with the "Old Law" of social-political activism, which had previously "blinded" and "crippled" the intelligentsia. Although, he later writes that "the purpose of these pages is not to overturn the old commandment , nor to give a new one. The movement about which I speak…has already begun, and I am merely bearing witness to it." This is more a case of modestly resisting any claim to a prophetic role or any claim that he himself is somehow launching the new movement of self-consciousness. However, this does not alter the fact that he holds out great hopes that "the new commandment" of self-consciousness will indeed replace the old sterile commandment. While these "old" and "new commandments" are, of course, not Judaism and Christianity, the thrust of Gershenzon's philosophy shared with Merezhkovsky, Rozanov and others the belief that this new gnosis was indeed a type of third testament for humanity.

As far as the first quote is concerned, the elision of identities allows one to forget that a member of Gershenzon's spiritual *narod* would hardly be likely to overlook this intellectual's Jewish face and accent, which he would not confuse for a Russian face at all, and indeed might be likely to place closer to a Turk's. From the lofty perspective of creative self-consciousness, such an elision of old distinctions might be par for the course – however, Gershenzon's dispute with Berdyaev shows that even amid the top echelons of the new spirituality, things were not quite as developed as might be hoped.

The second quotation, likewise, gives the impression that the writer of the article had also been steeped from childhood in old-world Christian pieties – which, though in a different way from Bunyan, he had burst out of. Were if not for the writer's unchanged surname ("Gersh" and his fondness for Slavophiles), that elision, too, might be allowed to remain. Once again, there were enough reminders, even from the "real" world of literary relationships (Rozanov, being the most brutal case in point, as we shall see) to demonstrate that for all the apocalyptic potential of the new age, spiritual revolutions on the page did not immediately correspond to fact.

Not everyone would agree with these judgments, of course. Perhaps, therefore, the last word on Shestov, Gershenzon and Berdyaev should be given to another remarkable contemporary of theirs, the priest and philosopher V.V.Zenkovsky, who adds a different perspective to this evaluation[153].

---

[153] Another interesting alternative view of Gershenzon can be found in the views of the influential "neo-patristic" theologian G.Florovsky. In his *Puti russkogo bogoloviya*, Florovsky cites Gershenzon's research on the Slavophiles, Gogol, and other Russian figures with respect and approval, especially admiring his novel methodology which resulted in a series of "talented" and "valuable" articles, especially on the Slavophiles "to the philosophical teaching of whom he draws close." Florovsky also approves of Gershenzon's psychological approach to intellectual history: "Gershenzon with good reason reminded us that 'the key to the history of ideas always lies in the history of feelings.'..." However, he disagreed with both Berdyaev and Gershenzon in one regard: "It is least of all possible to see in Slavophilism some sort of immediate or organic manifestation of the 'elemental force of the people' (as Gershenzon in particular did). And Berdyaev is completely wrong when he writes that 'it is the psychology and philosophy of aristocratic estates, of warm and cozy nests.'..." On the other hand, Florovsky writes of Gershenzon's "moral nihilism" in his exchange with Ivanov, and his own opinion that Slavophilism is the "voice of reflection" of the troubled intelligentsia,and not the "bared soul of the primitive" is also an implicit reproach of Gershenzon's own adapted Slavophilism which we examined above. Florovsky also significantly revised Gershenzon's interpretation of the Slavophiles. As M.Raeff puts it: "Florovsky [reinterpreted] the traditional (and Gershenzon's) view of Russian intellectual history... He concluded that their [Soloviev, Tolstoy, Tiutchev, Fedorov] major 'mistake' consisted in accepting an evolutionary framework...and in following the lure of utopia as the end product of the historical process." Cf. Marc Raeff, *Russia Abroad: A cultural history of the Russian emigration 1919-1939*. New York: Oxford University Press, 1990.In this, as well as in his emphasis on the Orthodox and Russian spiritual roots of Slavophile

V.V.Zenkovsky: the dialectic of Jewry and Christianity

As far as Gershenzon was concerned, Zenkovsky also detected in him a silent resistance to Christianity, which ignored the real historical dynamic that drives the destinies of Jews and Christians. For him, the mysterious root of that dynamic was unveiled – as for other Russian Christians – in St.Paul's words in Romans that "all Israel will be saved."

He was, however, aware of the fact that it was not just Jews but gentiles[154] who resisted these words. Still, "Jewry, for other motives, also does not want to accept the hints of Paul and builds a metaphysics of its own enigmatic history without reference to the dialectic connection of the destiny of Israel with the work of Christ and Christianity. An example of this was seen in the meditations of Gershenzon…"[155] What Zenkovky's own interpretation of Paul was, we will see shortly.

With respect to Shestov and Berdyaev, Zenkovsky's judgment differs to some extent from the one just given – especially as regards Shestov. In sum, Zenkovsky accepts Shestov's own claim to be more Christian than Berdyaev. In the Jewish thinker, he sees a return to the Bible and a genuine rebirth of faith: "In essence, Shestov is a religious thinker, he is not at all anthropocentric, he is theocentric – as perhaps no one else in Russian philosophy…."[156] And unlike Bulgakov, Zenkovsky read Shestov's references to Christ as the fruit of his own inner inspiration, concluding that: "We do not know enough of the content of his belief, but it would not be a great error to say that he accepted both the New and the Old Testaments; in any case, we find a number of cases which speak of his acceptance of the Christian revelation."

Berdyaev, by contrast, is criticized by the priest-philosopher in Shestov's own terms: he is too humanist and too immersed in Gnostic philosophy. Zenkovsky further reproaches Berdyaev for his lack of grounding in the Fathers and Church tradition, and his attempt to found a neo-Christianity for a new epoch, which is connected with the spirit of Merezhkovsky. For these reasons, he concludes that Berdyaev's reputation in the West as the representative of Orthodoxy was undeserved.

Given this judgment on Berdyaev, it is not surprising that Zenkovsky's interpretation of Jewish-Christian destinies is different. Perhaps of all the interpretations of Paul's enigmatic comments in *Romans* that we have examined so far, his is the most conciliatory towards contemporary Jewry. This is a result of his own Christian philosophy of history.

---

thought, Florovsky confirms the criticisms of Berdyaev and Struve.

[154] In chapter four we will see how Rozanov and Florensky interpret these verses anti-Semitically.
[155] Vassily Zenkovsky, "Na temy istoriosofii." *Sovremmenie zapiski* No 69. (1939):280-293.
[156] Vassily Zenkovsky, *Istoria russkoy filosofii. Tom 2.* Paris: YMCA-Press, 1989: part IV, ch.2: Religiozny neo-romantizm (Berdyaev). Irratsionalizm (Shestov).

For according to Zenkovsky, the subject of history is not separate nations (as the preferred focus of Bulgakov sometimes implies), and not individuals (as Berdyaev in essence believes[157]) – but all of humanity. Thus for Paul, Jewry is connected even in its rejection of Christ with the salvation of the rest of humanity – now, and not just in the future. For through its continuing non-acceptance of Christ, Jewry holds up the curtain so that the nations can enter the Church.

Thus Jewry's task, in a strange dialectical way, is as much of a contribution to the salvation of the rest of humanity as those whom God chooses to let into the Church. For this reason, again *contra* Berdyaev, "the supra-historical mission of Jewry *is still not finished* and...Jewry is still the mystical yeast of world history" until all the nations come in. Indeed, non-Christian Jewry is a partner with Christendom in the salvation of all humanity – a position which very nearly verges on an acceptance that Jews do not need to, and indeed must not, convert.

Given this acceptance of Jewish resistance to Christ, Zenkovsky was not compelled – for the sake of conscience – to see in Shestov a Christian believer. Paul's "all Israel will be saved" would seem to apply for him both to the "resistant" Gershenzon, as well as the "melted" Shestov. One may differ with regards to his evaluation of Shestov, but one can only applaud his bold reading of Romans even if it perhaps "lifts the veil" a little too thoroughly, dispersing rather too concisely with the essential mystery – in a dialectical way that would have offended Shestov's irrationalist sensibilities.

---

[157] The comparisons with Bulgakov and Berdyaev are not part of Zenkovsky's analysis.

Four

Vasily Rozanov (and Pavel Florensky): The sacred and the secrets of the Jews

Four

'Sinful slave Vasily.…'
Vasily Vasilievich Rozanov was born in 1856, that is, three years after Vladimir Soloviev. He is close friends with the philosopher and a far-off worshiper of Soloviev's late-found friend, Fyodor Dostoevsky. In a strange turn, but only the first of a manifold series of strange events in Rozanov's life that will be explored here, he will marry Dostoevsky's former lover, Anna Suslova, in the very year that his idol dies. The term "idol" is rightly chosen: Rozanov considered himself to have been spiritually fathered by Dostoevsky and liked to refer to himself as the real-life incarnation of the writer's fictional Underground Man. Perhaps not surprisingly, then, his marriage to his spiritual father's wife was bitter and painful, and would overshadow him for the rest of his life. And that life continues for another eighteen years after Soloviev's death. Rozanov lives through the apocalyptic events that Soloviev intuits with dread in the final years of the nineteenth century. His last work is entitled *Apocalypse of Our Time*. Shortly after finishing it, he dies in 1919 of starvation and exhaustion in Sergiev Posad, the holy heart of Russia, one of the many victims of famine and deprivation brought on by the first groundswell of the Revolution and Civil War.

Rozanov is Soloviev's contemporary, and twenty odd years older than Bulgakov and Berdyaev. But it is perhaps fitting to discuss him somewhat out of chronological turn, for he is truly eccentric, that is, off centre, out of kilt, at an angle to any carefully calculated schema. In looking at Rozanov, we will see aspects of Berdyaev and Bulgakov foreshadowed, as it were. In addition to his own self-designation as the living Underground Man, Rozanov has been called the "Marmeladov[1] of philosophy" (S.A. Levitsky's masterful epithet), a Little Judas Golovlev[2] (according to Soloviev during the years of their quarrel). Zenkovsky and others called him the Russian Nietzsche.

In a telling phrase of Levitsky, "what Rozanov let drop by chance would later become the starting point for systematic development by more professional philosophers and writers." Rozanov coins the term "sacred flesh," which Merezhkovsky develops in depth, and which permeates much of Bulgakov's thinking too. But as far as Jews and Judaism is concerned, Rozanov plunges us into an analysis of Judaism that is both enlightening and appalling by – seemingly unpredictable – turns. Even more so than Berdyaev, Rozanov hovers

---

[1] Of course, after the garrulous drunk with a penchant for home-spun philosophizing from Dostoevsky's *Crime and Punishment*.
[2] A well-known character from Saltikov-Schedrin's *The Golovlev gentlemen*, a contrary, ill-tempered, stingy old man who preached the obvious to all and sundry with didactic tediousness.

on the peripheries of Christian orthodoxy, and very often storms out beyond the walls of the Church, before rushing tearfully back in again. If Bulgakov came to decipher the mystery of Judaism through the prism of "sacred blood," Rozanov anticipated this, probably influenced it in roundabout ways, through his attraction to and then growing obsession with the *secretness* of Jewish blood, of Judaism and of Jewry. More than anyone, Rozanov embodies the troubled relationship between Judaism and Christianity, between Russia and Jewry – and, as will become clear, between all these and paganism.

Rozanov's analyses of Jewry are not directly Christian; sometimes they are manifestly and self-consciously anti-Christian, and yet he has a relationship to the Russian Church and the church life of his day. What is more, Rozanov just like the other figures who have been examined has re-entered the stream of modern Russian literary, cultural and Church consciousness. Like them, he is not a figure of the past, but a figure whose frozen form has come to life again now that the ice of seventy years that had encased him has started to thaw out.

In Rozanov's case, this rediscovery of a pre-Revolutionary figure by post-Soviet Russia is particularly lively and problematic. This is due to Rozanov's essential duality, or as some have seen it, duplicity. There seems to be a "left" Rozanov and a "right" Rozanov, who – to make matters worse – often inhabit one and the same space at one and the same time. Shortly after his death, efforts were being to collect the heritage of the "left" Rozanov for publication in Soviet Russia, but this came to nothing.[3] The effort to disseminate his heritage was taken up again only in the 1990s, and critics are still trying to make sense of the chronology and interrelatedness of his works and the development of his thought,[4] and of who the "real" Rozanov is or was.

These efforts are a continuation of the unfinished business of the first two decades of the twentieth century when Rozanov moved in a semi-permanent cloud of scandal, causing provocation to left and right by turns. He wrote prolifically for the conservative, nationalistic as well as the liberal, reforming press. Articles issued from his pen in praise of Orthodoxy and autocracy, as well as pieces that excoriate Orthodoxy, praise paganism and celebrate the 1905 revolution as a slap to a dying regime.[5] One of the most influential figures of both

---

[3] By Grzebin, who tried to enlist the support of Jewish philosopher A.Z. Steinberg and writer Ivanov-Razumnik, cf. Steinberg's account in Aaron Steinberg, "Filosofskoe sodruzhestvo," in Steinberg A. *Druzya moikh rannikh let (1911-1928)*, (Paris: Syntaxis, 1991), ch.2. Rozanov himself asked for his reactionary anti-Semitic books of 1911-1914 to be destroyed after his death, which would have partly, but certainly not fully, demolished the twin "right" Rozanov.

[4] Cf. Leonid Katsis, "Kastratorskii kompleks publikatorov, ili Rozanov v menjajushchemsja supere," in *Nezavisimiy filologichsekiy zhurnal* No.61(2003). Katsis is appreciative of Respublika's publication of new and unknown volumes of the writer, but critical of the ordering of the contents of various collections, maintaining they obscure the real line of Rozanov's thinking.

[5] Cf. the collection *Kogda nachalstvo ushlo*, (Moscow: Respublika, 2005).In that

the intellectual and political life of the time, P.S. Struve, denounced Rozanov in print for his shameless duplicity. For Struve this welter of contradictory views existed because Rozanov simply wrote for money what the readers of different journals wanted to read; he was a man shamelessly lacking in principle.

For the present purposes it is germane that the greatest scandal of Rozanov's scandal-strewn life erupted due to his views on Judaism and Jewry. For Rozanov's name and reputation came to be inextricably linked with the Beilis trial of 1911-1913. Indeed, Struve's angry denunciation of Rozanov was written as a result of this debacle. We will examine Rozanov's attitude to the Beilis trial more fully below. The bare facts of this "Dreyfus affair" of Russia, however, are these[6].

The Jewish Mendel Beilis was a superintendent at a brick factory in Kiev, who was arrested in 1911 and charged with the murder of thirteen-year old schoolboy, Andrei Yushchinsky. The Russian government, to the consternation of liberal Russia, prosecuted Beilis on the charge of ritual murder and brought its most able lawyers to make the charge stick. Not by chance, the case against Beilis was opened a month after the Third State Duma began debating a law that would ratify the abolition of the Jewish Pale of Settlement. This provoked a furore among right wing elements in Russian politics and cultural life, including high-up officials in the government close to the tsar.

The police investigation of the murder of Andrei Yushchinsky took a different turn under pressure applied from these sources, and attention was switched from a criminal band to whose activity Yushchinsky had become privy to Mendel Beilis. The unfortunate Beilis was now forced to assume the role of causing some rethinking among liberal campaigners for the abolition of the Pale. He spent two years in prison before being acquitted. During this time, the case against him was again and again revealed as a farce, causing even well-known anti-Semites to come out in favor of his innocence.

During those two years an existential battle for the identity of Russia – medieval throwback or emerging liberal nation-state – was waged in the national and larger European press. And Rozanov came out in favor of Beilis' guilt. However, as for many others in his camp, Beilis' guilt was not even the main point for him. Whether or not this Jew was guilty of ritual killing, there was the larger question of whether Jewish ritual murder existed, and whether it was a tool in the hands of the Jews, who were waging a sinister international conspiracy to undermine Russia. For liberals and progressives, merely to state such a charge was to bring shame and ridicule on Russia. And for black-hundreds extremists and reactionaries of different shades, to deny the truth of

---

year, Rozanov had emerged from a Slavophile phase, and was turning to liberal, pro-Revolutionary thoughts. In this snapshot of time, he thus presents an opposite picture to Sergei Bulgakov who had thrown off Marxism for monarchy under the pressure of the same events.

[6] For more details, see, eg. Feliks Kandel, *Kniga vremeni i sobytii. 2. Istoria rossiiskikh yevreev.* (Moscow-Jerusalem: Gesharim-Mosty Kultury, 2002), 781-808. Bernard Melamad's famous novel *The Fixer* is based on the events of the Beilis case.

the accusation was a sign of liberal naivety, atheism, and was anti-Russian and anti-Orthodox. These forces gleefully looked to Rozanov as their unashamed and most notorious spokesman.

The upshot for Rozanov, in addition to Struve's denunciation, was that he was excluded from the St Petersburg Religious-Philosophical Society, at a vote called by Dmitriy Merezhkovsky, a long-time friend. Thus the "Beilis affair," as it came to be called, can be seen in concentrated form in the figure of Rozanov. The exclusion amounted to an excommunication from liberal-thinking Russian intellectual circles. And of course, the revolutionary circles that were shortly to take Russia's fate into their hands were just as condemnatory of the clerical, imperial stooges who repeated the blood libel against Beilis. Rozanov in his final years thus managed to make himself a pariah with all but those forces in the life of Russia that were already taking their last, dying breath.

The main problem of this chapter can now be seen in outline: how to reconcile Rozanov's poisonous anti-Semitic writings of his "Beilis period" with his earlier writings in 1903-06 which are full of praise for Jews and Judaism, and later statements from 1917-18 where similar philo-Semitic sentiments are expressed? At first, one is tempted to appeal to chronology. Did something happen in Rozanov's life that made him revise his views on Judaism? Perhaps it was the reaffirmed Christianity of this period that was a causal factor in his new anti-Semitism?

This brings us to another of the major concerns of this chapter: to investigate how Rozanov's Christianity influenced his views on Judaism. Once again, this is to address the question of whether Christianity takes, must take, and historically took a leading role in encouraging anti-Semitism in different forms. Of particular concern in this respect is the influence of Fr. Pavel Florensky on Rozanov during the Beilis trial. This question has been investigated quite extensively by L.Katsis[7], who discusses recent archival evidence showing that Florensky was an active collaborator with Rozanov on the 1914 anti-Semitic work *The Olfactory and Tactile Relationship of Jews to Blood*, which had previously been ascribed solely to the pen of Rozanov.

The question is a deep and troubling one. In Russia, the debate over the publication of Rozanov's works and their meaning for contemporary Russia proceeds apace. But another aspect of the "defreezing" of the Silver Age heritage is the gradual translation of works of these Russian religious thinkers into English and other languages. One such beneficiary of translation is Pavel Florensky, whose works *Iconostasis*, *The Pillar and Foundation of Truth*, and *Salt of the Earth* are already available in English. The flourishing of Orthodoxy in the West depends on such works. But this means that if an Orthodoxy that is free of anti-Semitism is to flourish in the West, the same critical spirit must be applied to these translated works and their historical origins investigated.

While the question of Florensky's anti-Semitism will not be the main focus

---

[7] Leonid Katsis, *Krovavy navet i russkaya mysl: istoriko-teologicheskoe issledovanie dela Beilisa* (Moscow: Gesharim/Mosty kultury, 2006), esp. chapters 10-14.

in what follows, the eventual conclusion of this chapter regarding Rozanov's "Christian phase" anti-Semitism and the anti-Semitism of the Orthodox priest Florensky can be summarized in advance. This is that a determining factor in the anti-Semitic writings of both thinkers was not their Christianity, but rather their well-known attraction to paganism (as defined and idealized by each), and in the case of Florensky, an attraction to the occult, magic and Gnosticism. Florensky's occultism and paganism were roundly criticized by Bulgakov, Berdyaev, Florovsky and other Christian thinkers of the period. However, the connection between a certain type of anti-Semitism (for as we have seen, Bulgakov and Berdyaev themselves struggled with temptations in this direction) and a paganized Orthodox Christianity was not made.

The distinction is important, however, before a direct equation is made between Orthodox Christianity and anti-Semitism.[8] If this thesis is right, then at least on occasions an anti-Semitic Orthodox Christianity is not troubling merely because of some peripheral blemish called anti-Semitism. Rather, anti-Semitism will be a surface sign that something deeply non-Orthodox is afoot in the nether regions of such thinking. Alternatively, to take another approach it can be read as a sign of an eternal temptation within Christianity to abuse *legitimate* pagan elements in its heritage so that such a Christianity becomes defaced and distorted. We have already touched on this debate in considering Bulgakov and Berdyaev. In this chapter, the question will take on an even more acute form. For the more obviously heterodox Rozanov is a key figure in understanding the more Orthodox Bulgakov (and to some extent Berdyaev). Comparing their "paganisms," we can try to elucidate what is "Christian paganism" and what is "demonic paganism." It helps that Rozanov and Bulgakov were in correspondence and discussed the matter themselves.

In many respects, Bulgakov and Rozanov shared a common concern, or at least they did in the periods in which their thought overlaps, when Rozanov was writing from within the fold of the Church. That task was to bring Orthodoxy back into touch with life, to rescue it from clericalism and nationalism, to save it from sterility and ritualism. And along with Berdyaev, on whom in fact he exerts an influence, Rozanov calls for freedom of human self-expression, of the human personality in Christianity. That is why Zenkovsky, a philosopher with a deep Christian sensibility, esteemed Rozanov as a valuable religious thinker, one of the pantheon of greats produced by the Silver Age. He was convinced that beneath his disparate and scattered journalistic output, there was a serious philosophy.

In his *History of Russian Philosophy*, Zenkovsky argues that Rozanov is indispensible for Russian religious thought if it wishes to work out a theory of Christian culture, that is, of the interaction of the Church and "secularity." Moreover, Rozanov with his deep love of nature, of the cosmos, and of man's

---

[8] Katsis himself seems to ignore certain non-Orthodox and anti-Orthodox aspects of Russian thought which underpin Florensky's and Rozanov's anti-Semitic discourse; see below for full discussion.

rootedness in the cosmos through the mystery of his sexuality, though not overtly sophianic like Soloviev, Bulgakov or Florensky, is sophianic in sensibility.

On the other hand, Florovsky – whose judgments about Russian religious philosophers often tended to harshness, skeptical as he was of their Platonizing tendencies – certainly captured a truth about Rozanov when he wrote: "Rozanov is a psychological enigma, enticing and terrifying."

Both these evaluations need to be taken into account. There is a geniality, an openness, an attractiveness, a bold straightforwardness about Rozanov – as he appears on the page of his writings, which are full of intimate personal references, and in the recollections of acquaintances and friends. And yet that surprising, duplicitous or dual, element is always burning somewhere in the background. From a Christian perspective, Rozanov is instructive not just for what he writes but who he is: a man of the nineteenth century thrown into the horrors of the twentieth century who takes with full seriousness the truth claims of the Gospel, and will not settle for agreed-on platitudes and hand-me-downs. Scientifically, postivistically (despite his horror of positivism), he takes the Gospel to pieces, refines it into its constitutive elements – the pagan, the Judaic, the apocalyptic – and lives each of these tunes to the full. But when it comes to putting them together again, he fails; and they lie scattered and broken, and Rozanov ponders the ruins with a genuine grief.

The account of his death is illustrative. Many testimonies have it that after his blasphemous attacks on the Church, Rozanov took the last rites of extreme unction and communion on his death bed. Levitsky[9] recounts the story of how when Florensky offered to hear his confession, Rozanov demurred. "No. What place could you have hearing my confession? You'll approach me with 'psychology', seeing Rozanov, and that's not allowed. Bring me a simple village *pop* who has not heard about Rozanov and who will hear the confession of 'sinful slave Vasily.' It's better that way."

A similar story appears in Lossky, who also recounts that before his death Fr. Florensky and two other members of the Moscow Theological Academy approached Rozanov and told him to stop his blasphemous attacks on the Church. Rozanov, "obviously recognizing in himself or near himself some demonic force, answered them: 'Don't touch Rozanov, or it will be the worse for you.' And indeed in the following year, all three of them encountered serious misfortunes."[10]

The final moments, it would seem then, were full of piety. However, Steinberg reports a sequel to this account of reconciliation, which turns everything upside down again. A friend of the Rozanovs recounted to Steinberg in Berlin that after the priest who gave him communion had left the room, Rozanov exclaimed to his eldest daughter: "You think that's the end of it? And I tell you that when I'm dead I'll stick my tongue out at you all!" After her father had passed away, his daughter

---

[9] *Ocherki*, 286.
[10] *Istoria*, 459. Such misfortunes are perhaps not surprising given the precarious circumstances of theologians in the turmoil of the new Soviet Russia.

went into the room and removed the sheet from his face to look at him. "With horror she saw her father's tongue: it was as if he was sticking his tongue out at her." The pious daughter was so horrified that shortly after this she committed suicide, hanging herself. If this account is indeed true, it would not be the first time that Rozanov had confounded expectations in a dismaying way.

So: Christian or pagan blasphemer? Philo-Semite or anti-Semite? And crucially: Christian anti-Semite or Gnostic-pagan anti-Semite? To answer these questions, it is necessary to understand in outline the chronological development of Rozanov's thought, as well as the way in which the different periods of thought have a way of crashing back into each other again, giving rise to an increasingly familiar "Rozanovesque" confusion and consternation.

In the following section, we will summarize the different stages of the thinker's career, following the divisions given by Skorodumov[11], who starts with and then builds on Sukach's division of Rozanov's life into five periods. A brief review of these periods, and an exploration of those periods when Rozanov wrote most extensively about Judaism, will highlight how Rozanov fits into the fabric of Russian religious thought that we have seen so far, despite undeniable departures from this general tendency and a lone and odd-ball eccentricity that would get him into trouble with these thinkers. In this respect, it is instructive that Skorodumov opts to place Rozanov on the "extreme right wing of Russian religious philosophy," despite the fact that strictly speaking all but Rozanov's early works were more journalistic than philosophical[12].

One must also bear in mind that the five-fold division given below is not water-tight, or the paradox of Rozanov would disappear. Rather like Heraclitus, for whom the only constancy was the law of inconstancy, Rozanov developed for himself what he called a "manifesto of antinomianism"[13]:

> "How may opinions can one have about a subject?"
> "As many as you like. As many thoughts as there are in the object, for there is no object without thoughts, and sometimes without the multitude of thoughts inside yourself."
> "But where is the Truth then?"
> "In the fullness of all thoughts. Straightaway. To choose one with terror. In the vacillation."
> "But surely vacillation is not a principle?"
> "The first in life. The only solid one. That by which everything flourishes and lives. Once solidity arrives, the whole world turns to stone, freezes over."

---

[11] S.V. Skorodumov, *V.V.Rozanov. Filosofia zhizni i sushestvovaniya. Uchebnoe Posobie.* (Yaroslav: Yaroslav Ushinsky Government Pedagogical Institute, 2005).

[12] This is another reason why Rozanov is often not included in histories of Russian philosophy, religious or otherwise. In Russian he was called a 'publitsist'.

[13] In 'Fallen leaves:" Vasily Rozanov, "Opavshiye listya. Korob pervy. Korob vtoroi," in *Apocalipsis nashego vremeni*, edited by A.N.Nikolyukin, Moscow: Eksmo, 2008.

Rozanov's intellectual development.
Rozanov's first period takes in his Hegelian dissertation at the University of Moscow, which he entered in 1878. The dissertation was called *On Understanding*, and was more than seven hundred pages long, and the fruit of five years work. In it, Rozanov outlined a distinction between understanding and knowledge. The former is internal, deep, penetrating to the *noumenon*; the latter is external, superficial, remaining at the level of the phenomenon[14]. In this thesis, Rozanov defends a general non-denominational Christianity as the key to the true understanding of life. The groundwork for Rozanov's favorite themes of genuineness, truth to life and the role of Christianity has been laid.

The second period is his Slavophile phase, stretching from 1890-1898. Here a conservative string is added to Rozanov's bow, though at university he had already reacted negatively to the young professorate, the radical men of the 60s and 70s, preferring instead the older teachers with their doctrines of the establishment. (One is tempted to see here a quest for paternal guidance, given the early death of both his parents).

He abandoned provincial school-teaching and joined the Inspections department of the civil service in St Petersburg where he fell in with a circle of Slavophile civil servants gathered round T.I. Fillipov, "a zealot for Orthodoxy." Here we find the red-haired and still schoolmasterly ex-schoolmaster ("what a typical teacher, annoyed because a pupil had given the wrong answer...with a morose and irritable face" in P.P. Pertsov's recollection of their first meeting at this time[15]) repeating doctrines of Slavophiles like Kireevsky and Khomiakov.

The latter's doctrine of the superiority of Eastern Orthodoxy over Western

---

[14] When he was a student at Moscow University, Rozanov had a mystical experience one morning while gazing out over Sparrow Hills, in which the two aspects of the world suddenly divided before him: the divine, underlying definitions of things, and the overlaid goals ascribed to these definitions by humans. "For two years, I have been happy with 'that hour', for two years I have been 'in Easter', 'with the pealing of bells'....for I saw the destinations, eternal, ascending from the earth to heaven, and as the plants the tops of which were held by God, the Holder of All." (Rozanov, as recounted by Ernst Gollerbach: *A Critico-Biographical Study*, p.11 in Vasily Rozanov, *Solitaria. With an abridged Account of the Author's Life, by E.Gollerbach. Other biographical material and matter from The Apocalypse of Our Times*. Translated by S.S. Koteliansky (London: Wishart and Co.,1927)). Later, Rozanov would say of this core mystical experience of his religious psychology: "Christ completely passed me by, or more accurately, I completely passed Him by." [XXIII letter to E. Gollerbach, 8 August 1918: Vasily Rozanov, *Pisma V.V. Rozanova k E.F.Gollerbakhu* (Berlin: Gutnov Press, 1922)]. As with many Silver Age thinkers, it seems Rozanov's initial religious inspiration was pantheistic, connected deeply to nature. But for Rozanov what is interesting is that this pantheistic nature mysticism was immediately overlaid with a Christian veneer, so that one gets a Christian mysticism of a pantheistic nature – without Christ; what Soboliev and others have called "Orthodox positivism."

[15] P.P. Pertsov, "Vospominaniye," in *Novy Mir* No.10, (1998).

Catholicism found especial favor with Rozanov. Orthodoxy was harmonious, integrated, intuitive, holistic, while Catholicism was legalistic and coercive. In Orthodoxy, life (a concept that came increasingly to occupy Rozanov's attention) and religion have merged. The Orthodox Church contains the softness of the New Testament, Catholicism the law-centredness of the Old Testament.

These familiar dichotomies are given biographical grist by developments in Rozanov's life. Abandoning the unhappy union with Dostoevsky's lover Suslova, a beautiful but proud and torturously difficult woman, he marries V.D. Butyagina, the widow of a priest, in 1891 and the satisfaction he experiences with her causes him more and more to focus on the family as a cornerstone of human life and the core of human identity. Orthodoxy's married clergy, as compared with the life-denying celibacy of the Catholic priesthood, looks like another piece of evidence in the Slavophile case against Western Christianity.

This Slavophile cast of mind enters deep into Rozanov's psyche. It goes hand in hand with an admiration of the synergy of the Russian Church and government: in the West, the church is the enemy of the world and thus of politics; in the East the government and the world are churched and consecrated, creating a harmony. It is in this period that Rozanov becomes friends with Konstantin Pobedonostsev, the reactionary Ober-Procurator of the Holy Synod, and the incarnation of Byzantine church-state fusion, famous for his tongue-in-cheek proposal of a solution to the Jewish question: one third to emigrate, one third to convert, and one third to die.

It was in this period that the conservative and reactionary elements in Rozanov's thinking were developed. He quarreled with Soloviev at this time. The latter had abandoned his Slavophile ideology and friends, complaining that Slavophilism had degenerated into chauvinistic nationalism. Nonetheless, Rozanov's unpredictability was already apparent and towards the end of the 1890s – alongside his conservative and reactionary pieces – he begins to converge on some of Soloviev's opinions, refusing to toe the party line exactly.

He writes of the worship of the letter in Nikonian Orthodoxy, of the spiritual superiority of the Old Believers[16]. Though within the conservative camp, he declares that, all the same, Orthodoxy is inflexible, formal, and ignores the needs of individual believers. Moreover, he starts to write against Slavophilism: it is bookish, not a universally true philosophy, merely a phase in the development of Russian educated society – which needs complementing with some of the insights of the Westernizing camp.

---

[16]   In the 16th century, Patriarch Nikon excommunicated those who refused to incorporate his changes to Orthodox liturgy and ritual, which brought the Russian church into line with Greek practices. Those who resisted the changes developed into a schismatic sect known as the Old Believers. Rozanov, like Soloviev before him, bucks the view that it was only the Old Believers who were obsessed by the letter and ritual, rather than faith and spirit, seeing Nikon's reforms as equally motivated by a slavish and most unspiritual obsession with the letter of Greek rituals, rather than any deep spirituality.

Finally, Rozanov's growing focus on the importance of family in human identity leads him to criticize Christianity itself, to accuse it of ignoring the life-embracing roots of the Old Testament. Indeed, some of the life-denying aspects of Christianity need to be complemented by aspects of paganism, which it has suppressed.

Rozanov ends his "second" period as a critical Slavophile, who directs harsh criticism at some of his own fundamental beliefs. This simultaneous embrace and criticism of a belief raised hackles and evinced confusion as to what side of the fence Rozanov was on. In the next stage of his development, however, this criticism of conservative beliefs gradually gains the upper hand over the core beliefs it was responding to. Internal criticism of Orthodoxy and conservatism becomes wholesale denunciation. Before, the butt of Rozanov's Slavophile criticism had been cold Western Catholicism. Interestingly, in the third period, which Skorodumov places between 1898 and 1905, Orthodoxy itself replaces Catholicism in his critical attentions. All the complaints that had been directed at Western Christianity are now showered down on Orthodoxy[17].

Here, we already glimpse a clue as to the dynamics of Rozanov's evolution and how it will affect his treatment of Judaism. From 1878-1898 (his first two periods), Rozanov saw in some form of Christianity an all-embracing world-view. From early on for Rozanov, such a world-view had to be all-encompassing. Here we are reminded of Soloviev's and indeed Khomiakov's quest for unity and *sobornost'* and his own quest for true, noumenal knowledge. However, slowly it dawns on Rozanov that Christianity is an ascetic religion, and that it therefore has a negative attitude towards sexuality and the family. But he takes comfort in the idea that Orthodoxy is not as life-denyingly ascetic as Catholicism.

His own treatment at the hands of the Church, however, soon convinces him that Orthodoxy too is essentially monastic. Thus it is no surprise that his idealized Russian Orthodoxy soon succumbs to the same assault as Catholicism previously. In his third period, Rozanov turns with desperate curiosity to the Old Testament heritage of Christianity, as well as to the pagan religions of antiquity (and especially Egypt), seeking there a fullness, an all-encompassing embrace of every aspect of Life that first Catholicism and then Orthodoxy were missing.

This soon turns into a championing of Judaism, though not always of Jews – for the shadow of his old nationalism has been carried over from the past. Rozanov's immersion in Judaism, we can speculate within this general scheme of his development, is thus at this stage not a love-affair with Judaism for its own merits. Rather, it is part of Rozanov's ambition to recover an atrophied part of Christianity. Once this is restored, Christianity will be whole – and will correspond to that wholeness of which Rozanov had a vague but enticing vision.

---

[17] As we will see, it is a pity that Rozanov never turned his critical attentions on Judaism, the heir in his thought to discredited Catholicism and Orthodoxy. If he had been more realistic about Judaism (and Jews), then he would not have suffered from that self-confessed envy which eventually turned him vehemently against them.

The theme of a restoration, a reinvigoration, a Russian reformation of Christianity is, of course, found across the board in Russian religious philosophy. In Rozanov's case, it takes the form of an exploration of Judaism. Again, looking ahead to the next two stages that followed this third stage, we see that a Hegelian-style synthesis was not achieved. That is, his immersion in Judaism did not lead to the possibility of integrating the advantages found there into Christianity.

More and more, in the following stages of his life Rozanov was to come to the conclusion that Judaism/the Old Testamant and Christianity/the New Testament could not be integrated. His exploration of genuine "Old Testament religion," in other words, may have had the opposite effect to integration, leading him further in his conviction that Christianity could not be reformed. Consequently, despite the periodic announcements of a return to the fold of the Church (such as the death-bed episode recounted above), Rozanov's conclusions all seemed to be that wholeness, Life, noumenal understanding were not contained in either of Judaism (or paganism, which was closely related to Judaism for Rozanov), or Christianity.

From the point of view of Orthodox (with a big or small 'o' for that matter) Christianity for which there is nothing above Christ, Rozanov's dream of something bigger than Christianity should caution a reader of his works against being surprised at this pendulum-like return to and then vehement rejection of Christianity. Furthermore, his dream of something *deeper* than Christianity is fundamentally Gnostic: that is, Rozanov ultimately thirsts for an as yet secret knowledge which will transcend Christianity. It is this attraction to secretness as the essential marker of sacredness, which marks – and, as is the case with Christianity, also distorts – his investigations of Judaism as well.

To backtrack, however, our examination of his writings on Judaism must start with Rozanov's third stage (1898-1905), his post-Slavophile flirtation with liberalism and the harsh critique of Orthodoxy. This period is focused mainly on the themes of family and marriage. The bliss which these two institutions inspired in Rozanov was overshadowed by Suslova's refusal to grant him a divorce, thus depriving his new family of legitimacy in the eyes of the State. Skorodumov quotes from a work of this period, which poignantly conveys the personal reasons why Rozanov became an ardent advocate of reform in family law:

> …We live happily. We have five children, who have never argued once. My wife is obedient to me in everything, and I am still more obedient to her than she is to me. We went through a period of terrible poverty, and one (the sixth) child died – but we survived it by taking shelter next to each other. Now there's one thing left to do – work for the children and their upkeep, minimal though it may be: seeing as by law they do not get from me a pension, nor a surname, nothing in fact. In general, by law our family does not exist. The children were born thanks to 'some fine fellow of a stranger'; my wife is a whore, and I am worthy of Siberia. Everything is foul in the extreme. And how is it for God? And why?

This personal grief and rage at the Church's refusal to recognize a happy, fruitful marriage as legitimate Rozanov ascribes to the Church's inability to come to terms with human sexuality. This is due to its Manichean tendencies, which are an alien strain within true Christianity. The Church has focused too much on Golgotha, and not enough on Bethlehem. The latter is a symbol of core family warmth.

Rozanov presents an interesting contrast in this period to Merezhkovsky. Merezhkovsky also used the term "sacred flesh" and wished to replace dead Christian monastic asceticism with a bond of love between new Christians who would reach their God through erotic union. He even far outstripped Rozanov in sacrilege. His 1902-1905 trilogy *Christ and Anti-Christ*[18] praised Egyptian sacred bestiality in which the priests communed with their zoomorphic deities by having intercourse with them, and the novels are filled with rather stomach-turning descriptions. But despite Merezhkovsky's bold new religion of sexual liberation, there was a rather odd paradox at the heart of it: for Merezhkovsky detested the institution of marriage and was repulsed by sex! His love of the third testament was intended to be based on Platonic love, which is how he modeled his own relationship with his wife, Zinaida Hippius.

Rozanov, with his five children and his devoted wife, was certainly not persuaded on this score. This represented a turn in the direction of more ethereal "spirituality," and was precisely what Rozanov was against. Christianity had had enough of this bloodless spirituality. Going back to Judaism, Rozanov was seeking blood (the blood of sacrifices and circumcision, as we will see), flesh (and the purification of flesh in the Judaic ritual bath), family (which grows through sexuality), and bodily community (the people of Israel in the flesh, not the spirit). Still, he retained enough continuity with his previous self to condemn Merezhkovsky on the more dogmatic grounds of concentrating on the Spirit at the expense of subordinating the other members of the Trinity.[19]

Nonetheless, Rozanov along with Merezhkovsky, Gippius, and Minsky is one of the founders of the St Petersburg Religious-Philosophical Society in 1900. This is important: Merezhkovsky's later exclusion of Rozanov from the Society he helped to found was extremely hurtful to Rozanov, coming from a long-time friend. One of his responses to his exclusion was to repudiate the Society and its goals, and indeed to launch an attack on the converted Jew, Minsky, in one of his cascade of anti-Semitic articles from 1911-1914.

This is in the future, however. At this time, Rozanov is perhaps more hopeful than the other members of the Society that Christianity can return to its roots, and specifically that Russian Orthodoxy can be revived. In "Near the Church

---

[18] Dmitri Merezhkovsky, *Khristos i antikhrist. Trilogia.* (Moscow: Pravda-Ogonyok, 1990).

[19] Merezhkovsky in turn accused Rozanov of retrogressing to the religion of the Father.

Walls" he writes of how he is expecting a new Cherubic hymn from the church, where the laity will fall to the ground in a new prayer, not at the command of a deacon or priest, but of their own accord, and this new prayer should be dedicated to family, to living life, to marriage.

The major work that we will examine from this period in detail below is called *Judaism*, and was written in 1903.

The next, fourth period lasts from 1906-1917, and it is in this period that Rozanov – for long stretches at least – really leaves Christianity behind. He continues the searing critique of Christianity that he had begun even in his Slavophile period, but whereas before Rozanov was happy to return with one hand to the defense and propagation of the religion he was busy tearing apart with his other hand, such sorties back become rarer and rarer. There is such a moment of return to Christian sensibilities in the original and successful work *Solitaria* (1911-12), where Rozanov laments that he has dedicated his whole life to destroying what he loves most and takes himself to task for not going to church more often.

But the way he recalls his Christian religiosity in these episodes of "reconciliation" is always rather folksy: the beauty of the church walls, the memory of *kulich* as a child, and on those infrequent occasions when he went to a service, standing in church clutching candles to light. This all creates the impression that Rozanov is in love with precisely the non-dogmatic, behavioral and aesthetic aspects of Russian Orthodoxy. It is hardly surprising then that a year later he writes that this has all become alien to him.[20] When he does invoke Christianity again in *About myself and my life* (1918)[21], he views Christianity as an ideology that can save the Old Russia, protect the government, and the old way of life (Rus. byt'). Clearly, Christianity serves as a means rather than an end here[22].

It is in this fourth period that the Beilis trial falls. Rozanov's previous admiration of Judaism (albeit with latent anti-Semitic tendencies rippling close

---

[20] In *Fallen Leaves, Part 1* (1913). In *Solitaria* he had written: "May God grant me another 3-4-5 years: I will light a candle for the rite of healing and will not extinguish it till the grave. My previous life was madness." This momentary return to Christianity was triggered by the premonition of death he suffered due to his own and his wife's serious illness that year.

[21] Vasily Rozanov, *O sebe i o zhizni svoei*. Edit. V.G.Sukach. (Moscow: Moskovskii rabochii, 1990).

[22] Cf. S.V. Skorodumov, *V.V.Rozanov. Filosofia zhizni i sushestvovaniya. Uchebnoe Posobie*.(Yaroslav: Yaroslav Ushinsky Government Pedagogical Institute, 2005), ch.2.3, "'Sergievoposadskii' period tvorcheska V.V.Rozanova kak podvedenie itogov razvitiya filosofskikh vzglyadov filosofa." Having quoted extracts from Rozanov's writings of a later period in which the latter recalls his Kostroma childhood of kulich, candles, Easter eggs and church bells, Skorodumov writes of Rozanov's final attempt to return to Chrisatianity by relocating to Sergiev Posad in 1918, in the following terms: "alas, this time too, the conceptual 'return of the prodigal son' to the bosom of Orthodoxy did not succeed, and moreover Rozanov started to savage Christianity even more in his 'apocalyptic visions.'"

to the surface) morphs into sometimes crude, and sometimes – if one can put it this way – aesthetically creative anti-Semitism. At the same time, Rozanov continues to have contact, and warm ones, with Jews such as Gershenzon and Steinberg – another paradox we will examine.

Rozanov's "lapses" back into Christianity are fleeting, and the central element of the Orthodox faith, the Eucharist, oddly enough gets most mention not in his autobiographical writings, but in his anti-Semitic journalism. There it becomes a rather unfelt impersonal symbol in a contrastive polemic against the now murderous blood sacrifices of Judaism and the Old Testament. Otherwise, the general impression of Rozanov's non-Jewish writings in this period is of lukewarm, utilitarian Christianity, which is second to many other concerns.

Certainly, one does not get the impression of an active church life or a participation in the Eucharistic rite he so praises in his Jewish polemics. This must be borne in mind when we come to examine the voluminous and now anti-Semitic writings on Judaism of this period. It will, for example, give us good reason to disagree with the analysis of L.Katsis that Rozanov's (and Florensky's, for different reasons) analysis of Judaism is "particularly Christian" and that the wellspring of Rozanov's Judeophobia is the New Testament and Orthodox tradition.

The final period, the Sergiev Posad period, lasts from November 1917-February 1919. Rozanov moved from famine-stricken Petrograd to Sergiev Posad. The move was inspired mostly by practical reasons: Rozanov had friends there and a place to live. There may have been an element of cultural nostalgia, however. In the bitter aftermath of a Revolution which he despised, in the first years of Soviet government, Rozanov may have been seeking contact with that old Russia that was evidently dying or dead. His friend, Fr. Pavel Florensky, who was living there at the time, wrote an essay[23] in 1918 praising Sergiev Posad as the heart of Russia – in a manner close to Rozanov's own, that is, celebrating the folk pagan aspects of Russia and its national Christianity.

Florensky, who had collaborated and consulted with Rozanov on his anti-Semitic journalism of 1911-14 made an effort to bring Rozanov back to Christianity in that final year and a half. Rozanov was open to re-embracing his several times discarded faith, but one incident apparently scuppered his friend's missionary efforts: Rozanov one day caught sight of the key to a safe on the same chain as a monk's pectoral cross, and he began ruminating bitterly that he could not wheedle five hundred rubles out of old friends, while "such theologians" were stuffed with money and "the rage of paganism began to boil in me due to that."[24]

During this time, Rozanov was living in an unheated apartment with his

---

[23] Pavel Florensky, "Troitsa-Sergieva Lavra i Rossia," in *Voprosi religioznogo samosoznaniya*. (Moscow, Ast: 2001).

[24] In *O sebe i o zhizni svoei*. Quoted in Skorodumov (2005), "Sergievoposadskii period," p.2.

family, and they all suffered seriously from hunger. In November 1918, Rozanov wrote a begging letter to a friend with whom he had fallen out four years ago: "Dear, close, friend G., help, have mercy, get aid, a food subscription. I've no strength, a bottle of water, 6 litres costs half a kopek….Hungry, cold." The friend responded, pestered Maxim Gorky to send Rozanov money, and on its proceeds, he survived another few months before dying. The "G" of this letter is none other than Mikhail Osipovich Gershenzon, who had previously stopped answering Rozanov's letters due to the latter's increasingly rabid anti-Semitism in the press.

After the incident with the key, Rozanov gave full vent to his anti-Christian paganism. He wrote one last major work: *Apocalypse of Our Time*. That Apocalypse was certainly not the Revolution, which he dismissed in that book with the following words: "The Revolution has two dimensions: length and breadth, but no third dimension: depth. And due to this quality it will never have any mature, tasty fruit, will never be complete…The Revolution will always be a torture and will put its hope only in 'tomorrow'. And any 'tomorrow' will deceive it and turn into a 'day after tomorrow'…In the Revolution, there is no joy. Joy is too royal an emotion for this lackey."

Instead, Rozanov was dreaming of another apocalypse, not a social one but a metaphysical one. Rozanov began talking of a human spirituality that would transcend both Judaism-paganism and Christianity. He compared this development to the stages of a butterfly's life: the caterpillar was Old Testament Judaism, earthly and fleshly; the larva was New Testament Christianity, shrouded in darkness and death; and the yet-to-arrive butterfly was Apocalyptic Christianity which would transcend and negate Christianity – for the butterfly, which has no mouth and engages in copulation, sex and spirit will be one and the same, and the word will then have fully become flesh for each and every human.

There is no doubt in this schema that the death-obsessed Christian larva is meant to die, as Judaism died before it. With the usual taste for provocative paradox, in *Apocalypse of Our Time*, Rozanov accepts Christ's prophecy that the end-time will be marked by coldness of heart among mankind. But Rozanov adds that it is Christ Himself who has turned humanity cold: the scenario Christ prophesizes is fulfilled due to the death-obsessed and life-hating religion that follows in His wake.

And what is more, what will come after the butterfly's victory over Christianity, even God does not know: "What has happened no one knows from the beginning of the world, and this is not even understood by God Himself. And God Himself is also powerless to fight or win." Here, on top of a Hegelian "cunning of history" whereby Christ unwittingly causes His own words to be fulfilled, we have a convergence on Berdyaev's theodicy of divine powerlessness: the difference, here, is that while Berdyaev preaches Orthodoxy, Rozanov is unashamed of his Gnostic apocalyptic for the simple reason that he no longer claims to be Christian.

244   CHAPTER FOUR

In *Apocalypse of Our Time*, Rozanov also expressed regret for the madness of his "Beilis years" and his anti-Semitism. Already in 1914, he had written an article declaring that he had not really believed in the blood libel during the Beilis trial, but was adopting a pose in order to defend Russian honor. But now in his dying days, Rozanov turns to the Jews with a pushy philo-Semitism. Whether, had he lived longer, he would have turned anti-Semite again is perhaps impossible to say. However, it is noticeable that the philo-Semitic moments in *Apocalypse* are of a drunken, unstable, lurching – Marmelodovian – character, and as Gershenzon noted in a letter to Rozanov concerning his anti-Semitism, they have an exaggerated, fantastic quality, which is perhaps only a hair's breadth from turning into its opposite. The following somewhat manic extracts give the idea:

> The Jews are actually not only the preeminent nation of Asia, contributing not just a certain something, but the whole light of Asia, its whole meaning, - but with gigantic effort, tireless activity they are becoming bit by bit also the first nation in Europe. There! There! There! This has not been said by anyone about them, that is, about their unifying role between East and West, Europe and Asia. And – let it be. O, let it…This is – yes, yes, yes.[25]
>
> ….
>
> And they sang….'By the rivers of Babylon': - 'Oh, we will shatter your children against the stone, daughters of Babylon.' That's Nachamkis. Nachamkis shouts: 'Why did you strip him of the right to be Steklov, noble Russian citizen Steklov…?'[26]
>
> That's anger, rage; but isn't that why they live and cannot and do not want to die, because they are so hot?
>
> Be hot-tempered, Yid[27]. O, like Rozanov – and don't fall asleep, and

---

[25] In the height of his anti-Semitic publishing spree, Rozanov wrote to Gershenson, defending himself against charges of anti-Semitism as follows: "I somehow physiologically (almost sexually) and artistically love a 'Yid in payyos', and secretly in company always sneak a glance after him and admire him." (Cf. Vasily Rozanov, "Perepiska V.V.Rozanova i M.O.Gershenzona. 1909-1918," in *Novy Mir*, No.3. (1991): 215-242. Also at http://kosilova.textdriven.com/narod/studia3/ros_hersh.htm with introductory article by V.Proscurina.) Given his obsession with the theme of sex, this extract is probably meant to suggest a more than emotional excitation about the prospect of Jews being the first nation of Europe. A second point of interest here is that Rozanov hands to the Jews the role of mediator between Europe and Asia, which in Slavophile thought (and in early Soloviev) is played by Russia.

[26] Of a Jew who wished to conceal his Jewishness under a Russian name.

[27] The distinction in Rozanov, Bulgakov and Florensky (on which, see below) between "bad" *Yids* and "good (or better)" *Jews* seems to have been erased in a flood of forgiving tears here. Even the Yids are dear, even the revolution-makers: in another passage Rozanov says he admires Jewish socialism, that it is not sinister, but shows a touchingly naïve faith in human nature and in the world's conforming to simple,

don't fall eternally cold. If you nod off, the world will die. The world is alive and not sleepy just so long as the Jew 'with one eye at least looks at the world', - 'and how much are oats nowadays?' – And trade, Jew, trade, - just don't offend Russians. O don't be offended, my little dear. You're talented, a genius even at trade (the link of centuries, the link with the Phoenicians)…..give them 7-8%, take 100 for yourself, and the Russians will have to learn to live with that, they're not the inventors after all. Give to the Jew, give to the Jew, - he's the maker, he created it. But then give to the Russian as well, Lord: he's destitute.[28]

….

The Jews are the subtlest people in Europe.

Everywhere they take with them the noble and holy idea of 'sin' (I am crying), without which there is no religion, and humanity would be broken (by a righteous heaven), if they had not learned from the Yids to tremble and pray for their sins. Them. Them. Them. They wiped the snot from that celebrated European humanity and put a prayer-book in his hands: 'take it, dummy, pray.' They gave him the psalms. And the miraculous Virgin – was one of their Jewesses. What would we be, what sort of wild thing in Europe, were it not for the Jews.[29]

Two weeks before his death, Rozanov wrote in his will: "Believing in the triumph of Israel, I rejoice in it."[30] And he proposed to the Jewish community of Moscow that they acquire half the rights in the publishing of his works, on condition that they set up a farm with the proceeds to provide for his family. As the Russian Jewish Encylopedia entry on Rozanov comments on this extraordinary request, it is full of a typically perplexing mix of love, mistrust and mockery[31]. He also expressed the wish that his four anti-Semitic books of 1911-14 be destroyed.

This brings us to the end of our summary of Rozanov's life and work. In what follows, we will select and analyze the most interesting of Rozanov's works on Jewry and Judaism from the third and fourth periods of his life, exploring their relationship to his own Christianity and the Christianity of other Silver Age thinkers.

---

honest, good-humored calculations about happiness and good fortune. While this is hardly likely to make a Jew's heart glow, for Rozanov it is a philo-Semitic reconciliation, albeit of a still fantastic sort.

[28] Rozanov himself was destitute at this time.

[29] Tellingly, while other parts of *Apokalipsis* are filled with anti-Christian blasphemy, in his address to his darling Yids, Rozanov allows himself soft words for Christianity and the Mother of God.

[30] This recalls Bulgakov's comments on his trip to America: "But I won't yet trust to my first impressions, which are all tending in one direction – the factual conquest by Israel of the world…"

[31] КЕЭ, том 7, кол. 250-253.

Early Rozanov: Judaism over Christianity
Judaism (1903)

Rozanov's lengthy article (it is roughly 130 pages long), *Judaism*, was written in 1903 and was serialized in six installations over the year in the journal *Novy Put'* (New Way). This was the journal founded by Merezhkovsky as an organ for the expression of the ideas of the Religious-Philosophical society. Symbolists such as Balmont, Minsky[32], Ivanov and Blok were fellow contributors, and in later editions[33], Berdyaev, Bulgakov, Frank and Lossky used it as a platform to express their philosophical idealism. Rozanov was thus in progressive company after his Slavophile phase.

Several sources inform Rozanov's analysis of Judaism. Firstly, there was Pereferkovich's recent translation of the Mishna into Russian. This was a major event for Russian-Jewish understanding, and the volumes were sold out immediately. Pereferkovich's was the first complete translation of the Mishna into Russian: it was begun in 1899 and completed in 1904, a year after Rozanov used it to write *Judaism*. Evidently Rozanov devoured Pereferkovich's Mishna with great enthusiasm, and this translation endeavor triggered a whole new phase in his thinking, and thus in Russian thought at large. Rozanov follows a sort of personalist-symbolist methodology in his use of the Russian Mishna, scouring it for suggestive quotations which he then feeds to the exegetic talents of his intuition.

A second source was the reminiscences and meditations of two converted Jews, S. K. Litvin (Efron) and Semyon Iliich Tseykhanstein, whose *The autobiography of a Russian Orthodox Jew* existed only in manuscript form. These are also highly fascinating descriptions of the daily life of Judaism in mid-nineteenth century Russia. Though doubts have been expressed[34] as to the authenticity of Tseychanstein's manuscript, the details are so rich and accurate

---

[32] On whom, see below.

[33] The journal only existed for two years from 1903-4 – one of the reasons for its closure was the constant pressure of government censorship.

[34] By L.Katsis, *Krovavy Navet*, 415-416. Katsis contends that Tseykhanstein's manuscript is a fictional invention of Rozanov, consisting of extracts of compilations from Jewish lore, supplemented by Rozanov's own imaginings. He points to the similarity between "Tseykhanstein"'s father's breaking off of his engagement with his young bride, on seeing her immodestly wearing ribbons in her hair, and the identical andecdote found in *Shivkhei ha-Besht*, concerning the founder of Hasidism. This may well be so. Nonetheless, it is an interesting question whether *Shivkhei ha-Besht* had been transalted into Russian; even if it had, and even if "Tseykhanstein" is really Jewish lore and legend supplemented by Rozanov, this still shows that Rozanov had immersed himself in some sources that give striking details of the realia of Jewish religious ritual and life – as will become clear below. Thus for present purposes, the exact origin of Tseykhanstein's manuscript is not of overriding importance for the arguments to be made below.

that if Rozanov had invented or embroidered them this would only be stunning testimony to his intimate knowledge of Judaism. And indeed, a third source was Rozanov's own encounters and acquaintances with Jews and Judaism, which however are much less far-ranging than these manuscripts.

Finally, the fourth factor that guided and shaped all these was Rozanov's developing philosophy of the family and sex, which had turned to ancient Egypt for inspiration. In his 1901 anthology, *The world of the clear and the unclear*, Rozanov explored the ancient Egyptian cult of the life-giving Sun, and the concepts of fertility and family among the Egyptians. Following the hint in Acts 7, 22 that "Moses was taught all the wisdom of the Egyptians," Rozanov – rather like Freud some thirty five years later[35] – interpreted Judaism in parallel with the Egyptian religion that he believed had had a far-reaching influence on the Judaic spirit. Thus Judaism for Rozanov is deeply cognate with ancient paganism. Given his rebellion against first Western Catholic Christianity and then Eastern Orthodox Christianity, for him this is highly positive.

One quotation from the Mishna fires Rozanov's imagination and determines the shape of the whole essay: "circumcision, the Sabbath and ritual immersion are more important than the Temple, more precious than Jerusalem." These three elements are the key for Rozanov to the secret essence of Jewish being; Vespasian, who uprooted the Temple and destroyed Jerusalem did not realize that he had not cut to the root of Jewry and Judaism, for these three things remained and through them Jewish life not only survived but flourished.

Rozanov's choice of three highly ritualistic aspects of Judaism as an entry into the "essence" of the Jewish religion provide an interesting contrast to Soloviev, Rozanov's friend and sometime foe. Soloviev, partly for apologetic reasons and partly due to differing philosophical tastes, had focused on the ethical aspect of Judaism. Though he must have studied other tractates with Faivel Gets, he neglected them for *Pirkei Avot*. For all that Soloviev may have had greater good will towards Jewry, this imbalance certainly distorted his characterization of Judaism. While Rozanov suffers from other distortions, his interpretation of Judaism draws on a wider range of sources.

Of course, it seems odd that Rozanov (and *a fortiori* Soloviev) would have rejected the centre role of the Temple and its sacrificial system in his initial account of Judaism. However, this lacuna is more than compensated for by Rozanov's writings during the Beilis trial, when he will make much of the blood sacrifices of the Temple and the Jews' remaining atavistic penchant for sacrificial victims. But in the 1903 work, only circumcision is linked to blood, while the real meaning behind these three institutions is the mystery of sex and procreation.

Nonetheless, even at this stage there is a paradox. While much of *Judaism* is full of admiration for Judaism and Jews, the admiration is so extreme that – with true Rozanovian antinomianism – it can slide off the end of the scale

---

[35] Freud's *Moses and Monotheism* appeared (in a second revised edition) in 1936.

and end up as denigration. Judaism and its practitioners are portrayed as so wonderful that they become super-human. From there it is a brief flip to their inhumanity and sub-humanity.

Jews, one sometimes feels, in "early" philo-Semitic and "late" anti-Semitic Rozanov[36] have not essentially changed: in both stages they are aliens, slimy, green and stinking. And yet if one enters their world, the world of the alien, one realizes that the greenness and the slime are wonderfully bright and sweet, and that is our poor, colorless, sexless world which is the anomaly. It depends on the play of the light whether Rozanov places a sub- or a super- before the -human.

A case in point: three years after *Judaism* Rozanov wrote in a short article, *Jews and non-Jews*[37], that if he were told of the discovery in a Jewish house of a dead child drained of blood (!) nothing could convince him that the Jew, should the murder be linked to him, had acted out of Jewish motives. Only a perverted Jew acting non-Jewishly could perform such an act. Another five years later, and the Jew will be having the child for tea. One thing has not changed: the propensity for the Jew to attract to himself, like a moth to fire, strange and unusual occurrences that require the most creative imaginations to interpret them: enter Rozanov.

Another case: in 1905, to state the matter hyperbolically, Rozanov himself drank the blood of a living Jew and Jewess in a communion rite that took place in a secret convention after the clock had struck twelve. This incident of mystical cannibalism slipped his mind, until Merezhkovsky reproached him with it at the height of his Beilis furore, asserting that not only had Rozanov failed to prove that Jews use blood ritually, in fact he had only shown that Russians do so.

Rozanov responded in a letter published in the papers[38]: "Ba! Ba! Ba!...Yes, really, I completely forgot! At that time I looked upon the 'evening' as one of the manifestations of Decadent nonsense, and other than boredom, it created in me no other impression, which is why I completely forgot about it. But I remember the drawn-out and funny face of the Jewish musician N and some young Jewess, holding out their hands, from which, Minksy it would seem or someone 'by turns' extracted first with a safety-pin, then with a penknife 'a few drops' of his blood, as well as the blood of this Jewess, and then they shook it up in a glass and gave it to everyone to drink. There were 30-40 'guests', gathered 'in secret' and 'no earlier than 12 midnight'; the guests consisted of all sorts of musical, artistic, philosophical and poetic types...."

He also went on to suggest, in a move to distance himself from this embarrassing aspect of his past, that this Decadent ritual, part of the Religious-Philosophical

---

[36] Later, we will see that a putative division into early and late Rozanov as regards his anti-Semitism is more heuristic than substantive.
[37] Vasily Rozanov, "Yevrei i neyevrei," in *Russkaya gosudarstvennost' i obshchestvo: statii 1906-1907*, (Moscow, Respublika: 2003): 84-88.
[38] Vasily Rozanov, "V religiozno-filosofskom obshchestve (Pismo k redaktsiyu)," in In *Obonyatenl'noe i osyaznatel'noe otnoshenie yevreev k krovi*, edited by A.N. Nikolyukin. (Moscow: Respublika, 1998): 325-328.

society's endeavor to revitalize Christianity and its bloodless (in at least two senses) rituals, could only have been thought up by a Jew. Behind Minsky's prank-like ritual lay the atavistic forests of Lithuania, where Jews in reality do gather over slain but beloved children to reinvigorate their spiritual energies.

It seems that irony has reached its limits here. Life is stranger even than what Rozanov can conjure up. It is worth remembering that Rozanov's *Judaism* comes out of precisely that Decadent, symbolist milieu with its turn-of-the-century quest for genuineness and reality, its rediscovery of ancient truths and their reapplication to modern reality, the reality of the freshly dawned twentieth century.

It is also part of Rozanov's and Merezhkovsky's determination to push the boundaries of thought beyond even where Soloviev had taken them. There is something Nietzschean here: whereas Soloviev had always critiqued the amoral Nietzsche, his heirs found the also recently deceased German[39] strangely germane to the new century. They took it upon themselves to continue in the Nietzschean spirit of smashing convention, in this case the conventions that for centuries had been shackling and distorting the Spirit in state-sponsored Christianity.

This is not to say, however, that Rozanov's *Judaism* is tied inextricably to its place and time; as usual there are moments where Rozanov's genius transcends context – and local prejudice – and continues to speak to us a century later. In fact, the essay provides what was sorely missing in Bulgakov's approach to Judaism: an attempt by a Russian Christian (or quasi-Christian) to understand rabbinic Judaism, as it existed and continues to exist after Christianity. Rozanov is at his most scintillating when he is grappling with the Talmud; it is in fact when he turns to the mystical Kabbalah, which Soloviev and Bulgakov had also engaged with, that he becomes least mystical, and rather mundane.

There is another more global problem, as we shall see: that is that for all his local insights of brilliance Rozanov cannot unify them into a coherent whole. For him praise of the Old Testament is always denigration of the New Testament, and vice versa. And rather like Berdyaev and (and, as we saw, Shestov), Rozanov is too sure of his own intuition, and ignores centuries of Church interpretation of Biblical text.

With this in mind, we will see what Rozanov has to say about the religion of circumcision, Sabbath and mikveh[40].

The immanent church of conciliar Jewry
1. *Circumcision*
Each of these three is a portal into the mystery of sex and generation. The first point to make is that here Rozanov is the great irrationalist, struggling against the "scientific" interpretation of these rites. This would have it that circumcision

---

[39] Nietzsche, like Soloviev, died in 1900. Berdyaev, Frank, Shestov, Rozanov, Merezhkovsky, and Ivanov were all influenced by Nietzsche.
[40] Mikveh is the Hebrew word for a ritual bath.

was ordained for health reasons, the Sabbath introduced the notion of bodily rest, and the mikveh was also a transparently hygienic institution – it involves washing, after all.

Rozanov is insistent that there is something more sublime and ineffable than this utilitarian explanation would have it, and he turns to Jewish consciousness to prove it. He points to the resistance that Moses Mendelsohn, the founder of Reform Judaism, met when he proposed to abolish circumcision, by pointing out that its original rationale – unhygienic antiquity – no longer existed. Rozanov thus allies himself with Jewish traditionalists against Reform-Jewish rationalists. On a scale, by implication Jewish assimilationists with no religion at all are yet more contemptible. This is, in fact, not an unusual position for the conservative camp (in which Rozanov still has one psychological foot): as we saw Khrapovitsky and John of Kronstadt are most well-disposed to traditional religious Jewry. In this respect, Jewish and Christian religious traditionalism forms an alliance against rational and reforming Christians or Jews[41].

Circumcision, one can assume, was particularly attractive to Rozanov for a number of reasons. Firstly, the texts in the Old Testament that refer to it are indeed opaque, especially Rozanov's main textual starting-point – and thus an exegete's delight. An added bonus is that they are fairly guaranteed to offend rationalist sensibilities. Finally, the sexual organ is involved, which is perfect for Rozanov.

Rozanov, in fact, gives a convincing explanation of circumcision. The text which he starts with is Exodus 4.24-26. Zipporah, Moses' wife, is threatened with death by Yahweh after she has failed to circumcise their son. Circumcising him hastily with a flint, she announces: "You are my blood bridegroom," and she touches the foreskin to Moses' feet. This is proof for Rozanov that of the three major events in human existence – birth, marriage, death – circumcision is tied primarily to marriage, and constitutes a mystical marriage between Israel and God.

Once again, it is interesting that he rejects other explanations of this episode: Soloviev in a personal conversation with Rozanov had expressed the view that circumcision was a relic of human sacrifice: the part is given for the whole. Later, the structuralist Vladimir Propp would explain the episode as a case of sacrificial blood to expiate the blood of the Egyptian Moses had slain in Egypt. This too turns Zipporah's circumcision of Gershom into retributive quasi-murder of Moses' small child in return for the dead Egyptian.

Later in *Judaism*, Rozanov quotes Tseykhanstein's account of *matziza*, the ritual in which the *mohel* (circumciser) sucks blood from the end of the penis to seal the wound. Recently, Lawrence Hoffman has shown that the custom

---

[41] Rozanov shares with Shestov an inclination to irrationalism; the opaque ritualism of the Old Testament, and its sometimes opaquer interpretation in the Talmud are thus a great source of irrationalist inspiration. Shestov, for his own reasons, ignored the Talmud. It may have been irrational, but the great champion of irrationalism somewhat paradoxically preferred to take his irrationalism in more philosophical form.

of touching wine to the lips of the circumcised boy symbolizes an infusion of blood into the child to compensate for that lost in circumcision. Conversely, according to Hoffman, the action of *matsiza* is seen as symbolic of the imbibing of wine by the *mohel* – or it may even be that the very action of sucking the circumcisional blood is literally considered to be healing, for elsewhere he writes that the rabbis considered this blood to have special healing properties and "… adolescents about to enter puberty even [wash] their hands in the blood-water mixture, according to geonic testimony."[42]

Rozanov, in other words, could have had a field day with *matsiza*, connecting it to the Jews' lust for blood, and ritual murder - and later he did[43]. By contrast, this all goes to show that Rozanov's intentions are mostly benign at this stage. All the more thanatic elements are bypassed, and circumcision for Rozanov is a seal of marital intimacy between God and Israel, and of God's immanent dwelling in the body of each Jew.[44]

That Rozanov settled on this interpretation of the opaque text in Exodus[45] is

---

[42] Lawrence Hoffman, *Covenant of Blood: Circumcision and Gender in Rabbinic Judaism*. (Chicago: University of Chicago Press, 1996), 146. Hoffman notes that blood symbolism is deeply Jewish, but that many Jews feel uncomfortable with it precisely due to the blood libel. Certainly, one shudders to think how Hoffman's book would be construed in the wrong hands. But Hoffman's point is actually very important for Christians wishing to fight their paganism or anti-Semitism: he shows that Christ's blood sacrifice in the Eucharist is not a sign of Christianity's paganism, but emerges from the Jewish core of Christianity.

[43] In *Vazhniy Istoricheskiy Vopros*, where this is used to show the Jews' atavistic attraction to blood and thus persuade readers that it is perfectly possible that Jews killed Yushchinsky for his blood.

[44] He refers to the rabbinic legend that an angel descends on a Jew at circumcision. Drawing on the tradition whereby Yahweh and the angel of Yahweh are often one and the same, he concludes that circumcision brings Yahweh himself into the Jew's body. This is a nice explication of what could well be an implicit symbolism of circumcision. Unfortunately, Rozanov, unlike Bulgakov, cannot see that such Jewish immanentism is also present in Christianity.

[45] One should add that Rozanov's interpretation is fairly conventional for Jewish commentators. Yahweh attacks Moses because he has failed to perform the act by which the covenant with Abraham was sealed, promising the Land to the Jews. The promise is passed down from generation to generation – and inscribed on the organ of generation – and given that Moses is now leading the people to the very land of the Covenant, it is a serious oversight that he has not performed that generational sign of covenant on his own offspring. See Herz's commentary on Ex.4.24. Cf. Herz, Joseph (Rabbi). Edit. *Tora i pyatiknizhie i gaftarot. Ivritskii tekst s russkim perevodom i klassicheskim kommentariem 'Sonchino'. Kommentarii sostavil d-r I.Gerts, glavnii ravvin britanskoi imperii*. Moscow: Mosty kul'tury/Gesharim, 2008. (Incidentally, some anthropologists see in the phrase "and touched the foreskin to his (Moses') feet" a touching of the foreskin to Moses' own penis (feet is a euphemism): the blood of circumcision on the husband's member then looks all the more like a sealing of the marriage, recalling the virginal blood of the marital night. This is in certainly in

no doubt partly a function of his ongoing polemic with Christianity: "We wear a cross around our neck," he writes, "the Jews have their special type of cross down there. This shows how their theism contrasts with ours."[46] The point is that circumcision is the heart of Judaism ("circumcision is the Jew's 'I'"[47]), and it has a marital significance, and is concerned with reproduction. Christianity is fixated on the Cross, and has no thought for posterity; hence its shabby treatment of family. Judaism wins out fair and square. However, this victory of Judaism over Christianity is not very reassuring. As we will see later, it leads to what is the core motivation of Rozanov's later Judeophobia: envy. It is an envy that wreaks destructive effects.

However, other comments of Rozanov's in this part of *Judaism* show how distant he is from traditional Judaism or Christianity: Abraham is said to display passiveness in consenting with no argument to the command of circumcision, (and this passiveness is a trait he has passed down to modern Jews, along with his quintessential cunningness). Here his passiveness consists in the fact that he does not ask about the meaning of circumcision. And indeed, continues Rozanov, its meaning was hidden from the Jews – its mystery was only revealed fully to the Egyptian priests, who when Pythagoras visited them according to Herodotus, insisted he be circumcised before they told him their secrets. The Bible, furthermore, is merely "a verbal commentary to the mysterious, unfathomable operation," part of which Rozanov himself is uncovering in his essay. Again, as regards circumcision: the land, the kingdom, descendants are all promises – circumcision, says Rozanov, is the covenant and fulfillment of divine intimacy itself.

All of these points need to be exposed for what they are: unchristian neo-Gnosticism. Firstly, Abraham is a saint in the Orthodox Church – to talk about him as passive and cunning is to miss his saintliness. Rozanov also writes of the "Jewish tragedy" of Abraham's constant wanderings. But from a Christian point of view, Jews before Christ are the Old Testament Church, and certainly not tragic. The Jewish tragedy starts, from a Christian perspective, after the non-acceptance

---

the line of Rozanov's thinking.)

[46] Again, this has similarities with some Jewish interpretations of circumcision. Rashi (and other commentators) interpreted Abraham's command to Eliezer to take an oath by placing his hand on his thigh as Eliezer's placing of his hand on Abraham's "organ of circumcision" as the only object on which a *miztvah* (religious commandment) had been performed that was readily available. On this basis, some commentators have equated the organ of generation with a Torah scroll (on which, along with other sacred ritual objects like tefillin, oaths are usually sworn) in terms of sanctity. Cf. http://www.chabad.org/parshah/article_cdo/aid/2008/jewish/The-Breakthrough/htm

[47] Again, this chimes with certain Jewish interpretations: there is a midrash that David, when he was naked, panicked because he could fulfill no commandment and had no sign that he was a Jew. Looking down, however, he was reassured when he saw his circumcision (Babylonian Talmud, *Menachot* 43b).

of Christ. Again, Rozanov is theologically seriously "off" – if, that is, he has any pretensions to being Christian, or if his interpreters wish to make him so.

Secondly, Abraham's acceptance of circumcision was not passiveness, but a display of the Biblical virtues of obedience and faith, found in the Old Testament and then recommended as a model by Paul (using Abraham as the type) in the New Testament in Hebrews. Thirdly, the Jews have an interpretation of circumcision as a consecration of the sexual organ to reproduction for the sake of the fulfillment of the Promise that is pretty close to Rozanov's. Circumcision was and is thus not a complete mystery to the Jews.

Where Rozanov does depart from this Jewish idea of circumcision, he falls into idolatry. For the idea that circumcision *is* the Promise regardless of the land and so on is absurd. Circumcision in Judaism is a means – of dedication of the sexual act to God, of the family and the generations of Israel to God, and of the progression of the generations down the ages until God's Messiah comes. To say that the marking of the sexual organ is an end in itself, that the organ is an end in itself, regardless of the land, the generations and the Messiah – who for Christians is Jesus…is original, but not Biblical in the Jewish or Christian sense. Perhaps an Egyptian would have found it congenial.

But this brings us to Rozanov's desire to equate key elements of Judaism with Egyptian paganism. Even if that genetic link was there and could be proved, this is to be blind to the newness of the Sinaitic revelation and Yahweh's previous revelations to the patriarchs. What is Egyptian in Israel is transformed by God. This is clear from the narrative of the Exodus where Israel is commanded to spurn Egypt and its ways. Importantly, from an Orthodox Christian perspective, this Biblical emphasis is accepted fully by the Church Fathers, who uniformly see Egypt as unclean, and Israel's separation from it and departure from it as the type of the Christian's separation "from the world which lies in evil." Jewish separateness has a counterpart in Christian separateness. Rozanov goes completely against this grain in reinstating pagan Egypt and leading Israel back into Egypt[48].

Underlying all this – and part of the trip back to Egypt – is the fundamental idea that the Bible is a closed, secret text. This is partly true. Judaism has its oral law which gives the written text its living meaning; Orthodox Christianity has Church tradition. Rozanov – has Rozanov, who we may safely say, as of any individual, is not infallible. But the idea that there is a secret and hidden knowledge found neither in the Talmud, nor the Church Fathers – but rather in ancient Egypt – is firstly Jewishly Gnostic and then Christianly Gnostic. It is precisely this idea of a secret knowledge which appeals to Rozanov both here and in the later stages of his creativity. It no doubt explains why he consented to

---

[48] The penitential canon – among other canons – which is read before confession of sins and communion has as a theme this exodus of the Christian from the Egyptian uncleanness of his life, so the theme is woven liturgically into the rhythm of an Orthodox Christian's life.

be present at Minsky's "New Age" Eucharistic rite.

There is a paradox here. Rozanov claimed to despise positivism. But his own explanations of the Bible look like attempts to *objectively* trace the origins of Judaism. In his objectivity, he puts himself outside the explanation that tradition offers (both Jewish and Christian tradition, and the Church Fathers often looked to Jewish tradition to explain obscure parts of the Bible), in order to discover new, more "real" explanations. However, as Berdyaev wrote, it is not possible to look at the Church objectively, from the outside. As soon as one does so one ceases to belong to the living organ of the Church, to be within her. Thus Rozanov, for all his contemptuous criticism of science, has imbibed the scientism of his age, even while trying to transcend it.

What I have called Rozanov's neo-Gnosticism is a recurrent theme of his "theological" speculations. It is important, and a fairly simple matter in fact, not to confuse his neo-Gnosticism with Christian thought. Rozanov himself claimed that his anti-Semitism was Biblical and Christian in inspiration[49], and later when dealing with his strange later works on Judaism we will counter this aspect of his self-presentation, which for a Christian is more disturbing than his other, cruder Judeophobic seizures[50].

2. Sabbath

Rozanov next turns his attention to the Sabbath, which for him is connected to circumcision as a line is to a point: Sabbath is the rhythmic line which guards the Jew's circumcisional "I," that flesh in which God has been inscribed. In Rozanov's Gnostic words: "Circumcision is the seal of the Lord; but the text to which this seal is applied, is read on the Sabbath. The Sabbath is the fulfillment of the secret thought behind the 'covenant', which was not imparted to Israel; that which is brought forth by Israel is needed by God. But how can it be 'needed'?!"

Here Rozanov starts appealing to the texts of his Jewish informants: like a proto-phenomenologist he explores the categories of subjective experience to yield truth. There is a twist, however: given that the full truth "was not imparted to Israel" Rozanov himself must fill out the picture a bit. This building up of his ignorant informants' humble anecdotes to give a more global picture takes different forms, which will be commented on shortly. Rozanov's main conclusion regarding the meaning of the Sabbath is that, like the circumcision which it protects and expands, it is marital. Again, Rozanov has hit the mark: but this is hardly a secret for Jews, given that every Sabbath is welcomed with the song "Come, O Sabbath bride"[51].

---

[49] In "Ob odnom priyome zashchiti yevreistva," see below.

[50] Again, later we will discuss those parts of Katsis' analysis of Rozanov which miss this entirely, though Katsis has a good point that Christianity and anti-Semitism are often so intimately intertwined that it is forgivable to see a direct causal nexus in this situation.

[51] The Sabbath hymn "Lechah Dodi," whose opening lines are: "Come, my Beloved,

More informative than Rozanov's comments here is Tseykhanstein's description of how his parents spent the Sabbath day. There is a detailed account of all the blessings that are sung at table, the synagogue services and the three Sabbath meals. The remarkable impression for a Jewishly informed reader of these texts is how faithfully such customs have been transmitted to the present day.

One detail which particularly impresses Rozanov is Tseykhanstein's account of his parents' marriage. His father was thirteen, his mother eleven, and his father had fled Cracow when his child bride-to-be had worn ribbons in her hair on the morning of their wedding to impress her finally won suitor. Repelled by such frivolity, he had hot-footed it to more pious Warsaw[52]. Such seriousness, such chastity, such piety and self-sacrifice evoke a comparison with the Russian Christian saints Ambrose and Philaret, only among the Jews this saintliness can be met with in every family.[53]

When Tseykhanstein comes to his description of the second Sabbath meal (Saturday lunch), he describes how after a pot of heavy *cholent*[54], the pious Jews go to their rooms to sleep. Indeed, sleep is commanded on the Sabbath day. It is here that Rozanov steps forward in his role as Gnostic phenomenologist.

First, he indulges a little titter as to young Tseykhanstein's pardonable ignorance, ascribing it to the fact that he left the Jewish fold as a bachelor. For if he had not, he would have known that this sleep is *commanded* by Law in order to allow good Jews to catch up on the sleep they missed out on the night before. For on Friday night, there is an equally stringent command for spouses to engage in marital relations.

A Talmudic passage that Rozanov analyses earlier parses the redundant word "Sabbath" in the phrase "keep the seventh day, the Sabbath" as a reference to the fact the *night* is also part of the Sabbath. Rozanov, going beyond the exoteric meaning of this Talmudic verse, sees here an oblique and secret encoding of the fact – well-known to Jews but not broadcast around – that Friday night is the core and inner essence of the Sabbath festival. And generalizing his insight, he

---

to greet the bride – the Sabbath presence, let us welcome!" The "Beloved" here is God; the "bride" is the Sabbath, Israel's life-partner since creation. Alternatively, the "bride" has been interpreted as the Shekhina, God's indwelling Presence, separated from Israel after the destruction of the Temple and exile – except on the Sabbath. For further details, cf. Sherman, Nosson (Rabbi). *The Complete ArtScroll Siddur. Week/Sabbath/Festival*. Co-edited by Rabbi M.Zlotowitz and Rabbi Sheah Brander. (New York: Mesorah Publications Ltd, 1984): pp.316 ff.

[52] As noted by Katsis, there is a suspicious overlap here with the life of the Baal Shem Tov (Besht), the founder of Hasidism.
[53] A similar comparison is made between average Jews and John of Kronstadt in the Beilis-period "The Angel of Jehovah among the Jews." This will be commented on shortly.
[54] Bean stew, left on a low heat to self-cook to a state of density, to provide tasty fare for the Saturday lunch, while evading the prohibition against cooking on the Sabbath.

finishes with the well-known fact that Jews are night people, while Christians are day people. The evidence, again, is the fact that *all* Jewish festivals start in the evening[55].

The essence of the Sabbath, its unconscious one might say, is thus coaxed to the surface by Rozanov's probings. Just to make sure, Rozanov asks a Jewish acquaintance whether Jews have sex *only* on the Sabbath. His reply is that obviously not. With admirable scientific rigor, Rozanov is not put off by this contradictory data – it comes, after all form a Reformist Jew – and concludes: "However, I am certain that the *classical* Jew has relations only on the Sabbath, looking at everything else as debauchery and uncleanness…"[56]

The Sabbath has thus been uncovered: its peak, the *sanctum sanctorum*, is the nocturnal and hidden sexual act of the spouses. Again, in this it resembles Egyptian religion, where not a time for sacred sex was designated, but a place – the sacred temples. The thought is the same, however.

There is another aspect of the Sabbath which fascinates Rozanov – and this is the fact that even the slightest violation of its manifold ordinances was punishable by death. This would hardly have been the case if the Sabbath was meant merely to allow man to rest.

Rozanov's comparison of the Sabbath to an Egyptian sacred temple allows him to deduce that violating the Sabbath is equivalent to desecrating a sacred

---

[55] The hitch here, of course, is that Orthodox Christian festivals also start in the evening.

[56] The Talmud elsewhere lays down recommendations for the number of times a week a Jew should satisfy his wife, all depending on the strenuousness of his profession and the length of absence from home. Rozanov cites this text in a different context, but is not concerned to harmonize its ratification of non-Sabbath sex with his present assertion. Still, Rozanov's claim about the *special* holiness of Sabbath sex can actually be confirmed by Jewish sources: the twelfth century Kabbalistic text *Iggeret ha-Qodesh* (of disputed authorship) writes that: "the pious have not selected weekdays on which physical activity predominates; for their marital relations they prefer the Sabbath, which is spiritual and restful." Interestingly, according to Michael Stanislawski, an early Yiddish commentary on the *Iggeret* somewhat distorts and simplifies the rationale of the original, recommending Friday eve sexual activity on the basis that Jews are granted an extra soul on that night: the increased strength and divinity of that soul increases the chance of conceiving a healthy and intelligent child. Probably Rozanov must thus indeed have had an informant who was familiar precisely with folk Russian-Jewish notions of religiosity. Still, even here there is a certain prudishness which Rozanov does not take on board: even "holy sex" is for procreative purposes, and not for mere frivolity and pleasure, and its confinement to the Sabbath rather limits the Talmud's broader accent on sex as often as possible to satisfy the urge. Cf. Michael Stanislawski, "Toward the popular religion of Ashkenazic Jews: Yiddish-Hebrew texts on sex and circumcision," in *Mediating modernity. Challenges and trends in the Jewish encounter with the modern world. Essays in honor of Michael A. Meyer.* Edit. Lawrence Strauss and Michael Brenner. Detroit: Wayne State University Press, 2008.

temple, namely the temple of sexuality and procreation. "…The Sabbath is a way and a method of solving the great and even global problem of sex, which for example…has been solved by us through the millennial-old religious institution of marriage…" So while Jews have the Sabbath, gentiles have marriage – and if gentiles contravene marriage they also die.

Still, the Jews have the Sabbath *and* marriage – and they are the only ones to integrate the mystery of marriage into the mystery of religion: "In general, the mystery of true sexual intimacy is known only to the Jews and can only become known on the soil of 'To the Lord – of circumcision'; all other peoples are left only with the stench of this. The candle and tweezers that remove the wick: the Jews have the candle, and we have the tweezers, full of soot and wick."

It is extremely telling that even at the height of his sexual-familial prowess (by now he had been married twelve years and had sired a not inconsiderable six children), Rozanov can still feel he is on the periphery of true sexuality, while the Jews have penetrated – on their dark Sabbath nights – into the noumenon of the thing. Evidently, it is a question of integration: Rozanov's much-loved fertility is the exercise of a lone man who feels his God and his country are not with him on this. Hence the yearning for missing unity, the nostalgic gazing across to the fertile bands of the Pale of Settlement[57].

Aside from this personal dimension, however, Rozanov has surely hit on an important concept concerning the Sabbath: he throws much light on Jesus' conflict with the Sabbath as recounted in the Gospels. Why did the Pharisees object to Christ healing on the Sabbath? According to Rozanov, the rabbis reason as follows: "The blind man suffers; but if the Sabbath is broken for the blind man, then he will gain his vision, and all people will go blind in the eternal arena of marriage, and the day of healing will be a day of death for all, which we alone know in the world and which God taught us alone in the world, along with his prophet Moses, regarding this important secret."

This indeed captures a majestic truth about the Sabbath. It is not a utilitarian, humanistic institution designed to improve "quality of life." Rather the Sabbath is fenced around with death and is full of divine awe, terrifying and mysterious.

A confirmation of Rozanov's insight can be seen in the intensity with which rabbis discuss the Sabbath *halakhah* that forbids all but life-saving medical intervention on the Sabbath, if such intervention involves violating any of the thirty nine categories of work. To quote: "The *medrash* derives from a *posuk*

---

[57] While it is true that the Russian Jewish population was extremely fertile, increasing fivefold in just over a century, the Russian population also shot up after the emancipation of the serfs and improved economy brought on by industrialization. Indeed, between 1795 and 1910 the population of the Russian empire increased 5.5 times (from 29 million to 160 million) and from Rozanov's birth until the writing of *Judaism*, the population of Russia almost doubled (68.5 million in 1850 to almost 160 million in 1910). Social changes, resulting unemployment, migration for work, and crowded conditions in the Pale were some of the factors that led to social violence, including pogroms.

in *Parshas Lech Lecha* that one may violate the laws of *Shabbos* to save the life of a *choleh sheyesh bo sakanah* (an individual with a life threatening sickness). The Talmud clearly states that even when we are not sure whether there is a real danger to someone's life or whether the *chilul Shabbos* will save the life, we still declare that the *chilul Shabbos* is allowed. Rav Shimon Shkop, in his famous *sefer Shaarei Yosher*, points out from the *Gemarah* that even in a case of *sfek sfeka* we still allow *chilul Shabbos*."[58]

Here it can be seen that while the Sabbath can be broken for even a "sfek sfeka" (a doubt concerning a doubt), there are limits. A "sfek sfeka sfeka," in other words, if one could imagine such a thing using "pilpulistic" logic[59] would be forbidden. All this shows that the rabbis take the threat of death for violation of the Sabbath with utter seriousness and appropriate fear.

Only by understanding this can we understand the shock-effect of Christ's breaking the Sabbath to do non-life-saving healing (and thus "work") – which, of course, He could have done on any other secular day. The "Son of Man" is striding into the heart of this sacred Temple and proclaiming that his own edicts are equal to that of the deity of the Temple – or as Rozanov has it implicitly here, and explicitly in his later years (in his "Beilis works" and *Apocalypse*), that Jesus' edicts cancel that of the previous, and different, deity of the Temple. That is, because Rozanov understands the trans-human awe of the Sabbath, he understands that the Son of Man's cancellation of it institutes a new religion – which for Rozanov, however, is a religion of monkish denial and deathly infertility.

In this discussion of the Sabbath temple, we get a sense of this already: "In essence, in every 'I' there is the germ of the Christian and the Jew…and all of our 'I's'…live through this germ within of Judea, that is completely indestructible and destroyable only by eunuchs who have atrophied in their ascetical refuges or by hermit-scientists. But here the family has died; people do not carry on, humanity is dying out. Thus the 'Jew' in us is a sprout reaching into the future, is life, is being…."

That is, in *Judaism*, Rozanov thinks his "inner Jew" can, indeed should, live side by side with his "inner Christian," although he is not quite sure how this can be. Later, however, something more like civil war is the order of the day…with unpleasant consequences for real, "outer" Jews.

The next pillar of Judaism is the *mikveh*, where Rozanov really outdoes himself in interpretive genius.

3. Mikveh

His impressions of the mikveh come from Tseykhanstein[60] again. What strikes Rozanov is the great gulf between the common-sense rationale for the

---

[58] Hershel Schachter, "Shemiras Shabbos for Doctors and Medical Students," http://www.torahweb.org/torah/special/2007/rsch_shabbos1.html
[59] pilpul: the intense textual analysis used in Talmudic study.
[60] Or whatever meleé of sources may have lain behind the "Tseykhanstein manuscript," if one doubts the reality of that source.

existence of the mikveh and reality. For far from the waters of the mikveh being clean, Tseykhanstein describes how the water is not changed for months, so that it becomes rank and fetid with the sweat of hundreds of bathers[61]. Again, ritual immersion takes place on Friday evening just before the Sabbath night (!) comes in. On non-Sabbath days, it is used by women to purify (note, not clean) themselves preparatory to sexual relations.[62] The mikveh thus fits perfectly Rozanov's conception of it as a gateway into the sexual mysteries of the Sabbath.

Rozanov digs deeper, though. Why is it, he wonders, that in effect – as far as he understands Tseykhanstein – the dirtier the water is for the Jews, the holier it is?[63] How can it be that a Jewish man and wife can immerse themselves in this fetid sludge, while reciting "For the honor of the Sabbath (*lekhavod Shabbat*)"? They even rinse their mouths with this filthy water, according to Tseykhanstein. The reason is that, for Rozanov, immersion in the mikveh is a rite of unification: "with pre-emptive circumcisedness we immerse ourselves in the holy mikveh, so as to be one. How one?"

While all the contemptible "scientists"[64] of Judaism are out focusing on the bizarre rituals of the Temple cult, Rozanov in his humble journalistic endeavors has uncovered the *noumenon* behind the misleading phenomenon here: " 'We' are one, and not spiritually, not through belief, but bodily one. The secret[65] of secrets of the 'mikva' consists in the mysterious[66] all-common fleshly contact of each Jew and Jewess with all, and of all with each other. Everyone, just a little bit, and awesomely in their own way, takes communion (take a sip even!) of the being of all the others, of the entire body of the wholeness of Jewry[67] of a given location...."

In other words, Jews are immersing themselves in the literal body of Israel. This passage is probably as good a contender as any other to exemplify Rozanov's philosophy of "sacred flesh." The secret (*tainy*) mikveh is sacred, mysterious,

---

[61] Before mikvehs were made more hygienic in relatively recent times, this was indeed not far from the truth as concerns the cleanliness of mikveh waters, where tens of men can indeed immerse themselves in the tepid waters of the mikveh before rushing off to Sabbath eve prayer. Descriptions such as these heighten the sense that Rozanov must have had access to genuine descriptions of Jewish life.

[62] Rozanov is under the impression that one mikveh is used by men and women, which is not the case, and would run contrary to the strict separation of sexes in Judaism, not to mention the laws of *niddah* for women.

[63] This is all part of a recurrent theme where, as the Russian proverb has it: "What is good for a German is death for a Russian." Throughout *Judaism* Rozanov sees Jew and Christian as radically opposite: what is clean for Jews is dirty for Christians, what is an angel for Jews is a demon for Christians, and so on. See below.

[64] Contempt for scientists is part of Rozanov's irrationalism, and perhaps part of that "learned ignorance" which was cultivated in different ways by Shestov, Gershenzon, Florensky and, in a very different way, by Frank.

[65] *Taina*, in Russian.

[66] *Tainstvenni*, in Russian.

[67] *Tselogo yevreistva*, in Russian.

sacramental (*tainstvenny*). Soloviev's much-touted *tselnost'* (wholeness) which is meant to put Western abstract philosophizing to shame, is shown here to be more abstract cant (or Kant) of the same ilk. For what can be more whole than immersion in the fetid pool of the *whole* of Jewry at a given place. What Rozanov is giving is nothing less than an ecclesiology of the mikveh: welcome to the Jewish church, *here* is *sobornost*, brotherly gatheredness – Khomiakov, Fyodorov, eat your heart out! Jews, circumcised into Yahweh, and each little Yahwehs, take sips from the common pool of each other: they take communion from themselves, for they are divine, sexual creatures. This is *theosis*[68] in an entirely different register.

Even the phrase "the entire body of…Jewry of a given location" recalls Orthodox eccelesiology. According to this, the fullness of Christ is present in each local church, wherever believers are gathered. So here, not every single Jew can pile into a small *shtetl* mikveh, but all the locals and their discarded bodily filth together constitute a full manifestation of universal Israel – "Israel in the flesh," as the old and now much transfigured theological truism has it.

This reworking of the concept of fleshly Israel is, frankly, a *tour de force*. Rozanov takes the mikveh, which was one of the first institutions to be axed by the Reformers, and rehabilitates it for Jewry[69], shows its inner logic, its metaphysical beauty. Nonetheless, one is still left with the impression that Rozanov has got a bit carried away. As with his final request for the Jewish community to have a share in his literary estate, one feels along with admiration and love, something tongue in cheek, and even contemptuous. The super-human Jew, man of the moment is, we feel, tottering on the brink once again of sub-humanity. The slightest windfall will push him over into negativeness.

Nevertheless, even in his Beilis years Rozanov nursed a fondness for the mikveh. In *Solitaria*, which came out in 1913, he gives us another inkling of the ticklish methodology by which he extracted intimate information from his Jewish informants (we already saw how he quizzed an acquaintance about the timing of marital relations in Jewish households). One gets a picture of a cravated nineteenth-century gentleman putting questions to slightly put out men of society. However, in *Solitaria*, his informant is a young Jewish lady boarder, staying with him for an unspecified amount of time.

In reply to his queries about the mikveh, she blushes and replies that it is not proper to speak of such things. Her blushes, given the subject matter, are understandable: one imagines Rozanov cornering the poor girl at the bottom of the staircase, and then fairly scaring the living daylights out of her with the

---

[68] Gk. "deification" – the Eastern Orthodox mystical belief that it is the goal of Christian life to become God. "God became man so that man may become God," as Athanius the Great expressed it in the 4th century.

[69] We will see later that the Orthodox Jew, Aaron Steinberg, found Rozanov's *Judaism* and other Jewish articles to be deep insights into Jewish being. Thus, evidently for some Jews, these essays were benevolent. For Rozanov and Jewish reactions to him, cf. the later sections in this chapter concerning Steinberg, Stolpner and Gershenzon.

frank straightforwardness of an eccentric academic[70]. Not put off, Rozanov persists in his scientific inquiries, and is rewarded with new information which he integrates into an updated account of the significance of the mikveh:

> But the water must come from the ground – the water of a well. Thus, "to descend into the mikva" always means to "to descend to the bottom of the well"…The steps, as I observed in Friedberg, are "cyclopean"…and in descending one must "spread one's legs wide"…One does not walk, but proceeds by steps, "climbs," with great effort, great tension…The actual descent is very long, deep, and it takes ten minutes to get back up. Moreover, the woman is refreshed, joyful (the usual feeling after an immersion) – naturally, as she ascends bit by bit, she raises her head up: and before her eyes for ten minutes is the sight "of widely spread legs," rounded bellies, and smoothly shaved (a ritual) – completely bare – private parts. "Everything in a person is the likeness and image of God," it occurs to them in a flash as they ascend in that ecstatic, religious minute. "Kosher! Kosher!" the rabbis have pronounced…Thus panting and happy, they descend and ascend, they ascend and descend.

Here the mikveh has become the very type of Jacob's heavenly ladder, by means of which angels ascend and descend on the way between heaven and earth – only now these angels are human, biological, and all their unashamed physicality is allowed to them. Touching also is the male phenomenologist-journalist's adeptness at getting into the head of the lady bathers here ("it occurs to them in a flash…"). Despite this wonderful empathy, given the oddness of the passage it is perhaps not surprising that Rozanov can alternate in these later years between anti-Semitic libel and "philo-Semitic" passages of this sort.

By the time Rozanov has finished his interlocking description of circumcision, the Sabbath and the mikveh, the bulk of *Judaism* is complete. The picture of Judaism as an intimate, quasi-pagan chamber of sexual secrets has been deftly and lovingly painted. One should add that although our post-1960s sensibilities are somewhat dulled by the thrilling hints of revelations as to what occurs in the depth of the Sabbath night, to give credit where credit is due Rozanov is not being entirely prurient.

The press were constantly calling Rozanov "that awful pornographer," but he was sincere in his journalistic battle to make sex less dirty than his society with its norms would allow, and to combat the hypocritical attitude to illegitimacy which had so scarred his own family life. At this stage of his life, Rozanov really was fighting to lift some of the taboos around sex, and what is

---

[70] On the other hand, the incident is odd simply for the fact it brings us face to face Rozanov's contradictoriness again: the bugbear persecutor of Jewry has a Jewish woman staying over in his house and conducts friendly, exploratory chats with her. We will return to this theme when we consider his meetings with Steinberg and Gershenzon at the same time.

more interesting in the context of this exploration of Judaism – to find a way of integrating sex/biology and true religion, which for Rozanov is still, albeit obliquely at times, Christianity.

However, the fact that his admiration of Judaism is dependent on his seeing it through the lens of paganism has unfortunate consequences. There is a passage towards the end of *Judaism*, which reveals another side of Rozanov the phenomenologist, who enriches and theorizes his informants' experiential data with this dubious perspective. Only here, Rozanov's attempts to wear the philologist's hat fails miserably, and this is indicative of a larger malaise.

Astarte, Egypt and Judaism

Tseykhanstein's father, on waking would recite a series of blessings to God, one of which was called the "Asher Yitser"[71]. Rozanov does not give the first line of this prayer, but it reads: "Baruch atah adonai….*asher yatsar* et-ha-adam bekhokhma." Literally, this translates "Blessed (are) you, Lord….*who created man in wisdom*." Rozanov's focus latches onto the word "asher." He sees in this a Hebrew cognate of the Phoenician goddess Ashera, or Astarte. From this, he deduces that one of the Jewish God's names is that of a female deity, related to the pagan Phoenician goddess. A further step, and this is linked to the Shekhina and the Sabbath Queen, who is greeted in Sabbath hymns on that anticipation-filled Friday eve.

Rozanov goes further. Clearly, the Jews' familiarity and worship of Ashera raises the question of their prophets' castigation of Jewish worship of this very goddess. The prophets of the Old Testament constantly inveigh against this "idolatry." But Rozanov can explain this: it is the same as the Old Believers' invectives against the terrible deity *Iisus*, who is a devil compared to their own divine *Isus*[72]. Rozanov makes a similar point regarding the cognate etymology of the Canaanite "bel" or "baal" and the Hebrew "el." Both "bel" and "el" are the same; the Canaanite deity has a prefix "b," temporarily obscuring their unity.

The point of this philological excursus is to show that Judaism and the Phoenician religion are minor local variations on one and the same cult of Afro-Asian paganism found across the Mediterranean basin, the centre of which was the cult of sexuality and family. The link with Rozanov's 1901 Egyptian anthology, *The clear and the unclear*, is complete.

The bad news in all this for this Martin Bernal[73] of the early twentieth century is that the word "asher" on which Rozanov decides to build his house of cards is the humble relative pronoun, i.e. the Hebrew for "who/which." Likewise "bel" and "el" are no more cognate in any Semitic language, than "bell" and "el-

---

[71] In fact "asher yatsar."
[72] One of the points of contention in the Old Believer/Nikonite schism was the insistence of the former on preserving the old Russian spelling of Jesus with one 'i', when Nikon blasphemously introduced another 'i'.
[73] The author of *Black Athena*, who tried to prove the African origins of Athenian culture.

train" in English (though trains do have bells sometimes).

But far more dismaying than Rozanov's crackpot philology is the crackpot theology it is meant to support: namely that the Old Testament is on a perfect continuum with Astarte-worship and that the Old Testament God is the same (bar the odd orthographic trifle) as the Baal against whom the prophets railed with misguided, literalistic, sectarian fanaticism.

In the question of balance between paganism, Christianity and the Old Testament/Judaism which we examined in Soloviev, Bulgakov and Berdiaev, we can safely say that – in this respect at least – Rozanov has got it badly wrong. But worse, he has shot himself (or at least his Christian self) in the foot. All that is good, life-embracing, and unhypocritical in Judaism/the Old Testament is attributed to an Egyptian-Canaanite Yahweh. In other words, much that is good and life-embracing in Christianity due to its still living Jewish roots is siphoned off, leaving Christianity the parody of itself which Rozanov then rejects.

In fact, the metaphor is Rozanov's: at one point he refers to Christianity as drained of the blood of Judaism, a pale shell compared to the rich and detail-filled daily life of the Jews. In other words, to adopt a Rozanovian logic, for the Rozanov of *Judaism*, Christianity has ritually murdered Judaism and drained its corpse of blood. The later "Beilis" Rozanov's attack on Jewry for ritually murdering Andrei Yushchinsky is then simply agonized revenge – according to an "eye for an eye" – of one who was forced to inherit a bloodless religion from the princes of Christianity. You Jews, he shouts – unwilling to take the blame himself – , drain *our* blood.

In reality, Rozanov does not sound very convinced by his own shouting, and sure enough he later disowns this claim. For the fact is that Rozanov by tracing Judaism back to Egypt deprives Christianity of its Jewish heart. (In the analogy, he is the ritual murderer of Christianity). And it was in *Judaism* that he laid a solid groundwork for the Marcionite[74] theology – that is, a Christianity *sans* Old Testament – that he embraces in his Beilis years.

The agonies of Marcionism
The clearest example of this is his 1914 article, "Ob odnom priome"[75]. Here with an unhappy sarcasm, he mocks those Christians who have written to him

---

[74] Marcion of Sinope (85-160), an early Christian theologian excommunicated by the Church. He excluded the whole of the Jewish Bible from his Christian canon, as well as all the books of the New Testament apart from the letters of Paul and his own adapted Gospel of Marcion. He believed the Jewish god was demonic, and all that was Judaic in Christianity had to be extirpated. His name is synonymous with the most extreme rejection of Judaism by Christianity, and as we can see in Rozanov and Florensky, Marcionism has never ceased to be a recurrent temptation for Christians.

[75] Vasily Rozanov, "Ob odnom priyome zashchiti yevreistva," in *Obonyatenl'noe i osyaznatel'noe otnoshenie yevreev k krovi*, edited by A.N. Nikolyukin. Moscow: Respublika, 1998.

with the reproach that his anti-Semitism and anti-Judaism are unchristian on the grounds that the Jewish books of the Old Testament are Christian books.

Not at all, protests Rozanov. The books of Moses are in their entirety (bar a few ethical precepts) utterly contradictory to the spirit of Christianity, a pathetic rule-book of perverse and alien prescriptions, with a thoroughly carnal orientation. Christ (or "J.Christ" as Rozanov refers to Him[76]) rejected the Old Testament and the Old Testament Church in its entirety. He called Jews "sons of the Devil" and had to rid himself of them and their foul religion. He founded a new church with nothing in common with Old Testament perversity. All the priests and scientists who have written to Rozanov should read both Testaments of the Bible to see that this is so.

However, we have to remember Rozanov's antinomianism. "But where is the Truth then?" "In the fullness of all thoughts…To choose one with terror. In the vacillation." "But surely vacillation is not a principle?" "The first in life…."

In the same year, Rozanov was writing *Pered Sakharnoy*, a collection of aphorisms, random jottings, autobiographical trivia – a style which he had honed in *Solitaria*, and was his new pre-"post-modern" vehicle for antinomian expression. There, out of the gaze of the media, on holiday in the Crimea, taking a break from defending Russia's honor by Jew-baiting, he writes some of his famously throw-away lines (*pace* Levitsky), which outline the whole problem, as we have just described it:

> Was the Jews' guilt against J. Christ phenomenal or noumenal? I.e. only "that crowd" "couldn't understand," and most importantly, "now," well, "with the passage of time"? Or, at root, from antiquity, from Moses and even Abraham? Did the sickness come from the source, or only the mouth of the river? In the final analysis, i.e. if it's only "customs" and now – there was no good reason to abolish circumcision and the whole sacrificial cult, and Sabbaths and the Temple.
>
> In that case Christians would have preserved the Biblical family; would have preserved a living and animal feeling for the Bible, and not what we "sometimes read." The awful contradiction of the Old Testament and Gospel would not be giving us this heart ache.
>
> I don't understand anything. Oh, if only someone would explain.

---

[76] One periodically wants to use the word "demonic" when reading Rozanov. In an article supposedly written to defend Christianity, but more likely to defend Russian national honor, he uses this bizarre and quite horrific manner of writing Christ's name. Christ is reduced to an office clerk, or an obscure author, on the analogy of J.Smith, stripped utterly of uniqueness, cloaked with a mocking anonymity and mediocrity. One's mind leaps to his tongue-wagging antics on his deathbed. It is as if, in the very process of writing, he is already tugged by uncontrollable forces in an opposite direction, and winks at the reader, as if to say: "You see, I don't believe in this pathetic rascal J.Christ, but for the sake of honor, for the sake of honor…" The Underground Man *redivivus*.

We seem to hear the voice of (the later) Bulgakov, asking the very same questions, verging on a realization that a Judeo-Christianity is in principle possible… Some of the torturous confusion is brought on by Rozanov himself; but some of it is inherent in the subject-matter.

In *Pered Sakharnoy*, we hear another truth from Rozanov. Here is his private self, full of a measured appraisal of the Jewish-Christian paradox. Perhaps if with "terror…in the vacillation," he had chosen the other horn of the dilemma…

But as we will see, to have chosen that horn would have resulted in an abolition of his very self, of all his selves. And of course, the notion of the "private" Rozanov, heart on sleeve, is a very public construction. After all, thousands of readers would soon be drinking up the words of this public "private Rozanov" jotting his innermost ponderings down behind drawn blinds on the Crimean coast.

There is one friend, though, who was not part of that large anonymous public and in fact responded to the dilemma expressed so succinctly in *Pered Sakharnoy*: that is Bulgakov himself.

The two men were corresponding between 1911 and 1914[77] and Bulgakov gives his opinion of Rozanov's thought in this period, reacting to some of Rozanov's key works, in particular *Moonlight People* and *Solitaria*. Regarding the latter, Bulgakov comments directly on the "mikveh" passage that we cited at some length above. In sum, he gently formulates an objection to what he sees as Rozanov's pagan philosophy of sexuality, which arises from an idealized and distorted reading of the Old Testament.

Moonlight People was (before *Apocalypse*) Rozanov's most vitriolic attack on Christianity, in which he accuses the religion and its founder of encouraging sexual perversity. In a 1911 letter, Bulgakov chides Rozanov for confusing what the latter calls the "dark face" of Christ with what is in fact the "dark face" of the world. In particular, his positing of an antithesis between the Old and New Testaments does not stand up to scrutiny. Rozanov's "trouble-free world does not and has never existed, except for brief moments and out of a naivety regarding life. The crack is in the world and the human heart, including in the Old Testament world as well.…I love my family, friends, Russia, but the *dark face* of the world, to be more precise, of world evil, seeping into the soul, I cannot overcome except by looking on that *bright and gracious Face*. And you have seen a *dark face* in the wrong place…your half-sketched Old Testament world is a spectre…"

Although Bulgakov is talking of Rozanov's idealization of a non-existent perfect world of the Old Testament, the observation applies perfectly to the picture we get of Talmudic Judaism in 1903. As we commented earlier, it is an idealization which can only lead to disappointment.

Next, when *Solitaria* comes out in 1912 Bulgakov is charmed and touched by this intimate book, hardly believing that it can be sold in public bookshops. However, he once again takes him to task for his glorification of sexuality, and

---

[77] Sergei Bulgakov, *Neopublikovannie pisma S.N. Bulgakova k V.V.Rozanovu. Predislovie i kommentarii M.A. Kolerova*. Voprosi filosofii No.10, 1992.

explains his views on the Christian attitude towards gender and sex:

> You know, I find no savor in exaggerated sexuality, in the "mikveh." This is not a denial of sex, on the contrary, out of the recognition of the holiness of sex, "of the mystery in Christ and in the Church," there follows for me a feeling of the poisoned nature of sexuality: "in lawlessness was I conceived, in sin did my mother bear me."[78] And phallic sexuality bears within itself the natural, biological curse, that "undying fire" and "the worm that slumbers not." And this is regardless of the sacredness of "child-likeness," by which alone sexuality is sanctified and redeemed. And this feeling was in the Old Testament, and not just in the New. I do not think I will persuade you, but everyone nurtures in their own life their own "sexual" wisdom…

Then in a later letter of the same year Bulgakov writes:

> …And Christianity therefore is not asexual, but only supra-sexual in its higher strivings, but sexuality does not exhaust sex (gender). And the Old Testament is by no means as sexual as you make it: remember "in lawlessness was I conceived, in sin did my mother bear me." This inhuman wail belongs after all to David, and not at all to some "Urning"[79]. And how does this differ from the Christian prayer in the rite of purification after birth, where the Church implores: "and do not impute this sin to her," where she takes the child and draws attention to the sin! We are knitted of contradictions, and you want to overcome them through biology[80]! And were not the greatest Old Testament prophets Elijah and John virgins? And do we hear any mention of Zipporah when Moses is leading the people to Sinai?…

To put it in a nutshell, Bulgakov is underlining the continuity between

---

[78] Psalm 51, which Bulgakov discussed again in another letter cited below. The psalm is recited every morning during *Prayers on Rising* by Orthodox Christians.

[79] Urning (in German), or Uranian, in nineteenth century English usage: a term referring to a person of the third sex, a female in a male body, in other words one of the sexual misfits with which Rozanov equated Christian ascetics in *Moonlight People*.

[80] This is insightful. At this period, Bulgakov had not yet realized that Rozanov's spiritual father, Pavel Florensky, was obsessed by the same biological approach to the sacredness of life, and the anti-Semitic articles they wrote together during the Beilis trial contain a *racist* anti-Semitism that is in many ways a logical extension of the viewpoint expressed by Rozanov in *Judaism*. Bulgakov's (and Soloviev's) own "sacred materialism" does, of course, share an emphasis on the sanctification of the physical world and is to some extent cognate with and influenced by Rozanov. Nonetheless, there are crucial diverges, as Bulgakov's later negative re-assessment of Florensky shows. This will be discussed below.

the Old and New Testament, and reminding Rozanov that skepticism towards the world and its goodness was a part of the Old Testament heritage as well. Rozanov's false dichotomy for Bulgakov comes from a partial and thus false reading of the Old Testament, and this distortion of the Old leads directly into a perversion of the New Testament.

In the next section, we will see that this criticism is extremely accurate and we will attempt to apply it specifically to Rozanov's anti-Jewish writings of the Beilis period, where a partial and distorted reading of the Old Testament and then the New Testament leads directly to an anti-Semitic ideology that reaches new levels of perniciousness.

Bulgakov himself only made the connection between a distorted understanding of the Bible in Christianity and anti-Semitism at a later date, though we saw that he was interested in this problem even at this time.[81] Still, it is interesting that his relations with Rozanov remained warm despite Rozanov's blaze of anti-Semitic activity in the press. A sign perhaps that abstract theological appreciation of the Old Testament is still a long way from a lively concern with real Jews?[82]

In the next section, then, we will turn to the contemporary Rozanov of the right-wing press, a veritable one-man (or two-man as it later transpired) cottage industry of anti-Semiticana, heaping down curses on the head of Beilis for the salvation of a tottering Russia.

Middle Rozanov: Russia expels the Jew within

Rozanov's public "theology" of Judaism between 1911-1914 is, in one sense, quite different to that of his *Judaism* phase. His published letters and articles commenting on the Beilis case were gathered together in 1914 in a hefty volume entitled *The olfactory and tactile relationship of Jews to blood*[83].

---

[81] Cf. his comments about Schelling in *The Unfading Light*.

[82] We already saw this in chapter 3. *The Unfading Light* is written in 1917. In 1915, Bulgakov contributed *Zion* to Gorky's anthology of pro-Jewish articles, *Shchit*. In 1921, he was regretting the influence of Yids in the downfall of Russia. Most likely, Bulgakov and other Russians' division of Jewry into "Yids" and "Jews" ensured that there was little dismay over anti-Semitic sentiments in friends and colleagues – perhaps this could be attributed to anti-"Yid" sentiment. On the other hand, Merezhkovsky and others were precisely willing to break the friendship with Rozanov over just this issue. Still, it is even debatable whether breaking a friendship is a sign of concern for Jewry. In many senses Bulgakov was more sensitive to the concerns of Jewry than Merezhkovsky, as his *Shchit* article shows. In short, there are many complex factors at play.

[83] Recently reissued as: *Obonyatenl'noe i osyaznatel'noe otnoshenie yevreev k krovi*, edited by A.N. Nikolyukin. Moscow: Respublika, 1998. Along with Berdyaev's writings, at a rough volume count in Moscow bookshops, one can say that Rozanov's works are among the most popular representatives of Russian Silver Age thought. As far as his writings on Judaism are concerned, this is rather worrying – for one gets the sense that his anti-Semitic writings continue to fuel similar tendencies in contemporary

In general, as the title indicates, the focus of this "theology" replaces sex with blood. The latter, though, is connected to the former: both are core facts of that "sacred biology" with which, according to Bulgakov, Rozanov wished to transcend the contradictions and sin of the world.

The theme of secrecy, so connected to sacredness for Rozanov, is another link. And it is fitting, therefore, that there was in fact a secret force acting on Rozanov's thinking in this period, a force whose nature was only brought to light eighty years later. For it was only in the 1990s that the identity of Rozanov's anonymous collaborator on some of the articles in *Olfactory* was shown to be Pavel Florensky[84], who wished to conceal his participation in this scandal-stirring anti-Semitic volume, for fear of stirring up unwelcome attention to himself from the left and the right.

On the other hand, in what follows, it would not do to get carried away by the idea that Rozanov underwent a complete transformation in his attitude towards Jews, as if one can posit a pre- and post-Beilis Rozanov. That would be far too simple. Instead, there is a constant manic alternation between adumbration and condemnation of Jewry, sometimes taking place within the space of months.

Thus in 1898 Rozanov had written an anti-Semitic article expressing fear over the "power of Jewry" after Dreyfus' acquittal in France[85]. Most interestingly, in 1906, he wrote two articles denying that Jesus was a Jew and giving vigorous support to the just-published ideas of Houston Chamberlain concerning the Aryan origin of Christ[86]. Some of his arguments are echoed in the works we will examine below, such as the idea that the Solomonic Temple was built by Phoenician artisans and thus was essentially a Semitic pagan cult.

But then, a mere three months later, at the start of 1907, Rozanov went on to praise the Old Testament and the Jewish tradition of marriage, which "in the time of J.Christ was purely civil, and Jews who have not betrayed their traditions, to this day have no other form of marriage…"[87] That Jesus was a faithful Jew Rozanov makes clear by linking His presence at the wedding of Cana to the tradition of Jewish civil marriage[88].

---

post-Soviet culture; moreover, there does not seem to be much critical evaluation of these writings.

[84] See details in section on Florensky.

[85] Vasily Rozanov, "Yevropa i yevrei," St. Petersburg, 1914 (originally appeared in 1898); reprinted in *Tajna izrailja. 'Yevreiskii vopros v russkoi religioznoi mysli kontsa XIX-pervoi polovinoi XX vv.* (St Petersburg, Sophia: 1993), 269-290.

[86] V.V. Rozanov, "Byl li I.Khristos yevreem po plememi?;" "Eshcho o neyevreistve I.Khrista."

[87] V.V.Rozanov, "O kakom brake govoril I.Khristos?" All three of these articles can be found in *Okolo narodnoy dushi. Stati 1906-1908.* Ed. A N Nikolyukin. Moscow: "Respublika," 2003.

[88] The idea is that the fuss of a Church marriage with its State bureaucratic trappings makes Christians believe that marriage is the end rather than the means of the

Still, as we will see, while dividing Rozanov cleanly along the lines of the Beilis affair would be artificial, it does look as if that episode put the stoppers on Rozanov's rapid fluctuations for a time: instead of three-month alternations, between 1911-1914 Rozanov adopted the anti-Semitic persona for the most part, and would emerge into another fluctuation only after the whole affair had died down.

Before looking at this dynamic, however, one more comment is in order concerning the nature of Rozanov's anti-Semitism: while it was surely colored by the eccentricity of Rozanov's personality, the two articles we have just mentioned in which he pays tribute to Chamberlain highlights a disturbing fact. That is that one of the great literary figures of Russia's Silver Age was so taken with one of the architects of modern Western European anti-Semitism. For Chamberlain was to become the doctrinal inspiration of Alfred Rosenberg, the chief architect and propagandist of Hitlerite anti-Semitism. Rosenberg, in turn, as we pointed out in the discussion on Bulgakov, was born in Estonia, studied in Moscow and was a supporter of the White movement during the Revolution. Thus there are direct links between reactionary Russian anti-Semitism from the turn of the twentieth century and those tendencies which were later absorbed into Hitler's genocidal project[89]. And as we will see later, Florensky only deepens the impression of such a link.

Turning to the middle Rozanov now, articles from *Olfactory* that we will examine, some in detail and some merely in passing, include, by Rozanov: "A Jewish secret manuscript;" "Are there 'secrets' among the Jews (a reply to the 400 rabbis)?;" "Once more about Jewish secret manuscripts (a reply to Mr. Pereferkovich);" "The olfactory and tactile relationship of Jews to blood;" "Where do the divergences between the Greek and Hebrew texts of Scripture come from?;" "An important historical question;" "Andryusha Yushchinsky; an open letter to C.K. Efron (Litvin);" "About a certain reaction to a defense of Jewry;" "In the Religious-Philosophical Society;" "Reminders by telephone;" "A little bit 'about myself';" "The Old Testament temple had a mysterious secret;" "Sacrifice among the ancient Jews;" and by Florensky, or containing large extracts by him: "The affair needs to be transferred to a different plane (concerning the Yushchinsky affair);" "Prof. D.A. Chwolson on ritual murders;" "Jews and the fate of Christians (a letter to V.V. Rozanov);" "'Ekhad' – the thirteen wounds of Yushchinsky." All in all, the pair of them

---

marital institution: but marriage is merely the means for two people to get together and *reproduce*.

[89] One should not forget the following either: the genocide of Jews in Lithuania, Latvia, Belarus and Ukraine was facilitated by the fact there was an unnaturally dense concentration of Jews in that area – and that population distribution was, of course, a result of the Imperial Russia's policy of imposing a Pale of Settlement on Jews. Given that the Russian Church generally supported that policy, I believe the idea that the Holocaust is a non-Russian phenomenon that should primarily occupy the conscience of Western Churches needs to be rethought.

filled nearly a hundred and fifty pages in a furious flurry of activity evinced by the Beilis affair.

All of these articles are variations on a single thesis, namely that certain Jews murdered Andrei Yushchinsky and drained his body of blood so as to use it for purposes sanctioned by the Jewish religion. Whether Beilis' part was major, minor or non-existent in the larger mass conspiracy by the Jews was a secondary question to developing a comprehensive theory of why Judaism and Jewry require such ritual murders – for which purpose, the matter is traced back to the sacrificial system of the Old Testament.

The Jewish religion in Old Testament times had a clear relationship to blood, as evidenced by the Temple cult. However, the Jewish religion has an intimate relationship to blood in other areas, especially circumcision. But of course this is well-known to anyone who reads the Pentateuch. Therefore, getting from the Pentateuch to the contemporary Jewish ritual murder of Andrei Yushchinsky is the tricky part.

The second part of the thesis, then, is that the Hebrew Bible and even the Talmud contain "secrets" which are not known to gentiles, and even to many, perhaps the majority, of Jews. These secrets are hidden in code, and alluded to obliquely. In addition to a secret code, there is a mystical oral tradition among certain Jews (especially Hasidim[90]) which is not found even in coded form in the Talmud. Its existence can be deduced, however, by a scientific comparison of "secret" practices among ancient Semites who are cognate to modern Jews, as well as by a thorough examination of the Kabbala.

It is not the purpose of this chapter to engage in a serious "refutation" of this thesis, which would be a nonsensical endeavor and be a disservice to modern day blood-libelists, who would waste precious time refuting my refutations and thereby slow the traffic of information on the internet. And besides, Rozanov himself disowned these writings. More interesting is the task of uncovering the connection between these writings and Rozanov's earlier *Judaism*, as well as uncovering those Rozanovesquely antinomian moments, where the writer's determined anti-Semitism morphs tenderly back into philo-Semitism – in a reverse movement to that which we observed in his earlier work. The two sides of the coin are always flipping with Rozanov.

---

[90] The Hasidic connection came about due to the general effort to find "mystical" confirmations of the blood libel. But there was a more specific angle: there was a young trader called Faivel Schneerson, who used to dine at Mendel Beilis' house. He was a beardless and unobservant Jew, but his surname was the same as that of the well-known Lubavitch rebbe, Joseph Schneerson. The police interrogated the latter about his possible family connection with Faivel, and in the right-wing press the theme of sinister Schneersons and shadowy "tsadikim" became a popular theme.(Cf. Kandel (2002), p.804). Florensky, in particular, develops the connection between Kabbalah, Jewish-blood lust and Schneersonian conspiracies. Of course, as will be discussed below, the irony is that Florensky's own theological views regarding name-worshipping have distinct Kabbalistic congruities.

Nonetheless, towards the end of this section we will engage in a bit of gentle refutation of some of Florensky's claims, as he himself never owned up to these articles and – paradoxically therefore – never disowned them. In addition, his position as a priest has given some the unfortunate impression that his "Judeology" is somehow Orthodox.

Two Jewish encounters in the Beilis years

Before turning to an examination of the actual literature of this period, a deeper insight into the state of Rozanov's mind during the Beilis trial can be gained from examining two personal encounters with Jews at the time. By 1911, Rozanov had already been friends with Gershenzon for three years; in 1913, he met and started an acquaintance with the young Aaron Steinberg.

The fact that Rozanov could have friendly personal relationships with Jews at the same time as he was involved in public denunciation of Jewry is another paradox which an examination of these friendships will help to explain. In addition, the overlap in thought between these three figures sheds further light on what we have already seen of the Jewish and Russian heritage in Rozanov, Gershenzon and Steinberg[91].

Mikhail Gershenzon

Rozanov started a correspondence with Gershenzon in 1909, after reading the latter's *Lamdmarks* article. Shortly thereafter, he visited him at his home, where the pair spent two hours exchanging views and laying the foundation of a warm friendship that would last for five years. Rozanov's correspondence with Gershenzon lasted from 1909 until April 13, 1913 when their friendship came to an end, except for a brief revival in 1918.

The chronology of this break is somewhat remarkable if we compare it with the time-line of the "Beilis affair." Mendel Beilis was arrested on 12 July, 1911 and imprisoned until his acquittal, after a month-long trial, on October 28, 1913. During this imprisonment, Rozanov contributed his series of scurrilous articles to the right-wing press in support of its effort to secure a verdict of guilt by whipping up an atmosphere of innuendo and general anti-Jewish feeling. And yet, somehow, Gershenzon, who broke off his relationship with Berdyaev for the mere suggestion of anti-Semitism, continued to correspond with Rozanov for the better part of these two years[92].

We have already seen that Rozanov's account of Judaism in 1903 was positive. However, much in that positive evaluation was suspiciously and, as it were, self-defeatingly, generous – and thus already contains an undercurrent of anti-Semitism. Rozanov's correspondence with Gershenzon only confirms the

---

[91] Although the bulk of the analysis of Steinberg will come later in ch.5.
[92] Perhaps the erratic relationship with Rozanov made him more cautious in later encounters. Or perhaps, Gershenzon simply felt closer to Rozanov. The personal element in all this must not be overlooked: after all, Shestov and Berdyaev preserved a friendship despite similar scandals.

idea that, rather than going through a chronological development, his sympathy and antipathy towards Jews and Judaism is thoroughly mixed in all of his phases – although, in different periods, it is true that there are different emphases. This, then, partially explains how Rozanov could juggle vitriolic anti-Jewish journalism with Jewish friendships.

As far as Gershenzon was concerned, he also entered the relationship with a certain awareness, of Rozanov's dubious track record. However, he very quickly became captivated by Rozanov to such an extent that he was willing to forgive him things that he would not another: "if it had not been you," he wrote in 1912[93] to Rozanov, after the latter had questioned the Jewish Gershenzon's ability to truly understand Russian history, "but someone else who had ascribed to me such a mindset, I simply would not have answered. But you are a special person…."

It is true that Rozanov was often accused of duplicity: however, Gershenzon himself was not spared Rozanov's anti-Semitic ire in their letters. In that sense, it was not as if Rozanov put on a benign philo-Semitic face for his Jewish correspondent, while siphoning off the anti-Semitism to his public journalistic persona. Thus Gershenzon had the opportunity to defend himself and his Jewishness on the personal level – until, of course, he realized the futility of such defenses.

Nonetheless, towards the end of the correspondence when Rozanov was stepping up his anti-Semitic journalism, the theme of duplicity makes it appearance in Gershenzon's consciousness too. On 14 January, 1913, after receiving a letter in which Rozanov has contended that "the Jews will save Russia," he writes back: "But why don't you print *that*, why do you print the absolute opposite…how 'the Jews are bringing harm to Russia and Russians with their greedy attempts to seize everything in their hands'. Is that about mice or rats, or is it about people?"

Still, the extent to which Gershenzon had been sucked into the maelstrom of Rozanov's divided consciousness can be seen not only in the fact that he does not immediately break off his correspondence during the dark moments of the Beilis affair, but that he accepts Rozanov's defense of Jews at face value – ignoring, or choosing to ignore, the duplicitous foundations of that defense itself.

For even the exaggerated idea that the "Jews will save Russia" was actually wrapped up in an attack on Gershenzon himself, and formed part of a rhythm of attack and retreat, insult and copious apology, defamation and excessive praise, as the exchange proceeds. This attack was occasioned by a mix-up in delivery, due to which Gershenzon did not receive one of Rozanov's letters in which he had praised Jews for understanding that "God is in money, and that when God is in money – money will grow."

Taking Gershenzon's unintended silence on this theme as malicious, Rozanov had accused him: "Why did you not respond to that joy which I myself

---

[93] Letter 15.

felt returning to the Jews. Come-come: 'I thought G-n was better than other Jews, but it turns out – he is worse than them.' 'He has turned goy.' Jews are clear, better than you. A Jew shouts, gets angry, but looks you in the eye with a full eye, *totally direct…*"

The rhetoric then culminates in a paeon to the "Yidlet"[94], than whom there is no better or brighter person in the world, for Jewry "is the most human nation with a heart open to all good deeds." Further, "I think that Russians have corrupted Jews and not Jews Russians, have corrupted them politically and with revolution." The letter-writer then turns sorrowfully back to Gershenzon, the temporarily absent figure who had provoked his wrath: "Well, farewell. The Lord be with you, if you get angry too. You personally, a 'bad Jew' I forgive for the sake of the Jewish masses who are good, kind and desire the happiness of Russia."

This, then, is the "philo-Semitic" rhetoric with which Gershenzon had hoped to see his friend counterbalance his anti-Semitic journalism. And yet Rozanov had started his paeon by admitting that he had thought Gershenzon to be "better than other Jews," in other words, a good Jew who only proved the rule that Jews were bad.

Of course, Gershenzon at some level could not have been ignorant of the deep ambiguity of Rozanov's rhetoric. Eventually, he did break off the relationship; not to have done so would have been perverse, given Rozanov's public defamation of Jewry and his more subtle defamation of Gershenzon in their personal exchanges.

In this, he followed the example of B.G. Stolpner, a Jewish philosopher and sociologist who had also been a close friend of Rozanov. In 1909, he too had terminated their acquaintance, accusing Rozanov of being two-faced[95].

The figure of Stolpner, in fact, haunts Rozanov's correspondence with Gershenzon in the form of numerous, tender recollections of their friendship – starting from Rozanov's very first letter, in which he prophetically laments: "I am sad that Stolpner has stopped liking me…because of foolish things – as always with Russians."

In Stolpner, Rozanov had seen an ideal Jew in whom Russia's Jewish question had found a resolution – as he explained on several occasions to Gershenzon. For Stolpner was "a Jew *completely* and only a Jew" who was not corrupted by Russian education and the unclean atmosphere of Russian journalism; instead he "'remembers his father and mother': sometimes I compare him in my thoughts to 'the fathers of the Talmud', the great gaonim."

Thus Stolpner, according to Rozanov, was a model of the Jew who does not enter fully into Russian society and Russian psychology. This separateness and respect for the barriers between Russian and Jew is why he was "was needed and useful and a blessing for any Russian and for the whole of Russia, due to the fact that he brought it to himself and taught common redemptive mysteries

---

[94] zhidenka.
[95] Letter 2, fn.7.

for any 'I', which of course are contained in any ancient people who has seen the building of the pyramids."[96]

Of course, this vision of a joint Messianic task of Jewry and Russia depends in large part on the underlying idea that Jews must be denied any measures which could allow them to integrate or "penetrate" into Russian society – both for their own good and for the good of Russia. It thus perfectly captures the tension between Rozanov's idealization of Jewry in *Judaism*, and the – for him – entirely logical corollary that Jews must be actively resisted if they do not conform to this "Stolpnerian" archetype.

Rozanov had correspondingly little patience for writers like Sholom Asch and David Aizman who "depict the present Pale as a stupid, blind, hungry, petty 'ghetto' from which there is no escape"[97], or for other Jews who aimed at improving Jewish conditions in Russia. All this could only interfere with the "eternal Jew," who was the only legitimate collaborator with Russia in her world destinies[98].

Stolpner himself refused the oppressive accolade of Stolpnerian "true Jew," understanding long before the Beilis affair, that Rozanov's heavy-handed compliments concealed a simmering hostility. And it is probably not a coincidence that, in the same year that their friendship reached breaking-point, Rozanov initiated a friendship with another Jewish intellectual, who for the next few years would take Stolpner's place. Indeed, when Gershenzon in turn became estranged, Rozanov made overtures to Aaron Steinberg. In that way, Rozanov managed to secure for himself the close presence of a representative of that nation whom he loved to hate, and hated to love – and through whom, like Soloviev but in reverse, he could see Russian fate most clearly.

However, none of this explains why Gershenzon consented to adopt the role of "Rozanov's Jew" for five years, nor why despite the break in their

---

[96] Letter 26 to Gershenzon. After the Revolution, Stolpner's philosophy became overlaid with Marxism. Somewhat more oddly, Stolpner also became friends with A.Losev, who used this "learned Jew, who was quite familiar with kabbalistic and Talmudic literature" (as Losev refered to Stolpner in one of his Kabbalistic excursi) to give credence to his own Rozanovo-Florenskian anti-Semitic kabbalism. Thus Stolpner's own idiosyncratic views on Judaism and Jews were for a second time made grist to the distorting mill of a friendly anti-Semite. Cf. Konstantin Burmistrov, "The interpretation of Kabbalah in early 20th-Century Russian Philosophy. Soloviev, Bulgakov, Florenskii, Losev," in *East European Jewish Affairs*, Vol.37, No.2, August 2007:157-187.

[97] Letter 26.

[98] Again, there is a curious convergence between Rozanov's insistence on "doing business" only with a stereotypical archaic religious Jew, and the opinions of some traditional Russian Jews themselves regarding the desirability of not assimilating into the host society. The classic example is Chabad founder, R.Shneur-Zalman of Liady's confessed preference for the victory of Alexander I over Napoleon, due to the latter's wish to extend rights to Jews and thus hasten their integration and assimilation.

friendship, he responded to his final cry for help in 1918.

In answering this question, we need to turn back to the "real" Gershenzon (rather than Rozanov's projection) and his developing philosophy, which we examined in chapter three. Then we find that in one sense, at least, Rozanov was right to see in Gershenzon – Jew or not – a kindred spirit.

For already in September 1909 Rozanov had written to Gershenzon that "we have both become nihilists." The shared nihilism consisted in the fact that neither of them was content to accept the values of the past, but were bent on forging new values out of old religions that would be neither fully Jewish nor fully Christian. More interesting, however, was their shared *political* nihilism – if one uses that term to express the rather specific and odd point of view that they both shared towards the government of the day.

Initially, Gershenzon had attracted Rozanov's interest due to his *Landmarks* article. Along with others, he had seen in that article a political conservatism. This, in turn, thrilled Rozanov for it presented the tantalizing type of a *conservative* Jew, a Jew that is who might find his own "Stolpnerian" idyll amenable, might in fact become a new Stolpner in Rozanov's affections. Gershenzon's immersion in the Slavophiles, the joke making the rounds that "Gersh" was a Slavophile, can only have sharpened this curious image and offered up the possibility of a new marriage of minds with a real Jew.

Rozanov, for his part, was like Gershenzon an unhappily cast conservative. His own Slavophile past had imbued him with a worshipful respect for the monarch and his government; and yet he had managed to combine this with revolutionary sentiments in 1905.

Writing to Gershenzon in 1909, he expects to find a sympathetic ear when he writes that what he particularly liked in the last revolution was "that in it died 'Hellene and Jew'. Jews alone also lay with their bones on the Russian barricades. It is impossible not to remember this." Thus this shared perspective from eternity, or view from nowhere, which paradoxically mixes the categories of conservative and radical, is strangely germane to both Gershenzon and Rozanov.

Both expressed this agreement in different ways: Rozanov shortly after his confession of "shared nihilism" connects it to a Jewish propensity: "I also love Jews for the fact that they have an inborn religious sense of the deep nullity of things and human affairs and human personalities ('dust before the face of the Lord'), which gives them a depths and seriousness of thought, a spirit of life. By comparison with them all nations are 'brought low by the breeze' – except perhaps the Russians."

In this way, Russians and Jews (Rozanovs and Gershenzons) are seen as kindred nihilists – a point, of course, that had occupied other minds from Bely to Ivanov-Razumnik. And indeed, Rozanov's description of Russian-Jewish nihilism echoes down to the very phraseology Gershenzon's own portrait of nihilism in his much later *Wisdom of Pushkin*[99].

That this later echo is not accidental, that Rozanov's person and work both found an already existing echo in his thought when they met and further shaped it, can be seen in Gershenzon's own expressions of wonder at Rozanov's new book, *Solitaria*, his "most necessary book" to date:

> The abyss and lawlessness – that is what is in it; it is even incomprehensible how you managed completely to avoid attiring yourself in systems, schemes, and had the antique courage to remain as mentally naked as your mother bore you – and how much boldness has seized hold of you in the 20th century, where everyone goes round dressed in a system, in consistency, demonstrability, recounting aloud and publicly all about one's nakedness….You are not like anyone else, you really have the right to be yourself; even before this book I knew that and therefore I did not measure with the measuring-rod of morality, or consistency….

In this appraisal, we see just how deep is the affinity between the two writers' "spiritual nihilism." Again, Gershenzon's later remonstration to Vy.Ivanov that he wishes to cast off the clothes of civilization and bathe naked in "the waters of Lethe" makes one think that along with Tolstoy and the Slavophiles, Gershenzon had found in Rozanov another Russian spiritual father. For as he wrote towards the end of their correspondence: "You yourself know that your book is a great one – that when they come to enumerate the 8 or 10 Russian books in which was expressed the very essence of the Russian soul, they will not leave out 'Fallen leaves' and 'Solitaria'…"

In this "nihilism," we also find the key to how Gershenzon could have tolerated for so long Rozanov's anti-Semitic animosity against Jewry as a whole and against himself in person: in befriending Rozanov, Gershenzon entered right into the heart of that nullity that he had so praised as an escape from cold logic and dead systems. In Rozanov, it seemed that there was no logic and no system: one day he would praise you, the next excoriate you. Gershenzon could hardly object; rather he needed to learn to develop that tough spiritual demeanor which could withstand the seismic shocks of such Russian unpredictability.

Indeed, on January 24, 1913, meditating on the fact that the Jews' virtues are more terrifying for Russia's future than their faults, Rozanov wrote to Gershenzon: "Jews are now cold to me." Again, this will quite literally be part of Gershenzon's own later vocabulary.

In the *Wisdom of Pushkin*, part of Pushkin's prophetic greatness comes from the fact that he substitutes the ancient Avestan-Iranian values of "hot" and "cold" for the prim and recent monotheistic values of "good" and "bad." In *The Sermon on the Mount*, what is good in man comes from the "hot" subconscious; what is bad from the cold upper layer of the personality.

---

[99] See ch.6 for detail.

In the same letter, Rozanov once again seems to preempt Gershenzon's own thought remarkably, when he writes: "Of course, Jews are cleverer (because *historically* older) than Russians, and have a great upbringing in delicacy of feeling, and delicate methods of life – from the Talmud, the laws of Moses, and due to the fact that everything bad and weak has been beaten out by pogroms, which started in Spain…"[100]

So later, in *The Destiny of the Jewish People*, Gershenzon would describe how the Jewish Spirit had purified the Jewish people through its trial and tribulations, thus evolving in them a higher instinct of indifference to the world.

Both of these approaches are expressions of a belief in humanity's often cruel evolution according to the dictates of a higher Spirit; in *Apocalypse of our Time*, we can see the same Hegelian twist in Rozanov's version of this doctrine as we saw in Gershenzon's "heterogeneity of goals": in the latter, the Spirit deceptively lures human consciousness down paths which it has only partly chosen; in the former, Christ's repellent coldness is the unpredictable trigger of humanity's rejection of him in an advance to a third, transcending stage of spirituality[101].

Thus, in many ways Rozanov's and Gershenzon's worldviews overlapped. Rozanov, with his volcanic outbursts, his amoralism that went "beyond good and evil," his uncompromising genuineness, were all signs for Gershenzon of the prophet-genius. Rozanov, for his part, had seen in Gershenzon Russia's "greatest historian," and a man who despite his Jewish origins had managed to succesfully immerse himself in the thought of the Slavophiles.

And yet Rozanov's early judgment about "Russia's greatest historian" bore the same warning signs of dangerous hyperbole as his other judgments about Jews. And for all their similarities, it was odd – but telling – that Rozanov did not notice some equally significant differences in their worldviews.

After all, Gershenzon, like Merezhkovsky and Berdyaev, believed in a religion of the Spirit. Rozanov's own attempts to reinstate the value of sex and the flesh

---

[100] Later, we will see that Rozanov was also convinced that Jews also masochistically liked to be beaten up. Thus Rozanov's belief in a purifying spirit in Jewish history has its violent underside. But Gershenzon's scheme also contains the same amoral implications: we remember how for him the Jewish Spirit beckons to the gentile destroyers to decimate Jewish lives and property, all in order to strengthen the Jewish nation. Does this too not condone the tragedies of Jewish history? Are both not somewhat perverse instances of spiritualized social Darwinism?

[101] Interestingly, Shestov, while seeing in Rozanov an admirable struggler of the spirit and seeker after God, is less enamored of him than Gershenzon. He sees in Rozanov, as he had seen in Gershenzon, a submission to Hegelianism which ultimately prevented him from believing in the miracle of Christianity. This explains his anger at Christianity: though loving God, he was prevented by scientific blindness from truly embracing God, and thus unlike Dostoevsky he failed in his spiritual struggle. (Lev Shestov, "V.V.Rozanov," in *Put'* No.22, (1930): 97-103.) I believe Shestov is correct to see a certain unwilling scientism and positivism in Rozanov, and correct too in analyzing Gershenzon in similar terms. (The analysis is somewhat undermined by the fact that Shestov analyzed everyone in these terms!).

ran contrary to this, and he certainly found the time to criticize Merezhkovsky's hyper-spiritualized worldview.

In addition, Gershenzon was a Jew who had abandoned Judaism. He thus automatically represented a Jew who was trying to integrate into Russian society and entering the "unclean" world of Russian letters. This was in direct contradiction of Rozanov's sometimes tongue-in-cheek, but at other times, earnest depiction of the ordained path of the "sacred Yid" in Russia's own holy destiny.

Again, Gershenzon saw the Law, ritual and the grosser aspects of religion as relics of the past, with pure, ritual-free Spirit being the final Hegelian peak of Judaism's development; but Rozanov admired in Judaism precisely the bodily, fleshly elements of the Law which Gershenzon was so keen to reject.

Gershenzon talked of "abstraction from the world," was full of an ascetic world-denying ethic. Rozanov embraced the world, excoriated Christianity for its otherworldliness and believed in the goodness of human nature. In fact, one of his few gripes against Dostoevsky was that he placed too much emphasis on suffering as a route to God. Gershenzon, meanwhile, had a keen sense of the value of suffering. One might even sum up their differences according to the conventional dichotomies of the time: then it would emerge, somewhat ironically, that the Russian Rozanov was more Jewish in his sensibilities than the Semitic Gershenzon[102].

Gershenzon's position as a Jew in the heart of Russian letters soon led Rozanov to express his worries openly. For shortly after congratulating him on his historian's talent, he goes on to lament the fact that Russians could not have found one of their own to do the job. This segues into the lament that Gershenzon with his talent must secretly be spitting on Russians and laughing at them for the fact that a Jew can write their own history better than they can.

Not surprisingly, then, when the opportunity arose, Rozanov attempted to "defend Russian honor" by pointing out errors in Gershenzon's Jewish understanding of Russia. Thus in January, 1912, he writes: "My dear, please believe that Nicolas I did not 'buy off' the Decembrists. Ach, you 'yid, yid' (don't get angry): why not believe that he was a father to them? Without that, Russian history is incomprehensible." Later in the same letter, he accuses Gershenzon of "contempt for the government."

Not coincidentally, the same letter contains a reference to the murder of Stolypin, the Chairman of the Council of Ministers assassinated in 1911 by the Jew, Dmitri Bogrov. A year later and Rozanov is still "set against the Jews

---

[102] In the chapter on Semyon Frank, we will see that Frank depicted Franz Rosenzweig's philosophy of Judaism as too naturalistic, and critiqued it as being opposed to the Christian spirit, in terms that call to mind Rozanov's religion of the world and redeemed nature. Again, the Jewish convert Frank rejects a Judaic philosophy of religion that resembles that embraced by the gentile Rozanov. One is tempted to think, in a wistful counterfactual, that if Rozanov had been born Jewish (substitute –zon for –ov) he would have been an excellent philosopher of Judaism.

(whether they killed Stolypin or not, it's no difference...) and I have a feeling like Moses had when he saw an Egyptian kill a Jew"[103]. Thus, Rozanov's charge is, in effect, that Gershenzon is infected with the same Jewish revolutionary contempt for the government as the assassin Bogrov and cannot objectively write the history of "father" Nicolas I (the more so, probably, as he was one of the most oppressive tsars as far as Jews were concerned).

In sum, "Russia's greatest historian" is led into making gross errors about nineteenth-century Russian history – to Rozanov's great relief. Russian honor has been defended, and Gershenzon cut down to size – with one minor drawback, however: namely, that Rozanov must have been perfectly aware that Gershenzon had made no such error, and on the contrary, had been defending the same pro-Nicholine point of view against the Marxist, M.N.Pokrovoski. Thus this episode is a miniature version of the Beilis affair: Rozanov libels Gershenzon on known false grounds and bluffs his way with much bluster through to the bitter end.

However, Rozanov's attack on Gershenzon's alleged historical inaccuracy is revealing for a completely different reason: for of all the errors in Gershenzon's historical interpretation, he picks a spurious one. Frank, Struve and Berdyaev had all made genuine criticisms when they pointed to Gershenzon's de-Christianization of Slavophilism. But, for all his protests against the treacherous nature of the "Semitic spirit" Gershenzon is breathing into Russian historiography (which is "more worrying than their control of the banks"), Rozanov's own nihilistic, anti-Christian tendencies are so strong that he cannot even see in this potential artillery with which to attack Gershenzon.

For in the case of Stolpner, the latter's alleged hostility to Christianity had not been allowed to pass without comment. With provocative lack of self-consciousness, the arch-calumniator of Christianity had written of him that "it

---

[103] Notice in this simile that Rozanov (in fact, a Russian) is a Jew (or Hebrew), and Bagrov (in reality a Jew) is an Egyptian. We saw how Soloviev and Bulgakov referred to themselves as "Jews," and how Soloviev contrasted good (holistic) Old Testament Jews with bad (nationalist) Old Testament Jews, comparing the latter to Russian neo-Slavophile nationalists. My argument in this chapter is that Rozanov's anti-Semitism is anti-Christian; still, it must be admitted that the patristic claim that Christians are the New Israel, and hence the "real Jews," does influence Rozanov here: he claims for himself the title of "real Jew," like Soloviev and Bulgakov – thus relegating contemporary Jews to the status of Yids. However, as we will see, this is more the exception that proves the rule: for this simile is somewhat unusual – more often than not, Rozanov claims for himself the sobriquet of Egyptian (or Hellene), and contrasts himself with Old Testament Jews/Hebrews, thus condemning Jews in toto, be they "Old Testament" or contemporary. If, for the sake of argument, we label as anti-Semitic both the patristic claim to be the "New Israel," and the Rozanovian claim to be a neo-Egyptian who is higher than ancient and modern Jews, it emerges that the latter neo-pagan anti-Semitism is far more vindictive and aggressive than the former ("neo-Christian" anti-Semitism). This can be appreciated if we consider that according to this rubric, Soloviev is a neo-Christian anti-Semite, and Rozanov (like Florensky, cf. below) in his more hateful phases, is a neo-pagan anti-Semite.

is also sad that he ever so slightly and almost unnoticeably hated Christ and Christianity…and Jews on their path should really abandon it, and while not converting to Christianity, (although I also know very touching instances of conversion), sort of forget about him completely and not be hostile to him." By contrast, there was nothing "unnoticeable" about Rozanov's attacks on Christ when he got into his stride.

Gershenzon, meanwhile, took such criticisms seriously, and for a long time seemed naively immune to the calculated duplicity of Rozanov's assaults. Indeed, his Jewish consciousness really was awakened by Rozanov's attacks, even those in bad faith, and he attempted to justify himself[104].

To begin with, he admitted that "his Jewish spirit" did indeed bring "an alien element through my literary activity into the Russian consciousness," but that this should not be a cause for worry as "any effort of the spirit is for the benefit of people." He assures Rozanov that there is no need to cry for the Russian people on this account, as there are plenty of other things to bemoan, namely "the vulgarity, emptiness, selfishness of all these lawyers, journalists, politicians, professors – on the left and right – among whom we live…"[105].

Thus, for a time at least, Gershenzon managed to vindicate himself in Rozanov's eyes, and to bring them back to what united them. Indeed, Gershenzon's comments about Russia's "lawyers, journalists, politicians, professors" betrays a skepticism about the institutions of bourgeois society which is not only close to Rozanov, but to Florensky, who at this time was Rozanov's spiritual father and collaborator on his anti-Semitic works. Thus, in this unity there is a rather unpleasant irony: for at one point, Rozanov, sensing their shared spirit, even offered to introduce Gershenzon to Florensky. Somehow, Gershenzon had enigmatically managed to involve himself in a layer of Russian society that was deeply opposed to his very presence there[106].

As the correspondence neared its decisive rupture in April 1913, however, Gershenzon began to sense the futility of his efforts to persuade Rozanov. Before,

---

[104] In this sense, he presents an interesting contrast to Vladmir (Ze'ev) Jabotinsky, who conducted an implicit polemic with Rozanov in the Odessa newspapers over the Beilis affair. In an article called "Instead of an apology" he outlined his belief that the only reaction of Jews to blood libellists should be a refusal to engage in any self-justification at all, which would only dignify such charges. This was a turning-point in Jabotinsky's Zionist awakening. See discussion in L.Katsis, *Krovavy Navet*, ch.14: Vasili Rozanov i Vladimir Jabotinsky do, vo vremya, i posle Beilisady.'

[105] Letter 15.

[106] Florensky was a monarchist who nonetheless, when the time came, found much to admire in Soviet society. In this sense, he presents something of a similar enigma to Gershenzon, the quasi-Slavophile turned quasi-Bolshevik. Both Florensky and Rozanov railed against the "bowler-hatted" lawyers of the Beilis trial, associating them with bourgeois greed and mendaciousness. The rhetoric is highly similar to Gershenzon's comments of the same time, with the sole exception that for Gershenzon these undesirables have no connection with the Yids.

he had tried to reason with him, to show him that "to poison the government against [the Jews] again and again is a great sin" for "the mass of Jewry lives in such terrible poverty, with such inhuman sufferings." He had pointed out that the Jewish spirit was not as "*ganz accurate*"[107] as Rozanov made out, that Jews too were capable of spiritual spontaneity, that he himself was deeply in love with Russian culture…and so on.

Eventually, however, he decided that Rozanov's "judgments about Jews are so unreal that not for one minute do I doubt that the mainspring of your behavior is not in your logic, but in something psychological."[108] And then he encouraged Rozanov to dig deep into himself to find that psychological knot which surely lay at the base of his antipathy. Then his relationship to Jews could be clarified, if not necessarily improved.

However, that was not to be and, seeing no change in the rhythm of their exchange, Gershenzon eventually cut it short with a refusal to reply[109].

Interestingly, in the just quoted letter, Gershenzon added a brief comment which points to another vast difference between the two men, and which ultimately highlights an important divergence in what each saw as the basic element of humanity. In a seeming non-sequitur, he had written: "Rochko told me about your theory of 'sodomism' – but that is a big fantasy, and unreliable." While that judgment may have been correct, this curt dismissal of "sodomism" betrayed an insensitivity to a central premise of the Rozanovian worldview: the explanation of all things according to the sexual principle.

This "sodomism" of which Gershenzon writes is probably not a reference to Rozanov's well-known theory, outlined in *Moonlight People*, that the great Christian saints were secret sexual perverts and hermaphrodites who founded an unnatural religion. Instead, it is more likely to refer to a more directly Jewish version of the "theory" that Rozanov only outlined in public in his 1914 article "In the neighborhood of Sodom."

In that article, Rozanov portrayed Jewry as a feminine nation, a nation of *babas* – old women, or sissies – who were always trying to please their male host nation. He found evidence of this sissy nature of Jewry in the Pentateuch's story of Sodom and Gomorrah and the "perverse" Talmudic commentary on it. In the former, Abraham is keen to defend these cities of unnatural sexual proclivities; and in the Talmud, the rabbis go out of their way to emphasize that these cities were unusually successful, wealthy and happy. The conclusion: for sissy Jews, sodomy is not a fault – rather the reverse.

Thus, bringing the story up to date, Rozanov had concluded there that: "'Yidlets are cunning little girls, who run around among us, sweet-talk us,

---

[107] Again, as this epithet reveals, for Rozanov Jewishness and Germanness are related negative mentalities. We have already seen how the contrast of Germanicness and Jewishness as against Russianness was used to polemical effect in Bulgakov and Shestov. Cf. ch.6 for S.Frank's more "ecumenical" approach to European identities.
[108] Letter 25.
[109] In that sense, he did finally choose Jabotinsky's option.

seduce us, enter into intimacy and friendship with us…and conduct 'Russian politics' as their 'own Jewish politics' and in general turn all 'Russian affairs' into their 'own affairs'"[110].

All this shows that Rozanov's friendships with Jews fell for him into the category of forbidden sexual relationships, replete with the frisson of taboo that this entailed. But Gershenzon, with his focus on the Spirit, and his belief in the meta-physical compatibility of spirits, be they Jewish or Russian, was evidently blind to the fact that Rozanov in some sense had "courted" him, and was behaving towards him with a lover's hysteria and provocativeness – although he drew close to such an understanding as his rational remonstrations met with no response. Even Rozanov's comments that "I somehow physiologically (almost sexually) and artistically love a 'Yid in *peyyos*', and secretly in company always sneak a glance after him and admire him"[111] had not alerted him to the deep nature of Rozanov's "psychological knot."

However, in another respect, Gershenzon had been right: even if he or Rozanov had guessed the nature of the "knot," there is no guaranteeing that it could have been untied. Indeed, finally Gershenzon had only one option. To Rozanov's ever-growing protestations about the wonderful qualities of the Yids, coupled with his treacherous denunciations of them in public, Gershenzon chose eventually to reply with a manly silence. He thus defused the hysterical drama that Rozanov had been whipping up, putting Rozanov in the unfortunate role of the spurned "sissy," as Stolpner had before him.

And yet evidently, Gershenzon regretted the end of his friendship with the sick and erratic spiritual genius of Russia, as events five years later would show.

Rozanov went on to bad-mouth Gershenzon in a 1916 article[112], accusing him of partaking of that "stylized, imitative nature of Jewry, that penetrates from inside into Russian culture," and elsewhere repeating his old epithet about "Russia's greatest historian," but adding: "he is a little too great, something's 'not quite right', 'he is so Russian'.…I think he's a well-buttoned-up fellow, but not a good fellow. In the end, I am afraid of him, afraid for Russia. As I am of the Russian 'patriots', Stolpner and Hart."

But despite these bitchy comments about his old intimate – in which Rozanov gives enough flesh all by himself to his theory that Russia as well as Jewry is a feminine nation, so that the two are at each other's throats – Gershenzon never responded in kind.

Instead, in 1918 on reading the desperate preface to *Apocalypse* with its general address to readers to help its starving author, he wrote to Rozanov: "Most greatly respected Vasily Vasilievich, Your appeal to your readers went straight to my heart.…through [the Union of Writers]…I hope in the coming

---

[110] The transmutation of Russian into Jewish is, then, clearly a political and social equivalent of gender-switching perversity.
[111] Letter 11. This confession is preceded by the priceless phrase: "Anti-semitizmom, ya, batyushka, ne stradayu." (Anti-semitism, my dear fellow, is not one of my failings.)
[112] "Levitan i Gershenzon," in Russkiy bibliofil, 1916, No.1.

days to arrange something for you. I thank you greatly for your publication of *Apocalypse*. Your M.Gershenzon."

Gershenzon persuaded M.Gorky to send money to Rozanov – no mean feat, considering the latter was a sworn enemy of anti-Semites – and that donation contributed towards Rozanov's surviving for a few more months. Rozanov later expressed deep gratitude in his "Letter to his friends" for Gershenzon's "concern for me." Thus this final episode was a healing of sorts of the five-year silence that had, of necessity, reigned between the two Russian writers.

We already saw how Rozanov's sarcastic hysteria continued until the final moments of his death, and how in his will he had written that "believing in the triumph of Israel, I rejoice in it," along with his request that the Jewish community set up a farm to provide for his family in exchange for the publishing rights to his books.

In fact, a less melodramatic "triumph of Israel" did occur in the wake of his death: in 1923, two Jewish admirers of the Russian writer sent a parcel through a charitable organization to help support Rozanov's bereaved family. They were the two friends, Mikhail Gershenzon and Lev Shestov, and once again, their concern showed that all was not lost between Israel and Russia.

Aaron Steinberg

Equally illuminating is the visit of the next Jewish contender for Rozanov's friendship during the Beilis affair. The twenty-two year old Aaron Steinberg paid a visit to Rozanov in 1913, just before Beilis' exculpation, and thus in an interim period when Rozanov had no close Jewish friend to hand[113].

The young philosophy student, who was attending courses in St Petersburg as well as studying in Germany, had been a long-time admirer of Rozanov. Steinberg had read all those "in the highest degree original articles about Jews, explaining that Jews by nature were vegetarians, as according to the Biblical texts and Jewish customs, before consuming meat, they had to salt it and drain it so that not a drop of blood would be left. The articles of Rozanov produced a great impression on everyone, and on me in particular…"[114]

Steinberg was thus shocked to find that Rozanov was contending, such a short time after penning these arguments, that Jews now required and consumed blood for ritual purposes. With the self-confessed naivety of a young man, he picked up the phone and resolved to iron out what he took to be a logical misunderstanding:

---

[113] The following section contains extracts from Steinberg A. "Na Peterburgskom perekryostike. Vstrecha s V.V. Rozanovym." In Steinberg A. *Druzya moikh rannikh let (1911-1928)*, ch.6. Paris: Syntaxis, 1991.

[114] Again, Steinberg evaluates "early" Rozanov as philo-Semitic. Not all would agree. Steinberg even recounts that he used Rozanov's arguments to defend his own vegetarianism. The "great impression on everyone" that Rozanov's Jewish articles produced seems to indicate that many Jews too were persuaded by Rozanov's early vision of Judaism.

"'Can I speak to Vasily Vasilievich? 'Who's speaking?' 'A person who studies philosophy, a Jew, a long-time admirer of your works…'"

We get a wonderful sense of the small-town intimacy of St Petersburg in 1913 in all this. Indeed it seems the phone in those days was a far more intrusive instrument than screening has made it nowadays: responding to its tinkling bell, Rozanov on many occasions had had his ear subjected to a barrage of abuse for his Beilis shenanigans[115].

This caller, however, is not hostile, but anxious, serious. Rozanov listens politely, and naturally takes no time in deducing what the young Jew wishes to speak to him about: "Well, all right, all right, no doubt you want to talk to me about the Beilis affair. You know, that ritual has set all our teeth on edge, but I am at your service. Come on Sunday evening."

As can be deduced from this boldness, Aaron Zakharovich Steinberg was an unusual figure, and we will return in more detail to him in a later chapter, in connection with his friendship with Lev Platonovich Karsavin. Here it need only be said that from a young age, he gained access to the inner circles of the Russian intelligentsia and already at twenty two was writing articles for *Ruskaya Mysl'*. What is particularly interesting about Steinberg was that he combined this immersion in Russian thought and intellectual life with an observant Jewish lifestyle and Jewish Orthodox belief. He was highly conscious of and also highly secure in his religious Jewish identity.

In this, he presents a contrast with Gershenzon. The latter was at the boundaries of Jewish conventionality, held back from complete dissolution by loyalty to his mother and the memory of his suffering co-religionists in the Pale of Settlement. Likewise, Gershenzon's "Judaism" had been topologically shifted in the prism of Russian-Hegelian metaphysics and was as distant from mainstream Jewish belief as Rozanov's complex neo-Christianity was from folk Orthodoxy.

Steinberg, by contrast, was a "real live Jew," whose appearance in Rozanov's life caused great consternation and delight. On his arrival at the Rozanov residence Steinberg was surprised, and somewhat annoyed, to find a number of guests gathered for a soirée at Rozanov's, but he was received with great care and kindness and attended to by one of Rozanov's younger daughters.

Various other matters are discussed before Rozanov himself launches into the topic of "the ritual." Only a short while into the conversation, after Steinberg has explained himself, Rozanov is protesting: "Aha, so you think I do not believe in the possibility of such a ritual, but I do. I believe in it."

Steinberg sets out his views. Rozanov now resorts to empirical demonstrations of his point: "Look, my daughter has put down food before you and you won't

---

[115] In terms of Rozanov's philosophy of the body, we will see later that noses and mouths feature prominently. However, he is fond of ears too: information whispered into ears is a favorite image in his depiction of the transmission of Jewish secret rites. His own poor ears were subjected to more than whispers on the telephone: there was raucous background laughter when joke callers telephoned to mock him after Beilis' acquittal. Cf. Rozanov, "Reminders by telephone."

touch it because gentile food is abhorrent to you." Steinberg protests that he never touches ham even when it is not at Rozanov's table, that no slight is intended. But you Jews think we are second rate. Worse, Steinberg is trying to bewitch Rozanov with his dark-eyed gaze. And so on.

Steinberg by this time is holding back his anger and disbelief. Finally, in great disappointment he excuses himself, apologizing for disturbing Rozanov's intimate Sunday gathering. Rozanov shouts out at this point: "I believe in the ritual, I do!"

Steinberg is prevented from leaving when some other guests intervene in the conversation. One of them, Efron, is a converted Jew. He makes the point that Old Believers would not eat with "heretics" when they came to Petersburg university in Efron's youth, so this refusal to co-dine is not just Jewish, but Christian as well.

At this point Rozanov's daughter suddenly becomes upset and begs Efron to stop her father writing his articles as they will lead to pogroms[116]. Rozanov, relieved that the conversation has widened, reassures his daughter that no such thing will happen. The tone lightens: Rozanov's staccato recitation of the dogmas stated in his right-wing articles becomes softer. He explains to Steinberg that every time his youngest daughter comes home boasting of having made a new friend, he can be quite sure that the girl will either be a Rachel, a Rebecca or a Sarochka. Suddenly, Steinberg understands: Rozanov *doesn't* believe in the ritual. It's all about politics, and this fills him with disappointment. Once again, he resolves to make his excuses and leave.

At this point, Rozanov – evidently pained by any offense he may have caused to his guest – promises to show him something of great interest in his study. Steinberg is not persuaded, but the look of embarrassment for their father on the daughters' faces makes him consent.

In the hushed study a sick woman is lying on the sofa. Rozanov says: "You know, my friend[117] is very ill, we must not disturb HIM."[118] Steinberg is surprised by this way of referring to the person, who is obviously a woman, and as it soon transpires Rozanov's wife. Suddenly Rozanov in his tenderness is transfigured before Steinberg's eyes:

> In Rozanov's whole tone and behavior there was such a favorable disposition and such trust, unexpected in the circumstances, that I

---

[116] Efron – who real original name was S.K. Litvin, one of Rozanov's sources for *Judaism* – eventually did write an article criticizing Rozanov in the press to which Rozanov responded with the full bluster of his public persona.
[117] In Russian, *drug*, the male gender.
[118] Both Rozanov and his wife suffered from serious illnesses during this period. This was part of the reason for Rozanov's fleeting re-embrace of Christianity. He had always maintained that Christianity was a religion of death, useful and true only to the dying or sick (one of the ideas vacillation can grasp in its busy-bee journey from truth to truth).

experienced a dual feeling towards him. Instead of exposing a black-hundreds extremist, who was libeling the Jewish people, and stirring up the Russian population, and the clergy in a major way too against the Jews, I had as it were entered into the family of Vasily Vasilievich, and had become intimate with him for a short period. It was one of those incidents which allowed me to understand the originality, the great, ineradicable originality of the Russian character.

In the study, Rozanov shows Steinberg a death-threat he has received, in which the writer promises to sacrifice Rozanov and his descendants on the altar in the basement of the St. Petersburg main synagogue. After toying with various reactions, foremost of which is skepticism, Steinberg cautiously opines that he should show it to the police. Again, Rozanov's daughter wins Steinberg's warm sympathy when, having followed after them, she apologetically comments that Rozanov's guest is only saying this to be polite (evidently she is still embarrassed by her father's madcap antics).

Finally, Steinberg's feelings towards Rozanov are further rehabilitated when another guest, Buryakin, lays into Steinberg with various anti-Jewish sentiments, the chief of which is that Beilis' lawyer, Gruzenberg, is money-grubbing for taking 10,000 rubles royalties for the defense. Rozanov sharply reproves the man for being impolite to a guest under his roof, and curtly points out that he himself took 20,000 rubles for his articles in *Zemshchina*[119].

After this meeting, Steinberg ran into Rozanov's daughter in St. Petersburg several times. It emerged that Buryakin no longer visits Rozanov, who had insisted on defending Steinberg against his further attacks. The picture of Rozanov sacrificing a right-wing friendship in defense of a Jew should not be surprising, given what we have seen of his bivalent attitude to Gershenzon. Rozanov's daughter with evident sincerity also transmits to Steinberg her father's disappointment that he has not called on them again, and conveys to him her father's earnest desire to see him. This will be the first of several imprecations, whose urgency can partly be explained by Rozanov's need for a live Jewish presence near him.

Steinberg, for his part, is cast into a role as odd as that of Rozanov when he next meets this same daughter. This time he sees her weeping uncontrollably in the vestibule outside the hall where the Religious-Philosophical Society is conducting its vote to exclude Rozanov from the society he helped found. As the dethroning of the chief anti-Semite of St Petersburg proceeds apace behind their backs, the Orthodox Jew Steinberg tries to comfort the arch-anti-Semite's daughter. "When I think of what great friends Papa was with Dmitri Sergeivich[120]…Well, yes of course, Papa is acting wrongly, but why did it have to be Dmitri Sergeivich?"

The bell rings, giving news that Rozanov has been voted out of the society,

---

[119] The far-right paper in which Rozanov published his anti-Semitic articles.
[120] Merezhkovsky.

and Rozanov's daughter grabs Steinberg's hands: "Give me your word that you'll visit us again." Steinberg, deeply touched by her plight, says that he will, and even gives his word – a rarity for him, he emphasizes, "but I wanted to say and do something nice for her."

Steinberg never did return to Rozanov's house: he was trapped in Berlin by the outbreak of the First World War, and by the time he returned to Russia, Rozanov was dead. Nonetheless, there is a sequel.

A friend with whom Steinberg is staying is burning back copies of *Novoe Vremya* to stave off the cold, and true to his promise to Steinberg has torn out all articles by Rozanov. (Such a promise reveals the magnetic effect of even this brief meeting on the young man). One of the articles is called "Everyone lied then." Rozanov writes that only two people did not lie: a certain professor of Islam who genuinely believed in the ritual, and a certain young Jew called Aaron Steinberg, who genuinely did not. In the article, he admits that his own motivations were political, to defend Russia from the Jewish yoke.

While it is perhaps not a good idea ever to take a published opinion of Rozanov's at face value, this article – especially as we meet it in Steinberg's account of his encounters with Rozanov and his family – makes clear the political context of Rozanov's 1911-1914 Judeophobic seizure. For seizure it was – in intensity and (relative) brevity of duration – compared to what went before.

Rozanov's ambiguity about Judaism is magnified by the apocalyptic nature of these years. His constantly jittering personal hysteria is swept up in the sonic boom of the mass hysteria of the far right, which seemed to sense its impending doom with terrifying clarity. The abolition of the Pale of Settlement, the admission of Jews *en masse* into the heartland of Holy Rus, seemed to be the very symbol of the destabilization and disintegration of Russia.

In what follows, we will look more closely at Rozanov's great lie: a lie into which he poured all his literary talent, and his hysterically fervent rhetorical skills. It was a lie which was partly a tool used quite lucidly and rationally in the service of a political goal, namely to preserve a certain concept of the Russian state. But it was a lie by which, despite occasional hauntings of bad faith (*"I believe in the ritual, I do, I do…I don't"*), Rozanov came to be convinced and then possessed, till the mask became the face, the lie one of those many "truths" Rozanov had theorized about. In that sense, Rozanov consciously decided to overcome the dividedness and insecurity of the times by throwing himself fully into the lie – as if true dedication even to a false cause could cure the insufferable vacillation of the moment.

The odd, chattering dialogue with the hidden Florensky (who, by implication, was also lying), which took place in the sprawling footnotes of right-wing journals, also helped Rozanov construct a grandiose theology of the lie and for some time managed to give the impression that there was some fire beneath the smoke – to those, including Rozanov himself, who were willing to be drawn into the illusion for personal and political reasons.

Rozanov's Judeophobic outpourings (1911-1914)
One of the earliest articles Rozanov wrote was "Jewish Secret Writing." Here, Rozanov takes up the theme of Jewish mystique again, but this time with malicious intent. The Hebrew Old Testament is an indecipherable code to those not in the know, due to the absence of vowels. Only the secret whispers of the vowels make it readable, and even with the vowels sometimes that which is written is not what is read, for there is the difference between *qere* and *ketiv*[121]. Therefore any fool "can see the bones – but the blood let no one see." The inner meaning, the *noumenon*, the blood – is for Jewish eyes (and noses, which will make an entrance shortly) only. Vasily Vasilievich is warming himself up for a smooth transition to the "blood-drained" body of Yushchinsky.

At the end of "Jewish Secret Writing," we find Rozanov in a lyrically malevolent mood. We have already glimpsed ahead to *Apocalypse*, where Rozanov declares that European civilization could not have got where it was without the Jew. In 1912, Rozanov is expressing the same opinion, albeit less radiantly, but with the same lurid surrealness that we saw in his "theology" of the mikveh. Again, there is the same theme of dirt being transformed into holiness before our very eyes. He writes:

> Have you looked at their gait: a Jew is walking along the street, stooped, aged, dirty. A gabardine, *peyyos*; he doesn't look like anything else in the world! "He smells of garlic," and not just of garlic. The Yid in general "smells beastly."[122]…He walks somehow not quite straight, not with an open gait…. Cowardly, timid….The Christian looks on after him and ejaculates:
> -Pfu, disgusting, and *why* can't I get along without you?
> Worldwide: Why can't I get on without him?

(At this point, having delved into Rozanov's home life and letters, we are tempted to ponder on a few "secrets" of his own that form a mocking subtext

---

[121] The "read" and the "written." While Rozanov grasps the basic concept, the example he gives is wrong, as usual.

[122] Rozanov is fond of quotation marks. Like his hero Dostoevsky, in Rozanov's writing there is much "polyphony" (Bakhtin's term), or mingling of multiple voices, leading to a complex problem of attribution. *Who* says a Jew smells of garlic? Someone unspecified who is being quoted by someone else. In *Judaism*, Tseykhanstein writes that Jews stink and smell different from gentiles. Rozanov takes this up, and starts talking about stinking Jews. Soon the words have become Rozanov's own, but a doubt – the strength of which varies according to distance from the quotation – is always allowed to remain that Rozanov has not committed himself to them. This is part of what Nikolyukin calls Rozanov's constructions of literary "mythologemes" (A.N. Nikolyukin, "K voprosu o mifologeme natsional'nogo v tvorchestve V.V. Rozanova," in *Obonyatenl'noe i osyaznatel'noe otnoshenie yevreev k krovi*, edited by A.N. Nikolyukin. Moscow: Respublika, 1998.). See below.

here. For we cannot forget Rozanov's letter to Gershenzon[123], his Jewish mentor-rival at the same time: "I somehow physiologically (almost sexually) and artistically love a 'Yid in *peyyos*', and secretly in company always sneak a glance after him and admire him." Ah, but Rozanov is talking of the *Christian* reaction to the Yid in peyyos…)

Rozanov continues:

> But the Yid knocks on the door; the filthy hand has reached out and lifted the latch. Completely bent over – he creeps in there.
>
> Creeps in – the secret, and the secret place. And again, everyone is in agreement with everyone else: while you saw him outside, you were seeing as it were only the "consonants;" but once he's gone into the house – then the "vowels" in him are revealed. His very figure, fat, rounded, or on the contrary, excessively long drawn-out and ultra-thin (two *types* of Jews), his skin shiny with sweat, they have something about them that recalls an old, pot-bellied synagogue Torah, rolled round a stick.
>
> -Ah, if only we could get along without! But we can't!
>
> -We "beat" him, we do "business" with him, and – we "read his books."

So: the "filthy Yid" seen in the street by the horrified Christian, slowly metamorphoses into a Hebrew letter[124], specifically those excessively long or short ones from which the rabbis in the Talmud deduce a whole host of secret meanings[125].

Not to be outdone by the rabbis, with whom Rozanov is in close competition for interpretive originality, Rozanov latches onto his Yid-letter, who is the Word incarnate in a way that Christ never could be for Rozanov, and watches him depart from the street into his inner sanctum, leaving Rozanov gulping for more. Once he is inside, Rozanov (perhaps peering in through the window) sees the exoteric Yid-consonant blossom with sweet esoteric vowels into pure light.

---

[123] Can we speculate that there was a sexual frisson here? Rozanov's mother – in a shock move for the society of the time – married a man much younger than herself. Emulating the pattern, Rozanov married a woman much older than himself. Gershenzon (41) and Steinberg (22) were younger men than Rozanov (56). Is Rozanov an old woman falling for young men – or more likely, the older woman at whom these young men throw themselves? To his daughter, Rozanov had with gentle irony described Steinberg as coming to see the great Rozanov on a matter of wisdom. We recall his male *drug* on the couch during Steinberg's visit, i.e. his wife. Gender-switching was a matter of course for Rozanov.

[124] Typically symbolist poetics are at work here. Florensky will write an article "Ekhad" – low on scholarship and high on similar symbolist poetics – in which he tries to work the 13 (although in humble reality it was 14) wounds on Yushchinsky's temple into the shape of the Hebrew letter *shin*, from which a host of nonsensical Kabbalistic rigmarole is deduced. (See below). Rozanov is far more charming.

[125] On which Rozanov has just commented.

In other words, for all the grotesque anti-Semitic imagery[126] this attack on Jewry has somehow tripped up into being another paeon of envious praise for the Jew. Rozanov must try harder to keep his anti-Semitism on course[127].

The next effort we will examine is the title essay of the compendium, "The olfactory and tactile relationship of Jews to blood." Here Rozanov uncovers more Jewish secrets for his prurient reactionary readership. Gogolesquely, the Jewish nose also now makes an appearance in the Russian right-wing press. Jewish noses are not like the effete little *shtupsnasers* of the Russian, but instead great, heavy "bellies for sniffing." Jews' lips, too, are "fat, fleshy…: their taste, their smell is completely different than with Christians."[128]

It will be no surprise by now to find out that anti-Semitism segues logically into a Marcionite attack on the Old Testament. Shortly, we discover that God – or rather "god" as he becomes for long stretches – has a Jewish nose. The matter

---

[126] Such rhetoric is of course, not a prerogative of non-Jews. Perhaps the closest example of similar denigration of religious Jews can be found in contemporary secular Israeli perceptions of *doss'im* ("the religious," as secular Israelis somewhat pejoratively call the ultra-Orthodox, adopting Ashkenazic-Yiddish pronunciation of the Hebrew term). In Israel, it is not unusual to hear the charge that the *doss'im* sweat and stink in the confined space of buses during the summer heat. The reasons for this enmity are different (connected to the role of the Haredim in the Israeli political process). Nonetheless, there is a not dissimilar ambiguity: there is a sense that secular Israelis, like Rozanov, both dislike the Haredim, while at the same recognizing that they are an indispensable part of their identity. In passing, it might be observed that the ahistorical purity of the Haredim and ultra-Orthodoxy – so fascinating for Rozanov, and as we will see for a Jewish philosopher like Franz Rosenzweig – is seriously challenged by their inability to adapt to conditions of Jewish sovereignty, for which they have attracted the criticism of other Orthodox Jews. A cogent critique of ultra-Orthodox insularity in the Israeli context was made early on by the famous (modern Orthodox) thinker, Yeshayahu Leibowitz. Cf. his *Judaism, Human Values and the Jewish State*. Ed. Eliezer Goldman. (Cambridge: Harvard University Press, 1995): chapters 7, 8, 10, 11, 15, 16.

[127] Of course, there is a serious side to all this. Rozanov is trying to whip up a general hysteria over the "secret" nature of Jewish rituals, to undermine in the public eye the testimony of Troitsky and others at Beilis' trial that Judaism is an open religion. The polemic round Jewish Secret Writings continued in Rozanov's responses to a protest letter by 400 rabbis and a criticism by Pereferkovich himself, of whose Mishna translation Rozanov had so liberally availed himself. Suffice it to say that Rozanov's philological skirmishes with his critics are on the same level as his etymological excursus on 'asher/Ashera/Astarte-Yahweh. On a slightly lighter note, again, there is an interesting connection between Rozanov's obsession about Jewish secrecy and the hidden nature of the Jew/God Yahweh in the fact that among the many blessings(*b'rachot*) pious Jews are enjoined to recite on witnessing various pleasing and wondrous phenomena of nature, there is one which is to be recited on seeing 600,000 or more Jews gathered in one place: "Blessed are you, Lord, God of the Universe, Knower of secrets." One feels that Rozanov could have got much creative mileage out of this had he known of it!

[128] p.244.

of God's demotion to "god" is highly revealing. The Marcionite "theology" here is complete: the Old Testament deity is alien, demonic, entirely other to the God of Jesus. And what we learn about the Yiddish "god" is that he has no other organs *except* for a nose:

> "Invisible God?" – Yes! – "In the Bible?" Invisible! It's extraordinary, but by some clever law…some cumulative spiritual law – the Jews of the Bible gave "the invisible God" nostrils?!!
>
> "The steam from His *nostrils*' is the expression in the Bible. He doesn't have a face, nothing in fact, no head…. "But nostrils?"….The Jew is lost in thought, stubbornly silent, silent for a long time, then he whispers: "*God has got nostrils too.*" "For I wouldn't be able to sniff up the sweetest thing of all, sweeter than prayer even, ecstatically sweet, without nostrils; and I cannot take away from God that by which I myself live, have my being, and derive my pleasures…"[129]

Fee, fi, fo, fum – I smell the blood of an Englishman! Finally, we have come to the theme of blood and the Jew's thirst for it. But the tour-de-force of incarnational theology that Rozanov performed in *Judaism* makes it easier to understand that the Jew is Yahweh and Yahweh is the Jew[130]. Therefore if the Biblical "god" loved blood, then Jews love it. Why? The Jew wrote the Bible in his own image. We are straight back to the first philosophical atheism of Xenophanes here: the Ethiopians have black gods, the Sycthian god is red-haired and blue-eyed. The tedious patristic doctrine – adopted and adapted from the Jews – that the Pentateuch is of divine authorship, that the Bible has a universal meaning, that the Sinaitic revelation took place in the no-man's land of the desert and thus was intended not for one land or race but all humanity – all this is not deemed worth a mention. From Marcionism, we have segued into atheism. Jew-baiting is a dangerous sport.

In "The angel of Jehovah among the Jews," the theme of secrecy is continued:

---

[129] Actually, "god" has a tongue as well. Rozanov contends that when Abraham laid Isaac on the altar, god's tongue of fire came down and had a quick pleasurable taste of the boy before he was replaced by a ram.

[130] And yet there is something in this, a theme which Bulgakov explored in more dogmatic detail, and with less confusion. There is also a story by Bashevis Singer – which in this sense is Bulgakovian – where a pious heder boy is teased by a heretical tailor: "Maybe God's a gentile and not a Jew?" "God a gentile? One mustn't say such things." (Isaac B. Singer, *The Collected Stories of Isaac Bashevis Singer,* (Reading: Penguin, 1981), 534.) In the common folk, childish – and often adult – understanding of pious Jews, Xenophanes' thinking is right: God is a pious Jew, who lays tefillin, has a beard, studies Torah, and so on. If one hates Jews, one hates God. The problem with Rozanov's theology is that there is no asymmetry between the human Jew and the somehow divine though "Jewish" god. So while his insight is incarnationally profound, it is confused.

"And 'the Israelite god'[131] has always concealed from the eyes of science 'his dealings with Abraham, powdering it like sprinklings of earth with little humorous jokes. 'Scientists will never penetrate to what's funny.'" But Rozanov, of course, being free of the shackles of science penetrates straight to the humorous heart of the matter, which naturally is the circumcision of the Jew's fertile member.

Each Jew, carrying Yahweh's mark of circumcision on him is elevated straight to the spiritual level of Abraham. This is another great difference between Russians and Jews: a christened Russian is lowly compared to St. Vladimir, but an ordinary Yankel is just as close to God as Abraham, for the covenant with blood is repeated all over again[132].

All Jews, therefore, are spiritual heroes. This explains their amazing sense of well-being. Any other nation would have collapsed into depression being confined to the Pale of Settlement. But not the Jews: they are loving it. Among the Russians, Rozanov can only think of two men who were so tirelessly radiant, who deserved the name of "Russian Abrahams:" John of Kronstadt (who had recently died in 1908) and Seraphim of Sarov. He writes:

"This is 'our Russian Abraham', this John of Kronstadt. The sense of righteousness lifted his hands up, did not let his legs tire and gave wings to his whole old, mortal body.

"The source of this diabolic tirelessness in the history of Jewry consists in something similar...."

Here he seems to have got himself into a real bind. Each Jew is a John of Kronstadt. But Jewish radiance comes from a diabolic source, namely the aphrodisiac powers of circumcision transmitted to them by the Old Testament "Israelite god." By analogy, however, John of Kronstadt's Jew-like energy also comes from diabolic sources. Once again, we see the clear consequences of launching an attack on Abraham, the Old Testament, and Yahweh. Like a boomerang, it always returns to thump Rozanov in the back of the head. Perhaps one could call this "antinomian thinking:" with burning courage to choose the vacillating horn of the dilemma in the terror of pure thought, and so on. But from a Christian point of view, it simply looks like pitiable confusion.

Rozanov elsewhere takes a different tack. Before it was a case of "Jew, we cannot do without you." In footnotes to a letter addressed to himself from the awesomely pseudonymned Omega (Florensky), and bearing the title "Jews and the fate of Christians," Rozanov decides to try and "do without" the Jews once and for all. What follows is a painful divorce.

Now Rozanov openly declares that the Old Testament is not a Christian

---

[131] Both "god" and his people are vengefully lower-cased now.
[132] At the end of *Judaism*, Rozanov had included in a footnote the story of a Russian man who had undergone circumcision by some fortunate chance and wrote to Rozanov to tell him of the great improvement he was experiencing in his marital life. The letter ended with a promise to keep Rozanov informed of his progress. This aphrodisiac effect of circumcision is the heritage of every humble Jew and would go towards explaining the radiance he now writes of among them.

book and not a model for Christianty[133]. Not that it is not *true*: "Of course the Bible is a completely true book, but we must read it understanding that it was addressed to one people…" and has nothing to say to non-Jews. That is, according to Rozanov's relativism, the Bible is true and nice for the Jews, but false for non-Jews: "That's good and I am very happy for them, but what has this to do with us? We have our Pechinegs and Polovians, as they had their Amalekites and Moabites. The temple is their *local* temple, as there were similar ones…in Sidon, Tyre, and Egyptian Thebes…There is nothing special for the Russian, this must be kept well in mind…"

After Genesis, the Bible turns into the history of a local tribe, and certainly "…already before Christ the meaning of the Jews and Judaism had already somehow become narrow, and become less interesting, and e.g. their well-known Maccabees are heroes only 'on our street.'" Cunning Abraham, the parochial Maccabees, the unfortunate Exodus from sacred Egypt, and all the prophets – are all local events. But in the Orthodox Church, the Maccabees are saints; the prophets (Moses, Isaiah, Jeremiah, Elijah and so on) – are saints. Christ was transfigured in the presence of Moses and Elijah. But Christ is alone now, all these local Jews are gone – airbrushed out of the picture.

Well, at last we now have the Biblical canon according to Rozanov-Marcion: he is a tad more generous than his antique predecessor – who excluded the whole Old Testament. Still, it seems that Rozanov leaves only the first verses of Genesis, the "universal" account of creation, which has some meaning for non-Jews[134] - given that Jews and non-Jews do, after all, live on the same planet.

Luckily, all that Rozanov had savored in the Old Testament can be got elsewhere. For in "Jews and the fate of Christians" Rozanov declares that the magic secret of fertility was stolen by the Jews from Egypt, just as they stole the gold of Egypt. But enhanced fertility was a common Eastern secret, and indeed was known to all nations of antiquity, including Ancient Rus. Therefore, to his relief Rozanov has found a way of "doing without" the Jew. A bit of digging among the paganism of the ancient Slavs and Egyptians will restore Russia's broken families and fractured society. The Bible can be bypassed.

Here, it is instructive to recall how the Church Fathers interpret the stolen gold of Egypt, which is Rozanov's exegetical escape-route out of the Old Testament. This, of course, was the very gold that was used at God's command to build the Tent of Meeting where God chose to dwell among His people. For the fathers, this symbolizes the ability of a Christian to use pagan philosophers such as Plato and Aristotle in their building up of a Christian wisdom. The patristic license to use "pagan wisdom" in this transfigured way points to the gulf between

---

[133] This is done even more explicitly in *Ob odnom priyome*. See above and below.
[134] Rozanov's doctoring of the Bible is reminiscent of Shestov's tailoring of it for different purposes; Shestov, too, only ever referred to the handful of verses that supported his doctrine of the complete whimsicality and unknowability of God.

"Orthodox" Christian "paganism" and Rozanovian "Christian" "paganism." For Rozanov, Plato is a far-off and dull second best to the other pagan "secret" of enhanced sexuality.

All of the above has shown in ample detail that Rozanov's anti-Semitism was unpatristic and unorthodox and unchristian: in other words, in Rozanov's case anti-Semitism is tied inextricably to his violently anti-Christian metaphysics, which was so explicitly displayed in works like *Moonlight People*. It is the other side of the coin, a doomfully necessary consequence of it – rather than being a repudiation of it and a defense of Christianity.

Two questions remain. First, what did the Orthodox priest Pavel Florensky make of all this? Secondly, how could an analyst like Katsis have concluded that Rozanov's analysis was Christian?

Florensky: Rozanov's secret helper

In this section, we will consider only Florensky's joint writings with Rozanov on the Jews, although he also wrote – briefly – elsewhere about Jewry[135]. Such a consideration will show how Florensky's own philosophical views influenced the direction of Rozanov's new "Judeology," a point that L.Katsis makes in some detail[136]. It also raises in sharper form the question of the relationship between

---

[135] Interesting is his preface to the 1915 anti-Semitic collection "Israel in the past, present and future." (Pavel Florensky, "Predislovie k sborniku 'Izrail' v proshlom, nastoyashchem, i budushchem,'" in *Sobraniye socheniye v 4 tomax*, Tom 2, (Moscow: Mysl, 1996), 705-708.) Here Florensky accuses Jews of being directly or indirectly at the root of Satanic and Luciferian cults, and of being a "Satanic assembly." He also writes that both Judophiles and Judophobes are right: the former for recognizing that the Jews are the axis of world history among whom Christ was born, the latter for perceiving their cursedness since they rejected Christ. In an ambiguous passage, he writes that the alarm and sufferings caused by Jews in the hearts of Christians are relieved by the knowledge that the Lord in His love and mercy has determined a solution to the antinomy of the Jewish question, which "the greatest Judophiles and Judophobes…themselves Jews," St.John and St.Paul, wrote about. However, the idea that Florensky was here endorsing the idea that this merciful solution will be the salvation of all Israel, as Soloviev supposed, would seem to be excluded by the views that Florensky expressed in more detail to Rozanov in the passages we are about to examine. For the 1915 view is fully compatible with those earlier (1913) attempts to make Romans 11 yeild a reading that the Jews will be spiritually damned at the end time. Alternatively, one could hold that Florensky did not hold a systematic "metaphysical" view on the Jewish question, and like others, fluctuated according to political circumstances – so that he held a harsher view during the Beilis affair, so threatening to "Sacred Russia," and other – less vindictive – views during the First World War and later. Cf. below for another reference to Jews in his recollections about childhood.

[136] Katsis (2006): ch.12. This seems to be a plausible thesis. However, a reverse influence of Rozanov on Florensky's anti-Semitism can also seen. Katsis sees the "scientific" aspirations of Rozanov's Beilis-era anti-Semitism as showing Florenskian influence.

Christianity and anti-Judaism: if Rozanov was an eccentric from the Christian point of view, Florensky had just been ordained a priest of the Russian Orthodox Church in 1913.

Furthermore, Florensky was a central figure of Silver Age thought, a poet, philosopher and theologian. Like Bulgakov, he deepened Soloviev's sophiology and developed his own version of all-unity. Although twenty six years younger than Rozanov, the two men had become close friends and during this period Florensky was to become something of a spiritual father to Rozanov.

In *The Pillar and Ground of Truth*, published in 1914, i.e. just at the end of the Beilis period, Florensky had outlined a philosophy of friendship, in which "homophilic" union was to be the new model of Christian love, its spiritual basis to form a stronger bond than marriage between man and woman. Florensky himself attracted the deep friendship and admiration not only of Rozanov, but of Bulgakov too. The older philosopher, Nicolai Lossky, attributed his return to the Church to Florensky's influence.

In the context of our discussion, Florensky's theory of friendship provides a strange backdrop to the Beilis affair. Rozanov's terms of address for his wife, *drug*, is the launching-pad for Florensky's theory of *philia*, where he links the Russian word *drug* (friend) to the etymologically unrelated *drugoe* (other), using Hegelian logic: "The 'I', being reflected in a friend (*drug*), recognizes in the friend's I its own other (*drugoe*) I."[137]

Rozanov, it seems, partially found *druzhba* (which following Florensky's paronomasia, we can translate as "friendship, otherness") with a woman, his wife – for his philosophy of flesh put *eros* above *philia*, and his own view was that only sodomite ascetics would reject the pleasures of women completely. However, in light of our examination of his intimate and tempestuous friendships with three Jews, we can see Rozanov as being attracted to

---

But his admiring use of Houston Chamberlain in 1906 shows that Rozanov already had a soft spot for pseudo-science. In the two articles mentioned above, he dwells on Christ's being born in "Galilee of the gentiles," and moves from the concept of a distinctive Semitic philology to a Semitic mindset/culture and race. In one of their letters, Florensky confides that he found new grist for his thoughts on Jewry in the writings of Rozanov, so testifying to a mutual influence, and certainly Rozanov-Chamberlain's step from philology to blood was congenial to Florensky's way of thinking. A fuller treatment of how both their anti-Semitism relates to the development of academic-scientific thought in the Western academy and in Russia would take us beyond the scope of this chapter. For another article where Rozanov treats Judaism and the New Testament, and interestingly, Islam (this and not the New Testament is the true successor to Judaism), cf. "Kul'turno-religioznie voprosy," written three weeks after his Chamberlain articles. (Also in *Okolo narodnoi dushi*, 74-78). The arguments here resemble, for example, Florensky's later article about Chwolson, again proving that Florensky – like many other more mainstream thinkers – was indebted to Rozanov in several respects.

[137] Pavel Florensky, *The Pillar and Ground of the Truth*, translated by Boris Jakim. (Princeton, Princeton University Press: 2004), 314.

homophilic union precisely with *drugim,* "others" – and for Rozanov, there was no more Other/friend than the Jew.

In Rozanov's and Florensky's collaboration on *Olfactory*, however, we have the spectacle of two "Christian" friends forming an exclusive union against that Other, those lost friends of Rozanov, and indeed defining Christian humanity so that the Other becomes precisely the non-friend, indeed the enemy. Thus Florensky's etymological philosophy of friendship becomes utterly conventionalized again: the other really is the other, and beyond the bounds of love[138].

While no doubt much more could be written about the erotic-agapic aspect of Silver Age philosophy, what will interest us here primarily is once again the theological aspects of Florensky's writings on Jewry.

In so doing, it is impossible – as with Rozanov, indeed as with any thinker – to ignore the biographical elements of Florensky's work. A particular problem here is the high esteem in which Florensky is held.

Before the Revolution, he was a figure of fascination who moved from the monastery to the literary salon to the science laboratory with equal ease and grace, embodying the comfort of the new believer in the modern world. Rather as with Soloviev, his face, dress and mannerisms as much as his writings seemed to provide a living icon of the Russian God-seeker. Then, after his exile to Solovki gulag and his murder by the Soviet regime in 1937, the picture of a genius was complemented with that of the saint and martyr.

Testimonies to Florensky make it clear that he was a deeply spiritual man, with a love for his priestly service and a desire to serve people in the name of Christ. Nonetheless, this only heightens the question of how Florensky could have written so viciously against Jews.

In Russia, scholars have long recognized that the picture of the saint-genius is an idealization. In the West, distance has further exoticized the already exotic picture of Florensky. However, the German scholar M. Hagemeister[139] has also demonstrated the flaws in this portrait.

Some of Florensky's idealization comes from a corresponding idealization of Russian religious thought. We saw that Bulgakov's and Berdyaev's anti-Western rhetoric was sometimes excessive. Florensky is closer to V.Ern[140] in taking that tendency to greater lengths. In describing Kant's philosophy, for example, he wrote: "There is no system more 'slipperily evasive', more 'hypocritical', and more 'cunning' than the philosophy of Kant….it is all woven out…out of mysterious smiles and ambiguous vacillations between yes and no. Not a single term gives

---

[138] It would be interesting to trace the relationship between Florensky's philosophy of the Other, conceived in the framework of Russian all-Unity and the philosophy of the Other developed by the Russian-Jewish-French philosopher, Emmanuel Levinas. The latter's system is partially a rejection of overarching all-unity. Cf. Levinas, (1989), (1990), (1994).

[139] Michael Hagemeister, "Novoe Srednevekovye' Pavla Florenskogo." Zvezda, No.11, 2006.

[140] Cf.ch.5 for discussion of Ern, and esp. ch.6 for polemic between Frank and Ern.

forth an honest tone, but all of it is a howling….". The tone of such *ad hominem* attacks is worth bearing in mind when considering his anti-Jewish rhetoric.

Hagemeister also points to aspects of Florensky's work that scholars like Gavryushin and Khoruzhy[141] have already highlighted, such as his attempt to reinstate a geocentric Ptolemaic worldview using the theory of relativity and to locate the precise boundary between heaven and earth between Uranus and Neptune ("a stunning result" in Florensky's opinion). All of this casts doubt on his image as competent mathematician and scientist – or at least indicates a failure to prevent his philosophical hopes from intervening in scientific research.

Again, similar claims that "he…controlled all the European languages, classical and modern, as well as classical Hebrew, and a few modern Caucasian and Central Asian languages"[142] start to sound mythic, and indeed bombastic, when an examination on his writings on the Kabbalah reveal that he used French sources and did not seem to know the Hebrew word for "one"[143].

However, equally valuable is Hagemeister's clarification of the issue of whether Florensky has been canonized by the Russian Church[144]. He has not, and indeed at the beginning of the nineties "conservative circles of the Moscow patriarchate reacted to this [rumor] with indignation and pointed to Florensky's loyalty to the Soviet regime."[145] Florensky's odd relationship to the Soviet government will be commented on below.

Part of the filling out of the portrait of Florensky's person and philosophy has included a recognition of how his reactionary, anti-Western views expressed themselves in categories of racist anti-Semitism. Hagemeister writes about this too, and obviously this will be our main focus below.

Our approach differs somewhat from Hagemeister, however, in that he implies an equation between Florensky's anti-Semitism and that of other Russian religious thinkers when he writes that "the motives of Christian anti-Judaism, as well as the denied Jewish spheres of contemporary activity (materialism, capitalism, socialism, internationalism, masonry) are met in

---

[141] N.K Gavryushin, *Russkoe bogoslovie: ocherki i portrety*, pp.275-312: 'Borba za lyubeznuyu mne neponyatnost': svyashchennik Pavel Florenski. (Moscow: Glagol, 2005). Chapter on Florensky in Sergei Khoruzhy, *Posle pereryva. Puti Russkoy Filosofii*. (Saint Petersburg: 'Aleteia', 1994).

[142] Richard Gustafson, Introduction to *The Pillar and Ground of the Truth*, translated by Boris Jakim, ix-xxiii. Princeton, Princeton University Press: 2004.

[143] See discussion about his article on "Ekhad."

[144] Abbot Herman and Father Damascene make this claim in a translation of Florensky's *Salt of the Earth*, where the author is even called "St.Paul Florensky" on the book-cover. Herman (Abbot) and Damascene (Father). Introduction to *Salt of the Earth: Elder Isodore*, translated by Richard Betts. St Herman of Alaska Brotherhood, 1999. For another rather idealized English-language portrait of Florensky, cf. Donald Nicholl, *Triumphs of the Spirit in Russia*, London: Dartman, Longman and Todd, 1997. Cf. ch.4, "The scientist martyr: Pavel Florensky."

[145] Hagemeister, fn.5.

other Russian religious thinkers, like Vladimir Soloviev, Nicolai Berdyaev and Sergei Bulgakov."[146]

Florensky is certainly on a continuum with these thinkers; however, his "rabid hatred of Jews, that explodes into pogrom-inciting fever" (Hagemeister) is fed by quite different sources and is so intense as to make such a comparison of limited use.

Our own examination of Florensky's writings will consider them primarily from the point of view of Christian "logic" – that is, whether they correspond to patristic and Biblical teaching about Jews and Israel. In this, we respond to the work of L.Katsis, who has seen in Florensky's "Judeology" a particularly Christian ideology.

The second aspect of our examination will be to consider how Florensky's Jewish writings fit into his philosophy as a whole. Expanding the circle, we will then consider how Florensky's philosophy as a whole fits in with the thought of his fellow Russian religious thinkers, and how that thought, in turn, correlates with Christian Orthodoxy.[147] Only then, can we return to the question of how Christian Florensky's anti-Semitism really is.

Florensky's Jewish writings[148]

Florensky contributed to or wrote the following articles in *Olfactory*: "The affair needs to be transferred to a different plane (concerning the Yushchinsky affair);" "Prof. D.A. Chwolson on ritual murders;" "Jews and the fate of Christians (a letter to V.V. Rozanov);" and "'Ekhad' – the thirteen wounds of Yushchinsky."

These articles all focus on the cultic aspect of contemporary Jewish ritual sacrifices of gentile children. They are all written in 1913 (the year of his ordination). This is the same year when Rozanov's judeology turns to similar themes. The obvious conclusion is that Florensky, who was somewhat of a mentor to Rozanov in spiritual matters, pushed Rozanov's thinking in this direction.

---

[146] Ibid.fn.70.
[147] The shocking nature of Florensky's anti-Semitic writings and the relative ignorance concerning this aspect of his work – so heightening the shock factor – may, I am afraid, have cast an excessively emotional coloring on this section of the chapter. There is much to admire in Florensky's metaphysics, and in many ways his system shares similarities with the systems of Karsavin and Bulgakov, whose work I present more systematically. The obvious imbalance in approaching Florensky primarily through his Jewish writings, which are admittedly small in number, may have to be rectified in further work. For now, I leave it to those better acquainted with his larger work to make that judgment.
[148] The collaboration of Fr.Pavel Florensky on Rozanov's anti-Semitic journalism between 1911-1914 was only decisively established in 1998, by his grand nephew Hegumen Andronik (Trubachaev) on the basis of his discovery in the archives of corrections made by Florensky to drafts, letters and proofs. However, as early as 1925 Zinaida Gippius (*Zhiviye litsa*; see Hagemeister) had commented that Rozanov had attacked Jews in the far-right press "not without the help of Florensky."

As we saw, in 1903 and 1906, Rozanov had held the firm belief that the blood ritual was a blood libel. He also rejected the idea that Jews ate kosher food to spite gentiles. In "Jews and non-Jews" he admires the system of kosher slaughter and the kosher diet due to its evident respect for and tenderness towards animals: this is another positive "Egyptian" quality of Judaism. The Egyptian deities had animal features and animals were considered sacred; this was part of the ancient Egyptians' pantheistic love of the natural world, to which Judaism was heir. It was precisely this ideology of Judaism that attracted Steinberg's admiration, and precisely the volte-face in such attitudes that provoked his confusion.

In 1913, Rozanov writes "An important historical question," in which he tries to refute Troitsky's opinion that blood sacrifices to Moloch in ancient Israel were uprooted by the prophets and did not exist after the Babylonian exile. Rozanov maintains that such sacrifices did continue and were transmitted into Judaism through the rite of circumcision, where the knife of the *mohel* touches the living body of a child and draws forth blood. From this comes the secret requirement to obtain and ritually use the blood of a Christian child. After various other proofs, he concludes that his logic has the water-tightness of "algebra and the multiplication tables." And later: "The question of sacrificial murders by the heads of world Jewry of Christian boys can now be reckoned as solved in favor of a positive answer with the same fullness, exactitude and reliability as the proofs of geometric theorems."

The defamation of the much-lauded ritual of circumcision, the about-turn on Jewish diet and the sudden bewitchment with "mathematical" certainty would certainly look less schizophrenic if one postulates the impact of Florensky on Rozanov's thinking[149]. In addition, we recall Rozanov's previous contempt for "scientists" who try to deduce the noumenal essence of Judaism by banging on about arcane and bizarre Temple rituals. Now Rozanov is doing just that. It should be said however that another lengthy article, "Sacrifice among the ancient Jews," is simply a compendium of quotes from the Talmud about the arcane details of animal sacrifice in the Temple. Likewise, in the short article "The Old Testament Temple contained a secret" he pulls out one line from the Talmud about workmen repairing the Temple being carried past the Holy of Holies in a box, so as not to gaze on it. Conclusion: evidently some pretty nasty Semitic stuff was concealed there[150], at which point the article ends. It seems

---

[149] I follow Katsis (2006) in this analysis, with the provisos noted earlier about reverse influence.

[150] Another aspect of Rozanov's ignorance, or more probably, debonairly selective argumentation: he maintains the Jewish Temple had a secret section (true), while the Christian liturgy has no secrets (not true). This is to ignore the fact that it is only baptized believers, and not as yet unbaptized catechumens, who in the early Church were permitted to witness the second half of the liturgy where the Eucharist is performed. Till now the words "Depart catechumens" are pronounced by the priest, expelling non-initiates from the temple (as churches are called in Russian). In addition, women are not allowed up to the altar. Again, Rozanov here is pouring scorn

Rozanov cannot quite sustain the interest to build up a theory of his own: he copies out a few extracts from Pereferkovich, dashes down a comment or two, and retires to his smoking room, as if to say, "Well, ladies and gentlemen, I'm a busy man, you must make up your own mind about these animal-murderers and what have you…"

Florensky, by contrast, is much more committed to the task of proving a link between the ancient Jewish temple and contemporary Jewish ritual murders. In "Professor Chwolson on ritual murders," Florensky devotes five pages to disproving another Beilis defense witness. He digs up a previous article by Chwolson in which the professor talked about the existence of human sacrifice among the Sabeans. Without going into the details, some of which are quite scintillating, we can reproduce the structure of Florensky's syllogistic logic here, namely: the Sabeans were Semites and offered human sacrifices as recently as 600 a.d.; the Jews are Semites. Ergo, the Jews offer human sacrifices now.

Later in the article Florensky quotes Maimonides' commentary on the passages in the Bible which talk of "ob" and the "teraphim." Maimonides' opinion is that they are hollowed skulls, perhaps of first-born adults, used for necromantic purposes. Maimonides here is making use of rabbinical commentaries on these obscure passages, as well as glosses in the Aramaic targumim. Florensky cites one of the Mishnaic commentaries on the same subject: "What are *teraphim*: they slaughtered a person, who was a first-born, hollowed out his head, salted it with salt and oil, and wrote on a gold tablet the name of some unclean thing, and placed the tablet under the tongue of the head. Then they placed the head on a wall and lit a lantern before it, and bowed down before it, and the head spoke to them." Again, Florensky's point is that, given that the rabbis and Maimonides described the ritual in such detail, they must have known about it or, more probably, witnessed and partaken in it.

In general, the point of all this suggestive and little-known material is that the Jews have always had a propensity for magic and child-sacrifice. In Old Testament times, the prophets managed to prevent them from indulging their desires, but since the prophets ceased there are no controls on what the Jews get up to now. This is a much more energetic effort than Rozanov's rather feeble attempts, which boiled down to implying that if Jews could sacrifice animals all those years ago, there is no telling what they might get up nowadays.

---

on the ugly Semitic seraphim and cherubim: but a central prayer of the Liturgy (the Trisagion, Thrice-Holy) includes Isaiah's song of the cherubim to the Lord of Hosts. Hence more Marcionite foot-shooting. (Interestingly, the departure of the catechumens and the very term catechumen are now so poorly remembered and understood by some less well churched parishioners of the Russian Orthodox Church that the term "catechumen" is even associated with "bad spirit:" how else to explain the invocation "Depart catechumens." If Rozanov was similarly ignorant of the details of Orthodox liturgy, it would be no surprise that he could with a genuine and unmalicious ignorance overlook the parellels between the Jewish Temple service and the Christian liturgy).

Ritual murder and the eucharist

It is when Florensky turns to Christian sources to prove the existence of Jewish ritual murder that the picture becomes truly bleak. This can first be observed in "It is necessary to transfer the whole affair to a different plane," where Rozanov gives extracts from a letter written to him by his "friend from the Caucasus."

In this work Rozanov confronts head-on a rather obvious drawback in his accusations that Jews love blood and are cannibals: the fact that the central rite of Christianity is the Eucharistic consumption of the blood and flesh of the god-man Christ. This fact is pointed out to him by an anonymous correspondent, and Rozanov's first instinct is to reply that the words "This is my body, this is my blood" are not meant in a literal sense.

He then remembers in the nick of time that he is forbidden to think this by the Church, which insists the words have a non-symbolic meaning. Rozanov's dogmatic scruples here are rather breath-taking, considering that outside of his viciously anti-Jewish works, he is engaged in similar attacks on the Church. Still, part of this somewhat unconvincing adoption of a Christian persona is his appeal to an anonymous friend in "a mitre," to whom he now hands over the task of resolving this doctrinal difficulty. The fact that his friend wears a mitre is intended to add some hoary authority to Rozanov's proofs of the blood ritual.

Florensky takes over, but we will soon see that his orientation differs little from Rozanov's. The New Testament text with which Florensky launches his august theological exploration is Hebrews 9, 22: "Nearly everything according to the Law is purified by blood and without the spilling of blood there is no forgiveness." St. Paul[151] is pointing out in this letter that Old Testament religion required blood for purification. Blood was important in ancient Judaism, and it continues to be important in Christianity. Here Florensky admits a continuity between the Old and New Testament.

But Rozanov's efforts to inculcate in his readers the idea that the Old Testament is a secret book now come in handy for Florensky: what was the blood that Paul, that "great expert on rabbinism," was referring to here? At first glance, it would seem to be animal sacrifice and certainly not consumption of blood, animal or human. However, Florensky now explains that the blood taboo in the Old Testament was in place not as an absolute ban, but merely as a directive as to when to use this highly sacred substance.

He draws an analogy with ancient religion, in which a sacred animal was treated with great respect and love, but when the time of the festival came this same animal was slaughtered. Likewise in the Old Testament: "The blood of goyim, also animals, probably, should be considered as precisely this type of sacred food that is forbidden at normal times."

Florensky adds for the sake of plausibility: "But I imagine that very few, only the chosen of the chosen in Judaism, were initiated into this secret." Still,

---

[151] To whom Florensky attributes the Letter to the Hebrews.

given that the taboos around blood appear often in "non-secret" Old Testament texts, the implication here is that, in accordance with Rozanov's logic, the real meaning, the truly sacred meaning of the blood taboo is revealed in precisely this secret, esoteric aspect: namely, that blood is a sacred substance that is meant to be consumed on special occasions. As we will see, given that Yahweh instituted these taboos it is clear that Yahweh also endorses the sacred use of blood on special, secret occasions by his chosen people (who are expected to use the blood of the non-chosen goyim).

The meaning of the blood taboo in the Old Testament has thus been revealed as a regulation of blood consumption. Florensky is keen to point out that he has only admiration for this secret blood consumption of the Old Testament. In an odd way this makes him more "Orthodox" than Rozanov, whose whole endeavor has been to find as many reasons to reject the Jewish Old Testament as possible. It is through expressing admiration for ritual blood consumption that Florensky is trying to explain why Christian blood consumption is also a good thing. In this he distances himself from Beilis' atheistic lawyers who deny the very existence of a blood ritual in any shape or form. About this he laments:

> What can you do: religion is in essence tragic. Lawyers discuss thus: "Judaism is nonsense, Christianity is nonsense, and blood is nonsense – is there any point having an argument?"
>
> But I say: "Judaism is a religion and Christianity is a religion, and blood is holy and sacred, and ritual murder is a great affair."

This leads him to posit the following solution to Rozanov's troubled statement of the relation between the Eucharist and Jewish ritual murder:

> Christianity is opposed to Judaism as a religion, not as the negation of religion in general, but as a higher religion negates a lower one, as an overcoming of murder. The blood of lambs and goats and the blood of Yushchinsky are once and for all opposed to the blood of our Lord Jesus, poured out and still eternally being poured out. And eternally non-expiating ritual murder is opposed to the unique and eternal death of the Lord, Lamb and High Priest.

The message is clear then: Yahweh's Old Testament with the Jews consisted of animal sacrifice and on an esoteric but approved level, of ritual murder of gentiles. To put it mildly, the recognition of a continuity between the Old and New Testaments, so lacking in Rozanov, here takes on an even more grotesquely Marcionite form, if Marcionite is the right label now: for the Old Testament God is indeed a God of murder, and yet somehow this is all right.

Again, a little later we read in the same vein: "But of course you [Rozanov] are right to say that there is not a sharp difference between Moloch and the

God of Israel. To be precise, Moloch is the distorted image of that same God of Israel….." We will focus on how different Florensky thinks Moloch and Yahweh are later (not very), but in effect Florensky is in agreement with Rozanov at his more Gnostic moments: Yahweh and Moloch are fairly indistinguishable, and Yahweh-Moloch loves blood and blood sacrifices, and until He sent His Son to die was content with animals and humans.

The excerpt continues with a celebration of this God of murder:

"The God of Abraham, the God of Isaac, the God of Jacob - not the god of the philosophers and scientists" (the words of Pascal), not the "god" of the religious academies and seminaries, not the "god" of the newspapers and magazines….such a god does is not sensitive to the smell of blood and does not know its sacredness; *such a "god" does not establish the Eucharist, did not send His Son to die*, did not create "man and woman"…[italics, DR]

Here the link is made explicitly: Yahweh, the god who approved ritual murder as a path of salvation for his chosen people, is indeed the father of Jesus Christ. One can almost conclude that the difference between the Eucharist and ritual murder must be understood fideistically: ritual murder was sacred in times of yore, and a crime now, but not due to moral reasons; rather, only because the inscrutable God of mystery has changed His mind about the type of blood sacrifice that is pleasing to Him.

There is something rather stomach-turning in all this, but it is slightly trickier to work out quite why this account of the Eucharist and Christ's sacrifice is "off" from a Christian point of view. Certainly, Florensky is saying that God sanctioned human sacrifice and that Christ and Paul knew about this human sacrifice, Christ because He was replacing this type of sacrifice, Paul because he shows an awareness of the real meaning of Christ's shedding of His blood. The idea that Jesus and Paul knew of and approved human sacrifice as appropriate for its time is, to say the least, blasphemous.

Nor is it pleasant when Florensky himself expresses admiration of ritual murder, writing: "I am frightened by the Beilis affair not because ritual murders are committed, but because Christians are so oblivious that they have completely ceased to feel the significance of the idea of mystical murder and holy blood." And further on: "for those who basically and at root reject ritual sacrifice, can they really live as Christians and confess the saving effect of Christ's death on the cross?"

This gives the inescapable impression that Florensky welcomes the murder of Yushchinsky[152]. He makes a proviso that, certainly, his murderers must be hunted down and with all due process prosecuted…etc. But on the other hand, the

---

[152] According to Z.Hippius, Florensky once said: "If I had not been an Orthodox priest but a Jew, I myself would have acted like Beilis, i.e. have spilt the blood of Yushchinsky." Zinaida Hippius, *Zhivye litsa*. Moscow:Azbuka-Klassika, 2009, ch.4, "Zadumchivy strannik: o Rozanove."

murder proves that "religion" is still alive in the world, and this is a joyous thing. Clearly, this is not very reassuring coming from a Christian priest. Moreover, he is in effect stating that Christians cannot live without contemporary Jewish ritual murders: they are the proof of the Eucharist as it were[153].

The flaw in Florensky's two-tiered logic
At this point, it is worth exploring another way in which this account ignores and confutes Biblical logic. For, at first blush, Christ's sacrifice might indeed seem to be a type of "human sacrifice," thus supporting Florensky's claim that there is some deep meaning for the Bible in human sacrifice. A moment's thought will show that the New Testament has an altogether different take on the matter.

Paul, as well as Christ Himself and the other New Testament writers and the Fathers, is clear that Christ's sacrifice replaces the animal sacrifices of the Temple. After all, that is why Christ calls Himself the Lamb, who takes upon Himself the sins of the world. If one did believe that Christ's death on the cross was a type of human sacrifice, this would be to ignore clear stages in "sacred history" which form part of the Old Testament narrative, a narrative which is taken up in the New Testament. This narrative constitutes that very continuity between the Old and New Testaments, which Rozanov and Florensky miss, albeit in slightly different ways. The Old Testament logic, which Florensky utterly ignores, has the following structure.

An animal sacrifice is already a level of abstraction above human sacrifice: this first-born animal dies for your first-born son. Because of sin, all humans are mortal and deserving of death, but the animal sacrificial system, while graphically reminding humans of this, does not demand the lives of the sinners themselves. Abraham's testing can be seen as an object-lesson in this stage of religious development according to the Old Testament: the ram and not Isaac is pleasing to God, who formalizes this at Sinai.[154]

---

[153] He writes: "for those who…reject ritual sacrifice…can they really live as Christians?"

[154] Diodore of Tarsus (late 4th century) writes concerning God's command to Abraham to sacrifice Isaac: "Moses is going to narrate that God asked Isaac to be sacrificed to him, and in order that you, thinking correctly, be not suspicious about human sacrifice, he says 'He was testing': he was not asking earnestly, but was showing the notable faith of this man." Gregory of Nyssa, in a sermon to his congregation (*On the Nature of the Son*), imagines how fathers might react in Abraham's place, asking: "Why do you command these things, O Lord? On account of this you made me a father so that I could become a child-killer?....With my own hands I will slaughter my child and pour an offering of the blood of my family to You? Do You call for such things and do You delight in such sacrifices?" Gregory's lesson is that, in contrast to such fathers who are weak in faith, Abraham did not complain, nor have such similar thoughts. He was obedient and "gave himself up wholly to God and was entirely set on fulfilling the command." The idea is that faith and obedience are Abraham's inheritance to Christians; that it is not our place to second-guess God – however, the implication is that obviously God did not desire human sacrifice. Interestingly, St. Ephrem the Syrian wrote a poem including Gregory of Nyssa's

Christ comes after Abraham's testing and after the Law-directed Temple. He comes in "the fullness of time," when the Jews had already been trained in holiness by the Temple sacrifices and the Law. The first two stages are necessary to understand the type of sacrifice that Christ now makes.

For as the gospels, Paul and the Church Fathers teach, Christ's sacrifice relates to the heavenly sanctuary; the animal sacrifice of the Jerusalem temple was a copy of heavenly realities. (This is all in Hebrews, the book Florensky is interpreting). In the gospels, we learn of how Christ's "real," "heavenly" sacrifice results in phenomena that transcend earthly reality and are paradoxical in relation to our conceptions of body, time and so on. For example, even before Christ's death, He can distribute his body and blood to the disciples at the last supper – without physically dismembering Himself and "before" the sacrifice takes place. Similarly, after the Resurrection, while Christ can eat fish, He can also pass through doors. So He has a "body," which is not "not physical;" however neither is it purely physical.

This, then, is the linear course of sacred history: the Jews are weaned from idolatory, including human sacrifice. They follow the Law, are the Church in the world before Christ. Christ comes and "upgrades" the cult and the Law. Neither are abolished, but improved.

Now we see the far-reaching problem with Florensky. Human sacrifice was a primitive stage left behind by the Law – according to Christian belief, for here we are confining ourselves to Christian logic. Human sacrifice can never be inspiring, can never convince us of the "aliveness" of religion in the world. Child murder, even – especially – ritual can only be a cause for grief, and not as with Florensky, joy and comfort.

In contrast to this Biblical and patristic logic, Florensky would have it that Christ (stage three) was battling against primitive, concrete, non-abstract

---

insights, where he makes this more explicit: "For God is not pleased/by a dead sacrifice/offered to him/through ash and smoke,//But a living sacrifice,/holy, well-pleasing,/the reasonable worship/he seeks from us,//As the Apostle/clearly exhorts us all,/knowing that this/is well-pleasing to God./*For God did not wish/to make Abraham/a child murderer/ when he told him to offer his son,//*...[italics, DR]" Here, Ephrem is saying that the real sacrificial act was not the near-slaughter of Isaac, or even the actually slaughtered ram, but Abraham's inner process of faith – his willingness to leave behind the joys of nature (his growing family) to be obedient to God. This *spiritual* dimension of Abraham's test is the link with Christ's later obedient self-sacrifice. Diodore, Gregory and Ephrem all present a triple contrast to Florensky-Rozanov, who 1) try to penetrate to God's "real" intention in giving the command, 2) conclude that God *did* want human sacrifice, 3) miss the *spiritual* aspect of the command to Abraham. (Ephrem the Syrian,"Sermon of Our Venerable Father Ephrem: On Abraham and Isaac," translated by Archimandrite Ephrem: http://web.ukonline.co.uk/ephrem/AbrIsaac.htm ; for other church fathers on Abraham's sacrifice, cf. Mark Sheridan, ed. *Bibleiskie kommentarii otsov tserkvi i drugikh avtorov I-VIII vekov. Vetkhi zavet. II. Kniga Bytiya 12-50*. Transl. A.Bogatyrev and others (Moscow: Germenevtika, 2005):125-144.)

totemistic paganism (stage one). That this is simply not part of the discourse in any part of the New Testament is ignored by him: he applies Rozanov's hermeneutic of secrecy to interpret the New Testament Gnostically. He has made an effort to paper over Rozanov's Marcionite attack on the Old Testament, by applying the same logic to the New Testament. From an Orthodox point of the view, it is a disastrous move as now the rot begins to infect the credibility of that text and everyone in it.

One might also add – from a literary-critical point of view – that Florensky's hermeneutic is a betrayal of the literary Symbolism, of which he was such a prominent practitioner. In Symbolism, literary tropes are meant to point to higher realities. However, rather than seeing Old Testament figures as pointing upwards, everything is construed in reverse: Abraham and Isaac do not direct the reader towards God and His sacrifice of His Divine Son. Instead, they point to a more literal and concrete reality: that of God's desire for the real sacrifice of Isaac by his blood father, Abraham. Florensky's literary interpretations are thus by the standard dichotomy, Judaic, and "of the flesh"[155].

Once Florensky's letter is over, Rozanov takes the baton again. It has been proved to his satisfaction that the Jews eat blood because they want to "have communion in eternal life." This is fine for the Jews, but not for Christians: "With us, where the whole Old Testament is abolished and changed, where everything has been replaced with the 'blood and body of the savior', i.e. the God-man, naturally there is not and cannot be human sacrifice. But such a natural and ineradicable element must exist 'before us' in other religions."

We see that Rozanov has understood Florensky's logic and the two are in accord: Jesus' New Testament replaces the human (not animal) sacrifices of the Old Testament. "Christ, showing us and commanding us to eat His Body and

---

[155] Cf. the discussion in ch.3 about the correspondence between Gershenzon and the symbolist poet Ivanov. Gershenzon's Promised Land, is not literally Palestine – but some higher future reality, as yet unknown. To construe Gershenzon's symbolism in this exchange in a literalistic Florenskian manner would be – for example – to make Gershenzon a Zionist, i.e. to embroil oneself in nonsense and contradiction. This being said, Christianity is constantly in danger of falling into an excessively spiritualized "symbolism:" in some church Fathers, the typological approach actually denies the literal meaning of the text. A case in point is Gregory of Nyssa's contention that the blindess wrought on the Egyptians by the Lord was spiritual, and not physical. If one takes this approach consistently, then the Exodus will have been a purely spiritual ascent to a new faith. Ultimately, however Jesus Christ the Jew requires flesh-and-blood ancestors that culminate in His mother, otherwise he would never have got to be born. While we cannot say that Christian logic directly inspired Florensky's anti-Semitic and unbiblical reading of Hebrews and the Old Testament, there is a sense in which it indirectly inspired it: Christianity demands a constant need to reassert the literal meaning of the Old Testament, and in trying to fulfil that demand Florensky has gone several steps too far. In this he is part of that search for a "new Christianity" carried out in different ways with different degrees of success by Merezhkovsky, Bulgakov, Rozanov and even Shestov.

drink His Blood, did not mean to replace 'the blood of lambs and goats', but He precisely saved the human body in the future, abolishing forever human sacrifice, the true seed of the secret parts of the Jewish cult. This is frightening, but it is so."

To sum up, the Rozanov-Florensky picture in "It is necessary…" thus looks as follows. Christ was aware (as a Jew) that in the Temple[156] his Father had ordered human sacrifices, which was a satisfactory state of religious development for His people. But now he wished to help people, so that they could attain eternal life by eating His body, rather than people (presumably gentiles[157]) in the Temple. *That* was why he rejected the Temple, and said not a stone would be left unturned.

Florensky, Romans 11 and Jewish blood

The "judeology" put forward by Florensky in this article is further systematized in "Jews and the Fate of Christians." This is a letter to Rozanov from "Omega," i.e. Florensky. The main text belongs entirely to Florensky, but Rozanov has woven his footnotes at the base of the text, and often Florensky comments on Rozanov's footnotes, so that the letter begins to look like a page of Talmud.

Again, we cannot at this point assess the motives for Florensky's "theology of Jews," but one thing is clear: in this letter Florensky, the acolyte of Soloviev who in other works was developing the philosopher's conception of Sophia, pays homage to the master here too: the Jews are "the axis of world history," and the key text which can illuminate this is Romans 12.23, where St. Paul writes that "All Israel will be saved." In addition, as Bulgakov will later do in more depth, Florensky focuses on the concept of Jewish blood and its meaning for history. Once again, the revelation of the fact that "Omega" is Florensky, the gentle Soloviovian sophiologist, fairly whips the ground out from under one's feet. The text is not only utterly contradictory to Soloviev (and later Bulgakov); as in the previous texts, it is directly contrary to the Bible and the Church Fathers.

The discussion about Jewish blood and the influence of Jews in history and on Russia is launched when Rozanov in a footnote expresses the wish that Jews abandon their blood-thirsty religion.

Florensky answers that a Jew without religion is worse than a Judaic Jew. Here he deepens his distinction between Jews and Yids. Yids are the "so-so Jews," who do not care about religion. His point to Rozanov is that it is precisely the Yids who are more dangerous than "Jews" proper, as they enter into Russian institutions like the public school system, instead of keeping to themselves. In this respect, too much fuss has been about Andrei Yushchinsky's death, for: "Lord,

---

[156] Or secretly outside the Temple, sometimes it is not clear, but by Yahweh's command and according to his desire.

[157] Although in another argument, Rozanov draws attention to the fact there was a sign prohibiting gentiles to enter the court of the Jews on pain of death. Although come to think of it, perhaps it was those unfortunate straying tourists who ended up on the end of the priests' knives.

why don't people shout twice as loud about the thousands of similar Yushchinskys, in gymnasiums, schools and universities. Because these Jewish gentlemen are subjecting our soul to thousands of stabs. In them they poison the very source of sources of life – love of fatherland, family and world, of everything…"[158]

Rozanov's proposal that Jews give up their horrid religion is thus extremely dangerous from Florensky's point of view. At least lack of intermarriage limits the poison[159]. Rozanov tries to comfort Florensky in a footnote by assuring him that Jews are not as numerous as Florensky imagines: the best solution is to have faith that the Lord will keep the Jewish population down. Already God has done this to some extent: if he had let his promise to Abraham about Jewish populousness come to pass, the Jews – given their long history – should already have outnumbered the Russians.

Florensky now explains to Rozanov the danger of Jewish blood. Jews are having a baneful influence not just through core Jewry, but also by intermarrying. In this way, Jews marry into the surrounding nations, creating first half-Jews, then quarter-Jews, eighth-Jews, sixteenth-Jews and so on, until all nations will contain a preponderance of corrupt Jewish blood. "Consequently, there is little comfort to be had in the low numbers of Jews – that would mean to forget that the Jews do not have one trunk…but hundreds and thousands more side-branchings which are growing and multiplying at an alarming rate…"

The language about a Jewish trunk and branches in the gentile nations is interesting when compared to Paul's letter to the Romans, from which Florensky will soon quote: "Now suppose that some branches were broken off, and you are wild olive, grafted among the rest to share with the others the rich sap of the olive tree; then it is not for you to consider yourself superior to the other branches; and if you start feeling proud, think: it is not you that sustain the root, but the root that sustains you." Paul's metaphor of a life-giving Old Testament trunk and Jewish branches (even those broken off, i.e. those Jews who did not accept Christ) onto which gentiles are grafted is very different from

---

[158] Here Florensky claims that, for example, Rozanov's daughters' school-friends (the Rivkas and Sarochkas) are a worse phenomenon than the savage murder of a thirteen-year old boy. The thought is so grotesque that I believe it reveals something else: namely, that Florensky did not really believe in the murder of Yushchinsky by Jews, and that Yushchinsky has become a mere trope for him, a tool to make a political point. This is what Rozanov hinted when he claimed that he and all whom he knew were lying at the time of the Beilis affair.

[159] Later, in the article Florensky comes out in favor of the Jews having a state. The logic is not quite as generous as that of Bulgakov's Zionist article of the following year. It is based on a similar desire to keep the Jews separate from the rest of the world: "No! I say to you – 'no'. I am more frightened of 'just so' kikes. Any nation lives in its own particular Pale of Settlement; any nation sits in its ghetto. Let the Jews then also, the ones who say 'it's all right by me', and the one with 'peyyos', get for themselves some sort of territory somewhere on the earth and arrange for themselves their kingdom, their ghetto, any of them that wants to, but just let them leave us in peace."

Florensky's metaphor of a deathly trunk with poisonous branches polluting the gentile world. Again, the two Pauls are at loggerheads.

Florensky continues: "I repeat that although the relative percentage of Jews is growing, still with horrifying and dizzying speed it is increasing the implantation of Jewry into humanity. And sooner or later the percentage of Jewish blood in all nations will become so significant that this blood will decisively swallow any other blood, eat it up, as acid eats up paint. And for that, you yourself know, a significant percentage is not required…"

This then is Florensky's theory of Jewish blood. Oddly enough it corresponds almost exactly to that of Hitler's chief theorist, Rosenberg, against which Bulgakov later argued forcefully that to so construe blood is pagan, as it misses the role of blood as the locus of spirit. Quite how lacking in spirit this theory is we discover when Florensky remarks that the solution to the spread of Jewish blood would be castration – adding regretfully, "to implement which would be possible only if we denied our Christianity."

The last comment is, oddly, somewhat hopeful. If anti-Semitism is an illness, one can say that Christianity at least mitigates it somewhat. The path to a Hitlerite solution of the "problem" is blocked by Florensky's somewhat unwilling recognition that Christianity does not permit it.

Now Florensky comes to the famous quotation from a later section of Romans 11, that "all Israel will be saved." Comments Florensky: "Not 'spiritual' Israel, as the religious seminaries comfort themselves, alas, - *not* spiritual"[160]. No, Florensky understands the full mystery of this verse – that Israel in the flesh, St. Paul's blood family, will be saved as a matter of course, while "we will be saved – 'so', by the way." The promises of God are irreversible.

Are we about to see this same Christianity work wonders of mercy, hope and forgiveness? Will that gentle Sophianic spirit have a palliative influence? Is Jewry to be saved, in Florensky's books, and if so – how will he harmonize it with all he has said before?

Unfortunately, matters only get worse, and morbidly so. Yes, Jews will be saved – but in the earthly sense. That is, they will have world domination, which Christians will have to tolerate. This is the meaning of Paul's statement that all the previous promises to the Jews are in place. But these were *Old Testament* promises of earthly dominion – and apply only to the Jews. Florensky's task is to convince, and then comfort, his gentile Christian readers that the New Testament does not promise earthly domination, but only spiritual victory:

> The Old Testament talks of the future mastery of the earth by whom – the Jews. And the New? It is far from telling us Christians that this mastery will be transferred to us Christians, but only summons us patiently to bear our cross and promises salvation for that. One testament contradicts the

---

[160] Again there is an ambiguity here: "alas that it is not just spiritual Israel that will be saved;" or "alas that the religious seminaries think this."

other – but not because both say the same thing, but because they both say different things, and these different things are addressed to *different* people. And this deep and native divergence of both testaments, applied in the high heat of spiritual contemplation, as it was by the Apostle Paul, cuts and burns our wingless and flabby consciousness.

Thus, for Florensky Paul is saying that Israel will continue to have earthly world domination. By the "salvation" of Israel Paul understands fleshly dominion over the earth and spiritual damnation afterwards – for he is using his old Jewish concept of salvation which is utterly opposite to the New Testament concept of salvation. Again, we see the old polarity of the Testaments which Bulgakov criticized in his letters to Rozanov during these years.

The other problem is quite why Paul would be using this "Old Testament" concept of salvation here. After all, in the same chapter, he uses salvation[161] to refer to the gentiles finding Christ. In addition, even if the idea of a radically different Old Testament versus a New Testament concept of salvation were plausible, it is unclear why Paul, who is writing not as his old persecutory Jewish Sauline self but as Christian Paul, would be using his old conceptual artillery.

For all these reasons, it is hardly surprising that this interpretation whereby "Israel" refers exclusively to Jewry and singles out Jewry for a special type of non-spiritual salvation coupled with spiritual condemnation, is thoroughly opposed to the interpretation of these verses in patristic sources.[162]

Rozanov in his footnote, however, departs even further from the meaning of the Pauline text and its patristic interpretation. For him Florensky is too generous: he insists that Jewry is no longer chosen and will not be saved even in this limited earthly sense.

---

[161] Florensky's tortured interpretation of "salvation" here hardly needs refuting, but it may help to consider Rm.11:11-12: "The failure of the Jews has brought *salvation* for the gentiles, in order to stir them to envy. And if their fall has proved a gain to the world and their loss has proved a greater gain to the gentiles – how much greater a gain will come when all is restored to them!"

[162] Among the Church Fathers, to take four representative writers: 1. Cyril of Alexandria maintains that all of earthly Israel will be saved after the gentiles are called in; 2. Augustine says that all among the Jews and pagans who are predestined to be saved will be saved – i.e. for him "all Israel" means Israel out of the gentiles and Jews, who are destined to be called: thus while all Israel is not Jewry, Jewry has an analogous "salvational" destiny to gentiles. 3. Ambrosiast (mid-4th century) writes on this verse: "God will give back to the Jews the free exercise of its will, so that they will be purified and then saved, for their unbelief is not malicious, but due to confusion… He teaches that by the grace by which those Jews who believed were freed we too can become free – for it is not exhausted but is always running over." 4. John Chrysostom writes: "Inasmuch as you gentiles were called, the Jews became more stubborn. However, God even then did not cut off your calling, but is waiting until all of you have come in to whom it is given to believe, and then the Jews will come in as well." (Mark Sheridan, *Bibleiskie kommentarii*, 438.)

In all honesty, this dialogue between Rozanov and Florensky has to be read several times before the meaning sinks in. On first reading, one takes it that Rozanov is protesting against Florensky on the grounds that the latter is claiming spiritual salvation for the Jews. Then Rozanov would be saying that they will only be saved physically. The sheer mean-spiritedness of the discussion escapes one's attention to begin with. For, in fact, Florensky is saying that the Jews' salvation is merely earthly, and Rozanov wants to drag the stakes even lower, to deny them even that: "Not bodily, and not 'anyhow' will Israel be saved, but it will turn into bankers, in the hope, maybe that, in the house of Rothschild….their Messiah will be born…"

It is interesting to read a passage close to the end of the letter, where Florensky advises Christians on how to suffer this earthly domination of the earthly chosen people (taking it for granted that true Christians will be itching with mad envy to get their hands on this earthly salvation of the Jews).

Always "in the soul should be the joy of ultimate obedience" when confronted with Jewish success. In this sense, Christians find themselves in a Pale of Settlement of God's predetermination.

> We are the Egyptians, robbed and beaten and tortured; it is us whose "children's heads have been beaten against a rock" – and about this we sing *against ourselves* in our churches with angelic voices: "By the rivers of Babylon, there we sat and wept." We have but one comfort:
>> Though eternally with invisible chains
>> We have been shackled to these shores
>> Yet this circle we must complete ourselves
>> That the gods have determined for us.
> We must complete our circle of submission to Israel! Perhaps, you are the last Egyptian and I am the last Greek. And like hunted animals, we look on at "the triumph of the victors." Sooner or later they will take us beasts, perhaps the last beasts, and squeeze out our blood for kosher meat. But we must be obedient.

In sum, the old Gnostic-Marcionite themes are all there. There is the utterly disjunct Old Testament with its God making promises that Christ and Paul are unaware of (and yet elsewhere also somehow endorse). Then we find more Egyptian talk: the "robbed Egyptians" are the Egyptians whose gold (*pace* Rozanov) the Jews stole. In this Florensky ratifies the idea that the Jews in Exodus were thieves – as if God himself had not commanded them to take the gold for sacred purposes, while the Egyptians were the real heroes of the Exodus saga. Again, the super-sessionism of the Church Fathers had it the completely the other way round: the Church was the new Israel, and it was the Jews who were now Egypt or Esau. This is bold, and from a Jewish point of view, impudent – but its logic of a younger son replacing an older son emerges organically from the Biblical narrative.

Then there is the poem about "the gods," "determined" and Rozanov and himself being the last of the Greeks and Egyptians: this all shows a blindness to the message that St. Paul gives elsewehere: in Christ, there is no Greek or Jew, (let alone Egyptian). Paganness in *that* sense should have died in a Christian.

All this brings to mind the "consensus" we pointed to above concerning Florensky's Gnostic, occultist, pagan and non-Orthodox tendencies. The "mystery of Israel" that St. Paul referred to here is not even particularly mysterious anymore: with a Manichean dualism it has been cut clean in half – we Graeco-Egyptian gentiles good, them Jews bad – and left to dry.

Florensky's 'Kabbalistic scholarship'

By now, we have a full picture of Florensky's judeology. However, there is one more work of Florensky's that we will touch on: "'Ekhad': the thirteen wounds of Yushchinsky." Again, without going into Florensky's motivations in writing the text, it is a perfect example of arbitrary "scholarship:" all exotic, occult razzle-dazzle and no logic or argumentation. Details aside, all that needs to be said is that Florensky, applying "Kabbalistic" decoding to the thirteen (which in reality were fourteen) wounds on Yushchinsky's temple, manages to read on the boy's head the message: "This person was killed by blows to the head and chest as a sacrificial victim to Jehovah."

The text reads like a hoax, a parody of ill-informed pseudo-mysticism, and in another context with another goal in mind, the text could even have been humorous. Unfortunately, the dominant tone here is the sinister rather than the humorous element.

The article is illustrated with drawings of the murdered boy's profile, Hebrew characters, charts of the twelve sefiroth, and all the wonderful symbolist decorations that illustrate Florensky's magnum opus, *The Pillar and Foundation of Truth*, which came out in the following year. In other words, one can detect a certain common Florenskian style in this crypto-text of the philosopher, which lies like a shadow behind his public oeuvre.

In the thirteen (one gets lost) dots Florensky sees a three-pointed Hebrew *shin*; then he sees a geometrical pyramid. Linking the dots this way and that, and looking at the boy upside down, he gets the lower portion of a sephirotic diagram. From there, he manages to construct the other three quarters of that sephirotic tree and the letters for the sephiroth. A chart gives their word-meaning equivalent. And so on and so forth for twenty eight, time-consuming (for reader *and* writer[163]) pages…

With this, we have completed our examination of Florensky's judeology, and can return to the questions we started to discuss at the beginning of this section:

---

[163] In "It is necessary…" Florensky had complained of being tired and busy, thus not being able to express himself as well as he would have liked. (Rozanov, Vasily. "Nuzhno perenesti vsyo delo v druguyu ploskost'. (K delu Yushchinskogo)." In *Obonyatenl'noe i osyaznatel'noe otnoshenie yevreev k krovi*, edited by A.N. Nikolyukin. Moscow: Respublika, 1998.)

How do Florensky's "Jewish writings" fit in with his larger thought? Was Florensky, like Rozanov in this period, deliberately writing consciously false propaganda for political purposes? Are these texts an example of Christian anti-Semitism?

Florensky: the broader context
Occultism and magic

The answer can be given as follows: in many ways, a closer examination of Florensky's non-Jewish writings reveal that they do have a close relationship with the works just examined. Critical opinion in Russia has long been aware of Florensky's attraction to the occult, the Gnostic, the Masonic even, the pagan, and the neo-Platonic. As far as "loose scholarship" is concerned, Florovsky's appraisal of Florensky reads like a mild understatement when we consider *Ekhad*:

"His historical references are always accidental and arbitrary. With a sort of groundless aestheticism he weaves his theological crown. For him, questions of historical criticism are not important…" It is not surprising to find out, then, that *Ekhad* actually makes no reference to real Kabbalistic works; all the information comes from compilations in French translations[164].

The reason for Florovsky's harsh judgment becomes clearer when we consider some of Florensky's other works.

In *Names*, for example, Florensky ties a person's nature to their name. A person's nature is further determined by their constellation. The sounds of "a name and in general the verbal image of the name reveal the distant consequences in the fate of the bearer of that name."[165] The deeper meaning of

---

[164] This point is made by Katsis in ch.13, *Krovavy Navet*, drawing on various analyses of K.Burmistrov.

[165] A direct link between Florensky's "public" philosophy and his crypto-Judeology can be found in Section IV of his *Detyam moim. Vospominanya proshlykh dnyei*. There he recalls how a family of Jewish smugglers lived in the courtyard of his parental home. As a childish prank, he once yelled the insult "Yid" at one of the Jewish women. When the offended woman stopped to rebuke him, he contemplated with amazement the magical effect of that monosyllabic word, and the story so recalled offers more evidence of the magical power of words and their ability to go the heart of reality: "…I felt in her rage a confirmation of the fact that the word 'Yid' really was a special word, full of magical strength and power….[which captured, as the word 'Jew' does not] the blackness of the gloom, sorcercy and horrors" that he believed to exist in the house of that Jewish family. Further, one of the men of the house was called Yankel, which also fitted its bearer due to its "poisonous sounds." (Cf. Pavel Florensky, *Imena*. (Moscow, Eksmo, 2008), 777-779.) These recollections were written in 1923. Again, it seems that the Jewish smugglers were indeed dishonest and suspect characters, but Florensky's merciless generalization of their case to the whole of Jewry and in terms buttressed by magico-Platonist linguistic realism is dismaying – as is the fact that he sees his childish beliefs not as ignorant prejudice but as deep "intuitions" to guide the unrepentant adult.

these sounds can be deciphered by folk wisdom, occult experience (of which Florensky liked to boast) and true artistry.

Another indication that caution must be exercised in regard to Florensky's larger (and not just "Jewish") heritage comes from Sergei Bulgakov, whom we cited as a spiritual brother of Florensky's at the beginning of this section. Matters were not quite as straightforward, however. For by 1922, Bulgakov is writing in his Yalta diary that Fr. Pavel had ceased to be a church authority for him. This was because Florensky had expressed the view that historical Russian Orthodoxy was flabby and frail and needed to be supplemented with ancient Hellenistic and medieval sources that were peripheral to the Church. He wished to build a new Orthodoxy, his own type of Orthodoxy.

Bulgakov writes of Florensky's magnum opus *The Pillar and Foundation of Truth* – which was written during the Beilis years, and published in 1914 – that "indeed, in that book there is *his* own Orthodoxy... And his Orthodoxy – with such hopelessness, in the sense that these things have not been dissolved, and it would seem, cannot be dissolved, namely his occultism, neo-Platonism, Gnosticism, - is not historical Orthodoxy, and is not Church Orthodoxy, as I naively believed all the time."[166]

Of course, Bulgakov himself struggled with the place of pagan philosophy and religiosity in Orthodoxy, and attracted similar criticism of his own works. While the jury is still out on the finer points of Bulgakov's sophiology, however, Bulgakov's intellectual temptations were confined to neo-Platonizing tendencies. Occultism and Gnosticism, however, are facets that appear again and again in criticisms of Florensky.[167]

Another worrying trend in Florensky's larger work can be seen in his political writings towards the end of his life.

This is part of that general idealization of childhood embraced by the magical worldview.

[166] *Avtobiograficheskiye zametki*, C.106-7. For the sake of balance, it should be added that Vasilenko, commenting on these judgments of Bulgakov, qualifies them by pointing out that Bulgakov may have been prejudiced at the time of this writing, due to Florensky's rebuff of Bulgakov's attempts to develop a closer friendship with him. It is true that in 1943 Bulgakov wrote an article in praise of Florensky, and full of sadness at the unknown fate of his friend (S.N.Bulgakov, "Priest Fr. Pavel Florenskii," first printed in Vestnik RSKhD, 1971, No.101-102, and reprinted in S.N.Bulgakov, Dela i Dni, Moscow: Sobranie, 208: 287-298.).This adds to the impression that Florensky – like Rozanov in many ways – was a truly enigmatic character, capable of evincing love and mistrust or suspicion in equal measure, in the same people at different times.

[167] One particularly harsh critic of Florensky is Gavryushin, a contemporary professor at the Moscow Spiritual Academy, who sees Florensky's work as entirely beyond the pale of Christianity. Cf. N.K. Gavryushin, *Russkoe bogoslovie:ocherki i portrety*. 'Borba za lyubeznuyu mne neponyatnost': svyashchennik Pavel Florenski.(Glagol, Moscow, 2005), 275-312.

Political totalitarianism
In 1933, he writes a book called *A proposed political order for the future*[168]. The perfect government, it turns out, is a dictatorship under the leadership of a benign father of a prophetic character (Stalin has been in power for nine years by then):

> As a surrogate for such a person, as a transitional stage of history, there appear leaders like Mussolini, Hitler and so on. Their historical appearance is functional, inasmuch they wean the masses away from the democratic mode of thought…The future structure of our country awaits someone who will possess intuition and will, and won't be afraid to tear himself openly away from the paths of government, party factions, electoral rights and so on…Whatever he is called – dictator, ruler, emperor or something else – we will esteem him a true absolute ruler and submit to him not out of fear, but through a trembling consciousness that before us is a miracle and a live manifestation of the creative power of humanity.[169]

The dream of perfect earthly power, the neglect of the creative power of all other persons except the leader – all this has a pagan, Greco-Roman ring to it[170].

In the same work, he ponders Russia's future, concluding that as regards the current political set-up, the chaos of Kerensky's Provisional government and the consolidation by leaders since then must be built on: "the order achieved by Soviet power must be deepened and strengthened, but in no way loosened in the transition to the new order…" Once again, this displays a worrying admiration of Soviet methods of rule and a dismaying blindness to the nature of Christian history if the hoped-for "new order" is imagined as being consistent with the Soviet reality.

A preliminary judgment can now be made regarding the place of Florensky's anonymous "Jewish" works within his larger corpus, and regarding the Christian nature of these works. In sum, the conclusion reached about the Jewish writings when we examined them in isolation is not overturned. Zooming out to the large context of Florensky's work does not reveal them to be a moment of regrettable aberration; there seem to be no mitigating circumstances which could make them more digestible: radically contradicting as they do the Bible and patristic sources in letter and spirit, they cannot be regarded as a Christian response

---

[168] Pavel Florensky, *Predlogaemoe gosudarstvennoe ustroistvo v budushchem. Sbornik archivnykh materialov i statyei*. Compiled by Igumen Andronik (Trubachaev). Moscow: Gorodets, 2009.

[169] P.Florensky, *Predlogaemoe gosudarstvennoe ustroistvo v budushchem*, quoted in Gavryushin, p.270.

[170] Of course it invites comparison with Plato's Republic, that part of Plato's opus – political homogeneity – which Christianity with its recognition of a basic Church-state duality could never assimilate. In this, Florensky's totalitarian theocracy is also related to Soloviev.

to Jewry and Judaism. Instead, they must be judged a neo-pagan reaction to the same. This is merely confirmed by the neo-pagan tendencies in works like *Names*, *Pillar* and *A proposed political order*.

The other question of whether Florensky wrote these Jewish works sincerely, or whether they were political propaganda, is harder to answer. I would speculate that he almost certainly did not believe that Beilis murdered Yushchinsky. However, his belief that a shadowy kabal of mystical Jews were responsible for the murder may have been held with the same self-hypnotic sincerity that characterized Rozanov's embrace of a similar position. As with Rozanov, though, he probably came to disown such a belief after the furore died down. But I would posit that he could quite consistently have held onto the Judeology that he constructed to justify that belief, even after the "facts" on which that theologoumenon were built had been shown to be false. After all, this Judeology is woven out of a similar fabric to his other works of mystical, not to say sophiological, theology.

I would add a further speculation, too: Florensky, the great admirer of Plato, may well have justified his propagandizing against the "Jewish danger" by recourse to Plato's own belief in the necessity of myth to convince lower minds of higher truths: in that case Florensky's Judeology would be a crude, but necessary, propagandistic effort that nonetheless incarnated higher spiritual truths.

Florensky's Judeology in some senses was the theoretical working out of a very early visceral distaste for Jews, so that it is unlikely he would have had a reason to change his beliefs. Again, however, the mystery of Florensky's personality once again confutes full understanding: here I refer to his friendship with Lev Davidovich Trotsky (Bronstein) in the years after the Revolution: the two of them were often seen driving round Moscow together in an open-top car, Florensky in cassock beside the uniformed commissar[171]. Apparently, a shared interest in occultism brought them together.

Still, those positive evaluations of Florensky's devotion to Christ, his inspiration of other people (at least initially) in the same direction, the great suffering he underwent for his faith, his courage in the face of Soviet power (and who knows, maybe he was trying to bring Trotsky in his own way to faith, rather as he struggled to do with Rozanov?) – this cannot simply be ignored in light of what we have learnt.

The only conclusion we can make is that Florensky was a deeply complex

---

[171] Florensky also liked to wear a Caucasian dagger on a belt round his waist, while in priestly dress. Quite how the dagger and the cross go together in a cleric is unclear. As regards Trotsky, one can see the benefits of having kept his racist, anti-Semitic propaganda anonymous; presumably Trotsky would not have been impressed. As far as Paul is concerned, cf. the contemporary Jewish scholar, Daniel Boyarin, for a thoroughly Jewish portrait of the Pauline corpus, and a recognition that Paul's argument with Judaism and Jewry was intra-Jewish. Daniel Boyarin, *A Radical Jew: Paul and the politics of identity*. California: University of California Press, 1994.

and contradictory man, questing tirelessly, energetically for the Truth. His Jewish writings are scandalous and painful, but a Christian reaction, I would hazard, is not to judge the writer, while at the same time being quite unequivocal that these writings must be seen to dwell in a cold, dark place far outside the goodness and depths of Orthodox faith.

Katsis and Florensky's 'Christian exegesis'
This brings us to L. Katsis' judgment of Florensky's "theology of the Eucharist." In *The blood libel and Russian thought*, Katsis writes as follows:

> Essentially, Florensky is solving his own problem of the relationship between the bloodless sacrifice and Orthodox communion, and for this he needs a Jewish antitype, who not only believes in the literal existence of an ancient Judaic ritual sacrifice that was not carried out in the Temple, but who 'smells and senses' real human blood. Only then can people of *Florensky's type* convince themselves that in their chalice is not wine and bread, but the Wine and Bread of the Lord....Obviously in Florensky's case we have an example of a *certain type of Orthodox ecstatic* self-hypnosis concerning the reality of the transubstantiation of the wine and bread into the Blood and Body of their Lord [italics, DR].

> Once again, we remind the reader that at the root of similar discussions there lies *a particularly Christian exegesis*, and the opinion of Jews is deduced not from the opinion of high priest Saul but from the epistle of the apostle Paul, addressed polemically, moreover, to Jews.[172]

These passages imply that Florensky's views constitute an acceptable, normal and well-grounded Orthodox Christian theology of Jews and Judaism. Katsis is in effect proposing a *typology* of Orthodox theologies of the Eucharist – generalizing from Florensky. If one were minded to continue Katsis' scientific work we might expand the typology to include on the one hand Alexander Schemann's *Eucharist: Sacrament of the Kingdom*, and on the other Florensky's "judeological" blood theology.

This should concern any Orthodox Christian. Katsis is making an extremely important claim and he does not pull it out of thin air. His self-declared concern is not to engage in Orthodox theology, for he is not Orthodox, but to describe what he sees in Florensky and Rozanov. In this he takes them at their word: for they are indeed claiming to be writing as Christians a type of Christian metaphysics, or philosophy, or theology of blood sacrifice in Christianity and in Judaism.

They appeal, as Katsis notes, to the New Testament to develop this theology.

---

[172] L.Katsis, *Krovaviy navet*, 358, 371. Quite where Katsis gets the idea that Paul was "high priest Saul" is not clear. This is not found on Florensky-Rozanov.

Hopefully, it can be agreed that not everything a self-identifying Christian writes and does need be seen as Christian. Further, the whole of the above analysis should have shown that Florensky is indeed "solving his own problem," but that that problem is a grievous personal temptation and the proffered solution, to paraphrase Katsis, is particularly *un*christian.

The flaw in Katsis' evaluation of Florensky's "theology" is that he believes Florensky and the New Testament have similar views on Jews and Judaism. For him, Florensky simply lifts Paul's anti-Semitic ideology from Hebrews which is "addressed polemically to Jews." The latter statement is partially correct, and what is more, Hebrews is one of the most supersessionist books in the New Testament.

The fact, however, is that supersessionism rests on the idea that the Old Testament was valuable in its time. Indeed, Christ is so valuable because he is even more valuable than the very valuable divinely ordained Jerusalem temple. Paul the Jew understands this, which is why he understands just how great Christ is. It is precisely this theology that Florensky contravenes.

There is another strange misreading of the New Testament in Katsis. He quotes Florensky's introduction to the anthology *Jews in the past, present and future*:

> In fact, what decisions are we hearing? It's either philo-Semitism or anti-Semitism. But who would dare to argue with the philo-Semites that "salvation is from the Jews" (Jn.4.22) and that all that is most valuable in humanity's heritage – we mean Revelation, both New and Old Testament – was given through the "chosen people"? The Jews considered and consider themselves the core of the world and their destiny the axis of history. Can one argue with that?

Here Katsis detects a rare philo-Semitism in Florensky and he comments: "…here for the first time we see Fr. Pavel paying at least a little bit of attention to the position of Jews themselves, without being dictated to by one or another New Testament position of their accusers from the Christian camp."

The problem here is childishly simple. Katsis has overlooked the fact that the crux of Florensky's observation comes not from paying attention to "Jewish self-perception," but through quoting from what some consider to be the most anti-Semitic book of the New Testament, the Gospel of John. "Salvation is from the Jews" is quoted and attributed by Florensky precisely to John.

The fact is, of course, that John (and the other New Testament books) are all Jewish books. Thus Katsis' dichotomy is further flawed: the idea that "salvation is from the Jews" and that this salvation is Jesus Christ is also a part of "Jewish self-perception" of the end of the first century a.d.

Today there is a consensus in New Testament scholarship[173] that early

---

[173] Admittedly, there is a still a broad diversity in opinion regarding the origins of Christianity. On one end of the spectrum T.N.Wright sees even Johanine

Christianity was a Jewish sect whose fundamental doctrines and rites (including the Eucharist) were utterly Jewish. Furthermore, the anti-Jewish rhetoric in the New Testament is an intra-Jewish affair. Thus Katsis' "accusers" with their "New Testament position" are Jews engaging in polemic with Jews. The claim that (Jewish) Christians are the true Israel was on a par with the claim that the Pharisees and not the Sadducees, the rabbinites and not the priests, the Qumranites and not the Jerusalem priesthood, held the key to scripture. This is not an accusation from a position of power, but intranecine struggle for Truth. To equate this with the Florensky-Rozanov judeology is to seriously muddy the waters.

In mitigation, it must be said that gentile (and often Jewish) Christians have frequently forgotten this. But this very obliviousness with regard to the indisputably Jewish heart of Christianity is what leads to that gradual unraveling of the different strands of which Christianity is composed, until – with envy, pride and various other human failings added to the stew – the kind of pseudo-Christian ideology we find in *Olfactory* is born – the parasitic offspring of genuine faith, which to employ a slightly Florenskian metaphor turns round and cannibalizes its mother, leaving very little of Christianity left at all. Given the frequency with which this anti-Semitic degradation has occurred in Christian history, Katsis' analysis is a reminder to Christians to watch themselves – though of course his work will doubtless be a provocation[174] to those who cling to this type of poisonous and self-destructive ideology.

Florensky's position in Russian religious thought: 'name-worship' and neo-Platonism
This section on Florensky has labored the point that his Judeology is unchristian and anti-Christian, partly because both Jews and Christians again and again miss this.

However, in concluding, we will consider two separate insights from L.Katsis and S.Khoruzhy concerning the significance of two major events in Silver Age thought which both overlapped: the Beilis trial and the Athonite "name-worshiping" controversy. This will enable us to point to more widespread problems in the relationship of Russian religious thought as a whole to Orthodox Christianity, and the way in which Florensky's departures from Christian dogma,

---

Christianity as thoroughly related to Jewish institutions. But a writer like G.Vermes sees the Johanine language used to describe the Eucharistic rite as already far removed from Palestinian Jewish sensibilities. However, even Vermes accepts that Johanine Christians were predominantly of Jewish ethnicity, albeit of Hellenistic origin, whose polemic against "the Jews" was thus intra-Jewish. Cf. Vermes (2000) and (2003).

[174] Katsis's work has already stirred up predictable reactions in such elements. Cf. M. Nazarov, "Yevreiskie skazki: 'Krovavy navet' s sugubo pravoslavnoi tochoi zreniya. Retsenzia na knigu Leonida Katsisa 'Krovavy navet i russkaya mysl'." http://www.rusidea.org/?a=440406*navet

while extreme, can alert us to a broader tendency in the movement in Russian thought of which he was a central part.

The "name-worshiping" controversy lasted from 1911-1914. In essence, a doctrine concerning the powers of the divine name had reached the Caucasus and then Russia at the beginning of this period, and in the following years would ignite controversy over its theological significance.

The actual doctrine had originated among the Russian monks of Mt.Athos, who claimed that it was a development of the Palamite doctrine of the divine essence and energies. In the form in which they preached it, the doctrine quite simply held that "the name of God is God Himself." Thus pronunciation of the divine name, Jesus Christ, in the Jesus prayer guaranteed the unification of man and God, or what is called in Orthodox theology, deification.

Katsis correctly points out that many Silver Age theologians, including Florensky, supported those who defended the name-worshipping doctrine. Given the chronological overlap with the Beilis trial, he concludes that this arcane Christian mysticism is related to that mystical anti-Semitism which Florensky propagated in his Judeology.

However, Khoruzhy presents a quite different picture of the significance of name-worship for Russian thought. He sees in the support of Florensky, Bulgakov and Losev for name-worship a transitional moment where Russian all-unity moved from its Solovievian roots in a Platonic panentheistic orientation to a neo-Platonic "energetic-essentialism."

This seemingly technical change in philosophic outlook is, in fact, vastly significant for an appraisal of the relation between Florensky's name-worship, the magical and Gnostic trends in his thought that we have just examined, his relationship to Jews and Judaism, and finally, his – and other "symbolist" theologian-philosophers' – relationship to Orthodox Christian theology. The distinction will enable us to link common elements in the thought not only of Florensky, but also of other thinkers that we have examined, or will examine, in these pages: Gershenzon, Rozanov, Khodasevich, Bulgakov, Bely, Karsavin, Ern and Steinberg .

For as Khoruzhy shows in detail[175], by 1913 the name-worshiping doctrine had been rejected by the leading Greek theological institute, the Khalki theological school, for being an innovation incompatible with the Palamite doctrine agreed on at the local council of 1351 regarding the dogma of the divine energies.

That Florensky and other Moscow philosophers did not see "any difference between hesychastic practice and the pagan mysticism of neo-Platonism, between neo-Platonism and Orthodox energism, says a lot," according to Khoruzhy, about the state of that philosophy. In other words, in the given case, Florensky's support of name-worship is once again – *contra* Katsis – not a sign

---

[175] Sergei Khoruzhy, "Imjaslavije i kul'tura Serebryanogo Veka: fenomen khristianskogo neoplaotonizma," in Khoruzhy S.S. *Opyty iz russkoy dukhovnoy traditsii* (Moscow: Parad, 2005), 287-309.

of his particularly Christian orientation, but a sure sign of departure from Orthodoxy.

The distinction between the Palamite and the neo-Platonic outlining of the essence/energy relationship, which needs to be understood so that this departure can be appreciated, can be summarized as follows.

Neo-Platonism (in Plotinus' works) added to the Platonic concept of the divine essence the Aristotelian concept of the divine energy. The energy was said to be an emanation of the essence, and directly related to it. In the Christianized version propagated by the "Moscow school" (and having roots in the writings of pseudo-Dionysius), if the Divine name is taken to be the energy of God, then it can be assumed that this name contains the essence of God. By logical extension, the name contains the essence of God. Thus any repetition of the divine name in prayer involves a unification of the human essence with the divine energy (= essence). In short, repetition of the Jesus prayer involves a person's essence in unification with God's essence.

Losev and others justified this doctrine with reference to point 5 of the 1351 Council, which anathematizes those who assert that "The Name of Divinity is spoken only about the divine essence and…is not applied to the divine energy." From this they deduced that the divine energy is as fully divine as the divine essence (a true deduction that accords with Palamism), and that the Name of the Divinity is as divine as both – which is thoroughly unfounded, not only grammatically, but theologically, for the Divine name is a created reality.

Palamism, by contrast, makes several contrary assertions. Firstly, the relationship between essence and energy is different in the Trinity than it is in created being. In created being, essence and energy do not correspond. If a creature strives to unite with God, he can only do so by uniting his energy to the divine energy – and never to the divine essence. Furthermore, in doing so he must leave behind his fallen, created essence and become "de-essentialized."

His deified energy must then constantly strive to transform his fallen essence; there is no guaranteed process by which the human essence can once and for all become deified. In other words, the union of man's energy with the divine energy is at constant risk of falling back into sinfulness: and this is where the constant watchful *ascesis* of hesychast tradition can never be relaxed in the painful process of human deification.

In the new Russian Christian neo-Platonism, however, the essence of God meets the essence of man in verbal symbols. As Khoruzhy points out, this obviates the need for ascesis, for it assures man of an automatic union with God. In addition, the essence-energy fusion of pagan neo-Platonism erases the creator-creature gulf of Biblical theology.

In a conclusion which can only sound deeply ironic in the context of this chapter, Khoruzhy writes that Moscow neo-Platonism and name-worshiping ardor are based on a pagan fear of the Numinous, before which human freedom is radically reduced, so that "synergy" – the Eastern Christian term for free co-operation between man and God – simply becomes a mechanical, automatic fusion with the name of God as such. But this in fact deprives man of a real relationship with God which can only be found, as in the apostles, with a personal relationship with Christ.

As such, the impersonal, mechanistic name-worshiping philosophy

> as a cult of the Name departs from this initial foundation in the direction of other, more ancient images, that do not know the presence of the Divine Incarnation. The closest of these archaic images is of course the Old Testament one, as well as the later Judaic cult of the Holy Name. The rapprochement with this cult, which recognizes in name-worship a Judaic, or so as to recall the historical connection, a "Judaizing"[176] archaization of Orthodoxy, was demonstrated in my earlier works…

Name-worship and symbolism: a Judaizing, Hellenizing or syncretizing 'heresy'?

However, Khoruzhy merely adds admirable precision to what had already become apparent. Soloviev had admired the all-encompassing power of Talmudic theocracy, and even striven to implement something similar in his theocratic campaign of the 1880s. Florensky's all-embracing theocracy took on a totalitarian hue; in addition, in his neo-Platonist "worship of the name," he really did come to most closely resemble the more magical streams in Kabbalistic or Hasidic thought, whose *baalei ha-Shem* ("masters of the name") believed that through manipulation of the Hebrew alphabet they could move the divine spheres[177].

In the next two chapters, we will be looking at the work of Karsavin, Steinberg and Frank. In this respect, Khoruzhy's comments about the connection between philosophic pagan "energo-essentialism" and literary symbolism are highly suggestive, and should be considered in the same context as Florensky.

Khoruzhy quotes an extract from Andrei Bely's 1928 manifesto, "Why I became a symbolist," where the novelist describes the idea of "concrete monism, leading to the search for not even 'synarchy', but to a study of the rhythms of social syn-rhythmism or syn-ergy… - but syn-ergy is 'sym-bolia', or that symbolism on which my thought has been working." Thus Bely displays

---

[176] The word I have translated as "Judaic" is "iudeystvuyshchi," and the word I have translated as "Judaizing" is "zhidovstvuyushchi" (i.e.the name of the 15th century heresy).

[177] In the Lurianic liturgy, the worshiper recites a prayer for the unification of the two halves of the tetragrammaton so as to unite mercy and judgment in the fulfillment of the goal of creation; other Hasidic and Kabbalistic prayers aim to influence the workings of other *sephirot* (spheres) in the heavenly economy. Khoruzhy points to the contemporary French Christian movement of Alfonse and Rachel Goettmann, which combines name-worshiping theological elements with Jewish Name mysticism.

in literary form the strong belief that the divine Word is a "throwing together," or a "fusion," of the divine and human essences and energies: the divine Word *is* the human poetical word – the literary equivalent of the doctrine that "the name of God *is* God."

Bely is a central figure in the network of thinkers we are examining. In his student years, he corresponded with Florensky, and together they worked out a "concrete metaphysics" for the symbolist movement. But Bely was also friends with Gershenzon – whose own religion of the Divine Word and divine-human creativity shows obvious affinities with Florensky's philosophy of the Name. In addition, Bely was later to become friends and a close collaborator with Aaron Steinberg, who himself developed a philosophy of "concrete, or prophetic, idealism," which was based on a fusion of man with the divine Logos. To complete the circle, the poet Osip Mandelstam, born Jewish but then – in Averentsev's phrase – "baptized into Christian culture," was deeply influenced by Florensky's philosophy.[178]

Finally, Khoruzhy's thesis about the name-worshiping turn in neo-Platonizing all-unity must be applied back to Bulgakov, who wrote a tractate on the *Philosophy of the Name* at this time. Khoruzhy argues that Bulgakov's sophiology was another variation on energo-essentialism, for Sophia is depicted as "the unfolding world of the Divine energies"[179]. Moreover, for Khoruzhy the significance of the "dispute over Sophia" launched by V.Lossky and G.Florovsky is that "it was that field of meeting on which the departing stage of Christian neo-Platonism collided with the next stage of neo-Patristics that was coming to replace it" – thus, for Khoruzhy, returning Russian religious thought to its genuine Orthodox Christian roots[180].

---

[178] For further discussion of Mandelstam, cf. Konstantin Antonov, "Problema samosoznaniya yevreev-khristian." Diaspory No.3 (2004):168-190.

[179] In '*Ipostas i ipostasnost'*, quoted in Khoruzhy, "Imjaslavije…."

[180] Another contemporary attitude to the divide between (neo-)Platonizing Russian religious thought and the historicist rejection of this tendency in Florovsky's and others' neo-patristic synthesis is that of A.V. Sobolev. Although he accepts that the name-worshiping doctrine was false to historical Orthodoxy, Sobolev does not see a sharp conflict between the "wings" of Russian thought. He discusses the dispute between Florensky and Florovsky: in 1914, the former rejected the latter's "Orthodoxy in its essence" for his journal *Bogoslovskii vestnik*; the latter, as we saw, wrote a harsh review of Florensky's "groundless aestheticism" in his *Puti russkogo bogosloviya* twenty five years later. But for Sobolev, nonetheless, the two thinkers meet: "If Fr.Georgiy was moving towards the ontological centre from the direction of history, then Fr.Pavel approached it from the direction of language." [A. Sobolev, "Radikalniy istorizm otsa Georgiya Florovskogo," in A Sobolev, *O Russkoy Filosofii*. St Petersburg: Mir, 2008.] In our chapter on Bulgakov, we also mentioned the work of Nikolaos Asproulis (Asproulis 2009) who contends that Florovsky's neo-Palamite theology also blurs the distinction between God and world. If Asproulis and Sobolev are right to see a continuity between Palamas, Florovsky, and the "Moscow School," then some of the criticisms directed against "Symbolist pantheism" would have to

Khoruzhy makes the further point that the name-worshipping quasi-dogma was also embraced enthusiastically by certain sections of the monastic community in Russia – and he puts this down to the monks' infection by the same Russian folk-magic reverence for the word as a magical object. This magical tendency in folk Orthodoxy was something that Florensky glorified, but again, in its direct contradiction with Palamite dogma as established by the 1351 council, it is clear that its roots are not Christian.

Nonetheless, Khoruzhy's comments that Florensky was part of a "Judaizing" tendency in Russian thought, while they have a nice irony, would need to be qualified. Firstly, much Hasidic mysticism was frowned on by the *mitnagdim* (opponents of the Hasidim), as we commented in chapter one. Secondly, much of the Kabbalah contains Greco-gnostic and neo-Platonic influences: to that extent, it can be argued that it contains non-Judaic imports into Judaism. Thirdly, most of the distortions in Florensky's neo-Platonism are based on ancient pagan neo-Platonism – so to call them "Judaizing" is pejorative, as well as confusing for it implies a use of Jewish sources that has not yet been fully established.

Still, having said all this, through his Solovievian sophiology, and his own dabbling in – what he took to be – Kabbalah, there is at least some Judaic, or quasi-Judaic, element in Florensky's thought, which does distract from a

---

be directed at them too. Such an outcome would lead to yet another picture of the relationship between Jewish and Christian mysticism.

Another (massive and highly comprehensive) study of the Name-worshiping controversy is Hilarion Alfeyev, *Svyashchennaya tayna tserkvi. Vvedenie v istoriyu i problematiku imyaslavskikh sporov*. St. Petersburg: Izdatel'stvo 'Aleteia', 2002. Alfeyev devotes chapters to Florensky, Losev, and Bulgakov. Alfeyev points out that most (but not all) Church Fathers were opposed to an equation of God's name and essence; he believes that some of Florensky's and Losev's positions were acceptable and conducive to further, especially philosophical, development. He points out how there was much heated polemic in the debate, with ignorance of the real positions of opponents evinced on both sides of the debate. Stereotyping of opponents' opinions sometimes took place without the actual works having been read. Still, Alfeyev concludes that as regards Florensky, his position really was "much more radical in its essence" than other approaches held in the name-worshiping camp (this is an endorsement of a quote from another scholar) and that "the accusations of a 'magicalist' orientation made by Troitsky against the name-worshipers can seem fully justified if addressed to the name-worshipping position of Florensky." In his chapter on Bulgakov, Alfeyev shows that Bulgakov's own position was far more subtle, and indeed based on Palamas' distinction between the divine essence and energy. Thus, in this matter too, Bulgakov and Florensky diverged. (Alfeev, in the interests of fair-mindedness, quotes Losev's defense of Florensky's "magicalist orientation" – Rus. *magizm* – that the term "magic" in Florensky means not only "black magic," but the "white magic" of the Christian mysteries. Whether this is a plausible defense is a moot point, especially considering his explanation of the Eucharist explored here. Cf. *Svyashchennaya tayna tserkvi*, Tom 2, pp.111-129; 145-161.)

focus on Christ. However, whether this has any genuine relationship to Jewish mysticism as practiced by Jews is a different matter.

In fact, in this regard Burmistrov's[181] analysis of Florensky's Kabbalistic knowledge renders the situation somewhat odd. His conclusion, not surprisingly given what we have seen of "Ekhad," is that despite Florensky's claims in his lengthy bibliographies to be making use of original Hebrew works, analysis reveals that he in fact followed a narrow handful of poor second- and third-hand translations used by Western occultists who themselves had a meager knowledge of Jewish kabbalah.

This much we have seen. But Burmistrov shows that despite this garbled knowledge, as far as his name-worshiping mysticism is concerned, Florensky as it were *co-incidentally* converges on the 13th century "Name-mysticism" of Abraham Abulafia, and indeed of other Jewish Name-mystics, who as Scholem wrote, believed that the divine Name (the tetragrammaton) "represents the concentrated power of God himself, and this power is expressed in the name" so that (to use Burmistrov's expression now) "the one who contemplates the Name with inner sight communicates with the Divine itself."

This typological similarity of Florensky and the Athonite name-worshipers with Abulafian and Hasidic veneration of the tetragrammaton would need further investigation. However, scholars have long been aware that Abulafia borrowed some of his "sephirotic" terminology from Maimonides[182], who in turn was immersed in Arabic neo-Platonism. The influence of Greek numerology on Palestinian rabbis' use of gematria (Hebrew numerology)[183], another devise that Florensky resorts to, is also well-known. All of which shows that the above qualification must remain in place: to assert that Florensky was a "Judaizer" is to beg the question, when his sources were second-order, Christianized and occulticised versions of "Hellenized" Jewish mysticism[184].

---

[181] Konstantin Burmistrov, "The interpretation of Kabbalah in early 20th-Century Russian Philosophy. Soloviev, Bulgakov, Florenskii, Losev." *East European Jewish Affairs*, Vol.37, No.2, August 2007:157-187.

[182] For the sources of Abulafia's mysticism, see: Moshe Idel, *Language, Torah and Hermeneutics in Abraham Abulafia*. New York: State University of New York Press, 1989. Or Moshe Idel, *Kabbalah. New Perspectives*, esp. ch.1, for a survey of Jewish and non-Jewish scholarship on and reactions to the Kabbalah from the very first "appearance" of the Zohar in the twelfth century, claiming to be the work of second century mystic R.Simeon bar Yochai, up to the twentieth century.

[183] A good survey of gematria can be found on the Jewish virtual library, which points to the prior existence of the method of gematria among the Babylonians and Greeks, and quotes the Talmud to indicate that probably the first Palestinian Jewish gematria made use of Greek, not Hebrew letters: "Its use was apparently introduced in Israel during the time of the Second Temple, even in the Temple itself, Greek letters being used to indicate numbers (Shek. 3:2)." Cf. jewishvirtuallibrary.org, entry for "Gematria."

[184] Here, of course, I am making generalizations of a somewhat apologetic nature: I do not wish to imply that Jewish thought stops being Jewish if it contains Greek

Iosef Davydovich Levin: "I met Florensky once...."
We know little about the conversations Florensky shared with Trotsky as they drove round Moscow together. Rozanov's intended introduction of Gershenzon to Florensky never, it seemed, materialized as the two fell out before this. And yet some of our curiosity concerning what a Jewish conversation with Florensky might have looked like is satisfied by the brief reminiscences of a I.D.Levin[185], a thinker whose fate both shared and diverged from that of other Russian religious thinkers. In this section, then, we will briefly allow a somewhat different voice to express itself in regard to Florensky – a Jewish voice, that is, which unlike Steinberg, Mandelstam or Gershenzon, came to be separated from the orbit of his "concrete metaphysics" and his occasionally suspect mysticism of all-unity.

Levin recapitulates much of what was said later by Khoruzhy, Gavrushin and Hagemeister. But in the context of this book, Levin's critique is more interesting. For, firstly, he was a Jewish philosopher confronted with the challenge of Christian belief thrown down by Russian religious philosophy – there are thus continuities with Shestov, Gershenzon and Steinberg. But secondly, he lived in the Soviet Union until his death in 1984 – and this gave him a quite different insight into the destiny of Russian philosophy and life than his émigré fellow-thinkers.

Levin was born in 1901 into an Orthodox Jewish family in Warsaw, which was immersed in Jewish and non-Jewish culture: the family spoke Polish, Russian, Yiddish and Hebrew at home. In the nineteen twenties, after time spent in Odessa, he was studying philosophy at Moscow University, and visiting the formal and informal Moscow lectures of Shpet, Frank, Vyacheslavtsev, Berdyaev, Ilyin, Bely, and on one occasion, Florensky. His reminiscences of Florensky were set down in an article written a half-century later and called "I saw Florensky once...."

---

philosophic elements, or that Christian thought stops being Christian if it contains Greek or Judaic elements. The whole question of influence is extremely complex and, as concerns evaluation, goes beyond objective scholarship into the realm of faith values. Still, in this discussion I attempt to restore a bit of balance, for the "Judaizing" perspective assumes that Judaism and Jewish sources are monolithic and do not themselves contain multiple influences often from Greek and even Christian sources. This simplification is convenient both for Jewish and Christian purists. On the other hand, it would also be false to reductively assert that Kabbala is simply neo-Platonism: the roots of Kabbalah very likely go beyond its emergence in written form in the twelfth century to a native Jewish mysticism that stretches all the way back to Ezekiel's visions of the fifth century b.c, with their possible Chaldean input. In addition, of course, Jewish mystics contributed their own genuine mystical experiences to any sources they may have used, in the same way that Christians made use of Greek philosophical categories to articulate their faith and mystical experiences.

[185] Iosef Levin, "Ya videl P.Florenskogo odin raz," in *Russkiy Put': Pro i contra. Entsiklopedia russkogo samosoznaniya.* At: http://russianway.rchgi.spb.ru/

On that one occasion, Levin was impressed by the philosopher's icon-like face. But as soon as Levin became acquainted with his theories of Ptolemaic cosmology and the physical location of heaven, "unwillingly there arose in great confusion the almost blasphemous question….put forth by Florensky himself: face or mask?" Levin's own philosophical development was partly devoted to resolving this conflict between the seeming beauty of Florensky's philosophy and its acerbic attacks on the foundations of philosophy, and indeed, all of Western culture.

Unlike most of his august philosophical mentors, Levin did not leave the Soviet Union and lived and worked in Moscow until his death in 1984. His public career was taken up with teaching and researching jurisprudence. But even jurisprudence was not a safe avenue in Soviet academia: in 1949, he was stripped of his teaching post as being one of the leading "cosmopolitans" in jurisprudential science. Meanwhile, his private life was dedicated to the type of philosophy he had learned from the 1922 expellees. His disquiet with Florensky's contradictions would lead him eventually to converge on a metaphysics which differed considerably from the premises of Russian religious philosophy – of which, for Levin, Florensky was particularly representative.

By the nineteen sixties, Levin's thought had matured. Although he came from a religious family, he came to reject religion as the best means of seeking truth, seeing it as inferior to philosophy. But he was not hostile to religion, in either its Jewish or Christian form. His time spent among the Russian God-seekers had introduced him to Christian thought, and a life then spent under a fanatically atheistic regime had in fact given his regard for Christianity a positive and unambiguous edge, which, as we saw, was blunted in the outlook of Gershenzon and Shestov.

He also differed from Shestov and Gershenzon in maintaining respect for his native Judaic tradition. He thus achieved the rare perspective of looking with benign equanimity on both traditions, and indeed equating them. For him "the victory of Christianity in the Greco-Roman world was a great revolution of the spirit, which confirmed in the people's consciousness the superiority of the spiritual principle – both in man and in existence itself. This consciousness was based on an immediate experience of the spiritual principle by the prophets of the Old Testament (Zecharia's 'not by battle, or strength, but by My spirit'), and Jesus and the apostles."[186]

And yet that equanimity was based on a recognition that "the Christian, or more broadly, the Judeo-Christian (including the Pharisaic-Talmudic) worldview was and remained pre-philosophical, weighed down with a naïve materialism and mythology."

This is the viewpoint from which Levin eventually came to appraise Florensky, whose "ontology…remains in total at the level of pre-philosophical thought. Not of course because he did not mature to the philosophical level,

---

[186] Ibid.

but because he outgrew it, outstripped it, rejected it….." Florensky's rejection of philosophy was particularly connected to an attack on the Renaissance, and it is in this anti-Renaissance attack that Levin saw the most dangerous propensities of Florensky's worldview, and by extension, the worldview of Berdyaev, Frank and Bulgakov who also traced the incipient rot of Western society to this juncture.

Levin, writing in the Soviet Union of the 1970s, launched a piercing critique of this view. He saw in Florensky's rejection of the liberal society of the West the same totalitarianism that had spawned the society in which he was forced to live. Three premises attracted his dissent: firstly, he was not convinced that "the morality of the society of non-consumption, or even more so, of need, is purer" than that of consumer, capitalist societies. Secondly, Florensky's attack on scientism had turned into an attack on technology. But this assumed that enslavement to manual labor (where man and labor are cruelly identified) was better than enslavement to technology (a situation of alienation). While the latter enslavement may be damaging, Florensky's Luddism ignored the fact that manual labor was also a result of Original Sin, and the sentence for man to work by the "sweat of his brow."

Thirdly, Levin critiqued Florensky's idea that social problems could be solved by religious belief. But for Levin this was to turn belief into a tool for social engineering. In addition, the example of societies where traditional religion was still strong (the Muslim world and Latin America) did not show noticeably higher levels of morality than non-traditional societies. Finally, Levin accused the religious solution of elitism: mystical intuition and religious experience were after all the prerogative of only a small elite. In his own inability to believe (as a Christian, and as a Jew), one feels, he had felt the exclusive effect of Florensky's system.

His own solution was to accept the Renaissance revolution of the spirit which had produced an open society. Levin conceded that the West had suffered from religious wars after the Renaissance. But, by contrast, "Holy Russia turned into a country of mass atheism, while the countries who 'overcame' the Renaissance have nothing to repent of." Instead, those Slavophiles who rejected the West contributed to the stagnation which finally led to atheistic revolution; and their posture of rejection had nothing positive to teach Russia.

Looking back on the hopes of Russian religious philosophy, Levin saw it as growing out of the same dangerous soil. In those days, he recalled, there was too much emphasis on "sobornost," wholeness, and de-personalisation[187].

---

[187] It is interesting that Levin links sobornost' and depersonalization – usually considered by Russian religious philosophers to be inversely linked. This correlates with some of Asproulis' criticism of All-unity, under which rubric he places Florovsky's thought. For Asproulis, all-unity distracts from the person of Christ, and Christian personalism is better found in the thought of the Cappadocians. Berdyaev, on the other hand, is closer to Levin: he linked the flourishing of the person and freedom to a rejection of the architecture of all-unity.

There was an extremism in ideas: people demanded the absolute truth, and if they could not attain it, they went running to an equally extreme materialism. Hence Florensky's anti-modernist religious option and the Marxist option were connected for Levin – as they were for Bulgakov and Berdyaev, but in a very different way.

Thus Levin came to see in Florensky – standing in some sense for Russian religious philosophy as a whole – a dangerous elitism, and a rejection of realistic human goals, which shared an affinity to the totalitarianism of the regime that ultimately turned against him. Having rejected metaphysics, having rejected Descartes' Cogito for his own Credo, Florensky had failed to show that his own answers were any less subjective. And Levin was of the opinion that metaphysics was, at least, inter-subjective, depending as it did on the collaboration of fellow philosophers.

As for elitism, Levin maintained that metaphysics by keeping alive the eternal questions of human life, could eventually transform a whole society – as had happened to Germany in the time of Kant and Hegel. And he detected in the turn of positivism towards Platonism[188] a sign that in the West people had come to feel that need for the ultimate again. Why, he asked, should we believe Pascal's assertion that faith was given from above and that reason was human? Why not assume the reverse – that reason was given from above and faith implanted in themselves by humans? In sum, Levin concluded of the transformative powers of metaphysicians: "Ten righteous men could not convert Sodom, but their presence would have been enough to save it from God's wrath."

In this belated critique of Florensky, one cannot but see an oblique continuation of that Russian Jewish-Christian conversation that took place more directly in the earlier generation of which Florensky was part, and of which Levin was initially the child. Indeed, Levin's roots go all the way back to the Westernisers of the early nineteenth century, and form part of that heritage of Russian-Jewish Westernizing, whose partisans have often struggled to make their voices heard in the Russian arena. In a sense, some of Levin's critiques of the totalitarian orientation of the totalizing strivings of all-unity can be found – as an internal critique – in the work of Semyon Frank, whose work will be examined in chapter six.

In sum, while Levin's critique makes no mention of Florensky's anti-Semitism, his voice – the voice of a Jewish, liberal "cosmopolitan," as he came to be labeled by the totalitarian Soviet regime, in ways not dissimilar to how Jewish liberals were seen by some under the previous authorities – confirms us in the anxiety that the connection between mystical all-unity and exclusion of the Jewish Other, found most strongly in Florensky, but also to a lesser extent in Bulgakov, Soloviev, and other thinkers, may be too close for comfort.

---

[188] This is how he perceived Popper's positing of a "third world;" the movement in psychoanalysis from Freud through Jung to Fromm; and the reintroduction of metaphysical architecture in the existentialism of Jaspers and Heidegger.

And in that sense, Levin's critique of Florensky might be very useful for Christian thought even now. Indeed, a contemporary Orthodox theologian of eminence, Bishop John Zizoulias, has voiced concerns that even now pagan Hellenistic ontological monism may not have been adequately overcome in Orthodox thought. He asks whether "ontology can do anything more than rest on the idea of totality"[189]. While pointing out that the Greek Fathers made important steps towards solving this problem, he also opines that "here Christian theology can benefit considerably from E.Levinas' remarkable work *Totalité et Infinité*."

Zizoulias makes no reference to Russian thought, but the dynamic here is identical: he is appealing to a Jewish thinker (Levinas), who incidentally drew much inspiration from the Talmud, to rethink the concept of Otherness both within God (the relation between Persons of the Trinity), and as concerns the relationship of God to the world.

From this, we can only conclude that the voice of the "outsider" continues to be necessary for the well-being of the "insider" – in our terms, that an examination of the dialectic pull between Florensky and Levin can be of great interest for Russian Orthodox thought today. In the next chapter, we will provide further perspective on this assertion, when we examine the interaction of Karsavin and Steinberg.

Christianity and anti-Semitism: final words

All this still leaves the question of why Florensky and Rozanov were so vehemently anti-Semitic. Neither their Christianity, nor their neo-paganism fully explains it. Here, we have tried to defend a rather minimal thesis, namely that according to patristic and New Testament logic their anti-Semitism does not cut the ice.

But then an obvious objection arises: if Christianity is so philo-Semitic why have so many Christians hated Jews? We have seen one answer to this: primitive Jewish Christianity contains strong intra-Jewish anti-Jewish sentiment. This heritage has been used by later gentile Christians – due to self-doubt and envy – to construct a broad anti-Jewish ideology. Once the self-doubt and envy are absent (a tall order for humans, of course, as Christianity is the first to admit), there is little reason why one would want to create a wholescale *Christian* anti-Jewish ideology.

This, in turn, leads to the thought that if Rozanov's and Florensky's anti-Semitism cannot be derived fully from their Christian or neo-pagan beliefs (the latter in the case of Rozanov coincided with his pro-Jewish phase), then there might be a different underlying cause. To determine such a cause is far beyond the remit of this book. Nonetheless, the contemporary Israeli author A.B. Yehoshua[190], has offered the fascinating and controversial thesis that the

---

[189] John Zizoulias, *Being as communion*, London: Dartman, Longman & Todd, 2004: p. 86.
[190] Avraham B.Yehoshua, "An attempt to identify the root causes of anti-Semitism,"

root of anti-Semitism is to be found in the virtual or indeterminate identity that Jews possess in the non-Jewish mind. Yehoshua's starting point is the book of Esther, which recounts the genocidal anti-Semitism of a people and time that long predates the rise of Christianity and Christian anti-Semitism.

For present purposes, whether one accepts Yehoshua's thesis in full or not, the case of Esther should warn against explaining even the anti-Semitism of an Orthodox priest by reference to the dogmas of his religion[191]. There might be a far deeper process triggering such hatred, which a Christian merely justifies using those dogmas. As we have seen, however, the mismatch between that hatred and those dogmas is great; and the dogmas even serve to put a limit on the ultimate genocidal striving of such hatred[192].

Of course, if one were so minded one could try to create a more "Orthodox" anti-Semitism than Rozanov and Florensky managed. Perhaps one could say that the Jews, having rejected Christ, have fallen back to that stage of human sacrifice that the Law weaned them from. But how could one say this of Jews who continue to observe that Law? As for secular Jews, one would have to start resorting to theories of a genetic heritage that predisposes them to evil and so on and so forth, in which case one is already crossing over to that type of Gnostic all-knowing speculation that we have seen ends in misery and, to put it bluntly, is a waste of Christian time and energy. Better to hate, and not justify the hatred with a cooked-up ideology. At least that leaves room for repentance.

Probably, the lesson is that we should not expect an end to anti-Semitism any time soon – including the "Christianized" variety[193]. Berdyaev was no

---

AzureOnline, Spring 2008, No.32.

[191] Another influential Israeli figure to whom we made reference before, Yeshayahu Leibowitz, is more negative about the link between Christianity and anti-Semitism. For him, the Pius XII's refusal to intervene on behalf of the Jews was not due to a positive hatred of Jews: for him the Church clearly forbade murder. However, since its beginnings Christianity has had a wish that Judaism and Jewry disappear, and when Hitler appeared this wish could be fulfilled simply through inaction. Cf. Leibowitz, "Hochhut's error," in Leibowitz (1995). This point of view is thrown into question to some extent by Bulgakov's theology in support of Jewish continuity, and the activities of his spiritual children to put this theology into effect by rescuing Jews. Though, again, it must be admitted that Bulgakov's main concern is a revived *Christian* Judaism, rather than Judaism and Jewry *per se*.

[192] This cast doubt on Ruether's well-known thesis about the strong link between Christology and anti-Semitism.Cf. especially, Ruth Ruether, *Faith and Fratricide. The theological roots of anti-Semitism*. New York: The Seabury Press, 1974. It would seem that Christology is not the problem – though it can historically certainly be made a part of the problem, so that constant caution is necessary. Indeed if parishioners accept the Christian "justification," then *ipso facto* Christianity has contributed to anti-Semitism.

[193] Yehoshua posits in his essay that the state of Israel, by making Jews determinate

doubt right in several senses: anti-Semitism is a sin as is any hatred. He was right too when he said that Christianity is indeed anti-Judaistic, however this is construed: it is not surprising that this merges into an already existing anti-Semitism. Most probably, all Christians have to work through a phase of envy towards their elder brother, much of whose house they are inheriting without his full consent.

Again, some of the Church Fathers recognized this situation of fraternal rivalry but related to it with hope. When Jacob, having stolen his brother Esau's blessing and been driven out of the land by him, returns to Canaan he fears Esau's reaction. But Esau, seeing Jacob's great riches rejoiced for him and "ran to meet him and…threw himself on his neck and wept as he kissed him (Gn.33:4)." For Cyril of Alexandria[194] this is a prophecy of the day when Esau (the elder brother, now the Jews) will appreciate the wealth of the younger brother (the Christianity of those gentiles who usurped Jewry) and run to be reconciled with him. The encounter will end with a kiss of peace.[195] This interpretation, which reverses

---

and identifiable, rather than dispersed and anomalous, will end anti-Semitism. His critics have already pointed out that this implies a rather intolerant attitude to the existence of the diaspora, and one can only concur that to ignore the diaspora is to ignore vast chunks of Jewish history and identity, including the events surrounding the very birth of the Jewish people (i.e. Abraham's migrations).

[194] Cyril of Alexandria, the great defender of a mystical theology of Christ's incarnation and Mary's status as the Mother of God, lived in a mixed pagan-Christian-Jewish city where ethnic tensions were rife. His situation is not dissimilar to that of the Silver Age thinkers in the Russian Empire. He was also embroiled in a "Jewish scandal:" some historians have asserted that he led a mob to attack the Jewish community of the city; others contend that he headed a delegation which got out of his control. Considering this strife-filled background, his optimistic and hopeful comments regarding Jewish-Christian reconciliation could be looked at in different ways – either as an indication that theology does not impact on life, or – as I would prefer to think – that the temptations of the flesh (the deepest layers of one's self-identity, here ethnicity and confessional belonging) frequently confound good intentions. One must also remember that the imbalance of power between Jews and Christians was for various reasons (a third faction, pagans, made for a different situation) not as great then as in tsarist Russia, and the pattern of anti-Judaism morphing into anti-Semitism was not as clearly discernible as the intervening sixteen hundred years has made it.

[195] M. Sheridan (ed.), *Bibleiskie kommentarii*, 279-80. As the previous footnote indicates, the anti-Judaism of the Church Fathers who are here contrasted with the anti-Judaism of Rozanov and Florensky, is of course not free of problems itself. This is a separate question. However, if we take another patristic work, Justin Martyr's *Dialogue with Trypho the Jew*, whatever one ultimately want to say about Justin's anti-Judaism, it is still traceable to the Bible and is not directed against Jewry as a whole but only against Jewry's rabbinic leaders and their non-Christ-centred Biblical interpretation. He maintains the Law was given to the Jews because they were stiff-necked and sinful: but in Exodus, for example, it is indeed true that

the rabbinic identification of Jacob with Jewry and Esau with the gentiles, is – in our current age, before that end time – an impudence from the Jewish point of view. But as we said earlier, it must be admitted that it is Biblical impudence, i.e. a Jewish impudence.

For Christians, unlike say for those first secular Zionists, Jews will always be special. In that sense Rozanov and Florensky, even at their anti-Semitic lows, have not lost touch with Christianity.

And here we can add a final point. Florensky's writings about "Jewish blood" are certainly repulsive. However, if for a moment we try to abstract away from the hatred and read his Beilis writings as genuine attempts to understand passages of the Bible, we observe something interesting. Florensky really was grappling as a modern with texts of the Old Testament which are genuinely disturbing for any believer, Jewish or Christian. These texts – Yahweh's command to destroy the nations of Canaan, his instigation of animal sacrifice on a large scale, those portions of the Bible where there are indeed hints of a Yahwistic cult of human sacrifice – continue to provoke controversy and discomfort today.

The liberal answer, among Jews and Christians, was and is merely to dismiss these texts as belonging to another time. That answer infuriated Florensky, for it offended his sense of holism. Continued observance of religion while dismissing large parts of the foundation of one's faith seemed to him hypocrisy. Thus he found himself admiring those "real Jews" who continued to observe their traditional religion and took it with utmost seriousness. His own approach was also to take the Old Testament utterly seriously, and this then led him to return afresh, and with some shock, to the meaning of the New Testament.

From that point of view, his Jewish writings do contain that same ardent desire for truth, that same yearning for holistic purity which every modern dwelling in a disenchanted and alienated world world must feel. Florensky's

---

the mass of the people are not allowed to draw close to Mt. Sinai, they worship the golden calf, complain constantly and are not allowed into the land. This is a Biblical debate, therefore. Despite this harshness, it must also be remembered that: 1. for Justin the prohibitions of the Law are designed by Yahweh to counter specific Israelite sins, and Yahweh never at some esoteric-gnostic level condones what he prohibits; 2. Again, Christianity goes back to pre-Sinaitic Abrahamic religion, i.e. Justin looks to the Old Testament – with St. Paul – to find the real meaning of Christianity; 3. Justin is concerned for rank-and-file Jewry and opposes only the rabbinic leadership, even finding tolerant words for Jewish Christians who continue to observe the Law, as long as they do not encourage gentiles to do the same. All this shows that Justin's Christian anti-Judaism is a far cry from the racist unbiblical condemnation of the mass of Jewry and their Old Testament religion by Florensky-Rozanov. Cf. discussion in Mark Girshman, *Yevreiskaya i khristianskaya interpretatsii Biblii v pozdnei antichnosti*, trans. G.Kazimova. (Moscow: Mosty kultury, 2002).

yearnings were expressed in the form of that same philosophy of all-unity that other Russian thinkers embraced, and he shares much in common with them. The fact that his philosophy went so tragically awry can surely teach us something[196].

---

[196] The Romanian pre-War anti-Semitic Iron Legion, which grew out of the Brotherhood of the Archangel Michael, offers an interesting parallel to our Russian cases: as Shapiro recounts (Paul Shapiro, "Faith, Murder, Resurrection. The Iron Guard and the Romanian Orthodox Church," in *AntiSemitism, Christian Ambivalence and the Holocaust*. Ed. Kevin Spicer. Bloomington: Indiana University Press, 2007.) its leader, Codreanu, began to imagine himself in the role of Jesus Christ, and mixed this aura with an invocation of a cult of sacred Romanian ancestors protecting the nation. He quoted the poet Gheorge Cosbuc to the effect that Romanians were "descended from the Gods," and appealed to Legion members to use a sword against enemies of the nation. Ion Banea, one of the founder members of the Legion, hinted that the Legion was establishing a new faith, which though founded on Romanian Orthodoxy, was an improvement on it. All these elements indicate, on superficial inspection at least, that in the Romanian case, as well, anti-Semitism was a surface sign of a definite deep-rooted heterodox element in the Iron Guard's conception of Christianity, which tended in the direction of neo-paganism.

Five

L. Karsavin and A. Steinberg: Russia and Israel symphonically intertwined

Five

Two friends, two worlds

In 1928 the Russian emigration became privy to its own version of a public Jewish-Christian dialogue. The participants were Aaron Zakharovich Steinberg and Lev Platonovich Karsavin. The arena – for the debate was in print, not oral – was the pages of the recently founded Eurasian[1] journal *Versty*. Karsavin contributed his article "Russia and the Jews," and Steinberg's "Answer to L.Karsavin" followed on its heels.

Karsavin and Steinberg had both been living in Petrograd after the Revolution. However, while involved in similar movements (Steinberg was close to "Scythian"[2] circles and Karsavin was to become a Eurasian), they only became close in Berlin. In Petrograd, they had crossed paths only once when Steinberg introduced Karsavin as a speaker at the Free Philosophical Association (Volnaya Filosofskaya Assotsiatsia, or "Volphila")[3] of which he was academic secretary. Karsavin was ten years older than Steinberg, and as head of the history faculty at Petrograd University and author of a number of well-known historical works, he was more eminent and senior. Indeed, he was invited to lend weight to the budding Volphila's reputation. On the third anniversary of the October Revolution, he was asked to commemorate the birthday of Plato and discuss the work of the Florentine Academy in Renaissance Italy. This was a covert way of formally observing, while dissenting, with the official Soviet anniversary which it would have been perilous to ignore totally.[4]

---

[1] The nature of the Eurasian movement will be explored in some detail below.

[2] A movement which rejected the materialist orientation of Bolshevism and Marxism but saw the Revolution as unleashing the elemental spiritual energy of Russia's unique destiny. Literary theorist Ivanov-Razumnik and poet Alexander Blok were central figures. The latter's poem "Scythians" was a credo of the movement (it is prefaced by a quote from Soloviev: "Panmongolism – a wild name, but its sound is soothing to the ear!"). In exile, they set up a printing press in Berlin which was directed by Steinberg. Many of Volphila's members shared the Scythian inspiration.

[3] This should be distinguished from the Moscow-based Vol'naia akademia dukhovnoi kul'tury (Free Academy): the latter was founded by Berdyaev as an extension of a circle that originally met in his house and had included Gershenzon, Stepun and Aikhenvald. Frank later also partook in its activities. In 1921 A.Bely, G.Sphet and other professors founded a Moscow branch of Volphila, but Berdiaev's Free Academy was far more active in that city, drawing greater crowds from different sections of the population, and eventually its activity was what led Lenin to expel idealist-minded philosophers from the Soviet Union in 1922.

[4] Aaron Steinberg, "Filosofskoe sodruzhestvo," in Steinberg A. *Druzya moikh rannikh let (1911-1928)*, ch.2. (Paris: Syntaxis, 1991). For an overview of how the different spiritual and philosophical tendencies of tsarist Russia were faring after the Bolshevik

Two years later, the window of grudging tolerance extended by the Bolsheviks to dissenting voices had all but shut. Karsavin, after spending a month in prison, was exiled to Germany on the "Philosophy Steamer" in 1922. Steinberg had left for Germany of his own accord, sensing the growing hostility of the Soviet government to the Free Philosophical Association, which had led a precarious existence for five years. In Berlin, the two men met again and over the next fifteen years their friendship developed and deepened. Though Karsavin had not been a regular participant in Volphila, it turned out that there was much common ground between them. In particular, Steinberg and Karsavin were interested in philosophy of history as a way of arriving at metaphysical truth.

Both men debated the fate of Russia and Jewry in private conversations and the 1928 exchange was merely a public continuation of this personal dialogue. Karsavin's own philosophical-historical conceptions are not a bad way in which to understand the nature of this personal-public debate between the Russian and the Russian-Jewish thinkers. He held that individuals and institutions are both "personalities" that evolve through self-expression, disintegration and a reunification which incorporates aspects, or "moments" of the lost past. If that is the case, Karsavin had certainly synthesized Jewish "moments" from his conversations with Steinberg into his understanding of Jewry; and Steinberg was saturated with Russian "moments:" the sharing of "moments" was what made their dialogue possible, and what led the two men to continue it after the *Versty* exchange. That exchange is a cross-section of a debate within a debate within a debate: in order to understand the different layers of this debate, therefore, and to gain a sense not only of those who were debating but of those who were part of the natural circles of listeners surrounding the debate, a certain amount of excavation work is necessary.

Karsavin also wrote – somewhat controversially – of nations, societies, institutions, parties, and on a lower level even conferences or friendships as having a personalistic nature: the individuals who comprised them, for a shorter or longer period, were their embodied moments. In the 1928 debate, we see an intersection of several such corporate "personalities:" the Jewish and Russian peoples, and the national movements within those peoples that were struggling to determine the future of those peoples. But we will start our excavation at a somewhat lower level.

To begin with, then, Steinberg and Karsavin were both moments in the "social, or symphonic, personalities" of the institutions and movements to which they belonged and contributed from roughly after the Russian Revolution until the end of the twenties. Steinberg, by his own admission, had thrived in the atmosphere of Volphila where from 1919 to 1922, philosophers, writers and artists had tried to work out a different approach to the meaning of life than

---

victory in the Civil War, cf. ch.4 of Stuart Finkel, *On the ideological front. The Russian Intelligentsia and the making of Soviet Public Sphere.* (New Haven, Yale University Press, 2007).

that proposed by the sterile Marxism-Leninism of the new regime. Karsavin, in turn, had become the public theorist of the Eurasian movement in 1926 and would fulfill this role until 1929. In a certain sense, in the voices of Steinberg and Karsavin can be heard the larger voice of the creative collectivities which they represent. When Steinberg met Karsavin in Berlin, he expressed amazement and regret that the two had not developed deeper ties in Petrograd, as Karsavin seemed so close to the "spirit of Volphila."

Again, applying Karsavinian notions (and as we shall see, they overlap with Steinberg's own characterization of historical processes), the 1928 public exchange was also a "moment" destined to be lost to the disintegrating tide of history – both personally and socially. For since his emigration, Steinberg had begun to focus his energies on Jewish history and destiny: putting Russian matters to one side somewhat, he immersed himself in the task of translating Simon Dubnow's ten-volume *History of the Jewish People* from Russian into German. So when Karsavin tried to persuade him to take a more active part in the Eurasian movement, which in many ways was close to Scythianism and the "spirit of Volphila," Steinberg declined, saying he would only do what God sent him. Typically, with penetrating kindness Karsavin liked this answer and did not press Steinberg further[5].

Karsavin, for his part, was shortly to relinquish the uncomfortable and for him, as it turned out, deeply unsuitable role of theoretician-in-residence of the Eurasian movement. The movement itself took a sinister turn in the next few years, becoming increasingly pro-Soviet and finally ending its life as a propaganda tool of the Soviet government. By that time, Karsavin had already abandoned the hothouse atmosphere of Russian emigrant life in Western Europe for a teaching position in Lithuania.

Steinberg's parents were from Lithuania originally. Karsavin's move to Lithuania encouraged them to move from Moscow back to their home-town. Meanwhile, with the rise of Hitler Steinberg had moved to London, where he became more involved in Jewish communal and cultural activities. Until shortly before the Second World War (their last meeting took place in 1937), he combined visits to his parents with visits to Karsavin, and their friendship survived in this way until world events interrupted it.

The continuing friendship is another example of the way in which the "moments" of the past rearranged themselves into a slightly different configuration. Karsavin's own position on Jewry, as expressed in "The Jews and Russia" softened somewhat under the influence of his conversations with Steinberg. Indeed, the position put forth there is already a softening of the position towards Jews he had embraced before meeting Steinberg in the first place.

Before examining the 1928 *Versty* exchange between Karsavin and Steinberg, it is worth tracing the ideas of both men back to their origin in Russia, to those

---

[5] Steinberg also commented in self-exoneration that he was already a living Eurasian: in Europe he was an Asian, in Asia a European.

critical five years from 1917 to 1922 when thinkers, writers, artists, critics and dramatists of different stripes were still fighting for possession of the Revolution. For a time before the death of Lenin and the ascent of Stalin, it was just about possible to be dedicated to the Revolution, while not belonging to the Party and not espousing Marxism.

In an earlier chapter, we looked at how Nicolai Berdyaev rejected the anti-Christian false utopianism of the Revolution, and saw in Mikhail Gershenzon a typical Jewish embrace of a poisonous paradise on earth. For a while the trauma of the Revolution had caused him to converge on the position of Bulgakov, whose conservative views he generally disdained. For Bulgakov, the destruction of the sacred monarchy was the work of revolutionary "Yids" – by which he meant secularized, deracinated Jews who had succumbed to and were spreading rootless internationalism.

Steinberg and Karsavin partook in similar debates in post-1917 Russia and then in Germany. However, Steinberg's person and views confound the simplistic analyses of Berdyaev and Bulgakov. Here was a religious Jew, proud of his Jewishness and his Judaic faith, who combined traditional practice with a radical belief in the potential of the present to improve the lot of humanity. He was a Russian Jew whose memoirs and philosophical work is saturated with love and admiration of Russian literature and philosophy. He was a Jew who claimed to be the first Russian to hail Fyodor Dostoevsky as Russia's national philosopher. And he did it by denying Dostoevsky's anti-Semitism, and instead claiming him as an Old Testament prophet!

Karsavin is also a problematic figure for the Berdyaev-Bulgakov consensus (and they stated the consensus in relatively mild terms, compared to White propaganda). He made his reputation as a historian of medieval Catholicism. A historiographical expert in the Western middle ages, he nonetheless wrote extremely negatively about Catholicism, accusing it of being distorted Christianity.[6] He was an admirer of Soloviev's philosophy of organic all-unity, claiming Soloviev's Orthodox heritage over his Westernizing phase. With ironic self-referentiality, professor Karsavin used to lecture at St Petersburg University sitting below a portrait of Vladimir Sergeyevich – the irony being that Lev Karsavin bore a striking facial resemblance to his philosophical hero, replete with wild hair, beard, black eyes and Grecian profile.

And yet: this seeming Orthodox neo-Slavophile could write in his 1924 magnum opus *The Philosophy of History* that the Bolshevik government was "the best power out of those now possible in Russia."[7] Debating the interaction of personal and collective factors in the unfolding of the historical process, he poo-poos the idea that Bolshevism was a foreign import, a narrow cadre of revolutionaries far-removed from and violently opposed by the popular

---

[6] Lev Karsavin, *Katolichestvo. Otkrovenija blazhennoy Andzhely*. Tomsk: Izdatel'stvo 'Vodoley', 1997.

[7] Lev Karsavin, *Filosofia istorii*, (Khranitel', Moscow, 2007), 460.

spirit of the Russian people. He cites the idea that the Revolution really got going after the Germans sent dissatisfied exiles back to their homeland in "lead-coated trains," and dismisses it contemptuously as a candidate for real historical causality.

Bulgakov, we remember, was one such devotee of the "lead-coated" theory that holds that history is enacted by a few powerful personalities. Bulgakov was also keenly interested in the idea of a Jewish conspiracy, which was another variation on the theme, namely that a small coterie of (Jewish) individuals was driving the massive engine of history single-handedly. Karsavin's statements of understanding vis-à-vis the Bolshevik regime that had just exiled him did not go down well in certain sections of the émigré community: Berdyaev and I.Ilyin expressed the opinion that Karsavin was devoid of Christian sensibility; his application for a post teaching theology at Bulgakov's St Sergius Institute was rejected in favor of George Florovsky, perhaps due to the taint of such statements and his Eurasianism.[8]

However, Karsavin was not as distant from his elders (Bulgakov and Berdyaev, being ten years older, belonged intellectually at least to the previous generation) as this might indicate. As Steinberg recounts in his recollection of their friendship, Karsavin too had a weakness for denouncing the Bolshevik Yids in Moscow: Steinberg, however, saw these statements more as a case of *étaper le proletaria*t (to coin a phrase), i.e. speaking out against the ruling power that now controlled Russia. In Karsavin's own mind, too, this was a case of speaking truth to power rather than expressing enmity to Jews as such. Nonetheless, such statements earned him the reputation of a reactionary in other quarters and they indicate the extent to which Karsavin was saturated in the same cultural anti-Semitism as Bulgakov and Berdyaev.

This developing picture of Karsavin's and Steinberg's world view becomes still more complex when we bring into the equation Steinberg's own brother, Isaac-Nachman Steinberg. At first glance, he was one of those archetypical "Yids" whom Bulgakov must have had in mind in his diary pronouncements concerning the year 1917. Isaac Steinberg had been a long-time member of the Left Social Revolutionary party before 1917, and had been imprisoned numerous times by the tsarist regime for his activities, as well as exiled. For five months after the Revolution he held the post of "narkom" (people's commissar) of justice in Lenin's government, finally resigning in protest due to the signing of the Treaty of Brest. Having fallen into disfavor, he was exiled again, this time by the Bolsheviks in 1922, joining his younger brother in Berlin.

But was the brother of Karsavin's friend really a godless Jewish commissar, wielding power in Moscow and with a like-minded cabal destroying Holy

---

[8] Florovsky – a former pupil of Karsavin in St Petersburg – was one of the founders of the Eurasian movement, but had disowned it for its un-Orthodox orientation by the time Karsavin joined. Berdyaev also had a closely related philosophical bone to pick with Karsavin, regarding the latter's theory of collective personality, which he felt set up a series of hierarchical barriers between the free contact of the individual with God.

Mother Russia? Was he a revolutionary atheist who had fallen far from the tree that produced the religious Aaron Zakharovich, a destroyer of tradition and traditional values? Not all. In fact the intellectual biographies of the two brothers are fairly similar. In his own recollections, Isaac Steinberg recalls how when he was people's commissar, he would wait scrupulously for the appearance of three stars in the sky that marked the end of the Jewish Sabbath before returning to his work duties.[9]

The two Steinbergs thus confound the conservative[10] division of Jewry into a friendly, if misguided, religious core of "Jews" versus the dangerous, still more misguided, atheistic, assimilated "Yids" - a distinction made in different ways by Bulgakov, Florensky, Rozanov and Metropolitan Anthony Khrapovitsky. Here are two Jews, completely dedicated not only to Jewish religion (and as we will see culture), but also to Russian culture – and in the case of one of them, the Russian Revolution. Karsavin for his part confounds the neat picture of Orthodox intellectual who denounces the Revolution and its many Jewish supporters for its destruction of sacred Russian values. He sees the Revolution as coming organically out of the Russian people; and he also has room for a positive evaluation of some of its activities. This is why Aaron Zakharovich and Lev Platonovich found themselves occupying much common ground as their respective exiles kicked in in Berlin.

Of course, Karsavin and Steinberg were only anomalous from a certain point of view, which we dubbed the Bulgakov-Berdyaev consensus.[11] In fact, however, for the circles to which they belonged their positions were far closer to a mainstream position. To adopt Karsavinian language again, they were "moments" (or components, or "qualitations") in a wider whole, compressed expressions of that whole, and linked to each other by being part of that whole, or at least by partaking in the striving towards that whole. Again, à la Karsavin, it is interesting to note that the whole of which they were part has itself "disjoined," "distintegrated" under pressure of the world events that separate our epoch from their epoch. Whether it is in the process of regeneration, only time will tell.

Eurasianism, Volphila, Autonomism

Specifically, Aaron Steinberg was part of the Volphila in post-Revolutionary Petrograd. Karsavin became involved in the Eurasian movement. Both of these movements were "modernist" in that they saw the developments of the

---

[9] He was nicknamed "the narkom in a tallis:" no doubt for some this would have been an almost unbearable provocation, a symbol of all their deepest fears about Jewry.

[10] As we noted before, a distinction which to some extent united Russian conservative Christians *and* Jews.

[11] The label is merely for convenience; as we saw Berdyaev was himself later to depart from that consensus, drawing closer to Karsavin (and Gershenzon's) own position of limited toleration for some aspects of the Soviet Union. A similar continuity is seen in Florensky's anti-bourgeois monarchism and later "neo-Soviet" picture of a future totalitarian utopia – as G. Fedotov noted in his critique of Berdyaev's new post-1945 position.

twentieth century as presenting unprecedented opportunities for the spiritual, political and creative development of humanity. Both of them welcomed the fall of the old Russian imperial regime. Both of them cautiously saw energy and potential in the Revolution. Both of them thought it was not too late to put the Revolution back on track as a great tool in the historic service of greater (and not just Russian) humanity.

Both Volphila and Eurasianism were rather vague about what form a re-appropriated Revolutionary heritage should take, and both movements contained a great and often contradictory variety of opinion. Both, however, were certain that Marxism was a straitjacket and room had to be made for "spiritual" values, whether anthroposophic (as in the case of the Steinerian Andrei Bely), violently anti-humanist (Blok) or through post-Kantian "concrete idealism" (as in the case with Steinberg himself).

In addition, after Volphila's failure (in the sense that the Revolution ignored and crushed this fleeting attempt at diversity and re-appropriation), Steinberg put his energy into a Jewish movement which has to be seen as continuing his efforts at Volphila. He became the German translator of Simon Dubnov's *History of the Jewish People*. Dubnow was the spokesman for Jewish Autonomism, which believed that Jews should not emigrate to Palestine as the Zionists proposed, but staying in Europe retain the status of nation within a nation, which for all practical purposes was the position of Russian-Polish Jewry from the nineteenth century until the First World War.

Isaac Steinberg – after his expulsion from Russia – chose a similar ideological orientation to his brother, becoming spokesman for the Territorialist movement which advocated autonomous settlement of Jews in an uncontested corner of the world: as his moniker "the Australian doctor" indicates, it is clear where his choice settled eventually. Both brothers were therefore advocating cultural and religious creative development for Jewry in synergy with the surrounding nations, and without rejecting the contribution of the diaspora. The choice of literary language is indicative of their beliefs: both Steinbergs expressed their ideas in German, Russian and Yiddish. Aaron Zakharovich would later use Hebrew and English – after the war and the Holocaust – but this triad of languages speaks eloquently of their vision of an integrated, though distinct, diaspora Jewry.

Turning to Eurasianism, it becomes clear that it overlaps to some extent with Jewish Territorialism/Autonomism. It was started by four Russian exiles of roughly Steinberg's age in 1922 in Sophia, the Bulgarian capital: a theologian, George Florovsky; an economist, Peter Savitsky; a musicologist, Peter Suvchinsky (later Karsavin's son-in-law); and the world-renowned linguist, Prince Nicolai Trubetzkoy.[12] All four were scions of Russian aristocratic

---

[12] A friend and collaborator of the still more renowned Russian-Jewish structuralist linguist Roman Jakobson, who in a sense was forerunner of Chomskian generative linguistics, now so fashionable in North America.

families imbued with a long tradition of social conscience[13].

Trubetzkoy launched the movement with his article "Europe and humanity" in which he accused Western Romano-Germanic culture of aggressive Eurocentrism. Its patronizing, positivistic world-view was heartless and if followed as a model by developing or colonized nations would only distort their development. The solution was a regeneration of culture and an alliance between Russia and the nations of Asia against Western European liberal politics and culture[14]. Though all four of the first Eurasians were Orthodox Christians, Trubetzkoy always insisted that if the Russia-Asia alliance was to be real, religion should be left out of its platform.

Writing later in 1935, Trubetzkoy explained his position: including Orthodoxy in Eurasianism would have meant giving a foothold to Russian chauvinism which had always seen Orthodox Russia as a leader of servile dependents. Nonetheless, he intended for the movement to be permeated with a general "Eastern" religious spirit, consisting of: "self-limitation, consciousness of one's transient nature, one's connectedness with the order of the world, one's subordination to inscrutable laws prescribed by the will of the Creator, one's powerlessness in the face of His omnipotence, one's limitedness in the face of His infinity, and one's ignorance in the face of His omnipotence. Only on this basis can there be a unity of Christians, Muslims, Jews, Buddhists and shamanists."[15]

One can see why Aaron Steinberg would have seemed like a good candidate for Karsavin's Eurasian proselytizing in Berlin. In 1919 Steinberg gave a lecture at Volfila[16] called "Development and disintegration in contemporary art"[17], which was a critique of the practical reason of contemporary humanity, in words which strikingly anticipate Trubetzkoy's three years later. Steinberg's special target was also the "average European" petty bourgeois philistine, who has been made an object of technological and political manipulations. This "new type of man" strives towards pure objectivity and sees himself as a scientific fact, but has been

---

[13] See A. Sobolev, *O Russkoy Filosofii*, (St Petersburg: Mir, 2008), 163-220 (studies in Eurasianism).

[14] As far as democracy was concerned, Trubetzkoy thought it was fine for developed nations but that a stricter, centralized non-democratic form of government was better for non-developed countries due to the inefficiency of democracy.

[15] Letter of N.S.Trubetzkoy to P.N.Savitzky, 17 Nov.1935, quoted in Sobolev (2008), pp.223-4.

[16] In the following exposition of Steinberg's thought I draw on Vladimir Belous's three remarkable volumes editing the records and minutes of the Volphila sessions, as well as giving descriptions of people and themes discussed at Volphila. These are: *Volphila* 1. (Moscow: Tri Kvadrata, 2005); *Volphila* 2. (Moscow: Tri Kvadrata, 2005); and *Volphila, ili, Krizis kultury v zerkale obshchestvennogo samosoznaiya*. (Moscow: Mir, 2007).

[17] Aaron Steinberg, "Razvitie i razlozhenie v sovremmenom iskustve." Paper presented at 3rd open session of Volphila, 1 Dec.1919, in Belous V. *Volphila* 2, 591-608. (Moscow: Tri Kvadrata, 2005).

split into observer and observed, and ceased to see his own "I." The European has turned himself into a laboratory, examining not his free "selfness," but putting himself in the dock, judging himself with premature conclusions.

But since the First World War, the dream of positivism has crashed, and come to be replaced by pessimism. Nationalism has replaced internationalism; the fight against nature has degenerated into a fight of human beings with themselves. Only technology has triumphed, and it has turned not into a tool of creativity but destruction. The institution of the family has survived to some extent, though there are signs of decay there too. Humanity must find an organic, life-filled culture to face the present and the future. An intellectual basis for that culture can be found in Russian philosophy, especially as developed in the original, organic work of Russia's national philosopher, Fyodor Dostoevsky.

Steinberg, in fact, resisted Karsavin's overtures to involve him in Eurasianism. It should be clear, though, that this was not because of any lack of sympathy, but because his work with Dubnow took priority. In his 1928 *Reply to Karsavin*, he shows that he shares many Eurasianist premises, even disclaiming the need to work on the theory of Eurasianism, as being a Jew he is a Eurasian in practice: an Asian in Europe and a European in Asia. His decision to devote himself to "Jewish work" was thus not a rejection of Eurasianism or "Volphilism," but a continuation of it in different channels.

One could say that by working for the cultural revival of one Eurasian nation, Jewry, he was strengthening the larger "symphonic" body of Eurasia. The language I have chosen here, again, is somewhat Karsavinian, but the concepts Steinberg himself developed in Petrograd to describe unity, integration and historical development make it possible to switch between the philosophical dialects of each thinker while maintaining mutual comprehensibility. For Steinberg also wrote of a triadic development of humanity in his *The system of freedom of Dostoevsky*: the trajectory is from life (thesis) to consciousness (antithesis) to self-consciousness (synthesis). This is also conceived of as an initial plurality, followed by unity, and culminating in a synthesizing multiplicity-in-unity[18].

There are certainly differences in the philosophy of Steinberg and Karsavin, but what they share is also striking: a concern with all-unity (though Steinberg looks more to Dostoevsky, Karsavin to Soloviev) and a desire to transcend the merely objective as well as the merely subjective. The merely objective is the faux-certainty of Marxism, which hardly anyone at Volphila had time for. The merely subjective, however, was embraced by quite a few Volphilites and here Steinberg turned out to be closer to Karsavin.

Several of Steinberg's artistic and literary colleagues at Volphila gave priority to subjective, artistic insight and the prophetic knowledge of genius: the novelist Bely and the poet Blok are instances, but the literary critic Ivanov-Razumnik

---

[18] Vladimir Belous, "A.Z.Shteinberg o smysli istorii," in *Volphila, ili, Krizis kultury v zerkale obshchestvennogo samosoznaiya* (Moscow: Mir, 2007), 307-335; Aaron Steinberg, *Sistema svobody Dostoevskogo*. (Berlin: Skify, 1923).

also developed an approach he called "immanent subjectivism." Karsavin had attacked this trend in his 1921 article "The East, the West and the Russian Idea:" "Why should I believe the poetical intuition of A. Blok and his 'Twelve' (even without Ivanov-Razumnik's commentary)…Poets and publicists are an irresponsible people, who are not inclined to clarify the motives behind their intuitions. Perhaps it is all just subjective dreams…?"[19] Steinberg had retained enough of his systematic German philosophical training to be skeptical of this subjectivism as well: his and Karsavin's dialectical systems are united in their vision of a growth beyond the merely subjective; both of them see truth as being built communally. As Steinberg put it, true morality could only be collective – in Russian, *soborny* – morality.

This brief sketch of their philosophies shows how oddly similar their thought was even before they had become friends. And it is against this background of general agreement about fundamental concepts that the obvious disagreement about Jewry in the 1928 exchange should be understood.

In addition, given their philosophical belief in dialectical historical development, harmonic integration of parts, and the communal building of truth, it is no surprise that both men became involved in loosely political, or better, cultural-political movements with a trans-national orientation: Eurasianism and Autonomism. Nor is it surprising that it is possible to see the latter as a moment in the larger personality of the former. In principle both movements, the Jewish and the Eurasian, were integrated aspects of human All-Unity.

To state the matter in this way – in all its theory-laden glory, that is – is to come back down to earth with a jolt. A common criticism of metaphysicians of all-unity, from Soloviev to Frank to Karsavin, and Steinberg if one wants to include him here, is that they skate over the non-harmonious aspects of human existence. We will consider whether this is the case for Karsavin later. The criticism is germane here for a few reasons.

One reason is that co-operation between proponents of Eurasianism and Autonomism was not great *in practice*. This is because not many Autonomists were as immersed in non-Jewish culture as Steinberg. But there is another reason: while Eurasianism in its Trubetzkoyan form was open to Jews, Karsavin and others saw a place for Jews in Eurasia only once they had accepted Christianity. This is a point to which Steinberg responds in some detail in his "Reply to Karsavin." Finally, other forms of Eurasianism while accepting of Jews in the short term had a long-term vision of their ultimate assimilation: this was utterly in opposition to a basic tenet of Autonomism, which was to resist assimilation with all one's might[20].

---

[19] Cited in Beloous, 2007, p. 252.
[20] E.g. Svyatopolk-Mirsky, the "red prince," who was on the far left of the movement: he believed that Jewry would be regenerated through its "peasantification," which would lead to the removal of the economic causes of anti-Semitism, and hence to the complete assimilation of Jewry. He also considered Zionism the "most harmful type

However, another reason why the idea of a harmonious, higher co-operation between Eurasianism and Autonomism is somewhat fantastical is more brutal: both movements had evaporated by the end of the thirties. Eurasianism failed miserably to usurp the plans of Soviet ideology for Russia's (and the world's) future; and Autonomism was demographically and ideologically layed waste by the Holocaust. Its competitor, Zionism, replaced it completely in the attentions of the Jewish people.

So much then, one might imagine, for these grand visions of all-unity. And yet: Karsavin's triad of primal unity–disintegration-reunification, and Steinberg's triad of plurality, unity, multiplicity-in-unity make room for the notion of failure and dissolution – followed by resurrection and reintegration of dead moments of the past. In this context, it is interesting to note that Karsavin's work has attracted interest in contemporary post-Soviet Russia, both for its political and its philosophical aspects[21]. And recently, Steinberg's concept of a "Russian tribe of Israel" was the subject of an article by Russian-Jewish scholar, Nelly Portnova, in the Russian-Jewish monthly Lekhaim[22]. Given the constantly shifting geopolitical situation in the fates of Russia, Israel and the larger world it would surely be premature to conclude that the holistic philosophical-cultural-political ideas of Karsavin and Steinberg have completely seen their day.

If this is the case, then it is not just a matter of academic historical interest to inquire about the factors which prevented a harmonious integration of Jewish Autonomist philosophy into the Eurasian vision. It is also interesting to inquire why the transnational visions of Autonomism and Eurasianism did not survive the half-century mark. We can do this by finally focusing now on some details of Karsavin's and Steinberg's exchange.

The Karsavin-Steinberg exchange.
Karsavin
Much in the dialogue of the two friends recalls what we have seen in previous chapters. Karsavin's own position on the solution of the "Jewish question" recalls in outline Bulgakov's approach, hammered out more than a decade later. Steinberg's reaction to Karsavin turns out to show similarities to Franz Rosenzweig's analysis of the relationship between Judaism and Christianity[23]. What makes this dialogue more invigorating is that it was the fruit of eye-to-

---

of restrospective romanticism," overlapping with M.Gershenzon in this respect. On Svyatopolk-Mirsky, see Vadim Rossman, *Russian intellectual anti-Semitism in the post-Communist era*. Nebraska: University of Nebraska Press, 2008.

[21] E.g. V Kozhinov, "Chya Initsiativa?" *Nash Sovremmenik*, No.2. 2002; the work of S.S. Khoruzhy quoted in the present work; and the work of Y.Melikh.

[22] Nelly Portnova, "'Russkoe koleno izrailovo' Aarona Shteinberga,."in *Lekhaim* 4, April 2007.

[23] For a discussion of Rosenzweig's *Star of Redemption* and S.Frank's review of it, cf. ch.6.

eye contact. Indeed, one of Steinberg's opening comments is that "meeting is possible only when people do not glance to the side but look each other straight in the eye."

Certainly, Karsavin and Steinberg met eye to eye often enough, and while the exchange was in print, there is an "eye-to-eye" feel about it: it is not just Steinberg's epistolary format and intimate tone in addressing his friend (he starts his reply "Dear Lev Platonovich"), but one gets the sense of the spectators who were eyeing these well-known representatives of the different Russian émigré communities. Karsavin several times picks out sections of that audience, to explain an opinion or plead for tolerance and patience in letting him say his piece. "I beg the reader not to get overworked and ascribe to me a summons to pogroms," he adds at one point, after a call for Russia to resist cosmopolitan tendencies in Jewish culture.

The stalling of potential hecklers is understandable: the poet Bialik noted that in the early twenties Russian Jews and non-Jews mixed freely in Berlin; after the Civil War and the influx of White emigrants the lines between the communities hardened[24]. Karsavin himself was treading on sensitive ground in this respect, as he and the very first issue of the *Versty* journal had been the cause for a Jewish-themed mini-scandal, which makes his own opening words more comprehensible: "It is a fairly complex matter to mention Jews in the title and not to meet with accusations of anti-Semitism…"

What had happened was that the editor of another emigrant journal *Sovremenniye Zapiski* had written a review of the first edition of *Versty* and taken exception to Suvchinsky's declaration that Jewish participation in the socialist revolution would lead to a "splendid Jewish pogrom." He added that this was not very tactful in a journal whose editorial board included figures such as Efron, Shestov, Pasternak, and Lurie. The editorship of *Versty* denied any anti-Semitic intention or deed.

The debate then trailed off the pages of public journals and ended in a harshly sarcastic letter written by the histrionic poetess Marina Tsvetaeva – then residing in Paris with her husband Sergei Efron – to Karsavin and Suvchinsky, in which she contends that the two men's assertion that Efron was Jewish displays a greater keenness to sniff out a Jew than the tsarist military police. Sergei Efron, her husband, was baptized Orthodox and born to baptized parents[25], and grew up in a patriotic Russian environment. (Indeed he joined the White army).

---

[24] Semyon Frank, a baptized Jew, was himself the victim of such tensions in Berlin in the 20s; cf.ch.6.

[25] Tsvetaeva writes that Efron's father was Orthodox; without wishing to be tsarist it should be pointed out he was a Jew who converted to Lutheranism, a common choice of confession for Jews choosing baptism. Efron later became notorious for being an informer and spy for the Soviet secret service in France, becoming implicit in the assassination of a recruit who tried to leave the service. He was forced to escape to the Soviet Union where his family lived under constant persecution by the Soviet authorities.

By the logic of Karsavin and Suvchinsky, the Russian poet Balmont should be considered Scottish and Suvchinsky himself Polish, and so on. Tsvetaeva ends the letter: "P.S. I like Jews more than Russians and might have been very happy to have been married to a Jew, but – what is one to do – it wasn't to be."[26]

Tsvetaeva's charges and the motivations behind them are rather hard to fathom. After all, her husband was a member of the editorship of the very journal Karsavin was contributing to. What is more, it was the other journal that had labeled Efron Jewish. In addition, – Efron aside – the other members of this board were indeed Jewish and Karsavin and Suvchinsky were cooperating very amicably with them. Finally, as we saw, the Eurasianist movement of which the journal was a mouth-piece, was in principle also benignly oriented to Jews.

Against this background, it is clear that there were many toes on which Karsavin needed to avoid treading. Not everyone was as thick-skinned as Steinberg, who had voluntarily entered Rozanov's lion-den at the height of the Beilis affair. Perhaps in order to cater for his diverse readership, but also doubtless due to his historian's training Karsavin begins on a methodological note. He divides Jewry into three categories: core, peripheral-assimilating (half-assimilated) and peripheral-assimilated (completely assimilated). For him only the middle category of half-assimilated Jews is of real interest. These categories are ideal types[27], not empirical and Karsavin accepts that in reality they can mix. Later on, he blurs them more by accepting that the well-known unity of Jewish peoplehood, culture, history and religion binds representatives of these categories more closely together in real life.

He defines his categories as follows. At one extreme, core Jewry is immersed in religious-cultural Judaism. At the other, assimilated Jews belong to Jewry only due to the accident of a surname and facial features: other than that they have become Germans, Frenchmen or Russians, losing any cultural or religious ties with the Jewish people. Often they have changed their religion, and out of conviction, not cowardice. Really such people should not be called Jews and Karsavin will not discuss them. One can speculate that he had in mind men such as Semyon Frank, who was a Berlin acquaintance of Karsavin's.

This division is intended to avoid the sorts of problems we encountered in Bulgakov's writing on Jewry and in this sense are welcome. His discounting of assimilated Jews shows he does not believe in some Jewish essence that can never be escaped. He also – perhaps as a belated apology to Tsvetaeva[28] – makes

---

[26] Marina Tsvetaeva, "Pismo P.P.Suvchinskemu i L.P.Karsavinu," Bellevue, 9 March, 1927. At: http://www.tsvetaeva.com/letters/let_2ch.php
[27] Karsavin in his historical work invented the concept of the "average medieval person," "the average medieval charitable fund;" these are methodological idealizations of empirical realities. The French Annals school of history shares a similar historiographical approach. His division of Jewry seems to be similar.
[28] He also donated to her his large kitchen table before emigrating to Lithuania, a sign that this probably not untypical émigré spat had not ruined good social relations, and was not too out of the ordinary.

room for Efron to be a non-Jew. But the main advantage of his distinction, Karsavin believes, is that it exposes the absurdity of anti-Semitism directed indiscriminately at completely different types of Jews.

Karsavin points out that poisonous belief in a Jewish conspiracy, as exemplified in the forged *Protocols of the Elders of Zion* and the Beilis blood libel, is based on such category errors. Assimilating Jews who have rejected Judaism are depicted as holding to a stubborn belief in their own chosenness and superiority: but this is to ascribe to them a belief of core Jewry. On the other hand, religious Jews who reject materialism, are depicted as holding to the desire for worldly success and power which is characteristic of the assimilated Jew escaping the religious fold.

This distinction certainly provides a clarity lacking in Bulgakov, who ignored the existence of religious Jewry in his lament about Jewish materialism. On the other hand, as we will see, Karsavin's later comments on the nature of religious Jewry mean that he ends up with an analysis not so very distant from Bulgakov after all. One should add at this point that though he is very far from the tone and spirit of Florensky's writings, the core-periphery distinction is presented in a vulgarized form in the latter's distinction[29] between "Jews" (good, although/because blood-thirsty) and "Yids" (bloodless and bowler-hatted) – although Florensky is guilty under Karsavin's analysis of claiming that "Jews" commit their ritual sacrifices out of a desire for the world domination promised them by the Old Testament. In that sense, Florensky commits a cardinal category error.

However, as is becoming clear, once his categories are in place, Karsavin too has a bone to pick with Jews – just not the whole of Jewry, only assimilating Jews, who for him are the key to the Jewish question. These Jews are rootless: they have left behind the soil of religious Jewry and have not found firm ground in another nation. Core Jewry itself has its own national culture. Half-assimilated Jews have no sense of a national specificness, and instead become enamored with a false universalism in which mankind is more real than Russianness, Frenchness and so on. These rootless Jews thus become avid supporters of strict egalitarianism, radical democracy, socialism, communism – movements which undermine organic national cultures.

Having isolated "problem Jews," Karsavin now uses his previous distinctions to propose a surprising solution to the Jewish question.[30] In a future Eurasian state, the government policy should be to support core religious Jewry as much as possible. In so doing, Jewry will absorb its own dangerous renegades before they have a change to detach and harm other nations. Thus the "fight" against

---

[29] It might be better to say, his formalization of an implicit folk distinction that is present in a less explicitly stated way in Rozanov, Bulgakov and others.

[30] He considers it surprising. Despite the theoretical apparatus, the solution is not dissimilar to Khrapovitsky's policy of supporting religious Jewry and eschewing secularized Jewry with the support of religious Jewry. Again, this is reminiscent of early Rozanov, who favored religious Jews over secularized Jews. All of these thinkers have in common their political conservatism, of course.

peripheral Jewry must not take negative means – Pales, ghettos, quotas and so on: this would only encourage systematic corruption, lack of rights and injustice in the state. What is more, Karsavin emphasizes again that his types are not empirical individuals, but tendencies and potentials in an abstracted entity: and one cannot thus fight against a potential inclination that may or may not arise in an individual's breast. Therefore the only concrete measure must be the positive strengthening of the core Jewry which actually exists.

Returning to our earlier discussion, we see that Karsavin's solution shows a remarkable convergence on Dubnow's Autonomist position: the survival of Jewry must be assured through cultural and scientific work to encourage Jewish self-awareness in the struggle against assimilation. Dubnow too was fighting to strengthen the soil of Jewry, and the idea of Jews wholeheartedly engaged in developing the spiritual and intellectual vigor of their own nation (instead of pouring their energies into internationalist socialist experiments on Russia) shows that Karsavin was aligned with Dubnow and Steinberg.

The convergence of views goes further, however, and one cannot help thinking that Karsavin must have inquired quite deeply into Steinberg's collaboration with Dubnow. He makes it clear that core Jewry must be supported in its struggle for autonomy, which should not just be cultural but political. Touching on Zionism, he expresses the opinion that such a territorial solution does not coincide with the spirit of Jewry, due to its geographical and historical dispersal. However, he adds that if a Jewish centre were to be founded in Palestine it should be granted full autonomy, falling under no-one's protectorate (no doubt a dig at the British).

A better solution, though, would be a Jewish centre in Russia, where Jewry would be a full member of the future Eurasian state, possessing equal rights to other nations. As for those who fear an influx of Jewry to Russia, Karsavin chides them for their ignorance of the beneficial role Jewry has played in the development of mankind wherever they have settled: thus such an influx would be a cause for optimism. Moreover, such an autonomous Eurasian Jewry in the heart of Russia could be a centre and leader of world Jewry, strengthening it and providing it with positive influence. Once again, a prioritizing of the strengthening of Eastern European Jewry over the Zionist option coincides with the Autonomist approach.

Given all this, it is not surprising that Karsavin did actually find a Jewish Eurasian disciple, albeit not Steinberg – in the person of Jacob Bromberg. Following Karsavin's lead, Bromberg in his book *Russia and the Jews*[31] also posits an autonomous Jewish enclave in Eurasia, where Jews and Russians will live side by side harmoniously, joined by their common cultural features. Bromberg also developed Karsavin's other comments about the proximity between Russian culture and Russian Jewry, who had become "Eurasianised" over time.

Drawing on the anti-Western ideology of Eurasianism, Bromberg argued in his book that Jews are Asians who should not kow-tow to the superficial Western

---

[31] Cf. Rossman (2008) for more details on Bromberg.

critique of their culture (the well-known German and German-Jewish hostility to primitive *Ostjuden*). He went on to try and prove that Jewish history was intimately intertwined with Russian and Turkic history, as the Khazar kingdom showed. The development of Hasidism in South Russia was also no accident: it bears a native resemblance to the Russian Orthodox institution of eldership (*starchestvo*)[32]. Bromberg's critique of the West also targeted liberalism, which was leading to the assimilation of Jews as a culture. Finally, for Bromberg as for other Jewish Eurasians, Zionism was not an option, and indeed it was a threat as it could lure Jews away from the more integrationist vision of Eurasianism[33].

We have already commented that such convergence is a little too good to be true. And, of course, Bromberg's analysis bypasses a core aspect of Karsavin's analyis – and it is this aspect which led to Steinberg's courteous but firm disagreement with his friend. For having sung the praises of core Jewry and outlined the need for the future Eurasian state to give political support to Jewish cultural and religious development, Karsavin goes on to say that, in its own but different way, core Jewry is dangerous as well – and a bitter enemy of Christianity. One begins to understand why Steinberg was not so taken with Karsavin's vision. One also gets a sense of just how divided Jews and Russian Christians could be even within the boundaries of the trans-national, modernistically optimistic Eurasian movement.

Bromberg's willingness to ignore this key aspect of the master's thought is not a one-off. As Rossman[34] points out, there are other aspects of Bromberg's Karsavinian analysis of Russian Jewry which suffer from blank spots. For example, he maintains that the Judaizing[35] tendency in Orthodoxy was always looked upon benignly in Russian culture as a creative influence, whereas in fact it became symbolic of the worst type of heresy for Russian Orthodoxy, a constant threat to be combated. Bromberg also decried the Western Jewish intelligentsia for their false preoccupation with Russian pogroms, which supposedly obscures the real, organic unity existing between Russian and Jewish culture. Again, as Rossman argues, this goes too far in the direction of apologetics at the cost of a

---

[32] A comparison first broached by Karsavin in conversation with Steinberg, according to the latter's reminiscences.

[33] Interestingly, this perspective found a warm response among German Jews like Martin Buber, Hans Kuhn and Bruno Bettleheim, whose reaction to the fragmenting of Western society was to look to the Jewish east as a source of authenticity and regeneration.

[34] Rossman (2008), 32-36.

[35] One can also add that the Judaizing heresy had vanishingly little connection to real Jews, and was a cross-denominational Christian tendency among reformers to return to the purity of the Old Testament – rather than a specifically Russian affinity for Jewry. Also, as Rossman says, the picture of harmonious Russian-Jewish cohabitation is made meaningless by the fact that Jews were excluded from Russia proper by legislation until the Revolution – which is why there was such little real Russian-Jewish contact.

more sober appraisal of some violent aspects of Russian Jewish history.

As we will see shortly, one does not have to go far to find confirmation of this last point. A reader of Steinberg's reminiscences of his friendships with some of the seminal figures of Russian culture at Volphila[36] – men such as Bely, Blok, Ivanov-Razumnik, Bryusov, Berdyaev, Petrov-Vodkin – is struck again and again by the fact that they all display to a greater or lesser degree a deep and basic antipathy to Jews and Judaism, their association with Steinberg notwithstanding. And the Volphila was an enlightened environment, its members among the most cultured, creative and talented men of Russia. If there was such primal cultural hostility there, what would the wider picture look like? However, Steinberg is not dissimilar to Bromberg in this regard: he constantly expresses the belief that this antipathy is the unfortunate result of ignorance. Such ignorance will soon be dispelled by the activities of institutions like Volphila. That Blok and company did not change their prejudices seems not to have dissuaded Steinberg from his progressive belief in enlightenment, and he reiterates it again in his "Reply to Karsavin."

But to return to Karsavin's own belief about the threat of his previously lauded "core Jewry:" does this also place him in the ranks of the anti-Semites from whom he was constantly trying to distance himself in his essay? Does it unravel his previous hard-won distinctions? Not necessarily. Karsavin separates the political and religious aspect of the "Jewish question," as before he separated the layers of Jewry.

Writing as the chief theoretician of the Eurasian movement[37], he charts a new political solution to the position of Jews in the future Eurasian-Russian state that falls between that of imperial and Soviet Russia. In the former, Jews were deprived of civil rights; in the latter, as per the Napoleonic principle, everything was granted to the Jew as an individual, and very little to Jewry as a people[38] - or rather as a religious people: there were initial efforts to develop secular Jewish culture (Yiddish theatre, presses and so on), but eventually even that was deemed suspicious and un-Soviet. In Eurasia, by contrast, on the political level Jewry was to be granted autonomy and tolerance as a people and as individuals.

The political does not interfere with a deeper religious truth, however. Karsavin outlines this in terms similar to Berdyaev and Bulgakov, and indeed

---

[36] E.g. Steinberg, "Filosofskoe sodruzhestvo."

[37] Karsavin was approached by his future son-in-law P. Suvchinsky in 1924 with an overture to become involved in the movement. The other two founder members, Trubetzkoy and Savinsky, were far more ambiguous about Karsavin's recruitment, seeing his philosophical-theological essays as "semi-blasphemous." Cf. Sobolev (2008), 192-5. Trubetzkoy even wrote to Suvchinsky that he was advocating Karsavin merely because he happened to have fallen into the same circles as him in the "swamp" that was Russian émigré Berlin. Later, we will see the basis for this mistrust of Karsavin's intellectual work.

[38] The phrasing and interpretation of Karsavin is my own.

with echoes of Frank[39] that may have come from personal conversations or simply from reading Frank on the Jewish question. Judaism and religious Jews have rejected the Godman, their own Messiah who was sent primarily to Israel. Judaism is thus a dualistic religion, with God in His heaven and man on earth. Judaism is apophatic about the unknowable transcendent God. Due to the tension between eschewing any representation of God while constantly asserting the Being of God, Judaism's adherents often lapse into atheism, or the deification of man. Indeed "there is a tragedy in the fate of the religious Jew who is innately a fighter against God."[40]

Before Karsavin had denigrated the assimilating Jew who abandons the Judaic core. Now he admits that an assimilating Jew's internationalism and radical humanism is in fact organically connected to the core from which he disengages. The assimilating Jew's universalism is also connected to religious Jewry's belief in the Messiah. But, echoing Frank's analysis of the antinomy of a Jew who must make an impossible choice between the true Messiah (Jesus) and the truly chosen people (Jewry), Karsavin writes of the assimilating Jew's tendency, while becoming part of another nation to falsely universalize aspects of the new culture, to missionize and messianize that culture.

Becoming a German or a Frenchman, the assimilating Jew sells his birthright like Esau for a pot of lentils: he must combine his new belief that a Messiah has come (his new non-Jewish Messianism) with a rejection of the nation which produced the Messiah-concept, and to whom the Messiah was meant to come. "To overcome one's native Jewishnes and become a nationalist in the midst of another nation, to reject the Jewish Messiah and accept a Messiah who has come for others…yes, this is a most terrible tragedy which has not found its catharsis."

To some extent, then, Karsavin makes even core Jewry the purveyor of atheism and internationalism; the Jewish assimilationist's scientific communism is even replete with "false scientific Talmudism" – and we once again seem to be back in Bulgakov territory, where Judaic apocalyptic leads in a straight ahistorical line to the Russian Revolution. This is only true to a limited extent: in Karsavin's "solution," the lines are blurred – but at least there are lines to blur. This cannot be said of Bulgakov's more rambling analysis.

One other factor makes Karsavin's approach more realistic: he makes it very clear that the assimilationist does not act on his own. The assimilating Jew only has the power to destroy national culture because it is dissolving anyway: such Jews are merely a litmus paper which show up the process of disintegration more clearly. If European society is strengthened such Jews can have no effect. As regards the Russian Revolution, Karsavin is with (late) Berdyaev against Bulgakov: "Of course it is necessary to put an end to the silly fairytale (or the

---

[39] Cf. ch.6 of the present work.

[40] After his move to Lithuania, Karsavin revised this opinion about Jewry's and Judaism's limited vision of God, though this did not penetrate into his formal philosophy or any public pronouncements. See below.

new blood libel – everything changes its forms, even libel) that Jews invented and enacted the Russian Revolution. One would have to be a very historically uneducated person as well as contemptuous of the Russian people to think that Jews could destroy the Russian government…" Though they did partake in it, their role has been exaggerated.

Karsavin's article ends with the proposal to which Steinberg took greatest exception. In the ideal scenario, the political and the religious dimensions will meet. Having been granted autonomy and support in Eurasia, Jewry will of its own accord, free from the pressure of persecution, surrounded by the love of Christian Eurasian nations, make a choice in favor of Jesus Christ, the Jewish Messiah. For this is the only way out of the antinomy noted by Frank: individual Jewish conversions reject God's chosen people for God's Messiah. "Thus," writes Karsavin, "a Jew converting to Christianity should remain a part of his nation as a disciple and apostle sent to it by Christ. He should hope in a Jewish Christian church and not dissolve in the 'Hellenistic' church. (The words of the Apostle Paul in Galatians 3.27 on are usually interpreted incorrectly: he did not reject national-cultural particularities and their values)."

Even more so than Bulgakov, Karsavin rallies quotes from Matthew, Romans and Galatians to support a reading of Paul which leaves room for a Church in which Jews and Hellenes preserve their national identities. A special Karsavinian twist is added here though: he does make an effort to confront the problem that Judeo-Christianity has had a checkered and unfortunate history, admitting that "the ancient Church judged the ancient Jewish-Christians" adversely. This, however, "was not in the name of an abstract universalism but because it rejected their stubborn insistence on separateness."

Perhaps responding to the natural query of how the Jewish people, (who – we might add – in Balaam's prophecy were meant to be "the people that dwells alone"[41]), could abandon their separateness while remaining Jewish, Karsavin sees a way out of this paradox in the peculiar nature of Russian Jewry.

One can summarize Karsavin's thoughts as follows. Jewry consists of different sub-Jewries: German, Russian and so on, each with a slightly different character. Moreover, as a result of persecution and exile some aspects of Jewish culture have become distorted. Certainly, a Christian Jewry which had not abandoned the isolating tendencies condemned by the Fathers would not make a worthy national church, but repeat the same error of antiquity.

Russian Jewry, however, has a dual nature. It is (to use later Karsavinian terminology) a bi-unity of Eurasia and Jewry. One can see this in the deep affinity of Russian Jews for Russian culture, for instance in "the passion of Russian Jews for Russian religious philosophy (the Slavophiles, Dostoevsky unfortunately[42],

---

[41] However, cf. Jonathan Sacks' interesting interpretation that Balaam's prophecy was a curse, and that Jews should strive not to dwell alone, but to interact with other nations so as to be a light unto the nations. Jonathan Sacks, *Future Tense. A Vision for Jews and Judaism in the global culture*. (London: Hodder and Stoughton, 2009).

[42] This is an odd comment: later we will see that Karsavin took a hand in publishing

and V. Soloviev), and the particular fusion of this philosophy with Kabbalistic ideas[43]...." As a bi-unity, Russian Jewry can adapt and develop into the germ of the new Christian Jewry, slipping comfortably into the orbit of the Russian Orthodox Church.

On the Christian side, the Orthodox church is the best poised to embrace Christian Jewry: it spurns the leveling universalism of Catholicism where there is no room for national particularities, and is close to Judaism itself in its non-proselytizing respect for the identity of all the peoples of the world. Among the Orthodox Churches, the leading place among equals is held by the Russian Church: so the Russian Church would be the point where the remaking of a new Jewry could take place. From there, Russian-Christian Jewry can lead the remaking of other Jewries.

Karsavin sees two interpretations of the meaning of Russian-Jewry's dual nature: either it is a Jewry that has been reborn in Eurasian culture, and so more Eurasian really than Jewish. In that case, it would not retain its link with other Jewries and would be a poor guide for them. Alternatively, Russian Jewry merely expresses in itself a universal religious-cultural potential which in the other Christian nations of Eurasia is recognized as a shared fellowship and unity. Opting for the latter reading, Karsavin confirms his analysis that the Russianness of Russian Jewry consists in its already having opened up to that truly universal aspect of humanity of the type (one imagines) that Soloviev had talked about.

Thus, Russian Jewry, immersed in the universal qualities so well-expressed by Russia and her Church, is already on the brink of rebirth. Karsavin's political approach of laissez-faire, love and encouragement will provide the environment that will lead first to Russian Jewry's own choice to be consciously reborn, with other Jewries then following her lead[44].

Before turning to Steinberg's reaction to this thesis, it might add a certain vividness to this rather abstract and generalizing theory if we point out that

---

Steinberg's Dostoevsky book, and thought it a wonderful analysis of a great writer-prophet. Perhaps the "unfortunately" means that Jews will be offended by Dostoevsky's anti-Semitism; perhaps it means that for all his understanding of Dostoevsky Steinberg unfortunately did not respond the writer's core Christian message. Perhaps, it is a nationalist slip: Jews should not be meddling with our spiritual literature – Karsavin considered Steinberg Russian, but one of Steinberg's cousins remained for him non-Russian. This mysterious comment echoes Ivanov's comment about Jews' interest in Dostoevsky.

[43] An example might be Jacob Gordin, who became a noted French intellectual after the War. On Gordin, cf. Emmanuel Levinas, *Difficult Freedom. Essays on Judaism*. (London: The Athlone Press, 1990); and Vladimir Belous, *Volphila 2*, 720-726.

[44] Karsavin discusses the possibility that Jews could convert individually, but prefers collective conversion: the latter demands love for the whole Jewish nation on the part of Christendom, and the former does not escape the paradox that individual Jewish conversions embrace the chosen Messiah while rejecting the Chosen People. This contrasts with Berdyaev who rejected the idea of a chosen nation per se, Russian or Jewish, and had a highly individual-centered conception of Christianity.

Karsavin very much lived what he wrote in his relationship with Steinberg, which was a microcosm of the larger Russian-Jewish bi-unity, or symphonic personality.

A significant incident, recounted by Steinberg in his memoirs, encapsulates the paradox of Karsavin's (and Steinberg's, for that matter) attitude to the Russianness of Russian Jews. Karsavin had once written in a German newspaper that foreigners could never really understand Dostoevsky: to have a true understanding one must be Russian. Pressed by a German publisher to write something that foreigners could understand, Karsavin declined and recommended Steinberg's own book *Dostoevsky's system of freedom*.

If we follow Karsavin's logic here, we must say that for him Steinberg was a Russian, Russian enough to understand the most Russian of writers and interpret his work to non-Russians. Karsavin was so keen on the publication of Steinberg's book that he even hurried along its publication and found a translator for it: a certain Yakov Savlevich Klein, another Russian Jew and by implication a full-fledged cultural Russian.

But Karsavin's belief in the bi-unity of Russian Jewry went still further. Steinberg recalls how Karsavin confessed to him two secrets at their last meeting: one was that he wished to enter a monastery in his old age and take on the monastic name Lazarus. The other was that he had a hidden wish for his oldest daughter to marry a Jew. He had in mind none other than Yakov Klein. "She would be happy with a Jewish husband, and I would consider it a great fortune, please understand this."[45]

This is the ultimate fusion of the two entities: the Russian Jew will join Karsavin's own noble Russian family and become one blood with him through his beloved daughter. This is only one of several elements in Karsavin's thought and personality that recall Rozanov: Rozanov too had three daughters on whom he doted, and his relationship with Jewry had the same deeply intimate aspect: however, in his case, the desire to "fuse" with Jewry and Judaism was characterized by an equally strong force of repulsion. This, too, is a dynamic that is not alien to Karsavin. But this will be explored in more detail below.

Thus Karsavin's sense that Russian Jewry had been so transformed by its contact with Russian culture and its deep roots in Orthodoxy that it was culturally practically Christian was very personal. So much so that Steinberg had to defend himself from Karsavin's intimate attacks on his Jewishness, which took the form of an aggressive affection.

For Karsavin could not understand what to him seemed Steinberg's odd clinging to a religion which in spirit he had surely transcended. You are more Russian than anything else, he told his friend. Steinberg agreed and admitted

---

[45] Aaron Steinberg, "Lev Platonovich Karsavin," in Steinberg A. *Druzya moikh rannikh let (1911-1928)*, ch.8. (Paris: Syntaxis, 1991). It is worth noting that for some reason Karsavin did not consider one of Steinberg's relatives, Donsky, to be Russian. Thus there were Russian Russian Jews and Jewish Russian Jews.

that all his closest friends were Russian, that he got on better with Russians than Jews. Still, he defended himself, I am not Russian – a Russian Jew yes, but a Russian, no. For Steinberg agreed with Karsavin: the core of Russianness was Orthodoxy. Thus they would have to agree to disagree, while he could agree with his friend that the best traits of Russian Jewry do indeed come from the Russian environment. For Karsavin, this was still enigmatic and Steinberg reminded him of a member of the Judaizing tribes that lived on the Volga.

We know Karsavin's position. What is remarkable in these reminiscences of an Orthodox Jew is how very close Steinberg is to that position himself. If Russian culture is Orthodox, and if Russian Jews get their best traits from Russianness, then it may not just be logical casuistry to finish the syllogism with the thought that for Steinberg, too, Russian Jewry is saturated in Orthodoxy[46].

There is a final point that needs to be added to Karsavin's analysis before considering Steinberg's public reaction. While many Russian Jews had achieved a fusion of Russianness and Jewishness in 1928, it was not yet – even in Steinberg's case – the bi-unity that Karsavin was hoping would be a prelude to conversion. For that to happen, the Eurasian state would need to be founded, implementing the policy of Karsavin. And here we hit a snag.

Once again: Karsavin himself left the movement the year after he wrote this article. The Eurasian state was never to be. It was a utopian dream, its main activists frankly utterly unsuited for political activity. The plausibility of Karsavin's solution to the Jewish question thus suffers greatly from the fact that it is so embedded in a narrow fantastical schema.

In fact, the death of the Eurasian movement can be read rather ironically from the point of view of Jewish-Christian relations. Trubetzkoy, the founder of Eurasianism, left the movement in 1930, due to the launching of an openly pro-Soviet journal *Eurasia*. From then on, Eurasianism was infiltrated by the NKVD and became a propaganda tool for the Soviet government. Trubetzkoy had seen his conception of "ideocracy"[47] fully realized in Stalinist Russia – and it

---

[46] This is an interesting thesis. At stake is the extent to which Russian culture is Orthodox, and the extent to which aspects of the existence of Russian Jewry have been affected by Orthodox Russianness. Karsavin, Bromberg and Steinberg held the thesis in different degrees. Another example of Russian Orthodox-influenced Jewishness might be the following case. G. Fedotov in his *Saints of Ancient Russia* traces Populist and Communist idealization of labor back to the sacredness of the labor ethic of Theodosy Pechersky (Gyorgy Fedotov, *Svyatiye drevnei Rusi*. St.Petersburg: Satis derzhava, 2004.) Labor Zionism was definitely influenced by Russian Populism. We can thus say that much of the regenerative labor ethic of Russian Zionism has roots in ancient Russian monasticism. To cut out the intervening steps and state it provocatively: Zionism regenerated the Jewish people through a Christian monastic ethic. For more on Fedotov see later in this chapter. Further on, we will discuss the presence of Orthodox Christian motifs in Steinberg's own thought

[47] The idea that the task of government is not economic management as in liberal democracies, but ideological, cultural education of the people.

was a grim picture[48]. He came to the sad conclusion that Russia's Asian side was in fact its worst side and that Russia's hope lay in its European heritage. But it was nonsensical to defend and propagate a peculiarly *Russian* European culture. What remained? Only "to deny the limits of a nationally defined European-Russian culture and (*horrible dictu*) to work on common European culture, responding to the call of common humanity."[49] As a result, Trubetzkoy dissolved into the stream of Western European culture, becoming a Solovievian "universal man," so that few are aware that the great linguist was once a proponent of a separate Asian path for his homeland.

The irony lies in the fact that Trubetzkoy once compared emigrant Russians to Jews: both were uprooted, both disengaged from their host cultures and prone to nihilistic cynicism about values. While very tolerant of Jews and by no means anti-Semitic[50], this negative "émigré" aspect of Jewish culture meant that unlike Karsavin he had no vision of a way of preserving Jewish culture, and was assimilationist in orientation as far as Jewry was concerned.

In this sense, Trubetzkoy was true to his principles when it came to applying them to his own situation and nationality: for he put universal culture over the task of preserving émigré Russianness at all costs and assimilated himself out of existence, *qua* Russian messianic intellectual. He thus found himself in the position of one of Karsavin's Jewish internationalists disengaging from the soil of their own culture and country and working on a universal science. And indeed the science of phonology which he pioneered with Roman Jakobson was to become the forerunner of generative linguistics – which one might dub an international "Jewish" science, given its universalist premises and the Jewish origin of its founders.[51]

---

[48] Trubetzoy wrote in what must be one of the most thorough repudiations of a movement by its founder: "Stalin is not an accident, but a type who can be deduced from the concept of ideocracy in a purely deductive manner. Changing the content of the affair would not help. Stalin will remain Stalin regardless of whether he will act in the name of Orthodoxy. In which case, he might actually be more dangerous for the Church than now." Letter of N.S.Trubetkoy to P.N.Savitsky 8-10 Dec. 1930, in Sobolev (2008), p.218.

[49] Letter of N.S.Trubetkoy to P.N.Savitsky 8-10 Dec. 1930, in Sobolev (2008), p.217.

[50] Trubetzkoy (and Savitsky) categorically resisted and scorned the attempts of the somewhat farcical figure Baron A.V. Meller-Zakomelsky to fire up the Russian youth of Berlin with an ardor for Hitler by turning Eurasianism in that direction. His ideology was ecumenical and trans-national in essence. Cf. discussion in Sobolev (2008), including Trubetzkoy's correspondence with Savitsky over Meller-Zakomelsky's overtures.

[51] Generative linguistics argues for the existence of "universal grammar." The first work in generative linguistics was done in phonetics and phonology by Noam Chomsky, Morris Halle and Roman Jakobson. I do not intend seriously to label this science "Jewish:" while its main founders were Jewish, the truth of a science is not connected with the ethnic origins of its founders. Still, from a historical point of view of how the science developed as a discipline, how its problem areas were

Quite how Trubetzkoy's life would have developed as an "assimilated" Russian intellectual is not clear: he died in Vienna in 1938 at the age of 48, having suffered a heart attack brought on by Nazi harassment. Whether he would have continued Jakobson's path of further "assimilation" into Western culture by emigrating to the States cannot be known.

Karsavin, for his part, resisted assimilation – also following the same medicine he prescribed for Jewish exiles, to state the matter somewhat flippantly. Rejecting an offer from Oxford, he decided to accept a post in Lithuania in order to be nearer his beloved Russia. He achieved his dream of returning to Russia in 1950, as a prisoner on a convey shunting its way to a Siberian gulag. We will pick up his fate later.

Steinberg

There was much in Karsavin's article that Steinberg accepted and which many other Jews – especially those of a Zionist persuasion – would have rejected. He especially appreciated Karsavin's religious treatment of the Jewish question. But Karsavin went too far even for Steinberg.

Steinberg's argument is not difficult to state and it seems smooth and self-evident. Firstly, he picks up on the inconsistency of Karsavin's final words. He had chosen a story by Leskov to illustrate how Jewish fate might unfold in Russia. An old Jew had paid another Jew to take the place of his son in the Russian army. This Jew turned out to be a swindler and on receiving the old man's money promptly declared his intention to convert to Christianity, so escaping the draft. St. Philaret of Moscow solved the situation by refusing to baptize the swindler on the grounds that he was not worthy of holy baptism. Some time later, the old man chose baptism freely. The story is meant to represent the effect of Karsavin's policy of persuading Jewry of the truth of Christianity by means of support and love.

Steinberg points out that Karsavin himself had shown that individual baptisms were detrimental to Jewry. But he also contends that this is a poor turn-out by all accounts: the old man was not exactly honest himself, and his own conversion was more to "the Christians" than to Christ. On a larger scale, Steinberg asks rhetorically whether Karsavin has ever heard of a Jew who was satisfied with his faith converting to Christianity.

The answer to his own question is that no Jew sure in his faith has ever converted. Furthermore, "I will say straight out: I not only do not believe in such

---

selected, human history can have an impact. In this respect, Trubetzkoy – certainly in his own perception – shared a certain Jewish turn in his fate. In another sense, the exiled Trubetzkoy and Jakobson, who did much fruitful scientific work in exile, disprove Karsavin's assertion that science needs a firm national ground to flourish, which is why, Spinoza aside, he maintains there have been no good assimilationist Jewish scientists and philosophers. The old chestnuts Marx, Einstein, Freud, Popper, Jakobson himself and many others would seem to give the lie to this. His own fate as the founder of phonology outside his native Russia also throws his own assertions into question.

a conversion of Israel, but I believe that a Christian who believes in it shows a certain lack of faith in God. Forgive me, Lev Platonovich, for expressing my thought so sharply. But in reality I cannot imagine the conversion of Israel to Christ other than as a backsliding from the Father, as a betrayal of Him – and how could a Christian desire such a betrayal, such a breaking with faith?....For all Israel to be saved, all Israel would have to die."

The thought behind this seems to be the same as Rosenzweig's. In his earlier days Steinberg was a follower of Cohen and later of Rosenzweig's thought. He also lived and studied in Germany from 1909 to 1917 when the Marburg sage was most active. This philosophy, while no doubt made entirely his own, was probably inspired by them, therefore. Indeed, Cohen's development of a German-Jewish synthesis, his inspiration by the virtues and values of German culture finds a parallel in Steinberg's deep belief in the possibility of a Russian-Jewish synthesis[52] – which, however, stopped firmly short of the fusion Karsavin was pressing for.

There is a key difference between Rosenzweig and Steinberg, however. Rosenzweig is more negative about Christianity; he is also quite clear that the heart of his Star, the burning centre of the Truth is the place of Judaism. The weaker rays that emanate from the heart are Christianity. The Jew can see the Truth; the Christian follows the rays and is on the path to Truth – but he has not arrived. There is an honesty in this: after all, logically Judaism and Christianity can either be equal though different, or different and not equal. Steinberg's contention seems to be that they are different *and* equal and an honest Christian should be able to see this: hence Steinberg "cannot imagine the conversion of Israel to Christ other than as a backsliding from the Father, as a betrayal of Him – and how could a Christian desire such a betrayal, such a breaking with faith?"

The answer as to why a Christian could desire this is surely obvious: Christians believe that the Son and the Father are both God. To believe in Jesus as God is not a backsliding but the opening up of a new intimacy with God that was not accessible before God revealed Himself in the Son.

On the other hand if the Son is not God, then worshiping the Son as God is indeed a "backsliding." Technically, for Jews it is idolatry. But then if Steinberg allows that all but Jews may worship the Son as God, he is in effect saying that what is idolatry for a Jew is not idolatry for a gentile[53]. Then he is saying that

---

[52] Rosenzweig (and recently Wyschogrod, echoing him) saw a difference between Jews and gentile Christians in that the latters' religion did not stop Christians killing each other in the name of different nations. But Steinberg's identification of Russia as a spiritual Jewish ally, and Cohen's identification of Germany as particularly amenable to Jewish sensibilities in effect pitted two sections of Jewry, or two conceptions of Judaism, against each other – and while Cohen and Steinberg may have not gone to war with each other, vicariously their Judaisms did so through the nations they identified with.

[53] The doctrine that Christian *shittuf* ("association" of another together with God) is permissible for gentiles but not for Jews was first stated by Menachem Meiri, a 13th

Jews are ontologically, metaphysically different – superior – to gentiles; or else that Truth is relative.

All this does not take a long time to unpack and it makes one suspect that when it came to theology, Steinberg was not as adept as he was as a philosopher[54]. It makes his later statement that "it is easier for the Jew to have an attitude of love towards the Christian than it is for a Christian to love a Jew. (From which it does not follow that this is always the case.)" not entirely obvious: surely it is also not an easy task to fully love someone whom one does not take to be an equal. Sympathy, condescension, concern, pity perhaps – but without the key ingredients of admiration and respect, can there be true love?

This does not mean that Steinberg's opposite contention is not true: that Christianity in its very heart, at the core of its theology, does not accept Judaism. Karsavin says as much, and Russian religious philosophers who were seen to be liberal in other respects all reiterate the same point. But Steinberg joins the two statements: "Jewry knows only the empirical sins and failings of Christianity. Christians, though, have to accuse the people wedded to God and enamored of God of deicide and Godlessness…." Again, Judaism's judgment that Christianity is idolatry *tout court*, or an adequate religion for non-Jews has a metaphysical flavor every bit as sharp as Christianity's judgment on Judaism.

It is odd that Steinberg does not make this – after all, very old – conundrum explicit or at least provide another way of stating Judaism's attitude to Christianity – odd and worrying, as it may go some of the way towards explaining his extraordinary optimism regarding the future relations of Orthodox Russia and Jewry despite all his experience of anti-Semitism in Russian circles.

Steinberg is on firmer ground when he questions the consistency of Karsavin's advocacy of a Jewish Church. Having maintained that assimilating Jews are bad, but core religious Jews are good, Karsavin now accuses Judaism itself of being atheistic in spirit. Given that Jewish culture is permeated by Judaism what, asks Steinberg, could be left of Jewish culture once Jewry had accepted Christianity? That is, of course, the million-dollar question. Karsavin seems to imagine something like a nation of Steinbergs who have ceased observing the Sabbath and kashrut[55] – and Steinberg's lack of conviction in the vision is damning in and of itself.

On a more theoretical level, Steinberg is not convinced by Karsavin's attempt to paint a picture of a Jewish Church that will take its place beside the

---

century French Talmudist. Accordingly, Jewish Christians are idolaters, but gentile Christians are not. The doctrine became popular after medieval times, and Steinberg and Rosenzweig seem to subscribe to it.

[54] To be fair, his proposal of a third path out of the dilemma (different and equal) is not logically excluded, and later we will see that Steinberg allows that in some circumstances a Jewish conversion to Christianity might even be acceptable. However, he does not flesh out his proposition in a consistent way.

[55] Later, we will see that in an earlier article Karsavin had even toyed with the idea of Judeo-Christianity in which Jewish Christians would observe the Law.

Russian, Greek, Georgian and other national churches in the One Church that is the Body of Christ. Jewry and Christendom, he writes, are both awaiting the coming of the Messiah. For Jews this will be the first coming, for Christians the second. But when that Messiah comes and discloses his identity, "will there be a place for different faiths, for many churches, for the 'Jewish question'? In truth: 'they will not teach one another: recognize the Lord, for all will know Me, from the smallest to the greatest,' says the Lord, 'for I will forgive them their sin and their failings I will remember no longer.'"

For Steinberg, therefore, the coming of the Messiah will lead to the abolition of all churches and human differences. Jewish conversion to the Messiah will eradicate the difference between Jew and gentile and other human differences; all will be filled with the knowledge of God.

This is certainly a possible answer. In effect, he is saying that the "Jewish question" will be resolved beyond human time. But even if this is the case, and it is an alternative we have seen stated by Christians, the vision of a complete dissolution of human difference in the blinding light of God is not necessarily convincing. Both Steinberg and Karsavin, after all, had developed philosophies in which unity was composed of multiple integrated parts. Is this now to be abandoned?

Steinberg's comments are not developed enough to permit a serious engagement, but they raise as many questions as they answer: will the Torah then be abolished in the end-time along with God's own people? Is this not just supersessionism on a longer-term scale? And what is to happen to that Torah that the rabbis envision God studying in heaven, replete with its laws delimiting the difference between Jew and gentile? And what then was the role of Jews in human history?

One does not find the answers to these questions. But the last one is especially intriguing, especially given that Steinberg seems to place so much of the Messianic mission of the Jews on Russian gentile shoulders as we will see soon.

In short, one would have liked a more Jewish answer. And in this respect, Karsavin's philosophy of all-unity is more grounded in his own Christian dogma and theology than Steinberg's is in the Judaism which he practiced, but which intellectually seems somewhat cordoned off from his pan-unitarian world-view. Indeed, later Steinberg recognizes that in one sense Karsavin's approach is richer in *Jewish* content than his own. As Steinberg puts it, the Russian philosopher's condemnation of Jewish assimilationists looks odd coming from an Orthodox Christian, and would seem more comprehensible coming from a nationalist, religious Jew towards renegades of his own religion[56]. That Steinberg does not fit that bill can be seen when he states his own understanding and acceptance of assimilationists – a belief that got him into hot water with his fellow Jews.

For strange as it may seem for a self-professed traditional Jew, Steinberg

---

[56] Indeed, we have several times seen how a conservative position among Russian Christians leads them to a convergence on positions espoused by religious Jews.

views assimilated Jews who turn their back on Judaism as part of God's plan for the world. For him, such Jews deny their Jewishness in words but fulfill it in deeds. That part of Europeanised Jewry that is fighting for workers' rights can hardly be condemned in total, because concern for social justice has always been a part of the Jewish tradition and they are fighting to realize it. Therefore, they must be considered in a positive light[57].

Here Steinberg prefers a different metaphor to Karsavin's: not core-periphery, but "radioactive centre" and "centripetally discharged energy." The energy discharge is as much and as old a process of Jewish history as the preservation of the non-decomposing radioactive centre. In this respect, Paul of Tarsus – from Steinberg's perspective at the centre – is a typical representative of assimilated Jewry.

This recalls Semyon Frank's recognition of those who shun Christianity but profess it in their deeds[58]. Steinberg generalizes the achievements of the "radioactive energy" of the assimilationists as follows: "We have become accustomed to thinking that all major phenomena of Jewish history can never definitively lack meaning, which means that assimilation is needed for something. Likewise, the bend in our historical path which brought us to Russia is portrayed in the light of universal destiny."

This plea for tolerance for those who assimilate out of the Jewish people is certainly original. But one is still left with a feeling of inadequacy: for the assimilationist Paul was professing radically different ideas about what Jewry should be in relation to the gentile world than those proposed by the radioactive centre of Jewry. Tolerance for assimilationists does not address the respective truth claims of the centre and the radioactive element. Indeed radioactive breakdown can often distort the centre: are all assimilationists to be praised?

In this respect, Steinberg like Karsavin changed his mind about the core-periphery relationship. The poet Blok had once told him that during the Beilis trial he came near to Judophobia. The reason was the behavior of assimilated Jews who all their lives had denied Judaism, but now wanted him to write letters to the government denying that Jews engaged in ritual murder. Blok was put off by these Jews' denial of their identity except in times of personal threat to themselves. Steinberg replied that Blok should not judge healthy core Jewry by

---

[57] Perhaps there is still the influence of Herman Cohen's positive evaluation of socialism (Cohen greeted the October Revolution as a fulfillment of Biblical prophecies concerning the end-time; even his Russian-Jewish follower Matvei Kagan disagreed with him on this issue: on returning to Russia from Germany in 1918, he became deeply disillusioned by what he saw; cf. Matvei I. Kagan, *O khode istorii*. (Moscow: Yazyki Slavyanskoy kul'tury, 2004), 27.) The unfortunate implication would seem to be that Orthodox Judaism is not engaged in social justice, but must leave that up to departees from the fold. A similar accusation could be leveled at Orthodox Christianity, and Semyon Frank saw non-believers doing more Christian work than self-proclaimed believers.

[58] Cf. ch.6.

the actions of the assimilated periphery (using the same term "periphery")[59]. This flatly contradicts the assertion of an organic link between the two, and the defense of the periphery.

People can change their minds, of course. But this does highlight the problem – for Karsavin *and* Steinberg – of the value of Jewish assimilation: is it positive or negative? Surely, even Steinberg in his later phase would want a limit to complete assimilation: the very fact of his collaboration with Dubnow tells us this, as does his later work for Jewish communal organizations. Even this paradox has its boundaries, therefore.

Still, Steinberg's later defense of the periphery (and to be fair, in his conversation with Blok he did not go so far as to pass judgment on assimilationists) actually shows an underlying similarity with Karsavin's worldview: his concern for the meaningfulness of even seemingly lost moments of Jewish history parallels Karsavin's concern for the lost and seemingly unblessed moments of the individual life[60]. It also finds an echo in Bulgakov's vision of the hidden blessing in the depths of Judas' character, and in Frank's ecumenical tolerance for non-believers. Not surprisingly all these thinkers are bound by a vision of the unity of the world. Perhaps this is more evidence of Steinberg's Russianness.

Steinberg ends his "Reply to Karsavin" on a note of hope and agreement with Karsavin. While Russian Jewry can never become Christian, it does have a special place in world Jewry and it is called to fulfill a specific task: one for world Jewry and one for Russia. Service to Russia and service to Jewry do not contradict each other though: Jewry can only serve Russia because to do so coincides with the goals set down by the Jewish prophets. In sum, he ends on a note of Jewish-Eurasian consensus: "Russia's destiny as an unfading light from the East is also part of our path."

This idea that Russian Jewry has a special role to play in world Jewry was an idea that Steinberg clung to for the rest of his life even after Autonomism and Eurasianism had ceased to animate Jewish or Russian minds. As Nelly Portnova writes, it was in a 1937 letter to commissioners of an article about the crisis facing Jewry that Steinberg first used the expression "tribe" to refer to different components of Jewry.

The article decried the loss of unity among Jewry that had existed in former centuries, so that German Jewry had disintegrated into atoms of human dust, unable to bring themselves to concerted action. "Until the present crisis, however, to a lesser degree, one tribe always felt responsible for the past and future of the whole nation. In the last decades before the World War this recognition was worthily fulfilled in life by Russian Jewry."[61]

The editors who had commissioned the article refused to publish it, however,

---

[59]   In Aaron Steinberg, "Filosofskoe sodruzhestvo," in Steinberg A. *Druzya moikh rannikh let (1911-1928)*, Paris: Syntaxis, 1991.
[60]   See the later discussion of "Poem on Death."
[61]   Portnoy (2007).

saying that it was a call to the stone ages of previous centuries. Like his friend Karsavin, with whom he was still in contact at this time, he was accused of being a reactionary. The editors were German Jews: perhaps the Biblical notion of a Jewish tribe was too primitive for them due to their liberal sensibilities; perhaps they took umbrage at Steinberg's championing of Russia. And, indeed, the notion certainly has a Russian ring to it: both Russian anti-Semites and philo-Semites, and in the person of Rozanov both, commented on Jewish tribal solidarity with envy or admiration. However, despite the editors' negative reaction, Steinberg continued to use it with no shame.

In a 1971 article, he developed the concept of a "Russian tribe of Israel" in a truly "bi-unitarian" way, writing: "In the past, Israel was a community of communities, a kibbutz of kibbutzim, each with a special face, each one had its name…" If one considers that the Hebrew root of *kibbutz* is *kavatz* "to gather" one gets here a Russian-Hebraic calque of the Slavophile concept of *sobornost'* – also derived from the Russian verb *sobirat'* "to gather." Thus the tribes of Israel share a "*sobornost*-like" unity, which is a microcosm of that larger *sobornost'* preached from Khomiakov[62] to Soloviev to Karsavin.

We will conclude this examination of Steinberg's "Reply to Karsavin" by pondering on Ethan Finkelstein's article about Steinberg called: "The bad luck of Aaron Steinberg"[63].

Steinberg's bad luck, according to Finkelstein, was partly that he was always ending up in the wrong place at the wrong time. He lived in five different countries, constantly hounded from one to the other by war and persecution. But the other aspect of his bad luck was that he was always slightly out of synchrony with history. His embrace of Dubnow's Autonomism was undermined by the Holocaust. Dubnow, according to Finkelstein, had merely been the theoretician of what had existed in reality. Once that reality was gone the philosophy that in effect described it became an anachronism.

Steinberg's present bad luck is that Russian Jewry does not see itself as a unity, so that his Russian language works are mostly ignored by those who can read them. Again, German-speaking Jews and Germans have an entirely different cast of mind than Steinberg was originally addressing when he wrote in German.

Finkelstein's judgment is interesting. Obviously, only the Jewish community can decide the present relevance of Steinberg's work, but one would imagine that his idea of a Russian-Jewish fusion that can lead world Jewry has an uphill struggle in the competition with Hebrew-speaking Israeli Jewry and English-speaking American Jewry. The Russian Jewry that Steinberg had in mind is

---

62 Incidentally, Khomiakov was an ancestor on his mother's side of Karsavin's and another major source of inspiration to Karsavin.

63 Eitan Finkelstein, *Novoziye Arona Steinherga*, Forum noveishey vostochoyevropeiskoi istorii i kultury – russkoe izdanie, No.1, 2005. http://www1.ku-eichstaett.de/ZIMOS/forum/inhaltruss3.html.

vastly different after the Soviet period than the environment in which he was writing. The Russianness of his Russian Jewry lost its moorings in the same way as the Russianness of his fellow non-Jewish exiles. There is a parallel with the fortunes of that idealized German-Jewish fusion of Herman Cohen.

One can add, too, that in a "post-Christian" Europe, many of the implicit tenets of Steinberg's philosophy – imbibed from the ambient Russian Christian environment – have also aged badly. If, in Western Europe at least, Russian religious philosophy as a whole has lost the broader appeal it once enjoyed from the 1920s to 1960s – at least, for all but those engaged with theology – then Steinberg's heritage suffers from a double disadvantage.

The current dim prospective of Steinberg's thought aside, however, from the perspective of this book, what is more interesting and relevant is the nagging question of the place of philosophy in Steinberg's Jewish identity. His embrace of philosophy, specifically of Russian philosophy, is what brought him so close to the Russian Silver Age thinkers about whom he writes in his memoirs. The territory of philosophy once again turns out to be a meeting-ground for Jews and Christians, potentially a no-man's land in which strangers can meet and embrace. But this is partly because each one, venturing into this territory also attracts the suspicion of his own "side" and becomes somewhat estranged from his familiars.

It is to the question of Steinberg's encounters with Russians in philosophical territory that we now turn in more detail.

Inflected philosophy: Jews and Russians among the Greeks
Steinberg, Jewishness and philosophy: How strange that I am a Jew.

In 1916, Steinberg had written in his diary: "How strange that I am a Jew!" So attached had he become to "Lady Philosophy" that his universal self-consciousness was baffled by the intrusion of this historical particularity into its data field[64].

Karsavin also on several occasions was to exclaim how strange it was that Aaron Zakharovich was a Jew, and once Steinberg tried to explain the situation to him: "Dear Lev Platonovich, perhaps it will be clearer to you if I say that in Judaism there live the ideas of the Eleatic school, as they are expressed in Plato's Parmenides. Being is something which is completely indefinable, every definition of the ultimate reality already brings division to the fundamental essence." He went on to explain that this idea had appeared simultaneously in Asia Minor and Judea in the seventh to sixth centuries b.c.e.

In 1919, when the Soviet police did a round-up of Volphila members Steinberg found himself sharing a prison-cell with Alexander Blok. They had a deep and intimate talk about the Revolution, Blok defending terror and Steinberg against it. Steinberg also expressed his pity for the executed tsar and his family:

---

[64] Cf.N.Portnova (2007) for further details.

"...I belong to a non-Christian religious tradition, although it is considered harsher," he explained to his cell-mate. "[But] until now I cannot come to terms with the execution ....After all, we were all raised on the works of Dostoevsky and Tolstoy, especially Dostoevsky. Is it really a matter of indifference to us what a person experiences in his last moments before execution?" As in his explanation to Karsavin, so with Blok and so with himself: the Jew speaks with the voice of Kant, Parmenides, and – wonder of wonders – Fyodor Mikhailovich Dostoevsky![65]

A more provocative thesis would be hard to imagine – from almost any point of view, be it Russian-Jewish, Russian-Christian, or indeed German-Jewish. Before considering some other baffled reactions of Steinberg's contemporaries, Steinberg's "strange" blend of the Judaic and the Russian must first be described before it can be analyzed. Here is a Jew who observes the Torah and speaks the language of the philosophers fluently. More, it would seem: the language of Plato, Kant and Dostoevsky expresses the essence of the Torah Jew. Philosophic language is the perfect medium for the message of the Torah and, to some extent, the Torah is fulfilled through philosophical activity[66].

These views can best be understood by examining Steinberg's analysis of Dostoevsky in talks he gave at the Volphila, and in his 1923 book *Dosteovsky's system of freedom*, which constituted a kind of statement of faith for Steinberg in the Volphila years. Though Steinberg is original in the philosophy he derives from Dostoevsky, we can see the Russian sources of his Russian-Judaic philosophy in contemporary figures like Vladimir Ern, as well as Andrey Bely and Alexander Blok – to name only two of his colleagues at Volphila[67].

Steinberg read Dostoevsky as a Platonist whose characters are driven by ideas, which are themselves expressions of the Logos in history. Berdyaev arrived at a similar interpretation of Dostoevsky as a Platonic writer several years later[68], quite independently. But perhaps one can see both interpretations

---

[65] It was later in that conversation that Blok confessed his Beilis-era Judophobia. He went on to liken assimilated Jews to Isa Fomich, the Jew in Dostoevsky's *House of the Dead* who prided himself on being merely a mask and possessing no personality. Steinberg records the conversation himself, but as we have seen with Russian non-Jews, sees no irony in his appeal to Dostoevsky as a defender of universal values and an attacker of Jews in particular, or indeed his use as a Jew of Dostoevsky to support his "Old Testament" values. We will see this tendency on a more systematic scale shortly.

[66] As we will see later, comparisons with Maimonides suggest themselves.

[67] In addition, Steinberg is intricately bound up in that network of thought that includes Florensky and Gershenzon, the symbolist worldview which Khoruzhy linked to neo-Platonic "energo-essentialism." Indeed, Steinberg's choice of term to describe his philosophy was "concrete idealism," recalling Florensky's "concrete metaphysics." The latter term was worked out by Florensky in conjunction with Andrei Bely, later a close collaborator with Steinberg. An investigation of Florensky's and Steinberg's philosophies could also highlight interesting congruities

[68] Nicolai Berdyaev, *Mirovozreniye Dostoyevskogo*, Prague: YMCA-press, 1923. When he was preparing his Volphila lecture on Dostoevsky, Ivanov-Razumnik asked him

as being, directly or indirectly, inspired by the work of the prematurely deceased philosopher, Vladimir Ern (1882-1917) whose heritage had a strong influence on his contemporaries. His blend of Platonism, religion and Russian literature laid the ground for the concept of the unique "Russian idea" which was to be developed in different ways by Frank, Berdyaev, Bulgakov and others[69].

Ern's own philosophy of the Logos seems to resemble Steinberg's sketch of his Parmenidean inspiration. He called his system Logism, and urged a return to ancient Greek ontology: Parmenides, Plato, and the Platonized Aristotelianism of the early Church Fathers[70] were held by him to provide an alternative to the scholastic-rationalistic Western distortion of this tradition from Aquinas to Descartes and Kant. For Ern, Russian thought had always had a propensity to embrace the eastern Logos over Western "Ratio." Practitioners of Logism included the Slavophiles and Soloviev. Another interesting precursor in Ern is his inclusion of Dostoevsky's anthropology in this Logistic tradition – which suggests a clear analogy to Steinberg's analysis.

For Ern, the Logos had a cosmic (natural-aesthetic), divine (Christian) and logical-philosophical aspect. Thus, while he was clear that Logism was deeply connected to Orthodox Christianity, he also left room for a less dogmatic application of Logism. For example, despite his clearly anti-Western tendencies, he held that Catholicism was a stream of mystical Logism in the West[71].

---

in mock-trepidation whether he would not turn him into a Kantian. Not a Kantian, replied Steinberg, but perhaps a Platonist. When he met Berdyaev in Berlin in 1923, the latter expressed approval of this interpretation and handed him a copy of his own book in which he had made a similar connection.

[69] Though Dostoevsky himself too voiced the notion of a peculiarly "Russian idea" in his famous "Speech on Pushkin" and in another essay "The utopian understanding of history." Steinberg discusses this and takes his own inspiration from Dostoevsky's conception of the Russian idea as the "unity of multiplicity" in *Sistema svobody Dostoevskogo*, e.g. pp.42-3. (He also discusses Rozanov's development of Dostoevsky's Russian idea (ibid. p18), and in fact the title and inspiration of *Sistema* owes much to Rozanov's call to critics to "arrange into a system the intellectual treasures left behind by [Dostoevsky].").

[70] Below we will explore how Platonism and Platonized Aristotelianism also have a very Jewish pedigree in Maimonides, and Solomon Maimon's reinterpretation of Kant. This, of course, has a bearing on the question of just how plausible Steinberg's Judaic Logism without Christ-the-Logos can be – a question which was an implicit source of discussion for Karsavin and others.

[71] Ern's father was half-Swedish, half-German and a Lutheran; his mother was half-Polish, half-Russian and Orthodox. He was born in Tbilisi, Georgia. For a quarter-Russian born in Georgia, he was remarkably insistent on the strength of the "Russian Idea." On the other hand, this perhaps goes to show that "Russianness" in philosophy was interpreted in "spiritual" terms – hence, the ability of Steinberg, who had no Russian blood, to partake in it without qualms. (Razumnik-Ivanov was also from Tbilisi, and half-Armenian, like Florensky). Cf. ch.6 for discussion of Ern's argument concerning "nationalism in philosophy" with S.L.Frank.

In this sense, Steinberg can be seen as building a Russian Logism in which the Logos has all but the second Christian feature[72]: in other words, Steinberg's is a Russian-Jewish Logism, which has many familial features with Ern's system. Other points of convergence are Steinberg's belief in the catastrophic progress of history, the role of holistic personality or self-consciousness (as opposed to the Western abstract thinking "ego"), and ontologism (versus epistemology).

Another more concrete influence on Steinberg's "Logism" was his close Volphila friend, Andrei Bely. The ingenious novelist and poet was, by most accounts[73], fairly mediocre as a philosopher. But the speeches he gave at Volphila were mesmerizing embodiments of his belief that the writer became the Word. The musicality of his speech, intertwined with expressive gesticulations, were almost more important than the content of his lectures – as Steinberg himself recalls. In his book, *Symbolism as a way of understanding the world*, Bely writes: "…in the word, and only in the word, I recreate for myself what surrounds me externally and internally, for I am the *word* and only the *word*."[74]

As we will see, this echoes Steinberg's philosophy. But, more importantly, Bely was not just a practitioner of symbolism, but along with Blok, an incarnation of the idea of the writer-as-prophet and soothsaying decipherer of the times, himself a symbol who served to decode the world's symbols – and thus his value for Steinberg must have been more as a living demonstration of the truth of the Russian showing forth of eternal Truth, a living word whose actions could be read by Steinberg and given a more coherent form by his more philosophically educated intellect[75].

Ern and Bely thus constituted indirect and direct influences on Steinberg's philosophy. In the case of Bely, the influence was most probably reciprocal. And it is not surprising that Steinberg, who was more knowledgeable than anyone at Volphila about German philosophy, should have forged these influences into an original philosophy of his own, which also owed much to his Jewish heritage.

For while the Ernian Russian idea provides the background for his analysis,

---

[72] The "name-worshipping" neo-Platonism of Florensky, Bulgakov, Losev and Ern had in a sense already laid the ground for the further de-Christianization of "Logism" that Steinberg (and Gershenzon) contributed to, by blurring the boundaries between Christian religiosity and literary-creative inspiration, recast as prophetic activity.

[73] Stepun and Tsvetaeva, for example, though sympathetic to Bely had a low opinion of his philosophical output.

[74] *Simvolizm kak miroponimanie*, p.131. Cited in M.A.Maslin, edit.*Istoria russkoi filosofii. Uchebnik dlya vuzov*. (Moscow: KDU, 2008), 411. See Maslin, 491-495 for more on Ern.

[75] As we noted in chapter 3, Steinberg's friendship with Bely was similar to that between Bely and Gershenzon. Literary critics in a sense depend on artists for their secondary inspiration: Ivanov-Razumnik interpreted Blok and developed his own theories in conjunction with Blok's poetry. Still, it is tempting to see Bely as the Russian Word, midrashic interpretation of which allowed the Jewish outsiders, Steinberg and Gershenzon, to draw close to Russia's essence.

Steinberg also reads Dostoevsky as a prophet in the Old Testament style. For Steinberg, the prophetic aspect of Dostoevsky means that he is not simply a *timeless* Russian prophet of the Logos – as with any Biblical prophet the epoch in which he appeared in world history was crucial to his meaning and message.

But another original aspect of Steinberg's interpretation was to see Dostoevsky as a philosopher, as well as a prophet – indeed, Steinberg claimed to be the first to name him the national philosopher of Russia. So great was their connection that, in effect, Russia and Dostoevsky were synonymous. For Steinberg therefore, the boundary between prophecy – with its concrete call for immediate change in the face of peril – and philosophy, usually seen as the science of otherworldly abstraction – disintegrates in the Russian moment. Steinberg called this blend of prophecy and philosophy "concrete" or "prophetic idealism."

The concrete period in which the prophet-philosopher Dostoevsky emerged in Russian and European history has a crucial significance in Steinberg's Hegelian-style schema. According to this system, humanity passes through three stages of development: life, consciousness and self-consciousness. Dostoevsky appeared at a time when Russia, emerging from the primal stage of living merely in order to survive, had achieved consciousness. Dostoevsky lifted her up to the stage of self-consciousness[76]. That is, he managed to integrate all the conflicting tendencies in the mental life of Russia. He synthesized the ideas of the Westernizers and Slavophiles, the European-style socialists as well as the Russian Populists. In this respect, he built a system – not in the sense of Western systematic tomes on philosophy, but a system in which all elements are included and transfigured.

One work that Steinberg appeals to in his interpretation of Dostoevsky is the writer's *Dream of a Ridiculous Man*, which for him illustrates Dostoevsky's Platonic "idealism," his belief in "Ideas" as drivers of human personality, action and history[77]. After his unsuccessful suicide the hero finds himself flying towards a planet that look likes the one he has just left behind and he asks himself: "How can there be a similar repetition and for what? I love, can only love the world which I have left, upon which there remain the splashes of my blood, when I ungratefully shot myself in the heart and extinguished my life. But never, never did I stop loving that earth." The lesson is that there is no other earth, no other life, nothing repeats itself, life only happens once. "Kiss the earth and unceasingly, greedily love her…" the elder Zosima will later say in *The Brothers Karamazov*.

Thus all that is seemingly superficial and contingent in the world, what looks like failure and evil, is changed by contact with great ideas: "the Platonic idea of the universe, the idea of the world, the transfiguration of the superficial into a human-like face, is an integral part of Dostoevsky's metaphysics."[78]

---

[76] Steinberg once accused Shestov of being a quasi-Hegelian despite his protests to the contrary; his own system seems however also seems to echo Hegel, as is often the case in Russian philosophy whether of "left" or "right."
[77] *Sistema*, 43-44.
[78] *Sistema*, 136-7.

All of Dostoevsky's major characters are driven by such ideas, and these ideas are expressions of the Logos in history. They reveal how it is not a person who determines their worldview but that person's essential idea which produces their driving characteristics: their individual "philosophy" corresponds to their personality, behavior, and their self-consciousness. Each character is the incarnation of a transcendent idea. One need only think of Raskolnikov with his Napoleonic idea, Prince Myshkin the embodiment of otherworldly humbleness, Stavrogin in the grip of his devilish egotism (for there can be bad ideas too).

Dostoevsky was thus the great "systematizer of self-consciousness" and "a hero of all-human unity," whose work points the way forward in specific historical circumstances. He was among those great men who deserve the title of "ideologues, i.e. heralds of those ideas and that logic which are manifested as the logic of ideas and the teaching about the Logos." Such heroes connect all cultures because while immersed in their own culture they are out of time and space and connected with universal ideals beyond any division into periods or regions.

As the prophet of the Logos, Dostoevsky outlined a system of freedom, which if followed, would be able to liberate the world, especially Western Europe from its cultural and philosophical impasse. By developing and exploring that system Russia would be able to take further her national task of the "incarnation of the word in the deed," which is so far "the most revolutionary of human thoughts." Then "free self-being or being-for-oneself" will become "Being-for-the Whole, for the All-Unity." Transcendent thought will have turned into immanent activity; the "Russian system" will have provided humankind with a "system of searching and a searching out of the spirit." The mission of Russia, finally, will consist in the fulfillment of an international utopia, in the realization of "the philosophical recognition of the human race in the name of the transfiguration of humanity."[79]

It is evident that Steinberg saw himself and his colleagues at Volphila as fulfilling this incarnation-in-deed of the Russian Logos bequeathed by Dostoevsky. This puts a somewhat different spin on the claim Steinberg had made in his "Reply to Karsavin" that service to Russia and service to Jewry were complementary, because to serve Russia was to fulfill the ancient Jewish prophets.

For in light of the above, we see that Steinberg was not making a banal plea for tolerance on the grounds that the Jewish religion is peaceable, encourages patriotism, public morality, loyalty and so on. He was not talking of the platitudinous generalities of Jewish-Russian "co-existence." Rather his "prophetic idealism" was referring to the actual fusion of Jewish and Russian destinies in the concrete present moment that came after the Russian Revolution: in the year 1921 the Messianic impulse of Judaism can merge and synchronize with the Messianic mission of Russia – and create a new destiny for the whole world.

In other words, Steinberg's own activity at Volphila after the Revolution can be seen as embodying the Russian Messianic idea of "the incarnation of the word

---

[79] Ibid, 32.

in the deed" – for Volphila was to be the kernel of cultural activity that would kindle salvation in the ruins of destruction.

Indeed, timing was everything. The concrete or prophetic aspect that Steinberg noted in Dostoevsky's philosophy made it a revolutionary philosophy of history. Herein lies its superiority to Kantian philosophy[80]. The latter's transcendental scientific categories can only lead to generalizations about the world: they thus miss the concrete historical moment. There are those who attempt to bypass this problem by proclaiming the meaning of history to be beyond history. Only concrete idealism can seize and identify the significance of the present moment – and the clue to the direction history must take comes from examining the ruins of culture.

Culture can be resurrected and history redeemed through the activity of artistic and creative consciousness. Consciousness is a principle which can oppose the fragmentedness of time, weld together the broken pieces of history. It joins together these fragments into pan-temporality and pan-spatiality. In other words, it transforms atomistic reality into idea – the great unity, the all-one of which Parmenides and then Plato speak (and if we remember Steinberg's comment to Karsavin, we can infer a divinization of reality, as the Parmenidean All-One is the Judaic God).

The natural process of dissolution is thus not a tragedy, but an opportunity: it provides a window through the opaque universal categories of scientific consciousness, so that the here-and-now can be given a meaning, so that it can be drawn via human consciousness into the fabric of all-being. Using a biblical metaphor, which underlies the continuity for him between Greek and Judaic thought, Steinberg referred to history as a tree of life: the hidden roots of the tree are the concealed unity of being.

During the historical process the tree of life is transformed into a tree of knowledge. Destruction of some branches is inevitable for the growth of new ones. In fact, the infinite expressiveness of the root – which reveals itself through human consciousness – demands that some of the old branches give way for new incarnations of the infinite. In other words, the transformation of reality into idea is translated into the Biblical idea of the transformation of the tree of life into the tree of knowledge. Parmenides meets Genesis[81].

The drama of Dostoevsky's novels is also transferred to Steinberg's philosophy: man is defined by a choice between suicide, murder and power. Consciousness, the stage above mere life, is transferred into self-consciousness when a person faces the question of suicide. In the possibility of suicide man confronts non-being, nothingness, death: in rejecting the option of death, man

---

[80] Again, Steinberg's "national" hostility to Kantianism is cognate with Ern's and Florensky's – though the latter two expressed it in terms that would better be described as nationalistic. Cf. ch.6 for a discussion of Frank's argument with Ern regarding "nationalism in philosophy."

[81] There are definite echoes of pantheism here, specifically parallels with Spinoza and Nicholas of Cusa, which we will discuss below.

chooses life, but this time real life – not the mechanical, arbitrary life of natural being. This is freedom, whereby existence becomes not an imposition but a free choice[82]. Again, to highlight the Judaic aspect here, there is a direct reference to the passage in Deuteronomy where God enjoins the Israelites to choose between life and death, abandoning the Law or submitting to God's Law.

Finally, Steinberg deals with the appropriate life of a self-conscious being. Here murder must be eschewed and power used correctly. The self-conscious being cannot submit like a slave to a pseudo-objective truth and then impose it by terrorist means on others, so enslaving them (the case of the Marxists). On the other hand, Steinberg questions Kantian enlightenment morality with its emphasis on individual autonomy as the basis for a morality where the self and its goals are foremost.

For Steinberg, the free self which has faced nothingess is constantly open to the world. As a result, the world of common goals rather than the self's individual goals is more important for self-consciousness. Indeed, the only true morality is a collective (*soborny*) morality for in the "transcendental kingdom of ideas" "I" and "non-I" resemble each other. In the development of self-consciousness, the "I" is constantly crucified between pride and humility. Its goal – the only way self-consciousness can be attained – is to master itself and become a vehicle of the idea of the world, an incarnation of the Logos in deed. Freedom is thus a problem of consciousness.

Thus there can be no stultification of the self, no closure of history and final discovery of truth, for the development of self-consciousness is a permanent process of becoming, in which the self in fact constantly seeks to move outwards away from consciousness, and thus is personalized. Nonetheless, this permanent becoming transmits objective values from the world of ideas into each contingent moment of history, thus imbuing culture with value and meaning.

The personalization of human consciousness is in fact the filling of the self with a higher Personhood, so that consciousness becomes supra-personal, and turns into the vessel of a benign historical will. Ultimately, then, Steinberg's end vision of a Messianic future is one in which the world divides into Creator and creature, everything becomes a unified creative striving, in the uninterrupted flow of which all persons become vessels, boundary-points in the interpenetrating flow of living and meaning-giving life, true life, that is, and not merely biological life.

Having sketched Steinberg's Dostoevskian philosophy, it is time to consider reactions to it. Perhaps the first comments to be considered should be those of Steinberg's contemporaries, Alexander Meier and Israel Zinberg. The former was a central figure in a religious-philosophical circle which explored ideas combining anarchy, socialism and Christian spirituality. The latter was a fellow lecturer with Steinberg at the Jewish University of Petrograd, where he

---

[82] Just as Steinberg claimed to have preempted Berdyaev, in his memoirs he also notes that his existential reading of Kant preempted Karl Jaspers and Sartre.

taught Jewish literature and culture (Steinberg himself taught the philosophy of Zionism there).

Both were present at a two-hour lecture in which Steinberg gave an early presentation of his ideas concerning Dostoevsky. Steinberg followed this up with another presentation, which has not been preserved for posterity.[83] The literary historian-critic, L.Katsis, has uncovered in this work several Judaic references which he traces back to the discussions of freedom in the Talmudic tractate Pesach (concerning the liberation of the Jews from Egypt) and the Hagadah, the compilation read at Passover[84]. More overtly, a key point in Steinberg's 1921 presentation was his comparison of Alyosha Karamazov to Moses, and his brother Ivan Karamazov to Aaron. The former for Steinberg was the tongue-tied prophet whose head was lost in the kingdom of ideas; the latter was his interpreter to the world, incarnating the ideas in reality. Together, they are key figures in Dostoevsky's prophetic endeavor to unify the world of the Logos with the concrete and often grubby world of real-life particulars[85].

---

[83] Doklad A.S.Shteinberga. "Dostoevsky kak filosof" i preniya po ego dokladu na LXXXVIII-om zasedanii VFA 16 oktyabrya 1921 g., in Beloous, Volfila 1, 637-702.

[84] I have not been able to locate this work, which is refered to as in progress in Katsis' article, "Grad Kitezh yevreiskoi filosofii?" Lekhaim, No.12. (2007): 90-94.

[85] In addition to such Talmudic echoes, however, there is a theme that is equally compelling given our previous discussions of Rozanov, and the Rozanovian enchantment with the carnality of Judaism. Steinberg underlines how, in *The Brothers Karamazov*, the birth of ideas is always literally the birth of characters. The Karamazov father sires three sons, each representing different ideas. "In this sense in Dostoevsky relationships of blood-relatedness take on metaphysical meaning. And the so-called problem of heritability is turned from a biological issue into a logical issue – the logic of life itself, or the biological in this already metaphysical sense... (Doklad Shteinberga, 642)." Another example Steinberg gives is the relationship of Stefan Trofimovich Verkhovensky in *The Devils*, and his son Petr Stepanovich. The former represents the type of falsely abstract idealism, the latter the overcoming of this dualism. Dostoevsky has one of the minor heroines confuse the paternity of Petr Stepanovich, taking him to be the nephew of Stefan Trofimovich. In a sense, argues Steinberg, this is right: Petr is really the son of Stefan's brother, i.e. that better of half of Stefan's own self. Concludes Steinberg: "You see that all is a vision of the blood ties in the realm of ideas....(ibid.648)." This equation of concreteness with blood-genealogy is perhaps the most fascinatingly Jewish (at least in the terms framing the debate in our period) aspect of Steinberg's philosophy: the refusal to give in to a Christian dualism of flesh and spirit. Part of his all-unity is his unification of the two, and his discovery of this in Dostoevsky's novels. Other Judaic echoes can be detected when Steinberg refers to the all-humanity of people and their need to be ultimately responsible for one another: this may well be inspired by the Jewish belief in the unity of the Jewish people as the descendants of the 600,000 souls present at Sinai, as a result of which "kol-yisrael eveirin ze la-ze" (All Israel is responsible for one another). Or it might be inspired by the doctrine of Adam Kadmon in whom all humanity is present – a symbol, of course, that is found in non-Jewish Russian philosophers of all-unity. Whether Katsis makes the same connections, I am unable

However, this "Judaization" of Dostoevsky left both Meier and Zinberg unpersuaded. Meier remarked that if Steinberg was right in his analysis, then Dostoevsky was the first Russian writer to reject his Christian roots in favor of the Old Testament[86]. In addition, he saw Steinberg's attempt to squeeze Dostoevsky into the category of philosopher as also ignoring the writer's main aesthetic and religious inspiration in the person of Christ[87].

More recently, Katsis has come to a similar conclusion. For him, Steinberg's view of Dostoevsky as a prophet is not particularly original and coming from a Jewish writer can be seen as natural[88]. Nonetheless, he also remarks on the oddity of completely ignoring the Christian elements in Dostoevsky[89].

In addition to the problem of ignoring Dostoevsky's Christianity, there is of course the possibly related question of Dostoevsky's anti-Semitism. An American-Jewish scholar, G.S. Morson took the French-Jewish writer David Goldberg to task for his 1976 book *Dostoevsky and the Jews*, in which he claims that Dostoevsky's anti-Semitism was marginal and excusable[90]. For Morson this is a sad case of self-delusion, and more – a crucial misreading not just of Dostoevsky's journalistic works, but even of crucial themes in his literary oeuvre. What would Morson make of Steinberg's thesis of a Dostoevskian Jewish-Russian revolutionary fusion?

In fact, Steinberg explained and thus also excused Dostoevsky's anti-Semitism on the grounds that the writer's Russian Messianism led him to suffer an envy complex towards the Jewish people with their prior claims of Messianic chosenness.

But this is of course, once again, to beg the same question we posed concerning Steinberg's "Reply to Karsavin." If Judaism and Russianness – which Steinberg saw as being rooted in Christianity – are so compatible why did Steinberg's vision of a fusion leave Zinberg, Meier, and as we have seen Blok, unpersuaded? And why did Steinberg omit any reference to Dostoevsky's Christianity?

In this respect, more perplexity is triggered by Steinberg's brief account of another Volphila meeting, which took place in 1921. This was a Jewish-Christian debate between Steinberg himself and Andrey Bely – a prelude, one might say, to the later *Versty* exchange. A reader looking for clarification of the questions just raised will be disappointed, however. This is because Steinberg says vanishingly little about the actual content of the debate. But he is tickled by the fact that

---

at present to discover.

[86] See below for more on Meier in general, and for more detail on his criticism of Steinberg's 1921 presentation.
[87] See below for more details.
[88] Some might contend that it begs the question as to why this is "natural" for a Jewish writer.
[89] Cf. "Grad Kitezh yevreiskoi filosofii?" *Lekhaim*, No.12 (2007): 90-94.
[90] *Dostoevsky's anti-Semitism and the critics*: a review article, SEEJ, Vol.27, No.3 (1983).

people in the Russian provinces, hearing somewhat distorted rumors about the meeting, concluded that the end time must be coming as Jews and Christians in the capital were trying to convert each other to their own faiths. Given what we have seen of the apocalyptic atmosphere in Petrograd in these years, and the ambitions of the Volphilites' theological-philosophical-political vision, Steinberg's delight in the rumor could not have been purely ironical: for in a sense, the Volphilites *did* see themselves as living in the end-time.

But Steinberg, writing in his memoirs many years later, commented of the meeting that "the essence was not what we spoke about then, what was important was that Petrov-Vodkin openly declared his deeply rooted anti-Jewish beliefs, and Ivanov-Razumnik preferred to keep silent, as was often the case with him." Petrov-Vodkin, the famous painter of canvases that mix symbolism and pious Christian imagery in scenes that glorify Russia and – in these years at least – the Revolution was an artistic counterpart of Bely, Blok and the other creative Volphilites. The literary critic Ivanov-Razumnik, as we learn in Steinberg's recollections of Shestov, was a philo-Semitic anti-Semite somewhat on the Rozanovian mould[91].

While Steinberg's apocalyptic passion seems to have cooled with the years somewhat, one way of looking at his later cursory description of the meeting is to conclude that – like Rozanov, Meier, Bely and many others – he saw the actual differences between Judaism and Christianity as being swallowed up by a higher consciousness – how else to explain why he can see the essence of Dostoevsky's thought as "concrete idealism" shorn of Christianity?

Again, in Steinberg's own words we have it that the meeting was important not for highlighting the differences or similarities, or the respective truth value of Judaism or Christianity – but rather for showing up the essential antipathy of Russians to Jews. It would seem then that even Steinberg's higher, prophetic, Dostoevskian "revolutionary" Judaism striving for self-consciousness in the mold of Russian (Christian) thought could not appease the Judophobes[92].

Whatever one might say about this, it is legitimate to infer that this casts doubt on the validity of Steinberg's vision of the compatibility of Judaism and Dostoevskian or other Russian-Christian philosophies. After all, Steinberg's own refusal to accept Karsavin's vision of Russian Jewry as "de-facto Christians" pits Jewish self-perception against a forced interpretation by an outsider. *Vice versa*, Steinberg's appropriation of Dostoevsky as a "de facto Old Testament Jew"

---

[91] On which more below.

[92] Steinberg makes a fleeting reference to opinions that were expressed by different members of the audience: some were hostile to the official Church (Volphila often drew listeners from among local factory workers, as well as socialistically-inclined intellectuals). Others were of the opinion that the Church is invincible because it is not of this world. There was a Tolstoyan who advocated Christian rationalism with a Hellenistic component. Bely himself was in his Steinerian theosophist phase, and interpreted Christianity "purely mystically" – that is, presumably, without reference to the empirical ecclesiastical institutions of the world.

seems to be ignoring something essential in the writer's self-perception as well as in his interpretation by his Russian-Christian followers[93]. In this sense, Steinberg seems to be as bullishly recalcitrant to hearing the other, as Karsavin.

Still, one wants to know: what is it that makes Dostoevsky and his Christian devotees irreducible to "Old Testament" Judaism and it is to this question that we will now turn.

Jewishness and Russianness in philosophy

On a purely philosophical level, the components of Steinberg's "concrete idealism" could be seen as very Russian-Christian – at first glance. But this is a mistaken view, I would argue. That view seems to have been held by, or if we extrapolate, could have been held by, Karsavin, Berdyaev, Frank, Bulgakov and Florensky. Let us elaborate.

Karsavin saw Eastern Christian thought as characterized by Platonism and pantheistic tendencies – which contrasted with Western Catholic Aristotelianism and its emphasis on the transcendence of God[94]. Berdyaev, as we saw, also viewed Dostoevsky as a Platonist. Both of them thus saw Steinberg as one of their own.

Likewise, Semyon Frank criticized Franz Rosenzweig for his absence of a mystical spirit – specifically, his dismembering of all-unity into God, man, and world with no organic connection between them. That connection could be given

---

[93] Steinberg expanded his 1921 lectures on *Dostoevsky as a philosopher* into his 1923 book *Dostoevsky's System of Freedom*. It is clear that he stood by his previous "Judaization" of Dostoevsky as the comments on p.135 of the latter work make clear: "Dostoevsky's Christianity rests on a solid foundation of monotheism. The Gospel for him, as for Zosima, is a direct continuation of the Old Testament. *Out of all the Russian writers, he is the most Judaic* [italics, DR]; and his Christ most resembles the Biblical Messiah." The phrase in italics distinctly echoes Meier's skeptical quip that Steinberg wished to make Dostoevsky "the first confessor in Russia of the One and only One God. But then in my language that would mean that he was the first of all Russian writers to have converted to the Old Testament, and so to speak, to have betrayed those testaments which in general pertain in Russian culture (Belous, 696)." Meier's words reveal that he believes Steinberg to have made Dostoevsky un-Russian and un-Christian. And yet Karsavin embraced Steinberg's interpretation of Dostoevsky. I have to say that in this chapter I have not given a deep enough description of Steinberg's own philosophical system, and hope to treat his life's work in more appropriate depth in another work, addressing in particular how he viewed the role of Christianity in world history, and how his views of Russia fitted into his views on Jewish history and identity.

[94] The general consensus was that Aquinas's philosophy left room only for intellectual comprehension of God through logical and linguistic analogy, due to the fact that God's essence is so far removed from the world's being; while Eastern (Palamite) theology granted the possibility of experiential knowledge of God – through union with the divine energies, seen as intimately connected to God's essence. This Eastern criticism of Catholic intellectualism of course echoes the Russian critique of Judaic religiosity, also said to make God excessively transcendent and unknowable.

by the Neo-Platonic world-soul, Frank believed, which linked the transcendent and the immanent[95].

All three of these thinkers also considered Kant to be foreign to Russian sensibilities with his dualistic division between world and thinker and his iron categorical imperative in the sphere of ethics. Again, on this score Steinberg is a member of the club: he too believes man has access to Platonic ideals and that these ideals can be realized in history for the building of a harmonic "sobornost" that unites and fuses mankind.

Again, Steinberg talks explicitly of "the Platonic idea of the universe, the idea of the world, the transfiguration of the superficial into a human-like face"[96]. Moreover, the transformation of reality into idea, the integration of fragmented time and space into the pan-temporality and pan-spatiality of the One strongly echoes Bulgakov's doctrine of the sophianization of the world by man, first stated in his philosophy of economics.

No wonder then that Karsavin saw Steinberg as a kindred spirit and sponsored his book on Dostoevsky. No wonder he saw his friend as a de facto Christian.

And yet: if we consider Paul Franks' thesis in "Jewish Philosophy After Kant"[97], whether Steinberg or his Russian fellow thinkers realized it or not, there are good grounds for including Steinberg's thought in a worthy *Jewish* philosophical tradition that was started by the remarkable Solomon Maimon.

Jewish Platonized Kantianism

Kant famously called Maimon the most perceptive of his critics. As Franks shows, from the beginning (first Moses Mendelsohn and then Maimon) Jews had always been attracted to Kant's philosophy: its emphasis on the law as the ground of morality was congenial to Judaism. However, it is Maimon's seminal critique and revision of Kant's transcendental idealism that brings to mind Steinberg and other Russians.

Briefly, Maimon radicalized the Platonic elements inherent in Kant. Kant had made a difference between the ten categories[98] - which he derived from

---

[95] For further details, cf.ch.6.
[96] It is interesting that Steinberg combines all-unity and personalism, rather like Karsavin. Berdyaev, by contrast, felt that personalism was incompatible with a metaphysics of all-unity. However, the idea of the abandonment of biological individuality for spiritual personhood shares much with Karsavin's Christian personalism, and even perhaps with a Christian neo-Palamism that emphasizes deification through increasing abandonment of the human essence. However, the crucial criterion by which to judge Steinberg's proximity to the latter would be the role he gives man's fallenness and the asceticism needed to achieve this ascent to personhood. Cf. discussion on energo-essentialism and Khoruzhy at the end of ch.4.
[97] Paul Franks, "Jewish Philosophy after Kant: the Legacy of Solomon Maimon," in Morgan M. and Gordon P.E. *Modern Jewish Philosophy*, (Cambridge: CUP, 2007), 53-80.
[98] Space, time plus quality, quantity, modality, relation – and their subcategories.

Aristotle – and the three ideas of reason[99] - which he derived from Plato. The categories need to interact with the world to produce mental judgments; the ideas regulate the activity of the categories. The ideas are not innate, nor do they permit for judgments about reality independent of the categories. The ideas are merely extensions, "what-if" projections of the activity of the categories[100]. Hence, any metaphysical judgments, i.e. any theology, are impossible – for the ideas have no access to non-material objects.

Maimon objected that this opens up Kant's system to skepticism: Hume's explosive criticism of empiricism maintained that man cannot know anything about the world, merely about his conceptions of the world. Kant's "split" account of knowledge leaves epistemology sunk in the skeptical quandary: in other words not only theology but even physical science is impossible, as the judgments of the categories are not given any epistemological reality by the merely quasi-Platonic "ideas."

Maimon's solution is as follows: he introduces the notion of a higher intellect with which human intelligence is one, albeit in a limited way. "Between the human or finite mind and the divine or infinite mind, there is an identity-in-difference." Furthermore, form *and* matter[101] are said to originate in the infinite intellect – in which we partake – and as a result there can be a real physical science. In fact in the higher intellect matter *is* form. Thus when we perceive matter, we also receive true knowledge about its form.

Maimon's adaptation of Kant is based on his adaptation of elements of Maimonides' philosophy[102]. Maimon's medieval hero – from whom he took his pseudonym – adhered to the doctrine of a divine intellect consisting of perceiver, perception and perceived. From Maimonides too he took the idea that the human intellect is a mirror of the active intellect.

The notion that the human intellect can attain a true grasp of reality due to its "mirroring" a divine intellect appears in Steinberg, who writes that "the essence of consciousness is its infinite movement....I am conscious, I am conscious that I am conscious, and I am conscious of myself as being conscious that I am conscious etc. This is the mirror-effect of consciousness, I would say, the sphere of internal mirroredness, in the centre of which is an infinite light, and in this infinitely shining centre, consciousness is reflected in all

---

[99] God, freedom and reason.
[100] As Franks puts it: "An idea represents a *complete series of answers to why-questions*."
[101] Such a move is congenial to a "sacredness of matter" approach, a holistic approach to matter and the body which is often associated with "carnal" Judaism, but is present too in Bulgakov and Rozanov.
[102] For an interesting comparison of Maimonides and Palamas, see George Pappadimitriou, *Maimonid i Palama o Boge*. (Moscow: Put', 2003). An interesting project, which would help answer some of the questions posed below, would be to deepen this comparison of Jewish-Christian emphases in philosophy by comparing across different periods Maimonides/Palamas, Maimon/Kant and Steinberg/Karsavin.

directions, and transforms everything around it into complete limitlessness..."[103] The transformation of world and self into idea, finally, as we saw, results in the (limited) unity of self and creator in the transcendent world of ideas – the achievement, one might say, in Maimonian terms, of an identity-in-difference between creator and creature.

As Franks points out Maimonides' own neo-Platonic synthesis of elements of Plato and Aristotle was widespread among medieval Jewish philosophers. For all his Jewish heterodoxy, therefore, Maimon[104], was creatively adapting the Jewish sources he had mastered so well and using them to engage critically with Kant. As the passage just quoted shows, this "Judaized" Kantianism bears strong similarities to Steinberg's own later reworking of his previously held neo-Kantianism.

Of course, it is an open question whether Steinberg deliberately added elements of Maimonides or Maimon to his system. We know that he studied Jewish texts on a regular basis in Berlin, and Maimonides of course continues to be part of the core curriculum for religious Jews. Nonetheless, the question of direct influence is not crucial: Steinberg's uncontested immersion in Plato, acting on his previous neo-Kantianism, may have produced a typologically similar revision to Kant to that found in Maimon. The "Russianness" of Steinberg, and indeed of Bulgakov and company, is thus debatable.

Furthermore, there are two other important "Maimonian" or quasi-Maimonian moments in Steinberg's thought: the Spinozisitic pantheism of Maimon and Maimon's Messianic vision of history.

Kant and others – who were less well-disposed – accused Maimon of being Spinozisitic. The charge of Spinozism was often shorthand for a particularly Jewish heterodoxy, connected to atheism or pantheism. For anti-Enlightenment conservatives the term was pejorative, but for supporters of the Enlightenment (such as Lessing, Wolff and Goethe) it was a welcome epithet. For upholders of Protestant orthodoxy, the term expressed disapproval of any attempt to undermine the transcendence of God and his separateness from his creatures[105].

---

[103] Belous, Volphila 2, "Dostoevsky kak filosof," 657. Interestingly, in a footnote appended to this passage, Steinberg appeals not to Maimonides to confirm this vision of an infinite, mirror-like consciousness, but to Bely, who described his experience of consciousness as similar to "feeling like a sphere, multi-eyed and inward-looking...I felt only the 'inward'; and insuperable distances were sensed; from the periphery and towards...the centre." That Bely should have felt his consciousness to be spherical is also testimony to a certain Platonic sensibility, absorbed perhaps through his philo-Platonic mentor, Soloviev.

[104] Maimon had a deep knowledge of the Talmudic, Kabbalistic and medieval Jewish philosophical literature.

[105] If we try to define sides over "Spinozizing" tendencies a century or so later in the Russian context, the results might be seen as quite ironic. For one could argue that Soloviev and the sophiologists are Spinozizers (or Judaizers, if one Russifies the term). For some, such as Frank, who saw their philosophy as particularly Christian

Maimon denied that his system was guilty of this charge (as well as the charge that God and the world are one substance) but was willing to admit to a lesser count of modified Spinozism, namely that every finite thing is in some sense a limitation of God. Once again, Maimon was perfectly willing to "own up" to the Jewish origins of this belief. In this case he traced its origins back to the Kabbalah, which (as he writes in his *Autobiography*) "is nothing but expanded Spinozism, in which not only is the origin of the world explained by the limitation of the divine being, but also the origin of every kind of being, and its relation to the rest, is derived from a separate attribute of God."

Maimon expressed a preference for Cordovero's continuation of the Spanish tradition of philosophical rather than mythical Kabbalah. He understood Cordovero's idea of contraction (*tzimtzum*) as a variant of the rationalistic principle of plenitude: "God thinks himself as limited in every possible way." And in a letter to Kant, Maimon denied that this belief presupposes an identity of God and the world: such an identity for him is obviated by the existence of an intervening world-soul.

In short, then, Maimon's Platonic version of Kant, his rehabilitation of a neo-Platonic world-soul, his notion of the infinite outpouring of God into the world, and his positing of an identity between divine and human intellect, are all derived from Jewish sources[106] – and can all be found in Steinberg's "Parmenidean Torah Judaism." Furthermore, as we will see, many of these elements are present in Karsavin who derives some of them, like Frank, from Nicolas of Cusa[107]. In one sense, Steinberg was right then: a Jewish-Russian meeting is possible in philosophy, for it is a meeting of different variations on neo-Platonic mysticism. In contrast, Karsavin's (and others') identification of "Russian" elements in his friend's world-view may have been too hasty.

This brings us to Maimon's Messianism. Maimon remained aware that he had not demolished the possibility of skepticism entirely and held that even in his adapted Kantianism "reason finds that it and its activity are possible only under the presupposition of an infinite reason." Consequently, finite reason can only approximate infinite reason ad infinitum (asymptotically). In Maimon, then, as Franks puts it "the traditional Jewish view that the world is not yet redeemed but will be [turns] into the view that the world is always to be redeemed but never

---

when compared with Rosenzweig, this is an odd result. But the other side of the debate is no less odd: Florovsky, Lossky and others who opposed sophiology as too German, too Idealist, and thus "Protestantizing" and not adequately patristic, find themselves allied with the upholders of Protestantism. However, this ignores other important differences between Florovsky and Protestantism. We will take this question up again in ch.6, to further show the difference between Palamite vs. "Protestant-Judaic" transcendentalism.

[106] Which in turn of course have their roots in neo-Platonism.
[107] Cusa(1401-1464) predates Pico della Mirandola (1463-1494), the first Christian Kabbalist.

will be."[108] Human ascent to the divine is in principle unceasing.

The parallel with Steinberg is not exact. However, he too writes of the eternal becoming of self-consciousness. For if the tree of life has its roots in the infinite and is to be transformed by consciousness into the tree of knowledge, that process is surely unending. This also puts us in mind of one of Frank's criticisms of Rosenzweig, namely that this transformation seems to happen without divine intervention but according to the innate nature of man. The infinite nature of Maimonian-Steinbergian redemption also raises an eyebrow: for this is not only Christianly heterodox, but Jewishly heterodox. Maimon explicitly, and Steinberg implicitly, seem to have sidestepped the doctrine of a concrete, personal Messiah – which Maimonides encoded in his thirteen principles of the Jewish faith[109].

On the other hand, Steinberg departs from Maimon in his "revolutionary Messianism." In places he talks of the need to hasten the coming of the end, to overcome natural being through "creative evolution," and throw a bridge across the divide between existence and non-existence. But this raises in even sharper form the question of how human consciousness by itself can bridge the gap between the finite and the infinite.

Before taking up this more radical aspect of Steinberg's Messianism, it is worth returning to the question of Jewishness and Christianness in philosophy. Are Bulgakov and Karsavin Jewish? Or is Steinberg Russian? Paul Franks raises similar questions with respect to the different interpretations of Kant.

He comes to three conclusions regarding what he rather felicitously calls the Christian or Jewish "inflection" of philosophy. He maintains: firstly, Jewish philosophy does not presuppose the involvement of Jews (i.e. non-Jews could practice a "Jewish philosophy" if the term is defined independently). Secondly, what makes Jewish philosophy Jewish can also make it Christian. Thirdly, the Jewishness of a philosophy does not entail any positive relationship to the practice of Judaism.

---

[108] Just such a view of Jewish Messianism was stated by Yeshayahu Leibowitz, who sees in the notion of "asymptotic" redemption an insulation against eschatological disasters such as Sabbateanism and, for him, politicized religious Zionism. Leibowitz, also a Latvian Jew some ten years younger than Steinberg, thus adds another interesting strand to the debate about "Jewish utopianism:" on his reading, Christianity is particularly prone to false eschatologism, while true halakhic Judaism is particularly protected from that tendency. This is a nice reversal of Bulgakov's claim, and in fact, has more historical data to back it up, as I argued in ch.2 and ch.3, when I pointed out that all the example of Judaic apocalypticism come from Christian history. Cf. Yeshayahu Leibowitz, *Judaism, Human Values and the Jewish State*. Ed. Eliezer Goldman. (Cambridge: Harvard University Press, 1995):ch.10-11.

[109] In this sense, Steinberg would be as heterodox – despite his Orthopraxy – in respect to his own faith as his close friend Bely was with his theosophism in respect to traditional Christianity. On the other hand, Maimonides himself often came under attack from Jewish traditionalists for rationalizing the doctrine of the Messiah by depriving the Messianic era of miraculous elements.

Regarding the second point, if Jewish philosophy is defined as referring to messianism, divine unity, and law in Platonic and Aristotelian terms, then this of course does not distinguish it from Christian philosophy. Since the Renaissance even Kabbalah has infiltrated "Christian" philosophy, so even that is not a demarcation. We have several times encountered such a blurring of boundaries when considering Soloviev's heirs in Russian philosophy.

Regarding the first point, one would need to find some truly Jewish markers for non-Jews to be seen to be practicing Jewish philosophy. Franks suggests two parameters: whether divinity can be incarnate and the world thus knowable, and whether the Messiah has redeemed the world or not. "Jewish" philosophy would supposedly answer in the negative to both these options. Still, once again, as we have seen, things are not so simple here either. As Franks himself points out, Judaism has its own limited version of incarnation in the above examined Spinozism, which lessens the gap between God and the world[110]. And Maimon's adaptation of the Christian Kant is also a case where a Jew is arguing for greater knowability of the world[111].

To this one can add a further caveat: as Khoruzhy[112] showed, too *much* immanence results in paganism, or in his terms – which owe something to the pejorative language of Russian thought itself – Judaization. A fully immanent divinity, or divine power, diverts the believer from the necessary outward quest for contact with transcendent divinity. Thus the pagan worshiper of streams and

---

[110] Wyschgorod is an example of an Orthodox Jewish philosopher who emphasizes the incarnational aspect of Judaism: God dwells among his people and makes them holy. For him the notion of divinity and humanity dwelling in one person, Jesus Christ, is an intensification of Biblical incarnationalism. He gives the impression that the Christian doctrine of incarnation is not per se unJewish; for him more troubling and unconvincing is the idea that Jesus in His humanity is free of sin – it is this which comprises the doctrine of the Incarnation for Wyschgorod. Franks, too, points out that the famous Talmudic phrase "Israel, and the Torah, and the Holy One Blessed be He are one" even combines incarnationalism with triune structure.

[111] As we will see, Semyon Frank's central concept of unfathomability was seen by some as particularly Jewish. Was this his ethnic background making itself felt? Or is it better to say that this is the influence of Christian German mystical pantheism and idealism, with its roots in Gnosticism? Or simply his own idiosyncratic way of looking at the world? We will pick up this question again in the next chapter. It is interesting to consider how Shestov would fare by these criteria: he would be Jewish in not seeing the world as knowable, and in denying that the world is redeemed, despite occasions where he seems to accept God's incarnation in Christ. He would have rejected this label, of course, as he claimed that Maimonides and Talmudic Judaism, as well as Christianity, were equally corrupted by "Athens," and only the Bible was in "Jerusalem."

[112] Cf. Sergei Khoruzhy, "Imjaslavije i kul'tura Serebryanogo Veka: fenomen khristianskogo neoplaotonizma," in Khoruzhy S.S. *Opyty iz russkoy dukhovnoy traditsii* (Moscow: Parad, 2005), 287-309. Also, cf. discussion of this article in ch.4.

mountains commits the same error as the mutterer of Kabbalistic incantations – and both are similar to the Christian whose incomprehensible Slavonic (or Latin) liturgy is a thaumaturgy that replaces communication with Christ.

Indeed, the philosophic enterprise itself always contains the danger of including the all within the bounds of comprehensibility and thus of becoming a type of magic itself. This tendency is critiqued in the Talmud's repudiation of "Greek wisdom" as *apikorsos*[113], and in the Orthodox Palamas' denigration of the foolish and malevolent wisdom of Plato. In short, while there may be a Jewish and Christian "inflection" in philosophy, identifying such a difference is likely to be a matter of finding Wittgensteinian family resemblance rather than clear-cut binary parameters.

Regarding the future arrival of the Messiah, Franks points out that Lukacs, Adorno, Benjamin, and Bloch are Jewish in that they view redemption as always yet to come, and thus action in this world as justified. This is a good point. Steinberg too seems to have an "infinite" view of redemption, which like these German Jews does not stop him from expecting revolutionary activity – just not of the Marxist sort. But again, Franks' point is muddied by Christians like Meier and Fedotov (who we will examine more closely below), who were close to Steinberg in their support of a non-Marxist revolutionary spirit and belief in socialist action[114]. In this sense, action in the world is a prelude to the *second* coming of the Messiah. As a counterpoint, one also needs to remember Orthodox Jews who utterly eschew any this-worldly action (in the case of Neturei Karta even Zionist action).

Franks' third point concerning Jewish philosophy and Jewish practice is also important. He reminds us that Maimon was not buried in a Jewish cemetery, i.e. he died outside the fold of Jewish tradition. This was the heritage of his Kantianism. Kant himself was supportive of Jews as individuals but hostile to Jewish law; he saw Lazarus Bendavid's call not to grant Jews civil rights until they cease observing it as a welcome "euthanasia" of Judaism. Ultimately, Jewish *huqqim*[115] violate Kantian autonomy due to their irrationality. But without *huqqim*, Jewish particularity fades away. Kantianism and Jewish euthanasia thus seem to be logically linked.

Franks also makes the related point that Jewish Kantianism is ultimately dangerous to Judaism, and not just Jews – as in principle it makes possible a Jewishness without Judaism – which is what Maimon was engaged in. Whether such a Jewishness can transcend the individual, whether, as the traditional anxiety has it, it can guarantee that its practitioners will have Jewish grandchildren – is a moot point. In the case of Mendelsohn, Maimon and other Jewish Kantians or Kantian Jews, evidently not[116]. The euthanasia of Judaism would seem to be

---

[113] The Talmudic term for heresy, a mangled form of the name of Epicurus.
[114] One thinks of Latin American liberation theology as well.
[115] Those aspects of the Torah that have no rationale and are observed out of obedience to the inscrutable Divine will.
[116] It is becoming clear that even if we include Steinberg within a Jewish philosophical

linked to the euthanasia of Jews. As Franks makes clear, that phrase of course puts one in mind of a far more determined German euthanasia of Jews and Judaism, so that the stark question remains: "to recite, or not to recite, a blessing" over Kant – as Isaac Breuer, an Orthodox Jewish Kantian who had a picture of Kant over his desk once did, in fulfillment of the *mitvah* to say a blessing on seeing a non-Jewish sage.

The other famous Kantian Orthodox Jewish philosopher was Joseph Soloveitchik, who derived a philosophy of the *halakhah* out of Kantian premises. The example of Breuer and Soloveitchik goes to show that Kantianism is not necessarily a fatal impulse to Judaism. And if we relate this to Franks' third point, we can also say that there are Jewish philosophies that do entail a positive attitude to Jewish practice: i.e., philosophy and Judaism are not – as some Christians and Jews have thought – intrinsically inimical, an irreconcilable clash of the Hellenistic and Judaic. Soloveitchik's worldview, which he dubbed in Hebrew *Torah umaddah*, Jewish Law and (Greek) wisdom, testifies to this.

Steinberg and Jewishness in philosophy
However, with the exception of these last Orthodox Jewish Kantians, whose connection of Kantianism and Judaism is not unproblematic[117], Franks tends to confirm the sense of surprise we started out with at the beginning of this section – at the anomaly of Steinberg's observant lifestyle combined with his Volphilic Dostoevskian philosophy. Reading Steinberg anonymously, in the dark as it were, could one feel a way back to the unknown author's Jewishness and, more, to his Orthodox Judaism – just by using the grain of the text for guidance? Surely the path could lead to any number of Volphila's maximalists of the spirit?

In this sense Steinberg provides an interesting contrast to Breuer and Soloveitchik. These men were the founders of modern Orthodoxy, a movement within Judaism that is traditional but engages with contemporary Western culture. Steinberg is modern and Orthodox, but one would hesitate to call him "modern Orthodox." Though a scion of the eastern Lithuanian perimeter of the

---

typology, he is still rather odd: for his Maimonian, post-Kantian philosophizing in no way comprises his own Jewish observance – on the one hand. On the other hand, it is rather interesting that Steinberg's wish was to remain a bachelor, and that when he did marry, he married his best friend, and the two had a celibate relationship. Thus Steinberg's personal life is closer to that third-testamental spiritual asexualism preached by Merezhkovsky and embraced by Berdyaev. In other words, Steinberg too did not have any grandchildren, Jewish or otherwise – and this may be another indication that his Judaism and his philosophizing were not as harmonious as he believed. A fuller treatment of the relationship between Steinberg's life and his philosophy would have to be undertaken to give flesh to this assertion, however.

[117] For a mismatch between the two in Soloveitchik's philosophy, cf. Lawrence J. Kaplan, "Joseph Soloveitchik and Halakhic Man," in Morgan, Michael, and Gordon, Peter. Editors. *Modern Jewish Philosophy*. Cambridge: CUP, 2007.

German Jewish enlightenment[118], with his move east to Moscow he seems to have stretched the limits, to have gone beyond any homogenous movement.

In the case of Breuer and Soloveitchik their Judaic commitment can be read straight off the page of their philosophical writings. With Steinberg, this is not the case. Only once the reader knows that the writer is a practicing Jew, can he translate his "philosophese" back into Judaic. For example, when Steinberg talks of transferring reality into the transcendental kingdom of ideas - is that not what the halakhah does when it sanctifies portions of the physical world? The Logos incarnate: is that not God's Torah forging the people of Israel into a unity and rescuing them from historical dissolution? The decisive choice of Life of course takes us back to Moses' great recapitulation in Deuteronomy. And so on.

But there are moments of ambiguity, where it seems that the philosophese might get garbled in its retranslation back into Judaic. For example: that talk of man's consciousness being crucified; the tragic aspect of man's existence in which he faces nothingness and emptiness; the Logos incarnate; the supreme moment in human philosophical history which is the incarnation of the Word in the deed....? Do not these speak of the darkness of the Cross, the suffering of God's servant, the fallenness of the world? And suicide, murder, power: are these subjects for a good Jewish boy?[119]

The drama of these themes has obviously been taken from Dostoevsky. Dostoevsky with his deep internality has Christian roots which stretch right back to St Augustine's invention of the confessional genre. Thus while the Word incarnate

---

[118] Some of Steinberg's confidence in the fusion of Russian and Jewish culture comes from his own culturally "aristocratic" background. He was a scion of the most advanced layer of North-East Russian enlightened Jewry. His grandfather, Solomon Elyashev was the rabbi of Kovno, and an innate aesthete who read *War and Peace* in German translation. His uncle Isodor Elyashev was a Yiddish critic who translated Tolstoy, Turgenev and Herzen into Yiddish and devoted his life to expanding and deepening Yiddish culture and literature. Here we see the native roots of the Russian-German-Yiddish fusion that Steinberg was to make his own – or rather to inherit and re-make his own: for as he later said, "In order not to degenerate, one must consciously and unwaveringly guard one's noble heritage." Perhaps this heritage explains his brother's equally extraordinary fusion of revolutionary activism and Jewish observance.

[119] On an altogether less frivolous note, the theme of suicide in fact had a haunting presence in Steinberg's life. For several years when he was living in Germany, he was tempted by the thought of the absurdity of life and of killing himself. His wife's closest friend drowned herself in Lake Lausanne, and Steinberg tried to overcome his grief at his wife's own death by addressing a letter to her, written over several weeks. In it he grapples in torment with the thought that she herself tooks pills in order to relieve him of the difficulty of looking after her in his own frail state. The letter is painful to read, full of self-reproach for any actions in his own life which may have encouraged this mistaken self-sacrifice in his sorely missed life-mate. Cf. Aaron Steinberg, "'Dorogaya moya Sonyurochka…'. Pisma k pokoinoy zhene. Publikatisia, predislovie i kommentariy Nelli Portnovoy," in *Novy Mir*, No.1, 2006.

might find an Aramaic equivalent in the "memre" of the targumim, there are other aspects of Steinberg's thought which seem to be irreducibly New Testament.

Of course, Steinberg is silent regarding Christ and the presence of Christian influences. But this is not a neutral silence, but a very pointed one. He was also for that matter silent in his philosophical work about explicit Judaic parallels, except for a select audience. The meeting in which he outlined the congruity between Dostoevsky and the Old Testament vision of freedom is referred to Katsis as the only Jewish meeting of Volphila – but this was rather for the presence of Jews than of Judaism. Generally, Steinberg prefers to speak a universal Greek – rather than Judaic or Christian.

One might be tempted to see in this neutral philosophese another case of "Jewishness without Judaism" – were it not for the fact that Steinberg was deeply immersed in Jewish observance himself. That alone makes it tempting to speak of a "Judaism without Jewishness"! But one still wants to know why the Judaic language is so muted. Unlike with Shestov or Gershenzon, it seems that this cannot come from any ambiguity or negativeness about Judaism, nor – as in their case – ambiguity about the "Russian spirit" and his place in Russian culture. In fact, Steinberg's confident Judaic identity argues for the opposite.

Instead, one can see it as revealing an immense confidence in the *congruity* of Jewishness and Christianized culture. In this sense, Steinberg seems to be part of that bold appropriation of Christian symbolism by Russian Jews which we glanced at in our chapter on Soloviev. The most well-known practitioner was Chagall, with his image of a crucified Jew in a *tallis*.

I would speculate that Steinberg's underlying logic is this. While unable to relate dogmatically to the idea of the god-man or the crucified God, Steinberg feels none of the traditional Jewish squeamishness about employing such symbols as the essential building-blocks of his world-view. Perhaps this is because he feels that these symbols are ultimately Judaic: the suffering Messiah in Isaiah is a somewhat taboo theme due to historical circumstance but nonetheless it was never rejected totally by Jewish sources[120]. Furthermore, the notion of God suffering with His children is also common in Jewish tradition.

Thus in Steinberg Jewishness clothes itself in Christianity, but the two do not merge[121]. Steinberg's confidence in his Jewishness is such that he sees the Christian garment as woven from Jewish fabric, and thus a good fit for the Jewish body. He therefore uses the language that Russian revolutionaries of the spirit understood:

---

[120] Still, cf. the discussion in ch.6 regarding the difference between Herman Cohen's reading of the Servant in Isaiah and Semyon Frank's interpretation of suffering, which point to a clear difference in Jewish and Christian understandings of even common tropes and symbols. Steinberg's confidence about the congruity of the two religious worldviews, which underpins his whole analysis of Dostoevsky, thus does blur significant differences – as Katsis, Meier and Tzhberg noted.

[121] Rather as Karsavin will later claim that Christianity clothes itself in Greek thought while not merging with it. See below.

resurrection, crucifixion[122], incarnation – knowing that each of these terms has its own "dogmatic" locus in the Judaic/Old Testament[123] tradition. In this sense he adds a new category to Franks' list: a Jew who practices "Christian"[124] philosophy, while not adjuring his Jewishness or his Judaism[125].

---

[122] An exact quote will give an idea of how Steinberg uses Christian language: "We are nailed to the threefold cross of three dimensions, each of us in Time is constantly tormented, torn to pieces by all-dividing Time…And there, on the Golgotha of human consciousness each man in this same stream of Time recognizes himself as having an independent being, i.e. as an omnipresent and eternal creature whose annihilation would lead to the dissolution of the whole world…and thus we are free creatures inasmuch as this independent being manifests itself….(Doklad Shteinberga, 655)." An even more telling quotation from *Sistema* (p.132): "The image of the Mother of God is not accidental here: a real and truthful conception should be immaculate: it should be undertaken not in the name of human-divine ideas, but in the name of a divine-human calling…" The crucifixion of Jesus on the cross becomes an all-human type of man's search for meaning, and a legitimate symbol in Steinberg's Judaic philosophy of All-Unity; the dogma of the immaculate conception and the divine-humanity of Christ becomes symbols of pure artistic and ethical openness to the Logos. If we tease out the implications of this a little further, it becomes clear that Judaic All-Unity includes and transcends Christianity. The life of Jesus is a moment in the All-Unity of the Father, Whom Judaism worships directly. As Steinberg further implies in his "Otvet L.P.Karsavinu," Judaism also prays that the world, man and the Father can ultimately become One, thus further indicating that the Christian moment will be transcended. Thus Steinberg covertly develops his own version of Rosenzweig's "dual covenant" approach to Judaism and Christianity.

[123] He adapts himself to his audience to such an extent as to refer to his own tradition as Old Testament.

[124] Of course the term Christian would need to be defined. The present discussion is still not exhaustive.

[125] One should not forget that while studying Kant in Heidelberg, Steinberg also studied Talmud every day with a respected rabbinical teacher. In his other writings, he writes fondly of Jewish Lithuanian culture and language. Beneath his Russian self, there was a firmly rooted Jewish core. Portnova quotes Steinberg as saying that he had achieved an integrated personal identity consisting of "Jewish religiosity enclosed in the Russian element," with a European atmosphere and in the stream of general human movement. Incidentally, Isaac Steinberg's son and Aaron Zakharovich's nephew, is the famous American art historian Leo Steinberg. His book *The Sexuality of Christ in Renaissance Art and in Modern Oblivion* deals with the representation of the infant Christ's genitalia in Renaissance paintings, as well as the representation of the blood of the infant Christ at his circumcision as a pictorial representation of the dogma of full, fleshly incarnation. I do not know whether Leo Steinberg, who was born in Moscow in 1920, consciously derived these themes from his uncle, but he surely must have known of Aaron's visit to Rozanov to discuss precisely such themes, which had an even more inflammatory nature in pre-Revolutionary Russia. Whether he did or not, Leo Steinberg seems to be a true scion of the Steinberg family, judging by what we know of his father and uncle, and of its ability to clothe Judaism in the garb of the surrounding culture.

The reason he does this is clear too: he sees Judaism as having a universal mission. The presence of Jews in Russia and the baptism of Russia into a religion that has sprung from the Judaic core and is in a sense (as Steinberg said of St. Paul) a Judaic periphery is providential. A Jew can thus fulfill his universal mission of world redemption through the medium of peripherally Judaized (i.e. Christian) culture[126]. Thus Steinberg is engaged, as was his brother, in Messianic Jewish activity. His Judaism and what he in effect saw as the Russian "Judaism" of Dostoevsky are the yeast which will ferment the bread of political and ethical salvation.

That Steinberg's Jewishness could merge so comfortably – at least on the elevated intellectual plane – with the Russian culture of his day also points to a deep compatibility in the type of the Russian "host" culture. That was in part due not just to its ancient Judeo-Christian roots, and specifically its Eastern Christian mysticism, but also to the more recent efforts of Soloviev the "Jew." However, Florensky, too, for all his horror of the geometrically increasing infiltration of Jewish blood into the Russian body, also prepared the ground for Steinberg.

After all, should Florensky really have been surprised that his belief in all-unity would ultimately lead to the embrace of Russia's outsiders within her ever-expanding spiritual borders? Florensky clung to his hatred for Jews despite his love for "dear Spinoza," as he once called the philosopher. But the Spinozistic element in his own thought – and there were those who believed the half-Armenian priest with his long locks also bore a striking physical resemblance to the Amsterdam Jewish heretic – opened the gates to many Russian-born "dear Spinozas," who might be called his blood-brothers in the spirit, such as Gershenzon, Frank, and Steinberg. Perhaps the clinching example is Osip Mandelstam, whose wife spoke of the crucial influence on her husband's work of V.Soloviev and P.Florensky[127]. Of course, it is a different problem as to how he might have categorized these new guests at the philosophical table. Were they Yids? Surely not. Or Jews? Like Rozanov, he must have fluctuated desperately between the two extremes[128].

This leads on to an interesting conclusion regarding the disagreement between Karsavin and Steinberg about how to characterize the different "strata"

---

[126] It was Karsavin who called Steinberg a Judaizing Volga tribesman. But Steinberg could have used the very same epithet of Karsavin, adding that that was the reason why they could communicate.

[127] In K. Antonov. "Problema samosoznaniye yevreev-khristian." Diaspory No.3 (2004):168-190. Footnote 15. For more on the covert Judaic influence that one scholar detects in Mandelstam, cf. Epstein M."Khasid i Talmudist.Sravnitel'nii opyt o Pasternake i Mandel'shtame." Zvezda No.4. (2004).

[128] On the other side, Frank, to take one example of a philosopher of Jewish origin, was not enthusiastic about many aspects of Florensky's philosophy but he was respectful of his work, and included him in a collection of a dozen representatives of Russian philosophy that he edited shortly before his death.

of Jewry: as core-and-periphery or nucleus-and-discharge. In fact the difference between the two models are not so important in view of what we have argued above. For both models assume that the centre and the periphery are composed of different individuals, religious Jews and assimilating Jews respectively. But Steinberg himself is an example of a religious Jew whose job was to assimilate into Christian culture and so transform it: however, if we read him correctly, his type of assimilation was an immersion in the non-Jewish ambient culture which did not lead to the disappearance of the "immersee" (so that there is a difference here with Gershenzon). Not that the "immersee" will not himself be transformed: Steinberg is a catalyst who hopes to trigger a reaction, and himself be catalysed.

The boundaries between the believer and the world
Core and periphery, Orthodoxy and Revolution

This brings us to our next theme. This is the question of the extent to which Steinberg's "Messianic" belief in the Revolution, albeit in a spiritual sense, was "Jewish." We have already seen that Steinberg's Platonism and pantheistic inclinations endeared him to Karsavin and Berdyaev. We argued that this Russian "disguise" was perhaps not quite as Russian as might at first seem, but Jewish in a different sense.

The question is whether Steinberg's thought was "Jewish" in the sense that Berdyaev, Bulgakov, Florensky and others often decried, what we can now roughly equate with Franks' second feature of philosophic Jewishness: the belief in the unredeemedness of the world and the need for a near-future, eschatological redemption of the world, often through permanent revolution.

It is true that Berdyaev liked Steinberg's book on Dostoevsky. But there was a vital difference between Berdyaev and Steinberg's philosophy of history. Steinberg believed the revolutionary present could be seized and transformed through concrete idealism. For the task set by history to be achieved (namely the transformation of reality into idea), the whole experiential world must be pulverized to the last grain, and the quicker the wings of time flap – so hurrying on the process of decay – the more productive will be the work of its grindstones[129]. Steinberg was thus adhering to some sort of revolutionary idealism that wished to hurry on the future.

Berdyaev, by contrast, contended that eschatology can only be prophetic: "there can be no other philosophy of history than the prophetic…for in any knowledge there is not that reality of the present which we would like to know."[130]

---

[129] For this dramatic, eschatological language cf. Aaron Steinberg, "Razvitie i razlozhenie v sovremmenom iskustve." Paper presented at 3rd open session of Volphila, 1 Dec.1919. In Belous V. *Volphila* 2, 591-608. Moscow: Tri Kvadrata, 2005.

[130] N.A.Berdyaev, "Opyt eskhatologicheskoy metafisiki: Tvorchestvo i objektivatsia", in *Tsarstvo Dukha i tsarstvo Kesarja*, Moskva, 1995. Also, discussion in Belous (2007), "A.Z.Shteinberg o smysle istorii", 307-335.

Moreover, as we saw, for Berdyaev the main eschatological event of history is in the past: the incarnation and crucifixion of Christ, which spreads meaning and absorbs into itself all following events, so that what is truly eschatological in time is siphoned off into the timeless. Berdyaev may well fit into Steinberg's category of philosophers who make redemption trans-historical, and so fail to transform the world. We recall, too, that Berdyaev attacked Gershenzon for husking Slavophilism of its Christian core, leaving a Christless call to transformation through the "Spirit." Perhaps it was only because the two were not well enough acquainted that Berdyaev did not suggest a similar charge against Steinberg[131].

Turning to Bulgakov, who as far we know did not express an opinion about Steinberg's work, one cannot imagine that he would have been sympathetic to Steinberg's portrait of Dostoevsky as a prophet of spiritual revolution. His 1914 essay about Dostoevsky called "The Russian Tragedy" had hailed Dostoevsky as the great denouncer of Russian nihilism, socialism and false utopianism. True, Steinberg is no Marxist; he is an enemy of positivism. His utopia is a utopia of the Spirit. Nonetheless, his belief in the possibility of achieving this spiritual utopia in Russia in 1921 using the energies unleashed by the Revolution with Dostoevsky as its prophet would surely have struck Bulgakov as misguided, perhaps perversely inappropriate – on a par with fellow-Volphilite Alexander Blok's appropriation of Soloviev as the prophet of world revolution, a reading which necessitated discounting his last "reactionary" period when Soloviev turned his back on concrete political action.

However, here too, Steinberg needs to be seen against a background of Russian Christians who saw similar possibilities for spiritual growth in revolutionary Russia. The most compelling of these is Georgy Fedotov, who before exile was a member of Alexander Meier's religious-philosophical circle in Petrograd. (He was also a fellow-pupil with Karsavin of Ivan Greyvs, a magnetic and influential professor at the history faculty of St Petersburg's University who raised a whole generation of Russian historians.) A comparison of Steinberg, Fedotov (shortly we will examine Meier) and Berdyaev is instructive. As we have already seen, it was Fedotov who reproached Berdyaev in 1945 for his sudden enthusiasm for the rulers of their old homeland and his subsuming of communism under the aegis of the eschatological "Russian idea."

---

[131] And yet Berdyaev in his late eschatological phase converges with Steinberg, as he did with Gershenzon. Steinberg, too, emphasizes the wandering nature of the Russian thinker (*Doklad Shteinberga*, 645): "Remember how he [Versilov in Dostoevsky's *The Adolescent*] referred to himself: 'I am an eternal wanderer in Europe.' A Russian wanderer in Europe, wandering in search of what? The Russian idea, Russian thought. He flees Russia, so as to see Russia, so as to find Russia on other European tombstones..." The wandering Russian and the wandering Jew – with their eschatological obsessions – meet, and sometimes fuse, in the consciousness of Steinberg, Gershenzon and Berdyaev.

The case of Georgy Fedotov

There is an irony in this: Fedotov was regarded with suspicion even by the more liberal wing of the Russian emigration in Paris for his socialist political activity and writing. Right-wing, White circles regarded him with veritable loathing. This was due to his collaboration in France with Alexander Kerensky, the exiled head of the Provisional Government. Kerensky had been a member of the Socialist Revolutionary party when he was chosen to head the government that replaced tsarist rule. His policy of tolerance towards the more extreme Bolsheviks was believed by many to have facilitated their seizure of power in October 1917.

It seems odd that Fedotov with his socialist, democratic leanings should be the one to criticize Berdyaev, who in 1917 had found the Revolution so distasteful that his sympathies gravitated towards monarchism for a while. But as Fedotov pointed out, Berdyaev's critique of Western liberal society and his contempt for bourgeois values with their notions of gradual progress reveals a similar mindset to that of the Bolsheviks. Both of them share an eschatological impatience, an all-or-nothing approach to the world. Fedotov saw Berdyaev's utter rejection of political options in 1917 as rebounding on him in 1945.

Fedotov, by contrast, had always seen politics as integral to the Christian enterprise. While Bulgakov, Berdyaev and others made the transition from Marxism through Idealism to Orthodoxy, leaving each prior stage behind, Fedotov continued to be active in left-wing circles in emigration, and never rejected the social and political endeavors even after his return to Christianity and its growing centrality in his worldview. On leaving Russia in 1925, he found work at Bulgakov's St Sergius Institute where he taught hagiology and the history of Western Christianity. He also wrote for *Versty*[132] for a time. However, his main enterprise was always leftist politics and he felt uncomfortable in church circles.

It should be said that Fedotov's vision of socialism and democracy in no way aligned him with Soviet ideology. From the very beginning he detested the totalitarian nature of Soviet government, which he saw as immoral and uprooted from its socialist foundations. He refused to engage in any actions in his university teaching work which would give the impression that he supported the Sovietization of Russia. With this principle in place, however, he dreamed of a reform of Russian society that would be more in keeping with Christian notions of justice.

This meant that he vehemently rejected any right-wing politics that co-opted Christianity to supports its rule. He supported the Republicans in the Spanish Civil War, maintaining that the blood they spilt was the lesser evil when compared to Franco's massacres, carried out in the name of Christ and the Church – an opinion which he expressed in print, drawing the ire of both sides of the Russian émigré community. In another article he made ironic reference

---

[132] This was due to force of circumstance: he distrusted Eurasianism as like the Soviet idea it proposed to swallow up Russia in a larger artificial entity.

to Stalin's "supra-Christian sense of sacrifice." This led to a call for his expulsion from the St. Sergius Institute, which in the end did not take place.

His own intellectual work was devoted to examining Russian church history – with a view to building up the cultural resources that would facilitate the re-Christianization of Russia once the Bolshevik yoke had been thrown off. It is here that his political and cultural views are somewhat reminiscent of Steinberg. This is no coincidence: Fedotov absorbed much of his attitude to religion and politics from Alexander Meier, in whose *Voskreseniye* circle he was an active and deeply engaged participant. Meier, in turn, was one of the organizers of Volphila. Thus Steinberg and Fedotov were linked by a common intellectual spirit.

Like Steinberg, Fedotov believed that much good work could be done by people outside the core of the Church (or the synagogue, for Steinberg). The cultural life of society that went on beyond the walls of the Church had a positive value and could be a continuation in different, secular forms of the Church's message. This can be contrasted with the view of Florensky, for example, who theorized the relation between Church and society as that between the *cult* and (the etymologically related) *culture*. The job of the cult (Church) was to draw the whole of culture into itself and so redeem it; anything left outside was tainted. It is precisely this view that in our discussion of Soloviev we characterized as "Talmudic" and Judaic, for its theocratic tendencies, or as Frank was to put it, its underlying rejection of the division between grace and law.

Fedotov, in contrast, agreed that "the cult is the core from which cultures develop," but maintained that creators of culture who act outside the Church are expanding Christian truth. Like Steinberg, he was a devout believer who brought the principles of the Church to the periphery, thus churching what was beyond the walls of the Church. As we argued in respect to Steinberg, in his own activity he thus refused to believe that those "on the inside" should leave it to others, to renegades and heretics, to light up the periphery. Through his historical research and his political journalism, Fedotov was as involved in the periphery – and beyond – as in the centre.

While it would be forced to extend too far the parallel between the Orthodox Jewish revolutionary of the Spirit, Aaron Steinberg, and his brother the Social revolutionary commissar in Lenin's government, Isaac Steinberg, and the social democratic Orthodox Christian Fedotov, the aphorism which Fedotov formulated to express his view of Christian activity in a world between the two comings of Christ bears a striking resemblance to a similar aphorism in the Talmud[133].

---

[133] The following quote necessitates a timely self-correction. For it demonstrates that while the Talmud's overarching unstated premise is the reinstatement of all ancient Israelite laws in a perfect theocracy, at the same time it contains a recognition that such an implementation may not be possible in the real world, and quite evidently was not being realized in the real world. There is also a sense of the contingencies of human reality and their intersection with the divine will, which dilutes this picture of a crude "theocracy from above": for example, while recognizing the Sinaitic origin

The aphorism provides another take on how Christians can engage fully with the events of their times without giving in to false eschatological expectations. It reads: "Live as if you had to die today, and at the same time as if you were immortal; work as if history was never going to end, and at the same time as if it was going to end today."[134] The aphoristic form of this saying as well as its content brings to mind a similar recommendation from the Talmudic Chapters of the Fathers (*Pirkei Avoth*): "Rabbi Tarfon used to say: 'You are not required to complete the task, yet you are not free to withdraw from it.'"[135]

---

of the various tithing laws, the rabbis found ways to release Jews from tithing in times of famine, or excessive gentile taxation. In Christian dogmatic language this exegetic activity could be called a type of divine-human synergy.

[134] L.I.Vasilenko, *Vvedenie v russkuyu religioznuyu filofiyu. (*Moscow: PSTGU, 2006), 354 (from *Sudba Rossii*).

[135] Fedotov himself wrote an article on the Jewish question: "Novoe na staruyu temu: k sovremennoy postanovke yevreiskogo voprosa," in Novy Zhurnal, No.1, 1940. The first part of the article, told without any Russian philosophical "pathos" and more in the spirit of objective historical research, is an admiring account of Jewish achievements, and talent, honed by the tradition of respect for education developed in the ghetto. Fedotov expresses his hope that such a talented nation will never disappear through assimilation, viewing this as a tragedy for humanity. He also voices the opinion that Russian communism is doing more to destroy the Jewish people than Hitler and his camps: thousands of Jews have already disappeared in the "semi-Mongolian sea" created by atheistic communism. At the end, he broaches a more subjective approach, his own views as a Christian. He views the distinctive contribution of Jewry as its religion, and cannot help see the non-acceptance of Christ by Jewry as a misfortune. Nonetheless, he views thinkers like Buber and Cohen, as well as Jewish Jesus scholars like Klausner and Montefiore, as a sign that Jews are coming to a new attitude towards "Joshua." Writing probably from his experience of the Meier circle (as well as such friends and colleagues in exile like his friend and intellectual collaborator Ilya Fondaminsky), he also notes a new type of Jewish conversion of "pure and spiritually thirsty people." He also admits that for two thousand years pagans have crucified Jews, and now especially when Jews are accepting Christ a new gentile cry has arisen: "Crucify Him, He is a Yid!" Fedotov writes that while Christians can look with interest at the development of China or Islam, in the end they cannot but hope that these cultures will join "the universal sea" of Christianity. The same is truer of Judaism, which is an earlier stage of Christianity. A return to the religion of the Law is impossible for the modern religious consciousness and can only be tolerated out of a sacrifice by a nationalist instinct. Nonetheless, different people will make the decision about the relation of Israel and Jesus differently. Fedotov also once gave a talk called "Russian-Jewish friendship" to an audience of Russian-Jewish intellectuals. The title of the talk led to frothing denunciations of the writer in the right-wing émigré journal *Vozrozhdenie*. Still, in that talk too, Fedotov had stated that the Jewish lights of Russian thought had ultimately seen fit to depart from Judaism through embracing Orthodoxy. E.Fedotova, in her account of this episode (Introduction to *Litso Rossii*, p.xxiii) comments: "I don't think the Jews were offended because they did everything possible to help G.P.(Fedotov) escape to America with other socialists." It was indeed

While it is not the aim of the present discussion to make a final judgment regarding which approach to the relationship between religion and politics is best, one observation can be made. If we compare Fedotov to Florensky, Berdyaev, Bulgakov and Karsavin we find that he is the only one who sees an affinity between democracy and Orthodoxy. Karsavin expressed admiration for aspects of the Soviet system of government, which he thought resembled his own idea of a symphonic unity of the nation, councils, and people. Bulgakov, though believing in a similar churching or sophianization of the world, left Russia a mystical monarchist. Florensky's final utopian work, a continuation of his idea of the "theocratization" of society as we saw briefly in the last chapter, is barely distinguishable from Soviet totalitarian fantasies.

This brings us back to the question of how "negatively Jewish" Steinberg's involvement in Volphila was, not to mention his brother's more overtly political involvement in Lenin's government. The answer is that their support of a social-democratic or social-revolutionary politics, combined with a disapproval of Bolshevik totalitarianism, which was rooted in religious faith and practice is, unsurprisingly, not just a Jewish phenomenon. More importantly, it would be wrong, I believe, to see it as a negative phenomenon as well.

Often any combination of socialism and Christianity from this period of Russian history is condemned automatically by Russian Orthodox as "renovationism." The epithet refers to those groups of Christians (Rus. *obnovlentsy*) who collaborated with the Soviet regime, and were co-opted by the regime to produce a compliant façade that could be used to undermine and draw believers away from the real Church. Renovationists embraced an extremely liberal theology, gave their approval to communist ideology, availed themselves of privileges given by the government, and encouraged their parishioners to be obedient to the Soviets.

Unfortunately, the term is often used merely in a pejorative way to refer to anyone the speaker or writer disagrees with. It ignores the fact that there were many conservative Christians in high positions in the Russian church who also collaborated with the regime. It also ignores the fact that Fedotov and similar Christians embraced socialism and an (initially) experimental Christianity as part of a genuine search for truth under excruciatingly difficult conditions, which had nothing to do with a desire to please the authorities – to whom in fact they were opposed, and of whom they often became victims.

The case of Alexander Meier

Alexander Meier's circle is a case in point. A brief glance at it will add to our understanding of the atmosphere of the Petrograd where Steinberg was involved with Volphila. It will also further illustrate the concept of core/

---

the American Jewish Labor Committee that arranged Fedotov's visa and circuitous passage out of France and across the Atlantic in 1941. They had a list of socialist enemies of Stalin and Hitler, and Fedotov was one of them.

periphery in the Russian Christian and Jewish context.

Meier[136] had started a philosophical-theological circle (*Voskresenie*) in Petrograd shortly after the Revolution that conducted discussions somewhat in the spirit of the Religious Philosophical Society – in which he had also participated actively. The regular members (including the Merezhkovskys, Pumpyanski[137], Petrov-Vodkin, Bakhtin, A.V. Karteshev, Askol'dov-Alekseev and G.P. Fedotov) then formed the "Christ and Freedom" brotherhood, where discussion was supplemented by individual and church prayers. In a spirit of ecumenism, the Our Father was read in Slavonic, Latin and German.

The group was characterized by a breadth of political and religious opinion similar to Volphila. There were two communists who lived in the name of Christ, and one monarchist. There were several unbaptized Jews and even a Karaite. Most of the members were opposed to the Bolsheviks, but still hoped that the government would change its ways.

E. Fedotova[138] also recalls that the circle included quite a number of Jews who, "having been alienated for many years from the ruling church, in a fit of self-sacrifice strove towards the persecuted church which could promise them nothing but martyrdom."[139] In other words, the unresolvable paradox of Jewish

---

[136] In his youth, Meier – an Odessan of German origin – had also been involved in revolutionary circles. He started off as a Marxist who organized workers' meetings and was exiled to central Asia as a result, and then from 1906-1908 he turned to "mystical anarchism" (an article *Marx and Bakunin* was written at this time), i.e anarchism with a spiritual orientation. Later he took part in the Religious-Philosophical Society, where he propagandized for some combination of communism and Christianity – and became close to D. Merezhkovsky. In 1917, he participated in the Society's appeal to the Provisional Government to separate Church and State. He opposed the October Revolution, but recommended cultural and ethical resistance to save Russia's spiritual life, and initially believed the Bolsheviks could develop into a more benign force. His own circle thus shared many of the ideals of Volphila – which he helped to found and where he headed the History of Philosophy "faculty." He was arrested in 1928 for the activity of his *Voskreseniye* circle and sentenced to death; this sentence was commuted to ten years imprisonment. After serving his term as an engineer in different gulags, he died in 1939.

[137] A literary critic and baptized Jew who gave a presentation at Volphila, which caused consternation due to its deep anti-Semitism. He argued that the Jews were outside history and deserving of anti-Semitism; the historical task of humanity at present was to find a common ground for Jewry and Europe on which a new "real humanity" could arise. This would constitute a new Reformation and Europeans would find reality and Jews would become a part of humanity. Tzinberg criticized the presentation for its incoherence; Meier himself said: "I won't talk to anti-Semites. We do not have a common language – they are pagans." (Belous, *Volphila 2*, 703-720).

[138] Evgeniya Fedotova, Introduction to *Litso Rossii*, by G.P.Fedotov. (Paris: YMCA-Press, 1988): i-xxxiv.

[139] This description of baptized Jews in Meier's circle recalls Ilya Fondaminsky. He was a Russian Jew who lived in exile in Berlin and Paris. Attracted to Christianity and

conversion noted by Frank and Karsavin – to betray one's people or one's Messiah – was solved for some Jews in these apocalyptic times when the often man-made borders between people was erased. Conversion to Christ in those conditions no longer meant selling out for worldly gain[140].

This being said, Fedotova goes on to note an interesting tendency among the converted Jews: quite often their conversion would be a source of trouble for the group. For after baptism, the new converts would come under the influence of the priest who baptized them and turn their back on the circle, accusing it of Merezhkovskian heresies.

Certainly, in those days Meier and his circle were far from orthodox. But Meier himself drew closer to the Orthodox Church, as did a number of his circle. For Fedotov, the Christ and Freedom brotherhood remained the high watermark of his spiritual experience; he never found a similar intimacy in depth in exile in France or later in America.

This shows that in times when many were alienated from the state Church of tsarist times (including all the religious philosophers treated here), and when Russia was suffering so evidently from social injustice, circles such as Meier's did provide fertile ground for the nourishment of belief. They were fluid areas between heterodoxy and orthodoxy: nonetheless many who were nominally heterodox were imbued with a deep Christian spirit. Meier himself stayed in Russia even after the authorities broke up the circle in 1929. The depth of his convictions can be seen in the fact that he suffered death for his Christian beliefs in 1939. Likhachev[141] in his memoirs recalls how the philosopher continued to be a spiritual inspiration to the men he met in the various camps he was sent to.

The works of Fedotov devoted to Russian Orthodoxy found a wide readership outside of Russia and are being read again inside Russia. He too must be considered the fruit of this "peripheral" circle of Meier's. And once again, this

---

involved in Christian journalism he nevertheless refrained from being baptized out of loyalty to his family and his people. It was only when he was arrested, along with Mother Maria Skobtsova, and deported to Auschwitz that he took the decision to be baptized. He had thus lived as a Christian in spirit in the midst of his Jewish people, until the time to die came – when he died in Christ. He was later canonized by the Constantinopolitan Russian exarchate.

[140] These conversions are interesting from another point of view. The Jewish conversions of the 1960s to 1980s have been seen by some (e.g. Lyosov, Feingold) as a case of Jewishly uneducated Jews being unfairly poached by missionaries (specifically A. Men). See ch.7 for further discussion of Men. These conversions of the 1920s are somewhat different: Jews had not yet been "Sovietized," nor had Jewish (and Yiddish) culture been eradicated. In addition, anti-Semitism was no longer official government policy. Finally, the conversion brought no legal benefits, but the reverse. It would be hard to argue that these Jews were "selling out" for worldly gain. An honest onlooker can only conclude that they preferred Christianity to their native Judaism.

[141] Cf. Likhachev, *Vospominaniye*, SPB, Logos, 1995, p.225. [also: http://www.sakharov-center.ru/asfcd/auth/auth_pages.xtmpl?Key=13580&page=220].

goes to show that a tight sealing of the boundary between "inside" and "outside" is neither possible nor desirable Jewishly or Christianly[142]. The attempt to bring the "outside" wholly in (Florensky's utopian theocracy), or to hermetically seal the "inside" from the outside (a reactionary fantasy of a return to Holy Russia, for example, with consequent rejection of any intervening modernity) often ends up producing results opposite to those intended. Perhaps that is the lesson of Fedotov's and Steinberg's and other like minds' attempts to engage fully with their present moment in all its complexity – in ways which cannot be simply labeled intrinsically and predictably Jewish or Christian.

Karsavin: rootless Christianity

In the next part of this chapter, we will return to Karsavin and some moments where his thought engages with Jews and Judaism, forming an implicit commentary and contrast to Steinberg[143]. We will examine three aspects of his thought from three stages of his life. The first work is "A study in apologetics" which he contributed in 1925 to *Put'*. The second is "A poem about death," written in Lithuania in 1932 and considered by Karsavin (and Steinberg) to

---

[142] I don't mean by this that dogmas should be treated indifferently or adapted to the times, or that the differences between Judaism and Christianity can be overlooked – merely that judging the validity and fruitfulness of the unfolding life-paths of people in complex times cannot be a simple matter of measuring them against these dogmas with no concern for where they have come from and where they may be moving to. The unthinking and pejorative use of terms like "renovationism" or "Jewish" (or for Jews "Christian") can close our eyes to the riches of the ideas proposed by such people, and deprive us of the insights and answers they can offer to a later time.

[143] In several places in this section we mention Karsavin's relationship to the Kabbalah. However, this is not an aspect of Karsavin's "Jewish side" that we dwell on here in any detail. As Burmistrov (2007) has shown for Soloviev, Bulgakov, Florensky, and Losev a deep scholarly investigation of the exact relationship of Russian religious thought to Kabbalistic sources has not been carried out yet. As a preliminary observation, we can note that especially in *Noctes Petropolitanae* Karsavin joins these four figures in his use of Kabbalistic/Gnostic conceptions: "Adam Kadmon" is the name given to the concept of the all-man who is the centre of created being; "Sophia Akhamot" is that part of the divine wisdom that has fallen among created being. The positive sexual ethic that Bulgakov noted in the Kabbalah is also presented in *Noctes*: erotic love prefigures the fusion of Christ and the Church, and the Incarnation of the Logos in the Bride. Karsavin, who did not know Hebrew, probably derived these references from the same inexact translation of the Kabbalah, as well as Masonic or occultist sources, as Florensky. Indeed, *Noctes* in form and style owes much to Florensky's *The Pillar and the Ground of Truth*. However, perhaps more clearly than Soloviev or Bulgakov, Karsavin expressed himself clearly on the relationship of these Kabbalistic insights to Christian truth: they were interesting mystical approximations of Truth, which however were ultimately erroneous when compared to the Church's divine-human dogmas outlined by the Church fathers. See below for more detail.

be his finest work. The third work we will examine is a moving recollection of Karsavin's last years (from 1950-1952) in a gulag camp, "Two years in Abez." It was written by A.A. Vaneev, a self-professed disciple of Karsavin's who met him and became devoted to him in the camp; it contains both philosophical and biographical material.

"A Study in Apologetics"
In "A study in apologetics" Karsavin's aim is to clarify the relationship between Christianity and its sources, Hellenism and Judaism. Specifically, Karsavin is asking to what extent and whether Hellenism and Judaism have influenced Christianity. The apologetic genre testifies to the fact that Karsavin is engaged in a lively polemical defense of a certain vision of Christianity against contemporary opponents.

The first line of defense is against those who were arguing against excessive use of Greek philosophy in Christian theology[144]. Karsavin thus stands in the tradition of Byzantine theologians who were compelled to defend the use and adaptation of Plato and Plotinus in understanding Christianity, such as Michael Psellus in the 11th century up to Bessarion with his "Against the calumniator of Plato" in the 15th century[145].

The second line of defense deals with the relationship of Judaism and the Old Testament to the New Testament of Christianity. This aspect of the polemic is probably not a live defense against the attacks of contemporary critics. In large part it is historical, and does not address contemporary Jewry directly (unlike his "Russia and the Jews" three years later). Nonetheless, even this polemic has more than merely historical interest, for Karsavin devotes considerable attention to Philo and his attempt to reconcile Greek and Jewish wisdom.

This of course takes us straight into Steinberg territory and it is logical to infer that their three year personal and intellectual acquaintance must by then already have added some topicality to the question of the relationship between Philo's Hellenistic interpretation of the Hebrew Bible and contemporary Jewish "Hellenizers."

Indeed, Karsavin's discussion of Philo provides a felicitous entry into the essay, Karsavin's thought in general, and the relationship of that thought to Steinberg's Russian Jewish fusion.

Philo's concept of the Logos combines both sides of Karsavin's apologetics, and again raises the central question of influence, namely: if and how Philo influenced the similar concept of the Logos in the Gospel of John. This is part

---

[144] Interestingly, the two men who would later be most critical of the Hellenizing (and to some extent paganizing) tendencies in Russian religious thought were Georgy Florovsky and Vladimir Lossky: both of them were pupils of Karsavin at Petrograd University from 1920 to 1922 and Karsavin was the man who fired Lossky's interest in patristics and medieval history.

[145] See e.g. Jaroslav Pelikan, *The Spirit of Eastern Christianity (600-1700)*. (Chicago and London: University of Chicago Press, 1974), 242-252.

of the larger question of the extent to which Christian dogmas were shaped by Platonic and neo-Platonic thought, and thus of how "genuinely" Christian they are. (The other figure who dominates the essay the essay is Plotinus). The name of Harnack (who was still alive), while not explicitly mentioned, can be felt hovering in the background: the eminent Protestant theologian had devoted his life's work to stripping away Hellenistic accretions to Christianity to get at Jesus and the genuine core of Christian faith[146].

Karsavin states a general theory to dispose of Harnackian skepticism and it rests on an Orthodox understanding of the Church[147]. The Church as a divine personality bears the truth within her and thus she has eyes to recognize those things outside her which correspond to what she already knows. But the Church does not accept a new teaching because it was written by John or Philo; rather she examines a novelty and decides unerringly what this novelty means. If there is influence it is only in the sense stated by Socrates that a teacher is midwife to a thought that is already there – for if there was nothing there, there would be no resonance with the text and nothing would be forthcoming: if the midwife was father of the child there would be no freedom.

In this sense the knowledge that the divine-human Church possesses is above time; within time she responds to human thought and picks out the divine truths in it. Thus, even though the early Christians knew nothing of the eternal virginity of Mary and may have read the "brothers" of Jesus as referring to real brothers and not cousins, when that doctrine is proposed and discussed later in history, the Church finds that it corresponds to that which is within her. In this sense, the Church absorbs what is proposed by humans and in receiving it, she corrects it[148].

---

[146] Indeed, in attacking Harnack's thesis about the incompatibility of Hellenism and Christianity, Karsavin was also hitting a much closer target, Lev Shestov, who as P.P.Gaidenko points out was in agreement with Harnack. [Gaidenko: *Vladimir Soloviev i filosofia serebryanogo veka*, 133]. Although Karsavin recognizes the limits of Greek philosophy, and subordinates knowledge to faith in ways which sometimes recall Shestov, he disliked Shestov's irrationalism, and liked to repeat the ditty invented by one of Shestov's enemies that only "five fatheads read Shestov" (recounted in Steinberg's reminiscences about Shestov).

[147] Interestingly, Pelikan (cited in previous footnote) has recently been engaged in a similar and far more detailed defense of Christian dogma from the charge of Hellenistic distortion. Karsavin stands midway between those Solovievan philosophers who were not concerned to bring their all-unity into harmony with dogma (Frank and Nicolai Lossky, for example), and those who wished to church their philosophy – such as Bulgakov, who then abandoned philosophy – or claimed to have done. However, he never joined himself to the project of the "neo-patristic synthesis," which he in fact inspired through his former pupils Vladimir Lossky and G.Florovsky. Their embrace of Palamas' rejection of Plato's foolish and malicious doctrine was a step too far for his "Greek" heart.

[148] This theory of church and truth is very reminiscent of Rabbi Kook's idea that Torah-observant Jews can bring immanent "sparks" of Godliness that exist within the world

Karsavin discusses at some length how the Church recognizes truth in and corrects the thought of Plotinus[149], but it is his thoughts on Philo and John that interest us here.

Philo's thought is an "individualization of Judaic thought," meaning that Jewry/Judaism is a symphonic personality of which Philo is an instantiation. As a "moment" in Jewry, Philo is a vessel for one of the key ideas of Judaism: the unknowability of God. The pathos of Philo consists in the conflict between some of his own insights and the overarching "hierarchic personality" of which he is part. The conflict can be seen in how he vacillates and contradicts himself when trying to decide the status of his Logos concept and its relationship to the Judaic God.

His groping produces different descriptions of the Logos: variously, it is the "first-born son of God," "second God," but also "oldest angel" and "archangel," "shadow of God" whom God used as a tool for the creation of the world – and thus the Logos resembles God's angels, servants and powers who according to Jewish tradition also help God in creation. On the other hand, a higher status is assumed elsewhere: it is "not eternal (*agenetos*) like God, nor born (*gennetos*) like us, but in between these and participating in both." Thus Philo verges on a recognition that the Logos is God but draws back: the accessibility of the Logos cannot be ascribed to God Himself, for Judaism dictates that God must remain unknowable and inaccessible to man.

On the other hand, Philo lurches in the opposite direction when he talks of the emanations of God and the mystic union of the soul with God. Here he seems to reject the Judaic distinction between God and world and assume a continuity between them that comes from neo-Platonism. He thus "helplessly vacillates between Judaic dualism of God and man (world) and Gnostic pantheism. He is closer to gnosis and Plotinus than to the Gospel of John."

In John, these contradictions are resolved. John speaks of the unreachability of the Father, Who is nonetheless reached by the Son, and through the Son by anyone who comes to the Son. The gulf between God and creation is emphasized but only to show that it can be bridged, and not by ecstatic means involving leaving the body behind (a Platonic-gnostic aberration), but by anyone. Nor are there any naïve attempts in John to overcome non-continuity through the

---

outside the framework of Torah into the Torah framework after they have purified them of the worldly husks that obscure their light. Thus secular and other ideologies can be Judaized. Cf. Pinchas Polonski, *Kabbala i noviy etap v razvitii iudaima*,(Makhanaim, beyt ha-rav, 2006), who gives examples of how communism, liberalism, pluralism, Americanism can be reintegrated into modern Judaism. In that sense, Polonsky seems to be keying into a genuine Jewish mysticism of all-unity, which in Kook's case had Hassidic roots. It would be interesting to investigate and compare the genealogies of this Kookian all-unity with Steinberg's Russian-Jewish all-unity.

[149] He makes interesting comments about the difference between Plotinus' trinity (only the One contains the essence of God) and the Christian trinity (where all three persons share the essence).

continuity of emanations and powers, intermediaries and secondary powers. Everything is simply stated.

In what sense then is Philo close to John? In Karsavin's words:

> He knows the infinite perfection of the Divinity, surpassing any *human* understanding. And he *believes* that God is a Personal God, and that somehow man can be raised up to the fullness of unity with God. Searching for a solution, and awakened by the still unclear words of the Biblical revelation, as well as by the ponderings of the rabbis and the Greeks, he vaguely imagines some sort of medium, some Intermediary. But he cannot attain this, it is not in his strength to tell whether this Intermediary is God or not God. And in his dream of salvation he is ready to deny the created-human. We know that vague hopes can never produce that which does not lie within them, i.e. the hoped-for. Philo cannot be the "source" of John…After all, if he [the historical researcher] had not known John, he would never have "deduced" him from Philo….

For Karsavin, then, Philo comes closer to the Truth than Hellenistic Jewish philosopher Aristobulus, and even than Plato because he "strived fierily and because the Truth was closer in time, Her voice could almost be heard." But without revelation, it is impossible to philosophically "invent" a solution to the relationship between God and man, or to derive it through a careful comparison of sources.

Karsavin's consequent conclusion, for all that he is a historian who studies continuities, is rather radical concerning the "influence" of Hellenism and Judaism on Christianity. "Christ's Church is a special and unique personality created by God through the Logos and through Jesus Christ who partakes in the Divine-Personal Being. Christianity is not developed Judaism and Hellenism, and *Hellenism and Judaism are not a preparation for Christianity* (italics DR)." Christianity is radically new, that is, a new creation which is discontinuous with the old.

Tucked in a footnote is a sentiment which further radicalizes the idea of Christianity's discontinuity. Karsavin writes: "We consider it important to insist on the difference between 'natural' and 'supernatural' revelation. Any knowledge as something absolutely new in the world is a revelation. But only that which is linked with Jesus Christ, through real connection with Him, in knowledge, faith, and trust, is 'supernatural revelation.'"

This would seem to imply that both Judaism and Hellenism are revelations of the new, but that strictly speaking they are not *supernatural* revelations. Or at least, they are only supernatural inasmuch as their natural strivings can be integrated into and transfigured by Christianity.

This seems to be a correct reading of this slightly surprising equation of the Old Testament and Hellenism, for at the beginning of the essay Karsavin writes of how the Old Testament can no longer be read correctly by Jews. "Only the Christian has the power to understand the true meaning and fullness of the Old

Testament, which only in Christianity has been 'fulfilled'; to Jews this remains inaccessible. Each word of scripture speaks differently to a Christian than to a Jew, so that it is as much two words as one…"

Karsavin calls Christianity and Judaism a bi-unity[150]. But this is in the sense that the child and the man are two moments of the same person – from a certain perceptive they are two unrelated people, but from God's ultimate perspective they are one, and the child is contained in the man. Of course, one might criticize this idea of bi-unity as it breaks down somewhat due to the fact that Judaism still exists as a separate religion, so that it as if the child and the man are coexisting. This is a rather unsettling situation, reminiscent of the Stanislav Lem story in which avatars of the hero produced in a time-warp crowd out the real man.

Nonetheless, this Lemian state of affairs is not unprecedented for Karsavin. A feature of Karsavin's philosophy in general is that he believes even wrong and sinful moments of life are integrated into the all-unity, as well see in his *Poem on Death*. The sins of St. Peter, for example, when he arrives in heaven, will not be obliterated: he will always be the man who denied Christ thrice, and will always have cause to regret this. But close to Christ this moment in his temporal life, gathered into the pan-temporality of God, will become bearable and transfiguring.

Thus when Karsavin, ending his apologetic essay, expresses gratitude to the pagan philosophers for giving the Fathers the language in which to clothe the Christian truth, he does not see the pagan moment as dead and buried – but rather as a constantly living error of humankind that is redeemed through its offspring finding a place in Christ. Extrapolating, one can infer the same love and tolerance to the still living Jewish "error," which is justified by having produced that which made the statement and incarnation of the full Truth possible in the world.

Indeed Karsavin pays tribute to the period when the Judaic moment historically entered the Christian entity: "In the ancient Church a Jew who came to Christ did not reject the Mosaic law but 'fulfilled' it, i.e. transformed it by observing it. A Hellene who came to Christ did not have to accept the Mosaic law too, not in order, however, to forget his Hellenic law, but in order to – with all his Hellenism – become a child of God and by this enlightened Hellenism enlarge the earthly Church."

Here, Karsavin comes fascinatingly close to ratifying a Jamesian Jewish Christianity, namely a Jewish Christianity which combines faith in Christ with observance of the Law. Only the fact that this happened in the "ancient Church" indicates that perhaps Karsavin would not see validity in a Judeo-Christianity in the present day. The statement by itself could be read either way, and we have

---

[150] Individual Christians and Jews such as Karsavin and Steinberg would then be instantiations of this bi-unity. But instantiations do not necessarily perfectly instantiate the unities of which they are part, so that in empirical reality overlap and exchange is possible – i.e. Jewish Christians, Christian Jews and so on. We will return to this thought later.

to go elsewhere to see how he himself would have felt about a contemporary "Torah Christianity."

We can do this firstly by examining his more openly expressed opinion about the status of Hellenism in the contemporary Church. Karsavin was well-known for his belief that heresy served a useful role in the clarification of Christian truth, and he liked to quote St Paul's statement that "it is fitting that there be heresies too (1 Cor.11.19)." Once in the gulag, after they had already been studying together, with Karsavin in the role of teacher and Vaneev pupil metamorphosing into disciple, Karsavin asked Vaneev how he thought his own work fitted into the history of philosophy. "It would probably be most suitable to put you with the Gnostics," pronounced Vaneev. Karsavin, after a moment's pause for thought replied: "Well, that suits me well enough."

In this essay, too, Karsavin contends that "in fact, other aspects of the same Truth were brought forth by [Hellene and Jew], as other aspects were brought forth by heretics, and indeed as any person brings forth his own special aspect." Thus the Hellene, the Jew and the Gnostic should not abandon themselves but slowly be transfigured in the Church: without each of them with all their specificness, the full truth of the Church will not be uncovered – each one's slightly "off," slightly bent-out-of-shape truth takes a place in the infinite mosaic of the Church.[151]

That is why Karsavin is not ashamed to be called a Gnostic; that is his "face" in the Church, his own unique face in God's truth, which is drawing closer and closer to God. In this essay Karsavin himself writes that he *could* call himself a Christian neo-Platonist – but will refrain from doing so in order not to tempt people. Still, he says of Plotinus that for all his faults "he saw the single Essence and the Father and the Son and the Spirit, though he could not differentiate them, mixing them into a Unity and a Mind. Here he is again closer to Eastern-Orthodox thought than Aristotelian and Western thought. And not by chance do proponents of the latter, European philosophers, not see even a small measure of what the 'pagan' Plotinus saw, even though they have studied not only catecheses but the Gospel."

Thus Karsavin is somewhat sarcastic about the witch-hunt against Platonists in the Church. For, "with fateful inevitability the question about the influence of neo-Platonism on Christianity turns into a question about the influence of Christianized neo-Platonism, i.e. in the end of Christianity itself on Christianity, and thus the question destroys itself, leaving the 'scientist' in a silly position." Thus Karsavin permits himself considerable license, intimacy one might say, in his relationship to the philosophy of the Greeks: "To us they may be inaccessible but they were and are. However, through Christ's strength of Love we can so unite with them that, while not ceasing to be ourselves, we become them too, and are taught to look with their eyes…"

---

[151] Again, as with much of Karsavin this strongly recalls Kook and his integration of husk-coated sparks of Godly light outside the Torah.

This bold thesis, not surprisingly evoked and continues to evoke, different reactions reactions: Vaneev himself saw the master as a Gnostic, and today some[152] see his Trinitarian doctrines as tainted by heterodoxy (sometimes of a Catholic nature, ironically enough), while others[153] are more convinced by his Orthodoxy. Perhaps Karsavin would have applied to himself[154] the phrase he used of some of the excessively Platonizing early Church Fathers like Origen, who "hereticised but were not heretics," and whose "hereticizing" proved essential for the growth of the Church.

All of this can help us to understand what Karsavin might mean when he writes that "in the ancient Church a Jew who came to Christ did not reject the Mosaic law but 'fulfilled' it, i.e. transformed it by observing it." It is obvious that for Karsavin the temptation to observe the Law was not a pressing one. His own temptation, his own hereticizing "tic" was his attachment to the Greeks: indeed his family was said to be sprung from the noble Byzantine Paleologus family, and he was proud of his Greek appearance[155].

And yet as with our reading of Bulgakov, if we permit ourselves to extrapolate from Karsavin's words, we can imagine a kind of anti-Karsavin – who would be a Jew with an attachment to his Jewish ancestors, and a conviction that his Jewish ancestors and their contemporary instantiations, can sometimes see in the Bible more than contemporary Christians who have "studied not only the catechesis but the Gospel." In other words, the still living "child-avatar" can emerge from the time-warp and surprise the adult with his prescient wisdom. This anti-Karsavin would bring his Judaizing "face" into the Church and turn it towards God, not losing his uniqueness but, hereticising somewhat, while still being cleansed of heresy and leaving a pearl of unique truth in the bosom of the Church eternal.

That Karsavin was not such a Jew in love with his ancestors and contemporaries is quite plain, but Karsavin himself casts the shadow of such a Jew – as we will see in his *Poem about Death*. This is obviously why Karsavin has

---

[152] E.g. K.A. Makhlakh, "Triadologia L.P. Karsavina. Na material traktata 'O lichnosti,'" in *Nachalo*, No.5.(1997). Makhlakh sees Karsavin's triadology as dialectic, with the Father and Son being opposed to the Spirit in the same way as in the Roman Catholic *filioque*. P.A. Sapronov (*Russkaya filosofia. Problema svoeobraziya i osnovnie linii razvitiya*. St Petersburg: Gumanitarnaya Akademiya, 2008) devotes a chapter to Karsavin, grouping him with the sophiologists Bulgakov and Florensky, and leveling at him similar serious charges of pantheism and incoherence.

[153] Gavrushin (*Russkoe bogoslovie: ocherki i portrety*, (Moscow: Glagol, 2005)), usually hard on the sophiologists, comes out in favor of Karsavin's deep Orthodox sensibility, though he mentions him only in passing.

[154] A phrase which can usefully be applied to Berdyaev, and especially Bulgakov whose idea of a divine world-soul corresponds to Karsavin's reading of Plotinus' *nous*.

[155] We recall Rozanov and Florensky, also enamored of their roles as the last Greek and Egyptian. In Abez, people took Karsavin and his "students" for Jews – Karsavin being dark and intellectual, and there was indeed a Jewish circle. "My face is much more Greek," Karsavin pondered on this, "the Semitic type is altogether different. However, Russians typically suspect each other of being Jewish."

such tenderness for Greek hereticizing and does not develop his own hints about Judaic hereticizing[156].

There is a somewhat mysterious part in Steinberg's recollections of Karsavin which partly illuminates and partly obscures this issue. Steinberg writes: "The main wisdom of Lev Platonovich consisted in his understanding of the fact that the soil of Orthodoxy was not firm beneath his feet. Here he came face to face with Judaism. If Orthodoxy, in Lev Platonovich's analysis, could really draw a line between itself and its Judaic roots, then it would be able to stand and flourish on its own soil…"

Karsavin felt that in order to for such a "delimitation" to take place, an Orthodox Christian would need to know Hebrew; further, like Soloviev[157] who studied with a Jew, he would also need "inside" knowledge of Hebrew and the Old Testament. In that respect, Karsavin confessed to Steinberg that he envied him his ability to read the Old Testament in Hebrew. "You are my tongue," he said to him, showing that he undoubtedly quizzed Steinberg on a number of linguistic and theological questions relating to the Old Testament[158].

What did he mean by this? Steinberg commented that in this respect Karsavin reminded him of Rozanov.[159] Rozanov too had "an intuitive penetration into the essence of Jewry," but he also suffered from envy and an unreconciled attitude to Judaism. In his remarks to Steinberg, Karsavin seems to be expressing a belief that Orthodoxy's Jewish roots need to be understood so that the fruits of such understanding can be separated from the roots and planted on non-Jewish soil – thus obviating the need for contact with Jews and Judaism.

This, one might speculate, would be a universalizing – Hellenistic – operation: a process of abstraction, translation and generalization for the future. All Christians would be given a copy of the Hebrew key to the Bible, and from then on they would be independent, not needing Jewish tongues like Steinberg's to gain access to Biblical treasures.

Karsavin lamented to Steinberg that he was too old to read Hebrew and engage in such an operation. But one can only grin at the ridiculousness of such an assertion. Karsavin spoke and wrote fluently in several languages, and shortly after that conversation was to learn to fluently speak and write Lithuanian! Evidently something else other than linguistic obduracy was blocking the way

---

[156] Such a Judaic hereticizing, one can speculate, would draw its insights not so much from Plotinus, as from the Kabbalistic tradition of Jewish mysticism on which Karsavin himself – along with other Russian thinkers – drew to some extent.

[157] In his account of this conversation Steinberg states his belief that Karsavin was wiser than Soloviev in not wishing to discover a new theological idea that would bear fruit in his own lifetime. Karsavin's thought, for Steinberg was also less universal than Soloviev's – which in the context for Steinberg seems to be a good thing.

[158] And perhaps even the Kabbalah, as Karsavin makes occasional reference to it as we will see later.

[159] Shortly we will see that there are several other similarities between Rozanov and Karsavin.

to his embarking on a true expedition into the roots of Orthodox Christianity.

Karsavin evidently felt that he was not the one who would revive and reshape the Hebrew face of Christianity[160]. Instead, just as Berdyaev held out hopes that his friend Lev Isaakovich would eventually convert to Christ, so Karsavin constantly pressed Aaron Zakharovich to convert, perhaps hoping that he would fulfill this role for the Church. Somewhat slyly, Karsavin even asked Steinberg once – after a long conversation about why Steinberg had more Russian than Jewish friends and what it was that attracted him to Russians – whether he could accept his idea of a universal, symphonic church that would embrace all cultures and religions. "If you can, then you would not have to change anything[161], but you would be able to say that you belonged to the universal religion, that you are a member of the Orthodox Church."

Then as later, Steinberg replied that he saw no need for the Trinity. For all of Karsavin's profundity, this looks like an amateurish slip. In the grandiosity of his Hellenistic philosophizing about symphonic, world-embracing ecclesiastical "personalities" he had forgotten what the concrete Jew had quite rightly remembered in the nick of time – that in order to become a Christian, it is not enough to share philosophical tastes: one must believe in Christ.

Indeed this brings us face to face with an irony which has been building up throughout this section. Karsavin, in the essay we have been examining writes that "the value of a philosophical system can be measured by the degree of its Platonism" for reasons we have already examined. But if this is the case, it is no wonder that Karsavin respected Steinberg's philosophy and especially his work on Dostoevsky.

At the same time, however, Karsavin's disingenuous question to Steinberg is problematic. He seems to be asking him, as one Platonist to another, to recognize that to be a Platonist is in effect to be a Christian in all but name (as Augustine said of Plato). And yet: Steinberg (and many others as we have seen) was a Jewish Platonist. More, he was a Jewish Parmenidean, a Jewish believer in all-unity. More, he was a Jew who believed like Karsavin that Plato was tailor-made to fit him. Face to face with each other, the two Platonists seemed to have reached a mysterious impasse…[162]

---

[160] In an odd way, one could see Rozanov as "reviving the Hebrew face of Christianity." His *Judaism* and even some of his anti-Semitic articles sometimes do indeed seem to "penetrate to the essence of Judaism." To refer to Franks' categories once more, one could (a little frivolously) see this as an example of a non-Jew doing Jewish theology.

[161] One shouldn't put too much weight on conversational throw-offs, but this does imply that Karsavin envisaged a Jewishly observant Christian Steinberg – a proposition which suffers from the same problems we list immediately below.

[162] This had been, in fact, the essence of Alexander Meier's objection to Steinberg's presentation "Dostoevsky as a philosopher:" "…and that is why it becomes clear to me why Aaron Zakharovich did not mention [Dostoevsky's central concern with the *image* of Christ]. Of course, it is impossible to find room for this in a philosophical

But this should not be surprising. If we look at Karsavin's comments regarding Judaism, Hellenism and Platonism again, we see that Christianity is utterly new. It can take elements of Platonism if they correspond to Christ, but not otherwise. Without Christ, Plato is a mixture of the true and the false.

Here, we can make explicit what we only implied above. Despite Karsavin's conversational slip-up in which he assumed too much about Steinberg's Platonism, we see that he really was aware of the gulf between the Jewish and Christian follower of the ancient Greek. For all of Karsavin's comments about the Logos of Philo can really be directed against Steinberg's Logos.

For Karsavin, Steinberg's Logos must have been the same shadowy concept as Philo's. What does Steinberg mean when he talks of the (divine or semi-divine?) Logos being incarnate in the deed? What can he mean when he talks of the translation of reality into the transcendent kingdom of ideas? How is his Parmenidean One connected to this Logos, how is it connected to the kingdom of ideas (which are perhaps *logoi*)? At root, Karsavin must suspect Steinberg's whole scheme of a Judaic interpretation of Dostoevsky and Russian thought.

And yet such is his enchantment with his Greeks, that he is willing to forgive a Hellenizer anything. His affection for Plato spills over onto this modern-day Philo. No doubt this is why he was so enthusiastic about Steinberg's book on Dostoevsky. Oddly enough, though, this incident shows that for all his Platonizing, Karsavin comes close to a fideist position: one must first accept Christ, one must first submit to the authority of the Church. Only then can Plato, Philo and their Logos have meaning. Only then can faith seek understanding,

---

system." And slightly earlier: "This was definitely an *image*, a completely concrete image, and not an idea, and perhaps therefore, Dostoevsky is not a philosopher but, perhaps much more an artist." Belous, *Volphila 1*, 696-7. Furthermore, Meier made a penetrating point regarding philosophical all-unity *per se*. He saw Steinberg as interpreting Dostoevsky as such a philosopher, one interested in achieving a theoretical Unity; so Steinberg wished to make him "the first confessor in Russia of the One and only One God. But then in my language that would mean that he was the first of all Russian writers to have converted to the Old Testament, and so to speak, to have betrayed those testaments which in general pertain in Russian culture (ibid.696)." In a non-polemical manner, Meier is accusing Steinberg of de-Christianizing and Judaizing Dostoevsky. But in the context of the preceding discussion, a much larger point emerges: the All-Unity project in and of itself seems to be a systematizing endeavor that results in a focus on the Unity of God, and is thus automatically distant from Trinitarian Christianity and the Christianity that focuses on the *person* of Jesus. But if that is so, at least All-Unity looks more "honest" in the hands of a believing Jew! (Unfortunately, the majority of Steinberg's defense of why he did not mention Christ was missing from the stenographic minutes of the meeting). On the other hand, I argued above that Steinberg *did* covertly mention Christ, in his references to crucified human consciousness: it was simply that for him, as we discover later in his "Otvet L.P.Karsavinu," Judaic All-Unity included Christ and Christianity – and, as far as he was concerned, transcended them. That is, the Son for Steinberg was not divine, but a part of that humanity included in the truly One Father.

410   CHAPTER FIVE

pace Anselm – for whom, as it happens, Karsavin had a great respect[163].

However, in order to gain a deeper understanding of how Karsavin reworked Plato and Plotinus into a distinctively Christian philosophy – and where that left the Jew – we have to turn to his *Poem on Death*.

Karsavin: experiencing the Jewish vision of God (Poem on Death)
The tortured Jewess

Karsavin wrote the *Poem on Death* after he had moved to Lithuania. It is both a deeply personal piece, and yet a very public piece: Karsavin forges out of his private depressions and doubts provoked by this sudden geographical and emotional dislocation in his life a theological lesson for all of mankind. This combination of personal and public – which in certain respects echoes Rozanov's style – made the work especially dear to Karsavin. Steinberg, too, visiting his friend in Lithuania in 1932 was treated to a preliminary reading of the work and was also impressed, urging Karsavin to waste no time in publishing it.

The work is a watershed in another way, too: it was the last work Karsavin wrote in Russian. With extraordinary talent and adaptability, he would henceforth write all his major works in a language he had mastered in a mere two years or so. This move to Lithuania and Lithuanian will be commented on later: for a Russian Slavophile it was, to say the least, a paradoxical step. One might even suggest that it was a rebirth of sorts – and in that sense the *Poem on Death*, which is rich in such paradoxes, is a herald and even midwife of this new identity.

Turning to the *Poem* itself, we have already seen how Karsavin had a theatrical side to his character. He once provoked public outrage when he said in a lecture that God needed "to be taken by the horns." He shrugged off the controversy by asserting that God did not need to be defended by pedants. The *Poem on Death* is likewise a theatrical, hereticizing, and provocative exploration of God – which is at the same time carefully grounded in dogmatic theology[164]

---

[163] In *Dva goda v Abeze*. Vaneev summarizes the fascinating thumbnail sketch Karsavin gave of the history of Western philosophy (while lying in his hospital bed on which his two "students" perched too) in which he also offered an interesting version of Anselm's Ontological Proof. Concerning the proof's overgeneration of non-existent objects like centaurs, Karsavin held that centaurs do indeed exist, being non-verbal descriptions of the animal-human duality of man grasped by the mythopoeic imagination. (Anatoly Vaneev, "Dva goda v Abeze. V pamyat' o L.P.Karsavine." *Nashe naslediye*, III-IV, (1990).)

[164] In *On Personality* Karsavin grounds his ideas in a close analysis of patristic sources and the Christological statements of ecumenical councils. Khoruzhy (1994) notes that his thought is particularly influenced by Maximus the Confessor and Gregory of Nyssa. Khoruzhy also comments that Karsavin differed from Frank and even Bulgakov in his attempt to create a system of thought that was directly inspired by dogmatic theology. The two Western mystics whose influence Karsavin acknowledged were John Scotus Erigena and Nicolas Cusanus. These thinkers, of course, were

and Orthodox in spirit. It is, in effect, a more private and personal reworking of the system of philosophy that he developed in a more cautious, formal way in *On Personality* two years previously.

The *Poem* thus combines serious theological ideas with playful literary devices: Maximus the Confessor stands shoulder to shoulder with the flippant and mercurial wit of Vasily Rozanov, with Bernard of Clairvaux and Francis of Asssissi looking on[165]. In short, Karsavin is a sure master of profound erudition, personal boldness and literary creativity, and his juxtaposition of a vast range of disparate elements was, as usual, disconcerting to some and seemed to verge on the blasphemous.

For our present purposes it is the Jewish references in the *Poem* that will occupy our attention. While it would be foolish to argue that they are central, Karsavin's own Cusean philosophy that each part contains the whole means that focusing on the Jewish moments will allow us to understand the general message of the *Poem*; but on the other hand, in order to understand the Jewish moments we will need to have an overview of the whole work.

Nonetheless, we are not completely unjustified in approaching the *Poem* from a Jewish angle. The work actually starts with an odd Jewish reference: "… Over a fire they were burning a Jewess[166]. – The executioner is fastening her with a chain to the post. And she is asking him: Should she stand so, and is he comfortable….What is she worrying about the executioner's work for?" Indeed, this image is a gateway to the *Poem*. This Jewess from now on will turn up at intervals throughout the work, raising the same questions that Karsavin will address as the work progresses: what is suffering, what is the connection of the sufferer to the one who imposes suffering, what is worse – physical or mental suffering…and so on. These questions lead right up to the question of theodicy, evil and ultimately: the suffering of the Son of God on the Cross, and how it is connected to us.

Much later in the *Poem*, in the sixth section called 'Crucified'[167], there is

---

considered heretical in the West due to their pantheistic tendencies, and the former drew on Pseudo-Dionysius, Gregory of Nyssa and Maximus the Confessor – and thus was more Eastern in orientation anyway. However, more overtly Catholic influences on Karsavin were Bernard of Clairvaux and the Victorine monks with their mysticism of love for God, as well as St Francis' emphasis on the love of God for each individual. This provides the background for Karsavin's rhetoric of earthly love as an analogy for divine love, especially noticeable in *Petersburg Nights* and *Poem on Death*. Cf. Sergei Khoruzhy, *Posle pereryva. Puti Russkoy Filosofii*. Saint Petersburg: 'Aleteia', 1994. Chapter on Karsavin: "Zhizn' i ucheniye L'va Karsavina."

[165] For an account of Karsavin's relationship to medieval Catholic mysticism, cf. Pr.Mikhail Aksenov-Meerson, *Sozertsaniem Troitsy Svyatoi…Paradigma Lyubvi v russkoi filosofii troichnosti*. Kiev: Dukh i litera, 2007.

[166] Again, to make things odder Karsavin uses the pejorative "zhidovka" ("Yiddess") and not "yevreika" (strictly, "Jewess").

[167] There are seven sections: 1.From the author and about the author. 2. Sort of personal.

another Jewish image, this time even more perplexing than the first one[168], charming, perverse and strangely contorted. It is the story of a Spanish Inquisitor who gave his life in order to hound to death a particularly horrendous heretic.

The heretic was a baptized Jewess. Her heresy was believing that God would forgive Judas. The inquisitor considered his options: if he simply burned her, then her body would be destroyed but God might somehow forgive her soul – so unpredictable are the ways of God's mercy. He thus needed to ensure the perdition not just of her body – which he considered beautiful but mortal – but of her soul. The job demanded nothing less. He decided, therefore, to let himself be seduced by her: surely the seduction of the chief inquisitor would constitute an unforgivably mortal sin even for God. "But when the heretical Jewess in fleshly sin had almost slain her soul, the inquisitor himself cried out: 'Oh!...my love.' And he expired on the spot and went stiff."

Although the inquisitor died without repentance, he was taken to paradise. Three days later "he saw that she – whom through fiery hatred and unto sacrifice he had loved – was also in paradise, for they had unjustly burned her as a witch who had seduced and killed the Spanish inquisitor."

Although Karsavin does not say so explicitly, it seems that this baptized heretical Jewess is the very same one that we saw being bound by chains at the beginning of the *Poem*, kindly inquiring after the comfort of her executioner, who ignored her questions, but who "perhaps deep inside felt some tremor of sympathy that may have alleviated her final suffering."

In between these mysterious encounters with a gentle Christian Jewess – whose sin is an excessive belief in forgiveness, and a tendency to love too much – Karsavin ponders his own love and suffering in the five intervening sections of the Poem, one of which is called 'Israel'. Before dwelling on Karsavin's more explicit thoughts about Israel, however, it would be well to consider the overall movement of the *Poem* so that the place of the Jewess (and Israel) can be ascertained more clearly.

Contrary couples

After the opening encounter with the Jewess, the *Poem* moves onto Karsavin's melancholic reflections on his love for a woman called "Elenita." She was his lover many years ago, their affair ended, and she has since died – but her memory continues to live on within him and he is tortured with what might have been. His imagination tries to recreate the past, but all aspects of his past seem dead and indifferent; he chooses at random one moment for inspiration, but it falls apart, and only briefly can he deceive himself into believing in it. He is thus overcome with melancholy and aloneness.

At the same time, he cannot even fully believe in his own suffering and melancholy, or even in his love for Elenita and other people. Instead, he appears

---

3. Doubt. 4. Weakness. 5. Israel. 6. Crucified. 7. Beginning.

[168] Section 6, subsection 127.

to himself as solipsistic: his concern for others' suffering is really a concern for himself. When others suffer, he suffers sympathetically, fearing for himself, and his sympathy is thus selfishness.

On the other hand, Karsavin admits: "it is completely unimportant; am I suffering a lot or not. Let's assume even that having recourse to certain of my natural talents I only imagined the role of sufferer for myself – no matter. How else can one feel and understand our common torture?..." And here we get one of many clues that the *Poem* is a meditation on God and humanity through the medium of his own inner life, that reality which is closest to him. Karsavin's confessional outpourings become a type for humanity's discovery of itself.

As such, Karsavin's "I" – the first person narrator of the *Poem* – is both the small "I" of the individual man, and an inflated collective "I" of all humanity. (Later, we will see that this "I" even encompasses God.) Given the presumptuousness of speaking on behalf of the entire race, Karsavin is quick to underline the semi-fictional, conditional nature of his bold narrator-self: "The actor plays a tragic role. Why not play metaphysics? Only in games is the unalloyed truth revealed. The spectator must watch not the actor but the hero depicted by the actor."

We are not far into the *Poem* before Karsavin, true to his promise to play serious games, introduces a fictional reader to whom his fictional narrator-self (the "hero") can address his grandiose thoughts, a sort of counterpoint to this actor-narrator. He calls this companion his "lady-reader," and she becomes a third constant female presence in the *Poem* after Elenita and the Jewess. To her he appeals: "And you, lady reader, can do that better than anyone, inferring (not always, of course) the whole world from my 'I'. My 'I' is a mask."[169]

This fictive lady-reader thus lures out Karsavin's "I," leads his "I" into new pastures and away from old tortures – even though she is herself a product of that "I," and emerges from it. Karsavin's "I" changes, and the lady-reader changes. She even seems to take on some of the characteristics of Elenita (her blonde hair, her intelligent wit). Karsavin, by turns, writing the lines that will be read by her, expands to encompass her, the Jewess, the torturer, the world. He becomes Everyman in the writing of the *Poem*: all the many selves of humanity blended into his own self are distilled out by his illusory guide, who though she is an untruth leads her writer to come face to face with the Truth[170].

Already part of the place of the Jewess and her executioner in the *Poem* is

---

[169] The influence of Rozanov and Florensky on Karsavin's style is clear. However, an interesting difference between Florensky and Karsavin is that the role of homophilic "drug" (friend/other), by which the "I" dialogically discovers itself, is clearly given to a female, or females. However, as we will see later, the element of gender-indeterminacy observable in Rozanov and Florensky will be seen when Christ Himself takes the place of, and is compared to, these female lovers.

[170] Karsavin's poetic prose treatment of the relationship between art, truth and Christianity is strongly reminiscent of W.H. Auden's work, especially his *The Sea and the Mirror*. Auden also lived in Berlin during the late 1920s at the same time as Karsavin was a fellow foreigner in the city.

becoming clear. They are one of a series of strange pairs which illustrate a union of opposites[171]: lover-beloved, writer-reader, and torturer-victim. Karsavin even hints that husband and wife constitute such a pair: "It seems strange to you, fair-haired lady reader, to 'live so as to think and suffer.[172]' I am older and well know that for you too there is no pleasure without pain. I won't confuse you prematurely with a description of the internal contradictions of married life…." And, lest the point remain unclear, this is followed by a contemplation on the Marquis de Sade, who derived pleasure from pain but – says Karsavin – no doubt felt the pain of his victims and received pleasure from that. Thus, there are two more pairs – husband-wife, sadist-masochist – who, once again, are two sides of the same coin and contradictorily united.

It will be no surprise to discover that these types are illustrative of Karsavin's own version of the philosophy of all-unity. They show that for all its seeming contortedness and evil, humanity is woven from one material at a deeper level. For each weak and unstable member of humanity possesses a personality that contains within itself all of reality in different measure – which is precisely why all of humanity is linked to each other. Furthermore, all of humanity is a refraction of the one Person, the infinite Person[173] who is infinitely refracted in different degrees through humanity – the Son of God, the Son of Man.

This, in turn, leads Karsavin to perceive another paradoxical pair among human types, the crowning pair: crucifier and crucified. Looking into his cracked-open self he sees that "God suffers in me, I torture Him. I mock my self, and suddenly I hear my voice in the crowd on Golgotha: 'He saved others, but he cannot save Himself.' I drink cold golden wine. But the wine is already not wine, but vinegar, and I lift up on a reed the sponge soaked in it for Him to drink…" That is to say: in every misspent and foolish moment that the self spends, it mocks not just itself – but within itself that long-suffering better part of the self that is Christ, hidden and unobserved beneath the mantle of nature.[174]

---

[171] They thus illustrate Nicolas Cusanus' *unio oppositorum*.
[172] "I live so as to think and suffer…" is originally Pushkin's. There is thus a Pushkinian undertone to *Poem* as well.
[173] To whom in *Noctes Petropolitanae* (1922) Karsavin sometimes referred to as Adam Kadmon, revealing an interest in Kabbala even before his exile.
[174] Karsavin clearly belongs to the tradition of Russian kenotic theology, whose roots go back to developments in the 18th and 19th century "ecclesiastical tradition." One of the key figures in developing kenotic imagery was St. Philaret of Moscow, on whom cf. Ch.1. Its originality was to make a parallel between the self-emptying (kenosis) of Christ the Man, and the birth of the Son from the Father in a divine self-emptying, thus linking the inner life of the Trinity with the incarnational life of Jesus. Bulgakov significantly extended the kenotic idea within his sophiological framework, in ways critiqued by V. Lossky. This critique would apply equally to Karsavin, as we show below. For more on Russian kenotic thought, cf. Nicholas V. Sakharov, *I love therefore I am. The theological legacy of Archimandrite Sophrony*,

This does not exhaust the meaning of the image of the Jewess, the inquisitor and the executioner – for this is possibly the richest of all the images, and contains all the others. One would also like to know why exactly Karsavin chose a baptized Jewish heretic to be the suffering element in this particular pair. But the image has been placed in context and we will return to it later.

Meanwhile, we have reached a point where we can ask the questions that Karsavin is by this point posing: how can a person reach this Christ within? What is the relationship between humanity and God, between this Christ within and God? And what have all Karsavin's love-sick sufferings to do with the quest for God?

The answers to these questions involve understanding that this *Poem on Death* is a love-poem. It is a love-poem, however, which partially refutes an earlier "love poem" written by the younger Karsavin. This was the 1922 *Noctes Petropolitanae*, which in its blending of the theological and the literary is the nearest equivalent to *Poem on Death* in Karsavin's oeuvre. The 1922 poem was inspired by Elena Skrezhinskaya, of whom Karsavin said that "it was precisely you who connected metaphysics with my biography and life in general." She seems to have inspired the philosophy of love described there, in which earthly love is seen as a path to and a reflection of the divine[175], and anti-worldly asceticism is vigorously condemned – in terms that "share quite a lot with the sermons of Rozanov."[176]

The *Poem on Death*, by contrast, is – to put it in somewhat adolescent terms – all about "getting over" Elena. On a more adult plane, it is also about overcoming the idea that earthly love is a sure path to God. A decade later, and Karsavin seems to have outgrown that Pelagian-Rozanovian[177] optimism about the divinity of the flesh and the possibility of man approaching God by natural means.

Thus in the first part of the *Poem*, Karsavin follows his depression about the loss of Elenita (which is in fact a Lithuanian version of Elena Skrezhinskaya's Christian name[178]) to its bitter end. He considers that option which he rejected in *Petersburg Nights* – to turn to monastic asceticism and an embrace of death. But even now he refuses to deny the reality of the body and the bodily nature of love. And as for death: Karsavin launches into a morbid imagination of his own

---

New York: St Vladimir's Press: 2002 (esp. ch.4).

[175] We will have reason to consider the oddity of a love poem addressed to someone other than the author's wife of nineteen years.

[176] Khoruzhy's judgment, in his essay on Karsavin in *Posle pereryva. Puti Russkoy Filosofii*. Saint Petersburg: 'Aleteia', 1994.

[177] Pelagius, a disputant with St. Augustine, denied Original Sin, and emphasized that man could reach God through his own moral efforts. (This, of course, is to simplify matters).

[178] Another oddity concerns the fact that Elena Skrezhinskaya was still alive in 1932 and living in Leningrad. As Khoruzhy points out, Karsavin shares with Florensky this morbid literary device of addressing living friends as if they were dead.

death and subsequent decomposition. He sees his body underground, being eaten by worms for eternity, imagines his stomach swelling up, his face dripping off, and his brain becoming a liquid, slippery mess, which is sucked up with pleasure by red worms, even as he retains the ability to feel all this[179].

And yet, he concludes that even this thorough destruction of the body will never eradicate the fact that the body *was*. And because for God the past is always present, it seems there is no getting rid of the body. Furthermore, Karsavin imagines – in another image of all-unity – that even after this morbid decomposition is complete, particles of his old body will be reconstituted[180] in other suffering creatures so that suffering will carry on, for example, in the travails of a boiling lobster[181]. In sum, then, he reaches a point where earthly love cannot save and an escape into death is blocked, for it is really an escape into endless dying.

By mid-*Poem* then, Karsavin has reached an impasse. With fine writerly rhetoric, he has argued himself into eternal Hell and "now I am already being tortured in the whole world. I burn in the body of the unhappy Jewess, cry out pitifully in the black fly squashed by me. And I squash the fly, and burn the Jewess over the flame…simultaneously I am my own executioner and my own victim." However, Karsavin recognizes that in a sense this is what the writer deserves, for writers are demons, obsessed by themselves, constantly looking in the mirror with self-appraising vanity[182]; and he likens himself to the young Cossack in a Gogol story who only found out he was a demon when they brought out an icon of the Virgin.

This takes us up to the beginning of the fourth section of the *Poem*, where a turning-point is reached. This is the section entitled 'Israel', and it follows on immediately from 'Weakness'.

---

[179] In these Gothic images one can also see that Orthodox contemplation of death which brings a believer close to God.

[180] This draws on Gregory of Nyssa's writings about the resurrection of the body.

[181] Interestingly, this is the exact image of suffering Beckett used in "Dante and the lobster" in *More Pricks Than Kicks*. The story was first published in the same years as *Poem on Death* (1932). Karsavin adds a nice, "Beckettianly" ironic touch to his image, though, imagining the objection that only vertebrates feel pain. To which he replies: "All the worse for me, if I suffer in the lobster and he does not even sympathize with me." Is the choice of a lobster by Beckett and Karsavin coincidence, simply a shared mentality? Probably. But it is interesting that they were both living in Paris between 1927-1929, and that Beckett's first critical work was "Dante…Bruno…Vico…Joyce." The Italian Middle Ages and especially Bruno were also of central interests to Karsavin. They also share a common fascination with Christian doctrine: while both are ironic and original in this, of course Karsavin is ultimately an orthodox believer, while Beckett is a pained skeptic.

[182] Apparently, Karsavin was in real life rather vain, and once was extremely offended that he had been photographed with a beard rather than clean-shaven. (In Steinberg's *Reminiscences*).

Karsavin's and Steinberg's triadology

For those familiar with *On Personality* and other earlier works, this turning-point will be conceptually familiar. For Karsavin the human personality has a tripartite structure which reflects, albeit imperfectly, the inner life of the Trinity. By the time Karsavin reaches 'Israel', the first two stages of this process have – almost – been completed. At this point, we will sketch a more abstract overview of the philosophy behind this triadology of the development of the person. In so doing, we will have reason to once again pose the question of how – or if – it differs from Steinberg's "Jewish" triadology (notwithstanding the obvious use of Christian terminology in Karsavin).

For Karsavin, then, the model of the human personality is the Trinity. Within the Trinity there is a dynamic of primal unity (the unknowable Father), followed by disintegration (the Father's self-sacrifice of Himself in the birth of His Son), followed by reunification (the restoration of the God to Himself by Himself in the Holy Spirit)[183].

To expand somewhat on this: the Father goes out of Himself by eternally giving birth to the Son. This "dis-unification" of God from Himself, this birthing of the Son, is also a type of dying – in the sense that God the Father abandons Himself to give Word to Himself. The eternally dying Son, however, is restored to the Father by the Holy Spirit, and this process is the picture of sacrificial love. It is also shows, as will become clear, that the self-emptying of God becoming man in the Incarnation, and the death of God on the Cross are not disastrous aberrations – but an integral reflection of God's "difficult" inner life, his "self-consciousness" as reflected in his creation.

In humans, the development of personality is also tripartite, and an imperfect attempt to emulate the Trinity. A person consists of subject and object: inasmuch as a person analyses himself, he becomes the object of his own inquiry. By analogy with the Trinity, the human person, going out of himself, gives Word to himself. However, although it is theoretically possible to affirm the identity of the I-who-is-subject and the I-who-is-object, in fact for humans this does not reduce what is felt as a mutual opposition between parts of the self[184].

For despite asserting the unity of our self, we feel a disconnect between

---

[183] V. Lossky's comments in *The Mystical Theology of the Eastern Church* (p.45) seem directed against precisely such a dialectic interpretation of the inner life of the Trinity: "There is no interior process in the Godhead; no 'dialectic' of the three persons; no becoming; no 'tragedy in the Absolute', which might necessitate the Trinitarian development of the divine being in order that it be surmounted or resolved. These conceptions, proper to the romantic tradition of nineteenth-century German philosophy, are wholly foreign to the dogma of the Trinity." An analysis of whether Karsavin succeeds in making an analogy between the Trinity and human personality (as Augustine did) without violating the apophatic theology of the Fathers would take us too far afield.

[184] Of course, Karsavin is indebted to Fichte for the roots of this philosophy of the person.

the objective facts that our "I" produces and what we feel to be the real "I" that is the source of these facts. Thus, as the Spirit does for the Son in God, the human self tries to restore itself to itself. The self makes an effort to constantly assert the connection between subject and object; and this is the activity of self-consciousness. In the Trinity, of course, each "self" is a perfect person, and the three persons share the same essence: they are thus a "tri-hypostatic essence, or unity."

It will be seen that in the *Poem* Karsavin has been describing in concrete and graphic detail the travails of his own self-consciousness, the attempt to chase up and integrate the lost moments of his own past and bring them into harmony with his present self to form a unity. Equally graphically, in the *Poem* Karsavin shows how the triadic dynamic of primal unity, followed by self-disintegration, followed by self-reunification is full of dangers and falls far short of the trihypostatic unity of God.

In 'Israel', Karsavin begins to explore – again, in highly personal, concrete terms – what prevents the self-reunification of the human person and why man so differs from God in his person. To preempt, the problem for man is that he cannot reintegrate the infinity of his lost moments. Only in Him Who knows and *is* all the moments of the world could such a retrieval of man's consciousness be brought about. Therefore only by linking his self-consciousness to God's self-consciousness can man recapture and reunite his self[185].

Man's mistake is that he believes he can attain self-consciousness and Being on his own. At one extreme, he posits his own Being as independent from God, which is to say from perfect Being. But in a less hostile form, man recognizes God – but does not want God's Being enough, as it threaten his own being. The way Karsavin puts in the *Poem* is that a little "not," as in "I do *not* want God as He really is," separates his being from God's Being.

It is this little "not" that separates one man from another, giving each their precious self-identity, and each man's "'no' is a flea sucking the blood from God's little finger and refusing to budge. It is original sin." That is, God's blood (his Being) has already entered the flea (man) through that crack in his self opened up by his burgeoning self-knowledge. Because even a part of God contains all of God[186], man is thus potentially heir to all of Being. Like the flea, however, he only takes the small bit which suits him and which corresponds to his limited "appetite" for Being. The stakes here are high for the "flea": for if only one man

---

[185] Part of Karsavin's doctrine of all-unity is the idea of a connection between being and knowing. Being that does not know itself is the same as non-being. Man's efforts at self-consciousness are thus an attempt to attain perfect Being, an opening up towards Being, a self-disruption which permits the entrance of Being into the human person. And God's inner life consists of perfect self-knowledge, and therefore perfect Being. Thus man's self-consciousness/knowledge is a movement towards unity with Being, or God.

[186] Again, the Cusean idea that the part contains the whole, and that God being simple cannot be divided.

could overcome his "not," then all of humanity would have overcome it[187].

But to overcome this phantasmal "not" is singularly difficult: after all it involves the need to overcome one's desire not to desire God (to desire not to desire not to desire God!), and one's desire to desire one's own well-being. Resorting to zoomorphic imagery again, Karsavin describes the carnival of life lived through this "not": such a life "forgetting its unity, devours and savages itself through its very desire to live, when its creatures devour each other in order to survive. The lion eats the lamb and is killed in turn by some Tatar hunter from Taraskon. And the lamb does not understand that he is a sacrificial victim. This Life is not worth 30 silver pieces."

However in such a world, paradoxically enough, there is not too much but too little death and "evil is a shortage of suffering and death," the reason being that "pain is the vertebrates' way of avoiding self-sacrifice." In the struggle for what they consider life, which is merely self-preservation, creatures are prevented by fear from truly expanding their being. Pain drives us to compromise, to till the small patch of our own being and to limit ourselves.

As such what is needed is not less passion and appetite, but more passion and appetite. "Our passions too, in fact, are not passionate enough. They should be stronger: and then if we took away their little 'not' we would be borne straight to God." As Karsavin adds, using an image we saw developed at some length in Bulgakov: "Like Saul, when he removed the 'not' from his Christ-hatred."[188] Thus, albeit in modified form, Karsavin preserves his original *Noctes* diatribe against world-denial as a path into Being.

This call to passion will eventually provide the exit from the hell of infinitely disintegrating, solipsistic selfhood that Karsavin had sketched himself into in the first part of *Poem*. Here, however, it is worth stopping and comparing what we have seen of Karsavin's and Steinberg's metaphysics so far.

What is striking, now that we have examined each system in some detail, is how much they overlap. Steinberg also proposed a tripartite development of consciousness. If we juxtapose each stage of the Steinberg/Karsavin trajectories we see the following development: life/primal being; consciousness/disintegration; self-consciousness/reunification. While not exact, the following parallels can be made.

In both men's second stage, man faces the despair of nothingness – a disillusionment with one's own consciousness, which for Steinberg provokes thoughts of suicide and for Karsavin exaggerated fantasies of his own morbid death. This leads on to a third stage where man transcends his previous limited being and recognizes himself as being a creature of God. For Steinberg, this is exemplified in Dostoevsky's integration of the various streams of Russian

---

[187] Again, on the basis that in every man is contained all of humanity.
[188] To put this in chronological context: *Judas: Apostle-Traitor* was written in Paris in 1931; and this essay, which overlaps with it in its covertly sophianic sensibility was written in Lithuania in 1932.

consciousness into a harmonic self-consciousness. It is a period of crucifying choice between self-assertion and humility, which involves the acceptance of the unity of creation. For Karsavin, the process involves the retrieval of all the self's human moments through an openness to the all-unity of God.

If this analogy is correct, it once again raises the question of where the boundaries between Jewish and Christian philosophy and theology run. It remains then to propose some differences between Karsavin and Steinberg.

The locus for difference is the transition from the second to the third stage. While Karsavin and Steinberg both give a mixed evaluation of consciousness[189], for Steinberg the ascent to self-consciousness is made by the self in a painful but clear-cut choice between life and death. The new self that emerges is a "servant of the Logos" who incarnates the Word in the deed. Self-conscious people are vessels of the Logos, ideologues who can spread unity in the world by transmuting reality into idea, so that the world is transformed into the world-soul – sophianized, one might say.

In contrast, the colors on Karsavin's canvas are extremer: man and creation are both more hopeless, and the redemption of them he envisages is more ambitious.

So, firstly, for Karsavin, the transition to the third stage cannot be made by the self: it is impossible for the self to transcend the self; "desire to not" cannot be turned by the self into "desire to" love God. This is connected to how both perceive the world.

While Steinberg is aware of the dissolution and destruction inherent in the world, he sees this in a positive light. Moreover, man's consciousness is already raised above and immune to this destruction and from a higher perspective can use this destruction as a site for rebuilding the ever-diversifying tree of life, transforming it into the tree of knowledge.

Karsavin provides an almost polar contrast to this optimism (which was partly shared by his younger self). Instead, he sees man himself as – at least partially – immersed in that destruction, and worldly knowledge as a poisonous fruit that is powerless to suggest the correct path among all the possible exits. Thus in 'Doubt' (Part 3) he calls the intellect a serpent, who "feeds on dust, he makes the tree of life a tree of knowledge and death"[190] - a trope which directly

---

[189] The usual dichotomy that Christianity is world-denying, Judaism world-embracing does not apply here. Steinberg fully embraces Dostoevsky's idea there is only one world and that it is highly valuable. Karsavin decries ascetic rejection of the body and the world, and in words similar to Steinberg's (and Dostoevsky's) recommends fervent embrace of this world and the Truth it contains. In this he is a true exponent of anti-dualistic Christian Platonism such as is found – despite their other differences – in Gregory Palamas, who places high value on the body as fully involved in salvation.

[190] Again, whether these different evaluations of knowledge are Jewish or Christian is debatable. Much of Orthodox Judaism is deeply ambivalent to philosophy and worldly knowledge (Greek wisdom; "apikorsos"). Shestov is closer to Karsavin here

contrasts with Steinberg's transmutation of lower life into higher knowledge.

Secondly, for Karsavin the transition from consciousness to self-consciousness cannot be accomplished simply by facing the nothingness of createdness – and recognizing one's freedom[191]. The old self must actually embrace the suicide that Steinberg rejects – ontologically speaking. The self must die completely in order to terminate its infinite dissolution. The "not" must be negated by another "not" until a new self says: "I do not *not* want God."[192]

Thirdly, as we mentioned before, Steinberg's use of the concept Logos would no doubt attract Karsavin's criticism. For Karsavin, the self once reborn is not a "servant" or vessel of the Logos. Karsavin is in full agreement with Eastern mystical theology: man becomes the Logos, and the Logos is God. It is unclear what the Logos is for Steinberg, as it was for Philo – or what exactly it means that man incarnates the Word in the deed. The latter phrase seems to imply that man's actions can reflect God, while man himself in his nature remains distinct from God. Moreover, even if one took Steinberg to mean that the Logos is in fact God (rather than a power of God), man for Steinberg would still not be united with the Logos, but merely an instrument of the Logos, a conduit for the perfection that the Logos brings to the world.

To sum up, then, although Karsavin and Steinberg are not stereotypically Christian and Jewish philosophers (if such exist), unsurprisingly their different confessional allegiances certainly leave a trace on their thought systems. The boundaries between Jewishness and Christianness are blurred by the fact that both embrace an immanentist, panentheistic, and triadological view of reality. Steinberg's use of the Christian terms "incarnation" and "Logos" adds further confusion. But the differences are reinstated again by the degree to which each pictures the depth of man's fall, the means needed to rectify this, and the height to which he can rise[193].

Part of Karsavin's conviction of the truth of his own system consisted in

---

in his irrationalist rejection of the Tree of Knowledge. But is this due to his Jewish heritage, or his admiration for Lutheran and Pascalian fideism?

[191] Karsavin takes this point up specifically in 'Israel' as we will see shortly.

[192] In this sense, Karsavin parts company from Steinberg's self-described proto-existentialism, variations on which are seen in Heidegger, Sartre, and Jaspers.

[193] In Rubin (2009), I propose that Steinberg's need for self-dissolution, as a practitioner of Judaism, is less than that of Karsavin, the Christian. In quasi-Bulgakovian terms, I explain this by the idea that through the Torah Jews have a blood line to the unfallen Adam Kadmon; gentiles on the other hand must renege on their natural genealogy, and uniting themselves to the blood of Christ, attain to God through the New Adam. This schema is intended somewhat experimentally, as a development of themes that seem logically inherent in Bulgakov's and Karsavin's thought. I do not intend the analysis to be final, only suggestive towards a sophiological fleshing-out of the idea of a Rosenzweigian "dual covenant" for Jews and Christians – a conception of the relationship between Judaism and Christianity that Steinberg, too, seems to have held implicitly, and that as we will see Karsavin tends towards in some of his thought.

the belief that his philosophy of all-unity was broader than a Jewish system of all-unity that had no room for the doctrine of the Trinity. Steinberg, meanwhile, could not see the need for a Trinitarian conception of God. The pleasure he derived from listening to the *Poem on Death* must have come from those common moments (such as the struggle with nothingness) that ignited a response in his own religious and philosophical experience.

Karsavin for his part certainly found common ground with Steinberg's non-Trinitarian philosophy of self-consciousness. Indeed, we can speculate that part of that worldview can be found in the section of *Poem* called 'Israel', where Karsavin gives voice to an Old Testament/Judaic consciousness which must have resonated with Steinberg.

It is with this in mind that we will consider this part of *Poem*.

Israel and the living God

In 'Israel' we see the first movement out of eternal hell. This section of the *Poem* contains a number of multi-toned voices[194]. If we ask ourselves, for example, what 'Israel' signifies there are several possible answers.

Firstly, it is a stage in Karsavin's own development, as his first-person narrator continues his inner explorations. Secondly, that "I" as always is a mask that represents all humanity (as the Greek tragic masks represented human types) so that 'Israel' is a symbolic stage in general human development. But thirdly, 'Israel' is the concrete historical stage already passed by humanity in the experience of the people of Israel and recorded in the Old Testament. And fourthly, it seems fair to imagine that this section was enlivened by Karsavin's long-running experience with surviving members of the "old Israel," namely living Jews – of whom in addition to Steinberg, Karsavin had met quite a few since his move to Lithuania where the Jewish community was populous and thriving[195].

There is a further "overtone" in 'Israel', however. When Karsavin quotes from the Old Testament in this section, one is aware that for him the book is a "bi-unity," as it was for the Fathers – and as it was in less fortunate ways for Rozanov and Florensky. That is, it is two books – a Jewish-Hebrew book and a

---

[194] In Abez, a professor of physics suggested a physical analogy to Karsavin's idea of symphonic, hierarchic personalities. Each string on an instrument has its own tone, but it also contains a number of overtones. Depending on the method of stimulating it, one and the same string can produce a different composition of tones. Karsavin liked this analogy. Karsavin's multilayered writings can be thought of in a similar way.

[195] Steinberg recounts in his memoirs that Karsavin was greatly respected and admired by Lithuanian intellectuals, despite being non-Lithuanian and non-Catholic. A Polish professor shared this general admiration, but added one proviso – professor Karsavin's unfortunate infatuation with Jews. Later, we will look in more detail at just how deeply contact with Lithuanian Jewry changed Karavin's views on Jewry. The point is that Karsavin was sensitive to the living Israel in whose midst he had come to live when he moved to Kaunas and then Vilnius.

Christian book. Each letter bifurcates into two, depending on whether a Jew or a Christian reads it. In "Apology," Karsavin had stated quite severely that only the Christian reading was correct. In 'Israel', however, one can make a case for seeing each of the two readings as being legitimate in different ways.

The boldest idea in 'Israel' is Karsavin's rebellion against God – or a certain conception of God. Caught in eternal hell, he raises his fist to heaven and decries the injustice of his imprisonment:

> You don't imagine, Ancient of Days, that I could have <u>not</u> sinned, that I sinned freely?...But you called me out of non-being without asking: created a kind of lump, breathed a soul into it, and won't let me go back, and yet you call me free!

In the voices of the great Jewish strugglers with God – Abraham, Jacob-Israel, Job – Karsavin-Israel castigates the potter-God, who creates a weak lump of clay and then throws it into hell when it succumbs to temptation. With nothing to lose, he asserts his human dignity against this sham-God:

> "But who are you, man, to argue with God?" "I do argue. What's the point of a quasi-passionate piety since I am going to hell anyway? In non-recognition of such a God is the limit of his power and my freedom, my only treasure…"

But after he has hurled all his curses at this God, he hears only a silence – but a silence, it seems, like the one Elijah heard[196], in which the real God speaks out:

> "[Why are you silent?…Why are you crying?...] From joy? Because You love me? Did you hear in my curses my love for You? …. For these you call me Your son! So I didn't curse You? - …"

And that voice, which in a sense is his own voice, questions him in return:

> "- I myself did not want to be any stronger? It's me that does not want to live with all Your life?...So, it was not without my will? You created me: so – and exactly then did I too arise freely. I arose by Your power, but by myself?"

Thus like the patriarch Jacob, Karsavin wrestles with God and wins. God crumbles and concedes defeat. But in God's defeat Israel's eyes are suddenly opened to the real God, the God who lets Himself be defeated. Slowly, it dawns on Israel just what it means to fight against God and be allowed to defeat God.

Karsavin's voice, as it soaks up this realization, turns to address this emerging

---

[196] Karsavin does not mention Elijah; the comparison is mine.

God in the second person, as if in prayer. It fills with a new and bold intimacy and the image of God turns from wrathful old man to uncertain virgin:

> You dreamed of me as a girl dreams about her child, not knowing whether he shall come to be or not…You called me, a non-existent world, to live in Your Life, to be Your fullness. You retreated, You gave me all Your Life; begged me to become God instead of You. You wished to die fully, a terrible Death, so that I might live and instead of You be made God. Eternal Death horrified You, the eternal God. But for my sake, for the sake of the world You wished to die eternally and forever, to die completely, for with You everything is eternal.

Here we are brought up short: what business can 'Israel' have speaking of the death of God – and in terms which recall the Virgin – when surely he only bears an Old Testament knowledge? What is such intimacy doing in a section called 'Israel'? Why does it not appear in the following section, 'Crucified'?

The answer is that we are hearing two overtones simultaneously. The images of the young girl bearing a child, Mankind, and God dying so that Mankind can take his place and become God – all this refers, I believe, not (primarily) to the Incarnation and Crucifixion, but simply to Creation.

This is because for Karsavin, Creation and Incarnation are intimately linked; indeed they are really one and the same act, or different stages of one process. The Father's abandonment of Himself in the Word and restoration of Himself in the Spirit, when continued beyond Himself, is creation. So creation already involves God's self-sacrifice; that "creational" self-sacrifice is merely completed in the Incarnation, when God descends further, to bring back all of Creation into Himself.[197]

Thus even before Christ, God has "died" for Israel, so that Israel may exist. God has died, so Israel may become God. This is why what looks like Christian language is really Judaic.

Karsavin was well-informed enough about Jewish mysticism to know that the idea of God "dying" in creation had a near-equivalent in the Kabbalistic concept of *tzimtzum*[198]. This is the doctrine that states that God contracted His

---

[197] Here Karsavin is as bold in his extension of kenotic imagery as Bulgakov; he also runs the risk, as Lossky showed, of blurring the boundaries between the Creator and His creation. Further, as with Bulgakov, Karsavin implies that the Incarnation and Crucifixion would have happened even without the Fall; Lossky contended that this makes Christ's self-sacrifice not a free choice (a decision of the Will), but an ontological necessity.

[198] Vaneev records a conversation in Abez, where Karsavin expressed admiration for the doctrine of *tzimtzum* as "wonderfully conveying the essence of creation" as "the self-estrangement of God for the sake of the freedom of created being." On the other hand, he criticized it for not getting beyond the idea of Emanation, and stopping well short of the idea of Divine Incarnation. That is, he criticizes it on

infinity to create an empty space in which the world can be projected, existing freely somehow outside of, but also within, God. Thus for Israel, God's *kenosis*[199] is perceived as *tzimtzum*[200] and Israel is privy to a deep and intimate revelation of the divine.

This is why it is only by inhabiting Israel's mind that Karsavin can abandon his solipsistic moping, and his self-satisfied accusations of the deity, which amount to an abandonment of responsibility. Only in Israel, can humanity rise up to its true greatness by finding God within itself. Only now does Karsavin understand that in losing himself, he is losing God, that in some as yet unclear way he is responsible for God as well.

This, then, is one clear note in 'Israel', a deep and positive evaluation of the Old Testament and, indirectly, even of contemporary Judaism (at least mystical Judaism). It corresponds, as we saw before, approximately to Steinberg's own ideas about man's discovery of his deeper self in the nothingness of createdness – and this should not be surprising, as after all the radical doctrine of *creatio ex nihili* is found by rabbis and Fathers alike in the opening chapters of Genesis.

But Israel is not just the struggler with God who wins, who in his createdness is equal to God. Israel is also the people who receives the Law. And when Karsavin

---

similar grounds to Philo.

[199] The Greek theological terms for the self-emptying of God in His incarnation as a man.

[200] Lest there be any doubts that Karsavin is hinting at Israel's knowledge of God's death-in-creation, in the last section of the *Poem*, Karsavin makes the parallel quite explicitly:

> God compressed Himself into a little Hebrew "lamed" and made Himself a whole limitless world; He compressed Himself again and made Himself me, a little bug. But He remained the same, so that in the bug His Fullness appeared. And thus there is no way that the bug cannot grow infinitely and become the whole of God; I cannot not become the world; the world cannot not become the Fullness of the Divinity…

In terms of Russian appreciation of Jewish mysticism, this is paralleled by Bulgakov's belief that, in the Kabbalistic doctrine of the Son of Man, Judaism approached the mystery of Christianity. Karsavin makes a similar point regarding Philo's Logos. But here the contact is more intimate, as "contractio" (in effect, the Latin for *tzitzum*) is actually Nicolas of Cusa's term for God's method of creation. Whether Cusa derived it from Kabbalistic sources, I have not been able to determine. He lived just before the Italian Renaissance discovery of Kabbalah and the formation of Christian Kabbalah, which suggests another source for the concept. (Incidentally, it should be said that Karsavin's reference to "lamed" is slightly inaccurate. The Kabbalistic doctrine states that God contracts Himself into the *smallest* Hebrew letter, which is a *yod*. The *yod* is also the first letter of the Divine Name, the tetragrammaton *yod*-heh-waw-heh. Thus the first "point" of creation is also the first letter of the divinity. All the letters are ascribed meaning in the Kabbalah, but lamed's "profile" is not what Karsavin needs for his purposes.)

turns to the giving of the Law on Sinai, he has to contend with a God who once again seems to have reverted from shy virgin to angry sky-god. For Karsavin this contradiction is reconciled by seeing, not a change in God, but a change in man. God is perceived as fire and smoke at Sinai because the love of God is terrifying to those who are not ready for it.

He thus parts company from Steinberg for whom the Law was the core of the religious life, the ultimate revelation of the Logos after the liberation from Egypt. For Karsavin, however, the Law is merely God's initial drawing close to his beloved humanity. In that drawing near, the mountain smokes, there is thunder and lightening, it is not possible to see God and live, and Israel feels "the Immeasurable Divine Anger: 'It is awful to fall into the hands of the living God.'" God's people are huddled up in fear, knowing that "anyone who touches the mountain will be condemned to death," and even Moses is only allowed to see the back of God[201].

And God thus takes mercy, acceding to the people's request that he not address Israel directly but talk to them through Moses. This shows quite clearly that the God who breathes fire at Sinai is the same God who "stands with arms outstretched in painful disintegration, wounded, rejected by me, spat upon."

This God can only let Himself be consumed in morsels whose size is dictated by what the people can consume. His drawing close is dictated by what the people, who have chosen their type of createdness, want. Thus though God wants to embrace them, he must again contract Himself, hiding from them His real Being.

And contrary to what Rozanov and Florensky suggest, the real Being of the God of Sinai is not terrifying because it resembles some horror-story Semitic monster hungry for human blood. The God of Sinai is frightening because he is the self-sacrificing Word. For a world that is still frightened of being and half-hearted about the project of existence, this is unpalatable.

For God is the fullness of life without any hitches, doubts, qualifications. Moreover, God achieves His eternal Life through eternal self-sacrificing Death. And if the world neither wants to get on with the business of life, even half-life, it is even more afraid of death, and that dying which will open up the path to a fuller life. Thus the world cannot bear the vision of God in His fullness, and God in His mercy at Sinai keeps at enough of a distance so that the people will not be burnt up by His Life-through-Death.

Karsavin thus has no doubts that in the fire-and-brimstone of Sinai is the crucified God of the New Testament. At Sinai too, "God is Divine Love. He is the eternal birth of the Son in the bosom of the Father, i.e. His eternal dying and death for the sake of the Father, but also his eternal resurrection through the Holy Spirit."

Thus Karsavin gives voice to the dual-unity of the Old Testament. On the one hand, 'Israel' is indeed that segment of humanity that is blinkered by a typical Old Testament vision of a fiery and angry God. On the other hand, 'Israel' is that humanity whom God loves, and who is granted a vision of the Divine fire, is

---

[201] All these quotes/paraphrases from Exodus are Karsavin's.

permitted to hear the Divine voice, and is given the Divine Law. Though unable to grasp the fire entirely – yet – in Israel all of humanity is challenged to question the meaning of their existence.

The terrifying fire of Sinai hides in its core the Crucified God. While the crucifixion cannot be gazed on yet, that fire still speaks to mankind and inspires mankind to iconoclastic prophecy. The main message of that prophecy is not that God is crucified love, for it is too early yet. But the fire jolts mankind out of his complacent worship of a potter-god who makes man a mere lump of clay.

It enables man to see through the "various false prophets [who] assure unhappy people that God is punishing them justly for their sins. There are not enough human sins for the eternal fire: they think up new ones, accuse those who have lost their heads from fear of the sins of their fathers. With blasphemous lips they slander God's Love and substitute foolishness for the Divine Wisdom." Here one seems to see one part of the Old Testament pitted against another: Job's "pious" friends against the wiser Job.

For Sinai – and the whole Old Testament – seems to be triply ambiguous for Karsavin. At the deepest level, Sinai is Tabor[202] and Golgotha. At a lower level, it is Job and Moses and Abraham engaging with a loving and self-emptying creator-God. At the lowest level, it is the mistaken inspiration for the crudest recipients of that revelation: those who see it simply as terror and command.

Karsavin thus seems to be picking up on a strain of argument within the Old Testament itself. Of Moses, Karsavin says that "perhaps [he] was right and You were afraid lest I become like you, and in a fit of envy You chained me down so as to take pleasure in my weakness?" That is, the author of the Pentateuch who records his encounters with God, depicts a limited God. He records the frightening curses aimed at Israel in Deuteronomy. And yet, Moses gives a critical account of that God in a voice which Karsavin takes up, so we are to understand that the Old Testament prophets, being exposed to the fire of God, could also see through the fire to the paradox of love and freedom at the centre of the flames.

In that sense the Sinaitic flame – though subject to misinterpretation – at its best generates criticism of its own terror, burns away inadequate conceptions of the self. Karsavin, the admirer of Gregory of Nyssa, must have been sensitive to this: Gregory's *Life of Moses* started the tradition that saw Moses as the paradigm of the saint ascending through darkness to the light of God. In this way, Moses became a model for Christian sainthood, especially in the Orthodox East.

If it is correct to see Karsavin as implying a triple understanding of the Old Testament here, we can imagine how he would have reacted to Aaron Steinberg's Judaism. In his Orthodox Jewish friend's philosophy he will have seen that scalding criticism of consciousness, that encounter with Nothingness which gives rise to sacrifice of self and the birth of true freedom – which all flow from

---

[202] Karsavin does not make this parallel. But a patristic analogy links the lesser revelation of Mount Sinai with the higher, though continuing, revelation of the transfigured Christ on Mount Tabor.

Sinai according to its higher perception in the Old Testament.

And yet Steinberg for Karsavin – though teetering on the brink of seeing the *kenosis* or *tzimtzum* of God in the heart of Sinai – will not have been granted that final vision of God's Life-through-eternal-death. He would not have got gone beyond that Nothingness which is still a barrier to complete equality between God and man, creator and creature. He would not, in other words, have seen that the Logos of Sinai would finally, contracting still further, take on the slave's clothing of human flesh so enabling man not just to serve the Word but to become the Word, enabling the created to become uncreated.

The end of the Poem on Death

The idea of created man becoming uncreated through theosis is developed in Eastern Orthodox theology from Gregory of Nyssa to Gregory Palamas. Karsavin presents this doctrine in his own individual way in the garb of modern personalistic philosophy[203]. This was partly his way of making the Word live for the consciousness of modern man, and also his way of fulfilling his particular calling in Christ[204].

In this his work must be considered a success: Karsavin's literary implementation of ancient theological truth makes it live with a novelistic vivacity, even if in doing so he sometimes crosses the line into Gnosticism[205].

---

[203] As Melikh shows, to take only Western European philosophy Karsavin's personalism reveals influences and similarities with Schleiermacher, Kierkegaard, Scheller and Nietzsche. Apparently, like Frank and Shestov, Karsavin also met Martin Buber and appreciated his thought. His subject-object development of the self also strongly resembles a theologized version of Fichte's transcendental idealism.

[204] Karsavin's writings often elicited negative reactions from other Russian thinkers. I.Ilyin decried Karsavin's relativization of good and evil in his review of Karsavin's 1923 *Dialogues*, accusing the work of blurring the boundary between blasphemy and non-blasphemy; N.Trubetzkoy accused him of "making one statement, and then straight away making a completely opposite one…"; Berdyaev once called his philosophy unchristian. All of these reproaches recall the pained reactions to Rozanov (cf. Sobolev, 185-193). Nonetheless, Karsavin was also awarded a doctorate from St Petersburg theological academy, which was an extreme rarity for a layman, and he often preached in churches in emigration – thus despite these condemnations, clearly he participated seriously in church life and was taken seriously as a Christian figure by the church hierarchy.

[205] Again, Makhlakh's criticism seems to have some cogency: Karsavin's division of consciousness into subject/object, which somehow originates in the Father-Son distinction, does seem to introduce a Father/Son vs. Spirit opposition among the persons of the Trinity. It does seem like a not altogether comfortable conjoining of Fichte and the Eastern Fathers. As we discuss below, the use of adulterous love as a model of Trinitarian healing is also, to say the least, eyebrow-raising. One might even suggest that Karsavin's unapologetic use of such a transgressive love as an inspiration of his religiosity might be a result of an antinomian tendency in his Christianity. Perhaps that antinomian tendency itself is a result of his belief that Christianity

This brings us back to the series of odd and discomfiting allegorical pairs that culminated in the Jewess and her sexually ecstatic inquisitor-lover-executioner. Karsavin was nothing if not self-aware, as well as sensitive to the personalities of others. And he knew when he was treading a line. However, in *Poem* he explicitly states that jokes (for these and other images in the work are so extreme as to be blackly humorous) help build the walls of heaven, that "jesting is a necessary feature of that 'funny' hell [for] it relieves the unbearable pain and strengthens human freedom" by undercutting lies and theological crustiness.

These odd pairs then are partly tongue-in-cheek, but partly utterly serious in that they provoke us to examine the mystery of Christ again in a new light. In looking at the final pages of *Poem*, we will see how they were anticipated by the image of the Jewess and her executioner. Let us analyze, then, the encounter between the Inquisitor and the Jewess-heretic in more depth.

The Inquisitor and the Jewess-'conversa'

We already saw that this pair is one of several that illustrates the *unio oppositorum* of the Truth. The theme of hatred containing love, and of the lover who kills his beloved as the highest act of sacrificial love will reappear in the final drama of the soul later. But one seemingly incidental aspect of this allegory is, of course, the fact that the inquisitor is a Spanish Christian while the heretic is a baptized Jewess. In fifteen century Spain, such *conversos* were indeed objects of inquisitorial suspicion. Next, there is the odd heresy Karsavin attributes to the female *conversa*: the belief that Judas will be forgiven. All these details in fact add depth to the "spiritual" aspect of the allegory; but they also enable the allegory to be read as a commentary on the flesh-and-blood historical relations between Jewry and Christendom.

To begin with, the Judas heresy, especially as held by the Jewess in this context, can easily be seen as implying a belief that Jewry will be forgiven for rejecting Christ – even though she herself is a Jewess who has accepted Christ. Such a belief would be especially provocative to an inquisitor charged with the conversion of Jews and the investigation of sham conversions. And indeed the inquisitor is outraged by the idea that those formally outside Christ can come within Christ's forgiveness. So he resolves to kill the one who asserts this – for the sake of Christ's honor.

Indeed, the paradox deepens: for the Inquisitor here bears more than a passing resemblance to Bulgakov's Judas, who also intended to defend Christ's honor, believing that Christ was too weak to defend it Himself. By killing the one who asserts this truth, the inquisitor believes he can alter truth, and force Christ's hand from forgiving Judas/Jewry. Entering into the lion's den, he gives himself over to the Jewess's bed, and so bears the risk of losing his soul himself. Thus, though he looks like a cold fanatic, and indeed a Judas, the fieriness of his faith is

---

needed to overcome its Judaic, Old Testament roots – a real, rejuvenated Christianity could, after all, look with dialectical irony at the seventh commandment.

such that he is willing to lose his soul for what he takes to be Christ's honor.

His own arrival in heaven proves that, despite the depth of his belief about Judas' damnation, he was quite wrong: Christ does forgive the Judas-like inquisitor, fortunately for him. But in this way Karsavin shows how, in fully embracing his mistake, the inquisitor bursts through that mistake into the arms of Christ. There is also the clear implication that within the inquisitor's hatred of the heretic burns a sensual love, so that his choice of trap for the Jewess is not altogether free of self-interest. Again, that seemingly sinful passion is also the engine of his ultimate salvation[206].

The Jewess, on the other hand, is also not free from guilt. She is beautiful and sensual and perhaps her Christian conversion was – as Steinberg phrased it – more a coming over to the Christians than to Christ. Such was often the case among *conversos*. Perhaps she even did it for worldly gain, like Leskov's Jewish charlatan. Being a sophisticated woman, she has an easy faith: God will forgive everything, the world is not such an awful place. Taking her heretical belief in a wider sense, we might imagine that she believes that those among her people who did not convert to Christ can still be fairly sure of God's mercy. God finds room for all types, after all.

And so, without the attentions of the burning, repressed inquisitor who knows – given her lukewarm nature – what would have become of her eternal soul? But the inquisitor's actions throw her into the role of witch, and within three days of his death she is bound at the stake. This worldly, kind woman with a natural gentleness and sense of compromise is pushed to the extreme, allowed to taste death so as to become what by her own natural lights she could not have become: a martyr for Christ. She too breaks through her nature into the life of God.

On the one hand, for Karsavin, this is certainly a spiritual allegory. But on the other hand, it seems that it exemplifies a particularly telling historical moment in the history of Jewry and Christendom. Karsavin, so fascinated by Jews, has chosen to depict the inner drama of the soul using material from world history. What better colors to paint the inner mystery than by resorting to the outer mystery? This implies that the outer mystery has a corresponding logic of its own. But what is that logic? How do the Inquisitor and the *conversa* symbolize larger truths about the symphonic personalites of Christendom and Jewry? One might read them as follows.

Like the inquisitor and the Jewess, historical Christianity and Judaism are imperfect. Christianity knows the Truth: that life only comes through death. Judaism does not know this Truth, imagining that true Life can be birthed through the natural genealogies which will last until the world is transmuted into its End according to these same processes.

Yet Christianity's possession of the Truth has often led her to distort the Truth in a cold rage – with regard to the Jews. The untruth of Christians (rather

---

[206] Again we are reminded of the antinomian-flavored implication that Karsavin's affair with "Elenita" puts him on the path to Christ.

than Christ), in whom nonetheless the Truth lies deeply concealed, in paradoxical fashion has woken Jews to the Truth of Death – but it is a Death that they cannot ascribe to their God, while still remaining within the "Judaic moment."

Christians, on the other hand, who have often been the executioners of Jews cannot while remaining with their "Christian moment" see in the death of Jews for their non-Christian God a martyrdom for Christ. To human eyes, Jewish and Christian, the death of Jews at the hands of Christians is as far from Christ as could be.

Karsavin thus seems to reveal to us a moment which makes nonsense of all orthodoxies: the passionate embrace of Judaism and Christianity unto the death. Once this death is passed through, the historical imperfection of this encounter is transcended. Bulgakov showed how "Jewish zeal" contains the seeds of its own redemption. Saul, who was present at the stoning of Steven, became Paul. Here Karsavin, following a similar principle, seems to show us how Torquemada can become St John of the Cross[207]. Torquemada, despite himself, indirectly spreads Christ's light.

What should one make of this implicit meditation on Jewish and Christian fate through the lens of a representative moment from the Spanish inquisition? The picture is, of course, an uncomfortable one. We have seen similarly ambiguous meditations in Bulgakov, but in sensibility Karsavin once again approaches closest to Rozanov. In the gentle Jewess who loves her executioner, we almost seem to see the Jewish *baba* (the feminized Jewish male) in love with his *pogromshchik*. Indeed Karsavin himself once commented[208], in a less metaphysical context, that anti-Semitism is a sign of a healthy culture. By this, he did not intend to condone it but to indicate that a healthy national culture naturally resists cosmopolitan disintegration.

Still, even if this description of Jewish-Christian reality is not a *prescription* for violence, it does have that slightly amoral whiff which disturbed some of the critics of Karsavin's other works. For to ask Christians to recognize the religious sincerity of Jewish martyrs for God is one thing. But if one were to take this historical sketch with any seriousness, it would almost be like asking Jews to recognize the benefits of Torquemada – quite another proposition. It is true that since Biblical times religious Jews themselves have seen in anti-Semitism a divine instrument to keep them faithful to God's law[209] – but this is not the same as seeing anti-Semitism as a divine instrument to bring them through death to a different divine truth. The morality of this is questionable even in Karsavin's terms. For it would seem that the Jew in this way has truth foisted upon him in a way he does

---

[207] A Spanish saint who sharply criticized the activities of the Inquisition and was finally put to death by it. (Incidentally, Torquemada was actually not a simple figure: he shared many of the reforming passions of St John of the Cross, and was of part Jewish descent himself. This would of course all be grist to Karsavin's mill.)

[208] In *Rossia i yevrei* (second footnote, section III).

[209] A recent example of this from a Reform rabbi is Dan Cohn-Sherbock, *The paradox of anti-Semitism*. (London, New York: Continuum, 2006).

not have time to assimilate or practice anywhere other than in heaven.

And although we can safely say that Karsavin is not with any earnestness asking even Christians, let alone Jews, to recognize the moral benefits of Torquemada, there is a further reservation about this scenario. It concerns another tortured pair in the *Poem*, namely Karsavin and "Elenita." The nature of Karsavin's love for Elena Skrezhinskaya[210] is somewhat unsettling. Karsavin had already been married nineteen years when he wrote *Noctes Petropolitanae* in 1922 for his muse of love and life. He himself once joked that he was expelled from the Soviet Union in the following year, due to the fact that the NKVD confused article 27 of the criminal code with the seventh commandment. While one can only speculate about the complexities of Karsavin's marital life, this extended literary declaration of continuing love for a woman who was not his wife provokes considerable discomfort: deep metaphysical speculation and moral decency begin to look like uneasy bedfellows.

That is perhaps why Karsavin's metaphysics are best kept to the individual level – where self-willed executions and sado-masochistic orgasms of death are purely internal affairs of the developing self-consciousness. For it is here that Karsavin takes Rozanov's idea that all Christians bear the Jew inside themselves to levels that perhaps even Rozanov would have been surprised at. And again, there is a frisson of hellish humor in using such a perverse allegory to intuit the deepest mysteries of the Christian faith.

For if we switch back to the "inner mystery" represented by the inquisitor and his lover, we see their encounter is replicated in the final drama that Karsavin depicts between Christ and man's self-consciousness.

The final drama

In the Incarnation, Christ took on imperfect human nature. By uniting the human and divine natures in His Person, He made imperfection a part of the Divine. Henceforth, the human nature partaken of by Christ and all human individuals can be included in God. Created nature can become uncreated. This, however, is not the end of redemption but only its beginning. For in a new paradox, Karsavin now has man reject this gift of perfection. In an odd reciprocation of Christ's sacrifice for man, man now sacrifices the gift of perfection and embraces his imperfection, embraces the judgment previously laid on him for his imperfection (but now lifted) and refuses the rope offered to a drowning man, preferring instead to drown.

Why? Because to accept straightaway the gift of perfection and the union with God would mean that man could only give a small part of himself to Christ, the part that already fully accepts Christ's sacrifice. He knows that Christ can take that part and perfect his all from it – but this will only be in the future. This will not prevent his imperfection – which in part of himself he still feels after Christ's Crucifixion as a resistance to salvation – from always having

---

[210] "Elenita" is the Lithuanian diminutive for Elena.

existed, and which thus – in God – will always continue to exist.

So he resolves to withhold all of himself, the good *and* the bad from Christ's mercy: "I will not try to justify myself before you: all of me is evil. I won't separate evil out from myself, thus murdering You: I won't let myself bifurcate endlessly…"[211] To offer up a part and leave behind most of himself would after all be to reject that imperfection which Christ took on by assuming human nature, and which He died in order to redeem. To accept *tout court* Christ's sacrifice would be premature.

As Karsavin asks, in language which strikingly echoes – and parries – Rozanov's critique of dark-faced, world-hating Christianity with its sexual misfits, "how could I have cleansed myself if I only castrated myself? …God does not need eunuchs." But Karsavin, just over a decade after Rozanov's death, is offering a resolution of Rozanov's pained non-comprehension of Christianity: man offers all of himself up to Hell – thus preserving his unity, his life – so as not to belittle Christ and the world He embraced.

The drama takes on a further twist. For God is silent and it seems that He has rejected man's sacrifice of paradise, and his leap further into Hell. It seems as if nothing has changed, that man's hellish dying continues unabated. But things *have* changed. Dying continues, but now man embraces dying, wishes to speed it on. Having found the crucified Christ within himself, he has the nerve to do that now. The creature understands that he had to reject God, to say that little initial "no" to God – for in that "no" there arises the self which had to first exist before it could be left behind. In the same way the Father goes out of Himself in the Son. That "no" was the first tremulous assertion of being. Without that "no" it would have been impossible to approach God, to imitate God's own inner life, and ultimately to *be* God[212] - as God with His own sacrifice desired for man.

But that "no" took on a life of its own – just as the lady-reader acquired flesh and blood in the course of the *Poem*. To say another "no" – this time to the phantasmal first "no" – was beyond the creature's power: how could he destroy the only being he had? How could he be his own executioner? And indeed, as we

---

[211] For all that Karsavin differs from Shestov, he shares his agony over the tragedy of past events, refusing to accept them, and holding that God can, if not make them as if they had not been (as with Shestov), then redeem them.

[212] This is a radical idea. Elsewhere, in a conversation with Vaneev recorded in "Two Years," Karsavin used this idea to explain Adam's original sin. How could Adam, created by God, have sinned? If one answers that he was not perfect, for only God is perfect one insults God: could God not have made creation perfect? And if he made it imperfect, why punish it for its imperfection? Thus Adam's sin (his, our "no") was originally an act of love of creature to Creator: the perfect man, responding to God's self-sacrificing love in extending Himself beyond Himself in creation, freely posited his own imperfection as a reciprocal sign to his creator that he recognized the gift he had been given. Man chose sin to demonstrate his own inequality with God, within his own God-equality. Only then, held Karsavin, can man be held morally responsible for his sin; if man is imperfect due to being created weak, then in what could guilt consist of?

saw: self-execution is not what is needed. That would be too simple, and would amount not just to suicide but to deicide.

God provided the answer when He became incarnate. He showed plainly then to his weakly living creature that God is executioner and victim. God kills His beloved, but God *is* that beloved (the Father kills the Son). God kills Himself in a moment of self-love[213]: Jesus Christ dies on the Cross, and as a result God hands over his authority to man: it is up to man to do the same to himself; the model is there.

The model is there: but the only result seems to be that God has become man's slave, disabled, weakened, stripped of authority and compelled to follow man down to Hell and death where man makes his dwelling, like an obedient dog.

And yet having Christ the executed lover, and God enslaved and humiliated following him about silently at all times has its effect. The slave never opens His mouth (He does not kiss man, says Karsavin, as Elenita started their affair by kissing him first) to say anything: for that would be to force man's freedom. And yet His presence, the presence of God broken on the rack, finally allows man to ask himself why God got into such a state, what is the reason for all this, and what this might mean for his own unhappiness.

Thus God is silent, but man now begins to understand that he must become one with Christ in Hell, that he must bring Christ out of Hell, that he cannot repent and change his being without first becoming the One who will forgive him. The *Poem* ends not with Karsavin's salvation, for art and philosophy cannot bring that about, but a realization of what repentance might mean. And repentance, as Karsavin often emphasized, means in Greek a change of mind (*metanoia*). It this change of mind that we are witnessing in the *Poem*.

For at the beginning of the *Poem* "it seemed to me that I wanted to run away from meaningless suffering – only to live, only to have pleasure; and I was surprised that everything turned out to be nothing other than that, than one thing, only suffering." But at the end of the *Poem*, "it seems that I already do

---

[213] Again, there are striking parallels with Steinberg's own thought: "God as a suicide: this is the problem, I would say, which lies at the basis of the construction of self-consciousness for Dostoevsky….People have often thought that there can be no greater atheism than Nietzsche's, for he called himself a deicide. There lies the limit of atheism, and then Dostoevsky exposes a further limit: God as suicide." ("Dostoevsky kak filosof," 656.) Several questions arise concerning this similarity between Steinberg and Karsavin: was Steinberg, as A.A.Meier hinted, missing the fact that Dostoevsky mined such insights due to his sensitivity to the person of Christ, who for Dostoevsky – as a Christian – was indeed He in Whom God "killed" Himself? Or did this insight resonate with something already present in Steinberg's consciousness and which could be recast without excessive force in terms of Steinberg's own Judaic commitment? Finally, is the notion of God as a suicide in fact tolerable within Christianity anyway, or is this evidence of "deviance" in Dostoevsky, Karsavin and the neo-Christian ethos of Silver Age theology? Once again, to answer the first two questions, a more extensive study of Steinberg's life and work and its relationship to his Judaism would need to be undertaken.

not wish to have pleasure, but to suffer, not to live for myself, but to die for God. I want to suffer with eternal suffering, to love and feed even the graveyard worms and – all the rest…" And, there is the understanding that "God suffers innocently for me and in me. Do I not want to also suffer innocently for Him, for His fullness?....And won't I soon…die His Death?"

The role of the Jewess in the final drama
This then is the final drama of salvation: to reject life for death; to pass through death in order to find Life. So stated, we begin to understand that all those "pairs," starting with the Jewess at the stake, were anticipating the final pair: man and Christ. And this leads to an interesting conclusion when we go back and re-examine the dynamics of the inquisitor and his peculiar victim.

The inquisitor kills the one he (secretly) loves: rejecting love, he chooses death. And yet without the strong passion, there would have been nothing to reject. His imperfect passion is the first stage of his self, the sign of his humanity. He takes that sign, that passion and in killing the Jewess, he deprives his passion of its object, he kills passion itself[214]. The attempted murder of the Jewess turns out to be his own suicide, or at least the murder of his old self. In the death throes of passion, he himself expires and finds himself reborn by the side of God.

The role of the Jewess is harder to fathom, at first. She herself had also drawn near the fatal moment of passion which would constitute a sin against God, but the Inquisitor beats her to it. Thus she does not even sin through seduction. Next, she is burnt as a witch – unjustly. Moreover, her heretical belief that God will not forgive Judas in the context seems vindicated. Finally, when she is being bound to the stake, she asks with amazing humility after the well-being of her executioner – despite being fully aware that she is being executed unjustly. Instead, she has the power to see the common humanity of her torturer, and in a sense she, the victim, also dwells in the torturer's breast; she herself is the faint pang of concern there which is reflected back to herself.

But does this not lead to a rather shocking conclusion? Does not the Jewess most closely approximate Christ? Christ, on Karsavin's reading, is a bound, tortured, humiliated slave – the lowest of the low in humanity, so well does he take on humanity's imperfection. Christ has made His home in our souls, and there he waits silently, saying not a word, but through his very silence provoking us in his passivity to all manner of changes. He does not intervene, for to do so would compromise our freedom. He does not reach out to kiss us like Elenita, as Karsavin writes, thus making clear the femininity of Christ-within-us, his role of passive lover. Instead, he merely calls forth and reflects the quickly changing images from the inner drama of our own souls.

In like manner the Jewess, too, is – externally – an image of imperfection:

---

[214] This is made clear by another lover-beloved pair in the *Poem*: in this case the lover murders his beloved, seeing in this the highest sacrifice he can offer her – to live without her, to suffer her death, to lose his love.

that is, she is a person of dubious repute – a *conversa* among born and bred Christians, and always under suspicion. But she does not seem to undergo a drama of repentance: Karsavin puts all that onto the Inquisitor. Instead, it is the Jewess with her "heresy" of all-encompassing forgiveness who provokes that drama in the Inquisitor, who passes first through self-asserting passion, then to soul-threatening risk, and finally to a self-destroying explosion of love which culminates in his utter death. But that death, which explodes his passion, his coldness, his pride and leaves only pure love behind, is in fact his rebirth in God. These stages do indeed seem to reciprocate that last drama with which Karsavin finishes the poem. But if so, then who else then could this mysterious Jewess symbolize?[215] (And all this, of course, without even mentioning the rather obvious fact that Christ too was a Jew).

That, at least, is a possible reading. An allegory need not be confined to one reading, and this suggestive interpretation does not exclude the more human role for the Jewess as one who, lacking adequate faith, is herself paradoxically saved by the Inquisitor's attentions. In fact, the latter reading should in the larger context be foregrounded – for in general, all the "pairs" symbolize only the imperfect human dynamic of developing self-consciousness.

As Karsavin mentions several times, real closure is not achieved in this world, and certainly not in art. For "in the imperfection of the world one can comfort oneself only by sketching and playing at tragedy, inventing tragic poems which always turn into old-fashioned melodramas."[216] Nonetheless, though art and life only weakly hint at real Life, Karsavin also insisted with true medieval philosophical realism that the connection between the two is certainly present enough, so that echo of perfection emanating from the Jewess can indeed be taken as a weak hint in the direction of Christ, the Reality behind the symbol.

Jews and personality

This, however, takes us back to another paradox. Stepping outside the *Poem on Death* and back into the relatively real world of Karsavin's life, we see that the Christ-like Jewess really had her roots in his new life in Lithuania. Aaron Steinberg sheds light on this in two conversations that he recollects having with Karsavin.

While they were still both living in Berlin, Karsavin told Steinberg with admiration about his local Jewish grocer. The man had in a very tactful way extended him credit on learning that he was the father of three young daughters and a Russian professor. "You think that an attentive relationship to people is a special characteristic of yours," Karsavin told Steinberg, "but in my opinion it is

---

[215] Karsavin gives us in a Spanish conversa a shining example of Christianity. This is interesting for another reason: it was during the Inquisition that the connection between pure faith and pure blood was first made, with consequences reaching up until Hitler. Karsavin's metaphysics clearly rejects the connection between purity of blood and faith; while Florensky's metaphysics seems to allow room for just such a nexus, with Bulgakov's threatening at times to do so too.

[216] Section 7, 184.

a feature of the Jewish people in general." And he pondered that among gentiles, perhaps only a Nicholas the Wonderworker could have done such a kind deed. Once again, this echoes Rozanov's (albeit malevolent) characterization of Jewry as a nation of Seraphim of Savovs and John of Kronstadts.

The grocer had come up in conversation as a result of Steinberg's own insightful attentiveness into people. For Karsavin had sought his advice on how to proceed with a young Jewish girl from a Russified family who had approached him asking to convert to Orthodoxy. Karsavin had sent her away to think it over for a month. Steinberg now told him that he needed to consider other factors: did the girl have elderly parents? How would they take it if their only daughter changed her faith? Was she just converting in order to marry? Only if it was a life and death affair, he advised, should Karsavin tell her to proceed. Karsavin, who prided himself on his own insightfulness into people, was struck with admiration by this "Jewish sensitivity" to the human heart.

In Lithuania, according to Steinberg, Karsavin's appreciation of Jewry deepened further. He testified to Steinberg how his interaction with the ancient, traditional Jewish community of Kaunas had affected him: "I used to say that if you do not understand and do not accept the Trinity, then an understanding of personality (*lichnost'*) is not available to you. You answered me with a quotation from Ps. 145, first in Hebrew and then you translated: 'The Lord is close to all who call on Him, to all who recognize Him in truth.' This psalm is recited by all pious Jews thrice daily. But you did not convince me. Only when I moved to Kaunas and saw the old Jewish city of Kovno, and sensed the attitude of Jews towards me, a complete stranger, did I realize that I was wrong." And he told a story of another Jewish shopkeeper, a woman this time, whose eyes had filled with tears of genuine sympathy when she learned that Karsavin was separated from his family in Paris.

What is one to make of these anecdotes? After our analysis of the *Poem on Death*, it would be hard to see them simply as charming tales about Karsavin's new-found philo-Semitism and his rejection of his old unthinking Russian antipathy to Jews. Karsavin, not uniquely among Russian philosophers, maintained that a philosophy that was not lived was not true. But in this case, those small incidents in his life that convinced him that *lichnost'* could be attained without a belief in the Trinity have a simply stunning impact on our evaluation of his philosophy.

As we have just seen, true *lichnost'* comes from accepting eternal dying, and finally (ontological) death, and so being brought into the Life of the Son of God. *Lichnost'* arises through imitation of the Father's execution of Himself in the Son and His resurrection of Himself through the Life-giving Holy Spirit. Unification with the Trinity takes place within the Church, which is Christ, the eternally dying Son. How can a person outside the Church, outside Christ, attain *lichnost'*?

Thus when Karsavin told Steinberg that he now believed that "*lichnost'* is available to" Jews, what could he have meant? Could he have meant that *lichnost'* does not depend on partaking in the Trinity; that Man, the crown of creation, has an inner structure that does not reflect the Trinity? But this would almost amount to an empirical proof that the Trinitarian doctrine is off the mark!

In the *Poem on Death*, we noted that the Jewess is really a bright symbol of Christ. But I believe it is not merely a detail that Karsavin makes her a *baptized* Jewess. To have made her simply a non-baptized Jewess, like the one whose eyes filled with tears in the Kaunas shop, and then to have projected her straight into heaven after her encounter with the Inquisitor….That would have been to create a truly subversive symbol which would have threatened to explode this whole literary retelling of *On Personality*. It would have made the *Poem* just a tad more risqué than it already was.

There is, though, another way of conceiving how Karsavin could believe that Jews could remain without a doctrine of the Trinity and still partake in the Trinity (i.e. still be "personalities" in the technical sense). And that is the option we already explored when we considered Karsavin's treatment of Sinai. Was the section devoted to 'Israel', then, an attempt to grapple with how Jews, who were so obviously holy and close to God, could bear the marks of the Trinity without openly confessing this doctrine? Perhaps we can see Karsavin's hints at a fire of Sinai with Christ at its centre as his solution to this conundrum thrown up by his new life in Kaunas. In which case, he would draw near to Bulgakov's belief that Christ resides in the soul of Jews.

Still, the answer cannot be seen as altogether satisfactory. As we noted earlier, for Karsavin "repentance" was a conscious changing of one's mind to make it one with the Church. He lays great stress on how Reason and Thought are also imitations of the Life of the Logos. Being which does not think itself is the same as non-being. Perhaps this very gnostically-tinted emphasis on knowledge as a necessary path to salvation in the end works against him here[217].

In sum, the answer to this question must have been part of the continuing dialogue between Steinberg and Karsavin concerning the interconnection between philosophy and religion, and Judaism and Christianity. Steinberg's earlier contention that he saw no need for the Trinity in the development of personality was later vindicated by Karsavin's own admission that Jews could somehow come to God without confessing this doctrine. It seems that empirically the two had reached agreement – on Steinberg's home soil. In the domain of theory, however, a great many questions still remain – for Karsavin, at least, and those inspired by his work.

Nor should we let slip another detail in this exchange, however: Steinberg admitted that in "life and death" cases, it would be appropriate for a Jew to convert to Christianity. For an Orthodox Jew, who had declared himself unable to see the need for the Trinity, this is no less a stunning contradiction, and also

---

[217] On the other hand, the Inquisitor himself in his orgasmic death is explicitly said to die without repentance. And he was taken to Paradise. Somehow, in his actions he had effected a transformation which had changed him in the way that repentance does. His very actions and intentions were a form of repentance. I grapple further with how the contradictions in Karsavin concerning Judaism and personality might be resolved in Rubin (2009).

an admission of the multiplicity of personal being. For just as, grudgingly, and in defiance of his own theoretical ballast, Karsavin seems to accept that there may be a way to the heart of divinity that does not go by the Trinitarian path, so Steinberg seems to accept that a born Jew can have a calling that does not fall within the remit of the Torah. Both these admissions in these philosophers of different faith traditions arouse deep curiosity and warrant further exploration. They take us some way beyond each one's public statements in the *Versty* exchange of 1928.

Final years: London, Lithuania, Siberia
Karsavin and Steinberg met for the last time in 1937. Steinberg had fled Germany for London in 1934, where he dedicated himself to publicizing the work of Simeon Dubnow and working on the dissemination of Jewish culture[218]. In 1941, he became director of the department of culture for the World Jewish Congress, and founded a research centre to investigate genocide. After the Holocaust, Steinberg threw himself into administrative and communal activity on behalf of the Jewish people: this was his contribution to helping rebuild Jewish life after the catastrophe, and his own form of self-sacrifice for the sake of his people, for whom he put aside what might have been a stunning intellectual career.

Towards the end of his life, he wrote an autobiographical account of his years in Russia, which contains many valuable portraits of leading Silver Age figures. He also continued to keep his diary, in which can be found many touching and thought-proking insights – and which in future will surely merit research, meditation and wider dissemination for Jews and non-Jews in search of a model of a masterly and wise combination of the Greek and the Judaic, philosophical truth and the revealed truth. Steinberg's heritage, it can be said, surely contains valuable lessons for the whole expanse of Europe, from the Russian East to the Anglo-Saxon West, where he finally settled and died in 1975.

Karsavin's further fate is intriguing. His invitation to teach in Lithuania came from a former colleague who in 1926 had become president of the country. The offer had been conditional on Karsavin learning Lithuanian within three years. Karsavin moved to Lithuania in January, 1928, and having mastered the language much more quickly was soon writing his philosophical and historical works in it[219]. In fact, the *Poem on Death* was the last work he wrote in Russian.

This adds another note to our understanding of the work. The *Poem on Death*, as we have seen, was really a poem about a new type of Life and Love. It seems that a part of Karsavin's embrace of life-giving Death was that he died, in a literary sense at least, to his Russian self. But just as death is merely a way of achieving that recapitulation-through-abandonment of all one's past moments,

---

[218] He was a member of YIVO and the Internationl Jewish Congress from the mid-30s on.
[219] Karsavin's lectures in Lithuanian inspired Lithuanian linguists such as A. Greimas to take their native language with a new seriousness, and Karsavin was one of the central figures in developing a philosophical vocabulary in Lithuanian.

so through his Lithuanian identity he seemed to recapitulate in microcosmic form his past Russianness.

For Karsavin saw Lithuania as being part of Russia, a subordinate personality within the larger hierarchy of Russia. But the archaic Lithuanian language, with its retention of proto-Indo-European phonetics and syntax, had retained elements which the larger culture had lost. Steinberg recalls Karsavin enthusing about how even Lithuanian Catholicism differed from the Roman variant and had things to teach Russian Orthodoxy.

Thus we encounter Karsavin engaged in yet another impossible venture: the philosopher of Trinitarian personality who says Jews can do without the Church is now expressing himself in the role of Lithuanian nationalist[220] – even though he has not discarded his Russian Orthodox Slavophile identity. Is there not a parallel here with his admiration for archaic Jewry, with its retention of ancient Hebraic elements that the more universal culture of Christendom had lost? Was Karsavin not also saying that Jewry still had much to teach the gentiles, in the same way that his Jewess could teach her inquisitor? Both cases, dare one say it, seem to be yet more instances of that *unio oppositorum* that so occupied the philosopher.

The country he had chosen as his new homeland[221] was to suffer a series of abrupt political changes in the coming years. Its short-lived independence was crushed first by the German invasion, and shortly after liberation by the Soviet Union, it fell within the orbit of its ambiguous liberators.

This, too, is connected to the *Poem on Death*. Karsavin had chosen Lithuania over an offer from Oxford in 1926 much to the chagrin of his family in Paris. There were several reasons for his choice. Firstly, he wanted to be closer to his beloved Russia. Next, Russian émigré life depressed him: he saw it as full of bickering, pettiness and as he once lamented to Steinberg, "low morals"[222]. But finally, there may even have been an element of a death-wish in his move back eastwards towards his unstable homeland. Once, signing into a conference, Karsavin had listed his title as "confessor" – a pun on the expected "professor." The chances of fulfilling this wish, expressed once more through the medium of a serious jest, must have seemed greater at the end of the twenties, the closer he moved towards Stalin's domain.

But death did not come immediately. To begin with, there was a first Soviet occupation in 1940. After Hitler's declaration of war on the Soviet Union, the country was then occupied by the Germans, and Karsavin and the faculty of

---

[220] His earlier Eurasian dreams of a Russian-led confederation seem to have been abandoned: he publicly denounced the Soviet annexation of the Lithuanian republic in 1945.

[221] Karsavin was referred to for the twenty years he lived in Lithuania as the "Lithuanian Plato." He was instrumental in developing the philosophical vocabulary of modern Lithuanian. Even today he is a respected figure in Lithuania.

[222] In a conversation with Steinberg, Karsavin contrasted for the worse Jewish morals, as he had witnessed them in the behavior of his kind Jewish grocer, with Russian behavior in that city. We recall Trubetzkoy, who also lamented the Russian emigrant mentality, but put it on a par with permanently exilic Jewish morality.

Kaunas moved to Vilnius. During the Nazi round-up and annihilation of Vilnius' Jews, Karsavin managed to play a role in helping several people escape from the ghetto. When the country was incorporated into the Soviet Union after the war, Karsavin was stripped of his teaching responsibilities and instead given the post of director of the Vilnius Art Museum.

In 1948, he was arrested for anti-Soviet activities[223] and sentenced to ten years' labor in Siberia. Having fallen ill with tuberculosis, he was sent to the medical station at Abez of the infamous Vorkuta gulag, where prisoners worked in coal mines.

News of Karsavin's life reached the West only in sporadic fragments. Steinberg, who wrote his memoirs in 1967, finished his reminiscences of him with a speculation about what had become of his dear friend: "I would like to think that Lev Platonovich Karsavin ended his life as worthy brother Lazarus in his monastery." This was a reference to the wish stated in their last conversation together that he could end his life a monk. Karsavin, had already been dead more than a decade by this time.

Abez and a final Jewish encounter

We are fortunate that Karsavin's two years in Abez were recorded in detail by Anatoly Vaneev. Spared from harsh labor by his fatal illness, he spent two years dying slowly but with monastic patience and forbearance. Extraordinarily, his dying was – as befits the author of *Poem on Death* – also a creative period for him: he wrote nine more original works which Vaneev stored and smuggled out after his own release.

The Soviet gulags were strange worlds. In addition to the cruelty and harshness, there was the fact that they were a kalaidescope of dissidence, where the full variety of anti-Soviet opinion was gathered in one place: nationalists from different countries, monarchists, Christians, Trotskyites, and rabbis rubbed shoulders with criminals and bandits. Among the intellectual prisoners, Karsavin's presence caused excitement and people came to visit him. He was also taken good care of by the Lithuanians, some of whom had traveled on the same train as him away from their homeland, but back to his – a strange fulfillment of his dream to see Russia again.

It is in this environment that we can understand how a Yiddish poet could be thrown together with Lev Karsavin. This was Samuel Halkin, the translator of Shakespeare into Yiddish, and a well-known Yiddish poet in his own right. Through the good services of Vaneev, who for a while studied Hebrew and Kabbalah with this scion of an old Hasidic family, Halkin realized his desire to meet Karsavin.

This final meeting of Karsavin with another representative of Jewry was rather hurried and is more interesting for the impression that Halkin gave of Karsavin in

---

[223] In 1945, Karsavin publicly condemned the Soviet annexation of the Lithuanian republic. In 1947 he refused to participate in elections and openly called them a fiction. The official charges did not mention this but referred to his counterrevolutionary White activity in emigration and other fabrications.

the final year of his life: "I expected to meet a refined member of the intelligentsia, an intellectual, of the sort I had met before," he told Vaneev afterwards. "But I saw a person in whom what struck me was his spiritual concentration and inner greatness, so that I lost my nerve somewhat in front of him."

Due to this sudden loss of nerve, Halkin rushed through a recitation of his poems in Russian translation and Karsavin, though impressed by his verse, was a little disconcerted by his excitability. Halkin left in a flurry before Karsavin had had a chance to really express his opinion about his work.

Some time later, Halkin noted with regret that Vaneev's visits to him were becoming less and less frequent. "You appear so rarely now," he remarked, "as if coming to me was as difficult as getting from Russia to Israel. However, I know you. You are grazing in meadows where there is grass for you, and in my meadow, probably, there is nothing left for you."

This was indeed the case, as Halkin had ruefully noted. And although Karsavin and Halkin never met after that one hurried encounter, Karsavin took a fatherly interest in his protégé's "grazing" of Halkin's pastures.

When Karsavin's illness took a final fatal turn, he was moved to the sanitorium. Vaneev, after a few weeks, followed the master there – even though it meant having an operation that would make him fit for hard labor again. It was during this time of separation that Karsavin sent a message in the shoe of a devoted Lithuanian asking after Vaneev's spiritual progress, and expressing a concern that Vaneev, with his keen aptitude for dialectics, was not "being seduced by the arabesques of Kabbalistics."[224]

But Karsavin need not have been worried. In fact, Halkin had used "Kabbalistic arabesques" to prove that Vaneev was destined to become the disciple of Karsavin. Using *gematria*, he deduced – apparently in all seriousness – that since Vaneev's birth year totaled half of Karsavin's birth year, it was on the cards that their relationship should have developed as it did.

Thus even in the dissident "schools" of distant Siberia, in the middle of a Soviet wasteland, an old dialogue between Jews and Christians, Judaism and Christianity, continued unabated.

Death and burial

Karsavin's death, like his life, was full of literary echoes. Like Soloviev, Catholics claimed him as their own for a time. For in the absence of an Orthodox priest, Karsavin confessed and took communion from a Lithuanian priest –

---

[224] Karsavin's comments about Philo probably explain his sarcastic comments about Kabbalah. And yet his own use of the concept of Adam Kadmon in *Noctes Petropolitanae* to depict the universality of the human soul shows a debt to Kabbalah, as does his concept of divine contraction, and indeed the universal human soul, in *Poem on Death*. Thus some of Karsavin's heterodox, or "hereticizing," universalism can be traced to his use of this Kabbalistic or quasi-Kabbalistic doctrine. (It might be the case, as Burmistrov noted of Soloviev, that the idea of Adam Kadmon did not come directly from Jewish sources).

and the rumor went round that on his death-bed he had gone over to Rome[225]. The irony was that Fr. Peter, the Orthodox priest, though aware of Karsavin's imminent death, for some unknown reason failed to attend to him. To which Karsavin responded: "No matter. That, after all, is why he is Peter." Heir in many ways to the founder of the philosopher of all-unity, and a conscious if parodic imitator of him, in this odd circumstance he came by chance to echo an episode in Soloviev's last years – and its misinterpretation by outsiders.

His fate immediately after death was also not straightforward. When Karsavin finally expired from tuberculosis, he was buried in a way that was strangely fitting for this philosopher of the Word who had sought all those years before "to die His death." By arrangement with the chief surgeon, Vladas Shimkunas, a Lithuanian who was an admirer of Karsavin, Vaneev agreed that some way was necessary to identify Karsavin's body for posterity. The two agreed that Vaneev would write an epithet for his teacher and Shimkunas would insert it in the cut-open stomach of the corpse. In this way, Karsavin was buried with a flask in his stomach which contained a précis of his philosophy[226].

The Word, as it were, had quite literally come to dwell in the flesh – like the prophet Ezekiel consuming the words of his scroll. That rotting of limbs and consumption by worms, which Karsavin had imagined for himself, would at least be sweetened by fragments of his own metaphysics. The words inside Karsavin, a mini-creed of his life, read:

> Lev Platonovich Karsavin, historian and religious thinker. He was born in 1882 in St Petersburg. In 1952, imprisoned in a labor camp, he died from milarian tuberculosis. L.P.Karsavin spoke and wrote about the Tri-unified God, Who in His unfathomability reveals Himself to us, so that through Christ we may cognize in the Creator a Father who gives birth to us. And about how God, overcoming Himself in love, with us and in us

---

[225] A German fellow prisoner spread this rumor quite non-maliciously when he claimed in his memoirs that Karsavin had become a Catholic on his deathbed – a not unreasonable supposition by an outsider with no personal acquaintance with Karsavin. Karsavin's earlier hostility towards Catholicism diminished with age, but he continued to hold a dim view of scholasticism and the papacy. He also took with utter seriousness the dogmatic aberration of the *Filioque*, seeing it as the root of Catholic heresy. Karsavin, more than Soloviev or Frank, was thus never tempted by an ecumenical desire to blur confessional boundaries. The notion of him converting to Catholicism could only be accepted by someone unfamiliar with his work and life. See, for example, "Ob opostnostnyakh i preodolenii otvlechennogo khristianstva," in *Put'* No.6 (1927):32-49, for one example of his equation of Catholicism with an archetypically undesriable "abstract" Christianity.

[226] A less welcome but still Karsavinianly macabre element was also added by the fact that another patient in the sanitorium had his leg amputated on the day of Karsavin's death. The leg was thrown into Karsavin's grave. Someone comforted the distressed Vaneev by suggesting that it was a great privilege for the amputee to be at least partially united with the great philosopher.

suffers in our sufferings, so that we too may attain in Him in unity with the Son of God the fullness of love and freedom. And about how our very imperfection and the burden of our destiny should be recognized by us as an absolute goal. Attaining this, we already have a part in the victory over Death through death. Farewell, dear teacher. The grief of parting with you cannot be contained in words. But we too await our hour in the hope of being there where grief is transfigured into eternal joy.

One imagines that Steinberg, too, that philosopher – in another key – of the incarnation of the Logos, would have seen a certain appropriateness in this final union of word and flesh in his dear friend, whom he had imagined as dying in the role of "brother Lazarus."

Six

Semyon Frank: from *russkiy yevrei* to *russkiy yevropeetz*

Six

Frank: the Jew as universal man

Semyon Frank, born in Moscow in 1877 into the family of a Jewish doctor, differs from the other figures examined so far. He was born and raised Jewish, but converted to Russian Orthodoxy in 1913[1]. Subsequently, he was to propound his own version of the "Russian idea," a term which is avoided in his work, however, in favor of the "Russian worldview." Thus, whereas for Russian Christian and Russian Jewish thinkers, Jewish-Christian encounters were dialogues between different people, in Frank the encounter was – initially at least – an internal meeting.

There is something a little unfortunate about starting a study of Frank by focusing on his Jewishness. This is because he rarely mentioned this facet of his identity. In addition, Frank was a conciliator: by nature he tended to focus on the underlying similarities which bound people, rather than highlighting differences. In this respect, he differed from Berdyaev and Karsavin, his fellow philosophers and friends, with their fiery, confrontational personalities. Frank's desire to see similarity and continuity meant that when it came to his own conversion, he downplayed any sense of momentousness, or rupture. The sense of drama that one might expect from a converted Jew who became a leading proponent of Russian philosophy is resoundingly absent.

However, Frank's own understatement of his Jewish origins was often not reciprocated by the outside world. While in another epoch of world-history, Frank's desire for a quiet life might have met with more success, the twentieth century did not let him forget that he was at least born a Jew. In 1947, he renewed his acquaintance with Vyacheslav Ivanov, who had trodden a different path in exile. Summarizing the more than twenty years of his life that had elapsed since their last meeting in Russia, Frank comes to the war: "I spent the war years in France, hiding from the German occupying army, for – in view of my non-Aryanness – I was under threat of deportation and death in a gas chamber."[2]

These terse lines compress the three years of deprivation, hunger, cold and fear that Frank experienced while hiding in the hills near the Swiss border. After the war, he learnt of the death of Jewish friends and family members[3] murdered in the Nazi camps. He also visited in hospital a friend who had been liberated from Buchenwald, and was shocked by his skeletal condition. The possible

---

[1] The year of the Beilis trial, it might be noted.
[2] Frank, Semyon. *Russkoe Mirovozzrenie*, (St Petersburg: Nauka, 1996), 98.
[3] His sister's husband and son (Abram and Leonid Zhivotovsky) and Raisa and Michel Gorlin, Russian-Jewish poets. Frank was also close to Ilia Fondaminsky, who was murdered in Dachau along with Mother Maria. The friend he visited in hospital was Pyanovy.

consequences of his non-Aryan status were thus quite clear to him. And yet, Frank's choice of phrase is telling here: he prefers to refer to himself as a "non-Aryan" rather than as a Jew.

The problems of being a "non-Aryan" had been brought home to Frank much earlier, firstly in Russia where during the Civil War, there were round-ups directed at Jewish "hoarders" even in Saratov, where Frank had been appointed head of the university's philosophy department.

He was then exiled in 1922 on the "philosophy steamer" to Germany, where Hitler's rise to power had immediate consequences for Frank and his family. In 1937 his wife was taken to court by their landlady for subletting rooms to non-Jews: as the wife of a Jew, she was only permitted Jewish boarders. In the same year, Frank's Swiss publisher rejected his *magnum opus*, *The Unfathomable*, calculating that there would be no market for a book by a non-Aryan author. Frank had to rewrite the German original in Russian and find a Russian publisher. This episode led to serious problems with his health and psychological state[4], as well as his finances: from then on he became dependent on the welfare of friends and funds for refugees.

Again, the issue of Jewishness, the crux of the matter for his German persecutors, was a side-issue for Frank himself. When Hitler came to power in 1933, Frank had written: "I wish the Germans all the best with their national revival, but as a foreigner and even more someone of a different faith[5], I cannot be active on the ideological front, and would like to help the Germans in one way – by not burdening them further with my presence."

As regards the non-publication of *The Unfathomable*, Frank mourned not for himself and not for Jews, but rather for the German language: "My personal tragedy," he wrote to his friend, the existential psychologist L. Binswanger, "is that my book cannot be published in the language in which it was conceived and written…[however], this is trivial in comparison to the world-historical tragedy that philosophical thought in the foreseeable future will have to make do without the German language – the language of poets and thinkers."[6]

Finally, the gap between the outside world's willingness to see in Frank a Jew and Frank's differing conception of the matter, can be seen in his interaction with Jews themselves.

In Berlin, Frank was an object of suspicion among Russian-Jewish exiles. When he wrote an obituary of his friend Yuri Aikhenvald, the Russian-Jewish literary critic, he came under attack from the Jewish community. He described the situation in a letter to Berdyaev: "…recently they have started poisoning me, accusing me of calling Aikhenvald a person of Christian spirit[7], and even

---

[4] The non-publication of the book was partly responsible for a heart-attack he suffered in 1938.
[5] By which, of course, he meant Russian Orthodoxy.
[6] Phillip Boobyer, *S.L.Frank. Zhizn' i tvorchestvo russkogo filosofa* (Moscow: Rosspen, 2001), 203.
[7] As we will see below, Frank did in fact refer to Aikhenvald as a 'person of a

accusing me of voluntarily burying him in an Orthodox cemetery, and of forcing Jews to go to an Orthodox *panihida*. It's quite funny, but I can't say it's cheerful living in such an atmosphere."

A similarly painful incident for the non-confrontational Frank occurred two years after his conversion. The renowned German-Jewish philosopher, Herman Cohen, the leading proponent of the neo-Kantian school, visited Russia in 1915, partly as a gesture of support for Russia's beleaguered Jews. Frank approached him after his lecture, and in the middle of a philosophical conversation, it emerged that Frank was a Jew who had converted to Christianity. Cohen immediately expressed his distaste, turned on his heel and strode out of the hall.[8]

In the same year, Frank wrote a review of Cohen's philosophy, which will be examined below, in conjunction with his 1927 review of the work of Cohen's famous disciple, Franz Rosenzweig. Whether or not Frank was aware of it, the latter also expressed strong distaste regarding converted Jews. In particular, he begrudged any persecution a converted Jew might undergo, commenting that "he is not deserving of it."[9]

This hostility from Jews towards his Christianity and from non-Jews towards his Jewish origins did not leave Frank untouched. However, the racial categories of Nazi anti-Semitism impacted far less on his understanding of the philosophical-theological meaning of his conversion: Frank was close to much Russian thought in seeing this as symptomatic of the general cultural crisis of Western Europe.

The Jewish reception of his conversion was much more troubling as far as his own attitude to his "transition" to Christianity was concerned. This forced him, somewhat against his eirenic nature, to recognize that there was an element of tragedy in a Jewish embrace of Christianity, although he tended to see this in general terms – as applying to other people – rather than experiencing the dilemma as anything problematic in his own spiritual development.

For the concisest statement of his own attitude to his conversion was given in a brief autobiography written in Berlin in 1935[10]. There he recounts how his grandfather, Moses Rossianski, became the formative influence on his spiritual life when he invited his young grandson to study the Bible, Rashi, and the Talmud with him, as well as introducing him to the cycle of Jewish life in the synagogue:

"The reverential feeling with which I kissed the covering of the Bible, when in synagogue they brought round the 'scrolls of the law' became in a genetic-

---

Christian spirit.'

[8] A story recounted by Isaiah Berlin, and found in Boobyer (2001).
[9] In Nahum Glatzer, *Franz Rosenzweig. His life and thought*. (Indianapolis/Cambridge: Hackett Publishing Company, 1998.) This, despite the fact that Rosenzweig's close friend Eugen Rosenstock-Hussy was a converted Jew, and indeed had set him on the path to a rediscovery of Judaism.
[10] "Predsmertnoe: vospominaniye i mysli," in S.L.Frank, *Russkoe Mirovozzrenie*, 39-58. St Petersburg: Nauka, 1996.

psychological way the fundament of my religious sense, defining my whole life… My grandfather's stories about the history of the Jewish people and the history of Europe became the first basis of my mental worldview."

When his grandfather was dying, he asked Frank, then 14 years old, not to discontinue his studies of Hebrew and theology. In Frank's opinion, "I did not fulfill that request in the literal sense, however in a general sense I believe that – even while converting to Christianity and losing the link with Judaism – I nonetheless somehow remained true to the religious foundations which he laid in me…I always recognized my Christianity as a layer on the Old Testament base, as a natural development of the religious life of my childhood."

This contrasts somewhat with the aptly titled "The Religious Tragedy of Judaism," written a year earlier. Here Frank depicts Jewish conversion as involving an inevitable tragic split:

> either to reject one's nationality (the only basis of which is Old Testament belief), and despite the forecasts of the prophets to prepare for the Chosen People a definitive end; or to reject the Messiah and the greatest Divine revelation announced by him. One fateful circumstance makes impossible a positive resolution of this antinomy: after the Christian church became a ruling church both in political and secular life, and on the other hand, started to persecute the Jews for their belief, any act of conversion to Christianity must seem a betrayal of one's nation and belief for worldly benefits.[11]

The last statement, of course, accurately describes the situation of many Jews in the Russian empire for whom conversion was often a calculated step to attain equal rights, rather than a spiritual decision. Frank himself resisted converting for almost a decade, aware that his motives might be mistaken. In 1905, when his own conscience assured him that he was already Christian in spirit, he turned down the offer of a St Petersburg professorship that required the holder to be a Christian.

Three months after his baptism in 1913, he was offered – and accepted – another professorship. Some people saw this decision as a ploy to gain "worldly benefits"[12]. Extraordinarily, Nina Struve, the wife of his closest friend, Petr Struve, when she learnt of his decision to convert, entreated him to reconsider what she saw as a step of treachery against his people. If such was the reaction of a close friend, the interpretations of Cohen and the Berlin Jewish community of

---

[11] Semyon Frank, "Der religiöse Tragödie des Judentums," p.129. Quoted in Phillip Boobyer, *S.L.Frank. Zhizn' i tvorchestvo russkogo filosofa*.(Moscow: Rosspen, 2001): p.96.

[12] Lesley Chamberlain in *The Philosophy Steamer*, describes Frank as a Jew who converted for professional reasons. Lesley Chamberlain, *The Philosophy Steamer* (London: Atlantic books, 2006), 351: "Frank apparently converted to Orthodoxy for the utilitarian reason of getting a university job."

the successful philosopher's decision become easier to understand.

In sum, the explicit facts of Frank's conversion present an interesting dilemma. On the one hand, Frank describes his conversion as a "natural development" of his Judaic "Old Testament base." On the other hand, it is an irresolvable "antinomy" that "prepares a definite end for the Chosen people" in contradiction of God's own prophecies.

In fact, this discussion of Frank's Jewishness provides an excellent window into an essential aspect of his philosophy. As one of the four major philosophers of all-unity (along with Karsavin, perhaps closest to him conceptually, and Bulgakov and Florensky), Frank tends to diminish the boundary between God and Good, on the one hand, and the world, on the other. This makes it rather hard for him to find a place for evil in his metaphysical architecture.

This makes for a striking paradox. While empirically Frank came face to face with some of the major historical evils that the first half of the twentieth century threw up, his Platonic philosophy deals with evil almost as an afterthought – a frequent reproach of Berdyaev against Frank. In the case of his personal "Jewish question," Frank's natural tendency to see harmony, balance and order instead of chaos, evil and destruction seems to have led him to adopt a fairly serene attitude towards the "Jewish tragedy"[13].

Nonetheless, although he may have experienced his own conversion from Judaism to Christianity as a "natural" development, in Germany he came face to face philosophically speaking with representatives of the Weimar German-Jewish philosophical and cultural revival. He wrote reviews of the work of three prominent figures in this revival: Herman Cohen, Franz Rosenzweig and Oscar Goldberg.

One of the tasks of this German-Jewish renaissance was, of course, to strengthen Jewry and Judaism against assimilation, by testing Judaism against the highest standards of European culture. As Frank knew from personal experience, this also implied a corresponding rejection and critique of Christianity. The view that Christianity was a natural choice for a Jew was obviously anathema to these German-Jewish philosophers. Frank's reviews, which will be examined in some detail below, not surprisingly involve a rejection of this position.

Still, even when engaging in an open critique of Judaism Frank does his best to be fair-minded. Obviously, he was not compelled to publicly react to contemporary Jewish philosophy, and so it seems fair to assume that there is an element of self-justification in these engagements. However, these articles form a very small part of Frank's output and one still has the feeling that despite his personal background, the Jewish question held none of the emotional fascination and agony that it did for Bulgakov, Karsavin or Rozanov.

---

[13] Connected in this respect is his labelling of the situation a "tragedy": Frank's thought contains an element of Greek fatalism, which approaches the Stoical sometimes. The label here gives the impression that the Jewish situation is fixed by higher destiny, an immutable law of the world.

To a certain extent, one can even say that Frank's appraisal of Judaism contains nothing that one could not expect from a Russian philosopher, especially one who had gained a reputation for his clear statement of the Russian worldview. Did his own Jewish background not impact on his response to Jews who had taken a very different path in life to his own?

In fact, to the extent that Frank's whole "Russian worldview" bears traces of his Jewishness, it did. But the relationship between the Russian, the Jewish and (as we shall shortly see) the German elements in Frank's background is not entirely obvious. Nonetheless, we can see a clue here in how Frank elides together in his account of his grandfather's patrimony "stories about the history of the Jewish people and the history of Europe[14] (*yevreiskogo naroda i istorii yevropy*)."

The similarity in sound between the Russian words for "Jewish" and "Europe" is of course a fortuitous coincidence[15]. However, probably the best place to look for Frank's continuing Jewishness is not in the explicit statements he made about this aspect of his past but in the broadness of both his religious and political views. In the former case, this led to a rather ecumenical approach to Christianity; in the latter to an emphasis on Russia's larger European destiny.

The mention of universalism, of course, inevitably puts one in mind of Gershenzon, Shestov and Steinberg. We have already seen that the charge of "Jewish universalism" was often viewed in a treacherous light, and merges with the accusation of cosmopolitanism and rootlessness. Frank's universalism, of course, in one very obvious sense was bound to differ from that of these other Russian-Jewish thinkers: after all, he became a Russian Orthodox Christian out of conviction, and thus a member of the ruling religion and worldview.

Nonetheless, on closer investigation the "history of Europe" which he absorbed through his Jewish background created a sensibility that in many ways overlaps with his unconverted colleagues – especially, as we shall see, with Mikhail Gershenzon.

Moreover, like Steinberg, Frank's parents were from Latvia. Both sides of the family were German-speaking, and his maternal grandmother was from Tilsit, a town on the border of (Russian) Latvia and Germany. Frank thus grew up speaking German, as well as Russian; in addition his father's mother spoke French to her daughters, and was interested in the history of Europe's ruling families. Thus a crucial element of the family's Jewishness was not just,

---

[14] In his recollections, he also writes that the sound of the church bells formed another ingredient in the spiritual composition of his childhood.

[15] It is tempting, if only playfully, to develop the connection, however – perhaps in the following way. A rather unreliable etymology of the word Europe links it to the Phoenician word '*ereb*, West, where the sun sets. The word Jew or Hebrew, comes from '*eber*, to cross (the river) – said to refer to Abraham's crossing out of Mesopotamia towards the Promised Land. Both Semitic roots contains the same three letters, both refer to a Westward journey, both are in the sacred "Semitic language." Ergo: Jews have a sacred mission in Europe! While tongue-in-cheek, the underlying story may not be far off the mark.

and perhaps not so much the religious aspect, i.e. its adherence to Judaism. Perhaps more profound was its very Jewish retention of a familiarity with the different cultures through whose territories it had migrated, especially German high culture. This explains why Frank reacted with such personal chagrin to his publisher's refusal to publish *The Unfathomable* in German.

In that basic, factual sense, then, Frank was indeed heir to a "universal" blend of cultures that was bound to give him a different perspective on Russia. He shared this with Russia's non-metropolitan Jews, who were forced to live in the Western provinces which bordered the German-speaking lands[16]. While many Western Yiddish-speaking Jews picked up German due to its similarity to Yiddish, and studied in Germany to escape Russian university quotas (like Gershenzon, Shestov and Steinberg) Frank's family had originated in Germany itself only three generations back, and he still had relatives living in Berlin. As a student he also spent time in Heidelberg and Freiburg.

The importance of Frank's German connection in the formation of his political views can be seen in his reaction to the First World War. He was far less jingoistic about it than his colleagues. Frank's closest friend, Petr Struve[17], had written then that "the task of the war of 1914 is to bring to its end the external expansion of the Russian empire, to realize its imperial goals and its Slavic calling." For Bulgakov, the war showed that "Europe is the middle, Russia is the end. Europe is culture and government, Russia is in deep self-consciousness… The Russia era of world history is already approaching…We have again started to believe in Russia." And Ern collapsed philosophy and world-history into one with his belief that the German aggression was a direct result of Kantian philosophy: rejection of metaphysics and the belief in the categorical imperative had led to the German people's dedication to the cult of the German nation and government[18].

Frank himself rejected all this Slavophile-colored war-mongering. His reaction to the First World War was influenced by the spirit of harmony and tolerance that his philosophy breathes: "We must understand this war not as a war against the national spirit of our enemy, but as a war against an evil spirit

---

[16] Frank's father, being a doctor, and one who had been decorated in military service, had permission to reside in metropolitan Russia, so that Frank did not suffer from residential discrimination. Growing up in Moscow made him not only geographically but spiritually and linguistically closer to Russianness than, say, Shestov or Gershenzon.

[17] Struve himself was – a long way back – of German ancestry as his patronymic (Berngardovich) and surname testify. He considered retention of national feelings among minorities treacherous, and he certainly did not have proclivities for German culture over Russian culture. Perhaps the fact that Frank got his Germanness through a Jewish filter gave him a more devoted stance towards it: it was the German sphere that launched Jewish enlightenment, and German Jews were – before the Holocaust – much attached to Germanness.

[18] For these quotes and further details, cf. Boobyer (2001), ch.9.

which has overcome the national consciousness of Germany, and – in this very way – as a war for the restoration of those relations and concepts under whose aegis a free development of an all-European culture would be possible in *all* its national expressions."

Likewise, after the Second World War, Frank was remarkably balanced and forgiving in regard to Germany. In one of his last works, *Light in the Darkness*, he insisted in very similar language that Germany too was a victim of evil, for "the spirit of evil is not concentrated in any of its separate concrete bearers, [and] overcoming these bearers through military defeat does not mean conquering and destroying the spirit of evil itself: it has a secret capacity, like the spark from a fire, to jump from one soul to another…."[19]

In the face of Allied triumphalism, Frank – then a refugee on the soil of a victorious ally, Britain – went on to point out that the victors were not untarnished: "the fact [is] that the first application of warfare through artificial earthquakes and the instant death of thousands of innocent people belongs to the Anglo-Saxon world, widely recognized as the bearer of the principles of rights and respect for the human being."[20]

Thus, even while leaving the Jewish religion behind, we might not be far wrong in seeing Frank as continuing to be permeated by an undercurrent of secular, cultural Jewishness which informed his worldview. Of course, it is not yet clear how tolerant statements like these and a broad receptivity to different cultures and nations could be linked to Frank becoming a champion of the "*Russian* worldview," with which his name became associated.

We will address this question shortly below. A clue, however, can be found in a 1950 article on Soloviev[21] in which Frank admitted the unconscious affinity of their thought. He wrote that after Dostoevsky's 1880 speech in memory of Pushkin, Russians began to see themselves as universal men. For such Russians, noted Frank, this was a pretense; only for Soloviev was it real. Thus Frank connects his own predilection for universalism with something specific in Russian culture, noticed and developed by Soloviev – who, we remember, liked to refer to himself as a Jew. Thus Soloviev's metaphorical Jewishness seems to have come face to face with Frank's literal Jewishness.

Nonetheless, this answer is not fully adequate for an obvious reason: Frank really only discovered Soloviev's thought towards the end of his life, when he had already developed his own system. Frank's "Russian-Jewish-Christian" universalism must thus have traced a different route, and only converged on Soloviev's worldview from another direction. In fact, as we shall see, the subject of Dostoevsky's speech, Alexander Pushkin, is illuminating in this respect.

In the next sections, we will trace this trajectory of Frank's thought, paying

---

[19] Semyon Frank, *Svet vo tme* (Moscow: Faktorial, 1998), 35.
[20] Ibid, 34.
[21] Semyon Frank, "Dukhovnoe nasledie Vladimira Solovyova," in *Vestnik*, No.4-5, pp.2-10. Also in In S.L.Frank, *Russkoe Mirovozzrenie*. (St Petersburg: Nauka, 1996): 392-399.

attention to how Frank's cultural Jewishness led to some interesting convergences with the thought of his friend and fellow *Landmarks* collaborator, Gershenzon. This will also enable us to draw the line between equally crucial differences in their two worldviews.

Frank's philosophy

Here we will outline enough of Frank's philosophical development to enable a later comparison of his thought with that of Gershenzon, as well as that of the German-Jewish philosophers whom he later criticized on philosophical grounds.

Frank started off intellectually treading the by-now familiar path from Marxism[22] to Idealism, as well as experiencing the metaphysics-shattering hammer-blows of Nietzsche at about the same time as Shestov and Berdyaev[23]. After his Marxist phase, his political and religious formation was strongly shaped by Bulgakov, and especially Petr Struve: gradually his rejection of youthful Marxist materialism came to involve a search for a spiritual (but not as yet Christian) socialism that would steer a path between extreme liberalism and communism.

To this end, under Struve's guidance, he looked past the Russian radicals of the 60s towards the men of the 30s, such as Herzen, whose evolution he interpreted – contrary to Lenin[24] – as a gradual turning away from revolution to a liberalism informed with a spiritual sensitivity: "From that ferment of ideas is born Russian religious thought, pushed aside from the front stage of spiritual life in the 60s by materialism, positivism and atheism."[25]

His 1909 *Landmarks* article honed this rejection of the materialism of the

---

[22] In his case, involvement with Marxism and the social-democrats was due to the influence of his step-father, Vasily Zak (born Tsalel Izkovich), whom Frank named after his grandfather his second formative influence – one, however, which he would repudiate in favor of a return to his grandfather's spiritual values.

[23] In 1901, he had written a paper called *Friederich Nietzsche and the ethics of love for the far-distant*: as for Shestov, the combination of a failed love-affair and the discovery of the German nihilist had the effect of opening up hitherto unseen spiritual horizons for Frank, and henceforth he began to see himself as an idealist, only now "not in the Kantian sense, but an idealist-metaphysician, the bearer of a certain spiritual experience, that had gained access to the invisible inner reality of being." (*Russkoe Mirovozzrenie*, "Predsmertnoe," 54.)

[24] Lenin interpreted Herzen's last letter to Bakunin as a rejection of anarchism in favor of the Marxist internationale. Frank saw Herzen as discovering late in life a pantheistic sense of awe of nature and man's place in its hierarchical order, feelings which evoked in him a political conservatism, a gradualism, a distaste for forcing nature, including that of natural human society. This was a view that Frank by then also embraced.

[25] S.L.Frank, Introduction to *Istoria russkoi filosofskoi mysli kontsa XIX i nachala XX veka. Antologia*. Washington-New York, 1965. Quoted in A.A.Ermichev, *Russkoe Mirrovozzrenie*, footnotes (note 2), p.660.

Russian left intelligentsia, which he saw as arising out of a subjective utilitarianism that ultimately led to a denial of religion and culture. His view that the health of society should be fostered through culture and a sense of the spirit thus shows a convergence on Gershenzon's position in the *Landmarks* collection. The similarities would later be blurred, but not altogether erased.

However, Frank would not produce a truly independent work until the publication in 1915 of *The Object of Knowledge*, which established him as a philosopher. This work was preceded by three significant essays, which laid the groundwork: two essays were dedicated to the poets Goethe (1910) and Tyutchev (1913), and the third was a polemical engagement with V. Ern called "On nationalism in philosophy"[26] (1910). Each was significant for Frank's "coming of age."

The essays on the poets describe poetic perception as "one holistic, subjective-objective consciousness, something new, embracing feelings and concepts and an interpenetration that develops out of them." The essay on Ern took issue with the latter's chauvinistic dismissal of a Western philosophical journal *Logos*, which had come out in Russian that year under the editorship of the (Jewish) neo-Kantian, S.I. Gessen.

Together the essays constituted a justification for how Frank would do philosophy henceforth. His turn to poetry as a source of knowledge already shows a recognition of the limits of rational, discursive philosophy and a quest for "trans-rational" knowledge in the non-discursive, imagistic world of art. Later, the turn to poetry for philosophical inspiration would take Frank to Pushkin – as it would Gershenzon[27]. It is also of note that one of the poets is a German genius, the other a Russian genius, with a pantheistic sensibility for the divine in nature.

This is connected to Frank's rejection of Slavophile chauvinism, which was the subject of his rebuttal of Ern. The latter had written an article rejecting all Western philosophy as inspired by cold "ratio," and uttered a call for Eastern philosophers to philosophize according to the Logos. Frank quoted Soloviev's criticism that the Slavophile philosophers had not in fact achieved anything original: their work was deeply permeated by Hegelianism and French ideas,

---

[26] "O natzionalizme v filosofii" (1910); "Eshcho o natzionalizme v filosofii. Otvet na otvet V.F.Erna" (1910). The first appeared in Russkaya Mysl', 1910, Sept.Kn.IX; the second in a later edition, No.XI.

[27] In this chapter, we compare Frank to Gershenzon. However, it would be instructive to compare Frank and Steinberg: Frank's immersion in German and Russian romanticism pushed him towards Christianity. Steinberg's immersion in neo-Kantianism, Herzen, Lavrov, and Dostoevsky (slightly different, though overlapping, influences than on Frank) allowed him to find a philosophy which was compatible with his Judaism. Undoubtedly, Steinberg's Jewish background was far more solid than Frank's. Still, the trajectories of these two Russian Jews would also shed interesting light on the "national" question in philosophy – as Ern phrased it. Of course, here "national" would include ethnic, linguistic and confessional factors.

and any "mystical depth" really just consisted of quotations from Eastern ascetics that they had dusted off but not truly incorporated into their systems. Further, the so-called "ontological turn" was to be seen abundantly in Leibniz, Spinoza and Hegel (who also talks of the logos). In sum, Frank urged that it was possible to "respect the valuable aspects of eastern religiosity and the Russian national consciousness and still humbly recognize the weakness of Russian philosophical culture."

In a further "reply to a reply" of an unconvinced Ern, Frank reiterated that their debate was "not so much an argument between me and V.F. Ern as an argument between philosophical Slavophilism and the philosophical universalism of V.Soloviev." Henceforth, Frank would interpret this universalism as a license and necessity to incorporate Western philosophy into the Russian mystical search for a truth for all-humanity. In his view, the two methods of quest were complementary: Western philosophy gave rational understanding to the theological truths discovered in the East, and thus there was no conflict.

At the same time, however, Frank expressed his agreement concerning the "scholastic" emptiness and dryness of neo-Kantian philosophy, as well as his recognition that the Russian spirit was mystical-intuitive in nature, striving towards the whole and seeking not the good for the individual but for the collective (*sobornost'*). But for Frank, none of this negated the importance of rational and discursive logical thought. However, it certainly dictated the choice of Western and Russian philosophers to whom he would turn for inspiration to create a mystical-rational, Russian-Western philosophical system.

In "The essence and leading motives of Russian religious philosophy" (1925)[28] and "The Russian Worldview," both written in German, Frank lists these influences. On the Russian side they include: G.S. Skvoroda, Ivan Kireevski (with his concept of "living knowledge"), Soloviev, his contemporary N.Lossky, Lopatin, and Kozlov, the first Russian personalist. Frank also mentions Kozlov's teacher, Gustav Teichmüller, a friend and follower of Leibniz. He was a German who lectured in German at a Russian university in Estonia, and introduced neo-Leibnizianism to Russian thought. Interestingly, Frank calls him a "Russian-German metaphysician" – another indication that for Frank German and Russian thought, far from being at loggerheads as the Slavophiles contended, could unite into a harmonious "dual-unity"[29].

Frank's Western influences, both in *Object*, and then as he expanded his system included: Schelling and Goethe, as well as Leibniz and Hegel (at least as they were percolated through the first formal Russian philosophers). Another important and enduring influence was Spinoza, to whose pantheistic world-

---

[28] *Sushnost' i vedushchie motivy russkoi filosofii*. First in German in Gral, 1925, No.8: 384-395. Translated into Russian by A.Ermichev and A.G.Vlaskina, in Filosofskie nauki, 1990, No.5. Republished in *Russkoe mirovozzrenie*, 149-161.

[29] Another article where this opinion is expressed is "Rilke i slavianstvo" (1929), where Frank describes Rilke's own attraction to Russian culture as satisfying his deepest mystical intuitions.

view he had claimed to have been attracted since childhood. Later on, Frank would become fascinated, like Karsavin, by the philosophy of Nicholas of Cusa, and like Berdyaev would absorb the ideas of Eckhardt and Boehme concerning the "divine nothingness." However, the initial task of *Object* was to overcome the skepticism – and in his followers, the false romanticism – that Kant had let into philosophy.

Briefly stated, the thesis of *Object* is as follows. Frank defends the idea that humans have a direct access to Being, that as subjects immersed in Being they have a privileged access to reality, and are possessors of a genuine knowledge of reality. As such he denies the Kantian claim that knowledge of the thing-in-itself is impossible, which had turned into the subjectivity of romanticism. He champions a new realism, while avoiding the pitfalls of the rationalist realism (of Descartes and Leibniz) that Kant had overturned.

Frank's approach (which he dubbed "ideo-realism") accepts that some knowledge is merely reflective, analytical and secondary, i.e. a knowledge *of* being; but it champions the possibility of a knowledge *as* being, a knowledge which is the same as life and living, which Frank calls intuition: such knowledge when translated into "knowledge-of" inevitably trips up on paradoxes, as it comes from the trans-logical realm; as such artistic and creative language, which is more sensitive to paradox, is more fitting for presenting its insights.

This purely philosophical work was fleshed out to give religious insights in later works such as *The Soul of Man* (1918) and *The Spiritual Foundations of Society* (1930), which Frank grouped together with *Object* to form a trilogy. More detail was added in further major works, among others: *The Unfathomable* (1939) and *Reality and Man* (1949).

Unfortunately, while recognizing the quality of the work, not everyone was convinced that Frank had solved the Kantian dilemma. Gessen, the neo-Kantian whose journal Frank had defended a couple of years before, accused Frank of being a dualist, who posited two worlds of being, rather than a fusion of the two. For the rising star of pan-unity, this was a stinging criticism.

Bulgakov was more troubled by the religious consequences of Frank's new system. The "being," or reality, that Frank described is referred to as an "it," as something impersonal. It is also defined very indistinctly: sometimes it is the "Divine Nothingness" of apophatic theology, and sometimes it seems to be the world.

Both of these criticisms will prove to be extremely germane when we come to consider Frank's own critique of Cohen and especially Rosenzweig. Bulgakov's criticism, which amounts to a charge of pantheism – somewhat ironic, considering that Bulgakov's sophiology attracted exactly the same criticism regarding the relationship of the divine Sophia to the world – was reiterated by V.V.Zenkovsky in regard to Frank's much more mature version of his system in *The Unfathomable*.

The Unfathomable, written more than twenty years later than *Object*, is a systematic philosophical work that builds on that earlier work, as well as on the religious and political works that followed it. However, it is not just philosophy, which Frank had quite soon come to see as impossible in its current European form, but a work of "wisdom," a concept that would occupy Frank increasingly until the end of his life.

In this sense, it is a continuation of his earlier dispute with Ern. In *The Unfathomable*, Frank laid out what he called "a philosophy of respect and love, in opposition to the ruling tendency of contempt and hatred, to the destruction of one's opponent. ..." In other words, that initial impulse to combine the Russian and the Western is now given explicitly ethical meaning: recognition of the limits of knowledge and being have consequences for how one relates to one's neighbor.

As in *Object*, Frank starts with human knowledge and moves onto a classification of being. The types of knowledge recapitulate both main traditions of Western philosophy. For Frank recognizes the validity of empirical knowledge as well as rational knowledge. The latter is very similar to Kant's transcendental knowledge, a rationality which "determines" its object. However, Frank again goes beyond Kant: in order for transcendental knowledge to determine the object of knowledge, there must be a basis of knowledge "antecedent to its expression in concepts." Otherwise, there could be no reasoning with concepts or synthetic relations between determinations of different concepts.

This epistemological basis is trans-rational, that "living knowledge" of which he had spoken before. The sphere of being to which it points is "unknowable" being, also called "reality"[30] (as opposed to "being"), or the Absolute. The Absolute cannot be another object in the normal sense. For objects have a limited identity: an object A is known by contrasting it with not-A. But such a classification conceals the deeper connection between objects, on the basis of which, for example, the human mind – also an object – can perform its reasoning about seemingly unrelated things, thus baffling Kantian epistemology.

The Absolute is this underlying unity between objects. It is a unity outside of which no object can exist, for that would be to introduce further divisions of the type A and not-A. It is thus the ground of all knowledge and being. Whereas rational knowledge proceeds by the principle of negation (not-A), knowledge of the absolute involves the negation of this negation. Here Frank quotes one of the main inspirations of his system, Nicolas of Cusa: "The incomprehensible is comprehended through incomprehension," and the corresponding "intuitive" knowledge is Cusean *docta ignorantia*. As in earlier works, Frank reiterates that literature and art fare better than philosophy in this task of paradoxical comprehension. Hence, Frank's discovery means that strictly he is not engaged in philosophy, but something higher: wisdom.

For those like Bulgakov who had been troubled by the relationship of the

---

[30] Especially in his last work *Reality and Man* (1950). This "reality" indicates the extent to which Frank claims he has reinstigated a new epistemological and ontological realism in philosophy.

meta-logical Absolute to the God of Christianity, Frank weaves in a new strand of personalist philosophy. The Absolute, being beyond objective knowledge, cannot be objectified and thus knowledge of the Absolute "is expressed not in talk *about* God, but in words addressed *to* God (in prayer), and in God's words to *me*." Thus the Absolute (God) is always revealed through the seeker's being as a Thou. The concept of the "I-Thou" foundation of divine-human communication and knowledge is traced to (the German-Jewish) Martin Buber and Max Sheller.

In *The Unfathomable*, the personal nature of the Absolute is also reinforced by reference to the Christian concept of divine-humanity. Just as the possibility of rational and empirical knowledge depends on man being immersed in a level of being that includes the objects of his potential knowledge, so it is with religious knowledge: man belongs to a "collective whole of which each individual feels himself a part [and which] is itself a living individual… its limit is a kind of supra-temporal unity, the single collective organism of Godmanhood, the one great cosmic Man, as Pascal asserted…In this sense, organic togetherness coincides with the 'church', in the most profound and general meaning of this term…."

Having sketched the content of the *The Unfathomable* with its universal philosophy of all-humanity submerged in God, a comment should be made about the form of the work. As mentioned above, it was conceived and written in German, "the universal language of poets and thinkers." However, as the last quotation shows, the translation of Russian into Western concepts goes beyond language: the concept of divine-humanity, so central to Russian religious thought, is linked to Pascal rather than Soloviev.

In fact, in this and other major exilic works, this is an established tendency in Frank's exposition: where he can find a parallel with a Western philosopher, it seems that he will choose the Western thinker. In a sense, then, these works expounding Frank's wisdom-philosophy are pan-European works: in incorporating empiricism and rationalism, he is, as he implies in *The Russian Worldview*, integrating and synthesizing the national worldviews of England, France and Germany[31], or at least selecting the best of them.

However, the "Russian worldview" is underlyingly present, only somewhat anonymously. For these works demonstrate characteristics that Frank earlier outlined in his essays on the "Russian worldview:" Russians think intuitively; they are anti-rationalistic but not (as scientists like Lomonosov and

---

[31] "Empiricism…contains, as is well-known, the characteristic tendency of the English national spirit…In contrast, the French spirit is characterized…by an attraction to rationalism…" While some elements of German formal epistemology have tended to crush the Russian interpretation of philosophy as a means to create an all-embracing worldview, Frank mention Fichte, Hegel, Sheller and Hartman as thinkers who have shown that "the theory of knowledge is not a cold and formal 'police science', so to say, which keeps the metaphysical tendency in order…but is itself a part, and indeed a fundamental part of ontology and constitutes a positive penetration into the depths of the spiritual world." *Russkoe mirovozzrenie*, 165-6.

Lobachevsky show) *ir*rational; they put the "WE" before the "I;" from Eastern Christianity they have absorbed an ascetic mentality; Eastern Christianity, too, has made alien to them scholastic debates about grace and free-will, for the goal of their religiosity is to become one with God, to dissolve inner and outer in the godman[32]. All of these characteristics of Russian thought are, in fact, characteristic principles of the theo-cosmic system of all-unity found in *The Unfathomable* and later works.

The question then arises: if *The Unfathomable* is a book exemplifying and inspired by the Russian worldview, why are Russian sources so vanishingly rare? Part of the answer seems to be that this served an apologetic, expository function: where Russian and German thought converged he chose examples more easily digestible to his German audience. In that way, the main ideas of his Russian worldview could be absorbed more easily. One might say that he was a Russian apostle to the Germans. Fascist Germany's rejection of the German-language *The Unfathomable* was thus a devastating blow to this endeavor. Furthermore, if we see Frank's translation of a Russian sensibility into German categories as an attempt to harmonize aspects of his own identity, that rejection would have signaled an assault on the construction of his own person.

Of course, this harmonizing endeavor relied on his confidence in the mutual comprehensibility of the Russian and German worldview. And here Frank seems to have been steering a path between the traditional dominant Russian attitudes to Europe: Slavophilism and Westernization.

The latter was sometimes accused of aping the West, the former of rejecting it. But Frank saw even the Slavophiles as only rejecting what was decadent in the contemporary West and of venerating the depth of the European past. In that sense, Frank's Westernizing absorption of European sources and "light" Slavophile reworking of them according to values common to Russia and (old) Europe has a certain muted Messianic edge: the resulting philosophical fusion was both a call to Russia and Europe, "two branching of the same trunk," to return to the common values that lay at their common origin: "that alloy of Christianity and the spirit of antiquity"[33].

The general, but unnamed, Russian spiritual atmosphere was then the womb out of which sprung forth familiar names of an old European worldview cognate to it: Buber, Sheller, Eckhardt, Boehme, Angelus Silesius, Baader, Schelling,

---

[32] A concrete example of Frank's double translation of ideas can be found in the essay "Russkoe mirovozzrenie" ("Russkoe mirovozzrenie," in S.L.Frank, *Russkoe Mirovozzrenie*, 161-196. (St Petersburg: Nauka, 1996.))Having described how the Russian, due to his Eastern Christian heritage, bypasses Augustinian-Pelagian debates about nature and free will, seeing salvation in a unity with God, he concludes: "The individualism of inner subjectivism, no less than the merely external supra-individual objectivism, is overcome through an absolute all-embracing ontologism in the sense in which this is voiced by Goethe: 'Nothing inner, nothing outer – because what is inner is also outer.'"

[33] *Russkoe mirovozzrenie*, 194.

Hegel, Goethe and Rilke. The Russian worldview, like the all-encompassing Absolute enfolded these manifestations of being within itself – so that Frank's methodology mirrors his metaphysics[34].

Of course, not everyone was convinced that Frank had got it right with his depiction of the Russian worldview. Berdyaev[35], not surprisingly, saw Frank as essentially a German romantic: that is, the unnamed Russian background in which the German mystics were manifested forth was more of an empty vessel (and certainly it was some way from his own eschatological "Russian idea"). In addition, there were those who called into question Frank's depiction of Christianity, and for similar reasons, as we will see below.

Frank and Gershenzon

At this point, it will be interesting to step back and compare some aspects of Frank's world-view with that of Gershenzon. The purpose behind such a comparison is not to create another belated Berdyaevan polemic against Jewishness in philosophy, i.e. to show that because the two men were Jewish they "distorted" Russian thought. However, it seems possible to put Gershenzon and Frank on some sort of continuum, in which Jewishness played a role in their philosophical thinking. It seems artificial, after all, to claim that because Gershenzon did not convert to Christianity and Frank did, Frank's relation to his Jewishness was truncated, while Gershenzon's was not.

Obviously, there can be no question that Frank and Gershenzon engaged in overtly Jewish philosophy, that is, a philosophy that justifies Judaism – like Cohen, Rosenzweig, and Soloveitchik. However, it is a question of finding a place and descriptive apparatus for what Steinberg and Karsavin agreed on calling the peripheral, or "radioactive," element of assimilated-Jewish but still-Jewish activity.

Importantly, both Frank and Gershenzon acknowledged their continuing Jewishness, while rejecting their Judaism. Gershenzon explicitly wrote of "injecting his Jewish spirit" into Russian culture, and Frank saw his Christianity as a natural fulfillment of the promise to carry on with his childhood Judaism. Such self-definitions, of course, would be rejected by "core" religious Jewry (and sometimes by "core" Christianity), but that does not make them automatically

---

[34] Interestingly, in a 1912 letter to Gershenzon, Frank had described how a philosophical system can mould a philosopher's instinctive intuitions: "Spinoza had his pantheism, of course, before any acquaintance with Descartes – it was simply in his blood; still, the latest rationalistic form of his system added complexity and precision to his intuition, gave it a certain new coloring." If this is so, one could also say that Frank was using the latest German philosophical forms to give shape to his native Russian view, which was altered thereby.

[35] Review of *The Unfathomable*. Nicolai Berdyaev, "O knige S.L. Franka 'Nepostizhimoe,'" in *Tipy religioznoy mysly v Rossii*//*Sobraniye Sochenenii* 3, 650-655. Paris: YMCA-Press, 1989.

illegitimate. Perhaps, this is all the more so given that this Jewish immersion in Russian culture was a widespread phenomenon for the time.[36]

To begin with, Frank's "universalism" can now be detailed more explicitly.

Frank's universalism

First of all, Frank came to embrace a non-denominational Christianity – which at times became indistinguishable from a general pantheistic mysticism. Frank's own works, as well as his private letters, give the best picture of this.

A striking example is the quotation which served as the epithet for *The Unfathomable*: "To understand means not only to see things but to see how they are immersed in the absolute," which comes from the Persian Sufi, Al-Hussein ibn-Mansur al-Khalaji. Frank was reading his biography while he worked on the book, and in a letter to his daughter he called the Muslim mystic "the greatest religious personality after Christ."[37]

In a letter to his son Victor trying to dissuade him from converting to Catholicism, Frank himself writes that "in my conversion to Orthodoxy it was very helpful that from my childhood years, despite my Jewish upbringing, I got

---

[36] L.Chamberlain calculates that just under 20% of exiles on the "philosophy steamer"were Jewish. Cf. "Jews on the Philosophy Steamer," in The Jewish Quarterly, Spring 2006, No.201. Some errors which point to a need for deeper study of this Jewish-Russian fusion are her statement that Aikhenvald converted to Christianity; elsewhere in the actual book, as we saw she contends that Frank converted for a university position. (Frank's wife for some reason is described as "Catholic"). Also odd is the contention that Alexander Izgoev's pseudonym means "of the goyim." In fact *izgoy* simply means outcast in Russian. Hopefully, the present discussion will add some clarification to the motives and outlook of these Russian Jews, but much more work remains to be done on the nature of Russian-Jewish philosophy of this period.

[37] S.L.Frank, letter to Natalia in 1945. Quoted in Boobyer (2001), 199: "The Arab mystic, Al-Hallaj, the greatest religious personality after Christ, says: 'He who has suffered intensely, God has visited; in such a one God has built himself a dwelling.' This is awful and fearsome, but it is also a great attainment of the soul…" Frank underwent intense physical and mental sufferings, and he saw in Christianity a religion that was particular in tune with that aspect of human existence. Again, it is an interesting question why Aaron Steinberg, who was also tormented by thoughts of suicide and the meaningless of existence, still found succor in Judaism. (Indeed, the theme of suicide links Steinberg and Frank: during the War, Frank carried pills at all times, fearing he did not have the stamina to survive what the Nazis would put him through if they caught him. Steinberg also had a tolerant view to suicide, which however, tragically backfired on him, when he suspected that his wife had killed herself to relieve his own suffering – perhaps after being influenced by her husband's admiring view of "altruistic suicide." Christianity forbids suicide outright; Judaism permits it in extreme circumstances that are beyond a person's control. It is interesting that Frank's intuitive approach – during the War at least – to suicide seems closer to the Jewish view).

accustomed to the ringing of bells, the sight of churches, Russian holidays and so forth, and nonetheless, my conversion, I can say now, did not truly succeed. I have a different relationship to Orthodoxy, then for example, mama…I find spiritual ground only in the recognition that I am a 'Christian', a member of the universal Christian church, and not of one separate confession…"[38]

Thus, although "there is something very valuable in Orthodoxy, which is not clear to Europeans," Frank was convinced that the Christian truth was not and could not be contained in doctrine or dogmatics. In his briefly renewed correspondence with Vy.Ivanov[39], who had now become a Catholic, the poet tried to persuade Frank of the truth of the Roman Church (rather as he had earlier applied gentle spiritual pressure on Gershenzon). Frank himself recognized the leading role of the Papacy in the earthly church, but like Pascal, retained the right to "to appeal from the judgment of the pope to the judgment of Christ."

Indeed, Frank saw a providential role in the "existence of free Christian souls beyond the borders of the Church…[for] they are the only bridge that has been preserved between the Church and atheists." In addition, while the Catholic Church is "catholic," still "the Christian revelation, invisibly poured into souls, is still in a certain sense more universal than the historically unfolding face of the Church."

In that sense, Frank saw "invisible Christianity" where Christ was seemingly not present in name or even cultural influence: probably his veneration of a Sufi mystic over and above numerous Christian apostles, saints and martyrs is the clearest example of this trans-ecclesiastical faith[40]. However, closer to home, this attitude can be seen in his attitude towards Yuli Aikhenvald, in the obituary that provoked the fury of the Jewish community.

Here[41], Frank recognized in his unconverted Jewish friend a person with "an exceptionally morally gifted nature, of a truly Christian spirit." But more interestingly, Frank draws close to Aaron Steinberg's belief that in Russian culture there is incarnated the Word which gives spiritual force to the world. For Steinberg, this Word was universal, to be found in Judea and Athens, in the prophets and in Parmenides. Frank, too, sees in Aikhenvald's work on Russian literature a contact with the immanent Word.

Thus, although "a Jew by origin, [Aikhenvald] identified with his whole essence with Russian spiritual culture – at any rate in the form in which it was

---

[38] Boobyer (2001), 221.
[39] Frank, Semyon. "Dva pisma Vy. Ivanovu." In S.L.Frank, *Russkoe Mirovozzrenie*, 95-98. St Petersburg: Nauka, 1996.
[40] Indeed, such a faith is not only "trans-ecclesial" but "trans-national," given that in Russian Orthodoxy, many saints are associated with moments of nationl history and identity. I believe it would not be far wrong to see this veneration of anonymous Christians (in Rahner's terminology), in conjunction with the non-acceptance of dogma as a path to truth, as exhibiting a Jewish view on Christianity: one which goes back to before the division of the churches and their identification with particular nations and empires.
[41] "Pamyati Yu.I.Aikhenvalda," in *Put'*, 1929.No. 15. February.

incarnated in 19th century literature – and he could understand, as only a few, and communicate to others its spiritual beauty and significance…..the word was for him a revelation and as it were an incarnation of the divine principle in the human soul."

Although Aikhenvald lamented that he was not given the gift of faith, he "loved to repeat the opening words of the Gospel of John, 'In the beginning was the Word', and dimly felt its deepest meaning; in this relationship, in this contemplation of the force of the word, he overcame his own religious philosophical dualism[42], and albeit in a simplified and one-sided manner, believed in the genuine Incarnation…."

Of course, Frank is not unique here: Bulgakov too saw in Shestov an "almost-Christian." In a sense, for these philosophers of all-unity it was not just the boundaries between God and the world that were blurred, but that between Christianity and "pagan" culture. But in his attitude to Aikhenvald and al-Khalaji, Frank goes perhaps further than anyone in seeing philosophy (taken in its broadest sense to include spiritually inspired cultural creativity and the search for "wisdom") as a form of ecumenical ecclesiastical belonging.

The point is brought home in Frank's life-long veneration of Spinoza. In an article dedicated to his philosophy, Spinoza is characterized in terms not dissimilar to Aikhenvald, as another covertly Christ-believing Jew, who "could in his own way, recognize in Jesus Christ a 'son of God', because in him 'more than any other was incarnated the wisdom of God' (although on the other hand true incarnation seemed to him, because of his rationalism, as contradictory as 'the appearance of a curve in a triangle')….the whole life and thought of Spinoza was, albeit in mistaken and imperfect forms, a constant praise of God and a serving of Him."[43]

Of course, one must not forget that unlike for Steinberg or Gershenzon, the Word for Frank was a person, Jesus Christ; and the Incarnation, which was symbolic for non-Christian Russian seekers of wisdom, was for Frank a literal historical event. Still, there are elements in the deep structure of Frank's metaphysical system where these elements are blurred, so that once again the incarnation becomes symbolic, general and non-historical, and the Word seems to merge with the Logos of general philosophical wisdom.

The fault-line can be seen in the relationship between Frank's unfathomable, absolute "reality" and what he calls "being." Following Eckhart, he sometimes calls reality Deity (or Divine being[44]), distinguishing this from the personal God, the God of I-Thou relations. Like Eckhart the Deity is treated as a self-contained, impersonal[45] absolute. In Frank's system, it receives the name of All-unity, that

---

[42] As we will see in Frank's critique of Cohen and Rosenzweig, he associated "dualism" not only with German Kantianism, but also with religious Judaism.

[43] "Osnovnaya idyea filosofii Spinozy: k 300-letiyu dnya rozhdeniya 24 noyabrya 1632," in *Put'*, No.37.Feb. 1932.

[44] Rus. *bozhestvo*.

[45] To be fair, Frank argues that the terms "personal" or "impersonal" are inadequate

which is the ground of being. All-unity, by its very definition, cannot contain anything outside itself, for the "concept of something external to that unity… would constitute an internal contradiction"[46].

This, of course, leads immediately to the question of the relationship of the Divinity to the world. In *The Unfathomable*, this indefinable Divinity is a "metalogical unity…of the rational and irrational," the "transfinite" and the "potential," out of which all distinctions emerge. Thus "Being as a whole creates itself." This language, in fact, is reminiscent not only of pre-Socratics such as Anaximander (with his doctrine of the *apeiron*), but – as V.Zenkovsky[47] points out – of Spinoza: the Absolute resembles *natura naturans*, and the world *natura naturata*.

Frank himself vacillated in his conception of the relationship between God and the world, claiming that his doctrine "stood halfway between emanation and

---

when applied to ultimate reality, which transcends all labels. However, this itself may be problematic. See below.

[46] *The Unfathomable*, quoted in Zenkovsky, 861. See following footnote for more detais on exact sources.

[47] For this and other comments of Zenkovsky quoted here, see *Istoria russkoy filosofii*, Pt.4, ch.5. Metafizika vse-yedinstva L.P.Karsavina i S.L.Franka. Vassily Zenkovsky, *Istoria russkoy filosofii. Tom 2*. (Paris: YMCA-Press, 1989). The quotes in this section from *The Unfathomable* have been taken from Zenkovsky, and translated by myself. Frank's discussion in *The Unfathomable* of the relationship between God and the world, on which Zenkovsky's discussion is based, can be found especially in *Nepostizhimoe*, ch 9, "Bog i ya," and ch.10, "Bog i mir." (Semyon Frank, *Sochineniya*, (Moscow: Ast, 2000), 662-792.) While one could try to defend Frank against Zenkovsky's charges (and Frank, for example, makes an effort to distinguish his conceptions from Spinoza, (e.g. *Socheniya*, 742), and in other places is quite insistent that God does not emanate but creates the world (e.g. Socheniya, 738)), the effort to establish an absolute difference between world and God is, as Zenkovsky says, always blurred by Frank's constant recourse to his "transrational monodualism," in which no sooner has a difference been established with one hand, than it is erased with the other. The present discussion does not pretend to philosophical exhaustiveness, but for the meantime I am content to accept Zenkovsky's conclusions. One implication of that critique is that the fundamental terminology of Frank's system may, ultimately, not be very helpful: that is, perhaps the terms "transrational" and "monodualism" conceal an ultimate incoherence and unwillingness to accept the basic disparity between creation and creature. This recalls L.Jacobs' critique of Hassidic panentheism, which we referred to in ch.1. (Jacobs, (1973), pp.35-7). There is another way in which Frank's contention that there are two aspects of divinity, Reality – which is impersonal, the Deity or divine substance – and God, Who is personal, is deeply problematic. Trinitarian theology holds that there is no God without Triunity; Eastern Orthodox theology, especially, emphasizes that the "root" of God is the *Person* of the Father. Personhood ontologically precedes nature in God. (Cf. J. Zizoulias, *Being as Communion*). This personalistic foundation, seen abundantly in Karsavin, is missing in Frank – another sign of his lukewarm attitude to dogma.

creation."⁴⁸ The ambiguity is evident in the claim in *The Unfathomable* that "the world was not 'created' by God…in time the world continues infinitely…but the whole content and the whole being of the world rests on something 'completely different', on 'the supra-worldly'….and in this sense is not eternal, for it does not come from itself, is not a *causa sui*." Nonetheless, this "resting" of the world on the "supra-worldly" Absolute does not correlate to the complete break between Creator and creation that both Jewish and Christian orthodoxy insist on.

For Zenkovsky, these difficulties are entirely a result of Frank's embrace of the doctrine of all-unity, which asserts that true all-unity can have nothing outside of it. This is only persuasive if one does not posit an Absolute which is beyond Being as such. Bringing "genuine unity" within the sphere of all-unity is a voluntary premise, and "is in fact the imprisonment of Frank's thought to the idea of pan-unity and nothing more!" Of course, this criticism echoes that directed against Bulgakov's sophiology by V.Lossky and G.Florovsky – which the latter also directed against Frank, despite having admiration for the general religious spirit of his system.

Frank's pantheistic, or more forgivingly panentheistic⁴⁹, conception of God and the world spills over into his doctrine of divine-humanity. Again, it is V.Zenkovsky who highlights this most convincingly. In places, godmanhood becomes equivalent to man's natural immersion in the Absolute: here "god" is general Divinity, and "man" is a natural extension or showing forth of the divine. As we quoted earlier, godmanhood for Frank is then simply an "organic togetherness [that] coincides with the 'church', in the most profound and general meaning of this term…."⁵⁰

---

⁴⁸ *Nepostizhimoe*, in *Socheneniya*, 748.

⁴⁹ It would take us too far afield to compare Frank and Kabbalistic-Hasidic thought, but the congruence with Frankian panentheism and Hasidic pantheism is truly striking. Indeed, he himself – like Karsavin – explicitly recognizes this as the following quotes show: "[This is] the 'transition' from God to the world…it is as it were the clothing of the invisible God in a certain 'flesh', which is in relation to Him a sort of 'clothing'…..;""The mythological history of the creation or emergence of the world depicted in the Kabbalah in an extremely graphic way portrays this birth of the world from the bosom of the divine 'Not', describing how God, as the primal all-embracing eternal fullness, contracts Himself, departs within Himself, as a result of which there is formed around Him an empty 'space' – as it were, a Divine 'no' or 'not' – onto which he…projects the reflection of His own essence, precisely the image of the 'heavenly man' – and thus 'creates the world'. In this antinomian-dualistic unity with God, the world, while retaining its oppositeness to God, its being 'near' God, is still nonetheless a manifestation of God, a *theophany*." (Socheneniya, 750.) Frank faithfully describes the Kabbalistic account of creation, and by using his own terminology at the end of this account ("dualistic-antinomian") shows that his own account adds nothing essentially different to the Kabbalah. As Zenkovsky's criticisms indicate, this raises the question of what the person of Christ adds to a world which is already so highly valenced, and "theophanous."

⁵⁰ Below, we will consider how G.Florovsky, V.Lossky, K.Kern and their students like

This doctrine thus makes divinity "incarnate" in the world before the Incarnation of Jesus Christ. Furthermore, that divinity is a general divinity that exists outside of the personal Trinitarian God, and as it exists outside of Christ can be accessed apart from Christ. Moreover, Frank paints a picture of the divinity in which God recognizes his fullness in man: "God is not just God and nothing more but is in his very essence 'God and I'....just as the human in man is not just purely human but is a divine-human essence....so God is a true God precisely as the God-man." Again, the neglect of the patristic nature/will distinction yields a God who is compelled to create, or emanate, the world – an abstract Deity who perfects Himself as a personal God in His communication with man[51].

For Frank, then, human nature and the world is already the site of divine revelation and activity. Again, while this recognition is present in Bulgakov and Karsavin[52], both these men were also deeply interested in Orthodox dogmatics, Karsavin perhaps even more so than Bulgakov. Frank was surprisingly nominalist in regard to such disputes as the *Filioque*, seeing them as fruitless disputes about words, which did not and could not touch on the truth of religion. This also reveals a discomfort with historical Christianity and its exclusive claim to ongoing revelation through Jesus Christ acting through the Spirit in Church councils.

In this respect, when one returns to a consideration of his sources it becomes clear that both his Russian and Christian identity rest for the most part – as with Aikhenvald – on "Russian spiritual culture...as incarnated in the 19th century." While there are occasional references to the power of the Orthodox liturgy as a source of the ascetic spirit of this culture, there is no serious engagement with the history of Christian dogma.

The Russian Orthodoxy of "bells and...Russian holidays" has something in it of Rozanov's "Orthodox positivism," an embrace of the emotional exterior of church life, with an adogmatism as to the content of its belief. However, as Frank recognized, this superficial, cultural Orthodoxy not surprisingly was unable to compete for depths with his own philosophical investigations.

Indeed, Frank's depiction of a general divinization of man and humanization of God calls to mind Shestov's sharp condemnation of Berdyaev's Hegelian

---

J.Meyendorff embraced doctrines of creation, Christian existentialism, "sacred materialism" and personalism that resemble those of all-unity, but in taking their inspiration from St. Gregory Palamas and earlier Eastern fathers, avoid the pantheism of the philosophy of all-unity.

[51] While Frank's "unfathomable" Absolute reveals an apophatic element in his philosophy, Zenkovsky also points out that this apophaticism differs from that of Eastern Christian theology: "...the apophatic moment comes into its own, but only as an extreme limit in the unfathomable, different from, but not separate from that same unfathomable who 'enters' into communication with the world and man." (Zenkovsky, Vol II, p.810).

[52] And, of course, of theologians who reject all-unity.

Christianity, which he saw as a German, and indeed Judaic, metaphysical naturalism and rationalistic humanism, which diminished the freedom and mystery of God. For all its polemical edge, this judgment does coincide with both Christian and Jewish orthodoxy.

Frank and Gershenzon from Landmarks to Revolution
Given that in an earlier chapter we argued that Gershenzon absorbed much of his ascetic wisdom of the Logos-Spirit from the wellsprings of Russian Christian culture, it should no longer be surprising if a considerable overlap can be detected with Frank's Christian, but also universal-mystic, worldview.

The two men met during their collaboration on *Landmarks*. While there were differences in their outlook, they respected each others' opinions. Frank saw Gershenzon as a particular type of Tolstovian populist who desired a return of Russia to the organic wholeness of her previous spiritual culture. While Frank was less radical concerning the inadequacy of the intelligentsia's current spiritual state, they shared a belief that it would not simply be sufficient "to place Christ instead of Marx, and instead of socialism the kingdom of Heaven, for the reform of the intelligentsia's worldview and a new spiritual type to be ready…" as Bulgakov and Merezhkovsky, and somewhat later Berdyaev, were proposing. Instead, *"for us [DR]*, in contrast to this, it is extremely important to underline the necessity of an internal cultural-moral and religious re-education of the intelligentsia."[53]

In 1918, Frank and his family were living in a village near Saratov, trying to escape the horrors of the Civil War raging around them. He wrote to Gershenzon in Moscow, also living in deprivation: "Our weak intellectual souls are simply incapable of grasping the vileness and horror of such Biblical proportions and we can only fall into a frozen stupefaction. There's no way out, because there is no longer a homeland. We are not needed by the West, or by Russia, because she herself does not exist, but has turned out to be an unneeded figment. It remains to be locked in the loneliness of a Stoic cosmopolitanism, that is, to start living and breathing in an airless space."

Probably, in that "Stoic cosmopolitanism" they shared a spiritual link, a meeting-point of their two worldviews where common language was possible. Of course, part of the oddity of the *Landmarks* collection – as Frank and Gershenzon themselves had noted – was the absence of any positive platform. Frank's mentor, Petr Struve, was the man who had taken greatest exception to Gershenzon's populist mysticism, and who perhaps even more than Berdyaev was thoroughly unforgiving of his ex-collaborator's embrace of the Bolshevist "party of the heart."

Frank was in many ways close to Struve, which makes it more significant that he could continue to maintain friendly relations with Gershenzon. Both Struve and Frank apportioned blame for the Revolution on conservatives and

---

[53] Frank to Gershenzon, letter, 16 Nov. 1908. In Boobyer (2001), 90.

radicals. The monarchy's pact with the gentry, reaching back to Anna Ioannovna's co-opting of their support for autocracy in return for absolute rights over the peasantry, had delayed the institution of private property in Russia by a hundred years. This ultimately led to the isolation of the monarchy from the gentry, who lacked political rights, and the peasantry who lacked civil rights, and laid the ground for the 1917 Revolution.

On this analysis, a third catalyzing party in the disaster was the intelligentsia. Throughout the nineteenth century they had cultivated an antagonistic attitude towards the State, whose institutions were in fact no worse than those in the West. Against it, they had championed "the people" as a progressive class, while willfully ignoring "the anti-cultural and savage forces that slumber in the masses."[54] They had thus wholly neglected the potential of the only progressive element in Russia, the bourgeoisie, which had triggered the main revolutions in the West.

From this, it becomes clear why Struve had taken exception to Gershenzon's idealization of the masses and his championing of their spiritual instincts over that of the radical, but also even the liberal intelligentsia. Struve was very clear about the nature of his own positive platform: after the Revolution he threw himself into working for the White movement. His immediate practical goal was to re-establish the monarchy and the old government, which had had an organic link with the Russian people and which, once in place again, would through a conservative-liberal platform develop Russia's industry, commerce and social institutions.

A hint as to how Frank, who generally supported Struve's historical and political analysis[55], could nonetheless be more forgiving towards Gershenzon can be gleaned by considering the fall-out that marred Frank's relationship with Struve during their first years in exile.

Struve had become internal minister for the White government-in-exile. He supported military action against the Soviet regime, arguing that evil

---

[54] Pyotr Struve, "Istoricheskii smysl russkoi revolyutsii i natsional'nie zadachi," in *Vekhi. Iz Glubiny*. Edited by A. A. Yakovleva, 459-478. Moscow: Pravda, 1991.

[55] In "Bolshevizm i kommunizm kak dukhovnie yavleniya" (*Russkoe mirovozzrenie*, 137-149), Frank wrote of how the Russian government had cultivated "a fatal utopian-romantic theory of the patriarchal-collective peasant community," which had stifled economic development in the country and paved the way for the Bolshevist reaction. Interstingly, Burbank sees Berdyaev, due to his Slavophilism, as buying into a similar sort of airy idealization of Russian reality – only for him, it was the Russian intelligentsia that was in possession of some sort of mysterious secret from the East that would solve all of Russia's and then the West's ills. Burbank's analysis confirms our tendency to place Berdyaev and Gershenzon in similar "spiritualist nihilist" camps, and even in to attribute to them similar core political sensibilities. Cf. Jane Burbank, *Intelligentsia and Revolution. Russian views of Bolshevism, 1917-1922*.(New York: OUP, 1986), 193-208. See also Burbank, 143-154 for more on Struve.

needed to be resisted by force. All who lived in the Soviet Union had, in his eyes, compromised with the regime. Frank (and Berdyaev, by then) objected that Russia was not prepared for such a counter-revolution and they believed that Struve's embrace of practical politics was a betrayal of the *Landmarks* agenda of working for gradual change through education and "spiritual politics." They also saw the White movement as being infected by the same bloodthirsty revolutionary spirit as the Bolsheviks.

Unlike Berdyaev, who had had his moment of reactionary jingoism, Frank had never been attracted by the White movement. Living in hiding from the Reds and the Whites in Saratov during 1918, he heard of and himself witnessed the violence of the White army and its bands of marauding supporters, who were no less violent than the Reds. Frank's spiritual conception of evil refused to accept that good or evil could be identified with any one political grouping. A motto that he developed in 1917 was that "evil only engenders evil." In addition, of course, the number of Jews in the White movement was vanishingly small: part of their core motivating propaganda was the struggle against the so-called Jewish-Bolshevik take-over of Russia.

While Frank and Struve later reconciled (and Struve once sent a White neophyte to Frank to cure him of his excessive nationalism), the links with Gershenzon can be seen: a spiritual interpretation of revolution; a continuing general-spiritual interpretation of popular enlightenment, rather than a strictly Orthodox Christian conception; and even a concern that all the interests of the working class be defended and realized in a peaceful legal way. One can add, too, that in Frank's case his German-Jewish background once again steered him away from the more extreme nationalist conclusions that the pressure of events elicited in Berdyaev and Struve, and so prevented the sort of hostile split that occurred between them and Gershenzon.

Nonetheless, the lingering communication between Frank and Gershenzon soon dried up as well. After the exile of his fellow *Landmarkers*, and his choice to stay in the Soviet Union even Frank's position came to seem alien to Gershenzon.

However, Gershenzon maintained ties with Lev Shestov until his death. Perhaps Shestov's nihilistic abstention from positive explanation, analysis and philosophy accorded with his own apophatic attitude to the course of the Spirit and history. In 1923, Gershenzon – on a visit to Germany – expressed his disgust with émigré intellectual activity in a letter to his friend:

> Do you read the Berlin Russian papers? What trite and silly activities they are getting up to: Berdyaev, Ilyin, Frank etc…I am reading contemporary German thinkers with great interest now: there is a lot that is fresh and bold – and what really wins me over is the enormous fund of precise knowledge, whereas with us in Russia, metaphysical thought (like with Berdyaev) is not "weighed down" with any reserve

of knowledge – and the more easily it soars upwards.[56]

This picture of convergence and divergence is reflected more deeply in the growing attraction of each thinker to the thought of Pushkin – who is often, like Shakespeare, a mirror for the personality of the interpreter. In their encounters with Russia's founding poet, both of them defined essential aspects of their worldviews.

Gershenzon and Frank: the wisdom of Pushkin
Gershenzon's works on Pushkin were written from 1919 to 1922, during the hardships of the Civil War, and as we saw were viewed by several critics as being more expressive of his own worldview than the poet's. Frank started writing about Pushkin after his own philosophy had reached maturity, and he finds in Pushkin much that corroborates his own conception of the "Russian worldview."

Three of his six major articles[57] were written in 1937, the year of Pushkin's centenary. This was a tragic year for Frank: *The Unfathomable* was turned down for being non-Aryan, and Nazi harassment of his family finally forced him to leave Germany for France. In Russia, it was also the year in which the Stalinist terror reached eschatological pitch. And over Europe, in general, the clouds of war were beginning to gather. It was during that difficult year that Frank turned to Pushkin for guidance on the "spiritual path of Russia," as well as for thoughts concerning Russia's correct political route.

It goes without saying that Frank and Gershenzon were not unusual in their interest in Pushkin. Right at the beginning of the Silver Age thought, several poets – self-identified "Pushkinites" – had turned back to Pushkin's classicism as a reaction again Decadentism and romanticism. Towards the end of his life, Soloviev himself had championed this trend, worried by the path that Merezhkovsky and his Decadent followers were taking.

Sergei Soloviev, the philosopher's nephew and acolyte, quoted Pushkin's description of "'the friend', wife-like, sentimental, a deceptive and mendacious ideal, a demon magician…but beautiful" to critique Blok's and Merezhkovsky's quasi-Solovievan worship of Sophia, the "beautiful lady" – but an idolatrous and unchristian distortion of his uncle's sophianic thought, as he saw it. Yet Merezhkovsky himself – rejecting S.Soliev's accusation that his mystical movement was inspired by the anti-Christ – cited Pushkin as the source of his own project to create the first independent Russian culture. He claimed to be building

---

[56] Gershenzon to Shestov, 27.2.23. *Gershenzon M.O. Pisma k L'vu Shestovu (1920-1925)*. A d'Amelia and V.Aloya, Phoenix 1992. Quoted on: http://www.krotov.info/spravki/persons/20person/gershnzn.html

[57] "Religioznost' Pushkina" (1933); "Pushkin kak politicheskii myslitel'" (1937); "O zadachax poznaniye Pushkina" (1937); "Pushkin i dukhovniy put' Rossii" (1937); "Pushkin ob otnosheniyax mezhdu Rossii i Yevropy" (1949); "Svetlaya pechal'" (1949). Collected in Semyon Frank, *Russkoe Mirovozzrenie* (St Petersburg: Nauka, 1996).

on the achievements of Pushkin and Tyutchev, "the first Russian Europeans"[58].

Frank's essays are part of this long-running polemic. With typical tact, he pays tribute to his predecessors, no matter how vigorous their disagreement. Concerned primarily to uncover Pushkin's religious views, Frank cited Merezhkovsky and Gershenzon with approval as the only commentators to pay attention to this aspect of the poet's creativity. He especially recognized his affinity with Gershenzon's essays of a decade before, and in his series of studies paid tribute to him as one of the few Pushkinists who had tried to understand what they both agreed in calling "Pushkin's wisdom"[59].

Nonetheless, there was also an ambiguity in Frank's attitude to his predecessor's studies. Frank saw in Gershenzon's "Wisdom of Pushkin" a work that was, "despite its almost unbearable artificiality and the mannered nature of its positive construction, valuable for its lovingly attentive relationship to the spiritual treasury of Pushkin's work."[60] It is not quite clear what Frank had in mind with this uncharacteristically harsh reference to "unbearable artificiality," but given that their views differed on some crucial interpretations, most probably, like Khodasevich, Frank saw his readings as forced, and more indicative of "Gershenzon's wisdom."

However, in nearly every instance, Frank's interpretations are not strictly opposed to Gershenzon's; it might be better to see them as including them and altering them[61]. Of course, beyond brief comments of acknowledgement of Gershenzon's pioneering investigations, Frank was not concerned to compare and contrast their views; however, such an approach yields interesting results. In what follows, we will look at Gershenzon's depiction of Pushkin, and Frank's "amendments," before looking at Frank's own positive portrait of Pushkin.

Pushkin between Frank and Gershenzon

In Gershenzon, Pushkin emerges with the following traits. As we saw briefly in chapter 3, he is an ancient Ahasuerus, with "Arab blood," an Easterner who does not fully belong in Russia. His religious sensibility is pagan, he is a servant of the archaic and sometimes anarchic world-spirit, and is a nihilist in matters concerning the substance of God (God is pure non-being). In addition, he is indifferent to morality, substituting the ancient Avestan-Iranian values of "hot" and "cold" for the prim and recent monotheistic values of "good" and "bad." Nor does he believe in evolution, or progress, political or spiritual. He is passive, a vessel for the Spirit which fills him at its will, and in his passivity he does not strive for any goals.

---

[58] For discussion of S.Soloviev, Blok, Bely and Merezhkovsky, see P.P.Gaidenko, *Vladimir Soloviev i filosofia serebryanogo veka*, ch.10, "Sofiologia i simvolizm.Sergei Soloviev."
[59] It was Dostoevsky who first referred to Pushkin as "our teacher of wisdom."
[60] *Russkoe mirovozzrenie*, 251: "O zadachax poznaniya Pushkina."
[61] In this respect, he resembles Florovsky's respectful use of Gershenzon's historical insights into the Slavophiles, combined with significant reworking through the introduction of new themes, cf.ch.3.

All in all, this is a picture which Frank – not to mention others – cannot accept. Nonetheless, it contains echoes of strands in Frank's own portrait of Russia's founding poet, and has many points of contact with Frank's own mystical worldview.

Gershenzon writes[62] that for twenty centuries people have believed that sin can be healed, differing only in whether this could be accomplished through faith or deeds[63]. Pushkin believes sin cannot be healed. Frank disagrees with the last statement, but the first idea is strikingly reminiscent of Frank's own belief that the faith/deed dichotomy is alien to Russians due to their immersion and union with God. The same pantheistic sensibility unites these approaches.

Gershenzon dwells on Pushkin's famous reply to Metropolitan Philaret. Philaret had written a poem addressed to Pushkin in which he tried to comfort the poet in his despair at the darkness of life and the world. The poem talks of the world's darkness being a result of man's own sin, but then tells of the power of God's love to redeem from sin. Pushkin's rely to Philaret reads in part:

> And now from the spiritual heights
> You extend your hand to me,
> And with humble and loving strength
> Pacify my tempestuous dreams….
> By your fire the soul is warmed
> Rejecting the gloom of earthly vanities
> And the poet heeds the harp of the seraphim/Philaret (different versions)
> In sacred awe.

For Gershenzon, Pushkin's "sacred awe" is more evidence of his passive paganism: as in his poem, "The Devil," evil is permanent; occasionally, however, if it is passive and does not strive to escape its predicament, it can be lit up unexpectedly by contact with the angels. Here, Pushkin sees himself as the eternal "devil," whose life has been momentarily lit up by Philaret's angelic light; but he will soon sink back into his passive imperfection.

Frank is highly sensitive to Pushkin's Christian belief, as we will see; one can imagine that interpretations like this were "unbearably artificial" for him. Nonetheless, Frank's own harmonic sense of the goodness of all creation is a trait he finds in Pushkin. In his own study, he comments on Pushkin's ability to see the good in the bad. He quotes the poet's comments regarding an invitation to take part in a Moscow Schelling circle: "God knows how I scorn and hate German metaphysics; but what can you do? A group of people have got together,

---

[62] In this section, references are all to Gershenzon's "Mudrost' Pushkina." Translations of Pushkin and Gershenzon are mine.
[63] Gershenzon does not name the disputants: the faith/deeds distinction is a Protestant diatribe against Catholicism, but also a diatribe of both religions against Judaism. From Gershenzon's point of view, all three would be made irrelevant by Pushkin's archaic superiority to both.

warm, and stubborn: the *priest has a bit of me in him – and the demon too!*" [64] For Frank, however, this is not a sign of Pushkin's amoralism, just of his extreme receptiveness to the all-unity of God's world.

Gershenzon and Frank also meet and diverge in their interpretation of Pushkin's "Hymn to the penates"[65]. Both parse the same lines where Pushkin talks of the joys of privacy differently:

> They allow us to know the heart's depths
> In the power and weakness of the heart
> They love, coddle and teach –
> These undying, mysterious feelings.

For Gershenzon, these "mysterious feelings" are signs of the Spirit, which "Pushkin assures us…is an independent power and not obedient to consciousness, but obeys other laws."

Frank does not dispute that Pushkin received inspiration in solitude. However, he dwells on the larger context of the poem, which is a hymn to the household gods. Pushkin's solitude is only inspirational due to his connectedness to his native land, and Frank highlights this aspect by quoting another poem[66]:

> Two feelings are strikingly close to us
> In them our heart attains nourishment
> Love towards one's native hearth
> Love towards our fathers' graves
> On them is based from eternity
> By the will of God Himself
> The independent being of a person…

Thus these poems are not hymns to Romantic solitude, but express Pushkin's deep attachment to place as a key component in his personal identity. They demonstrate that for Pushkin personal identity is strongly linked to national, Russian identity, and are part of a series of poems expressing his emotional attachment to Tsarskoe Tselo, where he spent his adolescence and developed as a poet, and Mikhailovskoe, where he was born. For Frank, they are evidence that Pushkin was a man rooted in the soil of Russia, and thus a predecessor of the *pochvenniki* – not, *pace* Gershenzon, that he was ancient wanderer and a rootless vessel of the Spirit.

But as regards the pagan image of the "penates," and the numerous other references to pagan deities in Pushkin's poems, Frank and Gershenzon are not

---

[64] Frank, "Pushkin i dukhovniy put' Rossii," in *Russkoe Mirrovozrenie*, p. 276.
[65] Household gods.
[66] In "Religioznost' Pushkina," *Russkoe Mirovozzernie*, p.224.

so distant. For recent researchers, Pushkin's attitude towards Christianity has been a controversial issue. We have already seen that Frank's own Christianity contains a deep, pantheistic, and Hellenistic undercurrent – as with other Russian religious thinkers, the pagan does not automatically exclude deep Christian commitment.

One Hellenistic figure on whom Frank and Gershenzon converge is Heraclitus. In "About some tasks for an understanding of Pushkin," Frank's portrait of Pushkin seems to finally blend with that of Gershenzon, and this is all the more significant as in this brief characterization Pushkin also appears as the prophet of "unfathomability," taking the mantle that Frank had invested on Goethe and Tyutchev at the launch of his philosophical career:

> In view of the true, perfect quality of the poetry, this wisdom is a *revelation* of being – reality itself, acquiring a voice and declaiming about itself. It is that last living knowledge or life-knowledge, in which not the subjective knowledge of a given personality knows something and tells us about life, but life itself in the element of the word recognizes itself and reveals itself to us so as to be realized and identified. This living knowledge….is not exhausted by "thoughts" and "ideas"….it is a "union of opposites and a harmony of equals," as the ancient Heraclitus defined life itself.

Thus Pushkin is equally the prophetic receptacle of the ancient religion of the cosmic Spirit-Word embraced by Gershenzon, as well as the receptacle of the Word manifested by the divine-human Absolute. Nonetheless, the match is not perfect, for as Frank writes elsewhere: "Pagan, rebellious, sensitive and heroic Pushkin (as K.Leontiev defined him) along with all this appears to us as one of the deepest geniuses of the Russian Christian spirit."

To conclude this brief comparison, one can gain a sense of the fault-line between these two readings of Pushkin in what each man saw as the message of Pushkin for the present.

Pushkin's message for contemporary Russia

Gershenzon saw Pushkin's prophetic activity as a passive preaching of the word: he read "The Prophet" and "The Poor Knight"[67] in unison to produce a reading of a knight of the Spirit who abstains from social or revolutionary activity and "as long as activists fight evil and conduct reforms, he will perhaps shout out: 'Lumen coelum, sancta rosa!' and his cry will terrify the imperfect ones, threatening them with Judgment day."

The result of this reading is that ultimately, for Gershenzon, Pushkin is

---

[67] "The poor knight" is about a knight who falls in love with the Virgin Mary. Again, Gershenzon pays no attention to this at all. Likewise, "The Prophet" is full of Old Testament images of the calling of a prophet by the Lord, but this too is overlooked. Cf. A.S.Pushkin "Prorok" and "Zhil na svete rytsar' bedniy…"

a symbol of the Russian struggle[68] to combine nature and reason[69] without giving in to the slavery of reason, as the West had done. In this, despite the imperfection of his personality (which Gershenzon sees as lacking in will), he was a successful model: "He expressed more the thirst for freedom than the thirst for perfection (because he was more eastern than Russia, for in him there also flowed Arab blood); but with his tenderness, those prayerful prostrations before beauty and holiness, he also solved the antinomy practically, and actively attained *harmony in chaos;* in his personality imperfection was combined with wholeness...."[70]

Frank, as we saw, viewed Pushkin as mining insights from the Unfathomable. However, he also went much further in seeing Pushkin as having cultural, political and religious meaning for Russia, both in exile and in the homeland.

Thus, especially in "Pushkin and the spiritual path of Russia," Frank takes issue with the critique voiced by Gogol and Khomiakov (and repeated in a different form by Gershenzon) that Pushkin was somehow weak in personality, both in life and in his verses. For Gogol explicitly and Khomiakov implicitly, Pushkin was also not Christian enough[71]. However, Frank sees these readings as a function of an unfortunate turn in Russian literary and spiritual culture after Pushkin's death.

The dominant motif in the succeeding literary generation was the tragic mode; the main theme of Gogol, Lermontov and Dostoevsky was theodicy, the burning duty to reconcile the evil of the world with the justice of God. But whereas Pushkin stood for the type of truth which comes from mercy, these harsher writers stood for "justice-truth." That crusading truth, however, has a dangerous edge and can also turn into its opposite, malice and hatred. In a rather unexpected judgment, Frank even writes that "the path along which religious minds like Gogol and Dostoevsky led Russia, against their will, but with inexorable logic, brought Russia, in the final analysis – through that internal

---

[68] Gershenzon writes: "The Russian people, *it seems to me* [italics DR], is searching for a different way out and senses a different possibility..." We saw how Gershenzon, after Rozanov's attacks, abandoned the claim to understand the Russian mind. This looks like a proviso, therefore. When he adds a little later that Pushkin was not fully Russian, but "Eastern, Arab," this could be taken as giving Gershenzon the right to read deeply into the mind of this founder of the entire Russian tradition.

[69] For Gershenzon, Pushkin sees two types of knowledge: "damaged, discursive reason, which crawling in the dust, carefully dismembers, measures and defines laws; and the reason of wholeness, i.e. immediate, intuitive comprehension." This also echoes Frank's division of "intuition" and "reason," but unlike Gershenzon Frank does not advocate the abandonment of instrumental reason – Gershenzon celebrates those moments where Pushkin denigrates science in "The Gypsies" – but their measured integration.

[70] A theme which cannot be developed here is some of the striking overlap between Gershenzon's work and the sensibility of Karsavin. This is but one example.

[71] Frank quotes Gogol as saying of Pushkin that he is not a worthy model for his generation, for "a poet should be raised with a higher, Christian upbringing."

rebirthing which almost inevitably and actively occurred along that path – to Bolshevism."[72]

The Pushkinian spirit must thus be rediscovered if Bolshevism is to be overcome. Unlike Steinberg, Bulgakov and many other Russian intellectual exiles, Frank not only does not see Dostoevsky as the herald of a better Russian future and the bearer of the Russian vision. It turns out his type of faith shares the extremity of Bolshevism.

Frank is also keen to point out that Pushkin is not just frivolity and charm, though he was indeed a light-hearted personality in many ways. No less than his successors he had a Christian vision of life, and a tragic vision of life. And he was not, as his detractors aver, a pagan and he "certainly was not in the slightest bit a pantheist: he had a sharp sense of the 'indifference of nature' to the hopes of the human heart....he did not believe in the possibility of happiness; he well knew the 'the eternal contradictions of existence'; his whole oeuvre, no less than other Russian poets and thinkers, is full of the tragic worldview..."[73]

Nonetheless, this sense of tragedy is balanced in Pushkin, for his "main, defining religious-metaphysical basis...is different: it is a basis of sympathy to all that is living on earth, or to use his own term, 'good will'...The poetical genius of Pushkin coincided with a spiritual openness to the perception of the Divine origin and Divine meaning of world being."[74]

Pushkin is thus a figure of synthesis, harmonizing tendencies which would later diverge tragically in Russian history. Frank dedicated three essays to showing that this is true metaphysically. However, perhaps more interesting is his account of the poet's political beliefs and his attitude to the Slavophile/Westerniser controversy, which in the figures of Pushkin's friends, Chaadaev and Khomiakov, was contained in embryonic but already clearly discernible form. In both cases, Frank sees Pushkin as uniting tendencies which would later be split: politically Pushkin was a liberal-conservative; in his attitude towards the West, he was both a proto-Slavophile and a proto-Westerniser.

Frank traces Pushkin's development from a liberal with radical sympathies who supported the Greek liberation struggle to the man who in an 1823 letter to A.I. Turgenev disowned his 1821 Ode to Napoleon as "liberal nonsense," criticized the self-importance and verbosity of Russia's democratic liberals, and found in de Toqueville a kindred prophet against the leveling and stultifying effects of democracy.

Pushkin's mature political worldview is summarized by Frank as national-patriotic liberal-conservatism[75]. The liberal aspect of the formula is seen in Pushkin's concern for the rule of law and order, and respect for the inviolable

---

[72] "Pushkin i dukhovniy put' Rossii," 277.
[73] Ibid. 275.
[74] Ibid. 276.
[75] Cf. "Pushkin kak politicheskii myslitel."

independence of the individual; the conservative aspect in his support for the monarchy and the idea of an educated aristocratic elite who would protect the country from the whims of the democratic mob.

The national-patriotic part of the formula comes in Pushkin's frequent identification of the government and aristocracy with the interests of the country, for he often saw liberals as "standing in opposition not to the government but to Russia" – a critique he directed at Vyazemsky's support of the Polish Revolt in 1831. Pushkin by then was defending the governmental interests of Russia above the romantic aspirations of the Poles, and objecting to Western attempts to interfere in Russia's determination of her own interests.

Pushkin, furthermore, denied the liberal equation of monarchy, conservatism and a hierarchical class-system with backwardness, maintaining that the government had always been at the forefront of innovation in the life of Russia, while the masses had resisted progress and freedom. This aristocratic, hierarchical view of government was rooted in Pushkin's idea of "natural government." According to a friend, Pushkin once stated that "the rational will of a few individuals or a minority has always guided humanity…..in essence inequality is a law of nature….Individuals have achieved all the great deeds of history"[76].

Much of this recapitulates Frank's own liberal-conservatism, which developed under the guidance of his friend, Petr Struve. It was from him that Frank saw himself as having first learned to appraise government not from the point of view of the bitter, self-disenfranchised left intelligentsia, but as one close to the organs and ministers of power, whose view was imbued with practical realism.

Of course, this picture takes him, once again, further away from Gershenzon's Pushkin: from an irrationalist, Romantic, solitary poet fleeing to the woods so as to be open to the Spirit, we have an establishment patriot who felt comfortable close to power. Those moments when Pushkin did indeed speak of a desire to escape to his native village, Frank interprets as the occasional understandable outburst of an artist often forced against his will to remain on constant display in full uniform at the court of Nicholas I.

Again, Frank also places Pushkin firmly in the context of his times when he unravels his attitude to the emerging Slavophile controversy about the role of Russia in world history. He draws on Pushkin's letters and other historical material to draw a picture of his original view of this nascent dispute. According to Frank, Pushkin held a third opinion about Russia's destiny, which was, once again, a profound synthesis of these two views – rather than a superficial syncretism designed to conciliate both parties.

On the one hand, Pushkin thoroughly immersed himself in Goethe, Shakespeare, Byron and Voltaire and was a dedicated admirer of Western culture – despite never having set foot beyond the western border of Russia. He was also,

---

[76] Ibid. 240.

despite some misgivings, a supporter of Peter the Great's opening up of Russia to European cultural influences.

It is in the poet's attitude to Peter that Frank sees Pushkin's originality. Khomiakov saw in Peter's Dutch dress and beardless face a betrayal of Russia's authentic past and tradition. But Pushkin early on remonstrated that this betrayed a superficial understanding of nationality. The culture of ancient Russia in fact was based, as Khomiakov contended, on Byzantium. But Pushkin pointed out that this was, no less than Western culture, a foreign import into Russia.

Pushkin defined national culture by reference to geography, climate, and national customs. These defining elements could combine and evolve with external elements to keep ever fresh and new. In addition, Pushkin's sense of his own Russian identity was deep and secure enough to make room for such innovations: by reading Goethe Pushkin felt not a whit less Russian; nor did Peter stop being an essentially Russian type just because he did not wear a beard.

Pushkin was thus deeply dedicated to Russia, and yet also painfully aware of its shortcomings, not surprisingly for one whose life was constrained severely by the authority of the tsar. In particular, he sympathized with Chadaaev's proto-Westernizing attack on the isolation of Russia from the West due to the separation of the Byzantine Church from Rome. However, he was not convinced that Protestantism was more Christian than Russian Orthodoxy. But nor did he follow Khomiakov in claiming that the Eastern Church suffered from no ills.

To the latter's contention that the Eastern Church was more brotherly than the Western Church, Pushkin replied ironically: "Perhaps. I haven't measured the amount of brotherly love in the East or in the West. But I do know that it was over there that the founders of brotherly communities appeared, which we don't have. And they would be useful for us."[77]

Still, while recognizing that the Russian Church had indeed suffered due to separation from the West, he imputed to this a special meaning in the history of humanity. For Russia's suffering during the centuries of Mongol domination constituted Russia's special service to the tasks of European-Christian culture. Although this period weakened, exhausted and corrupted Russia, it protected Western Christendom from a similar time of crushing trial.

Frank quotes Pushkin at some length:

> There is no doubt that the schism separated us from the rest of Europe, and that we did not participate in a single one of the great events which so roused her; but we had our own special task…And by it Christian culture was saved. We had to lead a completely confined existence, which while leaving us Christian, unfortunately made us alien to the rest of the Christian world, so that our martyrdom gave Catholic Europe the possibility of an unencumbered energetic development.[78]

---

[77] "Pushkin ob otnosheniyakh mezhdu Rossiei i yevropoi," 286.
[78] Ibid, 287.

Pushkin then chides Chaadaev for his contempt for Russia and its isolated history, and in probably the earliest comparison of Russian and Jewish destinies in modern Russian cultural thought, he makes an explicit comparison with the scorned and contemned nation of Jewry and Russia, which many accuse of backwardness and isolation, including Chaadaev. Nonetheless, Jewry was chosen to give the world Christ, and Russia was chosen to protect Europe from the Mongol yoke.[79]

Here Pushkin, Gershenzon and Frank again converge. As Frank writes: "M.O.Gershenzon in his book on Chaadaev justly comments that if out of all Pushkin's works only this letter had come down to us, it would have been sufficient to get a picture of Pushkin's genius." Frank himself highlights Pushkin's Jewish comparison in a bracketed comment: "Pushkin aptly parries this thought [of Chadaaev regarding Russia's cursed isolation] by pointing out that Christianity also arose among Jewry, which was contemned by the whole world."[80] Thus while Frank does not make as much of Pushkin's unique "Eastern Russianness" as Gershenzon, he too sees in Pushkin a figure with the spiritual depth to transcend the dichotomies that traumatize Russian culture in its relation to Western Europe. As for Gershenzon, so for Frank Pushkin was a figure of transhistorical universalism, stationed at the well-spring of modern Russian culture.

Gershenzon himself did not explicitly mention the Jewish parallel in his essay on Chaadaev, but as we have already seen in his essay on Pushkin's wisdom, the poet's "Arab-Russian" love of freedom and perfection was for him a demonstration of how the Russian spirit and the Eastern spirit are in harmony, so that a person who is self-declaredly of the "Jewish spirit" is able to find his deepest aspirations reflected in the founding figure of Russia's literary-spiritual life. In Pushkin's openness to the foreign – be it Byzantine, or European, or in Gershenzon's mind, the call of his Eastern blood – Gershenzon was also able to find an authoritative answer to Berdyaev in their dispute about the universalism of Slavophilism. And in reading the "prophet" "slowly and attentively," according to his new hermeneutic, he sought to open up a path of Russian-Jewish synergy, magnifying the hints scattered by Pushkin.

Thus Gershenzon's essay on Jewish fate and his thoughts on Russian fate in the person of Pushkin converge: what he described as the Jewish desire for "abstraction" and escape from all earthly ties, achieved through extreme suffering, can synergize with Russia's long-suffering and eternal process of discovering a new form of perfection and freedom, a new way to combine reason and nature, which the easy-living West has not known.

And indeed, this is because Pushkin's defense of a "third way" is in effect a special universalism, a universalism of chosenness, which builds on and expands

---

[79] Nonetheless, by analogy this makes Western Europe Christ, while Russia receives a second-rate status as Jewry.
[80] Ibid., 287.

the old Biblical chosenness of the Jews. In this sense, in different ways, Pushkin is archetypically Russian and yet also all-human.

It is true that even despite his Easternness, and despite the extent to which Pushkin's wisdom overlaps with Gershenzon's own last testament as stated in *The Sermon on the Mount*, Gershenzon differend from Frank in ultimately rejecting him as a model for his own spiritual development. That is because, despite the fact that Pushkin uncovered the truth about the destructive evolution of the fiery Spirit-Word, towards the end of his life, he ceased to live by it. He did not succeed, that is, in allowing the raw kinetic energy of the world to enliven his personality. He was half-dead, living among the half-dead, and he wished for death. As his life drew to a close, he had become cold. Thus, for Gershenzon, "one must know about Pushkin, but it is forbidden to live by him."

Of course, this constitutes a final serious divergence from Frank. For it is precisely in the final stage of Pushkin's life that Frank sees the greatest expression of his maturity and the deepest stage of his harmonious synthesis of the Russian, the Christian, and the European, the spiritual and the political. But Gershenzon, with his horror of any idea or system as a hardened callus in the flow of world life, sees in this maturity little more than death. Pushkin's conservatism, no less than the national project of the Zionists, came to seem to him anathema, a strangulation of the spirit.

It is perhaps not surprising, then, that by 1922 Gershenzon had come to see Frank as engaged in "trivial and silly undertakings." After all, Frank – although nearly a decade younger than Gershenzon – had already developed his own philosophic system, which he would expand and deepen, as he saw it, over the coming years. Shestov, by contrast, though Gershenzon could not agree with his rejection of Hellenism, could not be accused of system-building.

Still, Gershenzon's horror of constructive systems, his embrace of the creative chaos that was raging in his homeland, with its Nietzschean rending asunder of the artificial knots of old culture, should not obscure those subterranean moments, just excavated, when his thought intermingles with that of Frank.

Russian-Jewish Wisdom

We saw how Gershenzon refused to print his final testimony, "Sermon on the Mount," in a joint anthology to be called *Russian Thinkers* due to the presence of Berdyaev. An anthology bringing together the worldviews of Gershenzon, Shestov, Steinberg and Frank was never proposed[81]. However, this comparison

---

[81] At the end of his life, Frank edited an anthology of 19-20th century Russian philosophy. In that volume Berdyaev was nearly placed under one cover with Gershenzon, but Frank finally decided to omit the latter. Instead, he chose Merezhkovsky and Ivanov as representatives of the "spiritual movement of the epoch….the former the originator of the 'new religious consciousness' and the latter as the representative of a type of refined subtlety of religious thought rare in Russia…However, unfortunately it was necessary to exclude from the anthology the literary critic and historian of Russian thought, M.O.Gershenzon, who while not a religious thinker in the strict sense, had

has indicated that Frank may not have been out of place alongside his more tempestuous and "maximalist" contemporaries[82]. For, in concluding this section, we can summarize a range of tendencies that these four Russian-Jewish thinkers shared.

All of them in different ways displayed a skepticism regarding dogma, and a belief in the "special universalism" of Russia which merged with the "special universalism" of Judaism and Jewry. All of them read the Bible, both Old and New Testaments, in a way which blurred traditional denominational lines between Judaism and Christianity so as to include outsiders. At the same time, they continued to see in the Bible, which they had absorbed first within the Jewish community, a continuing and central authority in their lives.

Apart from Shestov, all of them had a conception of God which departed from the traditional God of their childhoods in being immanent and very close to pantheistic. This God was especially manifest in the Logos, and the Logos for them reached its greatest expression in Russian literature. The God of their Jewish upbringing had thus become incarnate in the sacred texts of Pushkin, Dostoevsky and/or Tolstoy, and with the exquisite Jewish literacy, which was a function of Russian-Jewish multilingual culture, they interpreted and translated that prophetic word to give spiritual succor for their own and others' lives. In this sense they were engaged in a modern Jewish gnosis.

Shestov, of course, stubbornly resisted this gnosis and this incarnation of God in Greek wisdom – at least, according to his own doctrine. In fact, he too was an exegete of the divine Logos. For him, this word was not immanent in nature and history, but exploded sporadically in God's cryptic utterances in the revelation of the Bible – but also in the giants of Russian and, later, Western European literature. Shestov's divine Word, despite his protests, is also deeply philosophical and "wise" – and pan-European.

One word which especially links Gershenzon, Frank and Shestov is, in fact, "wisdom" – though it is not the theological Sophia of Soloviev, Florensky and

---

and preached his own original idea of the spiritual life." (*Russkoe mirovozzrenie*, 647). The juxtaposition of Merezhkovsky, Ivanov and Gershenzon as thinkers related by their immersion in the "new religious consciousness," spearheaded by Merezhkovsky, confirms the viewpoint adopted in these chapters. Frank included himself in the anthology, and thus by extension, in the genealogy leading indirectly to Merezhkovsky.

[82] A comment of Soboliev's is illuminating in regard to Frank's "calmness" in personality and philosophy: "Frank never possessed such solid social status to permit himself the quarrelsomeness which was typical of Berdyaev" (and, one might add, Karsavin in his earlier days) ["Chem nam dorog filosof S.L.Frank?" in Soboliev (2008)]. This is a point I made regarding Shestov and Gershenzon: while both joined in the general asssualt on historic Christianity that was the motif of the "left wing" of Russian symbolism, they did it in more discrete and anonymous ways than non-Jewish Russians. All three of these thinkers "trod carefully" in their philosophic careers as not fully Russian outsiders in Russian culture.

Bulgakov, or even of Bely and Blok, female wisdom personified as the beautiful lady, and indirectly related to Mary. Instead, it is a far less dogmatically defined wisdom, an Old Testament wisdom, perhaps one can say a more male wisdom, that of the Eastern sage.

This is reflected in how these thinkers were seen by others. Shestov and Gershenzon were looked upon by their Russian colleagues as "sages"[83] – which was certainly connected to their Jewishness. And in this respect, Frank too was not an exception.

Due to his "Eastern" appearance and his calm, sagacious nature Frank attracted that epithet to himself on numerous occasions. Of course, he also declared himself that his life's purpose was to find wisdom, rather than philosophy, and he had engraved on his tombstone the words from the eighth chapter of Proverbs: "Wisdom I loved and searched for from my youth. Realizing that I could never possess Wisdom unless God gave her to me, I prayed to the Lord."

For Frank, this wisdom was indeed something that he first found in his youth in the "covenant with my grandfather…[and] the religious foundations, which he laid in me" to which "I returned…in my mature years." This was different from the theological-philosophical wisdom which Bulgakov mined from his love of (Russian) nature and his immersion in the dogmas of the Orthodox Church. It originated not in the outer, but in the inner life of the heart, the experience which what Frank sometimes called a "spiritual empiricism."

Of course, it would not do to exaggerate this image of Frank as a "Jewish sage" – or, rather, one must remember that among the Russian intelligentsia the title of sage was bestowed respectfully on Pushkin, Dostoevsky, and Tolstoy as well. This Russian respect for writers as sages is, in turn, traceable to Russia's Byzantine heritage: the most influential sacred literature of the medieval period consisted of translations of Chrysostom's homilies and sermons, which along with the lives of the saints "remained for centuries the most edifying reading for Russians." Nor should it be forgotten that another crucial element in medieval Russian literature were the apocrypha on King Solomon, "whose wisdom eclipsed for Russian minds that of Aristotle and Plato"[84].

Thus while the roots of Frank's own "Eastern" wisdom may indeed be traced to a very empirical transmission of that wisdom in the person of his grandfather, it expanded "naturally" to meet the Eastern, and ultimately Old Testament, wisdom of Russia, and then the hidden wisdom of the German mystics. Finally, in encompassing Christ in the divine-human foundations of the world, Frank's Jewish wisdom merged with the Solovievian consciousness of the Russian as a universal man – and in becoming indistinguishable from it was swallowed up. There is an echo of Nicolai Trubetzkoy's situation here: the

---

[83] E.g. Khodasevich on Gershenzon. Ivanov-Razumnik on Shestov, and more recently Soboliev on Frank [in Sobolivev 2008 filosof-mudrets (o svoeobrazii filosofii S.L.Franka).]

[84] Both these quotes come from the introduction to *Medieval Russia's epics, chronicles and tales*, edited by Serge A. Zenkovsky, p.7. Meridian Books: 1974.

prince's Eurasian Russianness ultimately vanished, to his chagrin, through its utter immersion in European culture.

Frank also realized quite clearly that for many in the Jewish community, this type of ethereal Jewishness meant that he was no longer a Jew – not to mention, of course, the fact of his conversion. In fact, we started off with his own ambiguity about self-identifying as a Jew: it was to his "non-Aryan" status that he ascribed his persecution. Still, for Frank this ever-expanding Jewishness was a natural path. To have curbed its expansion would have been unnatural and counterproductive – much in the same way that Gershenzon theorized assimilation through dissolution in the Spirit as the apogee of Jewishness.

This is made quite clear when Frank turns to look at Jewish contemporaries who believed that the universalism of Judaism was best served by deepening Jewish identity and that to do otherwise was, to put it in no uncertain terms, a betrayal of God. This was the challenge thrown down by Herman Cohen and Franz Rosenzweig – a challenge that Frank, with his desire to encompass within his philosophy all that was true in life, felt compelled to meet.

Frank and German-Jewish philosophy

Frank wrote "The religious philosophy of Cohen" in 1915; "The mystical philosophy of Rosenzweig" appeared in Berdyaev's journal *Put'* in 1926; and "The Philosophy of the Old Testament world" appeared in 1929, also in *Put'*.

The basis of Frank's philosophical dispute with Cohen has already been touched upon. Frank's own philosophy was built on a rejection of Kantian transcendental idealism, which he saw as producing an abstract rationalistic knowledge, which despite its claims, had not succeeded in overcoming subjectivity. His own solution was to postulate the oneness of the human mind with the deepest, trans-rational layer of reality, which yielded the possibility of a "living knowledge" and not just abstract generalizations. This "oneness" of mind and reality was, of course, a variation on the philosophy of all-unity.

Here, in fact, can be seen the crux of Frank's later disagreement with Rosenzweig. The latter, too, had rejected Cohen's abstract rationalism and had originally held out high hopes of a more organic worldview in the philosophy of Hegel. His dissertation *Hegel and the State*, however, was destined to be the budding Hegelian's last work of philosophy – for in rejecting Hegel, Rosenzweig turned his back on all philosophy *per se*. *The Star of Redemption* expresses this rejection, and its particular target is none other than philosophical all-unity.

This philosophical dispute is enlivened by each of these thinkers' attitude to the relationship between Judaism and Christianity, and the relationship of these religions to the whole philosophic enterprise. Frank links neo-Kantianism and Judaism as two false transcendent, rationalistic worldviews; Rosenzweig links Christianity to Hegelianism and Hellenic ontologism in general, as two deceptive abstract mysticisms.

Nonetheless, these are different answers to the same question. For the

Russian-Christian and the German-Jewish thinkers have one thing in common: all of them, by including religion in philosophy, were trying to fight against dryness and abstraction in philosophy, and were responding to what they saw as Nietzsche's call to reappraise metaphysics. Thus in the larger picture, the Russian religious renaissance shared a central concern with the German-Jewish renaissance – and in the persons of Cohen, Rosenzweig and Frank different solutions to the same challenge can be examined and appraised.

Moreover, in a sense, both these responses to philosophic crisis were those of outsiders: both Jews and Russian Orthodox Christians were alien to the Protestant, and more rarely Catholic, matrix of German idealism, and both exploited this fact to give originality to their analyses.

Cohen and Frank

In his 1915 review[85], Frank detected in Cohen an unacknowledged debt to Hegel in his assertion that the "concrete-immanent expression of human consciousness…[is found]… in the fact of legal and social life" and that the "the only content of ethics…[is]…the realization of justice and common humanity in social relations." As such, despite himself, Cohen's adaptation of Kant constituted an implicit critique of the latter's abstract-formal ethics, which was "deprived of any link with concrete-historical incarnations of the collective moral consciousness of humanity"[86].

Nonetheless, Cohen's rational moralism still contained most of the flaws of Kant's system. Frank, in particular, could not accept Cohen's dismissal of mythical[87] thought in religion, or his conception that the Old Testament prophets were preachers of God as absolute Idea.

Here, with fair-mindedness he quoted a Russian-Jewish critic of Cohen, who agreed with Frank as regards this reason-centered view of religion, professor Gurland. The latter argued that all religions, including Judaism and Christianity,

---

[85] Semyon Frank, "Religioznaya filosofia Kogena," in *Russkaya mysl'* No.12. (1915): 29-31.

[86] Both quotes from Frank's review. (Steinberg's later replacement of transcendental idealism with concrete idealism came out of a similar criticism, and is similar to Rosenzweig's proto-existentialist reworking of philosophy resulting from a rejection of neo-Kantianism – as we will see in more detail below.)

[87] Later neo-Kantian thought did find a place for mythology in the work of Cassirer and others. Frank reacted to this development in "Novokantiaskaya filosofia mifologii (Ernst Cassirer. *Philosophie der Symbolisher Formen. Teil 2: Das mystische Denken.* Berlin 1925.)" Put' No.4 1926: 190-1.Briefly, he was unconvinced by the attempt of a man who had lost or did not have a religious sensibility to address a subject that fell outside the remit of his usual logical topics. For all the lofty talk of transcendental categories, Frank found Cassirer's basic assumptions positivist and permeated with psychological reductionism. Neo-Kantianism's inability to find a place for revelation condemns it to never being able to find a basis for the critique of practical reason, which the critique of theoretical reason found in science. Cohen's attempt to find such a basis in social and legal relations was an earlier failed attempt.

were mythopoeic. The God of the Old Testament was a concrete being who appeared before the eyes of men, and was not merely a mental concept[88]. The difference between Judaism and Christianity, according to Gurland, was that the Judaic myth is apocalyptic and eschatological, i.e. oriented towards the future, while the Christian myth is oriented towards the past.

Frank applauds Gurland's philosophical conclusions. But they only provide more fodder for the critique of Judaism with which he ended the review. Frank accepts the idea the Judaism is future-oriented – and as we have seen Gurland's depiction of Judaism ties in remarkably well with Berdyaev's and Bulgakov's view of eschatological Judaism – but links it to Cohen's portrait of a Judaism that rejects the personal and concrete for the abstract.

As a result, Judaism's "strict loyalty to the observance of cleanliness and the greatness of the Coming One can lead psychologically to the denial of the past and the present, to a sacrifice of the concreteness of the incarnate and alive for the purity of a dream which is abstracted of any real spirituality; and here religion turns into, or can turn into, a rationalistic moralism, a fearsome emphasis on the transcendence of God over everything realized and empirically existing – in a denial of His concreteness."

Thus Cohen and the unwillingly co-opted Garland provide – "to a certain degree," for Frank dislikes categorical language – an explanation of "the whole world tragedy of Judaic religious consciousness."

This brief critique which links rationalism and Judaism echoes Berdyaev's and Bulgakov's critique of Judaism as "tragic." Indeed, it overlaps with Shestov's (later) two-pronged critique of both historical Judaism *and* Christianity for ignoring the concrete in favor of the abstract and metaphysical. It must also be seen against a background of the Russian conservative critique of liberalism and rationalism in politics – which takes fanatical proportions in Florensky, for whom Jewry is a force that undermines the organic, holistic and even magical foundations of Russian existence.

Nonetheless, Frank's critique of Judaism here is more limited in scope and milder than that of his fellow Russians. For a start, Frank limits himself to religious Judaism. His reference to "the world tragedy of Judaism," for example, has a different orientation to Berdyaev's "world grief of the Jews," which he saw speaking through Shestov's tragic nihilism.

In fact, Frank's 1908 appraisal of Shestov highlights this: Frank concurred in many points with Berdyaev that Shestov was "a nihilist in the most genuine sense of the word," whose work was a "creativity for nothing." But he saw in this "a fateful Russian characteristic: an attraction to extremes…which makes any idea an empty abstraction and deprives it of a genuinely live strength."[89]

---

[88] In "The Philosophy of the Old Testament," Frank gives his most positive evaluation of Jewish thought, responding to Oscar Goldberg's reclaiming of mythical elements in the Pentateuch. See end of present chapter.

[89] "O Lve Shestove (po-povodu ego novoy knigi 'Nachala i kontsy," in *Slovo*, 1908, No.646.

Furthermore, in a review of Berdyaev's *The Spiritual Crisis of the Russian Intelligentsia*[90], a couple of years later, Frank took similar exception to Berdyaev's anarchistic, nihilistic rejection of Soloviev's metaphysics as a way of seeking truth. He concluded that despite his critique of the Russian intelligentsia for its love of abstract schemas, "Berdyaev himself…is a 'Russian *intelligent*', the main feature of whom is his inclination to condensed colors and a one-sided monistic tendency to schematize."[91]

For obvious reasons, then, Frank resists that tendency observed in Bulgakov and Berdyaev to find in Jewish thinkers archetypical bearers of Russian philosophical faults. Where the former observe nihilism in Russians and Jews, they are inclined – in places at least – to label it a Jewish nihilism; where Frank finds schematic monism and extremism in Shestov and Berdyaev, he labels it a feature of the Russian worldview[92].

The same is true for his rejection of Cohen's neo-Kantianism; it does not go on to launch itself into a "one-sided monistic" creation of a Germanic-Judaic religious-philosophic monster of the type we find in Bulgakov's (and others') Jewish writings. Frank retained an albeit strained respect for the Kantian avenue of research[93], if not for all its answers, and even more so, revered Hegel whom he continued to see as an indispensable guide in philosophy[94].

Nonetheless, for all that Frank's approach was more constrained and nuanced than other Russian critiques of Judaism, his conclusion that Judaism is abstract and future-oriented hardly seems a convincing characterization of the dense and historically-grounded texture of Jewish religious ritual. In picking Cohen as a Judaic sparring-partner, too many other factors intervene for Christianity and Judaism to enter into direct comparison.

For, in fact, Judaism and Christianity are not the deciding factors in Frank's disagreement with Cohen. Rather, each holds a worldview in which their attitude to religion is one part: both of these worldviews are deeply universalist in orientation, while finding an incarnation in the specific. Cohen's universal/specific dynamic involved his conception of the relationship between *Deutschtum* (Germanness) and *Judentum* (Judaism/Jewishness), just as Frank worked with Russianness,

---

[90] "Novaya kniga N.A.Berdyaeva," in *Russkaya mysl'*, 1910.Kn.4.C.136-141.
[91] This converges on Bulgakov's own self-depiction that we saw in ch.2 as a thinker insensitive to nuances and shades who can only see the broad picture.
[92] In a sense, Berdyaev's later philosophical "behavior" vindicated Frank. His embrace of eschatology as a typically "Russian idea" after the Soviet victory in World War Two was viewed by Frank as a particularly heinous example of that Russian "national self-love" condemned by Soloviev, and which "completely ruined Berdyaev," as he wrote in a letter to G.Fedotov ("Pismo G.P.Fedotovu," *Noviy zhurnal*.1952. Kn.28.C.288,289.).
[93] Which is of course why he celebrated the publication of Logos in 1915 by S.I.Gessen – a Russian-Jewish neo-Kantian.
[94] See particularly: "Filosofia Gegel'ja. (K stoletiyu dnya smerti Gegel'ja.)" Put' No.34. (1932):39-51.

European culture (especially German) and ecumenical Christianity.

Thus if we look at Frank's and Cohen's evaluation of *Deutschtum*, we see that already they are opposed. Cohen's representatives of "real" German culture are those religious and cultural figures who developed the rational: Luther, Leibniz, Mozart, Kant, Beethoven and the founders of social-democracy. Frank's Germans (Eckhardt, Boehme, Angelus Silesius, Baader, Schelling, Hegel, Goethe and up to Rilke and Sheller) are the mystics and pantheists.

Not only Germans, but Jews, criticized Cohen's headcount of "real" Germans. Jews, especially after the Holocaust, came to see Cohen's German-Jewish synthesis as having suffered precisely from ignoring the mystical, nationalist elements of German culture which viewed Judaism as incompatible with its deepest aspirations. Often the equation is made between mysticism and dangerous nationalism[95] - however, this is not an obvious argument, given that Russian thinkers during the First World War associated Kant's rationalism with German military aggression, and Kant too sometimes viewed reason as a prerogative of the white races.

However, even before that, Martin Buber – like Gurland – was a Jewish thinker who objected to Cohen's system on similar grounds to Frank. Despite attempts to reinterpret late Cohen as an existentialist[96], it seems that he never departed from his conviction that God is pure idea – and not a person. Schwarzschild[97] compares Cohen's efforts to "protect" God from concretization or personalization with the neo-Platonists' insertion of further degrees of emanation between God and the world.

Thus Cohen's God does not relate to man: rather the *idea* of God relates to the *idea* of man, or more precisely God is the *ground* of the relationship between the idea of God and the idea of man. As Schwarzschild puts it: "God is now the regulative idea of universal ethical reason….which is functionalized through the ideas of creation,…revelation,…and…redemption." As Cohen himself writes: "God is not real, and he is not alive. Maimonides put a clear stop to this. Only the truth is the valid value which corresponds to the being of God."[98]

Against this, Buber insisted that man enters into a real living relationship with God: man's "I" encounters God's "Thou." Buber charged that one cannot

---

[95] In this type of reductionist argument, Hegel's holistic politics is seen as a predecessor of fascism.
[96] An attempt started by his disciple Franz Rosenzweig.
[97] Steven Schwarzschild, "The title of Herman Cohen's 'Religion of Reason out of the Sources of Judaism,'" in Cohen H. *Religion of Reason out of the Sources of Judaism*, 7-20. (Atlanta, Georgia: Scholars Press, 1995).
[98] *Religion of Reason*, intro.Schwartschild, pp.16-17. This certainly makes God impersonal and abstract, in direct contrast to Buber's and Frank's philosophy of I-Thou/I-We. Still, we pointed out above that Frank's depiction of the Absolute, the Unfathomable, as the impersonal "higher aspect" of Divinity (a rather Solovievian aspect of his system) also shies away from making Personhood more central than nature, essence or substance in its depiction of God.

love an idea[99]; the Biblical command to love God presupposes, therefore, that God is a person. As we have seen, Frank's own analysis of the living relationship of man with the Absolute draws on Buber's (and Ebner's) philosophy of personal encounter with the Divine. In other words, there were Jews and Christians on both sides of the Kantian barricade.

It is, of course true that in their deep philosophical architecture Frank and Cohen differ. This does impact on their conception of Judaism and Christianity. If Cohen's system excludes – with extreme apophaticism – the possibility of God being real, alive and personal, it follows with geometrical "certainty" that Jesus Christ, a living human person, could not have been God.

A whole raft of conclusions follow from this concerning the meaning of Judaism and Christianity in world history. While they can be derived via a seemingly stringently rational chain of logic, it also seems to be the case, that once one has left the bedrock of philosophical system-building, many of Cohen's insights can be paraphrased in a more intuitive manner, and correspond to general "lay" Christian and Jewish self-perception.

Frank and Cohen on suffering

One area in which Cohen was particularly original was his explanation of suffering. The two men's views on this question, rather than the details of their divergence over Kant's philosophical heritage, most probably give a better idea of why the meeting between Cohen and Frank in 1915 resulted in the former's walking out – though, of course, these views were expressed in different philosophical language.

For Cohen, Judaism was a historical demonstration of non-eudaimonian ethics, i.e. the ethical idea that one does good for the sake of duty and not happiness or reward. Good must be performed regardless of the recipient or result. To achieve a non-bias goodness, one must have an abstract idea of humanity which ignores race, culture and class. This in turn depends on assuming an underlying ground of humanity that unites all people: this idea is God.

Ethics is thus a universal science. While science (truth) cannot be national, of all historical approximations to the science of ethics, Judaism has so far come closest. In the course of their history, Jews were stripped of the markers of specificity: land, language and kingdom. They thus became a symbol of that abstract, unified humanity which is at the base of and the ultimate goal of ethics.

This idea of an "all-human" Jewry which has lost its extraneous differential baggage is almost identical to Gershenzon's vision. However, while Cohen too once toyed with the idea that Jewry could now assimilate, mission accomplished, he ultimately drew away from this conclusion.

For until ethical monotheism has been achieved by all humanity, the example of Jewish non-particularity (!) must remain as an example to others.

---

[99] Cohen was not overly perturbed, for he maintained that even in love between people, a person loves the idea of the other person, the idealized conception of that person.

While Christianity is an ally with Judaism in this struggle, its compromising of some elements of ethical monotheism means that Judaism is still needed. Specifically, Christianity's idea of the Messiah compromises the idea of the relation between humanity and God. God's ideality is fulfilled by his uniqueness, and humanity's ideality is fulfilled in the Messianic process of drawing close[100] to an ideal morality of a united mankind. Christianity's claim that the Messiah is a person[101] rather than an event, and moreover, that he has already come, distracts humanity from its mission of moral unification.

This leads to Cohen's ideas on suffering. In *Religion of Reason*[102], Cohen focused on Isaiah's suffering servant as the locus for his thoughts on this issue. In this, of course, he deliberately faces the Christian interpretation of the same text and contrasts his own ethical monotheist reading as a truer alternative.

In these passages, Israel's Davidic king has become the disenfranchised servant. This is a natural development, for the idea of God shows that it is precisely the disenfranchised who most clearly show forth the non-face-favoring aspect of universal ethics. The suffering servant is thus a symbol of the people of Israel, who are themselves the symbol of a still-to-be-unified humanity. Through his unjust suffering, the servant shows the direction of history, and he thus gives meaning to suffering.

Cohen makes a distinction here between vicarious suffering and vicarious atonement. The servant endures suffering that should by rights have been endured by the guilty nations. However, he does not in this way take away the guilt of the non-sufferers – as in the Christian interpretation – which would contravene ethics. However, the servant – Israel, the humble man, any Jew connected to his people – is the vicarious sufferer, who takes on the suffering that rightfully belongs to the guilty nations,[103] and as such he is "the true sufferer, he is the representative of suffering. Only he is able to undergo suffering in its moral essence…[he is] the only true bearer of it."

Perhaps, one can speculate, this is why Cohen and Rosenzweig were offended by converted Jews. They had opted out of true suffering, the suffering which gives meaning to human history and had tied themselves to the safety of a historically particular religion and state.

Cohen's account of the suffering Messiah (the Jewish people) differs on one

---

[100] Cohen sees this as an infinite asymptotic approximation. Thus he conforms to Paul Franks' criterion that Jewish philosophy sees redemption as distant and unreachable.

[101] Of course, Cohen reshaped traditional Jewish doctrines, including that of the personal Messiah.

[102] *Religion of Reason out of the Sources of Judaism*, esp.ch.XIII: The idea of the Messiah and Mankind.

[103] Though he concedes the righteous among the nations can have some share in this suffering. He seems to have in mind especially the poor: "how could the poor man not know [the guilt] of men, since he suffers from the injustice of the world's economy."

more count from the Christian interpretation of Isaiah. For he does not see in suffering a good in and of itself. That is, suffering does not play as it does in Christianity, a cathartic role. Instead, the suffering servant plays a prophetic object-lesson in non-eudaimonian ethics; however, once the vision of that ethics is realized "it does not have to be the case, and certainly it shall be different in the future, that there should be only tragic representatives of morality. This is a conception of dramatic poetry to which ethics in no way has to consent."

This bold engagement with, and reclamation of, a crucial proof-text of the Christian Old Testament, not surprisingly, contrasts with Frank's own thoughts on the meaning of suffering. Frank, too, confronted Cohen's claim that it contravenes morality for Christ's sacrifice to atone vicariously for the sins of others. His answer emerged out his conception of humanity as an all-unity.

In *God With Us*[104], Frank depicts atonement through some form of suffering as a universal intuition across the world religions. Suffering oneself as a way of undoing error has an obvious meaning: the loss of property involved in sacrificing a lamb already points to ancient man's familiarity with that idea. However, in Christianity sacrifice must involve an act of love and not merely pointless abstention or morbid self-punishment.

Yet there are cases, where it seems that error and sin cannot be undone. The most global case is humanity's collective inclination to sinfulness, which presents a seemingly unresolvable paradox. It seems that humans cannot but sin and yet – in language that echoes Kant's optimistic maxim that "if one ought to then one can" – Frank affirms that we still feel that "if we know that we ought not to have done it, we know that we need not have done it."

A way out exists. Objectively, all men are guilty of general sinfulness and, objectively, they bear responsibility for their portion of sin. But subjectively, the picture can be different. Here, writes Frank, "the intensity of the sense of responsibility is by no means determined by the degree of one's personal sinfulness. It is indeed in inverse ratio to it, for it depends upon the degree of man's moral sensitiveness, and his capacity to experience other people's guilt as though it were his own, and to have compassion on people languishing under the burden of sin."

At its highest this passes into a desire to identify with such people, endure suffering and sacrifice for them. While a judge who judges from the outside must apportion guilt objectively, "in overcoming the boundary which morally divides one person from another, love overcomes the individual boundaries of responsibility and voluntarily takes upon itself the burden of another's guilt. This is the true and lofty meaning of *vicarious sacrifice*."

Christ's vicarious sacrifice takes this idea to its conclusion. For here "in the person of Christ, God in a mysterious way offers Himself as a redeeming sacrifice," and the sinner – tied to his own sin as well as knit into the fabric

---

[104] The following quotes are taken from Natalia Duddington's English translation: Semyon Frank, *God with Us*. London: Jonathan Cape Ltd.,1946.

of an erring humanity – has the possibility to really escape from remorse and sin. However, Frank adds, "any attempt rationally to explain this mysterious and gracious act would not be only futile, but blasphemous."

Of course, Frank sees another dimension in this vicarious sacrifice. It provides the only really convincing theodicy: for it shows that true reconciliation is not the work of a distant avenging God who requires compensation for the offense done to Him by a wretched and suffering humanity, but of a God, who out of love for mankind, voluntarily shares their suffering and takes it upon Himself, thus pouring into the world the saving power of redeeming love.

If we compare Frank's idea of vicarious atonement to Cohen's the following differences emerge. For Cohen, it is a human nation that takes up the suffering of others – not out of love but in order to convey an ethical lesson. The lesson can be understood by reason and indeed this Messianic suffering is a corrective to Platonic idealism: Plato does not let all classes have access to his philosophical truth, and Jewish Messianism with its vision of a unified humanity rectifies this.

In addition, for Cohen, "the holy spirit is the human spirit," and will fill every man and woman, and the superiority of Judaism lies in the fact that in the rabbinic continuation of the Bible "the extension of the revelation to tradition is unavoidably a *dissolution of revelation in knowledge*"[105], and thus of greater universalizability and accessibility to all of humanity.

Cohen would certainly not have been convinced by Frank's defense of vicarious atonement. No doubt, the notion that ethical failings can be brushed under the carpet due to the subjective love of an outsider would have seemed to him like a further distraction from the task of unifying humanity.

Indeed, this has a political aspect: Cohen's socialist politics looked towards a restructuring of society so as to relieve the suffering of the disenfranchised. Frank's hierarchical, conservative-liberal (as we have seen "Pushkinian") politics saw inequality as a natural feature of humanity. Cohen would no doubt have seen complacency regarding the effects of injustice and sin as stemming from the Christian certainty that God was taking the greater part of it on himself anyway. And Frank would have agreed that human effort can only do so much. Cohen's optimistic socialism would for him have looked very much like the "heresy of utopianism"[106] which he criticized in Russian revolutionary activity.

However, there is also a more personal angle in this debate: Frank had often experienced periods of psychological and physical frailty, and for him the Christian emphasis on suffering as somehow connected to the deep nature of the world and God was intuitively attractive, and in fact, he pointed to this aspect as a crucial dividing-line between Christianity and other religions, especially the Old Testament.

---

[105] *Religion of Reason*, 258.
[106] The title of a 1946 article by Frank: *Yeres' utopizma*, Novy zhurnal, New York, Kn.14.1946.

On his death-bed, in fact, he had a religious vision that arose out of the suffering brought on by his cancer. He recounted how he "was lying in great pain and suddenly I felt that through my tortures and sufferings I was communing in some sort of Liturgy, and in it I felt in myself, and at its highest point I partook, not just in the sufferings of Christ, but – audacious as it might seem to say so – in the very essence of Christ. The earthly forms of bread and wine were nothing in comparison to what I had then…How strange it was, what I experienced: it was beyond everything I had thought about my whole life. How did it come to me so suddenly?"[107]

Thus Cohen's and Frank's different views as to the meaning of suffering perhaps more than any other metaphysical concern highlight their different Judaic and Christian views of the world. It is hard to see how Cohen's heuristic view of suffering as an undesirable global object lesson in ethics could have satisfied Frank's intuitions about the meaning of suffering in his own life.

However, even on a more abstract theoretical level, Cohen's interpretation of suffering raises questions, not only from a Christian but even from a Jewish point of view.

Firstly, his view relies on an extreme variant of the "lachrymose version" of Jewish history. As for Gershenzon, that which is basic in Jewish history is suffering. Cohen was a bitter foe of Zionism, which to some extent is not surprising. On the other hand, it seems that his commitment to a doctrine of Jewish suffering blinded him to the possibility of relieving the suffering in this one case.

Secondly, the Jewish people seems excessively sanctified in Cohen's reading. It looks as if all Jewish suffering is undeserved, i.e. as if Jews are free of sin. This, however, contradicts the Biblical context from which Cohen has taken his source-text: in the Hebrew Bible it is quite clear, for the most part, that Israel is punished by God for the sins *she* commits.

Thirdly, while Cohen admits that some of the nations can suffer vicariously, it seems that the greater part of humanity suffers meaninglessly and randomly. While the idea of unified humanity is unfolding, the question of theodicy is as burning as ever: what meaning does the pain of non-Jewish humanity have in Cohen's schema?[108] And as with Frank's personal suffering, this extends to the suffering of the individual: if the individual is not poor, Jewish or somehow world-historically disenfranchised their suffering can have no meaning for God.

Finally, even if Cohen's doctrine concerning Jewish purity is correct, and

---

[107] Boobyer, 254.
[108] Christian self-congratulation on this point, however, needs to be tempered by the recognition that in Christianity, too, not all suffering is suffering for Christ. For example, the suffering of an adulterous lover pining for his beloved, could not be considered redemptive in Christianity, even though such subjects have often borrowed Christian metaphors of suffering, sacrifice and so on in literature and film (and Karsavin's philosophy has some of its origin here). Nor does much Christian theology see Jewish suffering (often at Christian hands) as having redemptive value – after all, the belief had it that Jews were dying for a false belief.

even if all other suffering is deserved, it raises the question of theodicy in another form: how can it vindicate (a rational) God if he merely pushes the suffering of some of his creatures onto other creatures, according to a choice that seems completely inscrutable – while also, presumably relieving the guilty of their burden of suffering? It is this point that Frank's contention that God Himself is the suffering servant who takes suffering upon Himself is designed to address.

Certainly, in this reconstructed debate, the Jewish and Christian elements of Frank's and Cohen's philosophy are clearly opposed. Even here, however, it is well to remember that some of Frank's rhetoric is directed at Protestant (and Catholic) Christianity: his description of vicarious suffering, as outlined in *God With Us*, was primarily intended to provide an alternative to the idea that Christ's sacrifice was a ransom paid by Christ to God to pay off humanity's sins, as first proposed by Anselm and then enthusiastically adopted by Luther.

Likewise, Cohen's arguments come from within Reform Judaism and would be unacceptable to Orthodox Judaism. In a moment of clearly Protestant inspiration, which is traceable to his Pietist mentor, Cohen comments that "the universalism of the church is not to be equated with Messianism because in the former the priest with his sacraments stands between God and the layman." As with his rejection of a personal Messiah, this flies in the face of Orthodox Jewish beliefs: Orthodox Jews, of course, pray thrice daily for the restoration of the Temple cult and continue to preserve the distinction between priest, levites and lay Israelites so that these divisions will be in place when that Messiah eventually restores animal sacrifice. Ironically, as the philosopher's surname shows, Cohen himself was of priestly descent!

In the next section, we will follow the debate between Frank and a Jewish philosopher who also took exception to Cohen's excessive emphasis on reason at the expense of religion.

Frank and Rosenzweig

Rosenzweig's path back to Judaism is well-known. He first decided to become a Christian, but for conscience's sake wanted to come to Christ as a Jew. He thus attended a Yom Kippur service for the last time. After that service, he wrote that "it no longer seems necessary to me and… *no longer possible*" to become a Christian. Some days later, he wrote to his converted cousin, Eugen Rosenstock, that while he understood that Christianity was necessary for the world, as no one can reach the Father except through Jesus, "the situation is quite different for one who does not have to *reach* the Father because *he is already with him*."[109]

Thus was conceived the well-known (but sometimes misinterpreted[110])

---

[109] In Nahum Glatzer, Forward to *The Star of Redemption*. Translated from the Second Edition of 1930 by William W. Hallo, (Notre Dame: University of Notre Dame Press, 2002): p.xix.

[110] Occasionally the doctrine is presented as if these were two different but equal paths to redemption. Rosenzweig makes it fairly clear, however, that Judaism is superior to Christianity. For example: "at the bottom of his heart any Jew will consider the

doctrine of the dual covenant, whereby Jews and Christians have different roles to play in God's plan for the world. Rosenzweig's embrace of Judaism was not just a rejection of Christianity: it was also a rejection of German philosophy as it had so far been practiced, as well as of the type of heavily philosophized Judaism that his teacher, Herman Cohen, had been developing.

In *The Star of Redemption*, written four years after his conversion on postcards sent home from the Balkan front, Rosenzweig set out to give rational expression to his experience. The *Star* was published in 1921, and thereafter, its author dedicated himself to Jewish education through teaching at and heading the Free Jewish House of Study in Frankfurt. There, he addressed himself to men, and not to scholars, those paeons of German culture, whom he now saw as possessed by "an insatiable, ever-inquisitive phantom which like a vampire drains him whom it possesses of his humanity"[111]. The meaningless technical questions of philosophy were to be replaced by the human questions of life, which were non-technical and often lacking in ready answers.

A year later, in 1922, Semyon Frank arrived in Berlin as an exile from Soviet Russia. Four years later he published "The mystical philosophy of Rosenzweig"[112]. The book and its author had already achieved fame and its concerns and arguments were both philosophically and religiously challenging to Frank.

Philosophically, the book claimed that the path to life and concrete existence led away from Greek and German Platonism into a type of existentialism. Religiously, it argued in effect that Judaism gave its practitioners an experience of "eternity in time," while adherents of Christianity were still traveling towards eternity in the wake of the fuller religious example of Judaism. Both these claims were a more radical assault on Frank's worldview than anything Cohen had proposed.

Thus Frank and Rosenzweig started out at similar places and finished far apart. Both were Jews of German origin who became captivated by German romanticism. Both then sought to critique aspects of this romanticism. Frank appealed to Russian-Christian sources, Rosenzweig to Judaism – and yet it is debatable to what extent either of them abandoned their initial premises.

The argument of The Star and Frank's critique: The Star
The first part of *The Star* argues that Parmenidean and Platonic all-unity is

---

[111] Christian's relationship to God, and hence his religion, a meager and roundabout affair. For to the Jew, it is incomprehensible that one should need a teacher, be he who he may, to learn what is obvious and matter of course to him, namely to call God our Father. Why should a third person have to be between me and my Father in heaven? This is no invention of modern apologetics, but simply Jewish instinct..." Franz Rosenzweig, "The Jew and the Christian. *From the Exchange of Letters with Eugen Rosenstock*," in Glatzer (ed.), 346-347.

[111] Glatzer, Forward to *The Star*, p.xi.

[112] "Misticheskaya filosofia Rozentsveiga. (Der Stern der Erloesung. Von Franz Rosenzweig. 1921)," in *Put'* No.2. (1926): 139-148.

false[113]. It deceives man by offering the eternity of the seamless whole in place of his own personal eternity. The individual has no ontological status, and thus his concrete death goes unnoticed. Rosenzweig looks to Nietzsche[114] as one who refused to accept this metaphysical prison in which God, dialectically derived from the whole by emanations, is indeed as dead a proposition as the whole artificial construct from which he is derived. He also preempts Heidegger in asking the individual to facilitate his escape by imagining his own concrete death[115]. No panacea of all-unity will then be able to cure the resulting anxiety of the awakened individual.

The second and third parts of *The Star* are dedicated to a reworking, or prizing apart, of this dead all-unity: being is replaced by "meta-being;" ethics by "meta-ethics;" and logic by "meta-logic." As far as God is concerned God is taken outside of the world: "The meta-physical in God makes physics a 'component' of God. God has a nature of his own, quite apart from the relationship into which he enters, say, with the physical 'world' outside himself."[116]

The end result is that, instead of world, man and God forming a whole, they now form separate parts. But this allows for a rupture between subject and object in which the individual can appear. The world is now seen under the Judaic aspects of creation, and man is seen under the Judaic aspect of revelation. (The third aspect, redemption, is dealt with separately).

Creation is constant: God's words "Let there be" do not cease to sound, and thus the world is ever renewed. Likewise, man is not immersed in the pantheistic, closed world of ancient Greek and Indian thought, but is woken to individuality by the fact of language, which is a miracle of God within him. Through language man finds God, as well as his fellow-man – a break-through in communication for the ancient mystic, who had been blinded to personal relations by immersion in the All.

The final aspect of this re-configuring[117] of the All is redemption. This turns

---

[113] It would be interesting to compare the relative success of Steinberg's Judaic-Russian Parmidean all-unity and Rosenzweig's "post-philosophical" Judaic rejection of all-unity.

[114] This highlights the partially parallel tracks of German-Jewish and Russian religious philosophy: Shestov, Berdyaev, Frank, Gershenzon, Bulgakov and others were also inspired by Nietzsche to rediscover a concrete and personal God. Karsavin's emphasis on the death of God and self can even be seen as taking its inspiration from Nietzsche's death of God. Steinberg, likewise, believed Nietzsche's "death of God" ultimately led back to a deeper conception of God.

[115] Steinberg and Karsavin were engaged in a similar contemplation of death at roughly the same time; the First World War and the Revolution were, of course, responsible for such thanatocentric meditations.

[116] E.Levinas traced his own rejection of metaphysics back to Rosenzweig's direct inspiration. In ch.4, we saw that J.Zizoulias has pointed to Levinas' proposal of an alternative to philosophical totality as useful tool for Christian thought about God and the world. Below, we will see how this aspect of Rosenzweig's thought compares to Frank's own system.

[117] The term carries some of the technical meaning of Cohen's neo-Kantian account of

out to differ from creation and revelation in being a two-way process: man redeems the world and the world redeems man. Both man and God already have essences, containing a "yes" in the core of their being, while the world is an unstable "no," a constant becoming. Man's work on the world, as the steward of creation, in which he uncovers the dynamic and alive goodness placed by God in the world constitutes man's redemption: in order to do this work he must come together with his neighbor to form a united "we."

The world in turn needs man's work in order to move from the false and closed unity of the Greek logos, to the real and all-embracing all-unity that is the end-task of creation. All-unity, true unity is achieved, not given, and lives in the unified "we" of mankind, as a work of art lives in its perceivers, and not in itself or even in its creator.

In this way the kingdom of the world becomes the kingdom of God, appearance becomes essence. The world is both humanized and divinized at the same time – and this mutual redemption of world and man in fact constitutes the redemption of God, for only when all-unity is achieved can God enter the world and transform it finally. Then there will be no separate God, man and world, but all will be all in all. God, who is light, will be revealed for what he is, and his first words will be fulfilled: "Let there be light!"

The critique

In principle, Frank was open to criticisms of all-unity. In 1932, he wrote a review of Hegelian philosophy[118] in which he accused Hegel of ignoring the personal, the contingent, and the irrational. Instead of Spirit and Substance, he argued that Hegel needed the term Life, for: "Reality is life; it relies on the irrational *secret* of being, on the unknowable – or more precisely on that ultimate principle which is philosophically knowable, but not through the concepts of spirit and idea, but only through the concept of the unknowable, by means of which we give an account to ourselves that it *is*, that we *are* , but which we cannot understand, i.e. express in concepts."

Thus, while Rosenzweig believed that Life only began where philosophy ended, Frank believed there could be, and must be, a philosophical approach which made room for Life within its portals. Refusal to respond to the challenge of dialectically correcting Hegel could only result in irrationalism[119]. Rosenzweig's

---

configuration – an indication that Rosenzweig's rejection of philosophy is not complete.

[118] "Filosofia Gegel'ja. (K stoletiyu dnya smerti Gegel'ja.)" Put' No.34.(1932):39-51. It seems probable that Rosenzweig's must have been one of the contemporary philosophical sources that forced him to give this re-evaluation of Hegel, as it seems to continue themes outlined in his response to *The Star* in 1926.

[119] In the article on Hegel, Frank may have had different targets in mind when referring to undesirable irrationalists. He may have meant Heidegger whose early philosophy he was not keen on; he may have meant Shestov; or he may even have meant the rise of the fascist movement in Germany, whose effects he was already feeling. Later, he explicitly connected the rejection of his type of universal European philosophy,

own evasion of this task, his contrary attempt to dismantle all-unity, for Frank was also a religious error, "reflecting a fundamental dividedness in the soul of the author." This dividedness is due to the absence of a concept of godmanhood, which is the "fundamental sin of Judaism," and forms "the experiential centre of the whole mystical experience of Rosenzweig."

For Frank, the all-unity of the world and God could be mystically intuited by everyone. He implies that while Rosenzweig has glimpsed this all-unity, he has somehow betrayed it in the telling. This is most evident, for Frank, in the disconnected and artificial structure of *The Star*.

The structure of *The Star* is, in fact, modeled on the two three-pointed triangles that make up the star of David, from which the book takes its title. The first star contains the unconfigured "Greek" world: man, world and God. The second star contains the configured Judaic equivalents: revelation, creation, and redemption. Man and the world, as we saw, correspond to revelation and creation. One might therefore expect God to correspond to redemption. However, as we saw, redemption is a two-way process involving man's work on the world and the world's corresponding effect on man.

Frank finds this rather shocking: Rosenzweig's third crowning point, redemption, turns out to bypass God completely. He also notes that Rosenzweig does not even include a reference to the Jewish Messiah. Instead, the third point of the triangle refers to an utterly natural process that has already been set in motion, in which God does not directly participate (if you exclude the permanent aspect of creation, which however has been dealt with under the previous "star-points").

Thus for Frank, Rosenzweig's complex six-pointed schema[120] obscures a

---

written in "German, the language of philosophy" with the rise of the new Hitlerite barbarism. Rosenzweig, in contrast, believed that precisely Frank's kind of philosophy was connected with a kind of cultural death.

[120] Rosenzweig does not help matters greatly with his distinction between a "configuration," such as the two superimposed triangles of a star, and the geometric "figure" of a triangle. In an attempt to get his reader to appreciate the meta-mathematical nature of the star as an instrument for uncovering truth, he writes in The Threshold: "For this is what distinguishes configuration from figure, that though configuration may be assembled out of mathematical figures, its assembly has in truth not taken place according to mathematical rules, but on a hypermathematical basis. This basis was here provided by the idea of characterizing the connections of the elemental points as symbols of real occurrences rather than as mere realizations of mathematical notion." (*The Star*, 256.) In other words, Rosenzweig claims to be escaping the mathematizing tendencies of philosophy and penetrating into reality by his use of a configuration that goes beyond mathematics. The threefold division of the book and the threefold division of each section of the book are all modeled on this tripartite nature of the star. One cannot help feeling that this is indeed an artificial pseudo-structural device to pull his insights together. Peter Eli Gordon, a recent scholar of Rosenzweig, hints at similar judgment ("Franz Rosenzweig and the Philosophy of Jewish Existence," p.122, *Modern Jewish Philosophy*), when he

basic similarity with Cohen's philosophy. Both systems posit a transcendent God, who stands outside redemption, and both posit a naturalistic account of redemption. In Rosenzweig, this naturalistic element is emphasized even more: for Jews, it comes from the natural, organic and worldly medium of Jewish blood and is thus not connected with repentance, but with the life of the tribe, with the transmission of divine-natural seeds from generation to generation, and with natural human building of the world. And like Cohen, Rosenzweig "even has words of sympathy for the contemporary constructors of the Tower of Babel, for those fighters for human (all too human!) principles of brotherhood, equality and freedom."[121]

In sum, Frank contends that Rosenzweig's new configured all-unity is no improvement on the old one. The figure of the self-centered, isolated human whom Rosenzweig had detected in the hero of Greek tragedy and philosophy is held by Frank to correspond more closely to the isolated Jewish "Old Adam," who thirsts for Christian truth but cannot grasp it. The Jew is ordered by the Law to love God, and according to Rosenzweig, is then imbued with love of his fellow-man.

Again, however, Frank contends that without the Incarnation the transcendent gap between man and God cannot be overcome by commandment: if God and man are isolated, there is no way for the isolation between man and his fellow man to be overcome. Only through Christ's words that he who "feeds the hungry feed Me," that is, God, can love open up between humans. In other words, humans must realize that they are immersed in the divine and already connected to one another.

Frank adds two further criticisms: the lack of a concept of Original Sin, which is connected to Rosenzweig's optimistic belief in natural redemption; and the fact that *The Star* lacks any mystical conception of a soul of the world, such as is found in Plotinus, or Christian Neo-Platonism, or even Kabbalah and Judeo-Arabic Platonism. The absence of this is responsible for the failure to overcome the isolation between human beings and between God and his creatures.

Evaluation of Frank's critique
An interesting way to consider Frank's critique of *The Star* is to compare it to that of a recent Jewish critic.

Michael Wyschgorod[122] pointed to the dangerous lack of clarity concerning

---

describes how redemption is presented in the Star: "It is necessary to live with some anticipatory sense of redemption if one's religious life world is to be structurally complete" – the notion of structural completeness, too, seems artificial; or else it hints at an abstract supposition of the necessity of redemption according to the demands of practical reason, i.e. in a neo-Kantian way that Rosenzweig was supposedly trying to avoid.

[121] Steinberg, too, had words of sympathy for socialists, seeing them as fulfilling Judaic, prophetic principles.

[122] "Franz Rosenzweig's The Star of Redemption," in Michael Wyschogrod, *Abraham's*

the genre of Rosenzweig's book: it hovers between philosophy and religion, but does not quite succeed in emancipating itself from the former. After all, two thirds of it is dedicated to a lengthy exposition of the Hellenic world of all-unity, and the place of "man" in that universe. Rosenzweig's conclusion is that the positing of such a universe does not correspond to the life experience of "man," so that while it is internally consistent and even persuasive, it must be abandoned in favor of the demands of life.

However, Wyschgorod contends that this assumption of a universal religious human type in a book whose goal is to argue for the inadequacy of universal categories is a contradiction in terms. The fact is that the universe described by philosophy served very well to ward off at least some men's anxiety concerning death (the classic case, writes Wyschgorod being Socrates – and one might add Boethius here, too). Thus Rosenzweig's argument that philosophy is inadequate to life, couched in his old Hegelian and Kantian philosophical concepts, can hardly be persuasive as an argument for anyone except Rosenzweig himself, and is certainly not adequate to overturn the whole universalizing project of philosophy.

In terms of the debate we have been following, the correct answer to all-unity would either be an irrationalist rejection of it, in Shestovian style; or else, one is within one's rights to question, as Frank does, the effectiveness of Rosenzweig's rejection of it and reworking of it in terms borrowed from philosophy itself.

Wyschogrod's second related point is that there can be no bridge from universal "man" to concrete "Jew" – of the type the author of *The Star* tries to build. In this regard, Rosenzweig provides a telling contrast to Karl Barth for Wyschogrod. The latter emphasized the adequacy of human philosophy, its complete inviolability to counter-proof *on its own terms*. Thus for Barth, the only hammer that could break philosophy was an eruption from the outside. Rosenzweig, however, tried – almost despite himself – to disprove philosophy from within, by having recourse to universal man and his so-called universal wants and needs. Revelation makes only the most fleeting of appearances.

This ultimately ties in with Frank's criticisms. For the picture of the Judaic reconfigured universe that we get at the end of *The Star* is indeed rather lacking in supernatural content. However, *contra* Frank, this may be more a function of Rosenzweig's lingering debt to all-unity, his ambiguous and inadequate break with philosophy, than to Judaism itself.

Indeed, this brings to mind the long-running debate between Aaron Steinberg and Lev Karsavin. The Jewish and the Christian adherents of all-unity were *too much* in agreement. Nothing, it seemed, in their system could give them the texture of their different real-life faith commitments.

In approaching Frank's critique from the Christian angle, however, one also finds a troublesome irony. Frank criticizes Rosenzweig for his transcendent God

---

Promise: Judaism and Jewish-Christian Relations. (Michigan: William B. Eerdmans Publishing Company, 2004), 121-131.

and for his naturalism regarding redemption. And yet, on both counts Frank's own system was subject to criticism by fellow Orthodox Christians.

Frank once quoted Tertullian's statement that "the soul is by nature Christian"[123], and he assumes in his critique of Rosenzweig that the Jewish philosopher's innate knowledge of Christianity is somehow distorted due to the philosopher's "national pride." Thus Rosenzweig's "book breathes simultaneously with enmity towards Christianity, as well as a passionate, unconscious anguish for it."

However, to quote Tertullian as a proponent of the idea that the soul naturally knows Christ is risky. It ignores Tertullian's other statements[124] regarding his own conversion that it was a sudden, sharp and unexpected break with his old pagan life – a dialectic repeated in Augustine.

Frank gravitates to one pole of this tension, and as we saw in Zenkovsky's criticism of Frank's adaptation of divine-humanity, he tends to assume that one can approach Christ through the natural world, that in a sense, every human is already a member of the divine body of Christ, simply by being a part of Absolute reality. In this sense, his own Hellenistic naturalism causes him to be too harsh in his assumption that Rosenzweig has encountered Christ but rejected him.

Thus Rosenzweig's insistence on a transcendent God, who has been separated from the all-unity of the world, is in fact a useful corrective to the idea that God, as in Frank's system, is linked to the world in an unspecified manner intermediate between creation and immanence, and is somehow accessible through immersion in the world and the acquisition of innate living knowledge of God through philosophical means.

Indeed, Rosenzweig's contention that "God has a nature of his own, quite apart from the relationship into which he enters, say, with the physical 'world' outside himself" reinstates that gap between God and the world on which even the mystical theology of the Eastern church in its Orthodox form continues to insist.

For Frank had indicated in his philosophy that Divinity only becomes personal when it relates to humans[125]. This is of course posits a dogmatically

---

[123] *Krushenie kumirov*, 97.

[124] Tertullian's statement about the "Christian soul" comes in *On the testimony of the soul*, an apologetic work defending Christianity against pagan attacks. His other well-known statement "Credo quia absurdum," a favorite of Shestov's, expresses precisely the non-pagan "foolishness" of Christian wisdom.

[125] From *The Unfathomable*: "God is not just God and nothing more but is in his very essence 'God and I'.... just as the human in man is not just purely human but is a divine-human essence....so God is a true God precisely as the God-man." And elsewhere: "What the language of religious life calls God is a form of observation or revelation of that which we mean by 'Deity'...God is the Deity as it is revealed to me and experienced by me....Deity is revealed as 'You' – and only as 'You' does God exist. The nameless or all-named Deity, when it addresses me, first of all takes on a name, the name of God." Here Frank seems to take account of God as ultimately

unacceptable and symmetric dependence of God on man, ignoring the doctrine that the triune God is a person before He creates the world. Frank's insistence on the immanence of God and man's ability to encounter God within himself echo Eastern patristic doctrines, such as the presence of the divine *logoi* within the world, which help man to see God in His creation. Further, for Eastern theology grace is a reparation of man's fallen, but still divinely created nature, bestowed in response to his own stirrings. It is not an accident randomly bestowed on an utterly evil creature (as the late Augustine would have it). In this sense, Frank's criticisms of Rosenzweig's transcendentalism are true to his Russian Orthodox faith.

It is also true that one of the most authoritative expositions of Eastern theology, that of Gregory Palamas, insists that Christ in His Incarnation is the fullness of God in the world. In addition, through the sacraments of the Church God works in man according to the divine energies. And the way that Palamas explains the energy/essence distinction makes it clear that the energies are not secondary to the essence, lower properties, but that they too contain the fullness of God as directed towards man by His Will.

However, contrary to Frank's pantheistic leanings, Palamas also makes it clear that God is not even to be limited to his essence – for God is above essence. Furthermore, God's act of creation is not linked to his essence but his will. Thus while God can act fully in the world and be known by humans, while humans can participate fully in the divine life and become "deified," there is no doubt that God is also outside the world, "before" the world, and has a personal life utterly unknowable to man[126]. In this sense, much of the apophatic architecture that separates the world from God is as present in Orthodox theology as it is in Cohen: the difference is that Palamas combines this with a doctrine of divine immanence, and even "sacred materialism," that does not compromise transcendence.[127]

It would take us too far afield to explore in detail how Frank and Rosenzweig differ with respect to Palamite doctrine. The immediate conclusion, however, is clear: both Frank's immanentism and Rosenzweig's transcendentalism are in their different ways distortions of Christian dogma, and Frank's own doctrine that the world is divine-human might be accused of the same naturalistic

---

Person; but, like Bulgakov, in linking the life of the Trinity and the Incarnation so closely, he makes the intra-Trinitarian life of the Logos and the incarnational life of the Logos, qualitatively similar, as if the Incarnation follows from the laws of God's essence, rather than being an act of will (or energy, in Palamas' terms). That is, there is a danger that the otherness of the divine Persons to each other within the Trinity, and the otherness of God to the world/man, come to be equated.

[126] As for the "logoi," they are not as in sophiology a part of God's nature, but willed interventions of God's energies in creation – the majority of which "lies in evil." Merely by participating in the world, then, one does not participate in God.

[127] Cf. Meyendorff, John. *A Study of Gregory Palamas.* (New York: St. Vladimir's Press, 1998).

optimism that he sees in Rosenzweig's belief that man and the world mutually redeem each other.

A final question that remains concerns Rosenzweig's so-called doctrine of a "dual covenant." Rosenzweig gives a clearly privileged status to Judaism, which is the intense core of the star, compared to the star's dissipated rays, symbolizing Christianity[128]. Judaism is closer to God, while Christianity is still moving towards Him. In addition, Christianity's doctrine of the Son as the path and the truth is contradictory. Judaism, too contains some errors, but as Rosenzweig explains in a section called "The harmlessness of the dangers," these are easily overcome, for "the Jew simply cannot descend into his own interior without at the same time ascending into the Highest....the more he finds himself, the more he turns his back on paganism, which for him is on the outside not, as with the Christian, on the inside."

Like Cohen's depiction of the relationship between Judaism and Christianity, this resembles a mirror image of the Christian teaching of contempt for Judaism. It depends on an idealized image of Jewish otherworldliness, in which Jews have never fought each other in opposing national armies, never partaken in the business of the world, and must never again found a state of their own[129]. As

---

[128] The first fission in the light of Christianity is a division of the divine light of redemption into the three proto-cosmic elements of man, world and God. This corresponds to the three temptations and historical divisions of Christianity (which have existed in Christianity from the beginning, though they emerged in time separately): Protestantism, which is skewed towards excessive humanization, idolization of *man*; Catholicism, which has tended to sacrifice the soul of man for the Roman juridical, governmental rescue of the *world*; and Orthodoxy, which with its excessive spiritualization has lost sight of the concreteness of *God*, and indeed of the physicality of the world, has spiritualized God, or in other words, deified the spirit. These stereotypes of Protestantism and Catholicism are, in fact, not far from Russian religious thought's characterization of these denominations. The characterization of Orthodoxy as excessively spiritual accords more with Merezhkovsky's neo-Christianity; but it is also a criticism of Orthodoxy that Bulgakov tried to repair through his "sacred materialism." However, this critique of Orthodoxy rests on a false view of asceticism, and also ignores the "sacred materialism" of Palamas, Maximus the Confessor, and other Fathers.

[129] Wyschgorod himself at times subscribes to such an idealized picture of Jewry: in "A Theology of Jewish Unity" (Wyschogrod (2004), 43-53), he argues that the foundation of Jewish unity is its election by God as the seed of Abraham in the flesh. He ends the essay: "Everything I have said will be proven false once and for all if, God forbid, a war among Jews should ever become possible. War among Christians has been and is a commonplace..." This repeats Rosenzweig's doctrine of the otherworldly nature of Jewry. However, it also relies on an absolutization of the tragic *galut*: in the Bible the two kingdoms of Israel and Judah went to war with each other; even separate tribes fought against each other. Thus there is ample precedent that Jews with political power behave the same as non-Jews. In addition, a war of the Jewish state against non-Jews also constitutes a type of worldly, "gentile" activity, not

with Cohen, once it is assumed that these conditions are met Jews are tacitly assumed to be above the world.

However, not far below the surface this conceals a very palpable sense that the real world – in which mysteriously only gentiles participate – is in fact a tragic place of blood and fury and historical contingency. Rosenzweig's attempt to protect Jewry from historical unpredictability – such as a new political existence in Palestine – once again seems to be a contradiction as unsettling as his recourse to universal man in order to undermine universal categories. By the end of *The Star*, he has re-created that stifling all-unity which encased the Hellenic hero in tragic dumbness. In rejecting both rabbinic and Biblical readings of exile and the destruction of the Temple as tragedies, and embracing these events as divine triumphs, Rosenzweig seems to meet Frank's charge that his Judaic hero is as cut off from the world as the Hellenic philosopher was assumed to be.

Thus while Frank himself may suffer from excessive philosophical immanence in his portrayal of the relations between God, world and man, it is nonetheless true that philosophy's use of the term "man" as a universal aimed at every human being can never be fully rejected by Christianity, even if it will sometimes be dialectically adapted – as in Tertullian's own contrary assertions regarding the naturalness and suddenness of Christian grace. This is equally true of Palamas, who ultimately rejected Platonic and Aristotelian metaphysics (referring to the "poisonous Plato"), but only after engaging with them and adapting their insights to the truths of revelation.

In that sense, Christianity can never abandon its conversation with Greek philosophy if it is to remain open to dialogue with humanity, even if it ultimately recognizes truths that lie outside its deepest categories. Karsavin expressed this paradoxical relationship well, when he wrote of the inclusion of that which is true in Greek philosophy within the Church – which, nonetheless, is utterly new beside it[130].

---

to mention the occasions in which Russian Jews have fought German Jews. To give an even more concrete instance: the Russian-Jewish neo-Kantian, Matvei Kagan, had a falling-out with his mentor Herman Cohen: the latter wanted him to engage in research on the Russian economy. As Russia was at war with Germany then, Kagan felt this would be unpatriotic. Cohen subsequently called Kagan "an enemy" after his refusal to do the work, and the relationship ceased. Thus Russianness and Germanness seemed to come above Jewishness for these two "Cohens" from different nations. (Cf. Matvei Kagan, *Ob iskhode istorii*, 27.) Interestingly, Rosenzweig's and Wyschgorod's "purification" of the Jews has odd parellels with a doctrine of the nationalist-Slavophile Aksakov: he argued that the early Russian tribes preserved a pure, organic union, a kind of pristine social contract that was free of the tainted authoritarianism of government, due to the fact that they invited the Vikings to rule them. Thus the Russian people had an eternal nature. In that sense they would resemble diaspora Jewish kehillim, which formed a state within the real "fallen" state of the gentiles. The problems start of course, once Russians and Jews form their own governments and start ruling other minorities!

[130] To be fair to Frank, he too recognizes that Christianity brings about a radical change

This, however, applies equally to Rosenzweig's Jewish Law, which he claims "is not alienated from the world but the key to the enigma of the world." One could try to claim that a "law" which explains only the Jew's existence and fails to explain the workings of the gentile world could not be a divine law – for it has limits. However, this might also be to philosophically generalize about God's inscrutable ways, in a way that Rosenzweig critiques.

One might further refer to the Bible's own references to the days when the gentiles will take a place beside the Jews – but again, that would be open to interpretation.

In sum, then, like Rosenzweig – at times – and more like Barth, and within the Orthodox tradition, like Gregory Palamas, one can ultimately only look beyond philosophical all-unity here. Only by referring to the New Law of Christ as it is preached in the Body of Christ can this doctrine of the dual covenant be "refuted," albeit on another plane. But it was precisely such a step beyond the circle of philosophy that neither Frank nor Rosenzweig could fully bring themselves to take[131].

After all, Rosenzweig's attempt to construct an intimate theological portrait, not only of his native Judaism but of Christianity too, betrays a continuing belief in the universal Logos, and in a universal *anthropos*, who in some sense supersedes the Jewish or Christian human immersed in his local revelation – and who will listen to Rosenzweig's voice of Reason. Not surprisingly, such an all-too human voice, while pretending to speak from a position of all-unity, can hardly outdo the voice of revelation which each Jew and Christian claims to hear.

In that sense, it is actually Rosenzweig's non-philosophical aphoristic comments about the relation between Judaism and Christianity that are more interesting than his quasi-philosophical discussion in *The Star*. In a letter to Rudolph Ehrenberg, for example, he succinctly encapsulated his response to St.Paul's thoughts on Jewish destiny in Romans, which formed the touchstone of so much contemplation among Russian thinkers, writing:

"The Church knows that Israel will be spared until the day the last Greek has died, when the work of love is completed, when the Day of Judgment…dawns. But what the Church admits for Israel in general, she denies the individual Jew. So far as he is concerned, the Church shall and will test her strength in the attempt to convert him."[132]

---

in Greek philosophy. While he defends Rosenzweig's Greek hero, he also recognizes that the pagan philosophy could not reach formulate a true synthesis between the divine-human soul on the one hand, and a divine cosmos, on the other. However, this differs from Rosenzweig's assertion that Greek consciousness was split into man-world-God.

[131] Bulgakov, as we saw, resembles Barth in wishing to move beyond the "tragedy of philosophy." And yet whether he escaped philosophical presuppositions was a question oft mooted by his critics. On a larger scale still at issue, for Christianity, is the ongoing controversy of the link between Christian dogma and Greek philosophical categories.

[132] "The Church and the Synagogue," from a Letter to Rudolph Ehrenberg, in Glatzer,

This formulation of the question is more striking than the answer Rosenzweig offers, and it draws close to Frank's own statement of the paradox of Jewish conversion as an unresolvable choice between "preparing for the Chosen People a definitive end, or rejecting the Messiah and the greatest Divine revelation announced by him."

Both men, therefore, no doubt felt this paradox and mystery in their own lives, from different angles – and yet, when it came to philosophizing, they added little to St. Paul's statement of the matter many centuries ago.

Frank and O.Goldberg

Frank wrote a last article[133] on Jewish subjects in 1929, his review of Oscar Goldberg's *Reality of the Jews*, which originally appeared in Hebrew in Berlin in 1925, and was then translated into German. Maybe because Goldberg's views posed less of a threat to his own worldview, Frank shows himself far more generous to Judaism, and his protest at the end of his review of *The Star* that, for all its faults, Rosenzweig's book was a remarkable and useful instrument in the fight against philosophical unbelief, ring more true of Goldberg's "philosophy of the Old Testament."

Goldberg led a Kabbalistic study circle in Berlin in the 1920s, of which the pioneering scholar of Jewish mysticism, Gershom Scholem, was a member. In his book, he combined the insights of German source-critical scholarship on the Old Testament with a living Jewish religious sensibility. Like *The Star*, the book was an attempt to outline a Jewish religiosity that takes note of but transcends the heavy hand of German historicism – which often killed the spirit with the letter of historical criticism.[134]

In fact, Goldberg rejects Welhausen's documentary hypothesis, and paints a far stranger picture of Pentateuchal Yahwistic faith. For him, this faith is not monotheistic in the modern sense, because the "gods" against which Yahweh, the Lord of Warrior Hosts, fights have full reality, and embody the destiny of the peoples among whom they dwell. Yahweh too is embodied among his people, or to put it another way, the Jews are an incarnation of Yahweh. But Israel's god differs from the gods of the peoples: "Hear O Israel, Yahweh your god is unique," because he is the only god who preceded the creation of the world. He is the centre of a system of being, which is empirically incarnated in the people. But in order to do battle with the other gods he has left the heavens and come to this world to live among his people. There he is open to attack and defeat by the other gods. The rituals and ordinances of the Old Testament are magical rites to ward off the influences of other gods; however, Yahweh lost access to his people in Egypt, and could only show himself to Moses in the desert.

Frank was rather enchanted with this primitivistic portrait of ancient

---

344.
[133] Frank, Semyon. "Filosofia vetkho-zavetnogo mira." Put' No.19,(1929):109-113.
[134] And in fact continues to do so in much Old Testament scholarship.

Judaism (which bears some resemblance to the incarnational Jewish theology of Michael Wyschgorod, whom we cited above). He sympathizes with the author's ironic contempt for what he calls the saccharine "dear God" of not just Jewish, but Christian tradition, and sees in Goldberg's portrait a vivid insight into the fact that the covenant between Yahweh and Israel was a mutually beneficent pact against mutual enemies: Israel and the Lord of Hosts offer help to each other.

This is welcome relief from the staid idea that God does everything for man, and man obeys, (that is, from the idea of a remote, transcendental God which Frank saw in Cohen's, and to a lesser extent, Rosenzweig's God.) Goldberg also expresses amazingly well, in Frank's estimation, that Divine materialism which Soloviev said was the essence of Judaism. And although in the final analysis, concludes Frank, it is not a satisfactory analysis for a deep religious view, a Christian one, it is highly useful for drawing attention to elements usually rejected or ignored in the conventional religious world-view.

Indeed, Goldberg's view of an incarnated god, a god who leaves his strength behind, and a god who is open to defeat find an echo in Frank's own later reading, in *Light in the Darkness*, of the verses in John: "A light shines in the darkness, and the darkness will not absorb/overcome (*katalaben*) it." Frank started this book with a close hermeneutic analysis of the Greek verb *katalaben*, concluding that both meanings, at first seemingly contradictory, are truthful. On the one hand, the verb gives assurance that the light will not be extinguished, a cause for optimism. But, on the other hand, nothing except hope offers the assurance that the dark forces of this world (which put us in mind of Goldberg's *elohim*, the gods) will relinquish their dominance. There is an affinity – stylistic, and conceptual – between Frank's scholarly parsing of John, and Goldberg's spiritual scientific immersion in the Hebrew Pentateuch.

Conclusion

As with Frank's final choice of a tombstone epithet from Proverbs, this buried continuity with Hebrew-Jewish sources should not be surprising. In the stream of Frank's worldview, after all, there flowed several currents that had their origin in his Jewish childhood. Even when that river had flowed a long way from its source, those Jewish streams could still be faintly detected – though Russian and European culture's embeddedness in Judaic origins sometimes obscures what is Frank's personal legacy and what is the legacy of the wider culture which his cosmopolitan outlook, itself a function of Jewish universalism in the worthiest sense, embraced.

In sum, while the tragedy and paradox of Jewish-Christian relations mean that Frank cannot be considered a Jewish thinker, although he was a thinker and a Jew, neither can the Jewishness of this Russian European heir of (the distantly "Arab") Pushkin be entirely neglected as a constituent part of his serene and all-embracing greatness.

For to ascribe those universalizing and "immanentizing" moments in Frank's thought exclusively to the German, Russian and Greek inspirations underlying his philosophy would be an error of attribution. In comparing Steinberg and Karsavin, we observed that since Spinoza and Solomon Maimon there has been a worthy tradition of Jewish immanentism in modern European philosophy. This is all the more so in the case of Russian philosophy, where all-unity is traceable directly to the Jewish (as well as Christian) Kabbalistic sources studied by Soloviev. Thus, from its very origin, the Russian worldview has "dual parentage."

Finally, another trait of Frank's that may also have dual Russian-Jewish origins is his optimism. This may seem paradoxical at first. After all, Florovsky wrote of Frank's *Light in the Darkness* that "Frank has no hope for history. For him, it is a tragedy without any immanent catharsis whatsoever," and Frank agreed in part. When Binswanger called him an optimist, Frank also retorted that it was his pessimistic belief that the victory of good over evil was not ordained, as God was an artist like any other and could not be sure of the success of his works.

Still, while he was in hiding from the Nazis in France, Frank railed against the dark outlook of Heidegger. He could not comprehend why the German philosopher placed fear at the centre of his system. For Frank it seemed more obvious to put belief, trust and love at the heart of philosophy. True, they might not triumph – but, according to his "practical theodicy," such an assumption was the only answer to evil.

This is, of course, paradoxical: Heidegger was living in comfort over the border from France under a regime that he had welcomed. Frank was living in straitened conditions as a refugee under threat of death from that regime. Even though *Light in the Darkness*, which he penned during that time does not foreordain whether the light will be "absorbed" or "overcome" – according to the constantly alternating current of the ancient Greek verb in John – Frank's continued immersion in the Word testified to a basic hope in the divine-human nature of the world and humanity.

In the foreword to *Light in the Darkness*, he also wrote:

> The proposed meditation was conceived before the start of the war and in outline was written during the first year of the war, when it was still not possible to foresee the entire scale and meaning of the demonic forces unleashed by it. Later events have not changed my thoughts, but rather strengthened and deepened them. But after everything that was lived through during those terrible years, it was necessary to express them in completely different words, and the manuscript was thus quite radically revised after the end of the war.[135]

While there is pessimism in that work, it is not the pessimism of Adorno and

---

[135] *Svet vo tme*, 16.

others after the Second World War, who declared that there can be no literature after Auschwitz. Perhaps in that sense, although the Second World War was more horrific that than the First, Frank had been prepared by his experience of the Revolution and Civil War. For, arriving in Berlin in 1922, he had written: "Now that we Russians have been impoverished materially and spiritually, have lost everything and are seeking instruction and understanding from the leaders of European thought…we see with amazement that we have nothing to learn from anybody, and that we can even teach others a few things now that we have had a full share of bitter experiences and suffering."[136]

The fact that Frank continued to philosophize after his experiences, and indeed continued to develop his philosophy in new directions (abandoning Platonism for a more Aristotelian turn, and insisting on a sharper separation between religion and philosophy), surely gives the edge to an optimistic interpretation of his work. The end of philosophy, one feels, would have meant for Frank a surrender to that irrationalism which fascism represented. Indeed, his continued creativity arose partly out of an urgency to contribute to the rebuilding of the European continent over which he had wandered for twenty years, and the currents of whose thought – from the Russian, to the "Western," to the Arabic, to the Hellenic, to the Judaic – he had absorbed into his own magnanimous synthesis.

Indeed, Frank's pan-European and even trans-European synthesis holds a suggestive fascination for the current European context. Today's Europe is different from Frank's: it often describes itself as "post-Christian," and certainly its religious and ethnic composition has radically altered even that troubled unity of Christian nations that Frank was familiar with. Still, if any philosophy is capable of pointing the way towards an underlying unity between the new Muslim immigration and the old Christian culture, it would have to take as its starting-point something like Frank's optimism regarding the compatibility and harmony of different European and non-European worldviews. What such a contemporary "worldview" would look like would no doubt depend in part on the national and religious identity of the philosopher forging it. But, for Frank, that initial national or confessional difference would only be observable initially: after entering into all-unity through a particular door, such a philosopher would, presumably, find themselves immersed in a larger mystical communal "all-human" heritage.

---

[136] Quoted in V.Kantor, "The Principle of Christian Realism or Against Utopian Self-will," in *Social Sciences*, Vol.31, No.1, 2000.

Conclusion
Soloviev's heirs: the third generation

Alexander Men: Bulgakovian Judeo-Christianity?
In the preceding chapters we explored in detail Jewish-Christian encounters in "Silver Age" thought from 1880 until 1950. The personality and life of each thinker was an important influence in how they assessed the relationship between Christianity and Judaism, and indeed in the shape of their own contribution to Russian religious thought. Nonetheless, while not homogenous, certain common features of their approach to Judaism and Jewry emerged.

One such feature which we will dwell on further here is the conservatism of Russian views vis-à-vis Judaism. This is a feature shared by pre-Holocaust Western Christian theological responses to Judaism. In Russian thought, however, this was combined with a deep, even urgent and topical, interest in Judaism that arose out of a particular historical circumstance: the fact that the world's largest Jewish population lived in Russia and that in the very period in which Russian religious thought was flourishing, its future had become a live political topic for Russian society. The question is: does this thought have relevance beyond its initial time and place for our contemporary world?

The thinkers examined in this study, from Soloviev to Frank, continue to be studied in Russia. Their way of doing philosophy is not dead. The mixing of boundaries continues apace between theology, literature, philosophy, journalism, and prophetic political commentary. Furthermore, during the Soviet period the smuggled copies of these philosophers' works provided an alternative to communist ideology, and with the fall of communism their works were fresh with the lure of the forbidden. Thus works that first saw the light of day in 1905, 1913 or 1921 can be read with an enthusiasm and topicality that is difficult to imagine in the Western context.

In terms of the then "Jewish question," which in its tsarist form was solved by the dissolution of the Pale and the granting of equal rights to Jews, history has also developed in ways that are divergent from Western Europe. In concluding this study, then, it will be useful to consider how those whom we might call "third-generation" "heirs of Soloviev," i.e. the heirs of the thinkers we have examined, reacted and continue to react to the Solovievian thesis of the Jewish question as a Christian question. In this regard, a central figure around whom attention must focus is Alexander Men.

Alexander Men was a "dissident" priest, of Jewish descent, who preached in Moscow during the late nineteen sixties, seventies and eighties. He was also a prolific author, who despite being cut off from the sources of scientific theological and Biblical research due to the repression of the Soviet regime, produced numerous books that were avidly read by his parishioners and in wider circles.

In many cases, they still continue to be used as standard books for catechetical classes or self-education by newly awakened Christians – at least among more liberal church circles.

In 1990, Men was attacked by an unknown assailant on the way to his church and murdered. Some saw the hand of the government in the murder: Men's religious propaganda was a thorn in the side to a dying regime. Others saw in it the work of conservative church circles, hostile to a Jewish priest with ecumenical leanings, whose books had been published by Catholic presses. Men had always had contacts in the West, and translations of his works were for many Western Christians a clear window onto the sometimes closed world of Russian Orthodoxy. With his death, the fascination with Men increased and he began to be viewed in almost martyr-like terms.

Among such Western admirers, Men's message is often seen as being liberal and ecumenical, and a beacon of the universal side of Orthodoxy. Thus non-Orthodox Christians in the West have also been attracted by the powerful figure of Men, seeing in him a fighter against totalitarianism and one of its victims.

However, within Russia opposition to the Soviet regime often concealed underlying differences which its collapse highlighted, thus scattering previous allies to different sides of the barricades. Men is a case in point. In terms of the contours that the Jewish-Christian dialogue has taken in the West "after Auschwitz," Men would be classified as illiberal and, in fact, saturated in a very Russian (and even Soviet) attitude to the issues. Part of this relative illiberalism can be traced to his immersion in Russian religious philosophy. His attitudes to Jewish-Christian dialogue thus form a fitting epilogue to this study.

Men several times stated his hope that there could be some form of Judeo-Christianity. In fact, his own parish consisted largely of hundreds of Jewish intellectuals who had, often due to his preaching, converted to Christianity. A recent study of Men's Jewish followers is Judith Kornblatt's *Doubly Chosen*[1]. The title indicates some of Men's theology: Jewish Christians come from the chosen Israel of the flesh, and have joined themselves to the chosen Israel of the spirit, the Church. Christianity for Men was a way for Sovietized unbelieving Russian Jews to reconnect to the faith of their ancestors, as expressed in the Old Testament, as well as deepening and extending that faith through the New Testament. As Kornblatt shows, that theology was absorbed deeply by Men's parishioners[2].

---

[1] Judith Kornblatt, *Doubly Chosen. Jewish identity, the Soviet intelligentsia, and the Russian Orthodox Church.* (Wisconsin: University of Wisconsin Press, 2004). Cf. also: Mikhail Meerson-Aksenov and Olga Meerson, "Yevreiskoe samosoznanie i pravoslavnoe khristianstvo," in *Kontinent*, No.111, 2002. For recognition of Men's Solovievan roots, cf. Mikhail Aksenov-Meerson, "Zhizn svoyu za drugi svoya," in *Pamyati protoiereya Aleksandra Menya*, 116-121. Moscow: Rudomino, 1991.

[2] In "Yevrei i khristianstvo," Men's "Bulgakovian" language is particularly strong: Jews' connections to Christianity is strengthened through their "relatedness in the flesh to the prophets, the apostles, the Virgin Mary and the Savior Himself, [which] is a great honor and a sign of double responsibility." Cf. Aleksandr Men, "Yevrei i

Men gave an interview to a samizdat Jewish journal in 1975, which was titled *Judaism and Christianity*[3]. He explained to its editor, A.Shoychet, his belief that conversion did not have to lead to assimilation. Just as Russians and Englishmen observe their national holidays, so there need be no contradiction in a Jewish Christian celebrating Hanukka – which after all commemorates the Maccabees, who are saints in the Orthodox Church. Men further expressed the hope that the small Hebrew-speaking churches that existed in Israel might eventually be the foundation of a Jamesian Christianity, that as in the early decades of Christianity, could fit into the spectrum of Jewish life in the Jewish state.

In 1973, Men had addressed a group of Jewish refuseniks. The talk was suggestively called "Is Judeo-Christianity possible?"[4], and he outlined his cautious belief that it was possible. Again, one objection that he had to overcome before describing this vision was the belief on the Jewish side that conversion was treachery. Taking forceful exception to this, Men expressed the view that the compulsory equation of ethnic Jew with the religion of Judaism was a type of Jewish "black hundreds" extremism. In Russian, that is, he denied that a *yevrei* need be a *yudaist*[5]. Men thus equated the Israeli situation with tsarist Russia: in both countries a state religion tried to dictate to the conscience of the individual.

Men's ideology was thus partly couched in the language of the anti-totalitarian dissident. On the other hand, the notion that a Jew (*yevrei*) can be a purely ethnic or even national category is itself partly a Soviet construct, which came to shape the reality of Soviet Jewish life, where Jewishness did indeed exist divorced from the synagogue, and even other markers like language[6].

Another Russian/Soviet aspect to Men's analysis can be seen when in one place, he refers to the "Jewish, German and Russian holocausts." A Western Christian writing in 1975 would have blenched at such a phrase: the term "holocaust" has come to be associated primarily with the Jewish catastrophe; to use the term of German suffering in the Second World War would seem odd, even immoral and provocative. But in the Soviet Union, where official "internationalist" ideology suppressed the facts of the ethnic component of the Nazi slaughter, such an attitude was more natural.

In addition, the fact that Men could speak to Jewish audiences, as a Jew –

---

khristianstvo," in *Vestnik RKhD* No.117 (1976):113-117.

[3] "Khristianstvo i iudaizm," Yevrei v SSSR, No.11, 1975.

[4] "Vozmozhno li iudeokhristianstvo?" Kontinent, 1995, No.8.

[5] *Yevrei* refers to an "ethnic descent" conception of Jewry; *Yudaist* refers to a practitioner of Judaism. The distinction between these categories seems to be sharper in Soviet and even late Imperial Russia than in Western Europe. In the Soviet period, where all religion was officially outlawed, *yevrei* was an official nationality (alongside Russian, Georgian etc). Here the disjunction between Jewish religion and ethnicity, alien to Judaism itself, reached its most acute form.

[6] In other words, I am claiming that Men's clear-cut division of *yevrei* and *yudaist* owes more to the historical circumstance described in the previous footnote. The question is, however, a complex one.

"This has often happened in our history, too," is one of several phrases where he identifies as a Jew – while simultaneously being a Russian Orthodox priest, and be published in a Jewish paper also says much about the times. In a sense, Karsavin's vision of a Russian-Jewish fusion was realized in a perverse way under the conditions of Soviet persecution, which temporarily made Christianity and Judaism allies.

Both religions became legitimate options for Jews seeking an alternative to Soviet emptiness. Thus conversion to Christianity could be tolerated as a worthy form of "internal emigration" even by Jews who rejected that path themselves. The conditions arising from the division between Church and State which led to the "honest" Jewish conversions in Meier's circle shortly after the Revolution were seemingly replicated in post-War Soviet society on a larger scale, creating just the right space for a Karsavinian fusion – at least, that is one way of looking at it.

The polemic against Men's Jewish Christianity
N.Feingold and S.Lyosov

However, many Jews objected to such a rapprochement and the circumstances which generated it. As with latent disagreements among Russian Christians that were smoothed over by the fact of common persecution by and opposition to the State, this uneasy alliance and odd ecumenism among Jewish Christians and "Jewish Jews" was sundered by changing circumstances.

Already in 1977, Natan Feingold, a Russian Jew who had emigrated to Israel, was writing an article called "Dialogue or Mission?"[7] in which – having broken out of this "peace from above" – he attacked Men's views as treacherous and deceptive. He accused Men of using the lure of Russian religious philosophy and Russian literature to seduce rootless Soviet Jews with no knowledge of Judaism into converting to Russian Christianity. His theology was false, and his claim that Jewish apostates to Christianity were reconnecting with the religion of their fathers, and thus contributing to some sort of dialogue between the religions was a dangerous lie.

Much more recently, similar charges have been made by Sergei Lyosov, a one-time friend of Men. Lyosov's views do actually correspond to what might better be called Western liberal Christianity, and he draws on Tillich's existential theology to outline a view of Christianity that is not absolutist, i.e. does not make demands or claims on parties beyond the believer's self. In two essays[8], one of which is subtitled "Notes towards a contemporary Orthodox liberalism," he outlines a Russian post-Auschwitz theology.

---

[7] N.Feingold, "Dialog ili missionerstvo? O 'dialogicheskoy' forme russkogo pravoslavnogo missionerstva sredi yevreev i o doctrine neoiudeokhristianstvo," in *Soyuz religioznoy yevreiskoy intelligentsia iz SSSR i vostochnoy yevropy*, Jerusalem, 1977.

[8] "Khristiansvto posle osventsima." (www.vehi./asion/lesev.html); "Yest' li u russkogo pravoslavija budushchee? (ocherki sovremennogo pravoslavnogo liberalizma)." (www.vehi./men/future.html#evr).

Lyosov's criticisms of Men are, if anything, harsher than Feingold's. Men's followers are depicted as having a drug-like dependence on communication with their pastor. Men's idea of Jewish Christianity is permeated by "racist categories." A passage in which Men calls Isaiah "the Old Testament evangelist" for his prophecies of Christ are relics of an outdated theology, for Men surely must have known that "Christianity needs to learn how to ask new, more human 'Jewish questions.'" Not only are Men's flock "captured children," that is apostates forced by Men into Christianity against their will in the non-freedom of the Soviet period where Judaism was persecuted more than Christianity and so was not a real choice, but Men himself is a forced apostate.

In sum, Men was a tragic and harmful figure whose death nonetheless arouses the sympathy of his friend: "Whatever the real motives of the murder were, I feel this loss, this nightmarish death of a person who was important for me, as the death of an unfortunate 'captured child', who had lost his way in an alien world. For to the end he never became his 'own' person in that social reality where he so energetically and successfully asserted himself, where his irresistibly victorious smile shone forth. He remained there an alien."

Lyosov correctly links Men's theology of Judeo-Christianity (as Men did himself explicitly) to the work of Sergei Bulgakov. Lyosov also sees a link with Karsavin, who for Lyosov is a straightforward anti-Semite. Again, Lyosov is entirely consistent with his "non-absolutist" approach in rejecting Men, Bulgakov, and Karsavin, along with Berdyaev as proponents of an "old" and anti-Judaic theology. Both Feingold and Lyosov are correct in seeing Men as an heir of these thinkers. The fact is also quite evident in the lectures that Men gave in the year of his death, which were later collected into a volume called *Russian religious philosophy*, where he examines all the thinkers considered here[9].

In particular, Men's vision of a cultural and ethnic Jewish Christianity is particularly close to Bulgakov and Karsavin. Like them, he clearly rejects the Law as a possible component of Judeo-Christianity, for it compromise the spirit of Christ. Christ's words about having come to "fulfill the Law," Men explains, are meant in the sense of giving fullness (*pleroma*, as the Greek has it) to the Law, which is by implication not yet full. Christ was therefore not referring to the observance of particular ritualistic commandments – like His Pharisaic predecessor Hillel, He was aware that the essence of the Law could be expressed as "service to God."

Moreover, Men believes that Jewish Christianity will still have a distinctive shape without the Law, because like Soloviev, he sees Jews as having a particular character, writing that "we are a tempestuous people, and 'stiff-necked'. God chose precisely such people, because quiet types would never have created a world religion….But one should not boast about one's chosenness. It looks very…unattractive…and between ourselves we can say

---

[9] Men, Aleksandr. *Russkaya religioznaya filosofia. Leksii.* Moscow: Khram svyatykh bessrebrennikov Kosma i Damiana v Shubine, 2003.

this." It is expressions such as this that Lyosov found racist.

Of course, a detailed examination of the views of Men and those communities that to this day revere him and to an extent practice his vision of a Jewish Christianity – primarily in Russia, Israel, and the United States – would be the subject of an entire book. Nonetheless, the basic point has been made: while there is much that is ecumenical in Men and Russian religious philosophy, in terms of contemporary Jewish-Christian debate Soloviev's present-day heirs might find themselves more closely allied with those groups, such as Evangelicals, who are generally not part of contemporary post-Holocaust Jewish-Christian dialogue.

Men in the context of post-Auschwitz theology

In that debate, it is generally accepted that Jewish Christians do not have a special seat at the table of Jewish-Christian dialogue, and indeed would be better excluded. Fritz Voll[10] expresses the opinion of the World Council of Churches when he writes that conversion and evangelism of Jews must be abandoned in favor of dialogue. He rejects Messianic Jews, Jews for Jesus and Hebrew Christians as groups based on a dispensationalist ("the time of the gentiles is coming to an end") and eschatological (the conversion of Israel at the end time has started) theology. The legitimate partners in dialogue must be the descendants of rabbinic Judaism and the official churches.

Some churches take this tendency to its logical conclusion and are willing to state that Judaism is a legitimate faith path in itself, without the need for Christ or Christianity. It is this theology that Lyosov hopes will be adopted by the Russian Church, linking it to her very survival.

Lyosov's approach finds a less strident echo in another figure in the Russian Orthodox Church, Fr. Sergei Haeckel, who also came close to that opinion. Haeckel, who in his youth was a member of the Russian Christian youth movement founded by Sergei Bulgakov, may have been influenced by Bulgakov's dictum that "it is forbidden to preach Christ to Jews" due to the inadequate testimony of Christian lives. In a 1998 paper entitled "The relevance of western post-Holocaust theology to the thought and practice of the Russian Orthodox Church," Haeckel pointed to the Catholic Church's renunciation of supersessionism as a model for the Russian Church to emulate[11].

How does Men's theology, and by extension that of the "Solovievan school," relate to these post-Auschwitz developments, which are finally trickling into the consciousness of Russian Orthodoxy? After the disintegration of the Soviet

---

[10] Voll, Fritz, "What about Jewish Christians or Christian Jews?" At: http://www.jcrelations.net/en/?item=961

[11] "Formerly, it would have been accepted that the Christian Church is the New Israel, which overshadows or displaces the Israel of old. More and more is it realised now that this theory was long ago rejected by its supposed originator, St Paul." In Fr S Haeckel, "The Relevance of Western post-Holocaust theology to the Thought and Practice of the Russian Orthodox Church." http://www.jcrelations.net/en/?item=937

space in which his Jewish-Christian theology flourished, has he lost relevance to the contemporary dialogue between Christian churches and Jewish groups? After all, this dialogue is built on very different assumptions and realities than Men knew. There are several points to be made.

Firstly, in 2008 Pope Benedict XVI shocked many when during Lent he incorporated an old but adapted prayer into the Lenten services: "Let us also pray for the Jews that God our Lord should illuminate their hearts, so that they will recognize Jesus Christ, the Savior of all men." Rabbi David Rosen, director of religious affairs for the American Jewish Committee, found the addition "disappointing" and a troubling abandonment of the previous prayer which called merely for the Jews' "redemption," without specifying the means[12]. He had believed that this implied a recognition of Jewish redemption through Judaism[13].

However, the Catholic Church's apparent abandonment of supersessionism was based on Paul's comment in Romans 9-11. As we have seen amply, it would be stretching this text, as well as Paul's entire theology, to make it mean that the Jews do not need Christ. Benedict's addition thus merely added honesty to an ambiguous lacuna. In reality, therefore, the Solovievan position (down to his final prayer for the Jews) and that of one of the main participants in Jewish-Christian dialogue does not differ.

A second point concerns the charge that Men was a "captured child," a Jew who never had the chance to experience Judaism, and was unfulfilled in Russia. This is also intended to question the validity of Men's theology and pastoral work. However, even disregarding the *ad hominem* nature of the charge, one might say that such an accusation is no less "racist" than Men was supposed to be: can Jews really only find fulfillment in Jewish culture and religion? What makes them incapable of fitting into other cultures? One can see the slippery slope open up before one's eyes.

Of course, this judgment also implies that all Jews who convert to Christianity (but not Buddhism, for example) are delusional – rather a dangerous judgment to make about a highly intelligent and dedicated man, in Men's case, one would think, not to mention people like Semyon Frank.

A related charge brought by Men's critics is that he was involved in "deception" in seducing Jews with the treasures of Russian literature and culture. This is seen as an idolatrous substitute for the Jewish religion. In the post-Auschwitz context, the further implication is that Men's type of theology contributes to "Hitler's posthumous victory," in leading to the assimilation of the Jewish people. Hence, Christians who wish to consider Jewish sensibilities should reject the Men

---

[12] New York Times, Feb.6, 2008.
[13] A more nuanced position was expressed by David Berger, who accepted that there was nothing unethical about Christians praying for the conversion of Jews at the end of days, but expresses concern when that desire is brought to the table of interfaith dialogue, so clouding the purpose of the latter. David Berger, "Let's clarify the purpose of interfaith dialogue," in The Jerusalem Post, Feb.16, 2008.

phenomenon no less than they do dispensationalist evangelicals.

However, the charge of Russophilic idolatry is also slightly odd. Zionism was a secular ideology. The devotees of Hebrew revival saw in the language a reassertion of the national spirit and were little concerned with the actual content of the writings of the ancient prophets; the self-termed Canaanites even looked to the pagan inhabitants of Palestine as their inspiration. Why should secular Zionism and linguistic revivalism be seen as less "idolatrous" than immersion in Russian culture and philosophy, whose roots – as we saw – are embedded in the religious and cultural concerns of Jewish culture itself? After all, this was an immersion that for both Christians and Jews (like Steinberg) was also an emergence into human all-unity.

In addition, as far as Hitler's posthumous victory is concerned, Jewish critics themselves have seen in Fackenheim's six hundred and fourteenth commandment to remain a Jew for no other reason than that Hitler wished to destroy Jews a paradigmatic case of putting nationality before God, i.e. of committing idolatry.

As far as Men's "poaching" of Jewish souls is concerned, the accusations made by Lyosov and Feingold (and Ella Graifer[14]) also echo accusations against Messianic Judaism that it lures Jews to Christianity under false pretenses. However, a closer comparison reveals a crucial difference– even beyond the fact that like Soloviev, Bulgakov and Karsavin, Men had no room for "Torah Christianity"[15].

---

[14] "O vykrestax i ob Alexandre Mene," where she compares Men to a particularly undesirable type of Jewish apostate who desires the harm of his former people. Thus Men and rabid Jewish anti-Semites like Jacob Brafmann seem to be equated. (The article can be found on http.berkovich-zametki.com). For a pro-Men persepective see: E.Levin, "Pochemu tak mnogo russkoyazichnykh yevreev obrashchaetsja v khristianstvo?" and an article written closer to the time of the Feingold-Men dispute: Yaakov Krotov, "10 Marta 1970 goda: Izrail' protiv yevreev-khristian." (www.krotov.info).

[15] Again, a serious discussion of the various theologies of contemporary Messianic Judaism would take us too far afield. One important point should be made in discussing Men. He refers to the Jerusalem Council of 51 a.d., in which a decision was taken by the Jewish Christian majority to permit gentiles to convert to Christianity without taking on the yoke of Torah observance. Men observes that this implies the prior legitimacy of Jewish Christians who do and should observe the Torah. He comments that this decision and the *status quo* regarding Jewish Christians endorsed by it was never abrogated by a council, and thus canonically still stands. In this he shows parallels with a contemporary Romanian Orthodox priest, Fr. Vasili Mihoc, who is the only member of JCII (Jerusalem Council II), a cross-denominational Christian group whose vision is for a second Jerusalem Council that will revive the decision to let Jews enter the church without abandoning their Jewish identity, and it would seem, religion. Both Men and Mihoc raise interesting questions. Men's mention of the Jerusalem Council implies that early "Torah Christianity" could be a model for a contemporary Judeo-Christianity. But he goes on to explicitly deny that Christianity is compatible with observance of Jewish ritual laws. Mihoc's

This lies in the fact that Men was not fundamentalist about his Judeo-Christian vision.

Men left room for Jews to return to Judaism in Israel, and expressed a desire only that Jews who chose Christianity should be allowed to practice it in freedom of conscience in the Jewish State: "The majority of people [in Israel] have fallen away from any faith, and live without religion. We should now consider it good if there is not imposed on these people some sort of official state religion…but that they should have a choice. If they return to Judaism, good; if they seek other options, that is also good. If they come to Christianity, they will not cease to be Jews, but will be connected more solidly with their tradition. But this will already be not tradition in the archaic sense of the term, not in the closed-national sense, but in the broad, universal, powerful sense, as with the very foundation of the Church."

Thus, like Soloviev and his heirs, Men was a "universalist realist." That is, on the one hand, he could not abandon the premise that truth is universal. He once asked a newly religious Jew whether he thought Judaism was true. The answer was that Judaism was true for Jews. For Men, truth had to be true for all humans. Thus, in his books, despite his evident fascination with Eastern religions[16] he ultimately presents them as precursors to the full truth of Christ. On the other hand, his strict realism was tempered by hope and mercy: he could not believe that the walls between Christian denominations could reach up to heaven, or that God would neglect the righteous of other faiths.

This universalism tempered by sensitivity to local detail may be the heritage of the philosophy of all-unity, as well as that multiplicity-in-unity preached in the Slavophile thought of Khomiakov, with his restated doctrine of *sobornost*. In this sense, another important difference between Messianic Judaism and Men's Judeo-Christianity is that, despite Lyosov's criticisms, Men was not inflexible or dogmatic about the relationship between Judaism and Christianity. His approach was not to weave a theology out of disembodied scriptural quotations. Rather, he looked to the realities of concrete situations.

If converted Jews wished to "become Russians," and this suited their path, he accepted that. Nor did he pretend that his own parish was an example of Judeo-Christianity. As he put it: "I fear that today Judeo-Christianity does not exist. That is a myth." For him Judeo-Christianity was a future hope, connected to the foundation of the State of Israel, where enough Jews with Jewish consciousness might gather to make it a real possibility. The process could not be unilateral. Men envisioned the co-operation of the apostolic churches and the approval of the Jewish community and State. As it turned out, towards the end of his life the

---

position about the compatibility of Orthodox Christianity and some form of Jewish observance has also not been articulated explicitly, so ambiguity remains in both cases. (I rely on personal communications for Mihoc's opinions; he has published nothing on the subject).

[16] E.g. Aleksandr Men, *U vrat molchaniya*. (Moscow: Fond Imeni Aleksandra Menya, 2002).

strength of opposition from the Jewish government in Israel began to tell on his hopes for such a realization[17].

But if Jewish humanity, and its no less important supporting partners, was not in a position to embody Christ historically in Jewish forms, Men was not so abstract or rigid as to see this as a lasting failure. That is, he was never tempted into sectarianism by his hopes, always maintaining a sense of the broadness of the Church and its embodiedness in any gathering of Christian humanity, including his work in Russia. In that sense, he was rooted deeply in the Orthodox understanding of the Church as a divine-human synergy.

Benevich: no Jew, no gentile – no Russian?

Here, it is interesting to compare Men's openness to historical options with a much more categorically stated option for Russian Jewish Christians voiced recently by Gregory Benevich in his article *The Jewish Question in the Russian Orthodox Church*[18].

Benevich, a Jew baptized into the Russian Church, argues that Orthodoxy cannot accept the categories "Jew" and "gentile" as referring to ethnic Jews and non-Jews. Instead, the only "Jew" is the New Israel, the Church. The other Jews are impostors, and the anti-Jewish rhetoric of Chrysostom and other Fathers is, indeed unpleasant, but "who ever said…that Christianity was established to bring us pleasure….the Orthodox Fathers' attitude towards Jews does not at all frighten those Jews who become Orthodox Christians in Russia." Thus anti-Semitism is a sort of spiritual ascesis for the converted Jew, which can help him on the path to Christ.

Benevitch is germane here too, for he also denies the need for a post-Auschwitz theology. In this sense, he is close to Men, due one feels to their

---

[17] The Catholic Church has expressed its support for Jewish-Christian communities. Cf. Elias Friedman, *Jewish Identity*. (New York: The Miriam Press, 1987). The Israeli State's decision to consider baptized Jews non-Jewish for the sake of immigration is part of the general non-acceptance of Jewish-Christians in the Jewish world.

[18] Grigory Benevich, "The Jewish Question in the Russian Orthodox Church." At http://www.ocf.org/OrthodoxPage/reading/jewish_1.html . As can be imagined, Men's assertion that Christianity was not incompatible with Jewish identity has spawned a large literature. Here I have selected a handful of figures to represent aspects of the debate. For an overview of other aspects, see the balanced assessment of Konstantin Antonov, "Problema samosoznaniye yevreev-khristian." Diaspory No.3 (2004):168-190. In passing, Antonov makes the good point that in many ways Russian-Jewish consciousness since the fall of the Soviet Union has not radically changed, so that the situation Men was addressing continues to have relevance. A recent interesting continuation of the debate can be seen in the conversation between Yakov Krotov (an Orthodox priest of Jewish background who allies himself with Men's heritage); Pinchas Polonsky (a Russian-born rabbi, whose recent book *Dve tysyachi let vmeste* argues that Judaism and Christianity are complementary faiths, thus departing from the hostility of Feingold and Graifer); and Gleb Yastrebov (a Russian Orthodox New Testament scholar). http://www.krotov.info/yakov/3_vera/3_radio/20090530.htm

common Russian-Soviet experience. Benevitch states his convictions more explicitly, though: "In Russia, we have no analogy to this theology....because the Russian people underwent a different experience. Instead of Nazism, we had communism...So, what we need is a post-Kolyma theology," even though in future "it would be essential to compare lessons from Kolyma and Auschwitz."

This puts Benevitch in direct conflict with both Lyosov and Men – for different reasons. As far as the latter is concerned, Benevitch would reject Men's continued assertion of his Jewish identity and his encouragement of it in his parishioners. He reads Paul's "no Jew, and no gentile" not as a relative diminishing of the distinction (after the model of "no man, no woman"), but as an absolute abolition of these categories. Men, with his sense of the survival of the individual parts in the all-unity, had come to a Bulgakovian approach to this Pauline verse.

It would take us too far afield to evaluate these different approaches, but a short comment can be made. Benevitch's approach about an ascetic approach to anti-Semitism is perhaps pastorally useful, given some Russian church anti-Semitism[19]. But his exclusive focus on Kolyma rather than Auschwitz perhaps assumes an excessive uniqueness of the Russian situation, and implies a belief that none but Russians will join the Russian Church.

In other words, having dismissed the categories of Jew and gentile – contra Men's continuing appeal to them – in a quest for universalism, he ends up with a new category: Russian. And, of course, his approach ignores the fact that many Russian Jews were deported to Auschwitz. Russia, still less the Russian Church, is thus not as hermetically separate from the rest of Europe as Benevitch would have us believe.

Nonetheless, for many baptized Jews outside Men's community, Benevitch's approach describes their theological self-identity quite well. Such Jews, having never experienced anything but the most marginal Soviet Jewishness, do not really see themselves as having much Jewishness to preserve. Their only Jewish

---

[19] Nonetheless, accepting and endorsing anti-Jewish rhetoric in the Church does a disservice not only to converted Jews but to anti-Semites. It is surely a truism that the Church is a place of love; to allow, and theologically approve of, statements attacking the basic humanity of groups or individuals is to give the message to the latter that hatred is not a sin, does not need repentance, and so on. The Church would then be failing in its mission of pastoral guidance, and in its task to bring souls to salvation. As regards Jews being required to deny their Jewishness, this equates Jewishness with sinfulness. There are, of course, aspects of Jewishness that include the anti-Christian parts of Judaism – and those would be incompatible with Christian faith. But there are aspects which are not. The same might be said for any ethnic identity, Russianness, Greekness, Americanness, and so on – though the blend of ethnic and religious in Jewish identity complicates matters. (As far as Greekness is concerned, the parallel is close: where Greek pride relies on aspects of the pagan Hellenic past, it too is incompatible with Christianity).

identity comes from external anti-Semitism. The Church for them is really an immersion into that deep universalism of the Byzantine-Russian tradition in which, as far as they are concerned, there is no Russian or Jew or Tatar.

Theologically, Benevitch's approach could be defended as well as Men's, and it avoids the complications of the "Judeo-Christian" dilemma – not, of course, that that makes it correct. However, while diverging from Lyosov's liberal theology, Benevitch is in fact allied with him and Goldfarb on one count: Benevitch is quite clear that a Christian with Jewish roots is in no sense a *bona fide* Jew. Thus Goldfarb, Lyosov and Benevitch can all agree that the Russian Orthodox Church contains no Jews, or people of indeterminate "dual" religiosity. They form a united front, in other words, against the theology of "double chosenness."

In this respect, despite its claim to be "ascetic," Benevitch's theology is more comfortable than Men's, and for all its boldly stated conservatism and insistence on the letter of tradition, it offers comfort to Jewish conservatives too: they can be assured that its harsh message will not lure Jews away from their fold, or confuse them, as the existence of a fluid, loosely defined parish of Christians of Jewish background and consciousness might do. Here is a clear-cut religion and ideology with comprehensibly pristine concepts that they can readily understand. For "gentiles," it also has the advantage of solving the Jewish question: a Benevitch-style "Jewish" Christian will not be tempted to "Judaize" through sentimental reversion to his roots. Boundaries are preserved all round[20]. In a sense, Orthodox Judaism and Orthodox Christianity make a pact in Benevitch's theology to divide humanity between them – even if that is not Benevitch's initial intention.

However, to explore Benevitch's approach further would take us too far afield, and as we saw Men and Benevich are not mutually exclusive, for Men too did not in practice reject the assimilation of converted Jews in the Russian church, if that is what they wished.

Conclusion: Russian Orthodoxy and Jewish-Christian dialogue – a note

In concluding, we will once more return to Men in the context of Russian religious thought – with the judgment still suspended as to whether his overall approach is the only one that can be adopted in forging an approach to Jewish-Christian relations. Having considered and responded to some of Lyosov's and others' criticisms regarding the inadequacy of Men's theology with respect to the post-Auschwitz turn in Jewish-Christian relations, we can ask again ourselves: does Men's approach have anything to contribute today?

---

[20] M.Agursky is a Jewish critic of Men who criticised Men for undermining both Russian and Jewish nationalism; he is thus a good example of how both Jews and Christians can agree on disagreeing with Men. M.Agursky, "Pamyati Aleksandra Menya," in 'Nasha strana', Tel Aviv.14.12.1990, p.6.

In answer to this question, I would suggest that like Frank, Soloviev, and Karsavin, Men shows that it is possible to embrace a realist theology of Christianity while still having a manifold sensitivity for the humanity of those who have chosen a different path. The Solovievian option is thus not entirely discredited, even after the tragedy of the Holocaust. Men also leaves open the possibility, also explored by these writers, that in the twentieth century Jewishness – especially as it encountered Russianness – might take forms that are not connected to rabbinic Judaism. This was, after all, an option explored by the Zionists as well.

Again, the dispensationalist and eschatological urgency of fundamentalist Messianic Judaism which has often led to a head-count approach to Jewish conversion, as well as a year-count approach to the devoutly to-be-wished end-time, is lacking in Men. Hence, even the partial, transient manifestation of Jewish Christianity that suited the human situation of his own place and time was valued by Men, even though strictly speaking he insisted that this experience could not be equated with Judeo-Christianity. In other words, Men's approach avoided many of the undesirable aspects of Messianic Judaism with its roots in dispensationalist fundamentalism.

Lyosov questioned whether the Russian Orthodox Church has a future. He proposed, contrary to Men, that it would not if it did not abandon core dogmas. However, such a move would result in an institution that resembled its historic forebear in name alone. It is thus better that Jewish partners in dialogue with the Russian or Roman Catholic Church be aware of what its core dogmas are. The ambiguity that survived in the Catholic Church's temporary omission of a prayer for the Jews did no service to Christian or Jew. Men's traditionalism in core dogmatic matters is thus an advantage.

However, within those parameters Haekel's suggestions that the Russian Church follow the Catholic Church in educating its members about the history of Christian anti-Semitism can only be enthusiastically endorsed. They include removing language that while not dangerous for sympathetic and theologically sensitive people can be a stumbling-block to the uninformed or malicious; considering the context of anti-Jewish rhetoric in the Fathers; and generally encouraging a non-idolatrous attitude to patristic writings.

As I discussed at length in the chapter on Bulgakov, there is no doubt that anti-Jewish attitudes mar the writings of many of Soloviev's heirs, and that such rhetoric is unacceptable as such (for all Benevitch's reverential approach to patristic anti-Judaism), and all the more so after the Holocaust, and indeed the pogroms that marred Jewish-Russian relations from the 1880s to the Civil War – not to mention of course the one and a half million Jews murdered on Soviet territory during the Second World War, often with the collaboration of the local Orthodox, or ancestrally Orthodox, population.

Of course, all of these tasks are part of the Church's endeavor to be true to the message she contains within herself – a statement which can only have meaning if one takes a realist approach to the dogma that the Church is the body of Christ on earth, a divine-human organism that offers salvation to all humanity, Jew or gentile, male or female, free or slave.

Meanwhile, in the enthusiasm for dialogue, the vast differences between Judaism and Christianity must not be ignored. Part of dialogue might consist in simply discovering what these differences are – a useful task for neighbors intending to live next to each other for the foreseeable future.

Thus, another Orthodox participant in Orthodox Christian-Jewish dialogue, Fr. Vitaly Borovoy, for all his good will made certain statements in a 1993 paper[21], which would need to be expanded. There he emphasizes many times that Judaism and Orthodoxy share common roots in the Old Testament, that both worship the same God. And yet, at the same time he states with admirable frankness and directness that the Old Testament is only a guide to bring children in faith to the New Testament. He also quotes Archbishop Nicanor's (1884) statement that the fullness of the truth of Christianity will only be complete once it includes Jewry, just as "the fullness of Jewry of the Old Testament will only become full once it becomes Christian."

Thus Borovoy embraces the stand held by most Russian religious philosophers and several bishops and priests of the nineteenth century Russian church. Many Orthodox Christians would not wish to dissent from these views. However, it seems to me that one must be prepared to acknowledge that while it might seem to such an Orthodox speaker that he is laying out the finest philo-Semitic gems of his tradition, Jews must still perceive these statements as insulting to their core beliefs – for they are none other than traditional supersessionism. In other words, even these statements should rather be delivered in an explanatory, reconciling way.

Elsewhere, Borovoy mentions Soloviev, Berdyaev, Bulgakov, Frank and Shestov as reconcilers and practitioners of eirenic Jewish-Christian dialogue. If heavily qualified, this statement could be accepted as true. It has been part of the purpose of this book, however, to explore those qualifications. For there is, of course, ample material in all of these writers to make Jewish believers think they are sitting face to face with yet another case of Russian Judeophobia. In this sense, Lyosov's criticisms of Russian religious thought, as well as Leonid Katsis's work on the anti-Semitic presuppositions of even some of those hierarchs who ardently defended Jews, should all be welcome criticism. In sum, Russian religious philosophy if approached rightly can be seen as an important source of inspiration for dialogue between Orthodox Christianity and Judaism.

One final point needs to be made – a crucial qualification of what has been stated above. To an extent, it is correct to see an opposition between two camps, who we can equate with Alexander Men, on the one hand, and Sergei Lyosov on the other. The former reject the possibility that Christianity can tolerate Judaism

---

[21] Protoierei Vitaly Borovoy, "Pravoslavnoe khristianstvo v sovremennom mire." www.golubinski.ru/russia/borovoy/soder_08.htm

as a legitimate faith path for Jews outside of Christianity. The latter see such toleration as the only possible path for Russian Orthodoxy. And yet, some of our in-depth analyses of the writings of Soloviev, Bulgakov and Karsavin indicate that this is, to some extent, a false dichotomy.

For the fact of the matter is that Soloviev and Bulgakov both drew extremely close to a recognition that it was not necessarily good for Christians to preach historical Christianity to Jews, or for the latter to embrace it. Karsavin went even further: although he nowhere put it down in writing, it seems that his experiences with Jews, including crucially his friendship with Steinberg, led him to accept – in practice, if not in theory – that Jews were assured of the presence of God within the parameters of their Judaism, so that conversion might not always be desirable. Finally, V.V.Zenkovsky came closest of all of these thinkers to stating in writing that Judaic Jews have a legitimate role to play in the salvation of all-humanity[22].

I myself argued in ch.2 that Bulgakov's "Judeology" already contains the seeds of a theology that could accept Judaism on its own terms. It is true that none of these thinkers state this view explicitly, and in their writings such "dual covenantism" sits uneasily beside their embrace of supersessionist presuppositions. Elsewhere[23], I have developed further the sketch of such a

---

[22] In this respect, another contemporary Orthodox voice that expresses tolerance for Judaism can be found in the remarks of the Serbian religious psychologist, Vladeta Erotich. He sets this tolerance in an even broader context, expressing support for Jewish and Islamic "fundamentalists" who exhort the believers of their own tradition to faithfully observe its Godly precepts. By "fundamentalist" he means those who are true to the fundaments of their religion, and he contrasts this tendency with that towards syncretism, which in his opinion weakens the divine basis of these revelations. He further expresses disapproval of "proselytism," which he interprets as a forced and artificial attempt to uproot people from their native faith – allowing, however, that there can be genuine conversions, but only on a rare and individual basis. In this context he writes (Erotich, 2007, p.93) that "among the world religions Judaism has been less inclined to proselytism than Islam and Christianity, and among Christian religions least inclined has been Orthodoxy." Thus, Jewish non-proselytism is a model that Christians should aim towards. It should be noted that his books have been published with the blessing of the Serbian Patriarch, and the Russian translation of his *Christianity and the psychological problems of our time* was published by the press of the Moscow Patriarchate, with the blessing of Patriarch Cyril. Erotich's inter-religious tolerance, no doubt partly a fruit of his Balkan background, could be theologically deepened by reference to Zenkovsky, Bulgakov and Karsavin. Cf. Vladeta Erotich, *Korabl' spaseniya*. Moscow: Sibirskaya blagovonitsa, 2007; Vladeta Erotich, *Khristianstvo i psykhologicheskiye problemy cheloveka*. Moscow: Izdatelskii sovet Russkoy Pravoslavnoy Tserki, 2009.

[23] Dominic Rubin, "Judaism, Christianity and All-Unity," paper presented at the International Conference on the theme of All-Unity and Universalism, Bose, Italy, 22-25 October, 2009. For other efforts to develop some of the thoughts in earlier

dual covenant theology based on Bulgakovian premises, but here there is only space to comment that there is still work to be done in studying what Russian religious philosophy can teach us about the relationship between Judaism and Christianity in the present age. However, it is too early to say what direction such research might ultimately take.

---

chapters, cf. also: Dominic Rubin, "Yevreistvo, iudaizm i Russkoe Pravoslavie v zerkale russkoi religioznoi mysli: k sovremennomu pravoslavnomu podkhodu k iudaizmu," paper read at St Andrew's annual readings of the St Andrew's Biblical Theological Institute, Moscow, 13 December 2009.

Bibliography

Ahad ha-Am, (Asher Ginzberg). "Al Shtei Ha-Se'ipim," in *The Collected Writings of Ahad ha-Am*. Jerusalem: The Jewish Publishing House, 1956.

Agurski, Mikhail. "Universalistkie tendentsii v yevreiskoi religioznoi mysli." VRKD No.140, III-IV.(1993):61-71.

-----. "Pamyati Aleksandra Menya." 'Nasha strana'. Tel Aviv.14.12.1990: p.6.

Akao, Mitsuo. "'Yevreiski' vopros kak russkii. (Obshchestvennoe dvizhenie russkykh pisatiley v zashchitu yevreev v poslednie desyatiletie tsarskoi Rossii.)" http://src-h.slav.hokudai.ac.jp/coe21/publish/no17_ses/11akao.pdf

Aksakov, Ivan. *Nashe znamya – russkaya narodnost'*. Moscow: Institut russkoi sivilizatsii, 2008.

-----. "Ne ob emansipatsii yevreev sleduet tolkovat', a ob emansipatsii russkyx ot yevreev." Rus' 15 July, 1867

-----. "Vozzvaniye Kremyo, obrashennoe k yevream ot litsa 'Vsemirnogo Izrail'skogo Soyuza'." *Rus'*, 1. Nov.1883.

Alfeev, Hilarion. *Svyashchennaya tayna tserkvi. Vvedenie v istoriyu i problematiku imyaslavskikh sporov*. St. Petersburg: Izdatel'stvo 'Aleteia', 2002.

-----. Official website: http://orthodoxeurope.org/page/11/1/1.aspx

Antonov, Konstantin. "Problema samosoznaniye yevreev-khristian." Diaspory No.3 (2004):168-190.

Arjakovsky, Antoine. "The Sophiology of Father Sergius Bulgakov and Contemporary Western Theology." Paper presented at the Sergius Bulgakov conference at the Russian House of Emigration, Moscow, Russia, March, 2001.

Asproulis, Nikolaos. "Creation and creaturehood. The neo-patristic alternative worldview of totalitarianism (all-unity, universalism). A brief approach to G.Florovsky's theology." Paper read at the conference on All-Unity and Universalism, Bose, Italy, 22-25 October, 2009.

Auden, Wystan.H. "The Sea and the Mirror." In W.H.Auden, *Collected Poems*. London: Faber and Faber, 1976.

Bar-Yosef, Hamutal. "Jewish-Christian relations in Modern Hebrew and Yiddish literature: A preliminary sketch." http://www.bgu.ac.il/~baryosef/Eng/research/jewish_christian.htm

-----. "The Jewish reception of Vladimir Solovyov." In *Vladimir Solovyov: Reconciler and Polemicist*, ed. Ewert von Zweerde, Peeters, Lewen, 2000.

-----. "Recreating Jewish identity in Bialik's poems: the Russian context." http://www.bgu.ac.il/~baryosef/Eng/research/jewish_identity.htm

-----. "Sophiology and the Concept of Femininity in Russian Symbolism and in Modern Hebrew Poetry." In *Modern Jewish Studies* 2/1, (2003):59-78.

-----. "Bialik and the Russian Revolutions," in *Jews in Eastern Europe* 1(29)(1996): 5-31.

Beckett, Samuel. *More Pricks Than Kicks*. New York: Grove Press, 1972.

Belous, Vladimir. *Volphila* 1. Moscow: Tri Kvadrata, 2005.

-----. *Volphila* 2. Moscow: Tri Kvadrata, 2005.

―――. *Volphila, ili, Krizis kultury v zerkale obshchestvennogo samosoznaniya*. Moscow: Mir, 2007.

―――. "A.Z.Shteinberg o smysli istorii." In *Volphila, ili, Krizis kultury v zerkale obshchestvennogo samosoznaniya*, 307-335. Moscow: Mir, 2007.

―――. "A.Z. Shteinberg." In *Volphila* 2, 581-648. Moscow: Tri Kvadrata, 2005.

―――. Edit. "Platon. 7 Noyabrya 1920." In *Volphila* 1, 385-402. Moscow: Tri Kvadrata, 2005.

―――. Edit."Pamyati F.M. Dostoevskogo. Oktyabr' 1921." In *Volphila* 1, 498-801. Moscow: Tri Kvadrata, 2005.

Bely, Andrei. *The Silver Dove*. Trans. John Elsworth. London: Angel Books, 2000.

―――. "Vospominaniya.Mezhdu dvukh revolyutsii." In *Andrei Bely. Izbrannaya proza*, ed. L.A. Smirnova, 297-439. Moscow: Sovietskaya Rossia, 1988.

Benevich Grigory. "The Jewish Question in the Russian Orthodox Church." At http://www.ocf.org/OrthodoxPage/reading/jewish_1.html

Berdyaev, Nicolai. *The Meaning of History*. London: Centenary Press, 1936.

―――. "Osnovnaya ideya filosofii L'va Shestova." *Put'*, No. 58 (1938-1939): 44-48.

―――. "Lev Shestov (po sluchayu ego semidesyatiletiya)." *Put'*, No.50, (1935/6):50-52.

―――. "Tragedia i obydennost'." In *Tipy religioznoy mysly v Rossii//Sobraniye Sochenenii* 3, 363-398. Paris: YMCA-Press, 1989.

―――. "Lev Shestov i Kirkegor." In *Tipy religioznoy mysly v Rossii//Sobraniye Sochenenii* 3, 398-407. Paris: YMCA-Press, 1989.

―――. "Russkii soblazn. (Po povodu 'Serebryanogo golubya' A.Belova.)" In *Tipy religioznoy mysly v Rossii//Sobraniye Sochenenii* 3, 407-413. Paris: YMCA-Press, 1989.

―――. "Novoe khristianstvo. (D.S. Merezhkovskii)." In *Tipy religioznoy mysly v Rossii// Sobraniye Sochenenii* 3, 487-516. Paris: YMCA-Press, 1989.

―――. "O knige S.L.Franka 'Nepostizhimoe'." In *Tipy religioznoy mysly v Rossii//Sobraniye Sochenenii* 3, 650-655. Paris: YMCA-Press, 1989.

―――. *Russkaya Ideya*, St.Petersburg: Azbuka-klassika, 2008.

―――. "Khristianstvo i antisemitizm. (Religioznaya sudba yevreistva)." *Put'* No.56. (1938):3-18.

―――. *Samosoznanie*. Moscow: 'Kniga', 1991.

―――. "Opyt eskhatologicheskoy metafisiki: Tvorchestvo i objektivatsia," in Berdyaev N.A., *Tsarstvo Dukha i tsarstvo Kesarja*, Moskva, 1995.

―――. "Tipy religioznoy mysly v Rossii"//*Sobraniye. Sochenenii*. 3, Paris: YMCA-Press, 1989.

―――. *Mirovozreniye Dostoyevskogo*. Prague: YMCA-press, 1923.

―――. *Sud'ba Rossii*. Moscow: Sovetskii pisatel', 1990.

―――. *Filosofia neravenstva*.Paris: YMCA-Press, 1990.

Berger, David. "Let's clarify the purpose of interfaith dialogue." Jerusalem Post, Feb.16, 2008.

Berlin, P.A. "Russkie mysliteli i yevrei." *Novy Zhurnal*, No.70. (1962):256-270.

Blok, Aleksandr. *Stikhotvoreniya i poemy*. Moscow: Khudozhestvennaya literatura, 1983.

Boobbyer, Phillip. *S. L. Frank. The Life and Work of a Russian Philosopher, 1877-1950*. Athens: Ohio University Press, 1995.

―――. *S.L.Frank. Zhizn' i tvorchestvo russkogo filosofa*.Moscow: Rosspen, 2001.

Borovoy, Vitaly. "Pravoslavnoe khristianstvo v sovremennom mire." www.golubinski.ru/russia/borovoy/soder_08.htm.

Boyarin, Daniel. *A Radical Jew: Paul and the politics of identity.* California: University of California Press, 1994.

Bray, G. ed. *Bibleiskie kommentarii otsov tserkvi i drugikh avtorov I-VIII vekov. Noviy zavet. VI. Poslaniye k Rimlyanam.* Trans.D.Afinogenov and others. Moscow: Germenevtika, 2004.

Budinitsky, Oleg V. *Rossiskie yevrei mezhdu krasnymi i byelami (1917-1920).* Moscow: Rosspen, 2006.

Bulgakov, Sergei. *Avtobiograficheskiye zametki.* Paris, YMCA-Press, 1991.

-----. "Chto dayot sovremennomu soznaniyu filosofia Vladimira Solovieva?" *Voprosy filosofii i psykhologii,* No.66 (1903).

-----. "Russkaya tragedia," *Russkaya Mysl',* Bk.IV.(1914): 1-26.

-----. *Dela i dni.* Moscow: Sobraniye, 2008.

-----. *Neopublikovannie pisma S.N. Bulgakova k V.V.Rozanovu. Predislovie i kommentarii M.A. Kolerova.* Voprosi filosofii No.10, 1992.

-----. *Dva Grada.* Moscow: Astrel', 2008.

-----. "Golosa khristianskoi sovesti v Germanii." In *Put'* No.43, 1934: 62-71.

-----. "Iuda Iskariot Apostol Predatel' (dogmaticheskaya)," *Put'* No.27, (1931): 3-42.

-----. "Iuda Iskariot Apostol Predatel' (istoricheskaya)," *Put'* No.26, (1931): 3-60.

-----. "Nekotoriye cherty religioznogo mirovozzreniya L.I.Shestova," *Sovromeniye Zapiski,* No.68, Paris, 1939.

-----. *Filosofia imeni,* Moscow: Nauka, 1998.

-----. *Tikhie dumy. Etika, Kul'tura, Sofiologia.* St.Petersburg: Olega-Obyshko, 2008.

-----. *Filosofia xozaistva,* Moscow: Astrel', 2008.

-----. *Malaya trilogia. (Kupina neopalimaya. Drug zhenikha. Lestvitsa Iakovlya.)* Moscow: Obshchedostupniy pravoslavnii universitet, osnovannii protoiereem Aleksandrom Menem, 2008.

-----. *O chudesakh yevangelskikh.* Moscow: *Russkiy Put',* 1994.

-----. *Khristianstvo i yevreiski vopros.*Paris: YMCA-Press, 1991.

-----. *Sion.* Moscow: Shchit' (1915):32-35.

-----. "Rasizm i khristianstvo," in *Tajna izrailja. 'Yevreiskii vopros v russkoi religioznoi mysli kontsa XIX-pervoi polovinoi XX vv.* (St Petersburg, Sophia: 1993), 352-406.

-----. "Sudba Izrailya kak krest' Bogomateri," in *Tayna Izrailya. 'Yevreiskii vopros v russkoi religioznoi mysli kontsa XIX-pervoi polovinoi XX vv.* (St Petersburg, Sophia: 1993), 348-452.

-----. *Sophia. The wisdom of God. An outline of sophiology.* Translated by Boris Jakim. Lindisfarne Press, 1993.

-----. *Svet Nevecherniy.* Moscow: Respublika, 1994.

-----. "Svyashchennik O. Pavel Florenskii," in *Vestnik RSKhD,* 1971, No.101-102. (Reprinted in S.N.Bulgakov, *Dela i Dni*, Moscow: Sobranie, 208: 287-298.)

-----. *The Bride of the Lamb.* Translated by Boris Jakim. Michigan: Eerdmans, 2002.

-----. *The Lamb of God.* Translated by Boris Jakim. Michigan: Eerdmans, 2008.

-----. *The Holy Grail and the Eucharist.* Translated by Boris Jakim. New York: Lindisfarne Books, 1997.

-----. *U sten Khersonisa* (manuscript, Yalta, 1923) reprinted in *Simvol*, Paris, No.25. (1991).

-----. *Put' parizhskogo bogosloviya.* Moscow: Khram svyatoi muchenitsy Tatiany pri MGU, 2007.

-----. *Towards a Russian political theology.* Texts edited and introduced by Rowan Williams. Edinburgh: T&T Clark, 1999.

Burbank, Jane. *Intelligentsia and Revolution. Russian views of Bolshevism, 1917-1922.* New York: OUP, 1986.
Burmistrov, Konstantin. "The interpretation of Kabbalah in early 20th-Century Russian Philosophy. Soloviev, Bulgakov, Florenskii, Losev." *East European Jewish Affairs*, Vol.37, No.2, August 2007:157-187.

Chamberlain, Lesley. *The Philosophy Steamer.* London: Atlantic books, 2006.
-----. "Jews on the Philosophy Steamer." The Jewish Quarterly, Spring 2006, No.201.
Cohen, Herman. *Religion of Reason out of the Sources of Judaism.* Atlanta, Georgia: Scholars Press, 1995.
Cohn-Sherbock, Dan (ed). *Holocaust Theology. A Reader.* Exeter Press, 2002.
-----. *The paradox of anti-Semitism.* London, New York: Continuum, 2006.
Coplestone, Frederick. *A history of philosophy: Russian philosophy (Vol.10).*London, New York: Continuum, 2003.
-----. *Russian religious philosophy. Selected aspects.* Search Press/Notre Dame, 1988.

Davidowicz, Lucy. *The Golden Tradition: Jewish Life and Thought in Eastern Europe.* New York: Syracuse University Press, 1996.
Davydov, Yuri.N. "Apokalipsis ateisticheskoi religii (S.N.Bulgakov kak kritik revolutsionistskoi religioznosti)." Introduction to *Dva Grada,* 4-51. Moscow: Astrel', 2008.
De Lange, Nicolas, and Freud-Kandel, Miri. *Modern Judaism. An Oxford Guide.* OUP, 2005.
Dostoevsky, Fyodor. *House of the Dead,* London: Penguin Books, 1987.
-----. *Crime and Punishment.* Harmondsworth: Penguin Books, 1983.
-----. *Dnevnik Pisatelya.Izbrannie stranitsy.* Moscow: Sovremmenik, 1989.

Eisenberg, Gilla, *De la rue Rollin à la rue Agron, à Jérusalem,* http://fondane.com/Gilla%20Eisenberg.htm.
Elior, Rachel. *The Mystical Origins of Hasidism.* Oxford/Portland, Oregon: The Littman Library of Jewish Civilization, 2006.
Epstein, Mikhail. "Khasid i talmudist.Sravnitel'nii opyt o Pasternake i Mandel'shtame." Zvezda No.4. (2004).
Epstein, Raya. "Post-Zionism and democracy." In Israel *and the post-Zionists: a nation at risk,* edited by Shlomo Sharan. Sussex Academic Press with ACPR publishers, 2003.
Erotich, Vladeta. *Korabl' spaseniya.* Moscow: Serbskaya blagovonitsa, 2007.
-----. *Khristianstvo i psykhologicheskiye problemy cheloveka.* Moscow: Izdatelskii Sovet Russkoy Pravoslavnoy Tserki, 2009.
Evtuhov, Catherine. "Bulgakov, Sergei Nikolayevich." *Encyclopedia of Russian History.* The Gale Group Inc. 2004. *Encyclopedia.com.* (October 4, 2009). http://www.encyclopedia.com/doc/1G2-3404100184.html

Fedotov, Gyorgy. *Svyatiye drevnei Rusi.* St.Petersburg: Satis derzhava, 2004.
-----. *Litso Rossii.* Paris: YMCA-Press, 1988.

―――. *Tyazhba o Rossii*. Paris: YMCA-Press, 1982.
―――. *Novoe na staruyu temu: k sovremennoy postanovke yevreiskogo voprosa*. Novy Zhurnal, No.1, 1940.
―――. "Berdyaev Myslitel," first published in Novii Zhurnal, XIX, New York, 1948. Also at: http://russianway.rchgi.spb.ru./Berdyaev/46_Fedotov.pdf
Fedotova, Evgeniya. Introduction to *Litso Rossii*, by G.P.Fedotov, i-xxxiv. Paris: YMCA-Press, 1988.
―――. "Vzglyady N.Berdyaeva na 'yevreiskii vopros', ix sootnesenie s traditsionnym khristianskim bogosloviem i novymi issledovaniyami." In *N.A.Berdyaev i yedinstvo Yevropeiskogo dukha*, edited by V.Porus, 132-142, Moscow: Bibleisko-bogoslovskii Institut sv. Apostola Andreya, 2007.
―――. "V.S.Soloviev kak predtecha iudeo-khristianskogo dialoga." In *Rossia i vselenskaya tserkov'. V.S. Soloviev i problema religioznogo i kul'turnogo edineniya chelovechestva*, edited by V.Porus, 237-247, Moscow: Bibleisko-bogoslovskii Institut sv. Apostola Andreya, 2004.
Feingold, Natan."Dialog ili missionerstvo? O 'dialogicheskoi' forme russkogo pravoslavnogo missionerstva sredi yevreev i o doctrine neoiudeokhristianstva." Soyuz religioznoy yevreiskoy intelligentsia iz SSSR i vostochnoy yevropy, Jerusalem, 1977.
Finkel, Stuart. *On the ideological front. The Russian Intelligentsia and the making of Soviet Public Sphere*. New Haven, Yale University Press, 2007.
Finkelstein, Eitan. *Neveziye Arona Steinberga*. Forum noveishey vostochoyevropeiskoi istorii i kultury – russkoe izdanie, No.1, 2005. http://www1.ku-eichstaett.de/ZIMOS/forum/inhaltruss3.html.
Florensky, Pavel. "Prof. D.A.Khvolson o ritual'nykh ubiystvakh." In *Obonyatenl'noe i osyaznatel'noe otnoshenie yevreev k krovi*, edited by A.N. Nikolyukin. Moscow: Respublika, 1998.
―――. "Iudei i sudba khristian. (Pismo k V.V.Rozanovu)." In *Obonyatenl'noe i osyaznatel'noe otnoshenie yevreev k krovi*, edited by A.N. Nikolyukin. Moscow: Respublika, 1998.
―――. " 'Ekhad'. Trinadtsat' ran Yushchinskogo." In *Obonyatenl'noe i osyaznatel'noe otnoshenie yevreev k krovi*, edited by A.N. Nikolyukin. Moscow: Respublika, 1998.
―――. "Chto mne sluchilos' uvidet'." In *Obonyatenl'noe i osyaznatel'noe otnoshenie yevreev k krovi*, edited by A.N. Nikolyukin. Moscow: Respublika, 1998. [Signed 'Pod zabralom' – under a visor, i.e. anonymously].
―――. "O terafimakh." In *Obonyatenl'noe i osyaznatel'noe otnoshenie yevreev k krovi*, edited by A.N. Nikolyukin. Moscow: Respublika, 1998.
―――. "Predislovie k sborniku 'Izrail' v proshlom, nastoyashchem, i budushchem.'" In *Sobraniye socheniye v 4 tomax*, Tom 2, 705-708. Moscow: Mysl, 1996.
―――. "Troitsa-Sergieva Lavra i Rossia." In *Voprosi religioznogo samosoznaniya*. Moscow, Ast: 2001.
―――. *Voprosi religioznogo samosoznaniya*. Moscow, Ast: 2001.
―――. *Salt of the Earth: Elder Isodore*. Translated by Richard Betts. St Herman of Alaska Brotherhood, 1999.
―――. *The Pillar and Ground of the Truth*. Translated by Boris Jakim. Princeton, Princeton University Press: 2004.

-----. *Predlogaemoe gosudarstvennoe ustroistvo v budushchem. Sbornik archivnykh materialov i statyei.* Compiled by Igumen Andronik (Trubachaev).Moscow: Gorodets, 2009.

-----. "Detyam moim. Vospominanya proshlykh dnyei," in *Imena*. Moscow: Eksmo, 2008.

-----. *Imena*. Moscow: Eksmo, 2008.

Florovsky, Gyorgy. "Rets.: Prof. N.N. Glubokovskii 'Pravoslavie po ego sushchestvu'. SPB.1914." In Sobolev A., *O Russkoy Filosofii*, 149-155.St Petersburg: Mir, 2008.

-----. *Puti russkogo bogoloviya*. Paris, YMCA-Press, 1983.

-----. *Creation and Redemption, The Collected Works*, Vol. III. Edited, Richard S. Haugh. Belmont, MA: Notable and Academic Books, 1989.

Fondane, Benjamine, *Entretiens avec Leon Chestov*: Mars 1935, Chez Madame Lovtzki, soeur de Chestov. www.angelfire.com/nb/shestov/fon/f_1.html

Fonrobert, Charlotte, and Jaffee, Martin, eds. *The Talmud and Rabbinic Literature*. Cambridge: CUP, 2007.

Frank, Semyon. *Russkoe Mirovozzrenie*. St Petersburg: Nauka, 1996.

-----. "Dva pisma Vy. Ivanovu." In S.L.Frank, *Russkoe Mirovozzrenie*, 95-98. St Petersburg: Nauka, 1996.

-----. "Predsmertnoe: vospominaniye i mysli." In S.L.Frank, *Russkoe Mirovozzrenie*, 39-58. St Petersburg: Nauka, 1996.

-----. "Eshcho o natzionalizme v filosofii. Otvet na otvet V.F.Erna." Russkaya Mysl', No.XI. (1910):130-137.

-----. "Filosofia Gegel'ja. (K stoletiyu dnya smerti Gegel'ja.)" Put' No.34.(1932):39-51.

-----. "Novaya kniga N.A.Berdyaeva. Russkaya mysl'." Kn.4.C. (1910): 136-141.

-----. "Novokantianskaya filosofia mifologii (Ernst Cassirer. *Philosophie der Symbolisher Formen. Teil 2: Das mystische Denken*. Berlin 1925.)" Put' No.4 1926: 190-1.

-----. "O natzionalizme v filosofii." Russkaya Mysl',Kn.IX. (1910):162-171.

-----. "Osnovnaya idyea filosofii Spinozy: k 300-letiyu dnya rozhdeniya 24 noyabrya 1632." Put', No.37.Feb. (1932):61-67.

-----. "Pamyati Yu.I.Aikhenvalda." Put', No. 15. February. (1929):125-126.

-----. *Sochineniya*. Moscow: Ast, 2000.

-----. "Pismo G.P.Fedotovu." Noviy zhurnal Kn.28, (1952): 288-289.

-----. "O zadachax poznaniya Pushkina." In S.L.Frank, *Russkoe Mirovozzrenie*, 248-273. St Petersburg: Nauka, 1996.

-----. "Religioznost' Pushkina." Put', No.40. (1933):16-39.

-----. "Pushkin i dukhovniy put' Rossii." In S.L.Frank, *Russkoe Mirovozzrenie*, 273-277. St Petersburg: Nauka, 1996.

-----. "Pushkin kak politicheskii myslitel'." In S.L.Frank, *Russkoe Mirovozzrenie*, 226-248. St Petersburg: Nauka, 1996.

-----. "Pushkin ob otnosheniyax mezhdu Rossii i Yevropy." In S.L.Frank, *Russkoe Mirovozzrenie*, 277-288. St Petersburg: Nauka, 1996.

-----. "Religioznaya filosofia Kogena." Russkaya mysl' No.12. (1915): 29-31.

-----. "Sushnost' i vedushchie motivy russkoi filosofii." First in German in Gral, 1925, No.8: 384-395. Translated into Russian by A.Ermichev and A.G.Vlaskina, in *Filosofskie nauki*, 1990, No.5. And in *Russkoe mirovozzrenie*, 149-161.

-----. *Realnost' i chelovek*. Moscow: Khranitel', 2007

-----. *Svet vo tme*. Moscow: Faktorial, 1998.

-----. *God with Us*. London: Jonathan Cape Ltd.,1946.

-----. *Zhivoe znaniye*. Berlin: Obelisk, 1923.
-----. "O L've Shestove (Po povodu ego novoi knigi 'Nachala i kontsi')." In S.L.Frank, *Russkoe Mirovozzrenie*, 574-578. St Petersburg: Nauka, 1996.
-----. *Rilke i slavianstvo* (1929). In S.L.Frank, *Russkoe Mirovozzrenie*, 609-613. St Petersburg: Nauka, 1996.
-----. "Svetlaya pechal'." In S.L.Frank, *Russkoe Mirovozzrenie*, 288-302. St Petersburg: Nauka, 1996.
-----. "Filosofia vetkho-zavetnogo mira." *Put'* No.19,(1929):109-113.
-----. *Nepostizhimoe*. In Semyon Frank, *Sochineniya*. Moscow: Ast, 2000.
-----. "Yeres' utopizma," Novy zhurnal, New York, Kn.14.(1946):137-153.
-----. "Misticheskaya filosofia Rozentsveiga. (Der Stern der Erloesung. Von Franz Rosenzweig. 1921)." *Put'* No.2. (1926): 139-148.
-----. "Tserkov' i mir. Blagodat' i zakon." *Put'* No.8. (1927):3-20.
-----. "Russkoe mirovozzrenie." In S.L.Frank, *Russkoe Mirovozzrenie*, 161-196. St Petersburg: Nauka, 1996.
-----. "Russkaya filosofia poslednikh pyatnadtsati let." In S.L.Frank, *Russkoe Mirovozzrenie*, 616-630. St Petersburg: Nauka, 1996.
-----. "Russkaya filosofia kontsa XIX i nachala XX veka." In S.L.Frank, *Russkoe Mirovozzrenie*, 645-659. St Petersburg: Nauka, 1996.
-----. "Lev Tolstoi i russkaya intelligentsia." In S.L.Frank, *Russkoe Mirovozzrenie*, 440-445. St Petersburg: Nauka, 1996.
-----. "Bolshevizm i kommunizm kak dukhovnie yavleniya." In S.L.Frank, *Russkoe Mirovozzrenie*, 137-149. St Petersburg: Nauka, 1996.
-----. "Eto ne russkii vzglyad na mir!" In S.L.Frank, *Russkoe Mirovozzrenie*, 196-205. St Petersburg: Nauka, 1996.
-----. "Dukhovnoe nasledie Vladimira Solovyova." *Vestnik*, 1950, No.4-5, pp.2-10.
-----. *Krushenie kumirov*. Berlin: YMCA-Press, 1924.
-----. *Smysl zhini*. Moscow: AST, 2004.
-----. edit. *A Solovyov Anthology*. London: The Saint Austin Press, 2001.
Frankel, Jonathan. *Prorochestvo i politika. Sotsializm, natsionalizm i russkoe yevreistvo. 1862-1917*. Translation by S.Ilyin of: Frankel J.*Prophecy and Politics: Socialism, Nationalism and the Russian Jews 1862-1917*.Edited by V.Levin. Moscow: Mosty kultury, 2008.
Franks, Paul. "Jewish Philosophy after Kant: the Legacy of Solomon Maimon." In Morgan M. and Gordon P.E. *Modern Jewish Philosophy*, 53-80. Cambridge: CUP, 2007.
Freud, Sigmund. *Moses and Monotheism*. New York: Vintage, 1955.
Friedman, Elias. *Jewish Identity*. New York: The Miriam Press, 1987.
Fry, Helen. Edit. *Christian-Jewish Dialogue. A Reader*. Exeter: University of Exeter Press, 1996.

Gaidenko, P.P. *Vladimir Soloviev i filosofia serebryanogo veka*. Moscow: Progress-traditsia, 2001.
Gavrilkin, Konstantin. "Mitropolit Filaret (Drozdov) i yevrei." Kontinent No.111. (2002).
Gavryushin, N.K., *Russkoe bogoslovie: ocherki i portrety*, pp.275-312: 'Borba za lyubeznuyu mne neponyatnost': svyashchennik Pavel Florenski. Moscow: Glagol, 2005.
Gershenzon, Mikhail. "Chtenije Pushkina" in *Russkaya kritika o Pushkine*, edited by A.M. Gurevich, 195-200. Moscow: Izdatel'stvo Moskovsogo universiteta, 1998.

—―――. "Nagornaya propoved"," *Simvol* 28 (1992).
—―――. *Griboedovskaya Moskva. P.Y.Chaadaev. Ocherki Proshlogo*. Moscow: Moskovskii rabochii, 1989.
—―――. *Izbrannoe. Tom 1. Mudrost' Pushkina*. Moscow: Gesharim/Mosty kultury, 2000.
—―――. "Delo pravdy i razuma!" Nevskii alamanakh. Zhertvam voiny.Petrodgrad, 1915.
—―――. "Tvorcheskoe samosoznanie." In *Vekhi. Iz glubiny,* edited by A.A.Yakovleva, 73-97. Moscow: Pravda, 1991.
—―――. "Yarmo i genii (o Byalike)." Yevreiskaya zhizn' No.14-15, 1916.
—―――. *Sudby yevreiskogo naroda*, Berlin, 1927. Also reprinted in *Tajna izrailja*. 'Yevreiskii vopros v russkoi religioznoi mysli kontsa XIX-pervoi polovinoi XX vv.* (St Petersburg, Sophia: 1993), 468-497.
Gershenzon-Chegodaeva, Natalya. *Mikhail Gershenzon. Vospominaniye docheri*. Moscow: Zakharov, 2000.
Gertsyk, Evgeniya. *Vospominaniya*. Paris: YMCA-Press, 1973.
Gippius, Zinaida. *Zhiviye litsa*. Moscow: Azbuka-Klassika, 2000.
Girshman, Mark. *Yevreiskaya i khristianskaya interpretatsii Biblii v pozdnei antichnosti*. Trans. G.Kazimova. Moscow: Mosty kultury, 2002.
Glatzer, Nahum. Edit. *Franz Rosenzweig. His Life and Thought*. Indianapolis/Cambridge: Hackett Publishing Company, 1998.
—―――. Forward to *The Star of Redemption*. Translated from the Second Edition of 1930 by William W. Hallo, ix-xviii. Notre Dame: University of Notre Dame Press, 2002.
Glouberman, Emmanuel. *Feodor Dostoevsky, Vladimir Soloviev, Vassily Rozanov and Lev Shestov on Jewish and Old Testament themes*. Michigan: Ann Arbor, 1977.
Gollerbach, Ernst. "V.V.Rozanov. A Critico-Biographical Study." In Rozanov, Vasily. *Solitaria. With an abridged Account of the Author's Life, by E.Gollerbach. Other biographical material and matter from The Apocalypse of Our Times*. Translated by S.S. Koteliansky. London: Wishart and Co.,1927.
Gordon, Peter. "Franz Rosenzweig and the Philosophy of Jewish Existence." In Morgan M. and Gordon P.E. *Modern Jewish Philosophy*, 122-147. Cambridge: CUP, 2007
Graifer, Ella. "O vykrestax i ob Alexandre Mene." At: http://berkovich-zametki.com
Gustafson, Richard. Introduction to *The Pillar and Ground of the Truth*, translated by Boris Jakim, ix-xxiii. Princeton, Princeton University Press: 2004.

Haberer, Eric. *Jews and Revolution in nineteenth century Russia*. Cambridge, CUP: 1995.
Haeckel, Sergei."The Relevance of Western post-Holocaust theology to the Thought and Practice of the Russian Orthodox Church." At http://www.jcrelations.net/en/?item=937 .
—―――. *Mat' Maria*. YMCA Press 1992, Paris.
Hagemeister, Michael. "Novoe Srednevekovye' Pavla Florenskogo." Zvezda, No.11, 2006.
Herman (Abbot) and Damascene (Father). Introduction to *Salt of the Earth: Elder Isodore*, translated by Richard Betts. St Herman of Alaska Brotherhood, 1999.
Herz, Joseph (Rabbi). Edit. *Tora i pyatiknizhie i gaftarot. Ivritskii tekst s russkim perevodom i klassicheskim kommentariem 'Sonchino'. Kommentarii sostavil d-r I.Gerts, glavnii ravvin britanskoi imperii.* Moscow: Mosty kul'tury/Gesharim, 2008.
Hippius, Zinaida. *Zhivye litsa*. Moscow: Azbuka-Klassika, 2009.
Hoffman, Lawrence. *Covenant of Blood: Circumcision and Gender in Rabbinic Judaism*.

Chicago: University of Chicago Press, 1996.
Horowitz, Brian. "A Jewish-Christian Rift in Twentieth-Century Russian Philosophy: N.A. Berdiaev and M.O.Gershenzon." Russian Review, vol.53, October (1994): 497-514.
Hollerbach, E. *The life and works of V.V. Rozanov*, in abridged version. Introduction to Rozanov V.V. *Solitaria. With an abridged Account of the Author's Life, by E.Gollerbach. Other biographical material and matter from The Apocalypse of Our Times*. Translated by S.S. Koteliansky. London: Wishart and Co.,1927.

Idel, Moshe.*Language, Torah and Hermeneutics in Abraham Abulafia*. New York: State University of New York Press, 1989.
-----. *Kabbalah. New Perspectives*. New Haven and London: Yale University Press, 1988.
Ilyin, Vladimir. "Khristos i Izrail." *Put'* No.11 (1928):59-75.
Ivanov, K. "Vaneev, uchenik Karsavina." Indroduction to Vaneev A.A. "Dva goda v Abeze. V pamyat' o L.P.Karsavine." *Nashe nasledie*, III-IV, (1990).
Ivanov, Vyacheslav. "K ideologii yevreiskogo voprosa." Moscow, Shchit': 1915.
-----. and Gershenzon M. *Perepiska iz dvux uglov*. St Peterburg, 'Alkonost': 1921.

Jacobs, Louis. *Judaism and Theology. Essays on the Jewish religion*. London: Valentine Mitchell, 2005.
-----. *A Jewish Theology*. London: Berman House Inc., 1973.
Judt, Tony. "The 'Problem of Evil' in Postwar Europe." Lecture given in Bremen, Germany, Nov.30, 2007 on occasion of award to Tony Judt of the 2007 Hannah Arendt Prize.
Justin (Martyr) *Dialogue with Trypho the Jew*. At: http://www.ccel.or/cel/schaff/anf01.toc.html

Kagan, Matvei. *O khode istorii*. Moscow: Yazyki Slavyanskoy kul'tury, 2004.
Kandel' Feliks. *Kniga vremyon i sobytii: istorii russkykh yevreev, 1*. Moscow-Jerusalem: Gesharim-Mosty Kultury, 2002.
-----. *Kniga vremyon i sobytii. Istoria rossiiskikh yevreev 2*. Moscow-Jerusalem: Gesharim-Mosty Kultury, 2002.
Kantor, Vladimir. "The Principle of Christian Realism or Against Utopian Self-will." Social Sciences, Vol.31, No.1. (2000).
Kaplan, Lawrence. "Joseph Soloveitchik and Halakhic Man." In Morgan M. and Gordon P.E. *Modern Jewish Philosophy*, 209-234. Cambridge: CUP, 2007
Karsavin, Lev. *Filosofia istorii*. Khranitel', Moscow. 2007.
-----. "Apologeticheskij etjud." *Put'*,No.3. (1926):29-45.
-----. "Noctes Petropolitanae." In *Put' pravoslavija*, by L.P.Karsavin, Moscow: Folio, 2003.
-----. "O lichnosti." In *Put' pravoslavija*, by L.P.Karsavin, Moscow: Folio, 2003.
-----. "Ob opostnostnyakh i preodolenii otvlechennogo khristianstva." *Put'* No.6 (1927):32-49.
-----. "Poema o smerti." In *Put' pravoslavija*, by L.P.Karsavin, Moscow: Folio, 2003.
-----. "Rossiya i yevrei." Versty, No.3.(1928):65-86.

-----. *Katolichestvo. Otkrovenija blazhennoy Andzhely*. Tomsk: Izdatel'stvo 'Vodoley', 1997.
-----. *Put' pravoslavija*. Moscow: Folio, 2003.
-----. *Svjatye otsy i uchiteli tserkvi (raskrytie pravoslavija v ix tvorenijax)*. Moscow: Izdatel'stvo Moskovskogo universiteta, 1994.
Katsis, Leonid. "Grad Kitezh yevreiskoi filosofii?" Lekhaim, No.12. (2007): 90-94.
-----. "Kastratorskii kompleks publikatorov, ili Rozanov v menjajushchemsja supere." Nezavisimiy filologichsekiy zhurnal No.61(2003).
-----. "Matvei Kagan – yevreiskii filosof. Filosofia i religia na fone pervoy mirovoy voiny." Lekhaim, No.3. (2008): 48-52.
-----. *Krovavy navet i russkaya mysl: istoriko-teologicheskoe issledovanie dela Beilisa*. Moscow: Gesharim/Mosty kultury, 2006.
Khodasevich, Vladislav. *Iz yevreiskikh poetov*. Moscow-Jerusalem: Gesharim, 1998.
-----. "O Bialike. (K pyatidesyatiletiyu ego rozhdeniya." In Khodasevich V. *Iz yevreiskikh poetov*, 33-35. Moscow-Jerusalem: Gesharim, 1998.
-----. "Bialik." Khodasevich V. *Iz yevreiskikh poetov*, 36-43. Moscow-Jerusalem: Gesharim, 1998.
-----. *Nekropol': Vospominaniya*. Brussels: Les éditions Petropolis, 1939.
-----. "Gershenzon." In Khodasevich V. *Nekropol': Vospominaniya*, 56-63. Brussels: Les éditions Petropolis, 1939.
Khoruzhy, Sergei. "Imjaslavije i kul'tura Serebryanogo Veka: fenomen khristianskogo neoplaotonizma." In Khoruzhy S.S. *Opyty iz russkoy dukhovnoy traditsii*. Moscow: Parad, 2005.
-----. *O starom i novom*. St. Petersburg: 'Aleteia', 2000.
-----. *Opyty iz russkoy dukhovnoy traditsii*. Moscow: Parad, 2005.
-----. *Posle pereryva. Puti Russkoy Filosofii*. Saint Petersburg: 'Aleteia', 1994.
Khrapovitsky, Anthony (Metropolitan). *Khristos spasitel' i yevreiskaya revolyutsia. Religiozno-istoricheskii ocherk*. St Petersburg: 'Literarturniy Vestnik', 1993.
-----."Yevreisky vopros i svyataya Biblija." In *Sobraniye Sochinenii*, tom 1, 884-900. Moscow: Dar 2007.
-----. "K kishinyovskomu bedstviyu." In Willem J. *Vavilon i Ierusalim. Blizhnevostochnii konflikt v svete Biblii*. Edited by D.Radyshevski, 14-20. Moscow-Jerusalem: MCF, 2002.
Kisilev, A. *Strana gryoz Georgiya Fedotova*. Moscow: Logos, 2004.
Kitsenko, Nadezhda. *Svyatoi nashego vremeni: otets Ioann Kronshtadtskii i russkii narod*. Moscow: Novoe Literaturnoe Obozrenie, 2006.
Klier, John, and Lambroza, Shlomo, eds. *Pogroms: anti-Jewish violence in modern Russian history*. Cambridge: Cambridge University Press, 1992.
Kochetkov, Gyorgy. "Genii Berdyaeva i Tserkov'." Paper presented at the First Berdyaev Lectures, Kiev, 28 May, 1991.
Kolerov, M. *Ne mir, no mech. Russkaya religiozno-filosofskaya pechat' ot 'problem idealizma' do 'vekh' 1902-1909*. St Petersburg: Aleteia, 1996.
-----. "S,N. Bulgakov v Krymu osenyu 1919 goda." Editing of "Vegetus. Nedelya o Bulgakove.(Pismo iz Simferpolya.)," first printed in Velikaya Rossiya. Rostov-na-Donu. No.339. Wednesday 6 (19). November 1919. No.2. Can be found at: http://russianway .rchgi.spb.ru/

-----. Ed. *Issledovaniya po istorii russkoi mysli. Yezhegodnik – 1997.* St Petersburg: Aliteia, 1997.
-----. Ed. *Neopublikovannie pisma S.N. Bulgakova k V.V.Rozanovu. Predislovie i kommentarii M.A. Kolerova.* Voprosi filosofii No.10, 1992.
Kornblatt, Judith. "Androgynous Sophia and the Jewish Kabbalah." Slavic Review 50/3 (1991):487-496.
-----. "Vladimir Solov'ev on Spiritual Nationhood, Russia, and the Jews." *Russian Review* 56/2 (1997): 157-77.
-----. *Doubly Chosen. Jewish identity, the Soviet intelligentsia, and the Russian Orthodox Church.* Wisconsin: University of Wisconsin Press, 2004.
Kozhinov, V. "Chya Initsiativa?" *Nash Sovremmenik,* No.2. 2002.
Kostalevsky, Marina. *Dostoevsky and Soloviev. The Art of Integral Vision.* New Haven: Yale University Press, 1997.
Krasil'shchikov, Arkady. "Shchipy yudofobii," in *Yevreiskoe Slovo,* 2008.
Kronstadt, John (Saint). "Mysli moi po povodu nasilii khristian s yevreyami v Kishinyove." In Willem J. *Vavilon i Ierusalim. Blizhnevostochnii konflikt v svete Biblii.* Edited by D.Radyshevski, 12-14. Moscow-Jerusalem: MCF, 2002.
Krotov, Yaakov, "10 Marta 1970 goda: Izrail' protiv yevreev-khristian." At: www.krotov.info.
Kuzmina-Karavaeva, Elizaveta (Mat' Maria). *Zhatva dukha.* St.Petersburg: Isskustvo-SPB, 2004.
Kuznetsov, P. *Lev Shestov i Nicolai Berdyaev: dva tipa russkoy religioznoy filosofii.* Logos, 2008.
КЕЭ, том 7, кол. 250-253. Jewish Encycolopeda.

Leibowitz, Yeshayahu. *Judaism, Human Values and the Jewish State.* Ed. Eliezer Goldman. Cambridge: Harvard University Press, 1995.
Levin, Evgeny. "Pochemu tak mnogo russkoyazichnykh yevreev obrashchaetsja v khristianstvo?" At: http://www.portal-credo.ru
Levin, Iosef. "Ya videl P.Florenskogo odin raz." Russkiy *Put':* Pro i contra. Entsiklopedia russkogo samosoznaniya. At: http://russianway.rchgi.spb.ru/
Levinas, Emmanuel. *Difficult Freedom. Essays on Judaism.* London: The Athlone Press, 1990.
-----. *Nine Talmudic Readings.* Bloomingston: Indiana University Press, 1994.
-----. *The Levinas Reader.* Oxford: Blackwell Publishers, 1989.
Levitsky, Sergei. *Ocherki po istorii russkoy filosofii.* Moscow:Kanon, 1996.
Likhachev, E. *Vospominaniye,* SPB, Logos, 1995, p.225. Also at: http://www.sakharov-center.ru/asfcd/auth/auth_pages.xtmpl?Key=13580&page=220].
Louth, Andrew. *Maximus the Confessor.* Oxford: Routledge, 1996
-----, and Conti, Marco eds. *Bibleiskie kommentarii otsov tserkvi i drugikh avtorov I-VIII vekov. Vetkhi zavet. I. Kniga Bytiya 1-11.* Trans.G.Vvodina and others. Moscow: Germenevtika, 2004.
Lovsky, German. "Lev Shestov po moyim vospominaniyam." *Grani* No 45.(1960) and No.46 (1961).
Lossky, Nicolai. *Istoria russkoi filosofii.* Moscow: Akademicheskii Proiekt, 2007.
Lossky, Vladimir. *The Mystical Theology of the Eastern Church.* Cambridge: James Clark & Co.Ltd, 1991.

-----. *Bogovidenie*. Moscow: Ast, 2006.
-----. "Spor o Sofii." In *Bogovidenie*, 11-94. Moscow: Ast, 2006.
Lyosov, Sergei. "Yest' li u russkogo pravoslaviya budushchee? (ocherki sovremennogo pravoslavnogo liberalizma)." (www.vehi./men/future.html#evr).
-----. "Khristiansvto posle osventsima." At: www.vehi./asion/lesev.html

Makhlakh, K. "Triadologia L.P. Karsavina. Na material traktata 'O lichnosti'.." *Nachalo*, No.5.(1997).
Markish, Shimon. "Vyacheslav Ivanov i yevreistvo." Paper delivered at the memorial colloquium for Vyacheslav Ivanov at Geneva University (10-11 December, 1982).
Maslin, M. Edit.*Istoria russkoi filosofii. Uchebnik dlya vuzov*. Moscow: KDU, 2008.
Meerson-Aksenov, Mikhail. "Zhizn svoyu za drugi svoya." In *Pamyati protoiereya Aleksandra Menya*, 116-121. Moscow: Rudomino, 1991.
-----, and Meerson, Olga. "Yevreiskoe samosoznanie i pravoslavnoe khristianstvo," Kontinent, No.111, 2002.
-----. Pr. *Sozertsaniem Troitsy Svyatoi...Paradigma Lyubvi v russkoi filosofii troichnosti*. Kiev: Dukh i litera, 2007.
Melikh, Y. *Personalizm L.P.Karsavina i yevropeiskaya filosofia*. Moscow: Progress-Traditsia, 2003.
-----. "O lichnosti L.P. Karsavina. K 125-letnemu yubileyu." *Vestnik MGTU*, tom 10, No.3 (2007):409-417.
Men, Aleksandr. "Khristianstvo i iudaizm," Yevrei v SSSR, No.11, 1975. (Reprinted as: Men A. "Yevrei i khristianstvo." Vestnik RKhD No.117 (1976):113-117.)
-----. Vozmozhno li iudeokhristianstvo?" Kontinent, 1995, No.8.
-----. *U vrat molchaniya*.Moscow: Fond Imeni Aleksandra Menya, 2002.
-----. *Vestniki Tsarstvo Bozhiya*. Moscow: Fond Imeni Aleksandra Menya, 2002.
-----. *Isagogika. Vetkhi zavet*. Moscow: Fond Imeni Aleksandra Menya, 2003.
-----. *Russkaya religioznaya filosofia. Leksii*. Moscow: Khram svyatykh bessrebrennikov Kosma i Damiana v Shubine, 2003.
Merezhkovsky, Dmitri. "Yevreiskii vopros kak russkiy." In *Shchit'*, 84-86. Moscow, 1915.
-----. *Khristos i antikhrist. Trilogia*. Moscow: Pravda-Ogonyok, 1990.
Meyendorff, John. *A Study of Gregory Palamas*. New York: St. Vladimir's Press, 1998.
Mindel, Nissan. *The Philosophy of Chabad. Vol.2*. New York: Kehot Publication Society, 1985.
Morgan, Michael, and Gordon, Peter. Editors. *Modern Jewish Philosophy*. Cambridge: CUP, 2007.
Morgan, Michael. "Emil Fackenheim, the Holocaust, and Philosophy." In Morgan M. and Gordon P.E. Editors. *Modern Jewish Philosophy*, 256-277. Cambridge: CUP, 2007
Morson, Gary. "Dostoevsky's anti-Semitism and the critics: a review article," SEEJ, Vol.27, No.3 (1983).
Moskovich W., Shvartzband S., and Alekseev A., eds. *Jews and Slavs*. Volume 1, Nauka, Jerusalem-St.Petersburg. 1993.
Moss, Walter. "Vladimir Soloviev and the Jews in Russia." *Russian Review*, Vol.29, No.2. (1970):181 191

Nazarov, M. "Yevreiskie skazki: 'Krovavy navet' s sugubo pravoslavnoi tochoi zreniya. Retsenzia na knigu Leonida Katsisa 'Krovavy navet i russkaya mysl.'" http://www.rusidea.org/?a=440406*navet

Nicanor, Archbishop. "Iz poucheniya pri osvyashchenii tserkvi Odesskogo komercheskogo uchilishcha." Willem J. *Vavilon i Ierusalim. Blizhnevostochnii konflikt v svete Biblii.* Edited by D.Radyshevski, 20-23. Moscow-Jerusalem: MCF, 2002.

Nicholl, Donald. *Triumphs of the Spirit in Russia.* London: Dartman, Longman and Todd, 1997.

Nikolyukin, A.N. "K voprosu o mifologeme natsional'nogo v tvorchestve V.V. Rozanova." In *Obonyatenl'noe i osyaznatel'noe otnoshenie yevreev k krovi,* edited by A.N. Nikolyukin. Moscow: Respublika, 1998.

Nivat, George. "Spyashchie i bodrstvuyushchie." Epilogue to A. Steinberg *Druzya moikh rannikh let.*

Okunev, Yuri. *Os' vsemirnoi istorii.* Moscow: Isskustvo Rossii, 2004.

Paperny, Vladimir. "O 'natsional'noi pochve' filosofii L'va Shestova (midrash kak filosofskii metod)." In Moskovich W., Shvartzband S., and Alekseev A., eds. *Jews and Slavs.* Volume 1, 161-176. Nauka, Jerusalem-St.Petersburg. 1993.

Pappadimitriou, George, *Maimonid i Palama o Boge.* Moscow: *Put',* 2003.

Pelikan, Jaroslav. *The Spirit of Eastern Christianity (600-1700).* Chicago and London: University of Chicago Press, 1974.

Pertsov P.P. "Vospominaniye." Novy Mir No.10, (1998).

Philaret, (Drozdov) Metropolitan. "Iz 'Slova v Velikuyu pyatnitsu.'" In Willem J. *Vavilon i Ierusalim. Blizhnevostochnii konflikt v svete Biblii.* Edited by D.Radyshevski, 9-11. Moscow-Jerusalem: MCF, 2002.

-----. *Prostrannii khristianskii katekhizis pravoslavnoi kafolicheskoi vostochnoi tserkvi.* Moscow: Sibirskaya blagozvonnitsa, 2005.

Poggioli, Renato. *Rozanov.* London: Bowes and Bowes, 1957.

Polonski, Pinchas. *Kabbala i noviy etap v razvitii iudaima.* Jerusalem: Makhanaim, 2006.

-----. "Sozdanie uslovii dlya yevreisko-khristianskogo dialoga v sovremennom mire." http://www.jcrelations.net/ru/?item=2315

-----. *Dve tysyachi let vmeste. Yevreiskoe otnosheniye k khristianstvu.* Jerusalem: Makhnaim, 2008.

Poma, Andrea. "Herman Cohen: Judaism and Critical Idealism." In Morgan M. and Gordon P.E. eds. *Modern Jewish Philosophy,* 80-102. Cambridge: CUP, 2007.

Portnova, Nelly. "'Russkoe koleno izrailovo' Aarona Shteinberga." *Lekhaim* 4, April 2007.

Porus, Vladimir. "Tragediya filosofii i filosofiya tragedii (S.N.Bulgakov i L.I.Shestov)." in *U Kraya Kultury.,* Moscow, Kanon, 2008.

-----. *U kraya kultury. Ocherki o russkoi filosofskoi mysli ot Vladimira Solovieva do Gustava Shpeta.* Moscow: Kanon, 2008.

-----. Ed. *N.A.Berdyaev i yedinstvo Yevropeiskogo dukha.* Moscow: Bibleisko-bogoslovskii Institut sv. Apostola Andreya,2007.

-----. Ed. *Rossia i vselenskaya tserkov'. V.S. Soloviev i problema religioznogo i kul'turnogo edineniya chelovechestva.* Moscow: Bibleisko-bogoslovskii Institut sv. Apostola Andreya, 2004.

Praisman, L., and Kipnis, M. main author and ed. *Istoria yevreev v Rossii*. Moscow: Lekhaim, 2005.
-----. "Ch.XI: Revolyutsia i grazhdanskaya voina.." In *Istoria yevreev v Rossii*, 395-451. Moscow: Lekhaim, 2005.
Pravoslavny molitvaslov. Moscow: Dar, 2006.
Preobrazhenskaya, K. *Bogoslovie i mistika v tvorchestve Vladimira Losskogo*. St Petersburg: Izdatelstvo S-Peterburgskogo universiteta, 2008.
Proscurina, V. "M.O. Gershenzon – istorik kultury." Introduction to Gershenzon M.O. *Griboedovskaya Moskva. P.Y.Chaadaev. Ocherki Proshlogo*, 3-26. Moscow: Moskovskii rabochii, 1989.
-----. "Neizadannaya statya M.O.Gershenzona." Simvol 28 (1992).
-----. *Vstupitel'naya statya, podgotovka teksta, premechaniya k* 'Perepiske V.V.Rozanova s M.O.Gershenzonom. 1909-1918.' at http://kosilova.textdriven.com/narod/studia3/ros_hersh.htm
Pushkin, Alexander. *Sobranie sochineniye v desyati tomakh*. Russkaya virtualnaya biblioteka. http://www.rvb.ru/pushkin

Raeff, Marc. *Russia Abroad: A cultural history of the Russian emigration 1919-1939*. New York: Oxford University Press, 1990.
Rashkovsky, Evgeny. *Istorik Mikhail Gershenzon*. Novy Mir No.10, (2001).
Reznik, Semyon, *Vmeste ili vroz': sudba yevreev v Rossii*. Moscow: Zakharov, 2005.
-----. "Krovavy navet v Rossii. Istoriko-dokumental'niye ocherki." *Vestnik*, No.22(229)-(237), 28 Oct, 1999-15 Feb, 2000. (Also at: http://vestnik.com/issues/1999)
Riasanovsky, Nicholas and Steinberg, Mark. *A History of Russia*. New York and Oxford: OUP, 2005.
Rosenzweig, Franz. *The Star of Redemption*. Translated from the Second Edition of 1930 by William W. Hallo. Notre Dame: University of Notre Dame Press, 2002.
-----. *Understanding the Sick and the Healthy. A New View of World, Man and God*. Harvard: Harvard University Press, 1999.
Rossman, Vadim. *Russian intellectual anti-Semitism in the post-Communist era*. Nebraska: University of Nebraska Press, 2008.
Rozanov, Vasily. *Obonyatenl'noe i osyaznatel'noe otnoshenie yevreev k krovi*, edited by A.N. Nikolyukin. Moscow: Respublika, 1998.
-----. *Sakharna*, edited by A.N. Nikolyukin. Moscow: Respublika, 1998.
-----. "Uyedinyonnoe" in *Apocalipsis nashego vremeni*, edited by A.N.Nikolyukin, Moscow: Eksmo, 2008.
-----. "Yevrei i neyevrei." In *Russkaya gosudarstvennost' i obshchestvo: statii 1906-1907*. Edited by A.N. Nikolyukin, (Moscow, Respublika: 2003): 84-88.
-----. "Opavshiye listya. Korob pervy. Korob vtoroi." In *Apocalipsis nashego vremeni*, edited by A.N.Nikolyukin, Moscow: Eksmo, 2008.
-----. *Apocalipsis nashego vremeni*, edited by A.N.Nikolyukin, Moscow: Eksmo, 2008.
-----. *V tyomnyx religioznyx luchax*, edited by A.N. Nikolyukin. Moscow: Respublika, 1994.
-----. *Vo dvore yazychnikov*, edited by A.N.Nikolyukin. Moscow: Respublika, 1999.
-----. *Lyudi lunnogo sveta*. Moscow: Azbuka-Klassika, 2008.

-----. "Ob odnom priyome zashchiti yevreistva." In *Obonyatenl'noe i osyaznatel'noe otnoshenie yevreev k krovi*, edited by A.N. Nikolyukin. Moscow: Respublika, 1998.
-----. "Iudeiskaya tainopis'." In *Obonyatenl'noe i osyaznatel'noe otnoshenie yevreev k krovi*, edited by A.N. Nikolyukin. Moscow: Respublika, 1998.
-----. Yest' li u yevreev 'tainy'?" In *Obonyatenl'noe i osyaznatel'noe otnoshenie yevreev k krovi*, edited by A.N. Nikolyukin. Moscow: Respublika, 1998.
-----. "Obonyatenl'noe i osyaznatel'noe otnoshenie yevreev k krovi." In *Obonyatenl'noe i osyaznatel'noe otnoshenie yevreev k krovi*, edited by A.N. Nikolyukin. Moscow: Respublika, 1998.
-----. "Vazhniy istoricheskii vopros." In *Obonyatenl'noe i osyaznatel'noe otnoshenie yevreev k krovi*, edited by A.N. Nikolyukin. Moscow: Respublika, 1998.
-----. "Nuzhno perenesti vsyo delo v druguyu ploskost'. (K delu Yushchinskogo)." In *Obonyatenl'noe i osyaznatel'noe otnoshenie yevreev k krovi*, edited by A.N. Nikolyukin. Moscow: Respublika, 1998.
-----. "Nasha 'koshernaya' pechat'." In *Obonyatenl'noe i osyaznatel'noe otnoshenie yevreev k krovi*, edited by A.N. Nikolyukin. Moscow: Respublika, 1998.
-----. "Khram vetkhozavetniy byl khramom zataeniya." In *Obonyatenl'noe i osyaznatel'noe otnoshenie yevreev k krovi*, edited by A.N. Nikolyukin. Moscow: Respublika, 1998.
----- V.V. "Zhertvoprinosheniya u drevnykh yevreev." In *Obonyatenl'noe i osyaznatel'noe otnoshenie yevreev k krovi*, edited by A.N. Nikolyukin. Moscow: Respublika, 1998.
-----. "Otkuda neskhodstvo grecheskogo i yevreiskogo tekstov Sv. Pisaniya?" In *Obonyatenl'noe i osyaznatel'noe otnoshenie yevreev k krovi*, edited by A.N. Nikolyukin. Moscow: Respublika, 1998.
-----. "Napominaniya po telefonu." In *Obonyatenl'noe i osyaznatel'noe otnoshenie yevreev k krovi*, edited by A.N. Nikolyukin. Moscow: Respublika, 1998.
-----. "Nedokonchennost' suda okolo dela Yushchinskogo." In *Obonyatenl'noe i osyaznatel'noe otnoshenie yevreev k krovi*, edited by A.N. Nikolyukin. Moscow: Respublika, 1998.
-----. "Angel Iegovy u yevreev." In V.V. Rozanov, *V sosedstve Sodoma. (Istoki Izrailya)*. St. Petersburg: 1914. Reprinted in *Tajna izrailja. 'Yevreiskii vopros v russkoi religioznoi mysli kontsa XIX-pervoi polovinoi XX vv.* (St Petersburg, Sophia: 1993), 257-269.
-----. "V sosedstve Sodoma. (Istoki Izrailya)." In: V.V.Rozanov, *V sosedstve Sodoma. (Istoki Izrailya)*, St. Petersburg: 1914. Reprinted in *Tajna izrailja. 'Yevreiskii vopros v russkoi religioznoi mysli kontsa XIX-pervoi polovinoi XX vv.* (St Petersburg, Sophia: 1993), 247-257.
-----. *Kogda nachalstvo ushlo*. Moscow: Respublika, 2005.
-----. "Levitan i Gershenzon," Russkiy bibliofil, 1916, No.1.
-----. *O sebe i o zhizni svoei*. Edit. V.G.Sukach. Moscow: Moskovskii rabochii, 1990.
-----. "Perepiska V.V.Rozanova i M.O.Gershenzona. 1909-1918." Novy Mir, No.3. (1991): 215-242. Also at http://kosilova.textdriven.com/narod/studia3/ros_hersh.htm with introductory article by V.Proscurina.
-----. "Yevropa i yevrei." St. Petersburg, 1914. Reprinted in *Tajna izrailja. 'Yevreiskii vopros v russkoi religioznoi mysli kontsa XIX-pervoi polovinoi XX vv.* (St Petersburg, Sophia: 1993), 269-290.
-----. "Byl li I.Khristos yevreem po plememi?" In *Okolo narodnoy dushi. Stati 1906-1908*. Ed. A.N.Nikolyukin. Moscow: "Respublika," 2003.
-----. "Eshcho o neyevreistve I.Khrista." In *Okolo narodnoy dushi. Stati 1906-1908*. Ed. A.N.Nikolyukin. Moscow: "Respublika," 2003.

-----. "O kakom brake govoril I.Khristos?" In *Okolo narodnoy dushi. Stati 1906-1908*. Ed. A.N.Nikolyukin. Moscow: "Respublika," 2003.
-----. "Kul'turno-religioznie voprosy." In *Okolo narodnoy dushi. Stati 1906-1908*. Ed. A.N.Nikolyukin. Moscow: "Respublika," 2003.
-----. *Iudaizm*. Novy Put', No.7-12. 1903. Reprinted in *Tajna izrailja. 'Yevreiskii vopros v russkoi religioznoi mysli kontsa XIX-pervoi polovinoi XX vv.* (St Petersburg, Sophia: 1993), 105-228.
-----. *Solitaria. With an abridged Account of the Author's Life, by E.Gollerbach. Other biographical material and matter from The Apocalypse of Our Times.* Translated by S.S. Koteliansky. London: Wishart and Co.,1927.
-----. *Pisma V.V. Rozanova k E.F.Gollerbakhu.* Berlin: Gutnov Press, 1922.
Rubin, Dominic. "Judaism, Christianity, and All-Unity." Paper presented at the International Conference on the theme of All-Unity and Universalism, Bose, Italy, 22-25 October, 2009.
-----. "Yevreistvo, iudaizm i Russkoe Pravoslavie v zerkale russkoi religioznoi mysli: k sovremennomu pravoslavnomu podkhodu k iudaizmu," paper read at St Andrew's annual readings of the St Andrew's Biblical Theological Institute, Moscow, 13 December 2009.
Ruether, Ruth. *Faith and Fratricide. The theological roots of anti-Semitism.* New York: The Seabury Press, 1974.

Sacks, Jonathan. *Future Tense. A Vision for Jews and Judaism in the global culture.* London: Hodder and Stoughton, 2009.
Sakharov, Nicholas. *I love therefore I am. The theological legacy of Archimandrite Sophrony.* New York: St Vladimir's Press: 2002.
Sapronov, P.A. *Russkaya filosofia. Problema svoeobraziya i osnovnie linii razvitiya.* St Petersburg: Gumanitarnaya Akademiya, 2008.
Schäfer, Peter. *Jesus in the Talmud.* Princeton: Princeton University Press, 2007.
Schiffman, Lawrence. *From text to tradition. A history of second temple and rabbinic Judaism.* New Jersey: Ktav Publishing House, 1991.
Schoemann, Roy. *Salvation is from the Jews. The role of Judaism in salvational history from Abraham to the Second Coming.* San Francisco: Ignatius Press, 2003.
Schwarzschild, Steven. "The title of Herman Cohen's 'Religion of Reason out of the Sources of Judaism.'" In Cohen H. *Religion of Reason out of the Sources of Judaism*, 7-20. Atlanta, Georgia: Scholars Press, 1995.
Seeskin, Kenneth. "How to read Religion of Reason." In Cohen H. *Religion of Reason out of the Sources of Judaism*, 21-43. Atlanta, Georgia: Scholars Press, 1995.
Sergeev, Mikhail. *Divine Wisdom and the Trinity: A 20th century controversy in Orthodox theology*, paper presented at the World Congress of Philosophy in Boston, August 1998.
Shakhavskoi, Ioann (Archbishop). *Ustanovlenie yedinstva.* Moscow: Sretinskii Monastyr, 2006.
Shapiro, Paul. "Faith, Murder, Resurrection. The Iron Guard and the Romanian Orthodox Church." In *AntiSemitism, Christian Ambivalence and the Holocaust*. Ed. Kevin Spicer. Bloomington: Indiana University Press, 2007.

Sheridan, M. ed. *Bibleiskie kommentarii otsov tserkvi i drugikh avtorov I-VIII vekov. Vetkhi zavet. II. Kniga Bytiya 12-50.* Transl. A.Bogatyrev and others. Moscow: Germenevtika, 2005.
Sherman, Nosson (Rabbi). *The Complete ArtScroll Siddur. Week/Sabbath/Festival.* Co-edited by Rabbi M.Zlotowitz and Rabbi Sheah Brander. New York: Mesorah Publications Ltd, 1984.
Shestov, Lev. "Poxvala gluposti." *Fakeli*, kn.II. (1907).
-----. *Martin Buber, Put'* No.39, (1933): 66-77.Shestov, Lev. "O vechnoi knige: v pamyat' o M.O.Gershenzone (1869-1925)," in *Sovremenniye zapiski*, no. 24 (1925).
-----. "V.V.Rozanov," *Put'* No.22, (1930): 97-103.
-----. *Apofeoz bespochvennocti.* Moscow: Ast, 2007.
-----. *Afini i Ierusalim.* Moscow: Ast, 2007.
-----. *Kirgegard i eksistentsial'naya filosofia.* Moscow: Progress-Gnosis,1992
-----. *Dostoevskii i Nitsshe.* Moscow: Ast, 2007.
-----. *In Job's Balances.* Translated by Coventry C. and Maccartney C. London: J.M.Dent and Sons, 1932.
Shkarovskii, Mikhail. *Natsiskaya Germaniya i Pravoslavnaya Tserkov'.* Moscow: Izdatel'stvo Krutitskogo Patriarchego Podvorya Obshchestvo lyubitilyei tserkovnoi istorii, 2002.
-----. "Otnoshenie Russkoi Pravoslavonoi i Ukrainskoi Greko-Katolicheskoi Tserkvyei k Kholokostu vo vremya II Mirovoi voiny." http://www.jcrelations.net/ru/?item=2932
Shochet, Jacob. *Chassidic Dimensions.* New York: Kehot Publication Society, 1990.
Skarsaune, Oscar, and Hvalvik, Reidar. eds. *Jewish Believers in Jesus.* Massachusets: Hendrickson Publishers, 2007.
Skorodumov, S.V. *V.V.Rozanov. Filosofia zhizni i sushestvovaniya. Uchebnoe Posobie.* Yaroslav: Yaroslav Ushinsky Government Pedagogical Institute, 2005.
Singer, Isaac . *The Collected Stories of Isaac Bashevis Singer.* Reading: Penguin, 1981.
Sobolev, A. "Radikalniy istorizm otsa Georgiya Florovskogo." In Sobolev A., *O Russkoy Filosofii.* St Petersburg: Mir, 2008.
-----., *O Russkoy Filosofii.* St Petersburg: Mir, 2008.
Soloveitchik, Joseph. *Halakhic Man*, translated by Lawrence Kaplan. Philadelphia: Jewish Publication Society, 1983.
-----. *The Lonely Man of Faith.* New York: Doubleday, 1992.
Solzhenitsyn, Aleksandr. *Dvesti let vmeste (1795-1995).* Moscow: Russkiy Put', 2001.
Soloviev, Vladimir. "Morality and Politics: Russia's Historical Responsibilities" in *The National Question in Russia* (1883).
-----. "A short history of the antichrist." In Frank S.L. edit. *A Solovyov Anthology*, 229-249. London: The Saint Austin Press, 2001.
-----. *Sobranie sochineniy. Tom 2. Kritika otvlechennykh nachal. Istoricheskiye dela filosfii.* Edited by Ernst L. Radlow. St Petersburg, 1901.
-----. *Veliki spor i khristianskaya politika.* In *Sobranie sochineniy Vladimira Solovyova, vols. I-XII, 3-114.* Brussels: Zhizn' s Bogom, 1966. Vol.IV.
-----. *Yevreistvo i khristianskiy vopros.* In *Sobranie sochineniy Vladimira Solovyova, vols. I-XII, 135-185.* Brussels: Zhizn' s Bogom, 1966. Vol.IV.
-----. "Talmud i noveishaya polemicheskaya literature o nyom v Avstrii i Germanii." In *Talmud s prilozheniem F. Getz 'Ob otnoshenii Vl Solovyovu k yevreiskomu voprosu.'* Berlin: Zarya, 1925.

-----. *Krizis zapadnoy filosofii*. In *Sobranie sochineniy. Tom 1*. Edited by Ernst L. Radlow. St Petersburg, 1901.
-----. "Novozavetniy Izrail." In *Rus'* No.24.(1885):7-9 and No.25 (1885):6-7.
-----. "Protest protiv antisemiticheskogo dvizheniya v pechati." In *Pisma Vladimira Sergeivicha Solovieva, Vol.2*, 160-161. St. Petersburg: 1908-1911.
-----. "Natsional'niy vopros v Rossii." In *Soloviev V.S. Sochineniya v dvukh tomakh. Tom 1. Filosofskaya publitsistika*. Moscow: Pravda, 1989.
-----. "Russkiy natsional'niy ideal." In *Soloviev V.S. Sochineniya v dvukh tomakh. Tom 2. Chteniye o bogochelovechestve. Filosofskaya publitsistika.* Moscow: Pravda, 1989.
Solzhenitsyn, Aleksandr. *Dvesti let vmeste (1795-1995)*. Moscow: Russkiy Put', 2001.
Stanchev, Krassen. "Sergei Bulgakov and the spirit of capitalism." In *Journal of Markets and Morality*, Volume 11, number 1, Spring 2008.
Stanislawski, Michael "Towards the popular religion of Ashkenazic Jews: Yiddish-Hebrew texts on sex and circumcision," in *Mediating modernity. Challenges and trends in the Jewish encounter with the modern world. Essays in honor of Michael A. Meyer.* Edit. Lawrence Strauss and Michael Brenner. Detroit: Wayne State University Press, 2008.
Steinberg, Aaron. *Druzya moikh rannikh let (1911-1928)*. Paris: Syntaxis, 1991.
-----. "Filosofskoe sodruzhestvo." In Steinberg A. *Druzya moikh rannikh let (1911-1928)*, ch.2. Paris: Syntaxis, 1991.
-----. "Na Peterburgskom perekryostike. Vstrecha s V.V. Rozanovym." In Steinberg A. *Druzya moikh rannikh let (1911-1928)*, ch.6. Paris: Syntaxis, 1991.
-----. "Lev Platonovich Karsavin." In Steinberg A. *Druzya moikh rannikh let (1911-1928)*, ch.8. Paris: Syntaxis, 1991.
-----. "Lev Shestov." In Steinberg A. *Druzya moikh rannikh let (1911-1928)*, ch.9. Paris: Syntaxis, 1991.
-----. "Razvitie i razlozhenie v sovremmenom iskustve." Paper presented at 3rd open session of Volphila, 1 Dec.1919. In Belous V. *Volphila* 2, 591-608. Moscow: Tri Kvadrata, 2005.
-----. *Sistema svobody Dostoevskogo*. Berlin: Skify, 1923.
-----. "Otvet L.P.Karsavinu." *Versty* No.3, Paris, (1928): 87-93.
-----. "Dostoevsky i yevreistvo." *Versty* No.3, Paris, (1928).
-----. "Dostoevsky kak filosof." Paper presented at Volphila Session 'Pamyati F.M. Dostoevskogo', 16th Oct. 1921. In Belous V. *Volphila* 1, 637-679. Moscow: Tri Kvadrata, 2005.
-----. "K filosofii istorii P.L. Lavrova." Paper presented at Volphila Session 'Pamyati P.L.Lavrova', 8th Feb 1920. In Belous V. *Volphila* 1, 174-183. Moscow: Tri Kvadrata, 2005.
-----. "O politicheskykh predskazaniyakh." *Znamya*, No.3-4, (1920): Columns 14-15.
-----. "'Dorogaya moya Sonyurochka…'. Pisma k pokoinoy zhene. Publikatisia, predislovie i kommentariy Nelli Portnovoy." *Novy Mir*, No.1, 2006.
Steinberg, Leo. *The Sexuality of Christ in Renaissance Art and in Modern Oblivion*. Chicago, University of Chicago Press, 1983.
Stolovich, L. "Yevrei i russkaya filosofia." http://www.lu.lv/studiju-centri/jsc/resursi/2-14.pdf
Struve, Pyotr. "Intelligentsiya i revolyutsiya." In *Vekhi. Iz Glubiny.* Edited by A. A. Yakovleva, 150-167. Moscow: Pravda, 1991.
-----. "Istoricheskii smysl russkoi revolyutsii i natsional'nie zadachi." In *Vekhi. Iz Glubiny.* Edited by A. A. Yakovleva, 459-478. Moscow: Pravda, 1991.

Sukach, V. *Vasily Vasilievich Rozanov*. Moscow: Progress, 2008.

Tabak, Yuri. *Sumerki shovinizma. Sbornik statyei*. Moscow: Akademia, 2006.
Terras, Victor. *A History of Russian Literature*. New Haven and London: Yale University Press, 1991.
Tertullian. *De Carne Christi*. Edited and translated by Ernest Evans. London: S.P.C.K., 1956.
-----. *On the Testimony of the Soul and on the 'Prescription' of Heretics*. Translated into English by T.Herbert Bindley. London: S.P.C.K., 1914.
Theophan, Metroplitan. "Iz tolkovaniya na XI Poslaniya k Rimlyanam svyatogo apostola Pavla." In Willem J. *Vavilon i Ierusalim. Blizhnevostochnii konflikt v svete Biblii*. Edited by D.Radyshevski. Moscow-Jerusalem: MCF, 2002.
-----. *O mere upotrebleniya yevreiskogo nynyeshnogo teksta, po-ukazaniyu tserkovnoy praktiki*. Tserkovniy Vestnik, 1876, No.23, 12 June, pp.1-5.

Van der Hoeven, Jan. *Vavilon i Ierusalim. Blizhnevostochnii konflikt v svete Biblii*. Edited by D.Radyshevski. Moscow-Jerusalem: MCF, 2002.
Vaneev, Anatoly. "Dva goda v Abeze. V pamyat' o L.P.Karsavine." *Nashe naslediye*, III-IV, (1990).
-----. "Ocherk zhizni i idyei L.P.Karsavina." *Zvezda* No.12.(1990).
Vasilenko, L.I. *Vvedenie v russkuyu religioznuyu filofiyu*. Moscow: PSTGU, 2006.
Velimirovich, Nicolai (Serbskii). *Skvoz' tyuremnoe okno*. Moscow: Izdatel'stvo Moskovskogo Podvorya Svyato-Troitskoy Sergievoy Lavry, 2006.
Vermes, Geza. *Jesus the Jew*. London: William Collins and Son, 1973.
-----. *The Changing Faces of Jesus*. London: Penguin Books, 2000.
-----. *The authentic gospel of Jesus*. London: Penguin Books, 2003.
Vissarion, Bishop. "Iz kn. 'Edinenie v Tserkvi Khristovoi iz iudeev i yazichnikov.'" Willem J. *Vavilon i Ierusalim. Blizhnevostochnii konflikt v svete Biblii*. Edited by D.Radyshevski, 24-26. Moscow-Jerusalem: MCF, 2002.
Volkogonova, Olga. "Religiozny anarkhizm D. Merezhkovskogo." At: http://www.philosophy.ru/library/volk/merez.html#_fn1
Voll, Fritz, "What about Jewish Christians or Christian Jews?" At: http://www.jcrelations.net/en/?item=961
Vorontsova, I. *Russkaya religiozno-filosofskaya mysl' v nachale veka*. Moscow, PSTGU: 2008.

Williams, Rowan. "Bulgakov and anti-Semitism." Appendix in *Sergii Bulgakov: Towards a Russian Political Theology*, texts edited and introduced by Rowan Williams, 293-304. Edinburgh: T&T Clark, 2007.
Wyschogrod, Michael. *Abraham's Promise: Judaism and Jewish-Christian Relations*. Michigan: William B. Eerdmans Publishing Company, 2004.

Yaffe, Leib. "Vladislav Khodasevich (iz moix vospominaniiy)." In Khodasevich V. *Iz yevreiskikh poetov*, 15-29. Moscow-Jerusalem: Gesharim, 1998.
Yakovleva, A. Edit. *Vekhi. Iz Glubiny*. Moscow: Pravda, 1991.

Yehoshua, Avraham. "An attempt to identify the root causes of anti-Semitism."AzureOnline, Spring 2008, No.32.
Yegorov, Gennady. *Svyashchennoe pisanie vetkhogo zaveta. Uchebnoe posobie*. Moscow, PSTGU: 2007.
Yernichev, A.A. "S.L.Frank – Filosof russkogo mirovozzrenie." Introduction to S.L.Frank, *Russkoe Mirovozzrenie*, 5-36. St Petersburg: Nauka, 1996.
Yovel, Yirmiyahu. *Spinoza and other heretics. The adventures of immanence*. Princeton, Princeton University Press: 1989.
-----. *Spinoza and other heretics. The Marrano of Reason*. Princeton, Princeton University Press: 1989.

Zakharov, Hieromonakh Dmitri. *Vsyo obretaet smysl*, Moscow: Fond "Khristianskaya zhizn'," 2000.
Zamaleev, A. *Russkaya religioznaya filosofia. XI-XX vv*. St Petersburg: Izdatel'skii dom S-Peterburgskogo universiteta, 2007.
Zander, Lev. "Tvorchestvo o. Sergiya Bulgakova. Etapy puti." Introduction to *Dela i dni*, 7-14. Moscow: Sobraniye, 2008.
Zenkovsky, Serge. edit. *Medieval Russia's epics, chronicles and tales*. New York, Meridian Books: 1974.
Zenkovsky, Vassily. *Istoria russkoy filosofii. Tom 1*. Paris: YMCA-Press, 1989.
-----. *Istoria russkoy filosofii. Tom 2*. Paris: YMCA-Press, 1989.
-----. "Na temy istoriosofii." *Sovremmenie zapiski* No 69. (1939):280-293.
Zhurakovsky, Anotoly. *My dolzhny vsyo preterpet' radi Khrista: zhizn', podvig i trudy svyashchenika Anatoliya Zhurakovskogo*. Moscow: PSTGU, 2008.
Zizoulias, John. *Being as communion*. London: Dartman, Longman & Todd, 2004.

Index

Adam Kadmon
    26-27, 48, 51, 80, 375, 399, 414, 421, 442
Ahad ha-Am (Asher Ginsberg)
    54-55
Aksakov, Ivan/Kirill
    16-18, 31-32, 505 fn129 (parallel with F.Rosenzweig)
All-Unity
    25-26, 28 (Soloviev), 35, 58 (Vasilenko on), 63 fn 6 (Florensky, Bulgakov and Jewry), 114, 157 (Berdyaev rejects), 209 fn 91 (Shestov and S.Trubetskoy dispute), 323 (Platonism and Orthodoxy), 326 (I.D.Levin critiques), 340 (and Karsavin), 345 (and Steinberg), 346, 363 (differences in Steinberg and Karsavin), 372 (Dostoevsky and Steinberg), 375 fn 85 (Judaic monism in Dostoevsky *pace* Steinberg), 378 (Frank vs. Rosenzweig), 389 fn 122 (Steinberg's Judaic version of), 401 fn 147 (and Kookian Jewish mysticism), 409 fn 162 (and Jewishness), 418 fn 185 (and Karsavin), 422 (Jewish vs. Christian), 451(Frank), 461, 465 (and culture), 466-467 (Zenkovsky's critique of in Frank), 485, 492 (Frank: atonement and human interconnectedness), 496-498 (Rosenzweig critiques), 500 (Frank vs. Rosenzweig), 519 (and Men)
Alfeev, Hilarion
    113, 324 fn 180 (on Name-Worshipping controversy)
Anti-Semitism (see also: Blood libel, Ritual Murder)
    17-18 (Aksakov and "new" anti-Semitism), 74 (Bulgakov on Marx's), 76 (Bulgakov on Schelling's), 91 (Bulgakov and Dostoevsky), 92-94 (anti-Semitic quotes from Bulgakov), 95-101 (Bulgakov controversy 1918-1922), 100-101 fn 99 (White movement), 106-107 (Bulgakov on Nazism), 107 fn 108 (Meller-Zakomelsky and Eurasianism), 110 fn 114 (Alfred Rosenberg), 140 fn 184 (Khrapovitsky), 131-132 (Bulgakov on Christian anti-Semitism), 141 fn 185 (Jabotinsky), 197 (Berdyaev's classification of), 264 (Rozanov on Christian anti-Semitism), 267-298 (and "middle" Rozanov), 298-313 (Florensky and Beilis), 330-334 (and Christianity), 341 (Karsavin), 346 fn 20 (Svyatopolk-Mirsky), 348 (Karsavin et al.), 349-50 (Karsavin against), 362 (Steinberg experiences), 376 (Steinberg excuses Dostoevsky's), 397 fn 137 (Pumpyanksi), 431 (Karsavin and cosmopolitanism), 449 (and Frank), 520-521 (Benevich and spiritual ascesis of), 523 (S.Haekel against)

Barth, Karl
    68 (and Bulgakov), 69 (Wyschogrod on), 105 (on Jews), 501 (on philosophy)
Bar-Yosef, Hamutal
    30 fn 34, 48, 50, 54, 55, 56, 57, 152
Beckett, Samuel
    416 fn 181 (Karsavin's lobster)
Belous, Vladimir
    344 fn 16
Bely, Andrei
    52, 56, 62, 65, 155, 158, 159, 161 fn 20, 163, 164, 170, 171 (Berdyaev's review of *The Silver Dove*), 173, 175, 194, 199, 222 fn 147, 322 (symbolist and Name-veneration), 323, 368 fn 67 (and Florensky), 370, 376-377, 381 fn 103

Berdyaev, Nicolai
    29, 47, 155, 157-161, 165-177, 183-188, 197-200, 207-211, 225 (Zenkovsky critiques), 243 (and Rozanov), 267 fn 83, 328 fn 187 and 379 fn 95 (against all-unity), 341 (critique of Karsavin), 368 (Dostoevsky and Steinberg), 386 fn 116 (and celibacy), 392 (and Steinberg on meaning in history), 393 (Fedotov's critique of), 428 fn 204 (critique of Karsavin), 448 (Frank's letter to about Berlin Jews), 451 and 462 (critiques Frank), 470 fn 55 (Burbank's critique of), 488 (Frank critiques)
Berlin, P.A.
    186 fn 61 (critique's Berdyaev)
Blood libel (ritual murder)
    17 fn 14 (and Christian sects), 21 fn 17 (and Y.Brafman), 109 fn 110 (and Florensky), 157 fn 6, 197 fn 86 (and Christian sects), 231-232 (Mendel Beilis), 244, 251 fn 42 (and L.Hoffman's research), 263 (Rozanov metaphorically), 270 (and Florensky's thought on Chwolson, Schneerson), 280 fn 104 (and Jabotinsky), 299 (early Rozanov condemns), 300 (Florensky's articles), 301-302 (and the Eucharist), 303-304 (Florensky, Judaism and Christianity), 317 (L.Katsis on Russian Orthodoxy and), 350 and 355 (Karsavin condemns), 364 (and Blok during Beilis Affair)
Blok, Aleksandr
    29, 52, 62, 65 fn 12, 159, 171 fn 36 (on Bely's Jewish temptation and "Twelve"), 246, 337 fn 2 ("Scythians"), 343, 346 (Karsavin critiques), 364-5 (to Steinberg about Judeophobia), 367 and 368 fn 65 (in prison with Steinberg), 392, 472, 484
Boobbyer, Phillip
    448, 449, 450, 453, 463
Borovoy, Vitaly
    524
Buber, Martin
    206, 352 fn 33, 395 fn 135, 428 fn 203, 460, 489
Budinitsky, Oleg
    89 fn 64, 91 fn 68, 97 fn 92
Bukgakov, Sergei
    61-66 (biography), 68 (and K.Barth), 66-69 (on Jews: summary), 69-82 (on Jews: early work), 82-90 (on Zionism), 91-101 (allegations of anti-Semitism), 101-105 (on Russian revolutions and Jews), 105-108 (against Nazi anti-Semitism), 108-112 (on Biblical theory of blood and nation), 112-123 (sophiology), 123-134 (Jewish chosenness after Christ), 134-138 (and religious value of Jewish religion), 138-141 (two-covenant reading of Jewish writings), 141-147 (on Judas, Russia and Jewry), 149-151 (Epstein and Okunev on), 212-214 (and Shestov), 265-267 (correspondence with Rozanov), 314 (critique of Florensky), 323 (critiqued by Khoruzhy), 324 fn 180 (Alfeev, on Name-worship of), 350 (analysis of Jewry compared to Karsavin's), 392 (contrasted with Steinberg on Dostoevsky), 419 and 429 and 431 (on Judas/Saul, compared to Karsavin), 424 fn 197 (and Karsavin's kenoticism), 453 (attitude to WWI), 458 (critiques Frank), 515 (and A.Men), 516 (and S.Haeckel)
Burmistrov, Konstantin
    26, 27 fn 28, 30, 48, 81, 325, 399 fn 143, 442 fn 224

Chamberlain, Houston
    268 (and Rozanov), 269, 295 fn 136
Chamberlain, Lesley
    450 fn 12, 463 fn 36

Index 549

Cohen, Herman
   361 (and A.Steinberg), 364 fn 57 (and M.Kagan on October Revolution), 449 (rebuffs Frank), 486-495 (and Frank's philosophy), 505 fn 129 (and M.Kagan during WWI)
Cohn-Sherbock, Dan
   431 fn 209
Coplestone, Frederick
   121 fn 144 (and Bulgakov, Sophia and pantheism)

Davydov, Yuri.N.
   70, 71
Dostoevsky, Fyodor
   18, 36 fn 43, 88, 90 fn 67 (*Diary of a Writer* and Jews), 103 fn 103 (*The Devils*), 179 (V.Ivanov on), 229 (Rozanov and widow of), 277 fn 101 (Shestov contrasts with Rozanov), 278 (Rozanov's reservation), 340 (Steinberg sees as Russian philosopher), 357 (Karsavin on foreigners' understanding of), 368 (Steinberg on moral value of), 371-374 (Steinberg on "prophetic idealism" of), 375 fn 85 (Steinberg on Judaic carnal metaphysics of), 376 (Goldberg and Morson on anti-Semitism of), 378 fn 93 (A.Meier vs. A.Steinberg on Old Testament qualities of), 391 (N.Berdyaev vs. A.Steinberg on), 392 (A.Steinberg vs. Bulgakov on), 392 fn 131 (Steinberg on Versilov as "wanderer"), 408 fn 162 (A.Meier vs. A.Steinberg on philosophic vs. artistic-religious nature of), 434 fn 213 (Steinberg on "God as a suicide" in), 477 (Frank on dangerous theodicy of)
Dubnow, Simon
   53 and 56 (on Soloviev), 339 (Steinberg works with), 343, 351, 365, 366, 439

Epstein, Raya
   88 fn 63, 130, 149-151
Erotich, Vladeta
   525 fn 22
Eurasianism
   107 fn 108 (Meller-Zakomelsky and fascism), 219 fn 143 (and Shestov), 342-345 (Steinberg and Karsavin), 346-347 (and Jewish Autonomism), 351-352 (and J.Bromberg), 358-359 (and N.Trubetzkoy), 393 fn 132 (G.Fedotov mistrusts)
Evtuhov, Catherine
   61

Fedotov, Gyorgy
   79 fn 39, 199 (on Berdyaev), 358 fn 46 (on sacredness of monastic labor), 393-396
Fedotova, Evgeniya
   395 fn 135, 397, 398
Feingold, Natan
   514
Finkelstein, Eitan
   366
Florensky, Pavel
   23, 47, 63 fn 6, 85 fn 56 (on Zionism and "kikes"), 107 fn 108, 126 fn 160 (vs. Bulgakov on blood), 186 fn 61 (and Berdyaev on Jewry), 242 (and Rozanov in Sergiev Posad), 280 (and Gershenzon), 294-298, 298-304 (writings on Jews), 304-307 (critique of Biblical

interpretation of), 307-312 (on poison of Jewish blood and world mastery), 312-313 (on Kabbalah and ritual murder), 313-317 (heterodox elements in the thought of), 317-319 (critique of Katsis' interpretation of), 319-326 (Name-worship, Symbolism, heterodoxy), 326-330 (I.D. Levin on), 332 fn 195 (contrast with Justin Martyr's anti-Judaism), 368 fn 67 (and Steinberg's philosophical relation to), 390 (influence on Jews in Russian culture), 394 (contrast with G. Fedotov on culture), 399 fn 143 (influence on Karsavin), 413 fn 169 (contrast with Karsavin), 436 fn 215 (and Karsavin's "conversa")

Florovsky, Gyorgy
76 fn 35 (and Bulgakov), 113, 119, 121-122 (and sophiology), 123 fn 151 (and Asproulis), 224 fn 153 (on Gershenzon), 234 (on Rozanov), 313 (critique of Florensky), 323 fn 180 (1914 dispute with Florensky), 341 (Karsavin and Eurasianism), 343 (founder of Eurasianism), 509 (on Frank)

Fondane, Benjamine
206, 207, 215

Frank, Semyon
24 fn 23 (on Soloviev), 28 fn 30 (on Soloviev), 29, 47, 168 (on Gershenzon), 213 fn 125 (on Shestov), 355 (on Karsavin on Jewish conversion), 447-455 (background and development), 455-462 (philosophical system), 463-469 (philosophical-religious universalism), 469-472 (and Gershenzon before 1917), 472-482 (and Gershenzon on Pushkin), 482-485 (and Russian-Jewish Wisdom), 486-495 (and H.Cohen), 495-507 (on Rosenzweig), 507-508 (on O.Goldberg)

Franks, Paul
379, 381, 382, 383-384, 385-386

Freud, Sigmund
217 fn 138 (and Shestov's sister), 247 (Rozanov preempts)

Friedman, Elias
520 fn 17

Gavryushin, N.K.
297, 314 fn 167

Gershenzon, Mikhail
95-96 (on Bulgakov), 155-156, 161-165 (general development), 166-169 (on I.Kireevsky), 172 (Berdyaev on), 173 ("Gersh" the Slavophile), 174-177 (and Berdyaev on October Revolution), 177-183 (and V.Ivanov), 188-191 (on Pushkin and Spirit), 191-197 (on Jewish destiny), 203-205 (Shestov on), 220-223, 224 fn 153 (Florovsky on), 225 (Zenkovsky on), 271-283 (friendship with Rozanov), 370 fn 75 (Bely and Steinberg), 462, 469-473 (and Frank, Landmarks, Revolution), 473-482 (and Frank on Pushkin)

Gertsyk, Evgeniya
155

Gippius, Zinaida
107 fn 108, 157, 240, 298 fn 148

Glatzer, Nahum
449 fn 9, 495 fn 109

Glouberman, Emmanuel
214

Gnosticism (Neo-)
113 fn 119, 114 (Bulgakov rejects), 159, 179, 215 (Shestov against), 252, 254, 303, 306, 314 (Bulgakov on Florensky), 324, 399 fn 143 (Karsavin), 402 (Karsavin on Philo), 405-406 (Vaneev on Karsavin), 428, 438

Gollerbach, Ernst
  236 fn 14
Graifer, Ella
  518,
Gustafson, Richard
  297

Haeckel, Sergei
  516
Hagemeister, Michael
  296-297
Hasidism
  49, 50, 51, 57, 116 fn 129, 120, 125 fn 156, 206-207 (Shestov and Buber), 246 fn 34, 270 fn 90 (Schneerson), 322 (baalei ha-Shem), 324 (versus Mitnagdim), 325 (and Abulafian veneration of tetragrammaton), 352 (Bromberg on), 441 (Halkin), 467 fn 49 (and Frank's mysticism)
Hegel (*Hegelianism*)
  74 fn 32 (Bulgakov on), 143 fn 86, 175 and 177 (Berdyaev and WWI), 192 fn 75, 203, 209, 211, (Shestov against), 219 (Steinberg accuses Shestov of tendencies towards), 236 (Rozanov's dissertation), 277 (tendencies in Gershenzon and Rozanov), 277 fn 101 (Shestov on Rozanov), 295 (in Florensky), 371 (in Steinberg), 456 (Frank on Slavophiles), 485 (Rosenzweig's dissertation), 486 (and H.Cohen), 488 and 498 (Frank on)
Herman (Abbot) and Damascene (Father)
  297 fn 144
Hoffman, Lawrence
  250-251
Horowitz, Brian
  16 fn 2, 169 fn 31, 172 fn 37, 174
Hollerbach, E (see Gollerbach)

Idel, Moshe
  325 fn 182
Ilyin, Ivan
  428 fn 204, 341
Ilyin, Vladimir
  82 fn 47
Ivanov, Vyacheslav
  90, 155, 170, 177-182 (*Iz dvukh uglov*), 203, 221, 246, 447, 464, 482 fn 81

Jabotinsky, Vladimir (Ze'ev)
  141 fn 185, 280 fn 104
Jacobs, Louis
  45 fn 50, 49 fn 59
Jewish Christians (Judeo-Christianity, Messianic Judaism)
  36-40 (Soloviev and Rabinowitz), 57 (among Soloviev's heirs), 127-129 (Bulgakov and Edith Stein), 133 (Bulgakov on the need for), 134-137 (Bulgakov and Messianic Judaism), 138 (possibilities in Israel), 148 fn 196 (Vasilenko on Karsavin and Bulgakov),

552

213 (Shestov and Bulgakov), 264-265 (Bulgakov and Rozanov), 333 fn 195 (and Justin Martyr), 355-356 (Karsavin on), 361 fn 53 (and "shittuf"), 404-405 (Karsavin on), 512-513 (and A.Men), 514 ff. (Men and Feingold controversy), 518 fn 15 (Men and Mihoc), 520-523 (Benevich and Men)

Jewish philosophy (see Judaism)
Judaism
17-18 (new Slavophilism against), 22 fn 18 (Bishop Nicanor praises), 30 (Soloviev studies), 33-34 (Soloviev praises), 36 (Soloviev criticizes), 40 (and Rabinowitz), 41-42 (Soloviev's ambiguity), 43-47 (Talmud a model for "integral" Christianity), 49-50 (and pantheistic mysticism), 53-54 (Ahad Ha-Am on), 71 (Bulgakov and rabbinic J), 74-80 (Bulgakov and Old Testament), 80-82 (Bulgakov and mystical), 92-93 (Bulgakov denies religious value of), 100 (Bulgakov's inconsistency about revolution and), 135 (Bulgakov on parasitic nature of), 136-137 (sophianic elements in), 139-140 (and Jewish identity), 140 fn 184 (and Khrapovitsky), 151 (and Wyschgorod), 162 (and Gershenzon's attitude), 185 (Berdyaev and eschatology), 193-195 (Gershenzon supersedes), 197 fn 86 and 199 (and Russian sects), 205-207 (Shestov on), 220-224 (and assimilated philosophers), 246-267 (Rozanov's essay on), 284-287 (Steinberg and Rozanov discuss), 291-294 (Rozanov on secrets and blood in), 301 (Florensky and ritual murder), 302 (Florensky and tragic religion), 324-325 (and Name-mysticism), 349-350 (Karsavin, Jews and), 353 (Silver Age antipathy to), 354 (Karsavin: dualistic and apophatic), 356 (and Orthodoxy non-proselytizing), 361 (and F.Rosenzweig), 362-365 (and Steinberg's defense), 367 (and Parmenides), 373 (Steinberg and Messianism), 375-377 (and Judaic elements in Dostoevsky), 379 ff (Kantianism, philosophy and), 384 fn 110 (incarnation in, and Wyschgorod), 386 ff (and Steinberg), 390 (and Russian culture), 404-404 (Karsavin, Philo, and), 425 ff (Old Testament, Karsavin and), 436-437 (and personality), 449-450 (Frank's childhood and), 483 (Jewish "sages" and), 486-487 (Frank and Gurland on), 490 ff. (H.Cohen, suffering and), 495 ff. (and Rosenzweig), 507-508 (and O.Goldberg), 513 and 519 (and A.Men)

Judaizing (heresy/tendency)
16-17 (fn 3), 104 fn 105 (and "Yid"), 145 fn 191 (Bulgakov, Russian chosenness), 322-325 (Khoruzhy, Silver Age Symbolism), 352 (J.Bromberg on), 325 (Steinberg and Volga tribes), 406 (and "face" of Christianity), 408 (Meier and Steinberg on Dostoevsky)

Justin (Martyr)
47 fn 54, 332 fn 195

Kabbalah
26-27 (and early Soloviev), 47-52 (and Sophia in Soloviev), 80-81 (and Bulgakov), 120-121 (Bulgakov and similarities to Hasidic doctrines), 312 (and Florensky), 324-325 (Florensky, Abulafia, Khoruzhy and "Judaizing"), 382 (Steinberg and Maimon), 399 fn 143 (and Karsavin), 425 fn 200 (Karsavin and *tzimztum*), 441-442 (Karsavin and Halkin), 467 fn 49 (Frank and panentheism)

Kagan, Matvei
364 fn 57, 505 fn 129

Kant (*Kantianism, neo-Kantianism*)
184 (and Berdyaev on history), 205 fn 106 (Shestov accuses Steinberg), 207 fn 11 (Shestov against), 210 (and Jews), 296 (Florensky attacks), 369 (Ern against), 373-374 (Steinberg critiques), 379-383 (and S.Maimon), 385-6 (and Jews), 457-459 (Frank critiques), 485 (Frank and Judaism), 486-490 (Frank and H.Cohen)

Karsavin, Lev

148 fn 196, 337-347 (background, and Steinberg), 347-360 (on Jewry), 399-410 (on Judaism and Christianity), 410-439 (Poem on Death and Jews), 439-441 (final years), 441-442 (S.Halkin in Abez), 443-444 (death and burial), 451 (similarity to Frank), 458 (Frank and Nicholas of Cusa), 466 fn 47 (and Frank), 477 fn 70 (similarities with Gershenzon), 497 fn 114 (and Nietzsche)

Katsis, Leonid
    242, 246 fn 34, 254 fn 50, 294, 298, 317-320, 375, 376, 388, 524

Khodasevich, Vladislav
    162 fn 21, 175 fn 46, 188 fn 64, 189, 190, 473

Khomiakov, Aleksei
    24, 25, 66, 86, 172, 366 fn 62 (Karsavin's ancestor), 478, 480

Khoruzhy, Sergei
    319-324 (on Silver Age and Name-Worshiping controversy), 410 fn 164 (on Karsavin), 415 fn 178

Khrapovitsky, Anthony (Metropolitan)
    20, 113 fn 119, 140 fn 184 (on Jews and Judaism), 161 (on Berdyaev), 250

Kireevsky, Ivan
    25, 166-169 (and Gershenzon)

Kochetkov, Gyorgy
    161 fn 19

Kornblatt, Judith
    30, 33 fn 39, 48, 512

Kronstadt, John (Saint)
    20, 292 (Rozanov on)

Krotov, Yaakov
    518 fn 14

Kuzmina-Karavaeva, Elizaveta (Mat' Maria)
    106

Levin, Iosef
    326-330

Levinas, Emmanuel
    330, 497 fn 116

Levitsky, Sergei
    145, 161, 229, 234

Lovsky, German
    206 fn 107 (Shestov's brother-in-law)

Lossky, Nicolai
    30, 178 fn 51, 234, 295

Lossky, Vladimir
    49, 113, 122, 323, 400 fn 144, 414 fn 174, 417 fn 183

Lyosov, Sergei
    514-516 (and A.Men)

Makhlakh, K.
    406 fn 152, 428 fn 205

Markish, Shimon
    90

Meerson-Aksenov, Mikhail
   411 fn 165, 512 fn 1
Meier, Alexander
   178, 374, 375, 376, 378 fn 93, 394 (and Fedotov), 396-398, 408 fn 162 (critique of Steinberg's Judaic Dostoevsky)
Melikh, Y.
   428 fn 203
Men, Aleksandr
   148, 511-514, 514-516 (polemic around), 515-520 (and post-Auschwitz Judeo-Christianity), 520-522 (compared to Lyosov and Benevich)
Merezhkovsky Dmitri
   62 fn 5, 65 fn 12, 70 fn 24, 81, 82 fn 47, 83, 83 (and Bulgakov), fn 49 (thought, career), 84-85 (*Shield* article), 157-158 (and Berdyaev), 159, 171 fn 35, 196 fn 83 (critique of Third Testament of), 200 fn 94 (on Shestov), 229 (and Rozanov), 232 and 248 (against Rozanov), 240 (sacred flesh), 386 fn 116 (Steinberg's affinity with), 397 fn 136 (and Meier), 482 fn 81 (Frank on)
Messianic Judaism – see under Judaism
Meyendorff, John
   468 fn 50, 503 fn 127
Morson, Gary
   376

Nicanor, Archbishop
   8, 524
Nikolyukin, A.N.
   288 fn 122

Okunev, Yuri
   149

Paganism (Neo-)
   33 (Soloviev, Jews and), 75-77 (Bulgakov on), 82 fn 47 (Bulgakov and Egyptians), 109 (and Nazism), 160 (and Merezhkovsky), 169-70 (Ivanov, Merezhkovsky, Bulgakov), 233 (and Rozanov's anti-Semitism), 238-239 (Rozanov, Judaism and), 243 (and Rozanov's anti-Christianity), 262-263 (Judaism, Christianity and), 293-294 (and Fathers' "pagan wisdom"), 330 ff. (and anti-Semitism), 384 (Khoruzhy and "Judaization"), 474 (Gershenzon on Pushkin),
Palamas, St. Gregory
   49, 50 fn 63, 122, 123 fn 151, 323 fn 180, 324 fn 180, 385, 420 fn 189, 468 fn 50, 503, 506
Pantheism
   48, 49, 79 fn 39, 121 fn 144, 123 fn 151, 323 fn 180, 381 ff, 406 fn 152, 458, 462 fn 34, 467 fn 49 (Frank and Hasidic panentheism)
Paperny, Vladimir
   206 fn 107, 214, 215, 219 fn 143, 221 fn 145
Pelikan, Jaroslav
   401 fn 147

Philaret, (Drozdov) Metropolitan
    18-19
Plato, (*Platonism, neo-Platonism*)
    35, 293 (Fathers and Christian wisdom), 319-325 (and "energetic-essentialism" of), 368-370 (Steinberg's interpretation of Dostoevsky), 378 (in Russian philosophy), 379-382 (Maimon, Kant and), 400-401 (Karsavin and Christianity), 405 (Karsavin and the Church), 408-409 (dividing and uniting Karsavin and Steinberg), 440 fn 221, 493 (H.Cohen critiques), 496 (Rosenzweig critiques)
Polonski, Pinchas
    88 fn 63, 402 fn 148
Pogroms
    20 (John of Kronstadt condemns), 21 (Khrapovitsky, M.Yedlinsky stop), 27 (and Soloviev), 37 (and Soloviev), 83 (and Bulgakov, 1915), 91-97 (and Bulgakov charged with incitation), 91 fn 68 (and Civil War), 100 fn 99 (and White propaganda), 102 (Bulgakov against Conservative "*pogromshchiki*"), 140 fn 184 (Khrapovitsky stops), 141 (and Jabotinsky), 155 (Kishinev and Gershenzon), 277 (Rozanov on beneficial effects of), 285 (Rozanov's daughter against), 352 (Bromberg and Jewish Eurasianism), 431 (in the imagination of Karsavin and Rozanov)
Portnova, Nelly
    347, 365, 389 fn 125
Prokurina, V.
    188
Pushkin
    165, 188-189 (Gershenzon on), 276, 414 fn 172, 472-484 (Frank and Gershenzon on)

Rabinowitz Joseph
    36-43 (and Soloviev),
Rashkovsky, Evgeny
    165
Revolution, 1905, 1917 (Feb), 1917 (Oct)
    55 fn 75 (1905 and Jewish conversions), 62-63 (impact on Bulgakov), 67-68 (Bulgakov blames Jews for), 71-74 (Bulgakov and Christian eschatology), 94 fn 81 (historians on role of Jews in), 101-105 (in Bulgakov's diary), 149 (R. Epstein and Jewish role in), 152 fn 203 (and Yevseksia), 156 (and Gershenzon's support of Bolsheviks), 169 (Gershenzon and Berdyaev on), 174-177 (Gershenzon and Berdyaev on), 177-178 (Gershenzon and Ivanov on), 182-183 (and Gershenzon's thought), 198-200 (Berdyaev, late reevaluation of), 243 (Rozanov about), 273 (Rozanov on Jews corrupted by Russian revolution), 341 and 355 (Karsavin on), 363-364 (Steinberg and Herman Cohen on), 391-399 (Christian and Jewish attitudes towards), 469-471 (and Frank and Gershenzon)
Reznik, Semyon
    94 fn 81, 99 fn 95
Rosenberg, Alfred
    110, 111, 112, 130, 269, 309
Rosenzweig, Franz
    125 fn 156, 278 fn 102, 361 (and Steinberg's affinity with), 495-507 (and Frank)
Rozanov, Vasily
    82 fn 47, 83, 99 (and Bishop Veniamin), 172, 176, 201, 229-236, 236-246 (career and development), 246-267 (*Judaism*), 267-271 (Beilis-era writings), 271-283 (and Gershenzon), 283-287 (and Steinberg), 288-294 (Beilis-era anti-Semitic journalism),

294-307 (and Beilis-era collaboration with Florensky), 310-311, 357 (and Karsavin), 369 fn 69 (influence on Steinberg's thought), 375 fn 85 (and Steinberg on Dostoevsky), 407 (Steinberg on Karsavin's similarity to), 415, 431 and 432 (Karsavin and), 433 (Karsavin and)

Ruether, Ruth
331 fn 192

Sacks, Jonathan
355 fn 41

Schwarzschild, Steven
489

Shestov, Lev
95, 96, 155, 156, 174 (on Berdyaev's politics), 189 fn 66 (Bulgakov on), 200-203 (background and career), 203-205 (and Gershenzon), 205-207 (on Buber and Judaism), 207-211 (and Berdyaev), 211-219 (Bulgakov and Steinberg), 220-224 (as Russian Jewish thinker), 225-226 (Zenkovsky on), 250 fn 41 (similarities with Rozanov), 259 fn 64 (and "learned ignorance"), 277 fn 101 (on Rozanov), 293 fn 134 (and Rozanov on the Bible), 371 fn 76 (and Steinberg), 401 fn 146 (Karsavin on), 433 fn 211 (affinity with Karsavin), 483 (Russian-Jewish sage), 487 (Frank on)

Skorodumov, S.V.
235

Singer, Isaac
291 fn 130

Slavophiles
24-26 (and Soloviev), 28, 36, 44, 53, 86 (and Zionism in Bulgakov), 103 (Bulgakov criticizes nationalism of), 165-173 (Gershenzon and Berdyaev clash over), 224 fn 153 (Florovsky and Gershenzon on), 236-7 (and early Rozanov), 275-276 (Rozanov and Gershenzon on), 328 (I.D.Levin against), 371 (Dostoevsky's synthesis), 457 (Frank and Ern dispute), 461 (and Frank), 505 (resemblance of doctrine of eternal Russian people to Wyschogrod and Rosenzweig on Jewry)

Sobolev, A.
323 fn 180, 359 fn 50

Soloveitchik, Joseph
386, 387

Solzhenitsyn, Aleksandr
94 fn 81

Soloviev, Sergei
63 fn 5, 65 fn 12, 472 (against Merezhkovsky)

Soloviev, Vladimir
24-29 (general development), 24-36 (Jews and Judaism), 36-40 (and J.Rabinowitz), 40-43 (and Judeo-Christianity), 43-47(and the Talmud), 47-53 (Sophia and Kabbalah), 53-58 (Jewish reactions to), 61-62 (Bulgakov influenced by), 62 fn 5 (Blok and Bely interpret), 64 (Bulgakov critiques), 76 (versus Bulgakov on Jewry), 81 (Bulgakov against sexual ethic of), 131 (and Bulgakov's approach to Jewry), 157 (heritage in Berdyaev and Bulgakov), 178 (V.Ivanov influenced by), 237 (Rozanov quarrels with), 238 (Rozanov and all-unity of), 250 (and Rozanov on circumcision), 279 fn 103 (and Rozanov on Jews), 295 (Florensky and sophiology), 307 (and Florensky on Jews), 320 (shift from Platonism to neo-Platonism in philosophical heritage of), 322 (theocracy of, and Florensky), 337 fn 22 (and pan-Mongolism), 340 (and Karsavin), 356 (Karsavin on enthusiasm of Jews for),

Sophia

26, 47-48, 51-52, 57-58, 63-66, 75-80, 112-123 (and Bulgakov), 136, 142, 323 (and Silver Age energo-essentialism, pantheism), 379 (and Steinberg), 399 (and Karsavin), 419-420 (Karsavin and Steinberg – sophianic sensibility), 472 (S.Soloviev, critique of), 484 (Frank's "non-sophianic" Wisdom)

Earlier entry (continued from previous page): 390 (and Mandelstam), 442 (similarities with Karsavin at death), 454 and 456 (Frank on), 511 (and "third-generation" heirs of), 515 (Men and)

Sophiology

48, 49 (and charges of pantheism), 50 (and Hasidism), 54-56 (and Hebrew poets), 79 (and dukhovnie stikhi), 112-123 (and Bulgakov, critique by Lossky, sacred blood, pantheism), 381 fn 105 (and "Spinozizing" tendencies), 467 (all-unity, and Zenkovsky's criticism of Frank)

Stein, Edith
    127, 128

Steinberg, Aaron
    171 fn 36, 205 fn 106, 215, 221, 234, 260 fn 69, 283-287 (and Rozanov), 337-342, 344-347, 347-367 (Jewish-Christian dialogue with Karsavin), 367-378 ("concrete idealism" and Dostoevsky), 378-391 (Jewishness, Russianness and Christianity in philosophy), 391-399 (Meier, Fedotov, religious orthodoxy and/vs. political involvement), 407-409 (Judaism and Karsavin), 417, 419-422 (triadology and Karsavin), 428, 434 fn 213 (Karsavin and suicide), 436-439 (Karsavin, Jews and personality), 439 (last meeting with Karsavin), 463 fn 37 (and Frank and suicide)

Steinberg Isaac
    178, 341, 342, 343, 394

Steinberg, Leo
    389 fn 125

Struve, Pyotr
    89 fn 64, 156, 164, 231 (denounces Rozanov), 453, 455 (influences Frank), 469-471, 479

Symbolism

56 (Shlonsky critiques), 57 (Bialik ironic about), 306 (and Florensky on OT), 322-325 (and Name-worshipping controversy), 370 (Bely and Steinberg)

Svyatopolk-Mirsky, Dmitri (Prince)
    346 fn 20

Tertullian
    75 fn 35, 502, 505

Theophan, Metroplitan
    20, 32 (and Soloviev)

Trubetzkoy Evgeniy (Count)
    52 (Soloviev's death)

Trubetzkoy, Nicolai (Prince)
    343, 344, 353 fn 37, 358, 359, 360 fn 51 (and linguistic science), 428 fn 204 (condemns Karsavin), 440 fn 222, 484

Trubetzkoy, Sergei
    201 fn 99

Tolstoy, Lev
    88 fn 61 (on Shestov), 163 (and Gershenzon), 179 (Ivanov on), 196, 368 (and Steinberg), 484 (as Russian sage)

Vaneev, Anatoly
    400, 405, 406, 410 fn 63, 424 fn 198 (on Karsavin on *tzimtzum*), 433 fn 212 (on Karsavin on Adam's Fall), 441-443
Vasilenko, L.I.
    24 fn 23, 29, 58, 148 fn 196 (on Bulgakov and Karsavin on Judeo-Christianity), 314 fn 166
Velimirovich, Nicolas (St.)
    145 fn 191
Vermes, Geza
    43 fn 49, 319 fn 173

Williams, Rowan
    149 fn 148, 150
Wyschogrod, Michael
    69, 129 (and Bulgakov, on Jewish unity), 151 (on secular Jews), 152, 361 fn 52 (compared to Rosenzweig), 501 (critique of Rosenzweig), 504 fn 129 (on Jewish unity, parallels with Slavophile doctrines)

Yaffe, Leib
    189 (on Gershenzon), 190
Yehoshua, Avraham
    330 and 331 fn 193
Yids
    43 fn 46 (Soloviev and secular Jews), 39 fn 79 (in folk songs), 74 (Marx, Bulgakov), 90 fn 67 (Dostoevsky), 100 (Vostokov's sermons), 100 fn 99 (White songs), 103 (Bulgakov on), 104 fn 105 (semantics of in Russian usage), 244 fn 25, 27 (and Rozanov), 245, 273, 278 (Rozanov, sacred), 281-282 (Gershenzon and Rozanov), 288-289 (alphabetic transfiguration of), 307 (versus Jews in Florensky), 308 fn 159 (Florensky, "kikes", Zionism), 313 fn 165 (Florensky, magical sound), 341 (Karsavin denounces), 342 and 350 (and core-periphery distinction), 390, 395 (Fedotov against anti-Semitism), 411 fn 166 (in Karsavin's *Poem on Death*)
Yovel, Yirmiyahu
    25 fn 26, 50 fn 64

Zionism
    54-56 (Ahad Ha-Am, Soloviev, Dubnow), 82-89 (Christian, mystical Jewish, Kook), 141 fn 185 (and Jabotinsky), 149-151 (R.Epstein and Bulgakov), 191-192 (Gershenzon against), 346 fn 20 (Eurasianism against), 351 (Karsavin's critique), 352 (J.Bromberg), 358 fn 46 (monastic influence on Labor Zionism), 375 (Steinberg teaches philosophy of), 383 fn 108 (Y.Leibowitz against eschatological trend in), 494 (H.Cohen against), 518 (as secular ideology)
Zenkovsky, Vassily
    178 fn 51, 191 fn 73, 225-226 (on dialectic relationship of Jewry and Christianity), 233 (on Rozanov), 466-468 (on Frank), 525
Zizioulas, John
    330

LaVergne, TN USA
14 September 2010
196920LV00002B/10/P